ENCYCLOPEDIA OF
COMMUNICATION and INFORMATION

ENCYCLOPEDIA OF
COMMUNICATION
and INFORMATION

Volume 3

Edited by Jorge Reina Schement

MACMILLAN REFERENCE USA

GALE GROUP

™

THOMSON LEARNING

New York • Detroit • San Diego • San Francisco
Boston • New Haven, Conn. • Waterville, Maine
London • Munich

Encyclopedia of Communication and Information

Copyright © 2002 by Macmillan Reference USA, an imprint of Gale Group

Macmillan Library Reference USA   Macmillan Library Reference USA
300 Park Avenue South   27500 Drake Road
New York, NY 10010   Farmington Hills, MI 48331–3535

Library of Congress Cataloging-in-Publication Data

Encyclopedia of communication and information/edited by Jorge Reina Schement.
        p. cm.
    Includes bibliographical references and index.
    ISBN 0-02-865386-6 (set : hardcover : alk. paper)-ISBN 0-02-865383-1 (v. 1 :
    hardcover : alk. paper)-ISBN 0-02-865384-X (v. 2 : hardcover : alk. paper)-
    ISBN 0-02-865385-8 (v. 3 :hardcover : alk. paper)
        1. Communication-Encyclopedias. I. Schement, Jorge Reina.
    P87.5.E53 2001
    302.2"03-dc21   2001031220

Printed in United States of America

10   9   8   7   6   5   4   3   2   1

■ PORNOGRAPHY

Major sources of information about sex include media such as magazines, videos, television, and movies. Some, but by no means all, of these sources are what most people think of as "pornography." The most common public perceptions of pornography include the "dirty magazine" that an adolescent has hidden under the mattress and the "X-rated" film that a group of men enjoy at a bachelor party. Although these examples may appear relatively harmless, almost an accepted part of societal curiosity about sex and images of beauty, this entry will demonstrate that not all types of pornography are harmless. In fact, some may have seriously adverse influences on attitudes and behaviors.

What Is Pornography?

When people speak of sexually oriented materials, they can be referring to a wide variety of sources. There are classes of materials, at least in the United States, that are explicitly labeled "erotic," "pornographic," or "sexually explicit." These come in the form of magazines, videos, films, and some notorious Internet websites. Such materials are marketed separately from nonsexual media, and their access is at least somewhat restricted with regard to distribution to children, although just how restricted it is, or should be, remains controversial. These materials are generally recognized as being for sexual purposes only and lacking recognized literary or artistic merit. One of the few exceptions is the comparatively tame magazine *Playboy,* which, practically alone

among sex magazines, also has some recognized literary respectability. It is also an exception because it refrains from explicit depictions of sexual acts and instead features nudity alone, which is often but not necessarily sexual in theme. Pornography is big business; about ten thousand pornographic videos were released in 1999. In the San Fernando Valley of Los Angeles alone, production of pornographic films provides ten thousand to twenty thousand jobs in a $4 billion industry (Gettleman, 1999).

Some sources (e.g., *Final Report,* 1986) distinguish between sexually violent material, which portrays rape and other instances of physical harm to persons in a sexual context, and nonviolent sexual material, which may or may not depict degradation, domination, subordination, or humiliation. Nonviolent and nondegrading materials typically depict a couple having vaginal or oral intercourse with no indication of violence or coercion. Research (reviewed below) has consistently shown more negative effects from viewing sexual violence than from the nonviolent, nondegrading material. Some materials include child pornography, which portrays minors and, although illegal to produce in the United States and many other places, still circulates widely through foreign magazines and personal distribution. For obvious ethical reasons, there has been little scientific research on its effects.

Sex also occurs in many other media outlets besides these explicitly sexual materials. For example, sex is rampant in advertising, particularly for products such as perfume, cologne, and aftershave, but also for tires, automobiles, and kitchen sinks. Sex in media is not limited to explicit portrayals of intercourse or nudity, but rather may include any representation that portrays or implies sexual behavior, interest, or motivation. However, the major focus of this entry is on the more explicit materials, most commonly what is generally called "pornographic." The term "pornographic" is highly value laden, however, and as such is rather scientifically imprecise. Although it is in many ways preferable to refer to such materials as "sexually explicit," the term "pornography" will also be used because it has some wide degree of common usage.

History of Sexual Art and Communication

Sexual themes in fiction have been around as long as fiction itself. Ancient Greek comedies were often highly sexual in content, for example, Aristophanes' *Lysistrata,* an antiwar comedy about women who withhold sex from their husbands to coerce them to stop fighting wars. Literary classics such as Geoffrey Chaucer's *Canterbury Tales* and William Shakespeare's *The Taming of the Shrew* are filled with sexual double entendres and overtly sexual themes, some of which are missed today due to the archaic language and the "classic" aura surrounding such works. Throughout history, the pendulum has swung back and forth in terms of how much sexual expression should be permitted in literature and how explicit that depiction should be. In contrast to what is normally thought of as pornography, sex in literature usually has some accepted literary purpose or merit, which makes it much more socially acceptable. This issue of "prevailing tone" is discussed in more detail below.

Since the advent of broadcast media, standards have usually been more conservative for radio and television than for print media because it is easier to keep sexually oriented print media from children than it is to keep radio or television from them. With the advent of widespread cable television and videocassette technology, a sort of double standard has arisen, with greater acceptance of more sexual materials on videocassettes and premium cable channels than on network television. The logic appears to be that premium cable and rented movies are "invited" into the home, whereas network programming is an uninvited presence wherever there is a television set. Even more controversial is the problem of the availability of pornography on the Internet, which has virtually no restrictions. The major issue is how to restrict legally the access by minors to sexually explicit materials, although there is disagreement about just how much sex is actually available on the World Wide Web (Glassner, 1999).

Sex is one area where some limits on the freedom of speech and press are clearly accepted. The difficulties arise, however, in deciding just where those limits should be. One important issue in the discussion of where the limits should be drawn is the age of the viewer or reader. There is far more concern about the effects of sexual materials on children than on adults. Even strongly libertarian people probably would not want their six-year-old children reading *Hustler.*

The Gender Bias

Explicit sexual materials have traditionally been designed by men for men. As such, they have a distinctly macho and hypermasculinized orientation. Although magazines and videos show all varieties of intercourse, they place little emphasis on associated foreplay, afterplay, cuddling, or general tenderness. Women are seen eagerly desiring and participating in sex, often with hysterical euphoria. There is little concern with the consequences of sex or the relational matrix within which most people experience it. Although there has been some increase in sexual materials developed primarily to be marketed to women (materials that show more emphasis on relationships, pre- and post-coital behaviors, and the woman's point of view overall), these comprise only a minuscule part of the $5 billion market worldwide (Day and Bloom, 1988; Hebditch and Anning, 1988; Weaver, 1991). Although men are much more active seekers and users of sexual material than are women, this cannot be assumed to be due to greater intrinsic male interest in sex; it may merely reflect the extreme slant of the pornography industry to the traditional male perspective.

Effects of Viewing Pornography

Although many people might wish it otherwise, sex apparently does sell, even very explicit sex. Sexually oriented print, video, and broadcast materials are highly profitable commercially, a condition that assures their continued presence. Although there is some increase in the production of "couple-friendly pornography," an estimated 71 percent of sex videos are watched by men by themselves (Gettleman, 1999). In examining the use of these materials, several specific effects have been identified.

Arousal

A fairly straightforward effect of consuming sexual materials is sexual arousal, the drive that energizes or intensifies sexual behavior. Sexually oriented magazines and videos do tend to arouse people sexually, both in terms of self-rating of arousal level and physiological measures such as penile tumescence (Eccles, Marshall, and Barbaree, 1988; Malamuth and Check, 1980; Schaefer and Colgan, 1977), vaginal changes (Sintchak and Geer, 1975), and thermography (Abramson, Perry, Seeley, Seeley, and Rothblatt, 1981). Sexual violence is particularly arousing to sex offenders and much less so to normal men, unless the victim is portrayed as being aroused by the assault. (These findings are discussed in more detail below.)

Sexual arousal in response to stimuli that would not naturally be arousing may be learned through classical conditioning. This process could account for the vast individual differences in which specific stimuli arouse people sexually. Through different experiences, individuals have all been conditioned to different stimuli as they relate to specific loved ones. For example, because of its association with a particular person, someone may be aroused by a certain perfume or cologne, type of clothing, or specific behaviors.

Contrary to what one might expect, the degree of arousal is not necessarily highly correlated with the degree of explicitness of the media. Sometimes people are actually more aroused by a less sexually explicit story than a more explicit one. A scene that cuts from the night before in a bedroom to the next morning may sometimes be more arousing than a more pornographic version with the intervening night uncut. Censoring out a sex scene may make a film more arousing because viewers can fill in their own images. Sexual arousal is highly individual. When people are allowed to use their own imaginations to construct the ending of a romantic scene, they are more likely to construct a reality that is more arousing to them personally than if they view someone else's idea of what is arousing. There is some validity to the old truism that the most important sex organ is the brain.

Attitudes and Values

Beyond arousal, sexual media may affect people's attitudes and values. In fact, sex is one of the most value-laden areas of people's lives.

Many concerns about pornography have to do with communicating attitudes and values. For example, pornography may encourage people not to take sexual issues as seriously as they should. When a sex magazine has a regular cartoon called "Chester the Molester" that features a child molester, many argue that this is an inappropriately light treatment of an extremely serious subject. Although few would probably argue that sex should never be comedic, there are for most people some sexual subjects that do not seem appropriate for light treatment.

One of the major social criticisms of pornography is that it is antiwoman in an ideological sense. It is usually women, not men, who are the playthings or victims of the opposite sex. Although this concern spans the gamut of sexual content in media, it is particularly leveled at violent pornography. When *Hustler* magazine runs a photo spread of a gang rape turning into an orgy (showing the women appearing to be aroused by the assault), what is being taught about women and their reactions to forcible sex?

Finally, with regard to values and attitudes, people sometimes complain that pornography, especially the more explicit varieties, removes some of the mystique, some of the aura, from what is a very mysterious, almost sacred, activity. This argument holds that sex is inherently very private and becomes less meaningful, perhaps even less enjoyable, if it becomes more public. This is a difficult concern to test or even to articulate clearly, but it is one that is often expressed.

A large body of research has shown effects on a variety of sexual attitudes and values after exposure to nonviolent sexually explicit materials. After seeing slides and movies of beautiful female nudes engaged in sexual activity, men in one study rated their own partners as being less physically endowed, although they reported undiminished sexual satisfaction with their partners (Weaver, Masland, and Zillmann, 1984). In another study, men reported that they loved their own partners less after seeing sexually explicit videos of highly attractive models (Kenrick, Gutierres, and Goldberg, 1989). Men who saw a pornographic video responded more sexually to a subsequent female

With the increasing prominence of the feminist movement in the 1970s, many women began to speak out and demonstrate against the pornography industry, claiming it exploited women and women's bodies and encouraged violence against women. (Bettmann/Corbis)

interviewer than those seeing a control video, although this result was true only for men who held traditional gender schemas (McKenzie-Mohr and Zanna, 1990). All of these studies show significant attitude changes in men after a very limited exposure to sexual media.

Such effects are not limited to men. Relative to control groups, both men and women who watched pornographic films on a weekly basis later reported less satisfaction with the affection, physical appearance, sexual curiosity, and sexual performance of their real-life partners (Zillmann and Bryant, 1988a, 1988b). They also saw sex without emotional involvement as being relatively more important than the control group did. They showed greater acceptance of premarital and extramarital sex and a lower evaluation of marriage and monogamy. They also reported less desire to have children and greater acceptance of male dominance and female submission. Also showing weekly films and then questioning the participants one to three weeks later, Dolf Zillmann and Jennings Bryant (1982, 1984) found that participants who watched sexually explicit films overestimated the frequency of sexual practices such as fellatio, cunnilingus, anal intercourse, sadomasochism, and bestiality in the general population, relative to perceptions of a control group that saw nonsexual films. This may reflect the cognitive heuristic of "availability," whereby one judges the frequency of occurrence of various activities by the ease with which one can think of examples (Taylor, 1982; Tversky and Kahneman, 1973, 1974). Recent exposure to vivid media instances thus leads to an overestimation of such occurrences in the real world and a perceived reality that is substantially at odds with actual reality.

Some such effects may depend in part on the medium. Participants in a study by Marshall Dermer and Tom Pyszczynski (1978) were told to think about their partners before reading some explicit passages about a woman's sexual fantasies. They later rated their own partner as more sexually attractive. This inconsistency with the Zillmann and Bryant results may be due to specific procedural aspects of the research, the particular materials used, or psychological differences in responses to print versus video material. It is possible that all-language descriptions of sex in print media (e.g., the advice column in *Penthouse*) may actually be more conducive to fantasizing about one's own partner, whereas photographic sex may encourage an unfavorable comparison to that person.

Behavioral Effects

The third major class of effects of sexual media is their effect on behavior. This area can be divided into the three areas dealing with the teaching of new behaviors, the disinhibition of known behaviors, and the relationship between pornography and sex crimes.

On the one hand, sexual media may actually teach new behaviors. One issue of *Penthouse* contained a series of photographs of Asian women bound with heavy ropes and hung from trees. Two months later an eight-year-old Chinese girl in Chapel Hill, North Carolina, was kidnapped, raped, murdered, and left hanging from a tree (cited in *Final Report,* 1986, p. 208). Of course, such examples are not commonplace, and definitively demonstrating a causal relationship in such cases is difficult, but the juxtaposition is nonetheless disturbing.

Some of the most extreme sexual violence includes very violent and offensive images, such as movies of women apparently being killed while engaging in sexual activity ("snuff" films). For obvious ethical reasons, it is difficult to study scientifically the effects of such extreme materials.

Besides teaching new behaviors, erotic material may also disinhibit previously learned behavior. For example, watching a pornographic video with oral sex or bondage may weaken the prior inhibitions of the viewer against engaging in such behavior. Watching a rape scene where a woman is portrayed as enjoying the assault may disinhibit the constraint against the secret urge of some men to commit such a crime. This is of particular concern given some evidence suggesting that large numbers of college men reported that they might rape if they were sure they would not be caught (Check, 1985; Malamuth, Haber, and Feshbach, 1980).

One of the main concerns about the behavioral effect of viewing pornography is that it may have a relationship with sex crimes. There have been many studies looking at rates of crimes such as rape, exhibitionism, and child molestation, relative to changes in the availability of pornography. In a careful review of such studies, John Court (1984) argued that there is in fact a correlation of availability of pornography and certain sex crimes. Most Western nations have experienced a large increase both in the availability of pornography and the rise in reported rapes since the 1960s. The relationship between the two, however, has been difficult to clarify. Court presented some data from two Australian states that showed a sharp increase in rape reports in South Australia, but not Queensland, after state pornography laws were liberalized in South Australia in the early 1970s. A comparable downturn in reported rapes occurred temporarily in Hawaii between 1974 and 1976 during a temporary imposition of restraints on sexually explicit media.

However, an interesting apparent counterexample occurs with Japan, where there is wide availability of pornography but very low rape rates (Abramson and Hayashi, 1984). Sexual themes in Japanese art and society go back centuries, although some restriction and censorship occurred after the Meiji Restoration in 1868 and even more occurred under the U.S. occupation that followed the end of World War II in 1945. Still, however, sexuality continues to be a strong theme of Japanese society—one not associated with shame or guilt. Although there are specific restrictions on showing pictorial representations of pubic hair or adult genitalia, sex is not restricted to sexual media in certain types of magazines, bookstores, or theaters, as occurs in the United States. Thus, depictions of nudity, bondage, and rape occur regularly on commercial television and in popular movies and magazines, even in advertising. Films often portray very vivid scenes of rape and bondage. Toward the end of the 1990s, a market surged for magazines that featured pictures of naked schoolgirls. It is legal in Japan for men to have sex with children as long as the girls are more than twelve years of age, and some schoolgirls earn extra money from prostitution or catering to the sexual fantasies of men in Tokyo's "image clubs." Some observers have concluded that the rising interest of Japanese men in child sexuality is a reflection of the men's feeling increasingly threatened by women's growing sophistication and demands for equality ("Lolita in Japan," 1997).

Why, then, is the incidence of reported rapes so much lower in Japan (which has an annual rate of 2.4 per 100,000) than in countries such as the United States (34.5), England (10.1), and Germany (10.7)? Paul Abramson and Haruo Hayashi (1984) argued that the answer might lie in cultural differences. Japanese society emphasizes order, obligation, cooperation, and virtue; one who violates social norms is the object of shame. Others have suggested that rape in Japan is more likely to be group instigated, perpetrated by juveniles, and greatly underreported by victims (Goldstein and Ibaraki, 1983).

Firmly establishing a causal relationship between the availability of pornography and the frequency of rape is extremely difficult, due to the many other relevant factors, including the different varieties of sexual material, changes in social consciousness about reporting sexual assaults, and changing norms sanctioning such behavior. Some evidence suggests a correlation of rape and the circulation of sex magazines, particularly those containing sexual violence. For example, Larry Baron and Murray Straus (cited in *Final Report,* 1986) found a high correlation (+0.64) between rape rates and the circulation rates of eight sex magazines in fifty states.

One sometimes hears the argument that sexually explicit material allows open expression of sexual urges and thus decreases the rate of sex crimes. This invokes the construct of "catharsis," the emotional release that follows the expression of an impulse. This popular idea comes from psychodynamic models of personality, notably that of Sigmund Freud. Applied to sex, the catharsis argument says that consuming pornography relieves sexual urges, with the magazine or video acting (perhaps in conjunction with masturbation) as a sort of imperfect substitute for the real behavior. Although this argument is sometimes used by libertarians to support appeals for loosening restrictions on pornography (e.g., Kutchinsky, 1973), the research support for catharsis is meager to totally nonexistent (Comstock, 1985; *Final Report,* 1986; Harris, 1999). Viewing pornography increases—rather than decreases—sexual arousal, and, after viewing, one is more motivated to engage in sexual behavior. Also, it is now understood that some violent sex crimes, most notably rape, are energized by a power motive, not a lack of sexual fulfillment (Prentky and Knight, 1991).

The Problem of Prevailing Tone

Responses to sexual materials are not entirely due to the nature of the material. They also depend on the perceived purpose and setting of the work, what is called the prevailing tone (Eysenck and Nias, 1978). The nature of this prevailing tone can make an enormous difference in the experience of using pornography. In fact, the nature of the prevailing tone often determines whether sexual materials are labeled "pornographic" or not. Typically, materials that lack some serious social, artistic, or didactic intent are labeled "pornographic," while those that have such merit are not. The surest way to disparage and devalue some piece of work is to label it "pornographic," as social critics frequently do with overtly sexual art, literature, or film.

Just because a piece of work is sexual in nature does not necessarily earn it the label of "pornography." For example, a documentary on rape or a "tasteful" drama on incest may be considered perfectly acceptable, whereas a comedy with the same theme, but which is far less sexually explicit, may be considered highly offensive and even pornographic. Although highly explicit videos, books, and magazines are used routinely in sex therapy to treat sexual dysfunctions (Quinsey and Marshall, 1983), few would consider such materials "pornographic." People react very differently to a sexually explicit drawing by Pablo Picasso than they do to one in *Hustler* magazine. Shakespeare, Chaucer, "The Song of Solomon" in the Bible, and serious sex manuals such as *The Joy of Sex* are seen to have serious literary or respectable didactic intentions, and thus the sex therein is considered more acceptable and even healthy.

The cultural context is also a factor in the prevailing tone. Some cultures do not consider female breasts to be particularly erotic or inappropriate for public display. Thus, most readers, at least those who are more than thirteen years of age or so, do not consider topless women from some exotic culture in *National Geographic* photographs to be erotic, sexual, or pornographic. Even within Western culture, standards have changed. In much of the nineteenth century, women's knees and calves were thought to be erotic, and the sight of a bare-kneed woman would be considered scandalous, even pornographic, as would a topless woman in the twenty-first century. As societies go, North America overall is moderate in what it considers to be allowable sexual expression in dress, media, and behavior. Many Western European and Latin American cultures are far more permissive, while many Islamic and East Asian cultures are far more restrictive.

The Special Case of Violent Pornography

Although neither sexual nor violent materials are anything new, the integral combination of the two has been increasing in prevalence. Cable, video, and computer-mediated communications technology have greatly expanded the capability of much of the public to view sexually explicit material privately and conveniently. Although many people are not willing to seek out and visit theaters that show pornographic films, the chance to view such material safely and privately in one's own home makes it much more accessible. While sex magazines are not new, some particularly violent publications are relatively new, and even more "established" publications such as *Penthouse* and *Playboy* have long shown evidence of increasing themes of sexual violence (Dietz and Evans, 1982; Malamuth and Spinner, 1980). Even the old genre of horror films has evolved into showing frequent and extensive scenes of violence against women in a sexual context (Weaver and Tamborini, 1996). Not generally labeled pornographic, these films can thus be heavily marketed to teenagers, in spite of their "R" ratings. With all of these materials, the major concern is not with the sex or violence in and of itself, but with the way the two appear together.

Effect Depends on How the Woman Is Portrayed

To understand the effects of sexual violence, the nature of the content must be examined carefully. For example, Neil Malamuth (1984) reported several studies in which men viewed scenes of violent pornography and afterward rated their attitudes on several topics. Men who saw those films showed a more callous attitude toward rape and toward women in general, especially if the women victims were portrayed as being aroused by the assault. In terms of sexual arousal, men were aroused by the violent pornography only if the victim was shown to be aroused. They were not aroused if the victim was shown to be terrorized.

Other studies have examined convicted rapists and found them to be aroused by scenes of both rape and consensual sex, whereas men who were not convicted rapists were aroused only by the consensual sex (Abel, Barlow, Blanchard, and Guild, 1977; Barbaree, Marshall, and Lanthier, 1979). An important exception to this occurred if the victim was portrayed as enjoying the rape and coming to orgasm; in this case, the men who were not convicted rapists were equally or more aroused by the rape than by the consensual sex (Malamuth, Heim, and Feshbach, 1980). The same did not hold true for women.

In further examining this question in regard to individual differences in men, Malamuth and James Check (1983) had men listen to a tape of a sexual encounter with (1) consensual sex, (2) nonconsensual sex where the woman showed arousal, or (3) nonconsensual sex where the woman showed disgust. Both force-oriented and nonforce-oriented men were more aroused, in terms of both self-report and penile tumescence, by the consensual than by the nonconsensual rape scene where the woman showed disgust. However, the nonforce-oriented men were equally aroused by the consensual and nonconsensual version in which the woman was aroused, whereas the force-oriented men actually showed more arousal to the nonconsensual (rape) version. Similar results were obtained by Malamuth (1981) using video stimuli.

Can such effects carry over to new settings? The answer appears to be yes. Edward Donnerstein and Leonard Berkowitz (1981) showed men a sexually violent film where a woman is attacked, stripped, tied up, and raped. In one version of the film, the woman was portrayed as enjoying the rape. Afterward, participants were given a chance to administer electric shocks to a confederate of the experimenter, the same confederate who had earlier angered them in an ostensibly unrelated study. Men who had seen the film where the woman enjoyed being raped administered more shocks to a female confederate but not to a male. This suggests that the association of sex and violence in the film allows violent behavior to be transferred to the target confederate in a new situation.

Although most of the research has been conducted on men, some studies testing women who view pornography have also found an increase in the female subjects' violent behavior toward other women (Baron, 1979) and a tendency to take rape less seriously and accept rape myths (Malamuth, Check, and Briere, 1986; Zillmann and Bryant, 1982).

In a meta-analysis of studies examining the relationship of exposure to pornography and the acceptance of rape myths, Mike Allen, Tara Emmers, Lisa Gebhardt, and Mary Giery (1995) conclude that experimental studies show a consistent positive effect between pornography exposure and rape-myth acceptance, while nonexperimental studies show only a very small positive or nonexistent effect. The relationship was consistently stronger when the pornography was violent than when it was nonviolent, although some experimental studies obtained effects in both cases.

Conclusions from the Research

Several conclusions emerge from the violent pornography research. One is that a critical factor is whether the woman is presented as enjoying and being aroused by the assault. Far more undesirable effects occur in men if the woman is seen to be aroused than if she is seen to be terrorized. This portrayal of women as being "turned on" by rape is not only a distasteful deviation from reality but also a potentially dangerous one. A second important conclusion is that violent pornography often affects individual men very differently, depending on their own propensity to use force in their own lives. Convicted rapists and other force-oriented men are more likely to become aroused or even incited to violence by sexually violent media, especially if the woman is portrayed as being aroused by the assault.

Some researchers have questioned the conclusion of sharply different effects of viewing violent versus nonviolent pornography (Weaver, 1991; Zillmann and Bryant, 1988c). Check and Ted Guloien (1989) found that men exposed to a steady diet of rape-myth sexual violence reported a higher likelihood of committing rape themselves, compared to a control group that experienced no exposure, but the same result was found for a group exposed to nonviolent pornography.

The Political Wild Card

What happens when political agendas to restrict or liberalize pornography start interacting with the scientific evidence? Politics has a tendency to undermine objective scientific analysis. For example, the U.S. Commission on Obscenity and Pornography was established in 1967 by President Lyndon Johnson to analyze (1) pornography control laws, (2) the distribution of sexually explicit materials, and (3) the effects of consuming such materials, and to recommend appropriate legislative or administrative action. It funded more than eighty research studies on the topic, providing important impetus to the scientific study of pornography. The final report in 1970 recommended stronger controls on distribution to minors but an abolition of all limits on access by adults. The latter recommendation was based on the majority conclusion that there was "no evidence that exposure to or use of explicit sexual materials play a significant role in the causation of social or individual harms such as crime, delinquency, sexual or nonsexual deviancy or severe emotional disturbance" (U.S. Commission on Obscenity and Pornography, 1970, p. 58). However, the composi-

tion of the commission was criticized for being overloaded with anticensorship civil libertarians. When the political winds had changed, it turned out not to matter anyhow in terms of policy. The conclusions were rejected by the new administration of the more conservative President Richard Nixon, who declared, "so long as I am in the White House there will be no relaxation of the national effort to control and eliminate smut from our national life" (Eysenck and Nias, 1978, p. 94).

Some years later, in the far more conservative political climate of the 1980s, a second commission was formed by President Ronald Reagan. U.S. Attorney General Edwin Meese charged this commission (the Attorney General's Commission on Pornography) in 1985 to assess the nature, extent, and effect of pornography on U.S. society and to "recommend more effective ways to contain the spread of pornography," thus clearly stating a political agenda. One of the major conclusions of the commission dealt with the effect of sexual violence: "the available evidence strongly supports the hypothesis that substantial exposure to sexually violent materials . . . bears a causal relationship to antisocial acts of sexual violence, and for some subgroups, possibly the unlawful acts of sexual violence" (Final Report, 1986, p. 40).

Groups such as these commissions typically have both a scientific and a political agenda (Einsiedel, 1988; Paletz, 1988; Wilcox, 1987). Sometimes, even if there is relative consensus on the scientific conclusions, there is often strong disagreement about the policy ramifications. For example, scientists Daniel Linz, Edward Donnerstein, and Stephen Penrod (1987) took exception to the way that their own work was interpreted by the Meese commission to support censorship. Linz and his colleagues argued that the call of the commission for strengthening pornography laws was not an appropriate policy change based on their research, because that call ignored the strong presence of sexually violent themes in other media not covered by such laws, for example, R-rated movies and soap operas.

Sometimes political agendas can guide pornography research in more subtle ways. Two of the most prominent pornography researchers, Linz and Malamuth (1993), have talked about how various normative theories have guided research and may be lurking behind the scientific evidence. The conservative–moralist position, very prominent in

Anglo-American history and culture, sees public portrayals of sex as disgusting, offensive, and especially threatening if occurring outside of monogamous heterosexual relationships. However, pornography is at the same time clearly arousing. There is an implicit belief that a heavy emphasis on sexual gratification and permissiveness encourages behavior that undermines other moral beliefs about women and sexuality and, ultimately, leads to the decay of family and other traditional societal structures. This position would tend to encourage research on sexual arousal, the materials that produce it, and how exposure to sexual materials undermines traditional beliefs and can affect later reactions.

A second normative theory is the liberal theory, which believes that sexual depictions trigger fantasies but that these fantasies are not acted out and thus no one is hurt. They may even be socially beneficial through liberating a person's excessive prudishness. Liberals believe that, if viewing of pornography is kept private, then the government should not restrict or regulate what is best left to the marketplace of ideas, which will naturally adjust to changing social standards. The liberal theory would tend to place a higher value on research that examined the physical and behavioral effects of sexual media in the real world rather than the laboratory, with a prediction of positive effects or a lack of negative ones.

The third normative theory, the most recent one, is feminist theory, which views pornography as a powerful socializing agent that promotes the sexual abuse of women and the social subordination of women as a group. Feminist-inspired research tends to focus on the arousal, or lack of it, in a woman in a rape scene. It also tends to look more at attitudes than behaviors, including differences between men with or without a propensity to rape.

Each normative theory has inspired some useful research, but it may be helpful to identify the ideological positions of researchers when evaluating their conclusions and the place of that research in the matrix of the overall research related to the effects of pornography.

Conclusion

What can be concluded from the research that examines the effects of consuming pornography? First, it is useful to reiterate the importance of the distinction between violent and nonviolent sexual media. While there are some negative effects of nonviolent pornography, especially on attitudes toward women, the research is much more compelling in the case of violent pornography. Sexual violence is arousing to sex offenders, force-oriented men, and sometimes even to "normal" young men if the woman is portrayed as being aroused by the assault.

Repeated exposure to violent pornography may lead to desensitization toward violence against women in general and greater acceptance of rape myths. Not only does this suggest that the combination of sex and violence together is considerably worse than either one by itself, but the nature of the portrayal also matters. If the woman being assaulted is portrayed as being terrorized and brutalized, desensitizing effects on "normal" men are less than if she is portrayed as being aroused and/or achieving orgasm through being attacked. There is nothing arousing or exciting about being raped in real life, and messages to the contrary do not help teenage boys understand the reality of how to relate to girls and women.

Finally, most individuals believe that "other people" are more influenced by advertising and news coverage than they are themselves; this is the "third-person effect" (Davison, 1983; Gunther, 1991). The same is true about the perceived effects of pornography (Gunther, 1995); individuals believe it affects others more than it affects themselves. However, as society accepts increasingly explicit sexual materials, no one is immune to the influences of pornography. These influences are much more far-reaching than the transient titillation of the adolescent boy who views a *Playboy* centerfold.

See also: Catharsis Theory and Media Effects; Gender and the Media; Internet and the World Wide Web; Pornography, Legal Aspects of; Sex and the Media; Violence in the Media, Attraction to; Violence in the Media, History of Research on.

Bibliography

Abel, Gene G.; Barlow, David H.; Blanchard, Edward B.; and Guild, Donald. (1977). "The Components of Rapists' Sexual Arousal." *Archives of General Psychiatry* 34:895–903.

Abramson, Paul R., and Hayashi, Haruo. (1984). "Pornography in Japan: Cross-Cultural and Theoretical Considerations." In *Pornography and Sexual*

Aggression, eds. Neil M. Malamuth and Edward Donnerstein. Orlando, FL: Academic Press.

Abramson, Paul R.; Perry, L. B.; Seeley, T. T.; Seeley, D. M.; and Rothblatt, A. B. (1981). "Thermographic Measurement of Sexual Arousal: A Discriminant Validity Analysis." *Archives of Sexual Behavior* 10(2):175–176.

Allen, Mike; D'Alessio, Dave; and Brezgel, Keri. (1995). "A Meta-Analysis Summarizing the Effects of Pornography II: Aggression after Exposure." *Human Communication Research* 22:258–283.

Allen, Mike; Emmers, Tara; Gebhardt, Lisa; and Giery, Mary A. (1995). "Exposure to Pornography and Acceptance of Rape Myths." *Journal of Communication* 45(1):5–26.

Barbaree, H. E.; Marshall, W. L.; and Lanthier, R. D. (1979). "Deviant Sexual Arousal in Rapists." *Behaviour Research and Therapy* 17:215–222.

Baron, Robert A. (1979). "Heightened Sexual Arousal and Physical Aggression: An Extension to Females." *Journal of Research in Personality* 13:91–102.

Check, James. (1985). *The Effects of Violent and Nonviolent Pornography.* Ottawa: Department of Justice for Canada.

Check, James, and Guloien, Ted. (1989). "Reported Proclivity for Coercive Sex following Repeated Exposure to Sexually Violent Pornography, Nonviolent Pornography, and Erotica." In *Pornography: Research Advances and Policy Considerations,* eds. Dolf Zillmann and Jennings Bryant. Hillsdale, NJ: Lawrence Erlbaum.

Comstock, George. (1985). "Television and Film Violence." In *Youth Violence: Programs and Prospects,* eds. Steven J. Apter and Arnold P. Goldstein. New York: Pergamon Press.

Court, John H. (1984). "Sex and Violence: A Ripple Effect." In *Pornography and Sexual Aggression,* eds. Neil M. Malamuth and Edward Donnerstein. Orlando, FL: Academic Press.

Davison, W. Phillips. (1983). "The Third-Person Effect in Communication." *Public Opinion Quarterly* 47:1–15.

Day, Gary, and Bloom, Clive, eds. (1988). *Perspectives on Pornography: Sexuality in Film and Literature.* London: Macmillan.

Dermer, Marshall L., and Pyszczynski, Tom A. (1978). "Effects of Erotica upon Men's Loving and Liking Responses." *Journal of Personality and Social Psychology* 36:1302–1309.

Dietz, Park, and Evans, Barbara. (1982). "Pornographic Imagery and Prevalence of Paraphilia." *American Journal of Psychiatry* 139:1493–1495.

Donnerstein, Edward, and Berkowitz, Leonard. (1981). "Victim Reactions in Aggressive Erotic Films as a Factor in Violence against Women." *Journal of Personality and Social Psychology* 41:710–724.

Eccles, A.; Marshall, W. L.; and Barbaree, H. E. (1988). "The Vulnerability of Erectile Measures to Repeated Assessments." *Behavior Research and Therapy* 26:179–183.

Einsiedel, Edna F. (1988). "The British, Canadian, and U.S. Pornography Commissions and Their Use of Social Science Research." *Journal of Communication* 38(2):108–121.

Eysenck, Hans J., and Nias, D. K. B. (1978). *Sex, Violence, and the Media.* New York: Harper.

Final Report of the Attorney General's Commission on Pornography. (1986). Nashville, TN: Rutledge Hill Press.

Gettleman, Jeffrey. (1999). "XXX = $$$." *Manhattan Mercury,* October 28, p. A6.

Glassner, Barry. (1999). *The Culture of Fear: Why Americans Are Afraid of the Wrong Things.* New York: Basic Books.

Goldstein, S., and Ibaraki, T. (1983). "Japan: Aggression and Aggression Control in Japanese Society." In *Aggression in Global Perspective,* eds. Arnold P. Goldstein and Marshall H. Segall. New York: Pergamon Press.

Gunther, Albert C. (1991). "What We Think Others Think: Cause and Consequence in the Third-Person Effect." *Communication Research* 18:355–372.

Gunther, Albert C. (1995). "Overrating the X-Rating: The Third-Person Perception and Support for Censorship of Pornography." *Journal of Communication* 45(1):27–38.

Gunther, Albert C., and Thorson, Esther. (1992). "Perceived Persuasive Effects of Product Commercials and Public-Service Announcements: Third-Person Effects in New Domains." *Communication Research* 19:574–596.

Harris, Richard J. (1999). *A Cognitive Psychology of Mass Communication,* 3rd edition. Mahwah NJ: Lawrence Erlbaum.

Hebditch, David, and Anning, Nick. (1988). *Porn Gold: Inside the Pornography Business.* London: Faber & Faber.

Kenrick, Douglas T.; Gutierres, S. E.; and Goldberg, L. L. (1989). "Influence of Popular Erotica on Judgments of Strangers and Mates." *Journal of Experimental Social Psychology* 25:159–167.

Kutchinsky, Berl. (1973). "The Effect of Easy Availability of Pornography on the Incidence of Sex Crimes: The Danish Experience." *Journal of Social Issues* 29(3):163–181.

Linz, Daniel; Donnerstein, Edward; and Penrod, Stephen. (1987). "The Findings and Recommendations of the Attorney General's Commission on Pornography: Do the Psychological 'Facts' Fit the Political Fury?" *American Psychologist* 42:946–953.

Linz, Daniel, and Malamuth, Neil M. (1993). *Pornography.* Newbury Park, CA: Sage Publications.

"Lolita in Japan." (1997). *Manhattan Mercury*, April 6, p. A7.

Lyons, John S.; Anderson, Rachel L.; and Larson, David B. (1994). "A Systematic Review of the Effects of Aggressive and Nonaggressive Pornography." In *Media, Family, and Children: Social, Scientific, Psychodynamic, and Clinical Perspectives,* eds. Dolf Zillmann, Jennings Bryant, and Aletha C. Huston. Hillsdale, NJ: Lawrence Erlbaum.

Malamuth, Neil M. (1981). "Rape Fantasies as a Function of Exposure to Violent Sexual Stimuli." *Archives of Sexual Behavior* 10:33–47.

Malamuth, Neil M. (1984). "Aggression against Women: Cultural and Individual Causes." In *Pornography and Sexual Aggression,* eds. Neil M. Malamuth and Edward Donnerstein. Orlando, FL: Academic Press.

Malamuth, Neil M., and Check, James. (1980). "Penile Tumescence and Perceptual Responses to Rape as a Function of Victim's Perceived Reactions." *Journal of Applied Social Psychology* 10:528–547.

Malamuth, Neil M., and Check, James. (1983). "Sexual Arousal to Rape Depictions: Individual Differences." *Journal of Abnormal Psychology* 92:55–67.

Malamuth, Neil M.; Check, James; and Briere, J. (1986). "Sexual Arousal in Response to Aggression: Ideological, Aggressive, and Sexual Correlates." *Journal of Personality and Social Psychology* 50:330–340.

Malamuth, Neil M.; Haber, Scott; and Feshbach, Seymour. (1980). "Testing Hypotheses Regarding Rape: Exposure to Sexual Violence, Sex Differences, and the 'Normality' of Rapists." *Journal of Research in Personality* 14:121–137.

Malamuth, Neil M.; Heim, M.; and Feshbach, Seymour. (1980). "Sexual Responsiveness of College Students to Rape Depictions: Inhibitory and Disinhibitory Effects." *Journal of Personality and Social Psychology* 38:399–408.

Malamuth, Neil M., and Spinner, Barbara. (1980). "A Longitudinal Content Analysis of Sexual Violence in the Best Selling Erotica Magazines." *Journal of Sex Research* 16:226–237.

Mckenzie-Mohr, Doug, and Zanna, Mark P. (1990). "Treating Women as Sexual Objects: Look to the (Gender Schematic) Male Who has Viewed Pornography." *Personality and Social Psychology Bulletin* 16:296–308.

Paletz, David L. (1988). "Pornography, Politics, and the Press: The U.S. Attorney General's Commission on Pornography." *Journal of Communication* 38(2):122–136.

Perloff, Robert M. (1989). "Ego-Involvement and the Third Person Effect of Television News Coverage." *Communication Research* 16:236–262.

Prentky, Robert A., and Knight, Raymond A. (1991). "Identifying Critical Dimensions for Discriminating among Rapists." *Journal of Consulting and Clinical Psychology* 59:643–661.

Quinsey, Vernon L., and Marshall, W. L. (1983). "Procedures for Reducing Inappropriate Sexual Arousal: An Evaluation Review." In *The Sexual Aggressor: Current Perspectives on Treatment,* eds. Joanne G. Greer and Irving R. Stuart. New York: Van Nostrand Reinhold.

Schaefer, H. H., and Colgan, A. H. (1977). "The Effect of Pornography on Penile Tumescence as a Function of Reinforcement and Novelty." *Behavior Therapy* 8:938–946.

Sintchak, G., and Geer, J. (1975). "A Vaginal Plethysmograph System." *Psychophysiology* 12:113–115.

Strasburger, Victor C. (1995). *Adolescents and the Media: Medical and Psychological Impact.* Thousand Oaks, CA: Sage Publications.

Taylor, Shelley. (1982). "The Availability Bias in Social Perception and Interaction." In *Judgment under Uncertainty: Heuristics And Biases,* eds. Daniel Kahneman, Paul Slovic, and Amos Tversky. Cambridge, Eng.: Cambridge University Press.

Tversky, Amos, and Kahneman, Daniel. (1973). "Availability: A Heuristic for Judging Frequency and Probability." *Cognitive Psychology* 5:207–232.

Tversky, Amos, and Kahneman, Daniel. (1974). "Judgment under Uncertainty: Heuristics and Biases." *Science* 185:1124–1131.

U.S. Commission on Obscenity and Pornography. (1970). *The Report of the Commission on Obscenity and Pornography.* New York: Bantam.

Weaver, James B. (1991). "Responding to Erotica: Perceptual Processes and Dispositional Implications." In *Responding to the Screen,* eds. Jennings Bryant and Dolf Zillmann. Hillsdale, NJ: Lawrence Erlbaum.

Weaver, James B.; Masland, J. L.; and Zillmann, Dolf. (1984). Effects of Erotica on Young Men's Aesthetic Perception of Their Female Sexual Partners. *Perceptual and Motor Skills* 58:929–930.

Weaver, James B., and Tamborini, Ron, eds. (1996). *Horror Films: Current Research on Audience Preferences and Reactions.* Mahwah, NJ: Lawrence Erlbaum.

Wilcox, Brian L. (1987). "Pornography, Social Science, and Politics: When Research and Ideology Collide." *American Psychologist* 42:941–943.

Zillmann, Dolf, and Bryant, Jennings. (1982). Pornography, Sexual Callousness, and the Trivialization of Rape. *Journal of Communication* 32(4):10–21.

Zillmann, Dolf, and Bryant, Jennings. (1984). "Effects of Massive Exposure to Pornography." In *Pornography and Sexual Aggression,* eds. Neil M. Malamuth and Edward Donnerstein. Orlando, FL: Academic Press.

Zillmann, Dolf, and Bryant, Jennings. (1988a). "Pornography's Impact on Sexual Satisfaction." *Journal of Applied Social Psychology* 18:438–453.

Zillmann, Dolf, and Bryant, Jennings. (1988b). "Effects of Prolonged Consumption of Pornography on Family Values." *Journal of Family Issues* 9:518–544.

Zillmann, Dolf, and Bryant, Jennings. (1988c). "A Response to Linz and Donnerstein." *Journal of Communication* 38(2):185–192.

Zillmann, Dolf, and Bryant, Jennings, eds. (1989). *Pornography: Research Advances and Policy Considerations.* Hillsdale, NJ: Lawrence Erlbaum.

RICHARD JACKSON HARRIS

CHRISTINA L. SCOTT

▓ PORNOGRAPHY, LEGAL ASPECTS OF

Sexually explicit expression has been subject to legal regulation in the United States since the earliest days of the republic. Until the last half of the twentieth century, legal sanctions imposed on sexually explicit expression were not thought to conflict with the free speech protections of the First Amendment. Beginning in the 1950s, however, the U.S. Supreme Court began recognizing that a large amount of speech containing sexually explicit content also had significant First Amendment value. The Supreme Court therefore began limiting the government's power to regulate or ban certain types of sexually explicit speech.

Under the Supreme Court's modern cases, what is popularly called "pornography" actually covers several different categories of speech. One category is "obscenity." Obscenity is defined very narrowly and is not protected by the First Amendment. The government may ban the distribution of obscene materials, but it may not criminalize the mere possession of obscene materials that do not include the depiction of children. Another category is "indecency." This term refers to sexually explicit expression that falls short of the narrow legal definition of obscenity. Indecent speech is constitutionally protected (and therefore may not be legally banned altogether), but it may be regulated in some manner to prevent both children and adults from coming into contact with it involuntarily.

The legal regulation of all forms of pornography is complicated by the growth of new communication media. The Supreme Court has traditionally been willing to permit greater legal regulation of all sexual expression in contexts such as radio and television. The Court has been less willing to apply similarly restrictive standards to cable television, and it is far less willing to uphold regulation of speech over the Internet. It remains to be seen whether the ease with which images and ideas can be transmitted over the Internet will eventually lead to a liberalization of free speech protection of pornographic materials in more traditional communications contexts.

History

The first reported case in the United States to involve the censorship of a pornographic drawing occurred in 1815. The first prosecution of a book on obscenity grounds occurred in 1821. The book that was deemed obscene in that case was John Cleland's novel *Memoirs of a Woman of Pleasure*, which is usually known by its alternative title, *Fanny Hill*. This book has been prosecuted repeatedly since its publication, and one prosecution made it all the way to the U.S. Supreme Court in 1965.

Despite the long history of regulating pornography in the United States, the legal doctrine related to prosecution with regard to sexually explicit material developed slowly. The early prosecutions related to sexually explicit texts and drawings were based largely on blasphemy and profanity statutes, which were not specifically addressed to sexually explicit expression. In addition, no First Amendment doctrine covered obscenity until well into the twentieth century. Prior to that time, most pornography prosecutions in the United States were guided by the standard set by the British House of Lords in the 1868 case *Regina v. Hicklin*. This case involved the prosecution of a sexually suggestive anti-Catholic tract. In one of the opinions for the court in *Hicklin*, Lord Cockburn asserted that expressive material was obscene if it tended to "deprave and corrupt those whose minds are open to such immoral influences."

The American legal system embraced the *Hicklin* immorality standard quickly, and soon after the Civil War, the states and the federal government began enacting the first statutes specifically directed toward the regulation of obscene materials. Many of these early statutes were attributable to the efforts of a dry-goods clerk and moral crusader named Anthony Comstock. Comstock started militating against the dissemination of pornography in New York in the early 1870s and later joined with the Young Men's Christian Association (YMCA) to form the Committee for the Suppression of Vice.

Comstock and the committee were instrumental in the enactment of a major federal anti-obscenity act in 1873, and the act soon became known informally as the Comstock Law. This law prohibited not only the distribution of obscene materials but also the distribution of materials related to contraception and abortion. Soon after the law's passage, Comstock was made a special agent of the U.S. Post Office Department, a post from which he would lead the anti-pornography efforts in the United States well into the twentieth century.

Although Comstock's personal influence waned in the years preceding his death in 1915, the zealous moralism that he embodied continued to define efforts to regulate pornography throughout the first half of the twentieth century. During this period, a range of now-classic literary works were subjected to obscenity prosecutions or other forms of legal regulation. These prominent cases involved the works of writers such as George Bernard Shaw, Theodore Dreiser, Erskine Caldwell, Edmund Wilson, and D. H. Lawrence. A 1933 obscenity case against James Joyce's novel *Ulysses* resulted in the first systematic attack on the *Hicklin* analysis by an American court. The case involved the seizure of the book by U.S. Customs officials. In his opinion holding that the book was not obscene, U.S. District Judge John Woolsey held that the artistic value of the book insulated it from a charge of obscenity. Obscenity, the judge ruled, was defined by the tendency of sexually explicit materials to excite sexual passions among those with normal sexual tendencies. This was a significant departure from the *Hicklin* analysis, which focused on the effects that obscenity had on those who were most susceptible to messages of sexual immorality.

The *Ulysses* decision was not appealed to the U.S. Supreme Court, and it took the Supreme Court another twenty years before it finally attempted to set forth a constitutional standard for regulating obscenity. In its 1954 decision in *Roth v. United States*, the Court announced the first of what would be several constitutional standards for obscenity regulation. In several ways, the Court moved beyond the restrictive *Hicklin* standard that had defined American obscenity prosecutions for almost one hundred years. The Supreme Court held in *Roth* that sexually explicit speech contained within otherwise intellectually valuable expression could not be deemed obscene. In addition, the Court rejected the notion that obscenity

Anthony Comstock. (Bettmann/Corbis)

should be defined by the sexual tendencies of the most susceptible portion of the population. Unfortunately, although the Court's opinion contained a broad statement of general principles pertaining to art and literature, the Court was unsuccessful in defining precisely where the realm of art ended and the realm of the legally obscene began. The *Roth* decision therefore resulted in almost twenty years of litigation in the Supreme Court over the factors that contribute to a finding of obscenity. This dispute over the general constitutional standard was finally resolved in 1973 in *Miller v. California*, a case that continues to frame discussions of the legal regulation of obscenity.

The Obscenity Standard

In *Miller*, the Supreme Court provided a three-part standard that governs both criminal and civil regulations of obscenity. Under the so-called *Miller* test, the government must prove that the sexually explicit material that it seeks to regulate (1) appeals primarily to the prurient interest as judged by contemporary community standards, (2) depicts sexual conduct that is patently offensive under contemporary community standards, and (3) lacks serious literary, artistic, political, or scientific value.

This standard is more protective of expression than earlier standards in several respects. First, when judging allegedly obscene expression, a judge or jury must consider the work as a whole. This diverges from earlier standards, which permitted judges and juries to consider obscene passages in isolation and out of the expression's larger literary or artistic context. Second, the reference point for the "prurient interest" and "patent offensiveness" components of the standard is the average person, rather than the person who is the most susceptible to influence by pornographic materials. Third, the inclusion of an intellectual-value component in the obscenity standard ensures that artistic, literary, and scientific works are no longer subject to the whims of local censors or customs officials—as has frequently been the case in the past. Moreover, unlike the first two elements of the *Miller* test, the intellectual-value element of the test is measured by a national standard rather than a local community standard. Thus, a local community can no longer deny its residents access to a respected literary work such as *Ulysses* simply because the work contains some graphic sexual passages that transgress local sexual mores.

Despite the more protective elements of the *Miller* test, several elements of that standard continue to create confusion in the regulation of allegedly pornographic materials. The first problem stems from the vagueness of the terminology used in the standard. The terms "prurience" and "patently offensive" are neither precise nor clear. The Supreme Court has subsequently suggested that these terms refer only to "hard-core" pornography, but the scope of that term is also subject to vigorous dispute. The fact that prurience and patent offensiveness is measured by contemporary community standards is another source of uncertainty in the *Miller* test. The Supreme Court has never defined the exact parameters of the relevant community; it has chosen instead to leave to local courts the exact scope of the geographic area covered by the term. At the very least, this localized standard produces significant variation in the application of obscenity laws throughout the country. What is obscene in Utah or Alabama will not necessarily be obscene in New York or California. This inconsistency can cause serious problems as the nation's communications industry becomes increasingly national and even international in scope, because tailoring content for the more restrictive communities will be difficult and expensive if not technologically impossible.

Despite the flaws in the *Miller* test, it has generally provided, in most communities, a broad protection for expressive materials that contain sexual content. The generally protective *Miller* test does not apply, however, to sexually explicit materials that include visual depictions of underage children engaged in sexual activity. The Supreme Court has held that materials of this sort may be regulated much more easily than materials that depict adults. Government authorities may regulate these materials without proving that they are prurient or patently offensive. The Supreme Court has clearly held, however, that the government cannot ban all depictions of nudity involving minors; thus, the lenient standard for prosecuting child pornography seems limited to relatively rare situations that involve visual depictions of live sexual activity by minors. The Supreme Court has also held that a work using a person over the statutory age who appears underage is not subject to the lowered standard for child pornography. Furthermore, it is unclear whether the Supreme Court would permit prosecutions over sexual depictions of minors in expressive materials that have serious literary, artistic, political, or scientific value.

One final aspect of the modern free speech standard involves the private possession of pornography, including material that may be deemed obscene under the *Miller* test. The Supreme Court ruled in *Stanley v. Georgia* (1969) that the possession of pornographic materials for personal use at home is protected by the U.S. Constitution even if the commercial distribution of the same materials could be prosecuted under the *Miller* test. The Court relied on a combination of privacy and free speech principles to justify this exception to the general rule that obscene materials are not protected by the Constitution. The Court noted that these principles could not be reconciled with the act of government officials sifting through an individual's library to identify contraband books or movies. Therefore, except in cases of child pornography, mere possession of pornographic materials is protected by the Constitution.

"Indecent" Speech

In the modern legal vocabulary, "indecent" speech refers to speech that contains sexual content but is not sufficiently explicit to fall within the definition of obscenity as defined by the *Miller* test. Except in the context of radio and television broadcasts, where special rules apply, indecent speech may not be banned, criminalized, or otherwise sanctioned by the government. However, the courts have permitted local governments to apply special zoning restrictions on bookstores and movie theaters that specialize in "indecent" adult entertainment.

These restrictions generally take the form of zoning laws that isolate such establishments in a few areas of a town—away from schools, churches, and residential areas. The theory behind upholding these restrictions is that although indecent (but not obscene) expressive materials are constitutionally protected, cities and towns may regulate establishments in order to protect against the "secondary effects"—such as prostitution and other crimes—that the distribution of indecent expressive materials can attract.

Regulating Sexual Expression on Radio, Television, and Cable

Another context in which regulation may occur is when materials are transmitted on radio or television. The Supreme Court has permitted the federal government to regulate both indecent speech (i.e., profanity) and other indecent sexual expression in both media. The theory behind permitting the stricter regulation of constitutionally protected speech in the broadcast context is that broadcasting intrudes into the sensibilities of unwilling listeners to a far greater extent than do other forms of communication. In a case involving a comedy routine that contained numerous expletives, the Supreme Court upheld a Federal Communications Commission sanction against a radio station that broadcast a tape of this routine at a time when children might be listening. Based on this theory, the government continues to require that speech containing indecent material must be broadcast at a time that is later than the time that is allocated to family-oriented programming.

The constitutionality of government regulation of indecent speech that is transmitted over cable television is less clear-cut. On one hand, the Supreme Court has permitted cable companies to ban indecent speech from leased-access channels that are controlled by the cable companies. On the other hand, the Court has invalidated federal regulations that require cable companies that agree to carry channels containing indecent speech to block, scramble, and segregate those channels in a way that permits subscribers to receive such channels only upon written request. The Court held that a simpler, less-intrusive blocking requirement was sufficient to protect unwilling viewers while still protecting the free speech interests of speakers and willing viewers. Although the decisions involving cable regulation are somewhat unclear, the standard seems to protect speech from government regulation more vigorously in the cable context than in the context of radio and "regular" television broadcasts.

Obscenity and the Internet

The Internet is the newest medium in which issues of pornography regulation have arisen. The Supreme Court invalidated the Communications Decency Act of 1996, which was a major congressional attempt to regulate pornography on the Internet. The statute prohibited the transmission of indecent material to anyone who was under the age of eighteen. The statute was premised on the theory that the Internet was intrusive into private homes to the same extent as radio and television broadcasts, and therefore, Congress could regulate speech over the Internet to the same degree. The Supreme Court rejected this theory on the ground that the regulation would severely limit access for adults who wanted to view sexually explicit materials. More broadly, the Court described the Internet as a vast democratic forum in which speech should be allowed to flourish in much the same way as it does in traditional public forums such as public parks. Although the Court did not foreclose the possibility of some regulation in the future, it did suggest that the First Amendment was incompatible with any regulation that significantly inhibited a willing adult from accessing sexually explicit material.

The Internet regulation case may indicate the future direction of law regarding the regulation of pornography. The Internet provides easy and quick access to materials from all over the world, and some of the materials contain sexual expression. This globalization of speech undermines the decentralized enforcement of the *Miller* obscenity standard, which relies on local community

As an example of the growing international concern over the influence of Internet pornography, Charles Winwood, Acting Commissioner of the U.S. Customs Service, held a press conference on March 26, 2001, and announced that the U.S. Customs service and the Russian police had teamed up to identify a group of Russian child pornographers, which led to five arrests in Russia and four in the United States in "Operation Blue Orchid." (Reuters NewMedia Inc./Corbis)

standards for two of its three basic components. The Supreme Court's Internet opinion may portend a shift by the Court to a standard that is defined by individual viewer interest rather than collective community standards. In other words, the world defined increasingly by the easy availability of speech over the Internet shifts to individuals the authority to decide for themselves the moral acceptability of pornographic speech. Under this analysis the government would have an interest only in ensuring that pornographic speech is not foisted on unwilling viewers. Under these circumstances, the government would no longer have the paternalistic responsibility of defining and enforcing a standard defined by the parochial perceptions of an isolated and morally homogeneous local community that no longer exists in the new world of global information.

See also: Broadcasting, Government Regulation of; Cable Television, Regulation of; Communications Decency Act of 1996; First Amendment and the Media; Internet and the World Wide Web; Pornography.

Bibliography

Adler, Amy M. (1996). "What's Left?: Hate Speech, Pornography, and the Problem for Artistic Expression." *California Law Review* 84:1499–1572.

De Grazia, Edward. (1992). *Girls Lean Back Everywhere: The Law of Obscenity and the Assault on Genius*. New York: Random House.

Dworkin, Ronald. (1981). "Do We Have a Right to Pornography?" *Oxford Journal of Legal Studies* 1:177–212.

Finnis, John. (1967). "'Reason and Passion': The Constitutional Dialectic of Free Speech and Obscenity." *University of Pennsylvania Law Review* 116:222–243.

Gey, Steven G. (1988). "The Apologetics of Suppression: The Regulation of Pornography as Act and Idea." *Michigan Law Review* 86:1564–1634.

Hawkins, Gordon, and Zimring, Franklin E. (1988). *Pornography in a Free Society*. New York: Cambridge University Press.

Henkin, Louis. (1963). "Morals and the Constitution: The Sin of Obscenity." *Columbia Law Review* 63:391–414.

Kalven, Harry, Jr. (1960). "The Metaphysics of the Law of Obscenity." *Supreme Court Review* 1960:1–45.

Kendrick, Walter M. (1987). *The Secret Museum: Pornography in Modern Culture*. New York: Viking Press.

Lockhart, William B., and McClure, Robert C. (1954). "Literature, the Law of Obscenity, and the Constitution" *Minnesota Law Review* 38:295–395.

Nahmod, Sheldon H. (1987). "Artistic Expression and Aesthetic Theory: The Beautiful, the Sublime, and the First Amendment." *Wisconsin Law Review* 1987:221–263.

Post, Robert. (1988). "Cultural Heterogeneity and the Law: Pornography, Blasphemy, and the First Amendment." *California Law Review* 76:297–335.

Richards, David A. J. (1974). "Free Speech and Obscenity Law: Toward a Moral Theory of the First Amendment." *University of Pennsylvania Law Review* 123:45–91.

Schauer, Frederick. (1976). *The Law of Obscenity*. Washington, DC: Bureau of National Affairs.

Stone, Geoffrey R. (1986). "Anti-Pornography Legislation as Viewpoint Discrimination." *Harvard Journal of Law and Public Policy* 9:461–480.

STEVEN G. GEY

■ PREFERENCES FOR MEDIA CONTENT

See: Attachment to Media Characters; Children's Preferences for Media Content; Parental Mediation of Media Effects

■ PRESERVATION AND CONSERVATION OF INFORMATION

Information has been recorded throughout time in a wide variety of formats as human knowledge, ability, and skills developed. Cave paintings, papyrus scrolls, handwritten manuscripts, and visual or sound recordings in various languages and formats provide information to people and allow knowledge acquired by one generation to be passed to the following generation. Along with the oral tradition, images, sound, and text have assisted in the transfer of personal, educational, political, social, or cultural information. These materials comprise our collective memory and are valuable and necessary to a society or group of people.

It has been impossible to save all information created throughout the history of humankind. The beginning of the twenty-first century represents an era of unprecedented growth in the creation of recorded materials. Consequently, institutions that serve as custodians of cultural and historical information must make decisions regarding its collection, preservation, and conservation. Candidates for preservation encompass a variety of formats, such as paper, books, photographs, and sound recordings. The decision to save information is based on criteria that considers the uniqueness of the information, its intellectual content, its historical or cultural significance, and its value to future research and education. In addition, valuable items that are in danger of being destroyed are also candidates for preservation and conservation.

Items that comprise visual or artifactual information, rather than written information, may also be considered valuable. Materials such as books, archaeological artifacts, paintings, and other artistic works may not provide direct information in the traditional sense, but still have value due to the knowledge that can be derived from studying them. It is not uncommon that an object may have informational value in the traditional sense, through words, images, or sounds, and as an artifact. For example, a book generally contains information in the text, but it may also be an important artifact in that its structure and format provide information on the process of its creation.

Objects that show value for the information they contain or for the information they can provide are collected and preserved by institutions such as libraries, archives, and museums. These institutions make every effort to preserve objects in their original form. In addition, objects that are in bad physical condition, and therefore at great risk, become immediate candidates for preservation and conservation.

Conservation and Preservation

Preservation involves maintaining an object or information in a format that ensures the continued use and accessibility of the information provided. It includes developing criteria for selecting materials that have cultural or historical importance and assessing their preservation needs; halting the deterioration of materials by providing a stable environment and proper supplies and equipment for storage; developing and implementing policies for the safe use of materials; and providing the resources necessary to engage in an on-going preservation program committed to the continued existence of valued materials. Preservation also includes preparing for potential disasters such as floods, fires, tornadoes, and earthquakes. Conservation is a vital aspect of preservation. The goal of conservation is to stabilize and restore an object in its original form through various treatment methods. Professional conservators are trained to apply conservation treatment methods and make recommendations for long-term preservation of materials in suitable environments.

Preservation and conservation decisions are dependent on a variety of factors, the most important of which is the value of the information or intellectual content an object provides. Other factors that are considered include the uniqueness or rarity of an object; its connection with significant events, individuals, or places; its significance in relation to an institution and the mission of that institution; whether the information provided by the object is available elsewhere; and the consequences of the loss of the item or the information it contains. The current condition of an object, including its fragility and level of deterioration or wear that has occurred during its use serves as an important factor in preservation and conservation.

Conservators and preservation administrators often work with individuals who manage collections held in institutions such as libraries, museums, and archival repositories. Collections managers strive to meet the recommendations from professional conservators and preservation administrators and provide the ideal conditions for the media and artifacts housed in various institutions. Private collectors and individuals may seek similar advice and follow guidelines developed by professional conservators and preservation administrators to protect and preserve items they consider to be of value and to safeguard the information they contain.

While various materials and formats have special preservation needs, there are a few recommendations that are common to the long-term preservation of nearly every type of item. These recommendations deal with temperature, relative humidity, light, and air quality. High temperatures, high humidity, or large fluctuations or changes in temperature and humidity can damage most materials. High humidity encourages the growth of mold and mildew and affects the chemical makeup of items such as film, photographic prints, and audiotape or videotape. High temperatures often speed up the deterioration of materials. Although individual items have specific requirements for temperature and humidity, generally, a stable temperature of 70° Fahrenheit and a humidity range between 30 percent to 50 percent is recommended for proper storage. Light can fade ink and paper, and alter the appearance of photographs, paintings, and other types of artifacts. Air quality is also a consideration because dust, dirt, and other airborne pollutants can contribute to the deterioration of objects and artifacts.

Paper and Books

Since the development of paper-making techniques, paper has been used to record and transfer information, and thus has influenced the cultural and social history of the world. Paper assisted in spreading ideas and information in a form that became increasingly prevalent as people became literate. The availability of paper led to the creation of books, which enhanced the spread of ideas and information. Books are considered one of the greatest achievements of humankind. The information in books assisted in the education of people and the dissemination of knowledge and ideas. Initially, books were handwritten, rare, and available only to the wealthy. However, with the development of movable type, books became available to all people who could read or sought higher levels of education.

Throughout time, as the demand for books and the information they contain increased, efforts were made to find cheaper components with which to create books. In the mid-1800s, in an attempt to lower production costs, paper manufacturers turned to the use of wood pulp (from trees) in the paper-making process instead of linen and cotton rags. The acids in wood pulp, however, cause paper fibers to lose strength, become brittle, and slowly disintegrate. A familiar example of acidic paper is newsprint, the paper used to print newspapers, which is highly acidic.

An awareness of the loss of vast amounts of printed information due to the acid content of paper resulted in an increased use of alkaline or acid-free paper by book publishers. The use of paper that is acid-free serves as a long-term solution for preserving information.

Institutions that hold valuable artifacts and maintain collections of rare and unique books or collections of primary source materials in the form of manuscripts and written records strive to maintain the ideal environmental conditions for long-term preservation of these materials. In addition to environmental controls, papers containing valuable information should not be subjected to direct sunlight, ultraviolet rays, or fluorescent light, all of which can weaken paper and fade writing. Also, paper should not be handled while eating or drinking, as food and drink near books can attract insects and rodents that may damage the paper. As with all types of media that contain valuable information, paper should not be stored in attics, basements, or places where mold and mildew may develop or already be present. Books should be stored on metal shelves or sealed wooden shelves and should be shelved upright. Retrieve books with care and use a bookmark, and avoid writing in books or using tape that can cause damage.

Photographs

Photographs record and store information regarding events, history, and people and provide through study a basis for the development of new

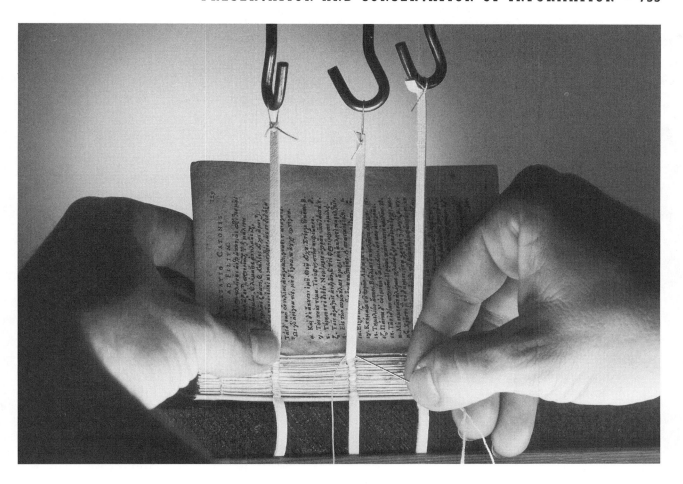

A restorer uses a sixteenth-century technique to rebind by hand an early Elizabethan book in the book restoration laboratory at the Folger Shakespeare Library in Washington, D.C. (Nathan Benn/Corbis)

information. Photographs are also an art form, comprising images created with a variety of techniques, such as the daguerreotype, tintype, and black-and-white and color prints. The process used to create each format is unique, however, the basis for producing photographs remains constant: exposing a mixture of chemicals on paper, film, or glass to light. The outcome of photography is both an image negative and a positive print image. Photographs and photographic paper are chemically complex structures and as such are more fragile and susceptible to adverse conditions than paper. Many steps can be taken to assist in the preservation of the information provided in photographs.

Photographs are susceptible to destruction caused by excessive exposure to light and physical and environmental fluctuations and hazards. They should be stored in an environment that does not have high temperature and high humidity or excessive fluctuations in temperature and humidity. An ideal temperature is 68° Fahrenheit with a relative humidity range from 35 percent to 40 percent.

Direct handling of photographs or touching the surface of a photograph should be avoided because oils and chemicals on human skin can permanently damage a photograph. Photographs should be protected from airborne pollutants, improper handling, as well as fingerprints, abrasions, dirt, pencil or pen marks, paper clips, and cracked surfaces. Photographs should be stored individually in paper that is acid-free or in plastic enclosures that are chemically inert. Paper enclosures protect images from light and avoid potential moisture buildup. Plastic or polypropylene or polyethylene enclosures allow an image to be seen without removing the image from the enclosure. Photographs are best stored in a dark closet on the first or second floor of a house, never in a basement or attic.

Slides consist of a transparent base, made from glass or film, that allows an image to be projected onto a screen. Both black-and-white and color slides are affected by the same environmental factors as photographs on paper. When slides are projected, the image is exposed to a great amount of both heat and light that adds to the deterioration of the slide. Slides are also affected by the acid content of cardboard sleeves or by the type of plastics used in the sleeves for the transparent image. Slides, as well as negatives, need to be treated with the same care and environmental considerations as print photographs.

Motion Picture Film, Audiotape, and Videotape

Films provide information in visual and audio form and are also considered to be artistic works. Motion picture film, both black-and-white and color, is composed of multiple layers that, due to their chemical components, can react to bad environmental and physical factors. Motion picture film is plastic that is made of nitrate, acetate, or polyester. Each of these types of film is coated with a chemical emulsion that holds the actual images.

Nitrate-based film, used prior to the 1950s on 35-mm format, is particularly unstable and can deteriorate rapidly in most storage conditions. It is highly flammable and the gasses emitted from the nitrate can invade and affect surrounding films. Because of these factors, nitrate film should be stored separately from all other materials in a collection. It should never be stored in an area that also serves as a living, working, or archival storage space for other materials. The deterioration of nitrate film can be slowed through stable cold storage at a temperature of less than 25° Fahrenheit. However, the best preservation option is to transfer nitrate film to modern, chemically inert polyester-based film.

Acetate has been used for 8-mm, 16-mm, and 70-mm film formats. Acetates are known as "safety" film because, unlike nitrate, they are not combustible. The plastic of the film can react with the atmosphere and create an acidic byproduct that gives off a vinegary odor, a form of deterioration known as "vinegar syndrome." This cannot be reversed and can spread to other films. Again, the best preservation method for nitrate-based film is transfer to polyester film.

Polyester is chemically inert and does not exhibit the same problems as nitrate-based and acetate-based films. All films are best stored horizontally, in chemically inert canisters, and in a controlled environment. High or fluctuating temperature and relative humidity can damage film by attracting mold, separating the emulsion layer of a film from its base, and accelerating chemical deterioration. Motion picture film should always be protected from light, dust, dirt, and fingerprints. All motion picture film is fragile and its base and emulsion layers can be easily damaged with improper handling or use in either a viewer or projector. For this reason, alternative copies may be produced for greater access to the information or content of the film.

Videotape, another common format for moving images and sound, may contain information that is considered highly popular, such as a copy of a popular movie, or may contain personal information, such as home videos. Videotape is an electromagnetic medium and as such is also highly affected by fluctuations in temperature and humidity, dust and dirt, use in poorly maintained playback machines, and magnetic fields. Videotape is not considered an appropriate medium for long-term preservation. Each time a videotape is played it loses some of the picture quality or signal. One way to ensure that the content of a videotape is not lost is to transfer it to polyester motion picture film and store it accordingly.

Audiotape, commonly found in cassette and reel-to-reel format, is subject to the same environmental and handling concerns as videotape. Analog reel-to-reel tape offers high-quality sound reproduction and is still considered the best preservation format for recordings on magnetic media. Audiocassettes, which also consist of a magnetized plastic ribbon, are more accessible and less easily mishandled that reel-to-reel tapes, but their sound quality is significantly inferior. The temperature and humidity should not fluctuate and a temperature range from 60° to 70° Fahrenheit and a range of 20 percent to 30 percent relative humidity is best for storage. As with any audiovisual format, the equipment used to play tapes should be maintained in proper condition, kept free of dust and dirt, and the tape ribbon should be aligned properly on the reels to avoid distortion. It is also best to create copies of original tapes for access and use.

Preservation of moving images on film and videotape and of sound recordings on audiotape is important due to the unique information these formats contain. Yet their chemical and magnetic components, and their dependence on machinery that may become difficult to maintain or become obsolete, makes the preservation of the original format a challenge. For these reasons, audiovisual materials become candidates for transfer to a new format.

Phonograph Records

Sound recordings or phonograph records preserve information through music and recorded voice and allow such material to remain accessible over time. Recordings have been made on wax and metal cylinders, and on disks made of aluminum, glass, and vinyl. The sound signal is stored within the grooves of recording and is released through a stylus or needle when it is played. It is particularly important to protect these grooves from dirt, dust, and oil, which act as abrasives. In order to protect the grooves of a record and to decrease abrasions, phonographs should be housed in inner sleeves made of either an inert plastic, such as polyethylene, or acid-free paper. They should be stored vertically to avoid warping. Phonograph recordings should be stored in an environment that has a temperature of 68° Fahrenheit (plus or minus 5° Fahrenheit), and a relative humidity that ranges from 40 percent to 55 percent. In addition, a record should be handled by supporting the edge of the record and the paper cover in the center. Phonograph records can be cleaned with a soft lint-free cloth or brush.

Computer Disks, Compact Discs, and DVDs

Computer disks and compact discs have superseded other types of recording formats for information and data. For example, compact discs (also knows as CDs) have essentially replaced phonograph records for recording and distributing music. DVDs (digital video discs or digital versatile discs) have been introduced as a replacement for videotapes and as a way to store large amounts of information. Computer disks, compact discs, and DVDs store information in a digital format. Compact discs and DVDs are created using lasers that burn a sequence of binary code (composed of 0s and 1s) onto the bottom of a disc. Lasers both record and read information from the compact disc or the DVD without direct contact with the surface of the disc.

Computer disks and compact discs are composed of a variety of materials that affect the permanence of the information they hold. They can be affected by high fluctuations in temperature and humidity, as well as dirt and dust. These types of environmental hazards can cause the loss of part of the digital code. Both should be stored away from high temperatures or direct sunlight, and should be housed in dust-free containers. For compact discs, a soft, clean, dry cloth can be used to remove dirt, dust, or fingerprints from the surface of the compact disc. Water, solvents, or sprays are not necessary in order to clean a compact disc. Care must be taken to not scratch or damage the surface of a compact disc or the surface of a computer disk. Compact discs, DVDs, and computer disks should be kept away from magnetic field sources that may corrupt or destroy the information that they contain.

As with video and audio media, computer disks, compact discs, and DVDs are dependent on machines to read or access the information they contain. There is also information or computer data that is dependent on a specific type of software for retrieval and access. This means that it is essential to preserve the media as well as the computer equipment and software necessary to access the information. Computer equipment is susceptible to an adverse environment. High temperatures, dampness, and humidity, as well as dust and dirt, can damage computer equipment and destroy the information or data it contains.

Computer technology is constantly changing and many storage formats are no longer in use or available; for example, punch cards and 8-inch and 5-inch floppy disks. An option to ensure survival of the information stored on a computer disk, compact disc, or other type of media dependent on a computer is to convert or migrate the information to a new format every three to five years without the loss of intellectual content or the integrity of the information. Creation of digital media mandates a commitment to the maintenance of the format over time.

Facsimiles and Reformatting

The artifactual value of an object, or its value in its original form, may make it a candidate for conservation and preservation through the creation of a surrogate or facsimile. The use of surrogates prevents further damage to the original item, in whatever form, by allowing the surrogate to be used in place of the original. An object presenting information often has historic or intrinsic value and must be preserved in its original form. Other issues that contribute to the preservation of an artifact in its original form are its age and rarity. Sometimes, and for many reasons, objects or materials cannot be maintained in their original format and in such cases it may be acceptable to copy the content onto an alternative format that preserves the information but not the original format.

Reformatting original materials onto a new media ideally provides an accurate and quality reproduction of the original and allows the information it provides to be accessible over time. This also assures that deteriorating materials are no longer required for use, and those materials that are of significant value but also have the potential to experience further damage will be protected.

Microfilm

If a source of information, such as a book or a paper document, cannot be maintained in its original format, conversion to another medium is considered an option. Microform technology is an alternative format that preserves information and the intellectual content of materials. Microforms are considered to be one of the most stable preservation mediums for long-term access to information and materials that are not intrinsically tied to their original form. These types of materials most often consist of serials or periodicals, newspapers, and books that are valued for research and scholarship.

Microforms include microfilm, microfiche, and microprint, which are composed of microimages that are magnified through a lens provided in a microform reader. Due to the size of the images on microforms, a large amount of information can be preserved on microforms, which require a limited amount of storage space. Microfilm used for preservation is composed of a photosensitive emulsion made of silver halides. Microfilm made with silver halide and kept in stable, environmentally controlled storage can last for several hundred years. The proper temperature for the storage of microforms is 65° Fahrenheit, with a relative humidity of 35 percent (plus or minus 5 percent). Preservation of microforms also includes the creation of several copies. Silver halide 35-mm microfilm, usually the master copy or first generation of microfilm created, is considered the archival or permanent copy. A printing copy of microfilm is also produced and this copy is used to provide additional service copies that can be distributed for use and access to the information it contains. Service copies of microfilm are made of diazo or vesicular microfilm, which allows the materials to be used at a greater rate, while the master copy is preserved under proper environmental conditions. Microfilm is also considered a relatively inexpensive preservation option.

Digitization

Almost every format and medium mentioned above, from books, sound recordings, videos, and microfilm, can be digitized. Digitization is recognized as a viable option for access to information and for the conversion of information into new formats. Transferring information from its original format to a binary code allows for greater manipulation of materials and the information they contain. Digitization provides greater access to information than any other type of format.

Reformatting and converting materials to a digital format assists in providing access to materials that are fragile, deteriorating, and still valuable based on the information or intellectual content they contain. Digitization provides a high-quality facsimile or surrogate of an original object or artifact. Transferring information to digital formats can assist in preservation because the original item, which is retained, is protected from additional handling that will further damage it. Digitization, however, does not constitute a long-term preservation method of information that is not preserved in its original form and it does not guarantee long-term access and authenticity of the information. It does not replace microfilming or other methods of preservation that can ensure long-term access and preservation. Digitization is preferred for improved access to materials rather than as a replacement of an original object or format that is best preserved in its original form.

Digital media, like magnetic media, requires machinery and software to read the binary code and present it to a user. Hardware and software components and human assistance is necessary to access digital information. Digital information must be migrated from outdated storage formats and software formats to current technology in order to ensure access to information considered to have long-term value.

Conclusion

Preservation assists in keeping information accessible and useful over time. Conservation treatments help to ensure the longevity of objects that have value for their content, so information can be learned from them as artifacts. Preservation and conservation efforts assist in research and scholarly activity but also affect daily life. Access to architectural records provides safety information for building and construction details that may prove useful during a natural disaster. State or municipal records that outline information on the storage of waste can ensure that housing developments are not placed in areas that once held waste materials. Photographs, maps, and other visual documents can help with the revitalization of neighborhoods and business districts. The records of organizations may help them plan community programs for the future.

The existence of information in its myriad forms, maintained or preserved over time, has benefits for all generations. It continues to provide the foundation for development of new information, knowledge, and skills. Societies and groups of people throughout history have sought to document their experience. It is from recorded information that we have learned about past cultures and peoples, how they lived, what they thought, what they placed value on, be it ideas or objects, and even what may have led to their demise. Information stored on paper, in books, through still and moving images, on sound recordings and electronic media, and in works of art, in original or surrogate form, help to define our culture and society, drives economic and political decisions, and should remain essential to our global heritage and cultures. Libraries, archives, local and state historical societies, conservation labs, museums, and related institutions serve as the custodians of these resources and as such make the effort to preserve information for generations to come.

See also: ARCHIVES, PUBLIC RECORDS, AND RECORDS MANAGEMENT; ARCHIVISTS; CONSERVATORS; MUSEUMS.

Bibliography

DePew, John N. (1991). A Library, Media, and Archival Preservation Handbook. Santa Barbara, CA: ABC-CLIO.

Feather, John. (1991). Preservation and the Management of Library Collections. London: Library Association Publishing.

Greenfield, Jane. (1988). The Care of Fine Books. New York: Lyons and Burford.

Higginbotham, Barbra Buckner, ed. (1995). Advances in Preservation and Access, Vol. 2. Westport, CT: Meckler.

Lesk, Michael. (1992). Preservation of New Technology: A Report of the Technology Assessment Advisory Committee to the Commission on Preservation and Access. Washington, DC: Commission on Preservation and Access.

Ogden, Sherelyn, ed. (1992). Preservation of Library and Archival Materials. Andover, MA: Northeast Document Conservation Center.

Ritzenthaler, Mary Lynn. (1993). Preserving Archives and Manuscripts. Chicago: Society of American Archivists.

Smith, Abby. (1999). Why Digitize? Washington, DC: Commission on Preservation and Access.

Swartzburg, Susan G. (1995). Preserving Library Materials: A Manual. Metuchen, NJ: Scarecrow Press.

Task Force on Archiving of Digital Information Commission on Preservation and Access Research Libraries Group. (1996). Preserving Digital Information: Report of the Task Force on Archiving Digital Information. Washington, DC: Commission on Preservation and Access.

M. E. DUCEY

PRICE, DEREK JOHN DE SOLLA (1922–1983)

Derek John Price was born on January 22, 1922, in Leyton, a suburb of London, England, to Fanny Marie de Solla, a singer, and Philip Price, a tailor. Both of his parents were descended from Jewish immigrant families. Price added de Solla as a middle name in 1950. His early interest in science was derived in part from reading science-fiction pulp magazines. In 1938, he became a physics laboratory assistant at South West Essex Technical College and received a bachelor's degree in physics and mathematics in 1942 and a doctorate in physics in 1946 from the University of London. During World War II, he did research in the optics of hot and molten metals and taught various adult education evening courses and armed forces training programs while completing his doctoral studies. He spent the 1946–1947 academic year at Princeton University as a Commonwealth Fund Fellow in mathematical physics and married Ellen Hjorth of Copenhagen, Denmark, in 1947. They had two sons and a daughter.

The period from 1947 to 1950 marked a shift for Price from work in physics to work in the history of science while he served as a lecturer in applied mathematics at Raffles College in Singapore. During that period, he read through the volumes (beginning with 1665) of the Philosophical

Transactions of the Royal Society and not only became aware of the evolutionary nature and the historical aspects of science and technology but also developed his theory of the exponential growth of the scientific literature. He first presented a paper on this theory at a history of science congress in 1950 in Amsterdam. His second doctorate (awarded in 1954) was in the area of the history of science, and it was completed at Cambridge University, where his earlier experience with laboratory apparatus led to an interest in the history of scientific instruments. In the 1955–1956 period, he received a Nuffield Foundation award for research in the history of scientific instruments and prepared a catalog of the instrument collection of the British Museum, as well as a catalog of all astrolabes known to him. In 1957, he moved to the United States as a consultant on the history of physics and astronomy for the Smithsonian Institution. He then served as a Donaldson Fellow at the Institute for Advanced Study at Princeton, studying ancient astronomy, and finally went to Yale University in 1959. At Yale, Price held the Avalon Chair for History of Science until his death on September 3, 1983. He was the recipient of the Leonardo da Vinci Medal from the Society for the History of Technology (1976), the John Desmond Bernal Award from the Society for Social Studies of Science (1981), and was elected a foreign member of the Royal Swedish Academy of Sciences (1983). He worked with the United Nations Educational, Scientific, and Cultural Organization (UNESCO) as a science policy advisor and was interested in exploring the social and policy dimensions of science and technology.

Price's background in mathematics led him to focus on the quantitative analysis of science and scientific development and laid the foundation for a new field of inquiry: the science of science (i.e., scientometrics). Two books of lectures, *Science Since Babylon* (1961) and *Little Science, Big Science* (1963), explored themes such as the growth and development of the publishing scientific community and caught the attention of a wide audience, including those interested in scientific information and communication. Through these and subsequent publications, he sought to turn the tools of science on science itself, measuring scientific personnel, literature, expenditure, and other indicators on a national and international scale. His research included establishing and interpreting the magnitudes of growth in the size of science, such as noting that of all the scientists throughout history, 80 percent to 90 percent were active in the twentieth century. He was an early user of the *Science Citation Index,* which records the links created when authors cite earlier works, as a source of data for investigating networks of scientific papers. He clearly demonstrated the broad patterns that scientists follow in referring to previously published documents and, by inference, something about the way in which new science builds on recorded knowledge. He suggested that relationships within and among disciplinary literatures could be identified and measured via their mode and degree of citation to one another.

In the realm of scientific communication, he explored the concept of the "invisible college" as a channel for informal communication among scientists. He observed that small groups of scientists at the forefront of a research area, but working at different institutions and possibly in different countries, stay in close touch through such mechanisms as conferences, summer schools, and distribution of preprints of papers. Price approached science as a social activity that can be modeled mathematically, and he sought to understand changes over time. His contributions included mapping the structure of science and measuring the size of science. His pioneering role—connecting the history of science, scientometrics, and information science—made a significant effect on the study of scientific communication.

See also: RESEARCH METHODS IN INFORMATION STUDIES.

Bibliography

Beaver, Donald. (1985). "Eloge: Derek John de Solla Price." *ISIS* 76:371–374.

Bedini, Silvio A. (1984). "Memorial: Derek J. de Solla Price (1922–1983)." *Technology and Culture* 25:701–705.

Kochen, Manfred. (1984). "Toward a Paradigm for Information Science: The Influence of Derek de Solla Price." *Journal of the American Society for Information Science* 35:147–148.

Mackay, Alan. (1984). "Derek John de Solla Price: An Appreciation." *Social Studies of Science* 14:315–320.

Price, Derek de Solla. (1961 [1975]). *Science Since Babylon,* enlarged edition. New Haven: Yale University Press.

Price, Derek J. de Solla. (1963 [1986]). *Little Science, Big Science . . . and Beyond.* New York: Columbia University Press.

LINDA C. SMITH

PRINTING, HISTORY AND METHODS OF

Printing consists of processes for preparing identical copies of a written or pictorial text. Writing, which dates from the beginnings of civilization, records messages and enables them to survive over the course of chronological time; printing enables the duplicated messages to move through geographical space as literary and political statements. The first printing dates from East Asia, just after the birth of Christ. Processes for duplicating written texts were invented anew in Europe around 1450, where it both reflected and profoundly stimulated an emerging Western culture.

The history of printing is a history of artifacts and events but also of crafts. Four objects are involved: (1) printing surfaces, determined by what is to be copied, (2) ink, which consists of a chemical vehicle into which are mixed other substances for pigment and drying, (3) presses to transfer the ink from the printing surface to a reading surface, and (4) reading surfaces (usually paper) to receive the printing in order to produce the objects that are distributed through the activities of publishing.

Based primarily on the printing surfaces, one of four prototypical methods may be involved for the presswork: printing from raised surfaces, printing from incised surfaces, printing from flat surfaces, or printing from perforated surfaces. Printing from raised surfaces (i.e., letterpress, using either movable type or blocks of wood, metal, or later often linoleum) is essentially what Johannes Gutenberg invented around the 1440s. It subsequently dominated the printing world for more than four centuries. Printing from incised surfaces (i.e., intaglio engraving, often known as copperplate) was also developed during the 1400s but under circumstances that are less well known. Because it is not tied down to the linear text sequences prescribed by movable type, engraving came to be particularly well suited for maps, music, and works of arts. Its history was soon expanded to include not only direct incision with a stylus (or drypoint) but also chemical incisions of the printing surface (e.g.,

This simple hand press is typical of the type of press that Johannes Gutenberg would have used. (Underwood & Underwood/Corbis)

etching, aquatint). Capable of fine detail, intaglio engraving has become the appropriate medium for modern "security printing" (i.e., money and stock certificates). Printing based on flat surfaces (stones at first, from which came the name "lithography") was developed around 1800. Slow to be appreciated at first, the method has become the most widely used for commercial work, thanks to transfer processes that copy the printing surface on a different medium for inking and printing. Printing from surfaces that are perforated (e.g., silk-screening) allows ink to pass through the perforations. This is the least common of the four methods. All four have been developed and refined to fill particular niches in a decentralized world that has endless special demands, deadlines, and resources.

The Hand Press Era

Gutenberg, as elusive as he is celebrated, worked obsessively over several decades to produce the first printed books. His monumental achievement is represented in two different printings of the Bible (both completed probably soon after 1450) and in other short texts. Behind his work lay the physical invention and visual conception of the movable type that is reproduced on the printed page. His invention also entailed the improvement of presses capable of exact pressure across a large surface and the preparation of ink of the right consistency and color. Gutenberg understood that only if his works were visually convincing would they be commercially successful; their appearance needed to rival handwritten copies in both elegance and detail. The movable type involved complex activities in its own right. First, the fonts needed to be conceived in models that would reflect local tastes (in a time when there were many local manuscript styles), and they needed to be impressive and readable wherever copies were sent. Over time, punch cutters became part of the picture, as they filed and shaped the conception of the letters on the hard metal surfaces of punches and then impressed them into matrices by striking the punches into soft, heat-resistant metal. The matrices were next fitted into molds, into which molten lead was poured to create the individual sorts of type. Gutenberg not only worked out such complex procedures, but having done this, he went further and prepared separate fonts for each of his two Bibles, with several different shapes for a number of the letters.

In the surplus labor market of the day, workmen and apprentices who had been trained in the Gutenberg shop soon moved out of Mainz and took their skills to other nearby German cities, including Strasbourg, Bamberg, Augsburg, and Nuremberg. The printing press was soon seen in Switzerland (in Basel in 1467), Italy (in Subiaco outside of Rome in 1465 and in Venice in 1470, and France (in Paris in 1470). Before long, printing presses could be found across most of Europe. William Caxton, who was active in Bruges around 1475, set up his press in England in 1477. His imprints include several major English texts that survive in no earlier manuscript copy. Each of these printers needed to do exactly what Gutenberg had done. They needed to construct the press, design, punch, cast, and set the type, and prepare the ink. They then needed to locate sources for paper (or often vellum) and work the press efficiently to produce copies that were impressive in appearance. All of this could only be done after they had secured the necessary patron-

age or working capital. They also needed authors, texts, and editors, along with visions of market demands in the form of readers who were likely to want the books and be able to pay for them. Under such circumstances, the perfection and elegance of their books are especially astonishing.

In hindsight, the historical effect of their efforts seems obvious; printing clearly became a driving force in the course of Western civilization. The trends were also subtle and tied in to other historical events, however, so that the effect is hard to describe. The first texts were mostly religious works, as well as the Greek and Roman classics; political and practical writings, and original texts in general, came later. The first letters naturally reflected countless local preferences, but a standardization of the alphabet soon emerged, following national and religious predilections. Black-letter forms were to survive in Germany until as late as the 1940s, and elsewhere in conservative areas into the seventeenth century. Roman-letter forms, as first revived by the Italian humanists, were adopted in the Calvinist world. They soon came to dominate the rest of Europe, except in those Slavic areas where Cyrillic forms were to reflect the importance of the Eastern Orthodox Church. Printing obviously played a major role in the events through which Latin came to be supplanted by the vernacular languages. It helped to codify the orthography of the vernacular languages and, more subtly, their grammar. Serious readers—including legal scholars and scientists— could compare variant texts more easily when printed copies could be seen side by side. Thus, the bibliographical study of physical evidence itself was enriched, and with it, the causes of standardization and of scholarship thrived. Thanks to printed copies, political tracts were distributed more widely in the sixteenth century; in the relatively literate environment of Germany, Martin Luther was quick to call on printed sermons to foster his theological agenda.

Well established throughout Europe by the beginning of the sixteenth century, the press found its first major commercial center in Venice, where beginning in 1501, Aldus Manutius issued small, portable editions of the Greek and Roman classics, the latter in handsome italic type. Around 1520, Paris emerged as a home of scholarly printing, thanks to the Estienne family, which was also venerated for lexicography. By the 1530s, printers, particularly in Germany and France, found themselves caught up in the religious battles of the Reformation. London printers, torn by the religious instability of the early Tudor era, worked together through the Company of Stationers to negotiate an exclusive patent in 1557. In exchange for their promise of loyalty to the crown, they received ownership rights to the works they printed, in an arrangement that amounted to one of the earliest forms of copyright protection. In Antwerp, Christopher Plantin produced important scholarly books; he also served as the major distributor of movable type. The Plantin-Moretus Museum, which preserves the shop, is preeminent as a historical showcase for the equipment and activities of the early printer. It was during the sixteenth century, and significantly in connection with Plantin, that many of the classic type faces that are still in use today were introduced and promoted, including fonts designed by the Franco-Flemish type designers Claude Garamond, Robert Granjon, Hendrik van den Keere, Guillaume LeBé, and Pierre Haultin.

During the seventeenth century, the quality of printing declined because of the political censorship and shortage of materials that accompanied the acceleration of religious warfare in Europe. Pamphlets and broadsides, often with political overtones, are well represented in this period, and it was out of these that the modern newspaper began to emerge. Intaglio engraving came to be used for maps during the great era of exploration, as well as for other pictorial printing and, around 1700, for music. During this period, printers became increasingly separated from publishers, and eventually from booksellers as well. Printing remained a craft, learned through apprenticeship, although its secrets slowly began to be publicly known. For example, Joseph Moxon's *Mechanick Exercises* (1683) provided an invaluable description of the workings of the early printing shop.

Printing was introduced outside of Europe by the church (as part of Protestant or Jesuit missionary efforts and in order to provide service books) and by colonial governments (in order to publicize laws and official notices). The first Icelandic printing, in 1534, was sponsored by Jon Arneson, the last Catholic bishop prior to the Reformation. In the New World, liturgies and other books for use with the native populations were printed in Mexico as early as 1540. In the

A 1592 type-founder's specimen provides examples of the typefaces created by the French publisher and designer Claude Garamond. (Bettmann/Corbis)

British colonies, Stephen Daye's press in Cambridge, Massachusetts (the first printing press in America), issued its *Bay Psalm Book* in 1640. The first books from India were printed by Portuguese Jesuits in 1675, while a British government press dates from 1675 and a Danish missionary press dates from 1712. A Dutch press in Indonesia dates from 1668, and one in Ceylon dates from 1719. Native presses were occasionally seen, one of the most provocative being the later Maori press and its readership in New Zealand.

Printing commerce stabilized in the eighteenth century. In England, modern copyright, vested primarily in the author, dates from the Queen Anne statute of 1710. The newspaper expanded in size, reflecting larger and more literate readerships, and there was a burgeoning output of pamphlets, many of them political. Because these publications challenged the national governments, they played a major role in the events that led up to the American and French revolutions. Other forms of books were first finding their markets and their readers. Printers were crucial to the advent of the earliest novels and to the specialty of children's books. Slowly, and most particularly in the Protestant nations, the printing press came to foster those elusive events through which nations with strong newspaper traditions also have strong library traditions.

In the United States, the press moved with the first settlers, across the Appalachians, prairies, and plains, following the rivers where there were no roads. Quickly, the new nation was blanketed with printing presses. The major publishing centers for books and popular reading materials were located initially on the East Coast, notably in Boston (where Isaiah Thomas first set up his shop), Philadelphia (where the firm of Matthew Carey was located), and New York (with the firm of Harper & Bro.). Local printers, in contrast, provided newspapers and pamphlets, along with state and regional notices and ephemera. From the ranks of the printers and their apprentices came such notable American writers as Benjamin Franklin, Walt Whitman, Mark Twain, and William Dean Howells.

What is known of the production of the early presses around the world consists mainly of books, mostly because books were thought of as items that should be preserved. The extent and importance of printed ephemera can only be guessed at, based on surviving copies (which are scarce) and secondary evidence (which is often ambiguous). Gutenberg is known to have printed indulgences, calendars, announcements, and other odd fragments. His immediate successors prepared a broadside listing the books they had for sale. Playing cards are known to have been printed even earlier. There are also surviving pamphlets and broadsides, which were sold by hawkers on the street. The literature was different from that of the established publishers who came to define the modern book trade and who worked mostly through the booksellers whose premises had slowly emerged out of the shops of stationers. Political tracts are known through the unrest they fostered. These include sermons that were widely printed and reprinted during the early phase of the Protestant Reformation in Germany, the news sheets printed during the time of the English Commonwealth and Restoration, and the pamphlets that stoked the controversy that led up to the American and French revolutions. Other printed ephemera that were probably published in considerable quantity include horn books and tutors for children, announcements, riddle books, songbooks, prayerbooks, almanacs and prognostications, trade cards, ledgers, and posters.

The Era of Mass Production

There is little reason to believe that the flat-bed platen printing press created by Gutenberg changed much between the time of its invention and the beginning of the nineteenth century. Around 1800, however, a growing demand for books, stimulated by a more literate populace, led to innovations that would transform the worlds of printing and publishing. The wooden press came to be made of iron, with its early forms named in honor of its patron, the third Earl of Stanhope. Its successors, among them the Washington, the Albion, and the Columbian presses, tell of a competition that reached across the ocean. Steam power was quick to be used in driving the press, and soon came the larger presses, among them the flat-bed cylinder presses that served the needs of nineteenth-century newspapers and other large editions that required timely delivery.

Other innovations affected the printing processes. Stereotype plates (i.e., castings of whole pages of type) had been conceived by William Ged in the eighteenth century but were fiercely opposed by the workmen who composed the type and distributed it after printing. By the nineteenth century, stereotyping had become a common option for printers, thanks in large measure to the support of the Earl of Stanhope. Meanwhile, the brothers Fourdrinier, working in London in the 1790s, invented the machinery for producing paper in continuous rolls to replace the cumbersomely produced handmade sheets. By the end of the century, stereotyped printing surfaces could be curved around a cylinder so they could be used on large rotary presses, which rolled the plates against a continuous roll of paper to produce modern newspapers and other large press runs. Also near the end of the century, the Linotype and Monotype further simplified the work of setting type by hand. Other machinery was developed at this time to distribute type and to justify the right margins on the printed page.

These inventions all served to provide more reading matter more quickly in order to meet and in turn to create growing public demands. Printed matter from outside the established world of the book trade was promoted, often by enterprising publishers. These materials included children's literature, gift books, sheet music, popular and local periodicals and newspapers, and organizational pamphlets. Books, previously sold in sheets for purchasers either to bind, lavishly or simply, or to leave unbound, were now sold as bound copies, with covers of boards often covered in cloth and, in time, with book jackets. Publisher's bindings quickly became so pervasive as to lead some publishers of the day to tout their work as cheaper for being in paper.

Lithography had been invented by Alois Senefelder at the end of the eighteenth century, but his wide ambition was not matched by capital and the process was slow to come into favor. Its ascendancy dates from the middle years of the nineteenth century, when chromolithography (i.e., color printing) was developed. This process was first accomplished by using different stones for each color, which was obviously very cumbersome. It was used primarily for maps and music, ill-suited as they were to movable type, and pictorial material, such as the famous prints of Currier and Ives. Still later the camera, another invention of the nineteenth century, was used to create lithographic printing surfaces, which led to the heralding of texts that had been reproduced by photolithography. Processes that shifted one printing surface to another one (i.e., lithographic transfer), helped make the process particularly appropriate to reprinting.

Paper, basic to the demand for reading matter, came to be produced more cheaply as grasses were introduced into the pulp and stronger acids were used to break down the fibers. The result was to make more printed matter available in an era of high commercial demand, although the cheaper paper has deteriorated more rapidly than has that of earlier periods, which has created major problems in preserving historical evidence in archives and research libraries.

As a device for attracting readers, printed pictures and decorative effects were also fostered in the nineteenth century. Illustrations, common in Renaissance books but seen less often in the word-bound writings of the seventeenth and eighteenth

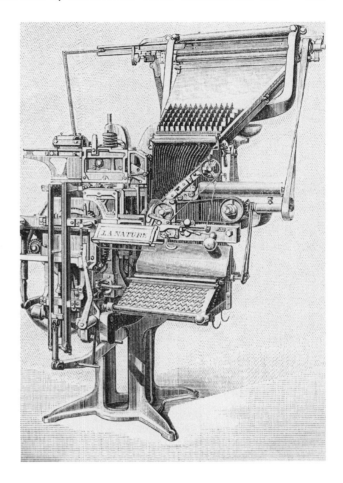

Ottmar Mergenthaler's creation and refining of the Linotype machine in the 1880s revolutionized the typesetting process. (Bettmann/Corbis)

centuries, returned to literary texts. Artists enjoyed a range of mediums for the creation of book illustrations. In addition to woodcuts and engravings, lithographs were now an option, and new processes were developed for metal cuts. For display work, the classic alphabetic forms were distorted with dramatic blackness and fine Victorian decoration, or they were reshaped to fit the fashions for gothic tastes.

Reacting against the "commonness" that resulted from mass production (and with a social agenda in mind), a group of passionate idealists at the turn of the twentieth century exerted a powerful influence on the design of printed matter. Working in London and for the most part socialist in their politics, William Morris, working at his Kelmscott Press (with the guidance of Walter Crane and Emery Walker), preached a return to Renaissance tastes and English folk art. Personal presses, including those of T. J. Cobden-Sanderson (Doves Press), Charles Ricketts (Vale Press), St. John Hornby (Ashendene Press), Lucien Pissarro

(Eragny Press), and Gwendoline and Margaret Davies (Gregynog Press) further helped to revitalize the design of printed books. The cause of public tastes was fostered through the political efforts of Sidney Cockerell and Stanley Morison and with publishing programs such as those of the Nonesuch Press and the Golden Cockerell Press in England and the Limited Editions Club in the United States. New type designs were fostered, based on classical models. Some of the best known of these new faces were created by Stanley Morison (Times New Roman), Bruce Rogers (Centaur), and Hermann Zapf (Palatino). Continental predilections of the futurist, dada, and Bauhaus movements strongly influenced the graphic design of nonbook materials, particularly advertising presentations.

During the twentieth century the printing industries flourished, widening their production of large newspapers and mass-media magazines, of bestsellers and bulk advertising, of an ever-expanding profusion of scholarly books, educational texts, and manuals, and of cards, forms, announcements, and other small job printings. As a surface for printing, paper came to share the press with a wide range of metals, cloths, glasses, and plastics, mostly for the needs of commercial presentation and packaging. New kinds of paper were developed, ranging from the coated stocks used for color illustrations to the alkali forms that promise to survive for library materials. These new and expanding applications have called for a wider range of specialty presses, commercial firms, and trained workers. Photography expanded from basic camera work in the nineteenth century into microforms and other kinds of image copying. Printing has also been obviously affected by computer innovations. For personal use, typewriters have been largely supplanted by dot-matrix and laser printers, while for formal publication, "hot type" (in which the metal itself is inked directly on the printing surface) has largely been replaced by, first, the Photon, and later, by other forms of phototypesetting machinery. The design of type itself has also been enhanced through the digitization of fonts, suggesting that the printing processes will continue to be redefined in order to continue to provide multiple physical copies of written material.

See also: BIBLIOGRAPHY; CATALOGING AND KNOWL-EDGE ORGANIZATION; CONSERVATORS; GUTENBERG, JOHANNES; JOURNALISM, HISTORY OF; NEWSPAPER INDUSTRY, HISTORY OF; PUBLISHING INDUSTRY.

Bibliography

Carter, John, and Muir, Percy H., comps. and eds. (1967). *Printing and the Mind of Man: A Descriptive Catalogue Illustrating the Impact of Print on the Evolution of Western Civilization During Five Centuries.* London: Cassell.

Chappell, Warren. (1970). *A Short History of the Printed Word.* New York: Knopf.

Gaskell, Philip. (1972). *A New Introduction to Bibliography.* Oxford: Clarendon Press.

Johns, Adrian. (1998). *The Nature of the Book: Print and Knowledge in the Making.* Chicago: University of Chicago Press.

McKenzie, D. F. (1999) *Bibliography and the Sociology of Texts.* New York: Cambridge University Press.

Steinberg, S. H. (1996). *Five Hundred Years of Printing,* 4th edition, ed. John Trevitt. Newcastle, DE: Oak Knoll.

D. W. KRUMMEL

PRIVACY AND COMMUNICATION

Privacy, as defined by Judge Thomas Cooley (1888, p. 29), is "the right to be let alone." As the electronic media expands its reach to all parts of the globe, and twenty-four–hour news services are increasing their desire for time-filling material, federal and state courts are seeing more and more lawsuits that deal with the violation of privacy. In their rush to beat the deadline, reporters may find themselves on the wrong side of a privacy tort. While libel cases make the news, and make newsrooms shudder, it is the tort of privacy that the journalist is more likely to be charged with in civil court.

Privacy entered the legal arena in 1903, when the state of New York passed a statute that made it a misdemeanor and a tort to use someone's name or picture for trade purposes without prior consent. The legislature was reacting to the case of a woman who had no legal recourse after her portrait was used in a flour advertisement that was tacked up in saloons, stores, and warehouses.

When media professionals talk about privacy, they generally mean the five tort actions of unreasonable disclosure of embarrassing private facts, intrusion upon seclusion, portrayal in a false light, appropriation for commercial purposes, and the right of publicity. These actions are referred to as the common-law invasion of privacy, although the courts are still refining the status of the right of publicity.

In the latter part of the twentieth century, plaintiffs seldom prevailed in their invasion of privacy lawsuits. However, that does not prevent someone from attempting to recover something of value from the reporter if that person perceives that the published stories have done harm to his or her reputation. Therefore, it is imperative that the reporter become familiar with the five torts of invasion of privacy. This will go a long way to ensure an adequate defense if the reporter winds up in court.

Unreasonable Public Disclosure of Embarrassing Private Facts

Unreasonable public disclosure of embarrassing private facts is the tort that is most often cited in cases that are brought before the courts. It is also the branch of invasion of privacy to which most definitions of privacy apply. Yet, even though the odds against winning are great, plaintiffs file embarrassing private facts lawsuits frequently; only false light actions appear to outnumber embarrassing facts among all privacy cases.

Why do plaintiffs almost always lose? The major reason is that the defense of newsworthiness, adopted early in the development of the cause of action, has almost completely negated the tort. Newsworthiness means different things to different people, but the majority of cases that have applied an analysis of the newsworthiness defense have relied on the definitions of the news media themselves in reaching conclusions. An editor or news director will likely consider any story newsworthy. Why else would the story have been published in the first place? At times, courts may apply a narrower definition—holding that issues that directly affect the audience members are newsworthy, but that facts that are merely interesting is outside the scope of the newsworthy defense.

The problem with this interpretation is that it focuses on the news *value* of the story, especially its political or social value, rather than the personal or intimate character of the information. Such narrow definitions of the newsworthiness of a story also fail to take into account the significance of entertaining or novel information. One of the ironies of the embarrassing disclosure of private facts lawsuit is the increased publicity that accompanies the filing of such a lawsuit. Not only

is the case brought out in the media, but also the original facts are brought forth again and again. Because the facts are now newsworthy, the lawsuit can only pertain to the original publication or broadcast. Once the lawsuit is public, the tort no longer applies.

In most cases, privacy rights terminate when a person dies or when their name appears in a court document or records of proceedings. Therefore, in these cases, the privacy tort cannot be used.

Two additional lines of private facts cases concern whether occurrences of the past that were then a matter of public record or public interest would be public if they were brought out again at a later date by the media. In *Roshto v. Hebert* (1983), it was determined that controlling weight on the decision should be given to the fact that the stories were true and a matter of previous public record. Past allegations, so long as they were made by law enforcement or government officials, are also protected from liability when published.

Newsworthiness by proximity to an event or to another person has been less of a concern. *Campbell v. Seabury Press* (1980) extended the public interest or newsworthiness defense to entirely private persons because of a "logical nexus between the complaining individual and the matter of legitimate public interest." *Campbell* dealt with the publication of remarks from a former sister-in-law in the biography of a civil rights leader.

Where can one draw the line between news and intrusion of someone's privacy? Taking into account what the public finds acceptable in its news and entertainment media, should there be a line at all? The courts are trying to decide the answer. Until they do so, one can see that there are fewer disclosure of embarrassing private facts lawsuits being filed, and of those that are filed, the plaintiffs are losing almost every time.

Intrusion

The tort of intrusion upon seclusion deals with newsgathering techniques rather than what is ultimately published. This tort seeks to protect the right of individuals to be left alone in places where there is a reasonable expectation of privacy—in other words, where someone would normally not expect to be observed by others. An act of intrusion occurs when someone intentionally enters a location where another has a privacy interest. In order

Carol Burnett testified on March 17, 1981, in connection with a libel suit that she brought against the National Enquirer *as a result of a 1976 story that alleged she had been drunk and rowdy in a Washington, D.C., restaurant. Burnett donated a portion of the awarded settlement to the Department of Journalism at the University of Hawaii in order to promote ethical reporting. (Bettmann/Corbis)*

for the tort to be applied, the intrusion must "be offensive to a reasonable person." Content of the news story or the permission of the owner or privacy interest holder is the complete defense for the tort of intrusion. By giving consent to enter, a person has waived their privacy interest, at least temporarily. Moreover, when newsgathering occurs in a public place, or a place where anyone could have gathered the same facts, a plaintiff has no reasonable expectation of privacy—similar to the "in plain view" defense in Fourth Amendment cases.

In reality, intrusion upon seclusion cases present little danger to the news media. Few suits are filed, and plaintiffs win still fewer. The only time that the media is in danger of violating the tort of intrusion is when the media also violates the common law of trespass—in other words, by entering onto private property without the consent of the owner or somehow interfering with the owner's right of exclusive possession. The property in question must be a place wherein the plaintiff has the right to exclude others (i.e., nonpublic, "private" property). As with intrusion, consent or permission serves as a complete defense.

Intrusion can also be closely related to nuisance laws, especially when surveillance reporting

through electronic or photographic means is involved. How a journalist obtains information may be just as offensive to a reasonable person as outright trespass. By using extraordinary means of newsgathering, reporters might find themselves on the wrong side of an intrusion complaint. Extraordinary means include persistent following of a potential news source, in addition to electronic or mechanical means.

The common element in all of these actions is control of one's own property or information about oneself. It is the interference with solitude or space, not the information that is gathered, that justifies the action. However, if the plaintiff cannot lay the claim of intrusion at first, then whatever harm may have come from the publication of facts gleaned during the intrusion is irrelevant.

Routine newsgathering in or from public places is almost always protected from a claim of intrusion. However, if newsgathering behaviors approach harassment, stalking, or public nuisance, the courts have occasionally been persuaded that intrusion or "tortuous newsgathering" has occurred. Tortuous newsgathering includes intrusion, trespass, fraud, harassment, and other related legal issues.

The proliferation of electronic communication devices, including cordless telephones, pagers, e-mail, computer software, and satellite telephones have caused privacy concerns to grow. Statutes at the federal level and in many states are designed to safeguard the privacy of private communications. However, some courts have held that there is no privacy interest in messages that are distributed over unsecured channels. Federal law has been interpreted as creating an interest in the security of communications, not of its confidentiality. In several cases that concerned privacy in the workplace, the federal courts have held that the owner of the communications system can tap into the network and monitor employee communications at any time, without the consent or knowledge of the employee. However, when a third party views the internal communications of a company without the consent of the company, then a tort of intrusion or trespass has occurred.

Is a reporter liable to charges of illegal wiretapping if telephone interviews are recorded without the source's consent? That depends on local state laws. Ten states bar one-party consent recording of telephone calls or of individuals in person. Broadcast news professionals are further barred from airing a recorded telephone call without the other party's consent. That consent must either be in writing or stated clearly by the source at the beginning of the conversation. However, the Federal Communications Commission (FCC), the agency that regulates the airwaves, has allowed exceptions to this regulation for reporters who were investigating crime. The FCC also prohibits the transcription or use of nonpublic radio broadcasts, such as broadcasts that are heard over police scanners, but the commission has not enforced that rule. It has, however, admonished broadcasters to respect that rule, reminding them of their public-interest obligation of not attracting crowds to dangerous situations.

If a reporter interviews someone from another state, is there a risk? Again, that depends on the courts. One might think that the state laws that are in effect in the state where the call originates would be applicable. However, *Krauss v. Globe International, Inc.* (1995) has indicated otherwise—at least where tort claims are involved.

Federal court decisions have interpreted the Omnibus Crime Control Act of 1968 to mean that if one side of a communication knows that the conversation is being taped, then no illegal wiretapping has occurred.

While wiretapping and bugging of private places by the media are illegal, eavesdropping or recording conversation that is taking place in a public or quasi-public location is legal for both print and broadcast media.

Portrayal in a False Light

Invasion of privacy by portrayal in a false light is the one tort that has fared the worst of all torts in the courts. In fact, false light is a legal hybrid. False light accusations concern either false assertions of fact or false implications of fact, just as in libel. The difference is that in false light, the errors need not be defamatory, only embarrassing. Because of that, false light is a privacy tort rather than a part of libel law in that the harm is considered to be against one's dignity rather than to one's reputation. Another way to look at the difference is that libel harms one in ways that can be quantified, whereas false light, while damaging, cannot be easily calculated. Where one lives could deter-

mine whether or not false light is even actionable. Ohio, Texas, and Massachusetts have all refused to acknowledge the existence of false light. These actions are libelous in those states.

The federal courts define false light in specific terms. According to the Restatement (Second) of Torts (section 652), false light is said to have occurred if "(a) The false light in which the other was placed would be highly offensive to a reasonable person and (b) the actor had knowledge of or acted in reckless disregard as to the falsity of the publicized matter and the false light in which the other would be placed." Part (b) reflects the "federalization" of both libel and false light under the First Amendment by the U.S. Supreme Court.

Filings of false light lawsuits are numerous enough to be a concern for the press. However, as with libel cases, false light cases are hard for plaintiffs to win. Plaintiffs might resort to false light claims rather than libel because the action, as defined in the Restatement of Torts, does not require the proof of defamatory meaning. Thus, this means that a plaintiff only has to prove that the defendant negligently (rather that with malice) overlooked an unfortunate meaning, resulting in embarrassment for the plaintiff. This makes false light cases easier to win for the plaintiffs, and it also invites criticism from legal and media experts.

The most typical instances of false light claims deal with coincidental uses of names, fictionalization, distortion, embellishment, and misuse or misidentification in pictures through unfortunate (not intentional) juxtapositions in otherwise legitimate news stories. If there is anything like a general rule to spotting a potential false light privacy invasion, it would be that some inappropriate interpretation or implication could be drawn from the news story.

Appropriation and the Right of Publicity

Using someone's name, picture, or distinctive personal characteristics without securing the permission of the individual was the first type of invasion of privacy tort to be recognized by the states. It is committed more frequently in promotions, advertising, and merchandising publications than by news personnel. Nevertheless, the tort is still of concern for the mass media.

To prove appropriation, a person must prove that they were used in an identifiable fashion for a commercial purpose without prior consent. In fact, the first appropriation case, *Pavesich v. New England Life Insurance Co.* (1905), involved an insurance company that used the plaintiff's picture and name and a phony endorsement. The two elements—identification and commercial use—remain the defining characteristics. The tort is designed to protect an individual's "persona" from noncompensated use for commercial purposes.

Starting in the 1950s, more and more appropriation cases have involved taking the name, likeness, or characteristics of famous people rather than unknown persons. From this line of cases has sprung a new tort, the right of publicity, which seeks to protect the monetary interests of those whose names, faces, or characteristics are marketable.

The obvious defense against a lawsuit that alleges appropriation would be a signed consent or release form from the person whose identity is used. Actually, consent forms are a defense against all invasion of privacy torts. However, the forms are rarely used in instances that are likely to provoke private facts, intrusion, or false light cases. Release forms are important tools where the famous or unknown are to be the subject of news or promotional events. If minors or the mentally incompetent are to be used, the parent or guardian must sign the form prior to the release of the materials. If the signed form accurately reflects the use of the name and picture, then it becomes the complete defense. In the case of celebrities, there is usually some form of payment that accompanies the signing of the form. Oral releases can be argued in court; however, the plaintiff usually wins.

Any major alteration of a photograph or substantial changes in treatment of the subject will void almost all release forms and may open the door to additional false light charges as well. Because the passage of time may nullify the reasons for consent, the media should seek an additional release form before using older images, or if the image is to be used for a different purpose than the originally agreed upon purpose.

The use of images of deceased celebrities will be entering the courts soon, as new digital technology can make long-dead movie stars interact with living actors. The appropriation tort states that the immediate family of the deceased owns the right of appropriation for fifty years beyond the date of death. If necessary, the rights can be renewed once through the copyright office.

While invasion of privacy torts should never be far from the mind of the media professional, common sense should dictate their actions. The public's right to know is almost always inviolate. However, when those rights interfere with an individual's right "to be let alone," the journalist should be ready with the consent forms or be ready to prove that the story was newsworthy and that the facts were gathered in a public or quasi-public place. The journalist should also be ready to show that he or she did not stalk the source or use some other illegal means of obtaining the information. This might not keep the journalist out of court, but will definitely increase the chances of winning the case.

See also: FEDERAL COMMUNICATION COMMISSION; FIRST AMENDMENT AND THE MEDIA; NEWS PRODUCTION THEORIES; PRIVACY AND ENCRYPTION.

Bibliography

Alderman, Ellen, and Kennedy, Caroline. (1995). *The Right to Privacy*. New York: Knopf.

Cooley, Thomas. (1888). *A Treatise on the Law of Torts*, 2nd edition. Chicago: Callaghan.

Ernst, Morris L., and Schwartz, Alan U. (1968). *Privacy: The Right to Be Let Alone*. London: MacGibbon & Kee.

Hendricks, Evan; Hayden, Trudy; and Novick, Jack D. (1990). *Your Right to Privacy: A Basic Guide to Legal Rights in an Information Society*, 2nd edition. Carbondale: Southern Illinois University Press.

Kupferman, Theodore R., ed. (1990). *Privacy and Publicity*. Westport, CT: Meckler.

Snyder, Gerald S. (1975). *The Right to Be Let Alone: Privacy in the United States*. New York: Julian Messner.

ERIC E. HARLAN

PRIVACY AND ENCRYPTION

Although privacy and its protection are hotly debated in the beginning of the twenty-first century, what is being debated is poorly defined. According to definitions of "privacy" and "private" in *Webster's Third New International Dictionary*, "privacy" denotes an element of being withheld from public view, of "belonging to oneself," of "freedom from unauthorized oversight or observation of others." Louis Brandeis and Samuel Warren, in a seminal 1890 article, called privacy "the right to be let alone." But whether privacy is a civil right, a property right, a market commodity, or all of these at one time or another is unsettled.

Concerns about privacy at the time of the Brandeis and Warren article focused on intrusive photographers and gossip columns, not the records of business or government. In the late twentieth century, the issue of informational privacy came to the forefront with the rapid development of electronic communication through distributed networks. Companies transacting business on the World Wide Web (WWW) must ask for at least minimal amounts of personally identifiable information in order to receive payment for orders and deliver them. Governments collect data about individuals in order to carry out functions such as collecting taxes, paying social security, and conducting the census. Information collected in the course of doing business or government is organized and stored; it can be readily accessed and used again to carry out additional transactions or for purposes beyond those for which it was gathered. This secondary use and the possibility of misuse of personally identifiable information have many people concerned about the protection of privacy with respect to electronic records. Encryption, or using a code to prevent unauthorized access to information transferred or stored electronically, is seen as one solution to the privacy protection problem.

Privacy

Privacy would not need protecting if people did not value it. The Universal Declaration of Human Rights, adopted by the United Nations General Assembly in 1948, declared, "Everyone has the right to the protection of the law against" any "arbitrary interference with his privacy, family, home or correspondence" as well as "attacks upon his honour and reputation." The coupling of privacy with home, correspondence, and reputation suggests that it is central to personal relations, some kinds of communication, and even identity. Although the Constitution of the United States does not explicitly claim privacy as a right, the Fourth Amendment addresses the "right of the people to be secure in their persons, houses, papers, and effects, against unreasonable searches

and seizures." There is also a "penumbra" of privacy in the First and Third Amendments. Therefore, many people find a civil right to privacy articulated in the Constitution as well.

Scholars theorize that privacy is necessary for the construction and maintenance of autonomy and integrity and a sense of identity. Within relationships people reveal themselves incrementally to others. They withhold information if they feel their freedom of conscience or of action or their safety would be compromised by self-revelation. The private, or Australian, ballot was instituted to protect voters from threats and pressures from vote seekers. Privacy is necessary to prevent people from becoming vulnerable to coercion or manipulation. For example, the rights of citizens to have free inquiry, association, and communication would be seriously chilled if their inquiries, associations, and conversations could not enjoy a certain degree of privacy.

The right to privacy, however, is not an absolute right. People give up a degree of privacy in exchange for intimacy or friendship. They give up information about themselves in order to achieve something they want or to be responsible citizens. For example, a college applicant divulges a scholastic record for the opportunity to get an education, and a patient releases medical records to an insurance company in order to receive needed care. Citizens reveal income and expenditures to pay taxes. They give up informational privacy.

Informational privacy, or privacy with regard to personally identifiable information, is, as the example of health care illustrates, inextricably bound with other types of privacy, such as privacy of the person. So closely bound are information about individuals and individuals themselves, that the theft and use of another's personally identifiable information is referred to as "identity theft." At least in the marketplace, personally identifiable information in sufficient amounts may equal personal identity.

Computers and Privacy

Widespread concern about privacy in both the United States and in Europe began with governmental development of large-scale computer databases to replace paper files in the 1960s and 1970s. Citizens became concerned that easy access to so much private information left them vulnerable to infringement of their civil liberties.

The result of this concern in the United States was the Privacy Act of 1974, which applied to "systems of records" held in government databases. The Privacy Act articulated what has become a widely accepted set of fair information practices, which have also been implemented by the European Data Privacy Directive of 1995. Subsequent legislation has attempted to address such concerns as data matching—the capability of computer systems to locate information about an individual across a number of databases using a common identifier such as a Social Security number.

In the 1990s, as electronic commerce flourished, concerns about privacy focused on the corporate, rather than government, sector. Distributed computing allowed personally identifiable information to be transmitted across networks and stored in hundreds of databases around the country or even the world. That information, easily sorted by any variable, becomes a valuable commodity, not only used internally by the company for tailoring services to its customers or improving its marketing, but also sold to others. Thus, informational privacy itself becomes a commodity, raising the issue of who owns information about an individual. In the electronic marketplace, for example, when information about which parts of a website a person visits is gathered without his or her knowledge or consent, the individual loses the ability to bargain over use of personal data. The market is asymmetric, with the individual at a disadvantage. These secondary uses of information have increased individual concerns about privacy. Because information can be shared without being destroyed, even one transmission of personally identifiable information across data networks means a person loses control over that information.

A growing concern is the vulnerability of networked computer systems to infiltration or "hacking." Technically skilled thieves can break into computer systems and steal passwords or by other means gain access to private information such as credit card or Social Security numbers, addresses, information about purchases, or health data.

The combination of distributed computing and the ease of searching electronic records makes discovery of personal information easier. A skilled Internet searcher can learn a great deal about an individual by aggregating information discovered legitimately. It is not difficult to find WWW sites that sell access to public records that would ordinarily be difficult to find. More than one company sells software to allow any individual to track another's use of the Internet without the other's knowledge, including seeing every message typed in a chat room.

Either authorized or unauthorized use of personally identifiable data can have deleterious results. For example, according to Paul Clayton and Jerry Sheehan (1997), medical records that have historically been poorly protected and widely spread could be used without an individual's knowledge to deny that person employment or access to health insurance.

If business and government are to be conducted on a large scale over the Internet, ways must be found to protect the privacy of records, especially those pertaining to personally identifiable information. In a poll, 80 percent of those who buy products on the Internet said they were concerned about privacy online, and 96 percent of Internet purchasers said that websites should explain how they use information (Maurici, 1998). In order for electronic commerce and government to succeed, privacy concerns must be addressed.

The European Union (EU) has chosen to address concerns over informational privacy, or data protection, with the Data Protection Directive of 1995. The directive incorporates and strengthens the fair information practices found in earlier U.S. legislation but directs its injunctions toward the private sector, whereas U.S. law deals only with data collection by the government. Organizations must state their policies on data collection, use, and transfer, which must conform to the following principles:

1. Collection limitation: Data collected must be limited to that which is relevant for its stated purpose.

2. Clear and conspicuous notice: Organizations must state clearly in a prominent place who is collecting data, for what purpose, and any third party to whom it might be transferred. Notice must include limits on disclosure of information and the appropriate party to contact to rectify data.

3. Informed consent: Before using data, an organization must get the consent of the data subject. Whether the consent takes the form of opting in (positive assent to sharing data)

or opting out (assent to sharing data by not acting to withhold it) depends on the sensitivity of the data.

4. Disclosure/onward transfer: Organizations must secure informed consent (opt in) before transferring data to a third party.

5. Records integrity: Information must be up-to-date, complete, and accurate; data not meeting these standards should be eliminated.

6. Security: Organizations must protect data from unauthorized use, manipulation, or modification.

7. Access: An individual has the right to review and correct personal data in a timely and affordable manner. The EU Directive also established a Data Protection Commissioner. A number of other countries have a similar official.

The United States, on the other hand, relies on self-regulation by private industry and commerce to protect data privacy, which concerns many privacy advocates. Many companies, however, understand that privacy policies and practices trusted by consumers are prerequisite to thriving electronic commerce. A good many participate in self-regulatory consortia such as Trust-e, which attempts to verify that the companies observe fair information practices. To ensure secure transactions such as the transmission of credit card numbers and other personally identifiable information over the WWW, companies use secure transmission capabilities, including encryption, one way to protect data from unauthorized use.

Encryption

Encryption is the use of a mathematical algorithm to encode any data transmitted or stored digitally, such as an e-mail message, a contract, or medical records. The code is a string of numbers or bits; the longer the string, the more complex the code, and thus the more computational power and time required to break it. Typical key lengths for strong encryption range from 56 bits to 128 bits. In order to receive and decode an encrypted message, a recipient must possess the right key.

There are two types of encryption: private key encryption and public key encryption. In private key encryption, the sender and the receiver must hold identical keys. Because the key is shared, it is less secure than is the key used in public key encryption. In that case, the sender uses the public key of the recipient to encrypt a message; the recipient uses a personal private key to decode the message. The private key is never shared. This type of encryption can ensure the security of a communication. Public key cryptography such as PGP (Pretty Good Protection) is freely available on the Internet.

The U.S. government has developed its own very powerful encryption system, the Escrowed Encryption System, or "Clipper Chip," which is an algorithm etched into a silicon chip. Because the government is concerned that encryption makes it easier for criminals or terrorists to use the Internet for criminal purposes, with the Clipper Chip the government holds a copy of the key in escrow, splitting it into two parts for security. This escrowed key would allow law enforcement, with proper warrants, to decode encrypted messages if they have evidence that a crime is being planned. Privacy advocates oppose such a system. They also oppose the Carnivore e-mail monitoring system, which was promoted in 2000 for law enforcement's use against organized crime and terrorist groups. Privacy advocates fear the misuse of such invasive technologies. It should be possible, they say, to encode data prior to its encryption by the Clipper Chip, thereby ensuring data privacy and decreasing the power of the government to monitor its citizens closely. Seldom addressed is the possible role of encryption in protecting against commercial misuse of personal data. Law enforcement, commerce, and personal freedom contend as the debate continues over encryption as an important tool to ensure informational privacy.

See also: COMPUTER LITERACY; DATABASES, ELECTRONIC; ECONOMICS OF INFORMATION; ELECTRONIC COMMERCE; INTERNET AND THE WORLD WIDE WEB.

Bibliography

Agre, Philip E. (1999). "The Architecture of Identity: Embedding Privacy in Market Institutions." *Information, Communication and Society* 2(1):1–25.

Agre, Philip E., and Rotenberg, Marc, eds. (1997). *Technology and Privacy: The New Landscape.* Cambridge, MA: MIT Press.

Brandeis, Louis, and Warren, Samuel. (1890). "The Right to Privacy." *Harvard Law Review* 4:193–220.

Clayton, Paul, and Sheehan, Jerry. (1997). "Medical Privacy in an Electronic World." <http://www4.nationalacademies.org/onpi/oped.nsf/(Op-EdByDocID)/C96108D0BD0B116A852566750073 B989?OpenDocument>.

Gellman, Robert. (1996). "Privacy." In *Federal Information Policy in the 1990s: Views and Perspectives*. Norwood, NJ: Ablex.

Kirchner, Jake. (1999). "Your Identity Will Be Digital." *PC Magazine* 18(12):142–143.

Lane, Carole. (1998). "KnowX for Public Records Searching." *Database* 21(5):31–33.

Lehrrer, Dan. (1994). "Clipper Chips and Cypherpunks." *The Nation* 259(11):376–379.

Maurici, Danielle. (1998). "E-Commerce & Privacy: What Net Users Want." <http://www.pandab.org/E-Commerce%20Exec.%20Summary.html>.

Shaffer, Gregory. (2000). "Globalization and Social Protection: The Impact of EU and International Rules in the Ratcheting Up of US Privacy Standards." *Yale Journal of International Law* 25(1):1–88.

United Nations General Assembly. (1948). "Universal Declaration of Human Rights." <http://www.un.org/Overview/rights.html>.

LOUISE S. ROBBINS

PRODUCTION PROCESSES

See: Film Industry, Production Process of; Magazine Industry, Production Process of; News Production Theories; Recording Industry, Production Process of; Television Broadcasting, Production of

PROGRAMMING

See: Cable Television, Programming of; Radio Broadcasting, Station Programming and; Television Broadcasting, Programming and

PROPAGANDA

"Propaganda" has been and continues to be a troublesome term. Many social scientists believe that the term is not particularly useful, since arriving at a workable definition of propaganda remains difficult. Other scholars are convinced that propaganda can and must be studied as a separate subject in its own right. No consensus on the definition of propaganda seems likely in the near future, but, after several decades in which almost no studies of propaganda were published, propaganda enjoyed a modest comeback in the 1980s and 1990s. Several important books and academic journal articles devoted to the subject appeared during those decades.

While labeling something as "propaganda" was widely perceived as pejorative through most of the twentieth century, the term did not always have an unpleasant connotation. While Garth S. Jowett and Victoria O'Donnell (1999) traced the systematic study and application of propaganda techniques to ancient Greece and Rome in the Western world, the earliest use of propaganda in a way resembling the word's contemporary meaning occurred on June 22, 1622, when Pope Gregory XV established what was commonly called the *Sacra Congregatio de Propaganda Fide* ("Congregation for the Propagation of the Faith"). This group was charged with evangelization in the "New World" of the Americas and with countering the Protestant Reformation by promoting orthodox Roman Catholicism. However, widespread references to propaganda did not become common until the twentieth century, when propaganda was increasingly associated with the trickery and deceptive mass communication that was employed by the governments involved in the two world wars and in the Cold War. Few people in the contemporary Western world would publicly describe their work as propaganda, since less controversial terms such as "information," "persuasion," and "communication" are available.

The Problem of Definition

The central problem of propaganda studies is one of definition. If propaganda cannot be distinguished practically and theoretically from other kinds of communication, then propaganda becomes nothing more than a disparaging label for a message that someone dislikes. The term is not very useful if it simply becomes an insult or epithet. Several possibilities for defining propaganda have been explored.

Source

One way to define propaganda is to suggest that it is a specific kind of persuasion that comes from a government or corporate source. From this perspective, a lone individual could not engage in propagandizing, but individuals working under the direction of the U.S. government or General Motors could be part of an organized propaganda effort. In the orthodox Marxism-Leninism of the Soviet Union, for example, propaganda was produced by well-trained professionals who worked for the state. This definition suggests that propaganda is ethically neutral, since government or corporate sources are not always or necessarily evil.

Critics of this source-based approach to defining propaganda would argue that this perspective creates another word for official persuasion and/or corporate advocacy and that an additional label is not particularly helpful. Also, some critics of this definition complain that describing propaganda in this way suggests a coordinated, secret, persuasive campaign that involves government and corporate actors, when no such plan exists in fact.

Technology

Another way to define propaganda is to emphasize technology and a variety of modern techniques that are used to reach large audiences. For some scholars, propaganda is in all important respects a synonym for "mass persuasion," whether in government messages or commercial advertising. From this perspective, studies of propaganda only became necessary in the twentieth century when new media technologies (e.g., radio, film, television) began to be used regularly by ordinary citizens. As with the source-based definition, a definition of propaganda that relies on technology is ethically neutral, since mass persuasion could be used for good or ill.

Critics of the technology-centered definition of propaganda would complain that mass persuasion is not inherently different from other kinds of persuasion and should not be given its own, unique label. This complaint is especially compelling when one recognizes that "propaganda" is a term with much negative baggage and that avoiding the term when possible has some intuitive advantages.

Intent and Purpose

A final way to define propaganda is to focus on the intent and purpose of the source that created the message and delivered that message to an audience. Propaganda from this perspective is ethically defective or troublesome because it puts the interests of the propagandist ahead of the interests of the propagandist's audience. Furthermore, propaganda relies on deception to secure agreement on the part of audience members. Even if the propagandist tells the truth, she or he does so as a strategy for facilitating attitude change, rather than because telling the truth is a moral obligation that is normally owed to all other human beings. While propaganda might happen to come from a government source and use mass persuasion techniques, the ethical problems that are inherent in propaganda separate it from more ethical forms of persuasion.

Concentrating on the intent or purpose of the propagandist distinguishes this definitional approach from the others described above. Specifically, while some scholars beginning in the 1930s sought to make propaganda an ethically neutral concept that was amenable to social-scientific analysis, others consistently maintained that propaganda was morally objectionable and, thus, could be distinguished from other kinds of persuasion. If a person who designs a message places her or his interests above those of the audience in the creation of that message, then, by definition, propaganda has occurred. While some versions of this definition compare (inherently unethical) propaganda with (ethical) persuasion, other variations make propaganda an unethical subcategory of persuasion.

Critics of attempts to ascertain intent and purpose in defining propaganda would complain that intent and purpose are hard to pin down since a speaker or writer may not be entirely forthcoming or honest when asked about her or his intent. Also, as was the case above, the justification for a separate label to be used for unethical persuasion is not necessarily compelling.

These three different approaches to defining propaganda illustrate the difficulty of finding a workable definition. Each of these approaches could be constructed as a subcategory of persuasion (organizational, mass, unethical) that does not require the existence of the propaganda label. While Jowett and O'Donnell (1999, p. 4) are right that a "definition sets forth propaganda's characteristics and aids our recognition of it," the need for the term "propaganda" itself is less clear, especially given the long, complex, and largely unhappy history of the term. Nevertheless, scholars who have studied propaganda, not surprisingly, have generally accepted that the references to and research on propaganda make sense given one or more of the definitional approaches described above.

Propaganda During and Between the World Wars

In the United States, the greatest degree of anxiety over the dangers posed by propaganda have involved the U.S. role in military conflicts, beginning with World War I and continuing after the end of the Cold War. During the world wars, preparation for and support of war efforts included extensive government attempts to create pro-war messages and promote attitudes and behaviors that would make victory in these wars more likely. The systematic efforts of governments to influence public opinion were widely characterized as propaganda.

During World War I, the Allied governments produced a variety of propaganda materials that denounced German motives and emphasized the atrocities that were committed by German soldiers. U.S. President Woodrow Wilson facilitated the creation of the Committee on Public Information, which among other activities offered assistance to the film industry and worked to see that pro-war films were created for U.S. audiences. The German government did not make effective or extensive use of propaganda during World War I, but the Nazis learned from the mistakes of their German predecessors and made frequent use of propaganda

FEED a FIGHTER
Eat only what you need—
Waste nothing—
That he and his family
may have enough

A 1918 World War I poster uses democratic propaganda to tell civilians that they can help with the war effort by conserving food. (Corbis)

during the 1930s and 1940s. Adolf Hitler's infamous 1926 book *Mein Kampf* would later be read as a "how-to" manual for propaganda.

In the years between the two world wars, propaganda was widely studied in the United States, despite the fact that references to propaganda had only been common in the United States since 1918. As the events of World War I were assessed, many scholars and public intellectuals described concerns about the public being misled by unethical communication practices. Driven by their belief that mass communication had a powerful potential to distribute messages that would alter audience attitudes and behaviors, these progressive propaganda critics, as J. Michael Sproule called them in his book *Propaganda and Democracy* (1997), wanted to educate the public about propaganda and to help people detect deceptive claims and faulty reasoning. The Institute for Propaganda Analysis (1939) identified several techniques of propaganda that are still widely taught. For example, "card stacking" by a propagandist provides evidence that favors one side of an argument while withholding the best evidence that supports the other side of an argument. Furthermore, "name calling" by a propagandist attempts to discredit a person or group by describing the relevant parties in highly negative terms, as when Vietnamese nationals were called "gooks" by some U.S. soldiers during the Vietnam conflict.

In the late 1930s, those people who favored U.S. neutrality during the early days of World War II recalled efforts by British propagandists to encourage U.S. involvement in World War I. In addition, pro-war messages during this time were often denounced as propaganda. However, once the United States entered World War II, propaganda efforts coordinated by the Office of War Information were again defended as a vital part of the total war effort. As explained in a War Department pamphlet, *What Is Propaganda?* (1944), which was prepared by the American Historical Association, there was a difference between democratic propaganda, which was truthful and provided the information that people need to make up their own minds, and enemy propaganda, which relied on lies in an attempt to fool ordinary citizens into following misguided, dictatorial policies. This pamphlet explained that democratic propaganda was a weapon of modern warfare and that it was vital for spreading accurate information about the war and for inspiring people to sacrifice in order to make victory possible.

Despite the insistence on a distinction between democratic and enemy propaganda, the practice of propaganda during World War II made this distinction difficult to sustain. For example, as described by Douglas Walton (1997), one 1939 newspaper article in London's *Sunday Times* recounted the bombing of a British fishing trawler in an exceedingly unbalanced and one-sided way. According to the story, a German submarine deliberately, rather than accidentally, bombed a civilian vessel and sank it, thus proving that Germany was an evil nation. Later, when the German submarine returned to the area to pick up survivors and give them water and shelter, this only proved that Germany was trying to deceive other nations, who would wrongly conclude that the Germans were not so bad after all. German behavior, whether in sinking the vessel or in tending to the survivors, was always interpreted in the most unfavorable manner. This democratic propaganda, even though published by an independent news source, did not provide for multiple interpretations of the same facts.

Additionally, enemy propaganda was not always deceitful during World War II. For example, some Japanese short-wave radio broadcasts during the war were designed for African-American consumption and argued that U.S. involvement in the war was designed to ensure white world supremacy at the expense of both the Japanese and African Americans. Japanese propagandists in this case were often truthful, since they had only to make reference to conditions in the Jim Crow South to support their claims about racial inequality in the United States. In short, conventional distinctions between democratic and nondemocratic propaganda did not seem entirely consistent with the actual propaganda messages of the period.

The Cold War and Its Aftermath

In the transition from World War II to the Cold War between the United States and the Soviet Union—the two great postwar military powers—both countries made extensive use of print and electronic media to disseminate messages that portrayed their economic and political systems on favorable terms. International short-wave radio broadcasts became a popular means of promoting

In 1949, U.S.-born Mildred "Axis Sally" Gillars was convicted of treason (and served twelve years in prison) because she made Nazi propaganda broadcasts on the German radio during World War II. (Corbis)

governmental causes. For example, U.S. broadcast services included Voice of America and a variety of other radio and television services.

The United States Information Agency published magazines and bulletins in several countries and, since the 1990s, it has maintained an Internet website. During the Cold War, attempts were periodically made to distinguish between totalitarian propaganda, which relied on central control of the content of messages and was intolerant of dissent, and democratic propaganda, which was truthful and allowed for expression of some differing perspectives. However, not surprisingly, democratic propaganda still sought to portray the experience of democratic political systems as being generally positive.

Despite the end of the Cold War at the conclusion of the 1980s, interest in propaganda was renewed by the sophisticated public relations operation of the U.S. military and the constraints on media coverage of military operations during the Persian Gulf War, as well as by the comparison of the independent news media in purportedly democratic nations with the state-controlled news media of Iraq. The Internet and international television broadcasts via satellite also were examined during the 1990s as new technologies that presumably would provide new capabilities both for the distribution of propaganda and for the challenging of propaganda.

Computer-Based Media and the Future

The future of propaganda and propaganda studies is not at all clear. With the creation of the Internet, access to mass media outlets is no longer limited to the wealthy. While nightly news television programming and commercial print, radio, and television advertising continues to have larger audiences than individual Internet websites, relatively inexpensive desktop publishing, electronic mail, and websites will provide convenient and cost-effective means for distributing information and challenging official sources of news. Unless a national government is willing to ban computers, facsimile machines, and other advanced communication technologies, that government will not be able to restrict the flow of ideas and information among its citizens.

When confronted with charges that some message is a kind of propaganda, perhaps the best response is to remember that those who create such messages are not the only individuals who have important duties to perform. Many communication scholars have argued over the years that, unless misled or intellectually incapable of making tough choices between two or more competing arguments, audience members—receivers of propaganda messages—also have an ethical obligation to think through and critically analyze those messages. In other words, if an audience member thinks that something she or he has heard might be propaganda, it is the job of the audience member to reflect on that message, to do research on it if necessary, and to act accordingly. Propaganda is only effective if audience members allow it to be.

See also: DEMOCRACY AND THE MEDIA; GLOBALIZATION OF CULTURE THROUGH THE MEDIA; INTERNET AND THE WORLD WIDE WEB; SOCIAL CHANGE AND THE MEDIA; SOCIAL GOALS AND THE MEDIA; SOCIETY AND THE MEDIA.

Bibliography

American Historical Association. (1944). *What Is Propaganda?* Washington, DC: War Department.

Bytwerk, Randall L. (1999). "The Failure of the Propaganda of the German Democratic Republic." *Quarterly Journal of Speech* 85:400–416.

Cunningham, Stanley B. (1992). "Sorting Out the Ethics of Propaganda." *Communication Studies* 43:233–245.

Doob, Leonard W. (1935). *Propaganda—Its Psychology and Techniques.* New York: Henry Holt.

Edelstein, Alex S. (1997). *Total Propaganda: From Mass Culture to Popular Culture.* Mahwah, NJ: Lawrence Erlbaum.

Ellul, Jacques. (1965). *Propaganda: The Formation of Men's Attitudes,* trs. Konrad Kellen and Jean Lerner. New York: Knopf.

Herman, Edward S., and Chomsky, Noam. (1988). *Manufacturing Consent: The Political Economy of the Mass Media.* New York: Pantheon.

Hitler, Adolf. (1943). *Mein Kampf,* tr. Ralph Manheim. Boston: Houghton Mifflin.

Institute for Propaganda Analysis. (1939). *The Fine Art of Propaganda: A Study of Father Coughlin's Speeches,* eds. Alfred McClung Lee and Elizabeth Briant Lee. New York: Harcourt, Brace.

Jowett, Garth S., and O'Donnell, Victoria. (1999). *Propaganda and Persuasion,* 3rd edition. Thousand Oaks, CA: Sage Publications.

Kellner, Douglas K. (1992). *The Persian Gulf TV War.* Boulder, CO: Westview.

Larson, Charles U. (1998). *Persuasion: Reception and Responsibility,* 8th edition. Belmont, CA: Wadsworth.

Marlin, R. R. A. (1989). "Propaganda and the Ethics of Persuasion." *International Journal of Moral and Social Studies* 4:37–72.

Masaharu, Sato, and Kushner, Barak. (1999). "'Negro Propaganda Operations': Japan's Short-Wave Radio Broadcasts for World War II Black Americans." *Historical Journal of Film, Radio and Television* 19:5–26.

Parry-Giles, Shawn J. (1996). "'Camouflaged' Propaganda: The Truman and Eisenhower Administrations' Covert Manipulation of News." *Western Journal of Communication* 60:146–167.

Pratkanis, Anthony, and Aronson, Elliot. (1991). *Age of Propaganda: The Everyday Use and Abuse of Persuasion.* New York: W. H. Freeman.

Qualter, Terence H. (1985). *Opinion Control in the Democracies.* New York: St. Martin's.

Smith, Ted J., III, ed. (1989). *Propaganda: A Pluralistic Perspective.* New York: Praeger.

Sproule, J. Michael. (1997). *Propaganda and Democracy: The American Experience of Media and Mass Persuasion.* Cambridge, Eng.: Cambridge University Press.

Walton, Douglas. (1997). "What is Propaganda, and What Exactly is Wrong with It?" *Public Affairs Quarterly* 11:383–413.

BRIAN R. MCGEE

▓ PROVIDER-PATIENT RELATIONSHIPS

Provider-patient relations is the study of interpersonal communication patterns and the resultant development of interpersonal relations between providers and consumers within a health-care delivery system. Both health-care providers and consumers depend on effective communication to seek and provide relevant health information in receiving and providing competent health care, and the relationships established between health-care providers and consumers have major influences on the quality of communication between these individuals.

Interpersonal Communication and Health Care

Interpersonal communication is a primary channel for information exchange for both consumers and health-care providers. For example, to diagnose health-care problems, doctors and other health-care providers depend on communication to gather relevant information from their clients about the specific symptoms these clients are experiencing. Without accurate diagnostic information, it is a hit or miss proposition to develop viable treatment strategies. Health-care treatments that are based on inaccurate or incomplete diagnostic information are unlikely to be effective. Health-care providers depend on communication to furnish consumers with information about how to carry out treatment strategies, such as the correct use of prescription drugs or therapeutic regimens.

Health-care consumers also depend on their abilities to communicate in describing their symptoms to health-care providers and in interpreting the recommendations of the health-care providers. Consumers use interpersonal communication with their health-care providers to gather relevant information about the diagnosis of their ailments, their prognosis for recuperating, the specific health-care treatment strategies that are recommended for them, and the costs and benefits of these treatments. Typically, patients have a lot of questions about health care that can only be answered if they can establish effective channels of communication with their providers.

Communication and Relationship Development

People develop interpersonal relationships to establish and maintain social agreements related to interacting with one another in cooperative and coordinated ways. The interpersonal relationship is the basic building block of social organization. People develop numerous interpersonal relationships in their personal and professional lives. These relationships range in their development from incipient (just beginning) to intimate.

All relationships are based on the development and maintenance of implicit contracts, mutually understood agreements to meet one another's (often unspoken) expectations for each other. In incipient relationships, these implicit contracts are few and are generally quite rudimentary, but as relationships develop, so do the agreed upon mutual expectations (i.e., the implicit contracts).

It takes a good deal more time and effort to develop intimate interpersonal relationships because of the many implicit contracts that govern how relational partners are expected to interact and cooperate. In intimate relationships, people learn over time to fulfill the many, often subtle, expectations they have for each other. Through the norm of reciprocity, which encourages individuals to respond in kind to one another, relational partners are encouraged to reciprocate with one another when their expectations are met. As more expectations are met and implicit contracts are established, the intimacy of the interpersonal relationship grows. This is known as the process of relationship development. When individuals fail to meet relational expectations, the norm of reciprocity encourages reciprocal violations of expectations, leading to a process of relationship deterioration.

Furthermore, individual expectations and cultural norms for role performances are continually changing, necessitating periodic updates in implicit contracts. To maintain effective interpersonal relationships, then, people must use interpersonal communication to continually identify their relational partners' different and emergent expectations, to let relational partners know that they intend to meet those expectations, and to share their expectations with the relational partners.

Relationship Development and Health-Care Delivery

Interpersonal relationships are central to providing health care. Consumers and providers must establish clear implicit contracts for coordinating activities in the health-care enterprise. Interdependent health-care provides, as well as support staff within the health-care system, also depend on the development of cooperative relationships.

It is critically important to develop and maintain effective health-care relationships between the many interrelated participants in the modern health-care system. However, relational development depends largely on the levels of communication competence that are engendered by health-care participants. Competence in relational health communication requires the ability to listen empathically, be sensitive to verbal and nonverbal cues, encode and decode messages, and manage interactions.

Complex health-care situations demand high levels of relational communication competence between providers and consumers if they are going to accomplish the goals of health communication, such as increased interpersonal satisfaction, therapeutic communication outcomes, cooperation between providers and consumers, social support, and health education. Insufficient competence at relational communication will surely limit fulfillment of these important health-care goals.

One of the most important competencies related to relational communication in the modern health-care setting is the ability to be sensitive to the two basic types of interpersonal communication. *Personal* communication (i.e., communication that demonstrates respect for others) is a humanizing form of interaction that encourages relationship development and cooperation, while *object* communication (i.e., communication that demonstrates disrespect for others) is dehumanizing, leads to relationship deterioration, and undermines interpersonal cooperation. There is far too much object communication in modern health care, and participants in the health-care system should work toward treating one another with respect to promote cooperation and relationship development.

For example, object communication can occur when a health-care provider conveys object-oriented messages to a client by spending more time looking at a patient's chart than providing direct eye contact during interviews. Providers can also express object communication by dominating the conversation during an interview. Lack of eye contact and failure to encourage participation are likely to suggest that the provider does not think highly of the client and believes the patient is not as important as his or her chart. Such behavior can discourage the client from speaking up during the interview and providing full and accurate information to the provider about relevant symptoms and health history. Failure to provide such information can limit the accuracy of diagnosis and the effectiveness of suggested treatments. By using a more personal interpersonal communication style that includes providing direct eye contact, engaging the client in conversation, and treating the client with warmth and respect, the provider can begin to establish an effective interpersonal relationship with the client, encourage the client to disclose relevant information, and gather pertinent data for making effective diagnostic and treatment decisions.

Patients should also be aware of the potential influences of their use of personal and object communication messages when communicating with health-care providers. It is not uncommon for patients who are in discomfort to be very demanding of their providers' time and attention, sometimes forgetting to use common courtesies (e.g., waiting their turn, speaking calmly, and using polite terms such as "please" and "thank you"). Demanding and tactless behaviors (i.e., object communication) can suggest a lack of respect for providers and may discourage providers' development of empathy and concern for patients. Expressions of courtesy and respect are more likely to encourage cooperation and concern from providers than are less civil discourse. It is a very good idea for patients to communicate in ways that will encourage cooperation and concern from their providers in order to promote the best possible health care.

Content and Relationship Messages in Health Care

Relational communication has both content and relationship dimensions; that is, every time people communicate with one another, they provide each other with both content information about conversational topics and relationship information about the nature of their relationship with one another. The relationship between the participants in the communication process affects how the message is interpreted. In a similar manner, the messages influence the development and interpretation of relationships.

Often people are so concerned about crafting the content of their messages that they neglect the monitoring and controlling of the relational aspects of their communication, especially since relational messages define the relationship being developed between the people. In fact, every time people say something to someone else they have a potential positive or negative influence on the development of the relationship with that other person. Messages that violate the cultural expectations of the recipient provide relational information that will inevitably lead to relational deterioration because these messages demonstrate a lack of respect for the relational partner. However, messages that validate the cultural expectations of the recipient enhance relationship development. Therefore, it is important for healthcare participants to be aware of both the content and relationship implications of the messages they send and to monitor how these messages influence the development of cooperative healthcare relationships.

See also: HEALTH COMMUNICATION; INTERPERSONAL COMMUNICATION.

Bibliography

Beck, Christina S.; Ragan, Sandra L.; and Duprè, Athena. (1997). *Partnership for Health: Building Relationships Between Women and Health Caregivers.* Mahwah, NJ: Lawrence Erlbaum Associates.

Cline, Rebecca J., and McKenzie, Nelya J. (1998). "The Many Cultures of Health Care: Difference, Dominance, and Distance in Physician–Patient Communication." In *Health Communication Research: A Guide to Developments and Directions,* eds. Lorraine D. Jackson and Bernard K. Duffy. Westport, CT: Greenwood Press.

Greenfield, Sheldon; Kaplan, Sherrie; and Ware, John, Jr. (1985). "Expanding Patient Involvement in Care: Effects on Patient Outcomes." *Annals of Internal Medicine* 102:520–528.

Jones, J. Alfred; Kreps, Gary L.; and Phillips, Gerald M. (1995). *Communicating with Your Doctor: Getting the Most Out of Health Care.* Cresskill, NJ: Hampton Press.

Kreps, Gary L. (1988). "Relational Communication in Health Care." *Southern Speech Communication Journal* 53:344–359.

Kreps, Gary L., and Kunimoto, Elizabeth. (1994). *Effective Communication in Multicultural Health Care Settings.* Newbury Park, CA: Sage Publications.

Kreps, Gary L., and Thornton, Barbara C. (1992). *Health Communication: Theory and Practice,* 2nd ed. Prospect Heights, IL: Waveland Press.

Query, James L., and Kreps, Gary L. (1996). "Testing a Relational Model of Health Communication Competence among Caregivers for Individuals with Alzheimer's Disease." *Journal of Health Psychology* 1(3):335–352.

Roter, Deborah L., and Hall, Judith A. (1992). *Doctors Talking with Patients/Patients Talking with Doctors: Improving Communication in Medical Visits.* Westport, CT: Auburn House.

Thompson, Teresa L. (1998). "The patient/health professional relationship". In *Health Communication Research: A Guide to Developments and Directions,* eds. Lorraine D. Jackson and Bernard K. Duffy. Westport, CT: Greenwood Press.

Watzlawick, Paul; Beavin, Janet; and Jackson, Don. (1967). *Pragmatics of Human Communication.* New York: W. W. Norton.

GARY L. KREPS

PSYCHOLOGICAL MEDIA RESEARCH, ETHICS OF

Research ethics are the moral principles and rules of conduct that guide research. In general, researchers must balance two major obligations: (1) contribute to knowledge through research, which ultimately should benefit society, and (2) protect the rights and welfare of research participants. Federally funded research must conform to the ethical guidelines of the U.S. Department of Health and Human Services. Many professional associations, such as the American Psychological Association, have ethical guidelines for research with human participants. Most academic institutions require that research proposals be reviewed for ethical standards by institutional review boards (IRBs). Applying ethical principles to research situations is a complex process that requires the consideration of many factors.

Assessing Risks and Benefits

Researchers must assess risks (e.g., costs, harms) and benefits when deciding whether and how to conduct a research study. Any risks to research participants must be carefully weighed in relation to the potential benefits of the research to the participants and to society. Risks of participating in research include the possibility of physical harm or discomfort, as well as psychological harms such as anxiety, embarrassment, reduced self-esteem, and invasion of privacy. The possibility of psychological harm is a serious concern in psychological media research, because studies often examine the harmful effects of media messages. Researchers are obligated to inform participants beforehand about any risks associated with the study and to remove any harms that may have been induced (e.g., fear) during the study. Researchers can reduce the possibility of harm by studying people who have already experienced an aversive state (e.g., interview people about past reactions to horror films) or by inducing minimal levels of stress (e.g., show children a mildly scary film rather than a graphic horror film).

Informed Consent

In general, individuals must be free to choose whether or not to participate in research, and must agree to accept any risks voluntarily. Researchers must avoid coercion, which may occur if someone in authority recruits participants or when large incentives are offered. According to the American Psychological Association (1992), before participating in research, individuals must be informed about the nature of the research, be told that participation is voluntary and that they may withdraw at any time, and be informed about any aspects of the study that might reasonably be expected to influence their willingness to participate (e.g., risks). Often, research participants are not fully informed beforehand about the purposes and procedures of a study, because this would compromise the validity of the research. For example, the responses that participants have to a public-service announcement about safe sex may be affected if the participants know that the source of the message (expert versus peer) was being manipulated. The key issue to consider is whether any concealed information would be likely to affect the decision of an individual to participate.

Occasionally, researchers actively deceive research participants about aspects of a study. Common forms of deception include providing a "cover story," or misinformation about the purpose of the study, using an experimental confederate who acts out a planned role, or providing false feedback during the study. For example, to create a more natural viewing situation, a study of memory for commercials may be described as a study of responses to the comedy program in which the commercials appear. Not all researchers agree on the ethics of using deception. Some feel deception is never justified, because it denies individuals the freedom to make an informed decision about research participation. Others feel deception is

justified when the research is meaningful and cannot be conducted any other way, when there is no deception about possible risks, and when participants are debriefed afterward.

Informed consent may not be required in certain field settings. These would include naturalistic observation in a public place and field experiments in which the treatment is within the range of normal experience and poses no risk. For example, a researcher who observed travelers watching television on airport monitors probably would not need informed consent.

Debriefing

At the conclusion of a research study, debriefing is used to inform participants about the full nature and purpose of the study, to explain the necessity for any concealment or deception, and to remove any harm created by the research. For example, research on the effects of violent sexual content in the media typically uses extensive debriefings, including researcher-led discussions. These procedures are designed not only to inform participants about the study, but also to ensure that any adverse effects of participating (e.g., increased acceptance of rape myths) are removed.

Privacy

All individuals have a right to control access to themselves and to information about themselves. Privacy may be protected, in part, through anonymity or confidentiality. Anonymity means that the researcher does not obtain any identifying information about participants. Confidentiality means that the researcher agrees not to reveal to others any information obtained from participants and that the researcher will disguise identifying characteristics when reporting the results of the research. Privacy issues are of particular concern whenever a researcher plans to film or record participants, gain access to personal records, or ask sensitive personal questions. These procedures can be used responsibly if the researcher is sensitive to the concerns of participants, obtains informed consent, and maintains anonymity or confidentiality.

Research with Special Populations

Special precautions must be taken when conducting research with any population that might be especially vulnerable to research risk or have a reduced capacity to consent to participate, such as individuals who are mentally disabled, ill, or victimized. Another special group is children (under eighteen years of age), who are the focus of much psychological media research. Research with children requires both documented permission from a parent or guardian and the child's agreement to participate. Children are more susceptible to coercion than adults and must be made fully aware that they are under no obligation to participate. Special care must be taken to limit the risks associated with the research. Developmental factors must be considered when judging how children of different ages will respond to research protocols. Debriefing, which must be age-appropriate may be unnecessary with young children who have a limited ability to understand the purpose of the research or the procedures that are involved. In any case, it is important that children leave the research setting in a positive state.

Reporting of Research

Researchers must also make ethical decisions about interpreting and communicating research results. The data must be analyzed appropriately, the procedures and results described fully and accurately, and those who contributed to the research must be given proper acknowledgment. Research reports typically undergo peer review to ensure the quality and significance of the research before being shared with the scientific community (e.g., through publications). Research findings should also be communicated to the general public (e.g., through the news media) when it is likely that the public may benefit from the knowledge. For example, research on children's responses to media messages can aid parents in helping their children become responsible media consumers. Psychological media research should contribute to scientific understanding, but ultimately it should also benefit society.

See also: AUDIENCE RESEARCHERS; CHILDRENS' COMPREHENSION OF TELEVISION; MARKETING RESEARCH, CAREERS IN; RESEARCHERS FOR EDUCATIONAL TELEVISION PROGRAMS; RESEARCH METHODS IN INFORMATION STUDIES; VIOLENCE IN THE MEDIA, HISTORY OF RESEARCH ON.

Bibliography

Allen, Mike; D'Alessio, Dave; Emmers, Tara M.; and Gebhardt, Lisa. (1996). "The Role of Experimental Briefings in Mitigating Effects of Experimental Exposure to Violent Sexually Explicit Material: A Meta-Analysis." *Journal of Sex Research* 33:135–141.

American Psychological Association. (1992). "Ethical Principles and Code of Conduct." *American Psychologist* 47:1597–1611.

Greenberg, Bradley S., and Garramone, Gina M. (1989). "Ethical Issues in Mass Communication." In *Research Methods in Mass Communication*, eds. Guido H. Stempel III and Bruce H. Westley. Englewood Cliffs, NJ: Prentice-Hall.

Kimmel, Allan J. (1996). *Ethical Issues in Behavioral Research: A Survey.* Cambridge, MA: Blackwell.

Littlejohn, Stephen W. (1991). "Deception in Communication Research." *Communication Reports* 4:51–54.

National Commission for the Protection of Human Subjects of Biomedical and Behavioral Research. (1978). *The Belmont Report: Ethical Principles and Guidelines for the Protection of Human Subjects of Research.* (DHEW Publication No. (OS) 78-0012). Washington, DC: U.S. Government Printing Office.

Sieber, Joan E. (1992). *Planning Ethically Responsible Research: A Guide for Students and Internal Review Boards.* Newbury Park, CA: Sage Publications.

Stanley, Barbara, and Sieber, Joan E., eds. (1992). *Social Research on Children and Adolescents: Ethical Issues.* Newbury Park, CA: Sage Publications.

CYNTHIA A. HOFFNER

■ PUBLIC BROADCASTING

Public broadcasting in the United States is widely seen as an important component of the media culture of the nation (Carnegie Commission, 1979; Twentieth Century Fund, 1993). Its programming and the terms of public support for it are not without criticism; it has its detractors from both the right and the left, and it regularly is a subject of debate. On the whole, however, public broadcasting tends to be endorsed as a social good; American society is seen as being better off for having it because of its role in broadening the base of information, education, cultural experience, and political discourse.

However, U.S. public broadcasting is much different from its counterparts abroad. By comparison with other major systems of public-service broadcasting (e.g., in Great Britain, Canada, Germany, Italy, Japan, and most other advanced "information societies"), the U.S. enterprise is not seen to be as central and as important to the overall national media culture. It is largely an afterthought, heavily rooted in a formal educational rationale and in some eyes serving principally as a palliative to the perceived shortcomings of the dominant commercial broadcasting system upon which it has been grafted.

Overview

Broadcasting began in the 1920s, and by the middle of the century, it had developed its various basic institutional structures and social roles throughout the world. In other industrialized, democratic nations, broadcasting typically began and grew around a model of itself as a cultural institution, as an extension of language, arts, and national identity. In contrast, U.S. broadcasting was considered at the outset to be principally a business enterprise, as a creature and promoter of commerce, and this has continued to be the prevailing view.

As in other countries, U.S. broadcasting has been subject to regulatory oversight. It is licensed under the assumptions of spectrum scarcity and related expectations about its public trustee obligations as a government sanctioned quasi-monopoly. In the United States, the fiduciary responsibilities of commercial broadcasting (to serve "the public interest, convenience, and necessity") were initially considered to be adequate to guarantee a broad range of services, such that no other major institutional alternative was seriously or widely contemplated. As a result, there was no commitment to a general model of a public-service broadcasting institution in the United States. The small, decentralized educational, noncommercial alternative that did emerge was considered to be only marginally necessary and was forced to begin life swimming upstream against the materialist currents of the dominant media structures and purposes.

Simultaneously, the modest educational broadcasting enterprise developed around a doctrine of localism and a resistance to the establishment of strong, national producing and programming entities. As such, it reflected the general public-policy structure for education in the United States, as well as the deeper constitutional debates about the structure of American government and politics.

During the latter third of the twentieth century, U.S. public broadcasting was given a new, seemingly firmer, public-policy mandate, plus public and private resources that were sufficient for it to build a system of local and national entities (i.e.,

stations, networks, and support agencies). That system was markedly larger and more stable than what had been imagined at the outset for noncommercial broadcasting. Nonetheless, at the beginning of the twenty-first century, it still remains a relatively small part of the overall broadcasting, media, and telecommunications nexus in the United States. Additionally, even as its existence seems more secure, it also is facing the substantial challenges of a new era of digital communications technology, marked by a widespread process of convergence and reconfiguration in media forms. Those developments are associated with increasingly rapid, broadband, multimedia and interactive forms of production and distribution, new business models, and changing regulatory assumptions.

History of Educational and Public Broadcasting

U.S. public broadcasting began in the 1920s and 1930s as a small collection of noncommercial radio stations that were licensed principally to educational institutions such as colleges, universities, and local schools. These stations were largely independent of one another, and they operated without any federal or even significant state or local funding. At the outset, public broadcasting had no special status under the relevant pieces of federal legislation (i.e., the Radio Act of 1927 and the Communications Act of 1934). Consequently, for its first twenty years, it also had no special regulatory protection through either the Federal Radio Commission (FRC) or the Federal Communications Commission (FCC), and for most of its first forty years, public broadcasting had relatively modest production capacities, little national programming, and no permanent interconnection (i.e., network) facilities. By the mid-1940s, noncommercial radio had been granted some reserved space in the emerging new FM (i.e., frequency modulation) band, though that status was never built back into the prior and then still dominant AM (i.e., amplitude modulation) band.

With the arrival of television in the early 1950s, interest in noncommercial broadcasting began to spread beyond school boards and colleges to national and community organizations that were seeking to develop broader-ranging social and cultural programming services that would be of interest to general audiences. The FCC also, in 1952, extended its spectrum reservation policy into the table of allocations for the very high frequency (VHF) and ultra high frequency (UHF) ranges. However, for most of its first decade or so and for most of its stations, the primary purposes of noncommercial television remained those of formal instruction (ITV) and education (ETV), and it had no major forms of national support and encouragement.

As with radio before it, certain dissatisfactions with the performance of commercial television began to emerge, and with them came increasing pressures for a more general-audience, public-service institution. This combination led to the activation of more stations and program exchanges in the noncommercial realm. The growth of the number of stations was stimulated by the direct aid of the Ford Foundation, which made capital facility grants to community and educational organizations throughout the country, and by the increasing interest of many universities and state agencies in building ETV capacities. By the mid-1960s, more than one hundred ETV and nearly four hundred noncommercial radio stations were on the air.

As their numbers, resources, and common needs had grown, the stations had formed a few of their own collective trade and service organizations at the state, regional, and national levels. The foremost of these, the National Association of Educational Broadcasters (NAEB), had roots dating back to the prewar educational radio days, and it had developed radio and television divisions that provided programming and other professional services. The Ford Foundation had helped create a rudimentary national production service and network, the National Educational Television and Radio Center (NETRC, later known as NET), which came to focus exclusively on television. It produced and distributed a regular but modest (and only videotape delivered) schedule of cultural and public-affairs programming. Meanwhile, as the number of stations grew, they formed new regional organizations, such as the Eastern Educational Network (EEN), the Central Educational Network (CEN), the Southern Educational Communications Association (SECA), and the Pacific Mountain Network (PMN), principally to provide more programming for exchange among the stations. Comparable regional associations also were created for radio.

The growing number of noncommercial entities and audiences created a critical mass of awareness, interest, and public support that led to more coordinated and explicit planning for the development of stronger national program production and networking capacities and for larger amounts of funding. Those interests began to focus particularly on the question of federal funding, and they culminated in the work of the Carnegie Commission and the passage of the Public Broadcasting Act of 1967. This act laid out the basic plan for completing the transformation from a relatively narrowly defined and unique U.S. educational broadcasting model to one that encompassed more of the general-audience purposes of public-service broadcasting, as reflected in similar institutions abroad.

Building on the tradition and imperatives of the largely decentralized, locally focused U.S. system of noncommercial radio and television, the 1967 act led to a series of actions that established the national structure and core dynamics that would define U.S. public broadcasting for the remainder of the twentieth century. The Public Broadcasting Act of 1967 chartered a new national, but theoretically nongovernmental, agency—the Corporation for Public Broadcasting (CPB). The act established a CPB governing board to be appointed by the president of the United States and confirmed by the U.S. Senate. It also authorized the corporation to receive federal funds and, in turn, to use those resources to create national systems of interconnection, to provide larger amounts of national programming, and to channel support directly to the noncommercial radio and television stations around the country.

Shortly after its own incorporation in 1969, working with the existing base of stations and other parties, CPB created two new organizations to manage the national interconnection systems—the Public Broadcasting Service (PBS) for television and National Public Radio (NPR) for radio. As a result of compromises with the stations, particularly with the larger producing stations in several major cities, national public television programming was to be produced by the stations themselves and other independent entities. PBS was to be the coordinator of the national schedule for public television, but it was not authorized to produce programs, and the stations were to retain considerable autonomy in decisions about when to carry the national programs. In radio, the stations had the same scheduling autonomy, but NPR

On July 30, 1970, Joan Ganz Cooney, president of the Children's Television Workshop, testified in relation to the benefits of educational television before a Senate subcommittee on Equal Educational Opportunities. (Bettmann/Corbis)

was given both authority and CPB resources for producing national programming.

Throughout the 1970s, the initial structure of U.S. public broadcasting solidified, though it also continued to change on the margins. In other countries, one or two organizations tended to lie at the heart of the public-service broadcasting enterprise. In the United Kingdom, for example, the British Broadcasting Corporation (BBC), founded in 1922, received the bulk of the funding designated for public radio and television; it operated several national networks and many local stations, and it produced nearly all of the programming that was carried on its networks. In the United States, such singular dominance never existed, even after the development of the new national structure. CPB was a sort of *primus inter pares* among the national organizations, but it had no direct operational responsibilities for production, programming, or distribution. It could only facilitate those functions through other organizations. Also, while its national funding mandate gave it certain responsibilities for speaking to the White House, the U.S. Congress, and the press on behalf of public broadcasting, that authority was never total, with many of the representation functions remaining with the stations themselves and with their membership organizations.

The multiplicity and divided responsibilities of those agencies, as reflected in PBS, NPR, the regional networks, and the vast diversity and sheer growing numbers of stations, meant that programming and policy authority in the United States was highly diffuse. Nonetheless, the funding, programming, and board appointment experiences during the early years of CPB led to concerns that its influence, and that of the president and the Congress through it, were too great. As a result, by the early 1980s, both PBS and NPR had been through major organizational and governance crises that had led to greater independence from CPB and more explicit station ownership and control. Those reorganizations also differentially affected the national representation functions in public radio and television. Whereas NPR had not had such responsibilities for the public radio system at the outset, it did by 1977. Alternatively, a new organization in public television—America's Public Television Stations (APTS)—was formed in 1980 to provide regulatory and legislative services independently from PBS.

This pattern of churning reorganization and constant, often inconsistent, debate about the roles and authority of the national organizations reflected the persistence of a strong local-station base in U.S. public broadcasting and the continuing debates over the appropriate extent of its federalist character. The newer national organizations had been welcomed as practical necessities if public broadcasting was to become anything more significant than a relatively small, dry, narrowly focused set of pedagogically oriented stations. However, there was little willingness within the system or in Congress and successive presidential administrations to permit the national organizations to coalesce and have the resources that would allow them to become strong centers along the models of commercial American broadcasters or public broadcasting abroad.

Meanwhile, although many licensees, particularly in radio, continued to be educational institutions, the newer stations and the growing number of state networks were increasingly licensed to nonprofit community groups. Unable to justify the costs in relationship to the value of their instructional services, and responding to the emerging emphasis on a more general-audience orientation, some school board and higher education licensees actually transferred station ownership to community organizations. In statewide systems, there also was a growing emphasis on governance by independent boards of directors made up of state and community leaders.

This public-service, corporate governance structure was similar to the pattern for other public U.S. cultural institutions such as museums, arts centers, and hospitals, and it had several consequences. It tended to draw to public broadcasting a powerful cross-section of professional, business, and cultural leadership well beyond the education sphere, thereby broadening its base of legitimization in the eyes of the public and state and federal political leaders. It opened the stations to a wider range of funding support, particularly in the private sector, and it also strengthened the authority of the local and state licensees relative to the newer and ever-growing national entities.

Meanwhile, other aspects of the public broadcasting system were continuing to change. In the mid-1970s, with congressional and CPB help, the interconnection systems had abandoned the conventional network structure of terrestrial land lines and microwave telephony for a new distribution system via geostationary orbiting satellites. As the newer national organizations developed, others waned. NET had been absorbed into one of the New York City public stations (WNDT, which became WNET) as a national program division. With the rise of CPB, PBS, and NPR, the role of NAEB became less clear. NAEB lost the financial and institutional support of the stations, which were now paying dues to the newer national programming and interconnection services. Increasingly defined as a professional association and therefore more dependent on the smaller revenues of individual memberships, NAEB finally went out of business in 1981.

Similarly, the regional television networks, now bypassed by the satellite system, began to abandon or substantially redefine their original roles as programming entities, with concomitant name changes and new charters. By the late-1990s, EEN had emerged as a general national programmer (i.e., American Public Television). CEN and SECA had added many aspects of the professional association work that had been lost with the demise of NAEB and changed their names to the American Telecommunications Group (ATG) and the National Educational Television Association (NETA), respectively. PMN

had ceased to exist as an operating organization altogether.

Although certain large-city public television stations, such as WNET in New York, WGBH in Boston, and WETA in Washington, D.C., continued to provide the majority of the programs on the PBS schedule, and did so in partnership with nonstation organizations such as the Children's Television Workshop (CTW), more stations and state networks across the country were offering programs for national distribution and competing for scarce national program dollars. Meanwhile, pressures for diversity of voice and access led in 1991 to the statutory creation of the Independent Television Service (ITVS) to promote program production and distribution outside of the normal process that had been developed by CPB, PBS, and the major producing stations. In radio, NPR remained the dominant producer and distributor, but over time, American Public Radio, later Public Radio International (PRI), grew up from within Minnesota Public Radio (MPR) and became a substantial competitor to NPR. In time, even MPR itself became a competitor to both NPR and PRI.

These changes were facilitated by the widening, more flexible distribution capacities of satellite and cable technologies and the steady, if small, growth of revenues in the public system. With an increasing demand for more diversity of service and the proliferation of program sources, the growth in the number of stations tended to shift away from the few remaining under-served areas in remote, rural portions of the country toward urban centers, providing an increasing number of communities with access to multiple public broadcasting signals. By the mid-1990s, well over one-half of the U.S. population was capable of receiving three or more public radio stations and two or more public television stations. To some people, this phenomenon became known as the "multiple services problem," which implied an unwarranted duplication of services and waste of scarce resources. To others, it was the "overlap opportunity" that provided capacity for a wider range of program streams and community services similar to the stronger public-service broadcasting institutions abroad and parallel to the differentiated, audience-niche program channels that were being developed in commercial radio, cable, satellite, and Internet telecommunications.

The institutional structure of public broadcasting by the end of the twentieth century reflected an uneasy amalgam of both its deep-set Jeffersonian, decentralized educational heritage and its post-1967 efforts to create a more coherent quasi-federalist model and a powerful, general-audience, national public-service media presence. The agencies that had been put in place by the early 1980s remained largely intact. Newer associations of stations and other interests, such as the Station Resource Group (SRG) in radio and the National Forum for Public Television Executives (Forum), the Program Resources Group (PRG), and the Hartford Gunn Institute (HGI) in television, had come into being to address issues and provide services that the existing agencies appeared to be unable to render.

However, the overall structure and the fundamental issues that faced public broadcasting remained. The substantial funding, technological, and overall policy problems that faced public broadcasting persisted. Individually and collectively, these matters had significant implications for the system, raising all the traditional questions about public broadcasting's own sense of itself and the public expectations for it. Additional national studies and task forces had tried to address them (Carnegie Commission, 1979; Twentieth Century Fund, 1993), but significant resolutions remained elusive. The continuing limits of public-policy commitment to public broadcasting were perhaps most clearly apparent when there was no mention of public broadcasting in the Telecommunications Act of 1996, the most sweeping piece of U.S. communications legislation since 1934.

Public Policy and Funding Patterns

The strengths and weaknesses of U.S. public broadcasting are reflected in the structure and amounts of its funding and in the associated legislative and regulatory environment.

The principal strength of the system's funding pattern is its diversity. Public broadcasting abroad tends to be supported by a combination of annual taxes for the right to own and use television sets (i.e., license fees) and limited amounts of commercial advertising. By comparison, the U.S. system has a much wider variety of revenue sources. This pattern of multiple public and private funding tends to protect it from direct control by any single social institution, such as government or business.

The financial situation of U.S. public broadcasting improved considerably after the Public Broadcasting Act of 1967. By the year 2000, that growth had led to the establishment of nearly eleven hundred CPB-qualified radio and television stations, a sophisticated satellite distribution system, two full-time national networks, various other national and regional services, thousands of hours of original programming every year (with much of it having exceptionally high quality), and a professional cadre of more than sixteen thousand employees. The infusion of federal funds also helped strengthen the other public and private sources of support.

However, a major weakness of the funding system was the relatively small amount of actual funding that it provided. Total funding for public broadcasting had reached $2.0 billion by 1998, but that amount was only 2 percent of the total revenues for U.S. commercial broadcasting and cable, which were about $95.8 billion in 1998 (*Broadcasting & Cable Yearbook,* 2000). In addition, the diversity of funding sources reflected ambivalence about responsibility for the institution. No single sector, public or private, had emerged to sponsor public broadcasting.

By the end of the twentieth century, the principal funding sources for public broadcasting could be divided into tax-based funding (which includes federal, state, and local funding) and private support (which includes sponsorship, underwriting, memberships, subscriptions, auctions, and special events).

Tax-Based Funding

Tax revenues for public television are provided at federal, state, and local levels, though the latter is small and insignificant. In virtually all instances, federal and state funding is appropriated from general treasury revenues.

Throughout the educational radio period and the early ETV years, there was no federal funding for public broadcasting. In the late 1950s and early 1960s, some federal support (e.g., the National Defense Education Act of 1958 and the Educational Television Facilities Act of 1962) began to emerge for instructional programming and the construction of noncommercial television facilities. However, such funding was modest and did not become significant and include support for programming and operations until after the Public Broadcasting Act of 1967 and the creation of CPB.

The total amount of federal support (for CPB, facilities, and special educational initiatives) grew from approximately $7 million in 1966 to approximately $400 million for 2001. The latter amount is still small when compared with funding for public broadcasting abroad. By the late 1990s, public broadcasting's per capita rate of federal support—the annual amount of national, tax-based public broadcasting revenue per citizen of the country—remained well below that of national government expenditures in all other advanced industrial, first-world nations (e.g., less than $1.20 in the United States versus $30 to $60 in Canada, Japan, and the United Kingdom) (Corporation for Public Broadcasting, 1999a). As a result, the U.S. public broadcasting program production rate, particularly in television, was far smaller than most other public-service broadcasting institutions around the world.

Additionally, federal funding has been consistently tenuous. The receiving-set license fees are widely employed in other countries and are relatively stable pools of funds, but in the United States, there are no special national funding mechanisms dedicated to public broadcasting. National task forces, study commissions, and leading political figures have at various times recommended the establishment of taxes on such things as the sales of receivers, the profits of commercial broadcasting and telecommunications, and the use or purchase of the spectrum. None of these ideas was ever implemented, and federal funding continued to come principally through appropriations from the general treasury.

There also have been serious limits on what is possible with regard to appropriations. Federal funding for public media has always been contentious in the United States. It lies at the heart of American ideological debates over the state of the arts, education, and communication (i.e., the "culture wars") and First Amendment issues about the role of government in such matters. As a result, even as federal funding for public broadcasting tended to increase, it was periodically reduced and regularly subjected to serious threats of elimination altogether. Such episodes occurred in the early 1970s, the early 1980s, and again in the mid-1990s. Those crises also undermined efforts to maintain a firm policy of multiyear advanced authorizations and appropriations.

The costs of overcoming such problems have been significant. To generate the appropriations and to recover from the reduction episodes, public broadcasters and their supporters have had to engage in constant, intensive lobbying, thereby exposing themselves to regular political oversight, similar to the process that is required of any federal agency or program. Those efforts also have required public broadcasters to divert considerable energy and resources from other essential tasks, such as the core mission of program planning and production and the longer-term strategic planning needs for service development in a rapidly changing technological world.

Taken altogether, state and local government support for educational or public broadcasting has always been a larger source of capital and recurring revenue than has federal income. That support has been channeled primarily through university licensees and state educational and telecommunications authority station boards. Increased numbers of stations licensed to such institutions, as well as support for various state and local instructional programs, accounted for a considerable portion of the system growth in the 1960s and 1970s.

Steady increases in such support during the late 1970s and early 1980s, when state government budgets were otherwise widely leveling off or dropping, did much to offset the reductions in federal support. That growth has remained remarkably solid, even through the fluctuations in congressional support during the mid-1990s. However, while state and local support was significant and even increasing, its growth remained slow and modest enough to guarantee only minor continued increases in public broadcasting facilities and program services.

State government funding also varied widely in type and amount across the country; many states did not make public broadcasting a high priority. Even where such support was substantial, it was typically annual or, at most, biennial, its overall levels showed no dramatic increases, and its actual proportion of overall public broadcasting funding was still shrinking. Proportionately, it declined from about 50 percent of overall public broadcasting revenues in the early 1970s to about 30 percent in the late 1980s and through the 1990s. By the end of the twentieth century, state support remained a substantial pillar of U.S. public broadcasting, predicated largely on the traditional belief in its instructional and educational potential, enhanced by its more contemporary Internet, distance-learning, and web-based instructional efforts. A large majority of the states had even committed to special funding initiatives to help public broadcasting make the conversion to digital technology. Overall, however, it was unclear whether state support could become the basis for anything more significant, such as providing operating support for the large increase in the numbers of noncommercial public-service channels and program efforts implied in digital conversion.

Private Support

In the absence of large amounts of federal and state funding, U.S. public broadcasting turned increasingly to private sources of support. In keeping with the pattern associated with other nonprofit institutions in the arts, culture, education, and health, public broadcasting came to rely increasingly on membership subscriptions, foundation grants, commercial underwriting, and special fundraising events. Altogether, these various forms of private funding grew at substantial rates after the early 1970s. Accounting for only about one-fifth of all public broadcasting revenues in 1970, they amounted to more than one-third by 1980. They more than trebled during the 1980s, and they accounted for well over one-half throughout the 1990s.

Up through the late 1950s, memberships and subscriptions were little used outside of a few listener-supported radio stations and the new community corporation ETV licensees. In time, particularly with the emergence of the stronger Carnegie Commission notion of *public* broadcasting, stations of all sorts began soliciting membership subscriptions; eventually, even school and university licensees began to seek subscriptions. Such patronage practices were already common in the arts and other cultural and social activities, such as symphony orchestras, opera companies, museums, and hospitals. The adoption of patronage practices for noncommercial broadcasting reflected expectations that public radio and television might play comparable roles in communities around the country. By the late 1980s, membership solicitation came to provide more than 20 percent of the total income for public broadcasting. That statistic rose to nearly 25 percent in the late 1990s.

The membership phenomenon was an encouraging sign of public loyalty and commitment to public broadcasting, and it reflected the institution's increasing acceptance in U.S. culture. It also was a source of largely unrestricted support that provided an important margin of extra capacity and independence for the stations individually and for the system collectively.

On the other hand, only about 10 percent of the audience contributed in this way, and generating such revenues had certain material and opportunity costs. The regular, frequent practice of soliciting subscriptions in special membership drives (derogatorily referred to as "begathons") required a large investment of staff and board time, and it disrupted program schedules, diverting stations and the national services from their core production goals and threatening to alienate viewers and listeners. Also, memberships turned over a great deal (a process referred to as "churning"), and their retention and replacement came to depend to a large extent on the value of the premiums that were offered, which themselves represented a considerable cost to stations. There also were questions about the frequently commercialized forms of pledge programming that stations were using. Those developments reflected an increasingly "transactional," goods-for-support character to the membership and subscription process that in some respects seemed to be at odds with the normal nature and purposes of public broadcasting.

Public stations also became creative in developing special fundraising projects such as auctions and the sponsorship of performances and other events in the community. These devices were similar to the ancillary revenue efforts of other cultural and educational institutions. Many of them became the responsibility of volunteer ("friends") groups, and they provided additional revenues, publicity, new audiences, and community grounding for the stations. As with memberships, however, these alternate devices also required considerable investment of staff time and energy, as well as an investment in inventories of material goods—all of which raised questions about cost–benefit ratios and their relationship to mission.

As with government funding, industrial and corporate support for public broadcast programming and operations is highly sensitive. The practice of underwriting was never explicitly defined and authorized in early legislation, and in many quarters, it was initially looked down on as antithetical to the educational mission. Nonetheless, the practice of soliciting underwriting developed early in the history of community ETV licensees, where appeals to foundations and various other private interests had become, like individual membership subscriptions, a material necessity and a symbol of public broadcasting's legitimacy as a particular kind of cultural institution. In time, as public broadcasting's popularity grew and its evening and weekend audiences took on a somewhat disproportionately upper-level, educational, professional, and politically significant demographic character, many national and local corporate interests began to recognize that there could be important public relations and political benefits in reaching such audiences. At first, identification of underwriters was possible only in brief, strictly regulated credits, but those practices became increasingly liberalized as program costs rose, federal funding proved to be continuously problematic, and corporate interests in reaching public broadcasting audiences grew.

Over time, federal policy actually began to encourage expansion of private, commercial support and even explicit sponsorship, particularly after the advertising experiments conducted under the auspices of the Temporary Commission on Alternative Financing in 1983. While that project did not lead all the way into the sort of limited spot-advertising provisions that exist for public broadcasting abroad, it did permit substantial movement in that direction by authorizing more liberalized sponsorship in the form of "enhanced underwriting." During the 1980s and 1990s, such support grew from less than 10 percent to approximately 15 percent of all public broadcasting revenues.

Public broadcasters, their friends, and their critics have remained sharply divided over this issue. There were strong concerns that any increasing commercialization of public broadcasting was unhealthy—that it was driving the institution ever closer to the programming and audience considerations that guide commercial broadcasting and against which it is assumed that public broadcasting must stand. At the very least, questions were asked about what programming efforts and voices went unheard when underwriting resources were unavailable. Another practical concern was that

increased commercialization would seem to threaten all the other significant forms of revenue generation and raise costs for such things as copyright and talent without any guarantee that it would offer sufficient replacement funds.

Other observers, however, felt that none of the other forms of financial support would ever provide the extent of revenue necessary for public broadcasting to survive, let alone to grow and substantially increase its range of services and appeal. From this perspective, there were no realistic alternatives to increased commercial revenues, and, although there were dangers associated with them, it was thought that they could be managed well enough to ensure that the better, unique characteristics of public-service programming would persist and even prosper.

A related issue was that of attempting to recover some of the profits on the public investment in programs that developed aftermarkets and ancillary commercial products (e.g., toys, books). There were mutually incompatible criticisms of public broadcasting for, on the one hand, allegedly not adequately exploiting such opportunities and, on the other hand, for being precisely that commercial and exploitative, particularly of children. In the end, such "deals" were never as potentially large as frequently represented, but they reflected the continuing pressure on public broadcasting to develop external forms of revenue and the confusions of public policy in that regard.

New Media and Digital Technology

As with all other media, the dramatic changes in telecommunications technology in the last quarter of the twentieth century had a substantial effect on the character and prospects for public broadcasting. Broadcasting had been built as an analog system of production and transmission, using open, "over-the-air" spectrum frequencies and serving generally as a mass medium. Beginning in the 1970s, the quickly spreading uses of and interactions among coaxial cable, fiber optics, satellite distribution, and computerization inaugurated a series of challenges to the conventional model and began to take broadcasting more explicitly into the complex welter of telecommunications. Those challenges became more significant with the rapid increase in the pace of digital technology development in the 1980s and 1990s, leading to a process of convergence and reconfiguration among media forms generally. By the end of the twentieth century, the very structure and associated industrial and service forms of traditional broadcasting were breaking down in the face of the much higher carrying and multimedia capacities of digital transmission, the Internet, and the World Wide Web. Public broadcasting was being challenged in similar ways.

Public broadcasting had been able to take creative advantage of the early phases of those changes, such as in its adoption of geostationary orbiting satellite services for distributing its national signals. In keeping with its ownership and fiscal base in the stations, it had been more open to the flexibility of that technology than had commercial broadcasting initially, where centralized network controls militated longer against such distribution options. It also had taken a leading role in the development of closed captioning for use by the hearing impaired.

In other respects, however, public broadcasting's reactions were more muted and uncertain. It had difficulty thinking through and effectively using all the multichannel capacity that was available to it in both conventional broadcast channels and the broader spectrum pipelines represented by coaxial and fiber-optic cable. In contrast, the commercial television responses of the broadcasting and cable industries to the newer program service opportunities seemed initially stronger, and by the mid-1980s, those industries were cooperating to develop new services that to many eyes resembled much of traditional public broadcasting.

Apart from certain limited efforts in its early days—the so-called golden years of radio (in the 1930s and 1940s) and television (in the 1950s)—commercial broadcasting had not demonstrated much of its educational and cultural service potential. The commercial marketplace seemed incapable of providing such programming on a continuing basis, and public broadcasting had come into existence largely in an effort to fill that need. However, the newer cable channels, such as Nickelodeon, the Discovery Channel, Arts & Entertainment, the History Channel, CNN, and C-SPAN, had much deeper funding resources than did public broadcasting, and they seemed to be providing much of the special educational, public affairs, and children's services that had been public broadcasting's traditional mandate. The true extent of the new channels' replication of the programming of public broadcasting remained debatable, and public broadcasters were quick to note that such services were available only on cable and direct broadcast satellite television, both of which involved a fee. These new channels were not free, over-the-air stations, and many of them were more commercialized than public-service models would permit. Nonetheless, their presence and persistence vexed the question of public broadcasting's special status as an institution deserving of continuing public funding by federal and state governments.

There also was the persistent problem of public broadcasting's small minority position in the overall structure of telecommunications and its concomitantly small audiences. Throughout the 1960s and 1970s, educational and public broadcasting stations constituted a minor but nonetheless noticeable share of the channel capacity of conventional broadcast radio and television (e.g., in television, the local ETV or public station was typically one of five or six locally receivable broadcast signals or of ten to twenty cable channels). By the 1990s, with the steady expansion of cable and direct broadcast satellite capacities, public broadcasting had not kept pace. The number of its stations continued to grow but at a much slower rate than had been the case during the late 1960s and early 1970s, and its relative share of the broadcast, cable, and satellite channel offerings had declined. In television, even with the development of new local stations, its presence amounted to no more than two or three signals in a sixty to one hundred cable-channel environment. Public broadcasting's audiences were likewise small, typically accounting for less than 5 percent of the viewers and listeners at any one time.

Despite proposals that it do so, public broadcasting had developed no master plan nor any clear, longer-term goal for maintaining and building a larger share of the nation's telecommunications carrying capacity. Throughout the growth of the cable and satellite era, public broadcasting therefore tended to be restricted in its thinking about the alternative service models that were available to it with increased numbers of signals and channels. Federal policy throughout much of the 1980s and 1990s, as reflected in the programs of CPB, the National Telecommunications and Information Administration (NTIA, which is a division of the U.S. Department of Commerce), and the Public Telecommunications Facilities Program (PTFP, which is a program within NTIA), actually contributed to that restrictive thinking, bowing to pressures within Congress and even among public broadcasters themselves that "overlap" stations and more diversity of signal and voice should not be encouraged. For many years, public broadcasting had the technical capacity to provide multiple streams of complimentary programming nationally and in every community, but with its continuing fiscal uncertainties, perhaps most dramatically exposed in the congressional calls for "zeroing out" of federal funding in the mid-1990s, public broadcasting tended not to press forward in the multiple-channel arena.

By the late 1990s, that issue began to be put into a new perspective, due in part to the decision by the FCC to convert all broadcasting to digital technology and by the steady growth and public acceptance of Internet, web-based online and interactive communications. Together, those changes provided a whole new set of opportunities for public broadcasting to supplement and even compete with its traditional video services. It was becoming increasingly apparent that, if public broadcasting did not position itself to take advantage of those opportunities by expanding the range, volume, and even forms of its services, it risked remaining trapped in the straitjacket of an obsolete mass-media model.

At the same time, it was uncertain if national, state, and local public policy would support all the implications of these new opportunities. The digital conversion process was an "unfunded mandate," something the federal government was requiring of public broadcasting but for which adequate federal and state funding was in doubt. Likewise, it was unclear whether the federal government was willing to continue supporting the traditional reservations, set-aside and must-carry policies that had done so much to help public broadcasting find and keep a toehold in the U.S. telecommunications system. The cable television industry had always resisted the FCC's must-carry requirements. As it was beginning to implement digital cable services in the late 1990s, much of that resistance was continuing, and FCC support for must-carry appeared questionable. Similarly, the direct broadcast satellite industry was resisting implementation of a "local-into-local" station carriage requirement, an equivalent of must-carry. Although that policy had been written into law in 1999 as the Intellectual Property and Communications Omnibus Reform Act, it had been vigorously opposed by the direct broadcast satellite industry.

Summary and Conclusion

By the turn into the twenty-first century, the institutional structure of U.S. public broadcasting that had been built on the original educational broadcasting model and put into place in the late 1960s and early 1970s remained largely intact. Public radio and television were much larger and more secure entities than they had been twenty-five years earlier, with solid, measurable, albeit, by commercial standards, still small sets of audiences.

However, public broadcasting also continued to be laden with an organizational complexity that was difficult to explain and understand. Without a clear national consensus on its appropriate goals, size, and structure, that complexity had increased throughout the 1980s and 1990s, making it difficult to describe the institution and the various roles of its many organizations. For similar reasons, it also was struggling with a continuing base of funding that was small by comparison with public broadcasting elsewhere in the world, and it was facing the challenges and opportunities of new interactive, Internet, and web technologies, as well as the federally mandated conversion to digital broadcasting, all without clear sources of adequate capital and operating funding.

The old debates about how much public broadcasting should focus on being an institution of formal education versus a high-quality general-audience service remained, as did the tensions over the relative balance of control between and among the stations and the national entities. Likewise, there was an even more intense phase of the debate over the extent to which the commercial telecommunications marketplace, in its new broad-spectrum environment, could provide the diversity and quality of alternative programming services reflected in public broadcasting.

By the beginning of the twenty-first century, there were signs that the stations and national services were making significant plans for creative uses of their impending new digital and multimedia capacities, and it appeared that many of them would be notably different from those that the commercial industries were proposing to use. However, the costs of digital conversion and the development of sophisticated Internet provider (IP) services were substantial, and it appeared they could not be met by existing funding sources. Additionally, it was unclear whether federal policy would continue to support the reservation of educational, noncommercial channels and require their carriage on the newer digital cable and direct broadcast satellite environments.

During the late twentieth century, U.S. public broadcasting had worked its way up to a relatively stable plateau upon which it had built a diverse funding system, a large local station infrastructure, and an active set of programming services and support agencies. It had a large corps of dedicated and effective personnel and a strong, if small, base of membership and public support. It continued to be seen as a public and social good and as more necessary than not. It therefore did not appear to be in danger of disintegrating and fading away. However, without adequate public-policy support and resources to fulfill its basic mission, public broadcasting was going to have difficulty moving up to the next plateau. Public broadcasting remained an important, some would say indispensable, element of U.S. telecommunications and culture, but it was still far from being central to those institutions. Public broadcasting was still swimming upstream against a swift, dangerous set of commercial and political currents.

See also: BROADCASTING, GOVERNMENT REGULATION OF; COMMUNICATIONS ACT OF 1934; DIGITAL COMMUNICATION; DIGITAL MEDIA SYSTEMS; FEDERAL COMMUNICATIONS COMMISSION; INTERNET AND THE WORLD WIDE WEB; OPINION POLLING, CAREERS IN; PIRATE MEDIA; PROPAGANDA; PUBLIC SERVICE MEDIA; RADIO BROADCASTING; SESAME STREET; SOCIAL CHANGE AND THE MEDIA; TELECOMMUNICATIONS, WIRELESS; TELECOMMUNICATIONS ACT OF 1996; TELEVISION BROADCASTING; TELEVISION, EDUCATIONAL.

Bibliography

America's Public Television Stations. (1999). "National Poll Finds Americans Strongly Support Public Television." Press release. Washington, DC: America's Public Television Stations.

Avery, Robert K., ed. (1993). *Public-Service Broadcasting in a Multichannel Environment.* New York: Longman.

Barnouw, Erik. (1966). *A History of Broadcasting in the United States,* Vol. 1. New York: Oxford University Press.

Blakely, Robert J. (1979). *To Serve the Public Interest: Educational Broadcasting in the United States.* Syracuse, NY: Syracuse University Press.

Briggs, Asa. (1979). *The History of Broadcasting in the United Kingdom.* London: Oxford University Press.

Broadcasting & Cable Yearbook. (2000). "Year in Review: Broadcasting and Cable 1999." New Providence, NJ: Bowker.

Browne, Donald R. (1989). *Comparing Broadcast Systems: The Experiences of Six Industrialized Nations.* Ames: Iowa State University Press.

Carnegie Commission on Educational Television. (1967). *Public Television: A Program for Action.* New York: Bantam.

Carnegie Commission on the Future of Public Broadcasting. (1979). *A Public Trust.* New York: Bantam.

Corporation for Public Broadcasting. (1999a). "Comparative Financial Statistics for Selected Public Service Broadcasting Systems in the World, FY 1997." *Research Notes,* No. 115. Washington, DC: Corporation for Public Broadcasting.

Corporation for Public Broadcasting. (1999b). *Public Broadcasting Revenue, Fiscal Year 1998.* Washington, DC: Corporation for Public Broadcasting.

Day, James. (1995). *The Vanishing Vision: The Inside Story of Public Television.* Berkeley: University of California Press.

Engleman, Ralph. (1996). *Public Radio and Television in America: A Political History.* Thousand Oaks, CA: Sage Publications.

Frost, S. E., Jr. (1937). *Education's Own Stations: The History of Broadcast Licenses Issued to Educational Institutions.* Chicago: University of Chicago Press.

Goldberg, Jonah. (2000). "Public Media, Stuff It." *Brill's Content,* April, pp. 53–54.

Goodman, Paul, ed. (1967). *The Federalists vs. the Jeffersonian Republicans.* New York: Holt, Rinehart and Winston.

Grossman, Lawrence K. (1997). "Introducing PTV Weekend." <http://www.current.org/weekend/wklg597.html>.

Grossman, Lawrence K., and Minow, Newton N. (2001). *A Digital Gift to the Nation: Fulfilling the Promise of the Digital and Internet Age.* New York: Century Foundation Press.

Gunn, Hartford N., Jr., et al. (1980). "In Search of the Formula: The System Planning Project Papers." *Public Telecommunications Review* 8(3):7–102.

Horowitz, David. (1995). *Public Broadcasting and the Public Trust.* Los Angeles: Center for the Study of Popular Culture.

Jarvik, Laurence A. (1997). *PBS, Behind the Screen.* Rocklin, CA: Forum.

Ledbetter, James. (1997). *Made Possible By . . . : The Death of Public Broadcasting in the United States*. New York: Routledge, Chapman & Hall.

Noam, Eli M., and Waltermann, Jens, eds. (1998). *Public Television in America*. Gütersloh, Germany: Bertlesmann Foundation Publishers.

Rossiter, Clinton, ed. (1961). *The Federalist Papers*. New York: New American Library.

Rowland, Willard D., Jr. (1998). "The Institution of U.S. Public Broadcasting." In *Public Television in America*, eds. Eli M. Noam and Jens Waltermann. Gütersloh, Germany: Bertlesmann Foundation Publishers.

Scheer, Robert. (2000). "Let's Protect Big Bird." *Brill's Content*, April, pp. 52–54.

Somerset-Ward, Richard. (1998). "American Public Television: Programs—Now, and in the Future." In *Public Television in America*, eds. Eli M. Noam and Jens Waltermann. Gütersloh, Germany: Bertlesmann Foundation Publishers.

Twentieth Century Fund. (1993). *Quality Time?: The Report of the Twentieth Century Fund Task Force on Public Television*. New York: Twentieth Century Fund Press.

Williams, Raymond. (1974). *Television: Technology and Cultural Form*. London: Fontana/Collins.

Witherspoon, John; Kovitz, Roselle; Avery, Robert; and Stavitsky, Alan G. (2000). *A History of Public Broadcasting*. Washington, DC: Current Publishing Company.

WILLARD D. ROWLAND, JR.

■ PUBLIC HEALTH CAMPAIGNS

Promoting public health and preventing the spread of dangerous health risks is an integral communication function in modern society. Whether the focus is on the prevention and control of acquired immunodeficiency syndrome (AIDS), cancer, heart disease, or community violence, a fusion of theory and practice in communication is urgently needed to guide effective promotion efforts. Public health campaigns involve a broad set of communication strategies and activities that specialists in health promotion engage in to disseminate relevant and persuasive health information to groups of people who need such information to help them lead healthy lives.

Public health campaigns involve the strategic dissemination of information to the public in order to help groups of people resist imminent health threats and adopt behaviors that promote good health. Typically, these campaigns are designed to raise public consciousness about important health issues by educating specific groups (i.e., target audiences) about imminent health threats and risky behaviors that might harm them. Health campaigns are generally designed both to increase awareness of health threats and to move target audiences to action in support of public health. For example, public health campaigns often encourage target audience members to engage in healthy behaviors that provide resistance to serious health threats. These behaviors can include adopting healthy lifestyles that include exercise, nutrition, and stress-reduction; avoiding dangerous substances such as poisons, carcinogens, or other toxic materials; seeking opportunities for early screening and diagnosis for serious health problems; and availing themselves of the best available health-care services, when appropriate, to minimize harm.

Frailty of Messages that Promote Health

Campaigns are designed to influence public knowledge, attitudes, and behaviors, yet achieving these goals and influencing the public is no simple matter. There is not a direct relationship between the messages that are sent to people and the reactions these people have to the messages. In addition to interpreting messages in very unique ways, people respond differently to the messages that they receive. For example, having drivers use their seatbelts when they drive might seem like a very straightforward public health goal. A very simple campaign might develop the message, "Wear your seatbelt when you drive!" For this message to influence the beliefs, attitudes, and values of all drivers, the campaign planner must take many different communication variables into account. Is this message clear and compelling for its intended audience? How are audience members likely to respond to this message? Will they pay attention to it? Will they adjust their behaviors in response to it? Campaign planners must do quite a bit of background research and planning to answer these questions. Effective communication campaigns must be strategically designed and implemented. In other words, they must use carefully designed messages that match the interests and abilities of the audience for which they are designed, and they must convey the messages via the communication channels that the target audience trusts and can easily access.

A refugee looks at an HIV/AIDS prevention campaign poster at a temporary refugee camp in Mae Hong Sorn province in northern Thailand, near the border with Myanmar. Thailand and Myanmar have agreed to cooperate on HIV and malaria prevention to help check the spread of the diseases, which increased substantially along their common borders during the late 1990s. (AFP/Corbis)

A primary goal of the campaign is to influence the way the audience thinks about the health threat. If the target audience already believes this issue is very serious and of great relevance to their lives, this will lead the campaign planner to craft messages that will support these preconceptions. If, on the other hand, members of the target audience barely recognize the health threat and are not at all concerned about it, the campaign planner must design communication strategies that will raise the audience's consciousness and concern about the topic.

Generally, campaign planners want to convince target audiences to recognize and take the identified health threat seriously. They want to influence the audience's beliefs, values, and attitudes about the issue to support the goals of the campaign. Only after a communication campaign raises audience consciousness and concern about the threat can it begin to influence (or persuade) the target audience to adopt specific recommenda-

tions for resisting and treating the identified health threat. The communication strategies used to raise consciousness and the strategies used to motivate action may be quite different.

Message Strategies and Communication Channels

Effective public health campaigns often employ a wide range of message strategies and communication channels to target high-risk populations with information designed to educate, motivate, and empower risk reduction behaviors. For this reason, modern campaigns have become increasingly dependent on integrating interpersonal, group, organizational, and mediated communication to disseminate the relevant health information effectively to specific high-risk populations.

Most campaigns use mass media (i.e., newspapers, radio, television, etc.) to convey their messages to large, and sometimes diverse, audiences. These channels for communication often have the ability to reach many people over vast geographic distances. In recognition of the multidimensional nature of health communication, the most effective public health campaigns develop information dissemination strategies that incorporate multiple levels and channels of human communication. To have the greatest potential influence on the health behaviors of the target audience, public health campaigns often employ a wide range of communication channels (e.g., interpersonal counseling, support groups, lectures, workshops, newspaper and magazine articles, pamphlets, self-help programs, computer-based information systems, formal educational programs, billboards, posters, radio and television programs, and public service announcements). The use of these different media is most effective when the campaign is designed so that the different communication channels complement one another in presenting the same public health messages to different targeted audiences.

Because effective use of communication channels is so important to the success of public health campaigns, research related to health communication can perform a central role in the development of an effective campaign. Such research helps campaign planners to identify consumer needs and orientations; target specific audiences; evaluate audience message behaviors; field test messages; guide message conceptualization and development; identify communication channels that have high audience reach, specificity, and influence; monitor the progress of campaign messages; and evaluate the overall effects of the campaign on target audiences and public health.

Strategic Public Health Campaign Model

Developing and implementing effective public health campaigns is a complex enterprise. Campaign planners must recognize that mere exposure to relevant health information will rarely lead directly to desired changes in health-related behavior. Edward Maibach, Gary Kreps, and Ellen Bonaguro (1993) address the complex relationship between communication efforts and campaign outcomes in their strategic health communication campaign model. This model identifies five major stages and twelve key issues that planners of public health campaigns should consider in developing and implementing their strategic campaigns. The major elements of the model are (1) campaign planning, (2) theories for guiding efforts at health promotion, (3) communication analysis, (4) campaign implementation, and (5) campaign evaluation and reorientation.

Campaign Planning

Campaign planning addresses two major issues, setting clear and realistic campaign objectives and establishing a clear consumer orientation to make sure that the campaign reflects the specific concerns and cultural perspectives of the target audiences. Realistic campaign objectives refer to the purposes of the campaign. Identifying an important public health threat or issue that can be effectively addressed by a campaign is a crucial first step. There must be an important health issue to address, and it must be a problem that poses significant risks for groups of people.

Is the identified health threat likely to be reduced through the implementation of a public health campaign? Are there clearly identified and proven strategies for addressing the threat that can be promoted by the campaign? Are members of the campaign audience likely to adopt the health strategies that will be promoted in the campaign? These questions must be answered before a public health campaign is started, or the planners risk wasting time and money on a campaign that will have a minimal effect on public health.

Adopting a consumer orientation means that the whole campaign is designed from the unique cultural perspective of the target audience and that members of the audience are involved as much as possible in the planning and implementation of the campaign. It is imperative that the campaign planners clearly understand the orientation and predisposition of the target audience in order to craft the most appropriate and effective campaign for that audience. Campaign planners must identify specific (well-segmented) target populations who are most at-risk for the identified health threats that will be addressed in the campaign. These populations of individuals become the primary audiences to receive strategic campaign messages.

Research related to public health campaigns focuses on the effective dissemination of relevant health information to promote public health. To develop and design persuasive campaign messages that will be influential with the specific target audiences, campaign planners must conduct audience analysis research to gather relevant information about the health behaviors and orientations of the target audiences. Audience analysis also helps campaign planners learn about the communication characteristics and predisposition of target audiences.

Theories for Guiding Efforts at Health Promotion

Once the basic campaign planning has been completed, it must be determined which established behavioral and social science theories will be used as guides for developing overall campaign strategies and materials. The best theories have been tested in many different contexts (with different populations) and provide the campaign planners with good advice in directing campaign efforts. Too often campaign planners are in such a rush to provide people with health-related messages that they do not carefully design their communication strategies.

Theory provides campaign planners with strategies for designing, implementing, and evaluating communication campaigns. There are a wide range of behavioral theories of communication, persuasion, and social influence that can be effectively used to guide public health campaigns. The theories that are adopted will direct the campaign planners' use of message strategies to influence key public audiences. For example, Albert Bandura (1989) developed an insightful theory concerning self-efficacy as a key variable in behavior change, which would lead campaign planners to develop message strategies that build the confidence of members of the target audience to implement and institutionalize campaign recommendations into their lives. Campaign planners who apply exchange theories to their efforts are likely to craft messages that identify the personal detriments of health risks and the benefits of adopting proposed behavioral changes. These theories direct the persuasive communication strategies used in public health campaigns.

Communication Analysis

Communication analysis identifies three critical issues in designing public health campaigns: (1) audience analysis and segmentation, (2) formative research, and (3) channel analysis and selection. Audience segmentation involves breaking down large culturally diverse populations into smaller more manageable and more homogenous target audiences for health promotion campaigns. The greater the cultural homogeneity (i.e., the more they share cultural attributes and backgrounds) of a target audience, the better able campaign planners are to design messages specifically for them. With a diverse target audience, the campaign planner is hard pressed to develop message strategies that will appeal to all parts of the population. It is far more effective to target an audience that shares important cultural traits and is likely to respond similarly to campaign message strategies.

After segmenting the target audience into the most culturally homogenous group possible, the campaign planners should, in order to guide the design of the campaign, gather as much information about the group's relevant cultural norms, beliefs, values, and attitudes. The more complete the audience analysis process, the more prepared the campaign planners are to tailor the messages to the specific needs and predilections of the target audience. Audience analysis can take the form of surveys, focus group discussions, or consultation of existing research results that are available and describe key aspects of the population of interest.

Formative research is the process used to guide the design and development of the campaign by gathering relevant information about the ways in which representatives of the target audience react to campaign messages. In essence, it is an early method of testing the effect of the developing campaign when changes, updates, and other refinements can still be made to reflect audience responses. Formative research can also help campaign planners make knowledgeable choices about which communication channels to use in the campaign because those channels are most likely to reach and influence the specific target audiences.

Campaign Implementation

Implementation involves the long-term administration and operation of the campaign. Campaign planners must carefully establish an effective marketing mix, which originates from the field of marketing and is indicative of the growth of social applications of marketing principles (i.e., social marketing) in public health campaigns. The marketing mix is based on product, price, placement, and promotion. In other words, campaign planners try to establish clear sets of campaign activities (products) to promote objectives that audience members can adopt with minimal economic or psychological costs (price). These objectives need to be presented in an attractive manner that is very likely to reach the target audience (placement), and the message must provide the members of the audience with information about how, when, and where they can access campaign information and programs (promotion).

Campaign planners should carefully evaluate the campaign process, which involves identifying macrosocial conditions that may influence accomplishment of the campaign goals and designing strategies for promoting long-term involvement and institutionalization of campaign activities with the target audience. Process evaluation is used to keep track and evaluate campaign activities in order to identify areas for fine-tuning campaign efforts. Since target audiences reside within and are interdependent with the larger society, campaign planners must attempt to involve these larger social systems, such as business organizations and government agencies, in the campaign activities. For example, planners for a campaign related to tobacco control used macrosocial factors to provide strong support for their efforts. They accomplished this by lobbying in support of government and corporate regulations that restricted smoking behaviors in public places and that corresponded nicely with their message strategies that encouraged people to not smoke. In this way, the macrosocial regulations on smoking supported the campaign goals of reducing smoking behaviors.

Furthermore, the campaign planner should design strategies for the long-term involvement of the audience with the goals and activities of the campaign in order to ensure that the audience members institutionalize the messages and make them a regular part of their daily lives. An excellent strategy for such institutionalization is to empower members of the target audience to get personally involved with implementing and managing campaign programs so they have a greater stake in achieving campaign goals and so the campaign activities become part of their normative cultural activities. For example, campaigns that support increased physical activity and fitness have benefited from efforts to establish annual activities, festivals, and sporting events to institutionalize their campaign goals.

Campaign Evaluation and Reorientation

The final process involved in the strategic communication campaign model is evaluation and reorientation. At this point, a summative evaluation (i.e., and evaluation of campaign outcomes) is conducted to determine the relative success of the campaign in achieving its goals at an acceptable cost, as well as to identify areas for future public health interventions. The information gathered through such outcome evaluations reorients campaign planners to the unmet health needs of the target audience. Such feedback is essential in leading campaign planners back to the first stage of the model (planning), where they identify new goals for health promotion. Through this evaluative feedback loop, the strategic communication campaign model illustrates the ongoing cyclical nature of efforts at health promotion.

Campaigns and Communication Research

As seen in the strategic communication campaign model, communication research performs a central role in strategic public health campaigns. Data are gathered (1) in the planning stage to identify consumer needs and orientations, (2) in the communication analysis stage to target specific audiences, evaluate audience message behaviors, field test messages to guide message conceptualization and development, and to identify communication channels with high audience reach, specificity, and influence, (3) in the implementation stage to monitor the progress of campaign messages and products and to determine the extent to which campaign objectives are being achieved, and (4) in the evaluation and reorientation stage to determine the overall effects of the campaign on target audiences and public health. The strategic communication campaign model suggests that to maximize the effectiveness of efforts at health promotion, research in the area of health communication must be used to guide the development, implementation, and evaluation of strategic public health campaigns.

See also: HEALTH COMMUNICATION.

Bibliography

Albrecht, Terrance, and Bryant, Carol. (1996). "Advances in Segmentation Modeling for Health Communication and Social Marketing Campaigns." *Journal of Health Communication: International Perspectives* 1(1):65–80.

Bandura, Albert. (1989). "Perceived Self-Efficacy in the Exercise of Control over AIDS Infection." In *Primary Prevention of AIDS: Psychological Approaches,* eds. Vickie M. Mays, George W. Albee, and Stanley F. Schneider. Newbury Park, CA: Sage Publications.

Kotler, Philip, and Roberto, Eduardo L. (1989). *Social Marketing: Strategies for Changing Public Behavior.* New York: Free Press.

Kreps, Gary L. (1996). "Promoting a Consumer Orientation to Health Care and Health Promotion." *Journal of Health Psychology* 1(1):41–48.

Lefebvre, Craig, and Flora, June. (1988). "Social Marketing and Public Health Intervention." *Health Education Quarterly* 15(3):299–315.

Maibach, Edward W.; Kreps, Gary L.; and Bonaguro, Ellen W. (1993). "Developing Strategic Communication Campaigns for HIV/AIDS Prevention." In *AIDS: Effective Health Communication for the 90s,* ed. Scott C. Ratzan. Washington, DC: Taylor and Francis.

Ratzan, Scott C. (1999). "Editorial: Strategic Health Communication and Social Marketing of Risk Issues." *Journal of Health Communication: International Perspectives* 4(1):1–6.

Rice, Ronald E., and Atkin, Charles K., eds. (1989). *Public Communication Campaigns,* 2nd ed. Newbury Park, CA: Sage Publications.

GARY L. KREPS

■ PUBLIC RECORDS

See: Archives, Public Records, and Records Management

■ PUBLIC RELATIONS

Varying in scope and duration, and differing in the methods used, all of the following examples have one thing in common—they were managed by practitioners of public relations and they would be recognized by any professional as public relations in practice:

- Fifty years after Thomas A. Edison invented the electric lightbulb, Edward L. Bernays convinces industrial leaders to finance and support "Light's Golden Jubilee," a year-long nationwide celebration involving school children writing essays, inventors contributing their machines to an industrial museum, and an event in Dearborn, Michigan, attended by Edison, Henry Ford, President Herbert Hoover, John D. Rockefeller, Jr., and a host of American inventors and presidents of corporations—a major "photo-op" if ever there was one.

- A coalition of environmental groups, concerned about pollution of drinking water, pushes a state legislature to call a public referendum on a bond issue to mandate stronger control of pollutants. A grassroots campaign—costing little but involving hundreds of volunteers and a speaker's bureau—succeeds in passing the law and funding cleanups.

- On the day of the initial public offering of its stock, the president of a software company rings the opening bell on the New York Stock Exchange while his employees toss T-shirts and baseball caps to those on the trading floor—an event that is seen by hundreds of thousands on the cable business channel CNBC.

- To raise money for a new pediatric wing of the local hospital, the mayor, city council members, president of the hospital, and other dignitaries agree to spend a day in mock "jail." They buy their way out of incarceration by phoning citizens and asking them to pledge contributions of money.

- The manufacturer of a spray that eliminates shoe odors stages the "America's Dirtiest Sneaker" contest for kids, with regional winners flown to New York City and the grand prize winner appearing on the *Tonight Show* with Jay Leno.

- Alarmed at the migration of manufacturing and service jobs from a decaying city center to suburbs and small towns, the city's Chamber of Commerce develops a partnership with labor unions, city government agencies, and the business school at a local university to implement an "It Pays to Stay" campaign, which includes a job fair, open houses at businesses, and a series of paid advertisements in the local news media.

In *Lesly's Handbook of Public Relations and Communications* (1998), Philip Lesly defines public relations by listing the following activities under the heading of public relations: publicity, communication, public affairs, issues management, government relations, investor public relations, employee relations, community relations, industry relations, minority relations, advertising, press agentry, promotion, media relations, and propaganda. Scott M. Cutlip and Allen H. Center, in their public relations textbook *Effective Public Relations* (1978, p. 37), provided a cogent definition of public relations: "Public relations is the planned effort to influence opinion through good character and responsible performance, based upon mutually satisfactory two-way communication." James E. Grunig and Todd Hunt, in their textbook *Managing Public Relations* (1984, p.6), further refined the definition: "Public relations is the management of communication between an organization and its publics [i.e., groups that can have consequences on the organization]." *Public Relations News*, an industry newsletter, defines public relations as "the management function which evaluates public attitudes, identifies the policies and procedures of an individual or an organization with the public interest, and plans and executes a program of action to earn public understanding and acceptance." The International Public Relations Association provides a slightly different perspective: "Public relations practice is the art and science of analyzing trends, predicting their consequences, counseling organization leaders, and implementing planned programs of action which will serve both the organization's and the public's interest."

The pejorative words "hype" and "spin"—often favored by detractors of the public relations profession—are not even hinted at in these definitions. None of them even mentions "persuasion" or "selling," although the concept of "influence" is suggested. Among academics and professionals, the emphasis is on management and on two-way communication that benefits both the organization and its publics—a concept referred to as "mutually beneficial outcomes." That may be an idealistic view, especially when one considers that sports promotion, show-business campaigns, product marketing, and even the packaging of celebrities and political leaders are activities that fit in the tent of public relations. But every profession should aspire to an idealistic mission, so when the members of professional public relations associations renew their membership annually, their signature on the renewal form signifies that they agree to abide by a code of ethics that grows out of these definitions.

Development of Public Relations

Academics who study the history of public relations are fond of pointing to examples throughout American history: the Revolution against England (with that foremost of pseudoevents, the Boston Tea Party); the campaign for the drafting of a *Constitution of the United States* (with the eighty-five *Federalist Papers* written by Alexander Hamilton, James Madison, and John Jay); newspaper editor Amos Kendall's efforts to turn the image of Andrew Jackson from that of an unschooled bumpkin to a man of presidential stature; the suffrage movement to give women voting rights; and prohibition campaigns with angry teetotalers storming saloons with axes. Indeed, public relations–like activities were part of all these movements—the making of slogans, the distribution of leaflets and pamphlets, rallies and parades, speeches, and letters to editors of newspapers. And, of course, one always can point to the legendary ballyhoo and excesses of press agentry used by showman P. T. Barnum to lure audiences to his freakish circus attractions. Some push farther back in history to argue that edicts published and publicized in ancient Egypt and Rome to gain the compliance of those living outside the cities were public relations campaigns, as were the successful efforts to marshal support for the Crusades aimed at reclaiming the Holy Land between the eleventh and fourteenth centuries.

It makes sense, however, to chronicle the history of modern public relations from the time when the actual phrase "public relations" was coined and came into sufficient usage that people knew what it meant. The clearest example of the movement of the term into the mainstream language was in 1908 when Theodore Vail, president of the American Telephone & Telegraph Co. (AT&T), titled the annual report of the firm *Public Relations*. Edward L. Bernays, in his book *Public Relations* (1952), said Vail was concerned that the company engage honestly and competently in practices that would pay a fair return to investors, thus assuring that there would be no basis for conflict between the company and its most important public.

Bernays, for his part, coined the term "public relations counsel" in the 1920s to describe a person such as himself who was more than a "press agent" disseminating press releases to the news media. The term "press agent" better described Ivy Lee, who in the early 1900s set up a "press bureau" to supply news that would provide publicity on the positions of coal mine owners during a series of bitter strikes against them by miners. In his Declaration of Principles, Lee laid the foundation for modern public relations by declaring certain principles. Among them was the concept that queries should be responded to promptly, that the

Edward Bernays, photographed in his Cambridge, Massachusetts, office in 1981, is known as the father of public relations. He was a strong supporter of licensing practitioners in the profession. (Bettmann/Corbis)

information provided be complete and accurate, that business leaders should be open and honest with the press and the public, and that the press bureau was not to perform any of the functions of an advertising agency. Lee is probably most famous for his ability to rehabilitate the public reputation of John D. Rockefeller, Sr., following the bloody suppression of a coal mine strike in Colorado, blamed on Rockefeller. Lee convinced the reclusive Rockefeller to be more visible as a family man and encouraged him to allow more publicity about the millions he was donating to charity, particularly to medical research that would benefit all citizens.

Bernays is referred to as the father of public relations. Born in Vienna in 1891, a nephew of psychologist Sigmund Freud, Bernays served during World War I on the Committee on Public Information—also known as the Creel Committee after chairman George Creel—which developed the notion that mass persuasion could be based on the principles of social science. In 1919, Bernays established a public relations agency, along with Doris E. Fleischman, whom he married in 1922.

Bernays wrote *Crystallizing Public Opinion*, the first treatise on public relations, in 1923, followed by *Propaganda* in 1928. His textbook *Public Relations* was published in 1952. In his books, Bernays argued that publics were not sheep to be herded; they could be persuaded to do only what was in their best interest. He counseled management to let him find out what the public liked about an organization, and then he shaped messages that reinforced these beliefs. "Engineering of consent" was the Bernays approach, meaning that the gradual application of psychological theory would lead from identification with a cause to intensified interest and eventually to the action desired by the client organization.

Bernays lived past the age of one hundred, and he could list more than two hundred clients he had served in virtually every field of endeavor, including retailers, trade associations, big business, hotels, government, public-interest groups, and trade unions. Keenly interested in social welfare, he helped the National Association for the Advancement of Colored People (NAACP) and similar organizations. On the other hand, those who consider him a master of "spin" point to gimmicks—like his promotion of cigarette smoking by women, accomplished by placing cigarette-smoking debutantes in New York's Easter Parade.

Colleges and universities began adding public relations to the curricula of journalism schools during the 1950s because corporations were hiring experienced newspaper and magazine reporters and editors to be in-house journalists, writing articles and placing them in the news media. In the 1960s, the growing focus on social responsibility and the consumer movement compelled businesses to switch from one-way message delivery to two-way communication, which meant listening to publics, responding to crises, resolving disputes, and maintaining relationships with key publics. By the 1970s, communication departments at many universities were taking on the role of training public relations professionals, using the tools of social science and preparing graduates to handle much more complicated tasks than publicity and public information.

The role of college preparation was examined in *Public Relations Education for the 21st Century: A Port of Entry*, the report of the Commission on Public Relations Education (1999). The group—which was comprised of forty-eight of the leading public relations practitioners and educators in the United States—summarized the status of public relations at the dawn of the millennium:

In recent years, public relations professionals have moved toward an emphasis on building and maintaining relationships and on becoming skilled active counselors at management's decision-making table. Driving the latest evolutionary movement are influential social trends: global business operations; mergers, acquisitions and consolidations; the empowerment of public opinion within the global village; segmented, fragmented audiences; the information explosion that has led to uncontrolled, gateless dissemination of messages; increased government regulation and oversight; issues of diversity and multiculturalism in the workplace, marketplace and town hall, and the introduction of technology, including automation and computerization [pp. 9–10].

Increasingly, the professional recognizes the need for education beyond the baccalaureate to handle this complexity. At the beginning of the twenty-first century, approximately seventy schools offer master's degrees or graduate emphasis in public relations. A handful of universities offer the doctorate in public relations for those seeking careers in academic research.

Who are the people who shaped the public relations profession? The trade publication *PR Week* assembled a panel of experts to select "The 100 most influential PR people of the 20th century" (1999) The top ten, in order, were judged to be Harold Burson, founder of Burson & Marsteller, the largest public relations agency in the world; Edward L. Bernays; Arthur W. Page of AT&T, considered the first vice-president for public relations in a large corporation; Larry Foster of Johnson & Johnson, a former newspaperman who built that firm's public relations operation and gained fame for steering it through the Tylenol tampering crisis in 1982; Ivy Lee; Daniel Yankelovich, the researcher who developed polling to determine public opinion; John Hill, founder of Hill & Knowlton, a vigorous proponent of research and the first to seek clients overseas; David Drobis, CEO of Ketchum, who has led or served on the boards of most of the influential professional organizations in the industry; Larry Moskowitz of Medialink, who developed the video news release; and Scott Cutlip, the foremost architect of university public relations education,

chronicler of the history of the field, and coauthor of a leading public relations textbook. The list indicates the variety of people who constitute the modern profession.

Settings, Structures, and Strategies

The four general settings in the field of public relations are (1) private and public corporations, (2) agencies and freelancers, (3) nonprofits, and (4) educational institutions.

Corporate public relations sometimes goes by the name corporate public affairs or corporate communications. In businesses, the chief public relations officer typically is a vice-president who sits on the management council and who has access to the chief executive officer in order to provide counsel and to receive information about any situation that may necessitate a communication program. As a senior officer of the corporation, he or she participates in planning and policymaking. The corporate public relations staff of anywhere from 5 to 250 people includes media relations specialists, investor relations people, speechwriters, publication directors, and videoconferencing specialists. Larger corporate operations have researchers, librarians, and special events coordinators.

This is not to say that all corporate communication is handled "in-house." Most businesses also use public relations agencies or freelancers to handle special tasks, such as running focus-group interviews, designing corporate brochures, making videos, or running a special community event on behalf of the corporation.

Public relations agencies may be worldwide in scope, with offices in half a dozen or more U.S. cities and as many places abroad. Those agencies often are allied with advertising and marketing groups so that they can provide complete communication services. There also are thousands of one-person agencies—often called John Doe and Associates or Jane Doe and Associates to indicate that the sole practitioner has support from freelance writers, artists, and photographers. Medium-size agencies of five to twenty-five persons may specialize in health care, product public relations, sports promotion, retail promotion, entertainment, travel and tourism, or fundraising, to name but a few areas of focus. Often, the principal person in a public relations agency has had prior corporate experience and left the corporate world to set up

Industries that fall on hard times sometimes resort to heavy public relations work, as the French beef industry did when in November 2000 they worked with the French government to launch a public relations campaign to sway consumers to start eating beef again after the threat of Mad Cow disease had dominated headlines. (AFP/Corbis)

the agency. And corporations, which prefer and can pay for people with several years of experience, often hire away agency employees who have worked on the accounts of the corporation and are familiar with the company.

Nonprofit organizations have a different culture and usually need professionals with a somewhat different mindset. Most nonprofit organizations—arts organizations, health groups such as the American Cancer Society and Project Hope, environmental groups, consumer organizations, and community improvement associations—have two primary tasks: fundraising to enable the organization to survive, and public information to accomplish the goals of the organization. Public relations specialists working for nonprofit organizations must work constantly on ways to attract financial support and volunteers, as well as on ways to get their stories into the news media at little or no cost.

Educational relations is a burgeoning field, as universities and colleges become more and more competitive for students, for research money, and for public appreciation of the complex roles educational institutions play in society. Whereas universities once satisfied their needs with a small news bureau and perhaps a speechwriter for the president, the top research universities now employ well over one hundred people in marketing, community relations, legislative relations, business relations, fundraising, and sports promotion. Little wonder that on those campuses public relations also is among the fastest-growing undergraduate majors.

Whatever the setting, public relations is now so vital to an organization and so complex in its application that creativity and inspiration—which might have carried the day in another era—are not the hallmarks of the field. Strategic planning is the key. Because public relations is a management function and because practitioners must be able to demonstrate how they support the mission and goals of an organization, practitioners must be able to explain how their tactics support strategic goals and objectives.

Any organization has a broad mission, out of which grow general goals—and goals are achieved by setting specific and measurable objectives. Heads of public relations departments must set communication goals and objectives. A goal might be to increase information-seeking behaviors among mothers concerning the need to have children vaccinated for certain diseases. Out of that goal might grow specific objectives, such as increase by threefold the number of mothers calling an information hotline or requesting a brochure or, in one year, double the number of mothers bringing children to a clinic.

By its nature, then, the public relations function in an organization is one of coordinating the many parts and programs of an organization to assure that internal publics (employees) and external publics (community, consumers, governments, suppliers) receive the needed information.

At a conference sponsored by a public relations professional organization, there are generally one or two large sessions that are attended by everyone and feature a major speaker on a general topic. The rest of the time, attendees meet in their specialized divisions to talk about their special interests: financial public relations, health communication, travel and tourism, or environmental communication and technology. There are generalists in the field, but as in many professions, practitioners tend to gravitate toward specialties.

The tools and techniques used by public relations practitioners to achieve communication objectives are limitless. The list that follows—

only a sampling—indicates many of the standard techniques:

- Prepare a press kit introducing a new product and explaining its uses.
- Disseminate a statement explaining the position of the organization on a public issue.
- Prepare the president of the organization to appear on televised public affairs programs.
- Design a program to encourage employees to volunteer for community organizations.
- Select a celebrity spokesperson to represent the organization at public events.
- Write a letter to the editor opposing the views expressed in an editorial of a newspaper.
- Attend a public hearing to support or oppose a referendum affecting the organization.
- Design a booth for the county fair to disseminate information about the organization.
- Participate in a career program at a local high school.
- Donate products or services to a local homeless shelter.
- Publicize a program designed by the human resources department to help employees quit smoking.
- Plan a one hundredth anniversary celebration for the organization.
- Help raise funds for a new state or regional museum of arts and crafts.
- Plan a campaign to introduce a new semi-professional sports franchise in the area.
- Write a crisis communication plan for the organization.
- Design a "letter to our consumers" advertisement on a controversial issue.
- Form a coalition with another organization to leverage the public relations power of that group.

Whatever the tools and techniques, it is crucial that public relations practitioners be able to demonstrate they had a reason for selecting the tactics, and that those tactics were able to deliver on the stated objectives. It no longer is sufficient to agree that everyone "felt good" after a public relations program was put in place.

Thus, as in the allied fields of advertising and marketing, research now is of increased importance in public relations. Management wants numbers to prove that programs and departments are performing their functions. One has no hope of winning a Silver Anvil award from the Public Relations Society of America if research was not performed. Judges are instructed to look for evidence that there was formative research before a program was put in place and evaluative research afterward to assess results. And counting the number of "media hits" or news clippings is not enough in the evaluative stage. If a survey of a target public was conducted as part of the initial research, a follow-up survey asking the same questions of the same public is necessary to demonstrate the effect of a communication campaign.

In the past, practitioners had few tools for real research and/or little preparation in performing research. At the beginning of the twenty-first century, public relations textbooks provide guidance on sampling techniques, conducting focus group interviews, and content analysis of messages. To some extent at the undergraduate level, and definitely at the graduate level of education, professionals are trained to do research. Publications such as *Guidelines for Setting Measurable Public Relations Objectives* (Anderson and Hadley, 1999) enable professionals to track objectives and results so they can be reported to management in a meaningful way. In practice, much research is performed by outside agencies that are hired for that specific purpose.

Maintaining Professional Standards

Professions related to areas such as medicine, accounting, engineering, and law have requirements that include higher education at an accredited institution, passage of an entry exam, certification by a board, and maintenance of credentials through continuing education. Most mass communication professions, including public relations, do not have these requirements. A simple explanation is that many in the field do not believe that rigorous special preparation and absorption of a specific body of knowledge are necessary for most public relations positions, and the public has never demanded the same accountability it desires for doctors and lawyers. Another reason cited by some practitioners is that licensing or credentialing could interfere with the First Amendment rights of freedom of speech that mass communicators hold dear.

Bernays advocated licensing, pleading with professional groups to embrace it. He argued it was necessary in order to bring respect to the field and to prevent charlatans from passing themselves off as public relations counselors. He never got far with his campaign, and some said he was not the best proponent for licensing, given some of the dubious promotions with which he was associated.

While the public and the profession may not see a need for licensing, many feel that public relations may not be a universally trusted profession, and thus some form of credentialing is necessary to help clients and publics recognize which practitioners have education and experience in the field.

Some employers favor hiring practitioners who have a college degree in journalism, communication, or business and have taken courses teaching public relations skills. And some employers also favor hiring practitioners who have joined one or more of the several professional organizations in the field. However, considering that as many as half a million Americans work in public relations—or in public relations–like activities—and the combined membership of the major professional organizations is about fifty thousand, many in the field do not feel association is necessary.

The two largest groups based in the United States are the Public Relations Association of America (PRSA), which has nearly twenty thousand members, and the International Association of Business Communicators (IABC), with nearly fourteen thousand members. There is some overlap in membership. In the 1980s, the two groups came close to merging, but the effort to create one dominant professional association foundered over issues of focus and identity.

Both organizations offer accreditation to professionals who take a day-long examination of their skills and knowledge. PRSA confers the distinction of APR (i.e., Accredited in Public Relations), and IABC awards the distinction of ABC (i.e., Accredited Business Communicator). Recipients of the designation usually identify themselves as John Doe, APR, or Jane Doe, ABC. Accreditation is not required of PRSA or IABC members, and it is most popular with counselors in small agencies who want the designation for their business cards. Some corporations automatically grant a raise to a public relations employee who achieves accreditation.

Examples of other organizations include the International Public Relations Association (IPRA), the Canadian Public Relations Society (CPRS), the Council of Communication Management (CCM), which caters to managers and consultants, and the Arthur W. Page Society, serving the needs of top public relations practitioners such as large agency heads and corporate vice-presidents of public affairs. There are organizations for many specialized fields, such as agricultural public relations and investor relations. All such groups enable practitioners to network, to benchmark with other organizations, and to enhance their skills and abilities. They accomplish this through publications, conferences, workshops, and award programs.

The field of public relations also benefits from a growing body of knowledge coming out of academia, and scholars are visible in the leading professional organizations. Foundations sponsored by both PRSA and IABC, along with the independent Institute for Public Relations (IPR), provide grants for campus-based research on public relations topics.

A study by three public relations scholars, titled "Influential Authors and Works of the Public Relations Scholarly Literature" (Pasadeos, Renfro, and Hanily, 1999), revealed that, unlike other disciplines, public relations is typified by a concentration of scholars, institutions, and topics. During the five-year period studied, James E. Grunig of the University of Maryland was by far the most cited scholar, and his coauthored textbook *Managing Public Relations* (Grunig and Hunt, 1984) was the most cited work in the field. The book *Excellence in Public Relations and Communication Management* (1992), edited by Grunig, has been heavily cited in the field, as has his theory-building work with Larissa S. Grunig.

The most heavily cited serial publications in the public relations literature, according to the study by Yorgo Pasadeos and colleagues (1999), are *Public Relations Review*, followed by *Journalism Quarterly*, *Journal of Public Relations Research*, *Public Relations Journal*, and *Public Relations Quarterly*. All continue to be leading journals in the field, except *Public Relations Journal*, which has been supplanted by other PRSA publications. Grunig was founding editor of the *Journal of Public Relations Research*, which is published in cooperation with the Public Relations Division of the Association for Education in Journalism and Mass Communication (AEJMC).

The scholars whose work is often cited—and who also are active in academic and professional organizations—include Glenn Broom, David Dozier, and Martha Lauzen of San Diego State University, whose work on public relations roles has been heavily cited and is the center of a major cluster of research. Robert Heath of the University of Houston had the largest number of published articles during the period of the 1999 study. He is the author of *Strategic Issues Management* (1997) and coauthor (with Richard Alan Nelson of Louisiana State University) of *Issues Management: Corporate Public Policy Making in an Information Society* (1986). Larissa Grunig, in addition to her theory-building work, is a leading authority on gender issues and research methods. Elizabeth Lance Toth of Syracuse University and Carolyn Garrett Cline of the University of Southern California are the editors of *Beyond the Velvet Ghetto,* an examination of women in the field of public relations. Judy VanSlyke Turk is the author of diverse articles and has examined the "information subsidy" provided to the news media by public relations practitioners in the form of news releases and videotape. Kathleen Fearn-Banks of the University of Washington is an expert on crisis communication, and Kathleen S. Kelly of the University of Southwestern Louisiana has been honored for her articles and books showing the relationship between public relations and fundraising. Douglass Ann Newsom of Texas Christian University was the first female academic to serve as president of PRSA. Debra Ann Miller of the University of Portland was the first woman of color to serve as PRSA president.

The Centrality of Public Relations

Say "television" or "radio" or "newspaper" or "magazine" or "book," and everyone knows exactly what is being talked about. People watch television, listen to the radio, and read the print media. It is very clear what these items are and what they do. Say advertising, and everyone has a clear idea of what that is: the paid messages encountered in the mass media—the main reason the media are free or cheap, because advertising is paying the bill.

Say public relations, however, and perhaps people are not so sure. It cannot be touched or felt. Most people cannot explain its role and purpose readily. So, does that mean it is a marginal form of mass communication? Hardly. Public relations plays a central role in much that occurs in the arena of mass communication. It is just that public relations often works best when its role is not apparent. Like a giant iceberg, seven-eighths of what goes on in public relations is below the surface in the sea of information we encounter every day.

Just as advertising provides important revenue to the media of mass communication, public relations provides a stream of information from which the media can select. Why did the local newspaper cover the grand opening of a new supermarket? Because a public relations agency hired a celebrity to cut the ribbon, and it informed the media that the celebrity would be available for interviews afterward. Why is a university professor appearing on a televised public affairs broadcast? Because the news service of the university included a profile of her and her area of expertise on a website where broadcast producers can find expert sources. Why is a town meeting on preventing crime being held at the high school auditorium? Because the mayor's public information department, aided by funds from the public relations departments of area businesses, has put the evening together and promoted it in the news media.

Professionals in allied fields often misunderstand the function of public relations and how it relates to their jobs. Certainly, publishers and broadcast executives understand the benefits of the "information subsidy" their enterprises receive when someone else foots the bill for pictures, text, and access to interview subjects. But reporters and editors may not appreciate the role of public relations in providing the raw material with which they work. That means public relations practitioners must be able to "pitch" their stories so the journalist sees the value of the information and feels aided in informing the public rather than pressured or annoyed into using material.

Similarly, advertising and marketing people are often not clear about what public relations people are doing. In an age when "integrated communication" is seen as necessary so that organizations speak with one voice and so that every message we see about a product or idea is consistent with other messages, public relations people need to work closely with the allied fields. One controversy that exists in the persuasive professions is whether advertising, marketing, or public relations people have the overarching perspective that makes them most central to a communication enterprise. Large public relations agencies either represent themselves as being "full service" or can tell clients they are associated with an advertising agency that handles creative work and media placement.

More and more public relations practitioners must take a global perspective because so many activities and enterprises have become international in scope. Most corporations do business abroad, so most large public relations agencies either have offices in major world capitals or they partner with local agencies in other countries. Even educational and nonprofit practitioners find themselves spanning national boundaries. Rescue and relief agencies in the United States regularly help other nations, and their fundraising is international. Educational institutions have exchange programs and distance education arrangements with universities in other countries.

The number one global priority for public relations practitioners in the twenty-first century is maintaining and strengthening support for the profession in the face of questions about the methods and the ethics of "PR"—the belief that if something is "just PR" it is not truthful communication. Counselor Chester Burger (1998) told professionals:

> Perhaps too many of our corporate messages are being framed in exactly the same way they were presented a quarter-century ago. We seem to pretend that the cynicism and changed values of a new generation don't exist. . . . If public relations advocacy is to be effective and persuasive, our messages should be quiet and civil, not angry and adversarial. And, in the age of the Internet, we must be ready to respond instantly.

Similar to lawyers, public relations practitioners are counselors and advocates. And, similar to lawyers, they must work hard to earn respect for their profession.

See also: ADVERTISING EFFECTS; ORGANIZATIONAL COMMUNICATION; ORGANIZATIONAL COMMUNICATION, CAREERS IN; PUBLIC RELATIONS, CAREERS IN.

Bibliography

Anderson, Forrest W., and Hadley, Linda. (1999). *Guidelines for Setting Measurable Public Relations Objectives.* Gainesville, FL: The Institute for Public Relations.

Bernays, Edward L. (1923). *Crystallizing Public Opinion.* New York: Liveright.

Bernays, Edward L. (1928). *Propaganda.* New York: Liveright.

Bernays, Edward L. (1952). *Public Relations.* Norman: University of Oklahoma Press.

Burger, Chester. (1998). "A Discussion of Truth and Credibility in an Era of Disbelief." Institute for Public Relations Distinguished Lecture, New York, Dec. 2.

Commission on Public Relations Education. (1999). *Public Relations Education for the 21st Century: A Port of Entry.* New York: Public Relations Society of America.

Cutlip, Scott M., and Center, Allen H. (1978). *Effective Public Relations,* 5th edition. Englewood Cliffs, NJ: Prentice-Hall.

Grunig, James E., ed. (1992). *Excellence in Public Relations and Communication Management.* Hillsdale, NJ: Lawrence Erlbaum.

Grunig, James E., and Hunt, Todd. (1984). *Managing Public Relations.* New York: Holt, Rinehart and Winston.

Heath, Robert L. (1997). *Strategic Issues Management.* Beverly Hills, CA: Sage Publications.

Heath, Robert L., and Nelson, Richard A. (1986). *Issues Management: Corporate Public Policy Making in an Information Society.* Beverly Hills, CA: Sage Publications.

Lesly, Philip, ed. (1998). *Lesly's Handbook of Public Relations and Communications,* 5th edition. Chicago: Probus.

"The 100 Most Influential PR People of the 20th Century." (1999). *PR Week,* Oct. 18, p. 26.

Pasadeos, Yorgo; Renfro, R. Bruce; and Hanily, Mary Lynn. (1999). "Influential Authors and Works of the Public Relations Scholarly Literature: A Network of Recent Research." *Journal of Public Relations Research* 11(1):29–52.

"Would You Ever Recommend that Your Son or Daughter Pursue a Career in PR?" (1999). *PR Week,* Nov. 1, p. 12.

TODD HUNT

■ PUBLIC RELATIONS, CAREERS IN

The wide range of career opportunities for people working in public relations include such jobs as media relations specialist for an insurance company, newsletter editor for an urban renewal agency, special events coordinator for a hotel, sports information director for a university, writer–editor for a public relations agency, community relations coordinator for a hospital, fund-raiser for the American Red Cross, speechwriter for a U.S. senator, and freelancer specializing in the preparation of video news releases.

In few other fields of mass communication would one find the range of job positions one finds in the area of public relations. As the above examples show, the array of possibilities available to a recent college graduate is vast. First, there is the varied choice of setting: public relations agency, government, industry, educational institutions, or nonprofit organizations. Then there is the range of endeavors: writing, editing, meeting the public, arranging events, replying to inquiries for information, distributing material to the news media, or coordinating campaigns with advertising and marketing people. Some public relations positions involve many or all of these skills.

Many public relations people begin their careers in other fields. Journalism has long been a starting place for careers in public relations because reporting, writing, and editing skills can be used not only by an employee of the news media, but also by a public relations person who prepares stories for a client and distributes them to the news media. The line between public relations and allied fields such as advertising and marketing gets blurred within the communications departments of many large organizations and in "full-service" agencies that offer advertising, marketing, and public relations services to their clients. The line does not exist at all in nonprofit groups.

The Public Relations Society of America has identified four levels of professional competence:

1. "Beginning professional" refers to a junior staff member who is using basic skills and is undergoing training. In an agency, the official title might be "writer," "researcher," or "assistant."

2. "Staff professional" refers to someone who, after amassing eighteen to twenty-four months of experience at the craft, takes on an initial supervisory role. In an agency, the title might be "assistant account executive."

3. "Professional manager" refers to someone with at least five years of experience whose activities include direction of staff and department operations, research, planning, budgeting, evaluation, and personal communication. In an agency, the title might be "account executive."

4. "Senior professional" refers to a top management position where the responsibilities would include running an operation, serving as adviser and policymaker, dealing with public affairs and issues management, and consulting with top management on communication policies. In an agency, the title might be "vice-president."

Alternatively, one can aspire to run one's own agency or become chief public relations officer (CPRO) at a corporation or chief information officer (CIO) in a government agency.

Unlike the field of medicine, where one attends medical school and then endures a long residency, the aspiring public relations practitioner can take many routes. If the career decision is made upon entering college, then majoring in journalism or communication makes sense. One or the other of those departments at most universities offers a sequence of public relations courses, and some offer full majors in public relations. Courses in organizational communication also provide a helpful background.

More than two hundred universities in the United States have chapters of the Public Relations Student Society of America (PRSSA). This means that each of the respective universities offers at least five courses in public relations, has a faculty member who belongs to the Public Relations Society of America (PRSA), and is affiliated with a local or state chapter of PRSA. PRSSA membership is an advantage because, in addition to sponsoring speakers and field trips, most student chapters run agencies that take on "real-world" clients from the campus and the community, which helps students build their resumes while in college.

Internships also are an invaluable way of getting experience while in college. If one is able to do more than a single internship, this provides the opportunity to try out different settings—perhaps working for a nonprofit organization and then moving to an agency or corporate position.

Lack of either a major in public relations or experience in multiple internships will not disqualify the late-bloomer who discovers public relations as a senior, after graduation, or even after sampling another career or serving in the military. For example, one can serve as a public information officer in the military and, upon discharge, present worthy credentials for employment by a civilian public relations employer. Majors in business, English, psychology, and political science can also lead to successful careers for those who belatedly discover the field of public relations.

The key to success in public relations is a skills-set that includes good writing and research abilities, strong interpersonal skills, imagination, and the ability to work in team settings. When the trade publication *PR Week* (1999) asked practitioners whether they would advise their children to pursue careers in public relations, the responses focused on such diverse issues as the pressures to perform, the ethics of disseminating information, the motivation needed, and the opportunity to shape the world of the future.

More and more practitioners are finding that they need to broaden their skills and learn new techniques and technologies as the field becomes more complicated and the pace of communication quickens. Membership in PRSA or the International Association of Business Communicators (IABC) provides the opportunity to hear professional speakers, attend workshops, and participate in conferences where new ideas and fresh approaches are discussed. Most universities offer continuing education courses (such as those focusing on the latest computer skills) that are of value to public relations practitioners. With all of this in mind, the consensus among those working in the area is that public relations demands a high level of professionalism from its practitioners.

See also: CHIEF INFORMATION OFFICERS; PUBLIC RELATIONS.

Bibliography

"Would You Ever Recommend that Your Son or Daughter Pursue a Career in PR?" (1999). *PR Week*, Nov. 1, p. 12.

TODD HUNT

▌■ PUBLIC SERVICE MEDIA

The term "public service media" is generally used to refer to a particular form of radio and television broadcasting that emerged in Western Europe in the 1920s, of which the British Broadcasting Corporation (BBC) is the best-known example and most common reference point. Public service broadcasting is still a mainstay in most of Western Europe, as well as in an array of countries as diverse as Canada, Australia, South Africa, and Japan. In various local adaptations, it is also an important model in the emerging media systems of Africa, Asia, and the former Soviet bloc. However, challenged by the pressures of diminishing public funds, the growth of commercial media, new technologies, and globalization, public service broadcasting no longer enjoys the dominant—even, in some countries, monopolistic—position that it once held. It is still nonetheless the most important existing mainstream alternative to commercial broadcasting.

Historically, the public service model dates from the early days of broadcast radio. Initial radio "stations" were established in many parts of the world as early as 1919 (Montreal's XWA and Pittsburgh's KDKA are generally considered to have been the first) by set manufacturers and other commercial organizations, as well as educational, labor, and public interest groups. The future shape of broadcasting was at first unclear. By the mid-1920s, however, sparked by the entrepreneurial initiative of networked programming pioneers such as David Sarnoff (later head of NBC), an advertising-supported commercial model was well established in the United States, Canada, and parts of Europe. Fearful that commercial broadcasting would soon dominate to the exclusion of all other models, educators and public interest associations began lobbying governments to recapture at least part of the new medium for public service purposes. In the United States, noncommercial broadcasting was quickly marginalized, but in Britain, the government created a national public service monopoly, the BBC, and put it in charge of all radio broadcasting.

The justification for this British move was spelled out by a 1923 committee chaired by Sir Frederick Sykes, which stated in its report to Parliament "that the control of such a potential power over public opinion and the life of the nation ought to remain with the State, and that the operation of so important a national service ought not to be allowed to become an unrestricted commercial monopoly." The BBC was created in 1926, and most European countries soon followed the British example, while Canada and Australia, among others, adopted "mixed" systems with both public and private-sector components. By the early 1930s, public service broadcasting was well established and began to be typified by distinctive program formats as well as its characteristic institutional structure. When television was introduced in the 1950s, most countries basically incorporated the new medium into the systems that they had put in place for radio, with some important variants, however. In Canada, for example, public radio is commercial-free, while public television depends to an important extent on advertising.

The notion of public service, at least in the Anglo-Saxon world, was strongly shaped by the BBC's founding director, Sir John Reith. Reith saw the public as an audience that was capable of growth and development, and he declared famously that the BBC would give the public what it needs, not what it wants. This kind of elitism would later return to haunt the proponents of public service broadcasting when audiences began migrating to private commercial outlets, especially after the introduction of private television. Be that as it may, the mandate of public service broadcasters inspired by the British example was to provide programming that informed and enlightened, as well as entertained. In many countries, this proviso was enshrined in broadcasting legislation. Depending on local circumstances, public service broadcasting was also typically mandated to provide service that would be accessible to all residents of a given national territory, to provide a range of programs that would be of interest to all social and demographic groups, and to contribute to building national cultural identity. Later, more specific objectives such as reflecting regional and linguistic diversity would be added to many official public service broadcasting mandates.

Public service broadcasting is typically organized in a national corporation, with varying degrees of autonomy from the state. In Britain and its former dominions, the public service broadcaster is deemed to operate at "arm's length" from the government, and this proviso at least nominally guarantees the independence of public service broadcasting. Public service broadcasting executives are named by governments but cannot be removed without cause. In France, however, political tradition called for the heads of public service broadcasting institutions to be replaced with every change of government. Generally, while public service broadcasters and the governments that created them have at times been at

TABLE 1.

Revenue Sources for Broadcasting for 1997

Country	Public Funding (%)	Subscription (%)	Advertising (%)
Canada	16	47	37
France	25	34	41
Germany	32	25	43
Italy	34	7	59
Japan	23	12	65
United Kingdom	21	30	49
United States	3	46	51

SOURCE: Organisation for Economic Co-operation and Development (1999).

odds over programming choices over the years, the main area of friction surrounds financing.

Public service broadcasting, following the British model, is funded by an annual "license fee," a charge akin to an automobile registration that must be paid by every household that owns a radio or television set. While this funding formula is designed to bypass government interference by providing a direct relationship between the broadcaster and its audience, the fee rates are inevitably set by the government, giving it obvious power over the broadcasting institutions. In some cases, such as Canada and Australia, public service broadcasters are funded by direct annual grants from their respective Parliaments, tainting the process with the potential for political interference even more. Many public service broadcasters also increasingly depend on commercial revenue for at least part of their income, making them reliant on the general regulatory framework in their countries as well. In just about every country with public service broadcasting, there is a lively and more or less permanent debate surrounding the appropriate level of public funding. In Germany, for example, the Constitutional Court ruled in 1994 that funding public service broadcasting appropriately was a government obligation. The figures in Table 1 show the comparative sources of revenue for overall broadcasting activities in seven countries for 1997.

National peculiarities apart, questions concerning the structures of broadcasting are increasingly global ones. In the new broadcasting environment, the issue of public service broadcasting can be reduced to the following question: What social and cultural goals that are attributed to broadcasting require a specially mandated, noncommercially driven organization that is publicly owned, publicly funded, and publicly accountable?

Broadcasters, politicians, media professionals, creative people, community activists, and scholars worldwide are wrestling with this question. While the diagnosis is global, the prescriptions are necessarily specific to context. When they are put together, however, the range of models, examples, and ways of framing the issues include the basis for a global portrait and a sketch of a solution.

There is no easy answer to the question "What is public service broadcasting?" However, a reasonably thorough one can be found in a 1994 document from the Council of Europe, which included a nine-point mission statement that reiterated, in a particularly European perspective, the traditional objectives of public service broadcasting. According to this body, public service broadcasting should provide

1. a common reference point for all members of the public,

2. a forum for broad public discussion,

3. impartial news coverage,

4. pluralistic, innovative, and varied programming,

5. programming that is both of wide public interest and attentive to the needs of minorities,

6. reflection of the different ideas and beliefs in pluriethnic and multicultural societies,

7. a diversity of national and European cultural heritage,

8. original productions by independent producers, and

9. extended viewer and listener choice by offering programs not provided by the commercial sector.

These goals led the Council of Europe to declare that the safeguarding of independent, appropriately funded public service broadcasting institutions is essential to the functioning of the media in a democratic society.

In 1997, the addition of a Protocol on Public Service Broadcasting to the Treaty governing the European Union (EU) highlighted the fact that what was originally a strictly "national" service, although similar in many countries, has become increasingly transnational in the context of glob-

alization. In light of the growing commercialization of all media, public service broadcasting continues to designate a strong value of social worth, the "last best hope" for socially purposeful media acting in the public interest.

The EU protocol considers "that the system of public broadcasting in the Member States [of the European Union] is directly related to the democratic, social and cultural needs of each society and to the need to preserve media pluralism." This in itself is important in terms of legitimating public service broadcasting at a time when its basis is under attack on both ideological and economic grounds. It links public service broadcasting to the question of democracy, emphasizes its sociocultural nature as a public service, and underscores the distinctive role of public service broadcasting in an otherwise uniformly commercial system.

The context of technological convergence and the accompanying policy debates can help to further clarify the concept of public service with respect to media generally and, hence, to develop a more appropriate conception of public service broadcasting. In telecommunication, for example, the concept of universal public service has been much more clear and straightforward than in broadcasting. The principle of universality has been tied to the operational provision of affordable access (not an issue in broadcasting as long as the main means of transmission was over-the-air, but increasingly so with the addition of various tiers of chargeable services).

The displacement of universal service by subscriber-based and pay-per-view services is the strongest factor favoring a shift toward the consumer model in broadcasting, and proponents of public service broadcasting feel that this needs to be countered by policy measures and institutional mechanisms that are designed to promote the democratic function of broadcasting. This can only come about through a rethinking of what is meant by public service broadcasting.

Traditionally, public service broadcasting has been expected to represent the national as opposed to the foreign. It may be time to refocus these conceptual categories in terms of the local and the global. Global cultural industries recognize this by developing products that are targeted to "niche markets." Public service broadcasting has a different role, which it seeks to fulfill principally by conceiving its audience as a public rather than a market. Some programs may speak to a particular national public, but on any given national territory there will be less-than-national broadcasting needs to be fulfilled. National networks can no longer be expected to be forces of cohesion; they can, however, be highly effective distribution systems for programs that are of importance to the communities they serve. For this to occur, public service broadcasting needs to be redefined in terms that are suitable to a new public culture, global in scope and experienced locally.

Nothing in the idea of public service broadcasting ties it intrinsically to that of nationhood; it is, however, necessarily linked to notions of community. In order to flourish in the future, public service broadcasting will need to be reconceptualized in the context of a changing role for the still-present, still-formidable (for lack of a structure to replace it) nation-state. As the alternative to the state becomes the market, the alternative to national public service broadcasting has been constructed as private sector broadcasting; this parallel is logically flawed as well as politically shortsighted. The globalization of markets is both global and local, in that global products are usually produced in a single place, distributed worldwide, and consumed locally, everywhere. As the nation-state struggles to find its way in this new environment, so does public service broadcasting. It is false to assume, however, that there is no longer a need for public service broadcasting, for this is the only established mainstream medium that can be said to place social and cultural concerns before the imperatives of the marketplace. Furthermore, as public authorities begin looking toward the capacity of national broadcasting systems as a whole to meet public interest goals and objectives, more attention may be paid to the overall ecology of broadcasting as a public service environment.

See also: CULTURE AND COMMUNICATION; CULTURE INDUSTRIES, MEDIA AS; DEMOCRACY AND THE MEDIA; PUBLIC BROADCASTING; SOCIAL CHANGE AND THE MEDIA; SOCIAL GOALS AND THE MEDIA; SOCIETY AND THE MEDIA.

Bibliography

Avery, Robert K. (1993). *Public Service Broadcasting in a Multichannel Environment.* New York: Longman.
Blumler, Jay G., ed. (1992). *Television and the Public Interest: Vulnerable Values in West European Broadcasting.* London: Sage Publications.
Broadcasting Research Unit. (1985/1988) *The Public Service Idea in British Broadcasting: Main Principles.* London: Broadcasting Research Unit.
Council of Europe. (1994). *The Media in a Democratic Society.* Prague: Fourth European Ministerial Conference on Mass Media Policy.
Council of the European Union. (1997). "Protocol on the System of Public Broadcasting in the Member States." *Draft Treaty of Amsterdam.* Brussels: Council of the European Union.
Graham, Andrew, and Davies, Gavyn. (1997). *Broadcasting, Society and Policy in the Multimedia Age.* Luton, Eng.: University of Luton Press.
McChesney, Robert W. (1993). *Telecommunications, Mass Media, & Democracy: The Battle for the Control of U.S. Broadcasting, 1928–1935.* New York: Oxford University Press.
McDonnell, James. (1991). *Public Service Broadcasting: A Reader.* London: Routledge.
Organisation for Economic Co-operation and Development. (1999). *OECD Communications Outlook 1999.* Paris: OECD.
Raboy, Marc. (1990). *Missed Opportunities: The Story of Canada's Broadcasting Policy.* Montreal: McGill-Queen's University Press.
Raboy, Marc, ed. (1996). *Public Broadcasting for the Twenty-First Century.* Luton, Eng.: University of Luton Press.
Rowland, Willard D., Jr., and Tracey, Michael. (1990). "Worldwide Challenges to Public Service Broadcasting." *Journal of Communication* 40(2):8–27.
Scannell, Paddy. (1989). "Public Service Broadcasting and Modern Public Life." *Media, Culture, and Society* 11(2):135–166.
Smith, Anthony. (1973). *The Shadow in the Cave: The Broadcaster, His Audience, and the State.* Urbana: University of Illinois Press.
Sykes, Sir Frederick, chair. (1923). *Report of the Broadcasting Committee.* London: King's Printer.
United Nations Educational, Scientific, and Cultural Organization. (1997) *Public Service Broadcasting: Cultural and Educational Dimensions.* Paris: UNESCO.
World Radio and Television Council. (2000). *Public Broadcasting. Why? How?* Montreal: World Radio and Television Council.

MARC RABOY

PUBLIC SPEAKING

The art of public speaking can trace its roots back to ancient Greece and the orators who proclaimed governmental achievements, entertained audiences, and debated political issues in public forums. In the *Rhetoric*, written in 330 B.C.E., Aristotle discussed the process by which a speaker prepares and delivers a speech. Much of this material is still applicable. For example, Aristotle wrote about three types of persuasive appeals: *ethos* (i.e., credibility of the source of the message), *pathos* (i.e., appealing to the emotions of the audience), and *logos* (i.e., the nature of the message). A contemporary advertisement in which a notable sports figure (*ethos*) telling a personal story about learning the negative consequences of driving while intoxicated (*logos*) to teenage athletes who have just learned to drive (*pathos*) illustrates the principles that Aristotle described.

History

Historically, public speaking was known as rhetoric and has a long history, both in terms of training people to become good rhetors (i.e., public speakers) and in analyzing what factors made a speech effective (i.e., rhetorical criticism or analysis). James McCroskey (2000) notes that the oldest essay ever discovered was written around 3000 B.C.E., and it consists of advice on how to speak effectively. McCroskey argues that the first theory of public speaking was developed by the Greeks and consisted of a theory about courtroom speaking. In the fifth century B.C.E., the Greek Sophists developed small schools to teach the concepts that are now included in the modern idea of debate. Good speakers were taught how to argue both sides of a proposition and were encouraged to write short, general messages that could be used whenever they were asked to speak in public. Isocrates, the most influential of the Greek Sophists, was recognized as an excellent teacher who also wrote orations for other people to deliver, much like a modern speech writer does. Isocrates emphasized rhetorical style (i.e., how to present a speech effectively) and how to train people to become effective public speakers. In 389 B.C.E., Plato wrote the *Phaedrus,* in which he discussed his theory of rhetoric. According to McCroskey, some scholars consider Aristotle's *Rhetoric* to be in response to the criticisms that were raised by Plato. Whether this is true or not, both theorists helped lay the foundation for the contemporary study of public speaking.

As discussed by McCroskey, the next major period for the development of the art and study of public speaking is the Roman period, during which the *Rhetorica ad Herennium* appeared around 82 B.C.E. This work includes information about style, delivery, and the six parts to a rhetorical message: introduction, statement of facts (i.e., narration), division, proof, refutation, and conclusion. Cicero also wrote several works about rhetoric during this period, as did Quintilian. As McCroskey notes, the most often quoted phrase from Quintilian is his observation that a public speaker is a "good man speaking well." Of course, this quotation would now be extended to include all people, not just men.

In the contemporary world, one of the most important areas of study for scholars of public speaking is analyzing and critiquing the rhetoric of significant public speakers. Sonja Foss and Karen Foss (1994) extend the traditional examination of famous public speakers by their contention that presentational speaking is an "invitation to transformation." Public speaking allows speakers to grow and change as individuals, and it helps others to do the same thing as well. Both the speaker and the audience have the potential to leave the interaction with new ideas and insights. Foss and Foss, among others, provide a reminder that the public presentations of Adrienne Rich, Audre Lord, Alice Walker, and Ursula Le Guin, for example, are as significant as the speeches of Abraham Lincoln and Thomas Jefferson in terms of scholarly study.

Basic Principles

The four principles of effective public speaking are both simple and complex at the same time. Effective public speeches are audience centered, organized appropriately, written clearly, and presented compellingly. Within each of these aspects of an effective speech, however, there are various ways to accomplish the task well.

Audience-Centered Speeches

The first principle, being audience centered, means that effective public speaking relies on understanding who the audience is and, once this is known, developing a speech that is appropriate to that particular audience. The most basic information that needs to be known about any potential audience is the demographic information (i.e., factors such as age, ethnicity, gender, education level) that may influence the audience's perception of the speaker's message. A young speaker who is talking about a historical topic such as the assassination of President John F. Kennedy, for example, needs to know how many people in the audience were alive when the event occurred. If most of the people remember the event, the speaker needs only to briefly mention historical details and then get to the main point of the speech, such as describing how contemporary teenagers view the event. If most of the audience consists of teenagers who were not alive when the even occurred, more time should be spent during the speech in describing the event and its aftermath. In fact, a speech on the Kennedy assassination for a young audience might have a very different purpose (e.g., convincing them that historical events are relevant to their lives) than it would have for an older audience (e.g., convincing them that modern teenagers are influenced by historical events). Thus, knowing the audience helps the speaker both to choose a topic and to develop it in a manner that is appropriate to the audience.

Appropriate Organization

Effective public speeches need to be organized appropriately both for the topic and for the potential audience. Traditional views of public speaking call for speeches to contain an introduction, body, and conclusion. In fact, some people have commented in jest that a good public speech consists of telling an audience what the speaker plans to tell them, telling it to them, and then telling them what it was that speaker just told them. While this is a bit of an exaggeration, an effective public speech may indeed contain more repetition than other forms of communication in order to assist the audience in remembering the main points that the speaker wishes to make. Stephen E. Lucas (1998) argues that the process of organizing a speech begins when the speaker determines a specific purpose (e.g., to inform an audience about a particular topic), identifies the central idea (i.e., what major issues are involved in the topic), and settles on the main points (e.g., three things the audience should know about the topic). Once this is accomplished, the speaker can then choose from a variety of traditional organizational patterns. These patterns include chronological (i.e., following a time pattern), spatial (i.e., following a directional pattern), causal (i.e., organizing points to show a cause-and-effect relationship), problem–solution (i.e., showing the existence of a problem and then providing a solution to it), and topical (i.e., dividing the speech into subtopics). Clella Jaffe (2001) points out

With the increased influence of media in the democratic process, it is crucial that candidates, such as Hillary Clinton and Rick Lazio in their 2000 battle over the Senate seat for New York, master the principles of public speaking for debates and other public appearances if they are going to be seen as valid contenders in the election process. (Reuters NewMedia Inc./Corbis)

three additional organizational patterns that she notes were explicated by Cheryl Jorgensen-Earp, who contends that they are less linear than the traditional organizational patterns. The patterns that Jaffe discusses include the wave pattern (i.e., a pattern where the crests of the waves are the major points that are developed through a series of examples; repetition and variation are key components), the spiral pattern (i.e., a repetitive pattern that has a series of points that increase in drama or intensity), and the star pattern (i.e., a theme that ties together a series of relatively equally weighted points).

One of the most famous organizational patterns for public speeches was developed by Alan H. Monroe and is called the "motivated sequence" (see German et al., 2001). It is particularly well suited to persuasive speeches. The motivated sequence consists of five steps: attention, need, satisfaction, visualization, and action. The attention step consists of the introduction to the speech, in which the speaker must gain the attention of the audience in an appropriate manner. A speaker may gain the attention of the audience by yelling loudly, for example, but this tactic may only alienate the listeners, not motivate them to pay attention to the speech. Introductions and attention steps must be tailored to a particular audience and fit within the purpose of the speech. For example, a startling statement, such as the number of teenagers who die each year as the result of drunken driving, would be appropriate for introducing a speech that is designed to persuade the listeners not to drink and drive. Many speakers feel that a joke is a good way to begin a public speech, but this tactic often fails because the joke is not well told, does not fit the purpose of the speech, or is inappropriate for a particular audience. The second step of the motivated sequence, the need step, consists of establishing the need for the audience to listen to the speaker's message by describing the problem to be discussed. Monroe proposed four parts to this step: statement (i.e., describe the nature of the problem or situation), illustration (i.e., give examples), ramifications (i.e., give support such as statistics that show the extent of the problem), and pointing (i.e., demonstrate a connection between the problem and the audience). In the satisfaction step, the speaker proposes a solution that will satisfy the need that has been established in the need step. This satisfaction step may include statement, explanation, theoretical demonstration, practicality (i.e., using facts and statistics), and meeting objections. The next step consists of visualization, in which the speaker describes the consequences of either adopting or rejecting the proposed course of action. In positive visualization, the speaker describes the favorable consequences that will results from following the proposed plan (e.g., how one's life may be saved by wearing a seatbelt in a car). In negative visualization, the speaker describes the potential negative consequences that will result from not following the proposed plan (e.g., asking the audience members to imagine what it would feel like, as a result of not wearing a seatbelt, to strike the windshield of a car during a collision). Contrast visualization can be used to compare the negative results of not adopting the proposed action with the positive results of adopting it. Finally, the action step consists of asking the listeners for specific action, which may include changing their beliefs about something, changing their behaviors, or changing their attitudes.

Knowing the audience will help the speaker to determine which organizational pattern is appro-priate. Audiences who already basically agree with the speaker's message (e.g., voters who support a particular political candidate) will not be as critical of a speech as will audiences who are either unfamiliar with the speaker (e.g., undecided voters) or opposed to the speaker's message (e.g., voters who support an alternative candidate).

Clear Writing

Effective speeches must also be clearly written. A well-organized speech is useless unless the audience understands the message that is being communicated to them. One of the most important ways to ensure clear writing is to make sure that the vocabulary used in the speech is appropriate for the particular audience. For example, it is possible to use highly technical medical jargon when speaking to physicians, but that would not be effective for an audience of college students. In the same way, sports terminology is useful for communicating a message and establishing credibility with a group of sports fans, but it would be ineffective with people who are unfamiliar with the nuances of a particular sport.

Compelling Presentation

A speech does not have to be overly dramatic or theatrical to be effectively compelling. Instead, an effective delivery should be sincere, honest, straightforward, and dynamic. Varying vocal pitch, speech, and volume are effective devices for keeping the attention of an audience. However, an overemphasis on these aspects can be disastrous and can make the speaker seem phony or insincere. It is a good rule of thumb for a speaker to remember to talk to the audience as if he or she were talking to one person at a time. A speaker should try to convince the listeners that he or she is competent to speak on the topic and that he or she is sincere in wanting the listeners to understand the message.

Much research has been conducted on ways in which public speeches can be presented effectively. The first step in effective presentation is rehearsal. In formal situations (e.g., important political speeches or theatrical presentations), dress rehearsals are held. This situation simulates the actual presentational situation as closely as possible. A mock audience may even be included to ask the speaker typical questions and test the answers to them. For less formal situations, the speaker may still want to simulate the situation (at least in his or her imagination) and check for things such as timing, familiarity with the setting (e.g., where the controls to audiovisual equipment are located), and knowing how the audience will be seated. It is extremely important for speakers to prepare a presentation that does not extend past the allotted time, and they must not be confounded by any technical difficulties, such as not knowing how the overhead projector works. Good public speakers make sure that they know how any audiovisual aids work and have alternative strategies prepared in case the expected technological aids do not function properly.

Presentational strategies should also be developed that can be used to respond to feedback from the audience. If the audience seems restless or confused, the speaker should be able to change the message to include more examples or to shorten parts of the planned presentation that seem to be repetitive. More interesting graphics or the use of more vocal variety may help get the audience more involved with the message. Again, audience analysis before the public presentation can aid the speaker in developing strategies to cope with various reactions from the "real" audience.

Good public speakers also often attend to other presentational elements before they enter a situation where they will be presenting a public speech. For example, dress can be a unifying strategy that links the speaker with the audience. Politicians are seen wearing caps that build a bridge between them and their audiences. Jackets with sports insignias are used to help the audience see a speaker as "one of them." Not all speakers endeavor to identify closely with their audiences, however. For example, religious leaders often wear special clothing that signifies their official capacity to conduct a religious service and to reinforce their role as spiritual adviser.

Ethics of Public Speaking

Given their potential to influence so many people, public speakers should have a heightened sense of ethical responsibility as they prepare and present their messages. Jaffe has identified three ethical guidelines that are important for all public speakers: courtesy, tolerance, and civility.

Courteous public speakers demonstrate their respect for the audience by responding politely to them and being considerate of their beliefs and feelings. Demonstrating courtesy does not mean that a speaker must agree with the audience. In fact, the speaker's job may be to persuade the audience that they are mistaken about a particular issue. However, disagreement should be expressed in well-presented ideas and in statements that are backed with supporting evidence, not in name-calling and making insulting statements to the audience.

Effective public speakers exhibit tolerance by understanding that neither they nor their audience may possess the total truth and that each party should be tolerant of the other's views. This does not mean that a speaker should refrain from vigorously arguing his or her viewpoint, but the argument should be framed within a recognition of the potential for legitimate disagreement from the audience.

Speakers who demonstrate civility rely on persuasion, compromise, and coalition building instead of coercion, deceit, or manipulation. A willingness to listen is a necessary prerequisite for civility.

Conclusion

Public speaking and the study of public speakers and their messages continue to evolve as technology changes the means of communicating to larger audiences. A modern speaker can deliver a speech on television and reach a vastly larger audience than could a speaker at any time in previous history. In this way, it is particularly crucial for public speakers to deliver ethical and responsible messages that further the dialogue between themselves and their potential audiences. Technology has given public speakers the ability to influence hundreds of thousands of people at one time, and these speakers must recognize their responsibility to use this power wisely.

In addition, the Internet has given speakers even greater access to a multitude of individuals who are able to gain access to documents, such as speeches, that are posted on the World Wide Web in text, audio, or video formats. The possibilities and potential dangers of this new access to information have not yet been fully explored, but they provide a rich source of data for new scholarly study in the future.

See also: APPREHENSION AND COMMUNICATION; INTERPERSONAL COMMUNICATION; MODELS OF COMMUNICATION; PUBLIC SPEAKING, CAREERS IN; RHETORIC.

Bibliography

Beebe, Steven A.; Beebe, Susan J.; Dreyer, Jennifer; and Patton, Gregory H. (1999). *Public Speaking: An Audience-Centered Approach,* 3rd edition. Englewood Cliffs, NJ: Prentice-Hall.

DeVito, Joseph A. (1999). *The Elements of Public Speaking,* 7th edition. Reading, MA: Addison-Wesley.

Foss, Sonja K., and Foss, Karen A. (1994). *Inviting Transformation: Presentational Speaking for a Changing World.*. Prospect Heights, IL: Waveland Press.

German, Kathleen M.; Gronbeck, Bruce E.; Ehninger, Douglas; and Monroe, Alan H. (2001). *Principles of Public Speaking,* 14th edition. Boston: Allyn & Bacon.

Hanson, Trudy L. (1999). "Gender Sensitivity and Diversity Issues in Selected Basic Public Speaking Texts." *Women & Language* 22(2):13–19.

Jaffe, Clella. (2001). *Public Speaking: Concepts and Skills for a Diverse Society,* 3rd edition. Belmont, CA: Wadsworth.

Lucas, Stephen E. (1998). *The Art of Public Speaking,* 6th edition. New York: McGraw-Hill.

McCroskey, James C. (2000). *An Introduction to Rhetorical Communication*, 8th edition. Boston: Allyn & Bacon.

Osborn, Michael, and Osborn, Suzanne. (2000). *Public Speaking,* 5th edition. Boston: Houghton Mifflin.

Zarefsky, David. (1999). *Public Speaking: Strategies for Success,* 2nd edition. Boston: Allyn & Bacon.

LEA P. STEWART

■ PUBLIC SPEAKING, CAREERS IN

Effective public speaking is a basic skill that is needed for a variety of careers in contemporary society. People who have completed undergraduate communication programs can be found working in occupations ranging from account managers and actresses to web administration directors. Typical careers for individuals skilled in public speaking include advertising executive, attorney, corporate communications officer, corporate trainer, customer service representative, human resources manager, organizational development specialist, public relations professional, sales representative, and television reporter.

Training in speech and communication is also important for individuals who desire employment as administrators, audience coordinators for television programs, business analysts, computer consultants, digital media specialists, entertainers, financial consultants, hospitality managers, insurance agents, librarians, marketing professionals, mediators, nonprofit development officers, project development specialists, retail buyers, social workers, telecommunications consultants, travel agents, and television producers.

From the above lists, it may seem that any professional career could benefit from training in speech and public speaking, and, in fact, that is probably true. Training in public speaking helps individuals develop organizational skills, the ability to be comfortable when talking in front of both large and small groups, and effective means to persuade others. These skills contribute to effectiveness in almost any career situation.

Basic Career Characteristics

In general, jobs that are pursued by people skilled in speech and public speaking involve three things: (1) dealing with the public, (2) organizing information, and (3) exhibiting individual responsibility.

Most people who seek training in speech and public speaking have a desire to work with the public in some fashion. For example, a talent coordinator on a television show is responsible for interviewing potential guests, persuading individuals to appear on the show, making sure guests are comfortable when they arrive at the show, and often writing questions for the host to ask the guests. A hospitality manager serves as the liaison between employees and customers to ensure a pleasant experience for customers. Much of the time of a hospitality manager may be spent listening to customer complaints and resolving them. Strong listening and negotiation skills, as well as patience, are particularly essential in this profession. Individuals trained in speech and public speaking are effective in dealing with the public due to their experience with presenting information to a variety of audiences and their ability to "think on their feet." Being at ease in public speaking situations easily translates into effective interpersonal communication skills.

Individuals who can organize information find these skills useful in a variety of careers. As part of the training process for public speaking, people find information through various research methods, analyze the credibility of the information, decide which information is most effective in a particular situation, organize the information into a pattern that will communicate the information in the best way, and use effective delivery skills to present the information to a particular audience. These skills have a direct benefit for people working as attorneys, librarians, small business managers, or sales representatives.

Finally, people trained in public speaking are able to be effective in jobs that require individual responsibility because they have been trained to use their self-motivation to formulate messages that can both inform and influence others. For example, a television reporter must first develop a story idea before researching, editing, and presenting the information to the public. The idea must be checked with editors and other decision-makers before it is approved for dissemination to the public. A software project manager must coordinate the efforts of a variety of individuals in order to develop a product and get it to market. Each step of this process may entail presenting the product to diverse audiences to gain their approval before the next step can be taken.

Important Career Skills

There are many important skills that can contribute to success in the careers discussed above, but three of the most important are (1) the ability to adapt to various audiences, (2) the ability to do research, and (3) the ability to exhibit a sense of personal integrity.

Training in speech and public speaking includes an emphasis on audience analysis and adaptation. This means that in order to deliver an effective public speech, the speaker must first know the audience in terms of who they are and what their needs are. It would be inappropriate and ineffective to address an audience of third graders in the same manner as one would address an audience of senior citizens. In the same way, individuals who have been trained in speech and public speaking know that they must adapt their message to the needs, understanding, and desires of their customers. A sales representative who uses the same message to describe a product to physicians, to government regulators, and to the general public will probably not be successful.

Public speaking training also includes the development of research skills, which are a necessary component of any public speech. In the broadest sense, research skills are essential in any career dealing with effective communication skills. Social workers need to gather information about their clients, marketing executives need to

gather research about the products they are selling, documentary filmmakers need to gather research about the topics of their films, and book sellers need to gather information about the latest books that might appeal to their customers.

Finally, effective public speakers need a sense of personal integrity. This may not seem like a skill that is equivalent to audience adaptation and research skills, but personal integrity can be developed just like these other skills and is essential to effectiveness in any of the careers discussed so far. Professional communicators are constantly judged by the credibility of their messages and their personal integrity. For example, a client service representative who has a reputation of assuming responsibility for solving problems and taking into account individual customer needs will be more effective than a person who fails to honor promises or effectively resolve conflicts with clients.

A prominent source of information regarding careers in the public speaking field is the National Communication Association. This is the largest professional organization devoted to serving the needs of both scholars and practitioners in the fields of speech and public speaking.

See also: INTERPERSONAL COMMUNICATION, LISTENING AND; PUBLIC RELATIONS; PUBLIC RELATIONS, CAREERS IN; PUBLIC SPEAKING.

LEA P. STEWART

■ PUBLISHING INDUSTRY

In the broadest sense, the publishing industry would include newspaper publishing, magazine publishing, music publishing, map publishing, government information publishing, comic book publishing, and book publishing. This entry, however, will be restricted to the modern book publishing industry.

Publishing may be defined as the commercial dissemination of literature or information in multiple copies and with the probability of multiple formats (e.g., paper, electronic, CD-ROM, microfilm, microfiche). Publishing is a business, and as such, it embraces the values of competition, sales, and profit. Publishers are as concerned with accounting, marketing and advertising, shipping and distribution, and inventory control as they are with their products—the intellectual, artistic, and cultural creations of the authors. The publishing business often operates under the tension of highly divergent interests. An author's creative works or specialized knowledge may not meet the market values of profit, popularity, and standardization.

Publishing requires authors to create content. Editors work with authors to improve the writing. Scouts look for authors who have stories that may be profitable for the publisher. Literary agents work with authors to represent and protect the interests of the authors. Lawyers work with both the author and the publisher to finalize contracts. A publishing house usually divides its operation into editorial, design, production, publicity, sales, distribution, contracts, rights (e.g., translation, foreign republishing, licensing), and administration. Publishers must also work with printers who create the multiple copies or printings of a work, information processors who make works available electronically, distributors who pack and ship the finished product, and consumers (e.g., booksellers, libraries, school systems) who buy the content to resell at a profit or lend as a service.

While publishing is a complex combination of commerce and culture, it is much more multifaceted than that. It involves controversy (such as censorship, whether for political or propriety reasons), ethical considerations (related to authenticity, libel, plagiarism, and copyright), value considerations (with regard to taste, propriety, and aesthetics), international issues (including translations, politics, diplomacy, and markets), social conditions (related to literacy and education), and philosophical concerns (over authorship, commodification, and commercialization). All of these are key factors in the publishing industry.

As for the physical product of the publishing industry, all books can be divided into the following categories: (1) trade books, which include both hardback and paperback publications that are available in easily accessible retail outlets, (2) religious works such as devotionals, scriptures, and prayers, (3) textbooks for students ranging from kindergarten through graduate or professional school, and (4) scientific, technical, and medical books. Trade books, which can obviously be divided into paperback publications and hardback publications, can be further divided according to the age of the intended reader and the specific content. Adult books are generally intended for readers who are nineteen years of age or older. Juvenile books, which are intended for those individuals who are younger than nineteen years of age, can be further divided into books for young adults and books for children. The broad content genres for trade books are non-fiction, fiction, drama, and poetry, but these can each be divided into more specific sub-genres. For example, fiction can be divided into romance, mystery, westerns, science fiction, fantasy, adventure, military, historical, horror, and thriller, as well as the emerging areas of splatterpunk, cyberpunk, and prehistoric epics. Within each of these sub-genres, there are also niches that satisfy specific audiences and interests, such as African-American romance, urban fantasy, glitz and glamour romance, and technothrillers.

Literacy, Education, and Libraries

Publishing depends on both writers and readers. People read books for many different purposes. Those readers who purchase or borrow a book for voluntarily reading may be looking for recreation or inspiration. Those readers who purchase or borrow a book because it is required reading are looking for specific information. Publishing is intricately tied to literacy, education, cultural institutions such as libraries and museums, and societal respect and support for education and an educated populace. Authors need safe environments for free expression; they need time to think, write, read, and revise. The social conditions of peace, stability, and security are helpful for a healthy publishing environment, but war, instability, and insecurity can sometimes create an environment that encourages an active authorship and readership. Access to literature through a free public library system can create a large reading public and a guaranteed outlet for selling certain publications. Although public libraries are often thought of as a triumph of democracy, communist countries have also been supportive of libraries. Vladimir Lenin and his wife were strong supporters of libraries, and Cuba, with its high literacy rate, has an official government library system as well as, since 1998, a system of "independent" libraries (which are not part of the official government system).

Literacy, education, and the right to opinion and expression are essential for human dignity. In fact, the United Nations, in its *Universal Declara-*

tion of Human Rights (1948) states: "Everyone has the right to freedom of opinion and expression; this right includes freedom to hold opinions without interference and to seek, receive and impart information and ideas through any media and regardless of frontiers" (Article 19). "Everyone has the right to education. Education shall be free, at least in the elementary and fundamental stages. Elementary education shall be compulsory. Technical and professional education shall be made generally available and higher education shall be equally accessible to all on the basis of merit" (Article 26). "Everyone has the right freely to participate in the cultural life of the community, to enjoy the arts and to share in scientific advancement and its benefits. Everyone has the right to the protection of the moral and material interests resulting from any scientific, literary or artistic production of which he is the author" (Article 27). Many nations have their own statements on the freedom to read, write, and disseminate information and knowledge. These political and social structures are important to the publishing industry.

Authors, Writers, and the Publishing Process

The term "author" can refer to many different situations in the publishing industry. An author can be a commodity, a name brand that sells titles to an eager readership, an individual or a succession of creators who contribute to a series. An author may be a ghostwriter—someone who writes for another person. In many cases, a pseudonym is an assigned name under which many different authors may write—for example, the Stratemeyer Syndicate, which was created by Edward Stratemeyer, chose a pseudonym for each of its series, including the Hardy Boys and Nancy Drew series, but multiple authors contributed to each series. An author may be a professional who makes his or her living by writing and may be under contract to one publishing house. An author may be an amateur who is defined by some other circumstance or occupation, such as a prisoner, student, teacher, policeman, doctor, lawyer, or housewife.

The relationship between a publisher and an author is defined by a contract, which generally stipulates what the content of the manuscript will be, how and when it will be submitted, who is responsible for proofreading, and what amount the author will be paid—in initial payments and in royalties. (Royalties are additional payments that are made to an author for each copy of the work that is sold.)

The publication process follows a standard sequence that is often modified according to the type of book that is being produced. The basic stages are as follows:

1. An author writes, revises (as many times as necessary), and then submits a manuscript to a publisher. This submission can be unsolicited (i.e., submitted directly to the publisher by the author) or solicited (i.e., submitted through a literary agent), but it should be noted that many publishers do not accept unsolicited manuscripts.

2. If a publisher agrees to consider a manuscript, it is then assigned to an editor for review.

3. The editor reads the manuscript and makes a recommendation to the publisher about publishing or not publishing the work. If the manuscript is essentially publishable, the editor and author work together to develop a contract and to polish the manuscript before sending it to the compositor.

4. The book is copyrighted and assigned an International Standard Book Number (ISBN).

5. While the manuscript is being polished, a designer develops specifications for an interior design and creates a cover that is appropriate to the manuscript and will attract the attention of potential readers.

6. A compositor typesets the polished manuscript according to the specifications that have been created by the designer and provides pages for proofreading, correction, and approval.

7. While the manuscript is being typeset by the compositor, the marketing department develops strategies to create interest in the book. Prepublication information is sent to bookstores and libraries to entice them to order the book. Advance copies are sent to reviewers so that information about the book—what it is about and how good it is—can appear in newspapers, magazines, and over the Internet around the time the book is actually published.

8. While the marketing department is busy creating interest in the book, the approved type-

set materials created by the compositor are sent to the printer/binder, who produces multiple copies of the work and prepares them for shipment.

9. An author tour is arranged where the author participates in radio and television interviews and reads portions of the book at bookstores, libraries, and cultural centers.

10. Sales representatives attend book fairs and trade shows and visit bookstores and other retail outlets to sell the book.

Publishing Houses

Historically, publishing houses were relatively small family-owned businesses, but they have evolved into multinational corporations, many of which are publicly traded on the various stock exchanges (e.g., Elsevier is listed on the Amsterdam, London, and New York Stock Exchanges). Some houses are subsidiaries of corporations that are centered on the entertainment industry. Other houses are minor subsidiaries of corporations that have little else to do with literature and publishing. The effects of corporate mergers and acquisitions are shaping the modern book industry in ways that are yet to be determined.

Some of the major houses in the history of publishing include Elsevier, Macmillan, Longman, Charles Scribner's Sons, and Harry N. Abrams. Elsevier, which was founded in 1583 by the Dutch family Elzevir (or Elsevier), is a publisher of scientific literature. It is often cited as the first important European publishing house. The Elzevirs were businessmen, and their business of printing and selling books grew as literacy increased across Europe. Macmillan was founded in 1843 by Daniel and Alexander Macmillan. These Scottish booksellers and publishers created one of the largest and most influential publishing houses of textbooks and works of literature and science. Longman was founded in 1724 by Thomas Longman when he bought a British bookshop and publisher. It is an imprint known for its textbooks and important monographs in the social sciences and humanities. Charles Scribner's Sons, one of the first important American publishing houses, was founded in 1846. It is notable for its legendary editor Maxwell Perkins, who assisted F. Scott Fitzgerald, Ernest Hemingway, Thomas Wolfe, and many other giants of twentieth-century U.S. literature.

Harry N. Abrams, an American publisher of art books, was founded in 1950.

These historic publishing houses, which represent just a small portion of the publishing houses worldwide, have not been immune to the corporate practices of buying, selling, and merging of companies and imprints. Longman is now a subsidiary of the publishing house Addison-Wesley, Longman. The Macmillan company operating in the United Kingdom has no connection to the Macmillan companies in the United States, and even the Macmillan companies operating in the United States are not all owned by the same corporation. In addition, Scribner reference books are no longer published by the same corporation that publishes Scribner trade books. New names that have grown in importance in the publishing world are Bertelsmann, Viacom, Time Warner, and Disney. Bertelsmann is a German publisher that has purchased American publishers such as Doubleday, Dell, and Random House. Viacom, a global megacorporation with entertainment interests in film, video, television, amusement parks, and sports teams, purchased American publisher Simon & Schuster in 1994 and subsequently sold off several of its imprints. Time Warner is a corporation that publishes books, operates book clubs, and owns large segments of the communication and entertainment industry. With the announcement of its merger with America Online, the synergy of publishing (production and distribution of cultural content) with electronic multimedia points to the future of the dissemination of information, ideas, knowledge, and art. Critics are concerned that these types of mergers and acquisitions will lead to the "corporatization" of culture. The prominence of the Disney Corporation, which owns movie studios, operates theme parks, and licenses characters that were not created originally by Disney (e.g., Winnie-the-Pooh, Pinocchio), has critics asking the question "Can companies own culture and thus control it?" With the foreign acquisition of publishing houses, those who study the publishing industry also ask if there are dangers in having foreign ownership of a nation's information outlets. For example, does it matter if Germany publishes American textbooks? Will content and editorial changes occur that may not be in the national interest of those people who are purchasing the books? Or will it make no difference to have foreign ownership of publishing houses?

University presses were initially created to publish the specialized works written by the faculty members of the respective universities. The presses later developed into publishers of scholarly works that were not restricted to those written by an institution's own faculty and students. Traditionally, university presses have not been expected to make a profit, but rising costs, diminishing resources, and shifting values regarding education and profitability are pressuring university presses to print books that have a wider popular appeal. For example, in 1999, Northeastern University Press published a new edition of *Peyton Place*, a popular 1956 novel about New England life. In other cases, university presses have been sold to commercial publishers. In July 2000, Iowa State University agreed to merge Iowa State University Press (founded in 1934) with Blackwell Science, an international scientific and technical publishing company. Some important university presses include Oxford University Press (founded in England in 1478), Harvard University Press (officially created in 1913, but Harvard has published faculty materials since the seventeenth century), and University of Chicago Press (established in 1891). The last press is also the home of the definitive work in manuscript preparation: *The Chicago Manual of Style*.

Vanity Presses are publishing houses that publish books at the authors' expense. Often considered unscrupulous, vanity presses rely on the authors wanting so strongly to see their works in print that they will pay all of the expenses of having the books published. However, book distributors, bookstores, and libraries generally do not purchase books printed by vanity presses, and reviewers do not accept them to review for journals, newspapers, and magazines. Therefore, although it is published, there is very little recognition of the work. Electronic self-publishing on the Internet is modifying how some authors get into print. Similar to the vanity presses, websites that allow for self-publishing are changing the avenues for new voices to be heard and read, but unlike vanity presses, websites are somehow not yet tainted with the association of narcissism. Other forms of electronic publishing mimic the traditional format of the publishing process with the exception that the author publishes the work online first and then has it picked up by a major publishing house. Websites that allow for authors

Charles Scribner. (Corbis)

and publishers to negotiate rights in an auction format are part of electronic publishing.

Publisher Associations

Publishers have organized international, national, and regional associations to protect their interests. They also collect statistics and follow trends in the field regarding technology, commerce, trade, taste, and new markets.

The International Publishers Association (IPA) was established in Paris in 1896 to serve as a worldwide organization of the individual national associations, which are recognized as representative of the book and music publishers in each country. The office of the secretariat is located in Geneva, Switzerland. The IPA has a statement on the "Freedom to Publish," collects and maintains statistics on publishing as reported by member nations, and celebrates "World Book and Copyright Day" every year on April 23.

The national book publishers associations include the Association of American Publishers, the Bulgarian Bookpublishers Association, the Canadian Publishers Council, the Den Danske Forlæggerforening (Denmark), the Cámara Ecuatoriana del Libro (Ecuador), the Egyptian Publishers' Association, the Syndicat National de l'Edition

(France), the Ghana Book Publishers Association, the Icelandic Publishers Association, the Federation of Indian Publishers (India), the Ikatan Penerbit (Indonesia), the Book Publishers Association of Israel, the Japan Book Publishers, the Fédération Luxembourgeoise (Luxembourg), the Malaysian Book Publishers' Association, the Cámara Nacional de la Industria Editorial (Mexico), the Nigerian Publishers Association, and the Philippine Educational Publishers' Association.

Book Fairs

Publishers, authors, agents, and scouts attend international, national, and regional book fairs. They show their wares, attract new clients (e.g., authors, translators, booksellers, book buyers), discuss trends, buy rights to works (e.g., foreign rights to publish or distribute a book in a country other than the original country of publication), make licensing agreements, and attend meetings, seminars, and training programs. Regional book fairs, such as those held in Frankfurt, Guadalajara, and Zimbabwe, are important for highlighting the works published in various countries. Given the large number of countries in the world, international and regional book fairs are important to the publishing industry. Some the most important fairs include the Frankfurt Book Fair, BookExpo America, the Bologna Children's Book Fair, the Guadalajara International Book Fair, the Zimbabwe International Book Fair, the New Delhi World Book Fair, the Asia International Book Fair, the London Book Fair, and the Havana International Book Fair.

The Frankfurt Book Fair was established in 1949 in Frankfurt, Germany. This annual six-day event, organized by Ausstellungs und Messe GmbH (a subsidiary company of the German Publishers' and Booksellers' Association), is the world's biggest international trade fair for publishing. This is an important event for publishers to attend if they wish to obtain information about the international publishing industry.

BookExpo America, formerly known as the American Booksellers Association Convention & Trade Exhibit, is another one of the largest fairs in the world. Usually held in Chicago, this event showcases books in all formats (e.g., paper, audio, comic books), presents new technology and services for publishers, and shows sideline merchandise such as greeting cards, calendars, stickers, and other non-book products for bookstores. It is

an education forum that looks at the business of books from many viewpoints.

The Bologna Children's Book Fair, which has been held in Italy since 1963, is uniquely devoted to children's publishing. Organized by the Bologna Fiere Group, this fair includes textbooks and reference works as well as picture books and works that feature licensed characters. Exhibited works exist in a variety of formats, including paper, electronic, and multimedia.

The Guadalajara International Book Fair was founded in 1987. Organized by the University of Guadalajara, it is one of the most important book fairs for Latin American and Spanish-language materials. Its goals are to promote and consolidate the Mexican and Latin American publishing industry and to contribute toward encouraging reading among children and young adults.

The Zimbabwe International Book Fair is the most important annual book event in Africa. Administered by an independent trust (comprising a broad cross-section of Zimbabwe's book industry) and attended by some of the major writers of the continent, this fair provides the opportunity for the free interchange of ideas and expression between those people living in North Africa and those living in sub-Saharan Africa—as well as between Africa and the rest of the world.

Organized by the National Book Trust at Pragati Maidan, New Delhi, the New Delhi World Book Fair occurs every other year. The fair highlights India's eleven thousand publishers, the multilingual publishing industry of India, and its world presence as the third largest publisher of English-language books.

Held in Singapore and organized by the Reed Exhibition Companies, the Asia International Book Fair is a trade event that serves the growing intellectual property rights market in Asia. It is a unique marketplace for the buying and selling of rights for publishing, reprinting, distribution, translation, and co-edition of books in print or electronic format.

The London Book Fair was established in 1970 and targets a wide variety of publishers, booksellers, and printing services. It also features a variety of non-book products that are of interest to readers and book buyers.

Since 1990, the Havana International Book Fair has highlighted the literary achievements and

A worker puts finishing touches on the Polish pavilion at the 52nd international Frankfurt Book Fair, which took place in October 2000. (AFP/Corbis)

strengths of Cuba. Although the United States has a trade embargo with Cuba, some of the larger U.S. publishers participate in the event regularly.

Book Festivals and Awards

Many cities celebrate books and reading by organizing festivals. Often these festivals account for a high percentage of a book's overall sales. For example, in the United Kingdom, it is estimated that 50 percent of all children's book sales are made through book festivals or school book clubs. Some festivals concentrate on local or regional authors or on authors who have a connection to the state, province, or city. Cities may hold many book festivals in the course of a year. Some examples of book festivals held in the United States include the Harlem Book Fair (New York City), the San Francisco Bay Area Book Festival, the Great Basin Book Festival (Nevada), Bumbershoot (Seattle), the Texas Book Festival, the Virginia Festival of the Book, and the New York is Book Country Festival (New York City).

Book fairs and festivals are not the only ways to recognize outstanding works. Publishers, professional associations, and governments honor authors by presenting awards for books of unusual merit. Often, awards are presented for works that are published in specific categories. For example, the National Book Awards given in the United States bestow honors in the areas of fiction; poetry; arts and letters; history and biography; and science, philosophy, and religion. These awards are important to both publisher and author because the honor raises their profile, attracts attention, and generates interest in reading and the exchange of ideas. Some of the other important book prizes and awards include the Nobel Prize for Literature, the Pulitzer Prize in Letters, the Caldecott Medal, the Newbery Medal, the Booker Prize, the Prix de Goncourt, and the Black Caucus of the American Library Association Literary Awards.

Censorship, Banning, and Embargo

Because publishing is the human communication of ideas, desires, information, and knowledge, publishers often face attempts to stop their dissemination of literature. The reasons may be political (e.g., if a ruling government wants to suppress publication of specific ideas), or the reasons may involve personal tastes (e.g., if a person or group believes that a publication contains obscene material).

Publishers vehemently protect the right to free expression and often provide support when a specific publisher's rights are being infringed. For example, in the United States, a joint legal defense fund was launched by what some may consider to be unlikely allies: the American Booksellers Association, the Association of American Publishers, Playboy Enterprises, and Penthouse International. These four entities came together in response to the 1985 Meese Commission, which sent letters to convenience stores saying that if they sold the *Playboy* and *Penthouse* magazines, then the commission would identify them as stores that sold "pornography." In this case, a Federal District Court ruled that the commission had overstepped its authority.

Sometimes publishers come up against national laws and international access. Adolf Hilter's *Mein Kampf* cannot be sold in Germany, but it can be (and is) published and sold in the United States. When Amazon.com, a U.S.-based online bookstore, was filling orders that German customers had placed for *Mein Kampf,* German officials objected and cited German laws for banning sales of hate literature. As a result, in 1999, Amazon.com stopped selling *Mein Kampf* to German customers. In 1989, the American Association of Publishers published *The Starvation of Young Black Minds: The Effects of Book Boycotts in South Africa* in an attempt to have books excluded from the economic embargo against South Africa under apartheid. The publication did not have the desired effect, and books remained part of the sanctions while they were in effect.

The notions of taste and what is acceptable are not universal. What may be acceptable in one culture may not be acceptable in another. In 1978, a Swedish sex education book for children was deemed obscene in the United States because of graphic nudity. Some governments, such as the Canadian government, subsidize cultural production, which is a practice that is praised by some and criticized by others as a form of government interference. All countries have unique characteristics, customs, and philosophies that shape their respec-

tive publishing industries. In spite of those unique elements that are related to specific countries, it is clear that all publishers still struggle with the concepts of free expression, social responsibility, cultural taste and propriety, and intellectual freedom.

International Publishing

While figures for new titles published in the United States generally fall between 55,000 and 75,000 books per year and the Publishers Association of the United Kingdom indicates that British publishers produced more than 100,000 new titles in 1997, these are not the only two countries in the world that have a publishing industry. In fact, the United Nations Educational, Scientific, and Cultural Organization (UNESCO) has reported that, for example, Egypt produced 2,215 new titles in 1996, while Iran produced 15,073 new titles, Israel produced 30,487 new titles, Japan produced 56,221 new titles, Argentina produced 9,850 new titles, and Peru produced 612 new titles. Specific international cities that are known for their strong publishing houses and communication industry include—in addition to the American cities of New York, Boston, Philadelphia, and Chicago—the cities of Buenos Aires, Toronto, London, Paris, Vienna, Florence, Milan, Zurich, Edinburgh, Frankfurt, Leipzig, Singapore, and Tokyo.

The global exchange of ideas and literature, however, is complicated by inequalities between developed and developing nations. Access to raw materials (e.g., paper, ink, glue) and technology, opportunities for authors to write, currency exchanges, diplomacy, politics, war, tariffs, taxes, and distribution systems (e.g., postal services, roads, shipping) are all key factors that can vary from country to country. Consider the variations that exist in Africa, Central Europe, Latin America, Asia, and North America.

The publishing of African authors by African publishers has continually grown since the 1960s. With the emergence of independent African nations after World War II, national pride and postcolonial scholarship fueled the publishing industry. However, challenges such as economic recessions, chronic foreign exchange constraints, war, famine, drought, and political unrest have impeded the development of a robust publishing industry for the African continent. In 1989, a group of African publishers organized to found the African Books Collective, a self-help initiative that was established to promote, sell, and distribute African books in European and North American markets and to promote an intra-African book trade. The African Books Collective is registered in the United Kingdom, and books are shipped from its United Kingdom warehouse. The Swedish International Development Authority supports the African Books Collective website, which helps librarians, educators, and general readers find African books to buy. African publishing still reflects colonial influences, so the industry may generally be divided into Francophone (French-speaking), Lusophone (Portuguese-speaking), and English-speaking markets, in addition to the markets for the native languages and dialects of the many African nations.

With the break up of the former Soviet Union, Central European nations (e.g., Bulgaria, Czech Republic, Hungary, Poland, Romania) moved from communism and state-owned publishing companies to free market economies and a new horizon for publishing. Challenges in Central Europe include foreign exchange rates, political changes, attempts to nurture local authors and increase interest in a nation's classic literature, and the need to balance the new influx of Western European and North American literature with indigenous literature so the culture is not homogenized. Still, there is a concerted effort to build the infrastructure of technology, expertise, and distribution and to re-create the publishing industry in the Central European nations.

Latin American nations are producers and consumers of Spanish-language and Portuguese-language works. Many of the region's nations have strong educational systems with fine universities that produce high-quality scholarship. Recognition of the importance of the translation process has allowed many Latin America authors and poets to reach readers in other countries around the world. More similar to Africa, or perhaps Central Europe, than to North America in terms of robustness of the Latin American publishing industry, the main Latin American book producers and exporters are Cuba, Mexico, Argentina, Colombia, Chile, Venezuela, and Brazil.

Asia, the world's largest continent, also features a large diversity in its publishing industries. Japan, with its high literacy rate and excellent educational system, has a strong publishing industry that is characterized by quality content and some of the highest standards for the physical aspects of publishing (e.g., paper, ink, binding, and color quality). China, on the other hand, has a long and strong book tradition, but a climate of suppression and government control stifles publishing and the import and export of cultural materials. Singapore, with its cosmopolitan population and British ties, has poised itself to be part of progressive Eastern–Western publishing activities. Western publishers and Australia look to Asia as a profitable marketplace. India, the third largest publisher of English-language works is a major player in Asian publishing and in worldwide publishing.

In North America, there is a shared popular culture, there is a shared language (i.e., English, although French and Spanish each have a strong presence as well), and there is a free trade agreement among Canada, the United States, and Mexico (although Mexico is culturally and linguistically more aligned with Latin American publishing). The face of publishing in the United States is changing. Entertainment industries (e.g., film, television, music, radio) are merging with the publishing industry. Many U.S. publishing interests are being purchased by European or Australian interests. Small publishing houses are becoming minor parts of large corporations. The context of publishing in the United States is one of free expression, regionalism, and corporate synergy. Also influencing publishing in the United States is an increase in the Spanish-speaking population and the need to create and provide materials in Spanish. Canada publishes in two languages (English and French) and supports the idea of multilingualism. Canadian publishing exists in an expansive country with a sparse population. There too is strong regionalism, which affects taste, content, and distribution. Canada's proximity to the United States and strong ties to the United Kingdom also affect what is imported, sold, and read. The Canadian marketplace is dominated by foreign products, but these connections also allow Canadian artists and scholars to have their works distributed throughout the world.

The Future in Publishing

In developed nations, time for reading books as a source for information, education, and recreation competes with television, the Internet, computer games, videos, music, and radio. In response, publishing has broadened its base and views the book as just one component of the cultural and educational whole. Multimedia productions of computer software, CD-ROMs, and maps are changing the definitions of publications, as is the development of e-books. The publishing industry is embracing the change.

Developing nations, however, continue to struggle to acquire the raw materials and technology that they need to produce works. They also face obstacles from developed nations that may resist purchasing the published works because they consider the printing to be inferior or because they question the intellectual value of the work.

Despite the inherent complications involved in the publishing industry around the world, as long as the fundamental human urge to communicate remains, publication of the expressions and findings of human endeavor will continue.

See also: EDITORS; INTELLECTUAL FREEDOM AND CENSORSHIP; LIBRARIES, FUNCTIONS AND TYPES OF; MAGAZINE INDUSTRY; NEWSPAPER INDUSTRY; PORNOGRAPHY; PORNOGRAPHY, LEGAL ASPECTS OF; PRINTING, HISTORY AND METHODS OF; PUBLISHING INDUSTRY, CAREERS IN; STORYTELLING; WRITERS.

Bibliography

Council of National Library Associations and R. R. Bowker Company. (annual). *Bowker Annual of Library & Book Trade Information*. New York: R. R. Bowker.

Greco, Albert N. (1997). *The Book Publishing Industry*. Boston: Allyn & Bacon.

Johnson, Deidre. (1982). *Stratemeyer Pseudonyms and Series Books*. Westport, CT: Greenwood Press.

Kobrak, Fred, and Luey, Beth. (1992). *The Structure of International Publishing in the 1990s*. New Brunswick, NJ: Transaction Publishers.

Korda, Michael. (1999). *Another Life*. New York: Random House.

United Nations Educational, Scientific, and Cultural Organization. (1996). *Statistical Yearbook*. Paris: UNESCO.

LORNA PETERSON

◼ PUBLISHING INDUSTRY, CAREERS IN

Publishing is the activity of commercially producing, distributing, and selling literature or information. It is both a business and cultural-intellectual enterprise that makes the work challenging, exciting, and rewarding. Associated with and crucial to the intellectual, cultural, and educational roles of society, the products of publishing (books, magazines, newspapers, online resources, and so on) inspire different feelings than other commodities produced by industry. Publishing is a business and, therefore, vulnerable to the vagaries of the marketplace of supply and demand, fashion and taste, capital, profit, and investment. The finding, nurturing, and supporting of authors with all of their idiosyncratic needs must be coordinated successfully with the bottom-line business concerns of marketing, competition, profit, and cost. International mergers of publishing houses, the development of the Internet and electronic publishing, and the blending of publishing with multimedia entertainment all point to dynamic growth in publishing careers.

Background

The major publishing houses, small or specialty presses, newspapers, and magazines hire employees to fill a wide range of positions. Many of the larger publishing houses and news agencies maintain offices in Europe, Asia, the United Kingdom, Mexico, or Canada, where employment requires a high degree of competency in the local language.

Specific careers in publishing are generally divided into two broad categories: creative and business. On the creative side of the industry are the editor-in-chief, editorial staff, designers, photographers, writers, researchers, multimedia producers, and translators. On the business side of the industry are the publisher, marketing staff, advertising staff, production staff, permissions coordinator, foreign and domestic rights manager, and literary agent.

Experience is essential in this highly competitive industry. One of the best ways to enter the field is to attend a publishing program to make contacts and learn the basics of the industry. Some of the best known programs of this type are the Dow Jones Newspaper Fund, the New York University Summer Publishing Institute, the Radcliffe Publishing Course, the Rice University Publishing Program, and the University of Denver Publishing Institute.

Creative Careers

Writers are generally self-employed or freelance. Depending on the circumstances, writers might submit their work directly to publishers or producers, or they might submit their work through literary agents who act as liaisons between the writers and the publishers or producers. Only in very select careers, such as a copy writer for an advertising agency or a reporter for a newspaper, are writers hired as full-time staff employees. Writers contribute to all aspects of the publishing industry. Scholarly writers, writers for children, screenwriters, writers for television, and technical writers have skills that are unique to the type of writing they do. For example, technical writers should understand the specialized area that they are working in, such as engineering, education, and telecommunications. Such knowledge is necessary to write effectively for the specialized market. The technical writer may also oversee technical operations such as preparation of illustrations, photographs, diagrams, or charts that accompany the technical material.

Editor-in-chief and managing editor are the top slots in the editorial track. The career path to a managing editor position requires comprehensive understanding of the editorial process, usually gained by starting as an editor at the entry level. Editors (who may work in either print, multimedia, or online environments) perform a variety of duties, such as overseeing the layout for the way the final product will look and revising the content of written material in preparation for final publication. These positions require an excellent command of the English language and an understanding of the communication and media industry. Writing comprehension, originality, sensitivity to problems, and attention to detail are the knowledge, skills, and abilities necessary for starting out on the editorial track. Since the managing editor directs and coordinates the editorial operations and formulates editorial policy, a person in that position must know about administration and management responsibilities, be able to manage personnel (i.e., the editorial team) effectively, and have a working familiarity with computers and electronics. As for specific education, a bachelor's degree in any area is appropriate, but most editors come to publishing with humanities and social science degrees.

Book design, particularly of the book cover, is a critical aspect of marketing, and most book designers have a degree in graphic or fine art. A publisher may have a book designer on staff to provide these services. Some designers and illustrators work on a self-employed or freelance basis or are hired on contract to illustrate, design, or supply technical drawings or photographs that are needed for a publication such as a technical manual or a children's book. The newspaper and magazine industry employs staff photographers in addition to using freelance talent.

In addition to writers, editors, illustrators, and graphic artists, there are opportunities in publishing for translators, researchers, fact checkers, copy editors, proofreaders, and outside readers of manuscripts of books, plays, scripts, and other material.

Business Careers

The publishing industry is a business and employs personnel who watch the bottom line of the business. Managing the business side is the president, chief executive officer, or publisher, along with the directors of departments concerned with marketing, advertising, and production. An education in business management, finance, or marketing plus an in-depth understanding of the publishing industry is essential.

Agents guide an author's career. They understand the industry, and they know which people should be approached with ideas. They negotiate contracts on behalf of the author, forward promising manuscripts to publishers or producers, and handle foreign and subsidiary rights. Literary agents have many contacts in the industry and understand the process, generally having worked within the industry itself before moving on to become agents.

Literary scouts, who can be either self-employed or publisher employed, seek out writing talent around the world. They do so by reading broadly and attending readings and book fairs, such as the Asia International Book Fair, the Frankfurt Book Fair, BookExpo America, the Bologna Children's Book Fair, the Guadalajara International Book Fair, the New Delhi World Book Fair, and the Zimbabwe International Book Fair.

With the increase in electronic publishing and desktop publishing, publishers hire technical support personnel to manage the technological aspect of publishing. Positions may include computer support personnel with skills in computer hardware, software packages, computer networks, telecommunications, and information technology in general. Knowledge of specific software packages for design, publication layout, and computer graphics is a trend in the industry, and employment opportunities will continue to grow in the electronic, multimedia, and web-based publishing environments.

Women, Minorities, and the Future

Conditions for women and minorities in the publishing industry could be improved. Although not a female-intensive profession, women have been traditionally better represented in publishing than in some other fields. The numbers of editors, journalists, and publishers from racial or ethnic minority groups, however, remain disappointing. To compensate for this and to fill the need for a minority voice in publishing, independent publishing houses have been founded by females and by members of minority groups.

Movies, videos, television, computer and video games, and the Internet compete for people's leisure time. Nonetheless, the outlook for publishing careers is strong, for there is no indication that the book-reading public is dead. The increasing numbers of magazines aimed at specialty markets and online "e-zines" indicate that there is a high demand for the technologically equipped and educationally prepared individual. International and national organizations also work to protect the right to read and to write so that free expression can exist. With free expression, there is publishing.

See also: EDITORS; MAGAZINE INDUSTRY, CAREERS IN; NEWSPAPER INDUSTRY, CAREERS IN; PUBLISHING INDUSTRY; WRITERS.

Bibliography

Greco, Albert N. (1997). *The Book Publishing Industry*. Boston: Allyn & Bacon.

Harlow, Victoria, and Knappman, Edward W., eds. (1994). *American Jobs Abroad*. Detroit, MI: Visible Ink Press.

Holm, Kirsten C., ed. (1999). *The Writer's Market 2000: 8,000 Editors Who Buy What You Write*. Cincinnati, OH: Writer's Digest Books.

Krantz, Les. (1999). *Jobs Rated Almanac*. New York: St. Martin's Press.

Petras, Kathryn; Petras, Ross; and Petras, George. (1997). *Jobs '98*. New York: Fireside.

LORNA PETERSON
DEBORAH J. KARPUK

PUBLISHING INDUSTRY, HISTORY OF

See: Printing, History and Methods of

PULITZER, JOSEPH (1847–1911)

Joseph Pulitzer was a Hungarian-born American journalist and innovative newspaper publisher of the late nineteenth and early twentieth centuries, but he is perhaps best known as the founder of the Pulitzer Prize.

Recruited by an American agent, Pulitzer immigrated to the United States in 1864 to serve for one year in the Union army during the U.S. Civil War. Afterward he drifted, arriving in St. Louis, Missouri, in the autumn of 1865. Pulitzer studied law and was admitted to the bar in 1867. That same year he became a naturalized citizen. He began reporting for the German-language newspaper *Westliche Post* in 1868. In 1869, Pulitzer was elected to the Missouri state legislature, where he gained prominence fighting graft and corruption in the St. Louis county government. He later bought a controlling interest in the *Westliche Post* and then sold it for a considerable profit. In 1878, Pulitzer bought the bankrupt St. Louis *Dispatch* and merged it with the St. Louis *Post*, which then became the leading newspaper of the city. In 1883, he turned the *Post-Dispatch* editorial duties over to subordinates and moved to New York City to purchase (for $346,000) and reinvigorate the financially troubled *New York World*, which had a circulation of 15,000. Within four years, Pulitzer turned the *New York World* into New York's leading newspaper, with a record-breaking circulation of 250,000. By the mid-1890s, the *New York World* was earning yearly profits estimated at $1 million.

Pulitzer's rise to journalism titan took place in the dazzling context of a burgeoning society. From 1870 to 1900, the U.S. population doubled. Immigrants flooded cities and mass-production techniques were stimulating commerce. Newspapers were becoming big business. Pulitzer appealed to the growing immigrant population by using simple language and clear writing. He published editorials of high character and verbally fueled crusades against poverty, crowded slums, and discrimination. Pulitzer urged the poor to educate their children rather than sending them to work. His determination to effect reform and be a voice for the underprivileged was reflected in his ten-point platform, which was published in 1883 and advocated the taxing of luxuries, inheritances, large incomes, monopolies, and privileged corporations. It also proposed a tariff for revenue, reforming the civil service, punishing corrupt officials, prosecuting vote-buying, and punishing employers who coerced employees in their voting behavior.

Pulitzer was responsible for many publishing innovations. For example, he attracted advertisers by reserving more space for advertisements and pricing that space on the basis of circulation. He used illustrations, banner headlines, and large display type. He introduced the sports page, a color magazine section, and the first color comics.

Pulitzer understood that news could be manufactured. Nellie Bly's sensational reporting was a popular feature. She went undercover as a patient in an insane asylum so she could report on the abuses that were going on there. She also managed to beat the fictional record of Jules Verne's Phileas Fogg by circling the world in less than eighty days—completing the trip in seventy-two days, six hours, eleven minutes, and fourteen seconds. Pulitzer cleverly promoted his paper with such content, but the *New York World* overall, under his leadership, was a paper based on news and service to the common citizen. Many journalism historians deem him to be the most innovative and effective newspaper editor in American history.

After Pulitzer was well established as a newspaper publisher in America's largest city, a younger imitator became his fiercest competitor. William Randolph Hearst, of the wealthy Hearst mining family, took over the *New York Journal* in 1895 after building a successful circulation track record as publisher of the *San Francisco Examiner.* Gene Wiggins, in *Three Centuries of American Media* (1999), put it this way: "Hearst did everything Pulitzer did, but on a grander scale. . . . Hearst had learned from the master and now was ready for a little oneupsmanship" (p. 161). According to Wiggins, "what Pulitzer did with genius, Hearst did with money" (p. 161). Pulitzer was the innovator; Hearst was the imitator.

James Wilson and Stan Wilson, in *Mass Media/Mass Culture* (1998), called this period of fierce competition between Hearst and Pulitzer,

Joseph Pulitzer. (Bettmann/Corbis)

which lasted into the early 1900s, "one of American journalism's most degrading circulation wars" (p. 135). It was thought to be degrading because the key weapon was sensationalism—news coverage that emphasized the lurid, emotionally riveting, and titillating, such as sex crimes, gruesome domestic violence, and gossip. "Yellow journalism" is the pejorative term that came to represent such content. The idea for the term was based on a comic strip character that wore a yellow, sack-like garment and was featured in Pulitzer's *New York World.* Hearst enticed the cartoonist, Richard Outcault, with higher pay, but Pulitzer hired another cartoonist to continue a strip featuring a similar character.

Media historians generally regard Hearst rather than Pulitzer as the most flagrant publisher of sensationalism during this era, but many of his tactics were already in use, some pioneered by Pulitzer and, before him, by Wilbur Storey of the *Chicago Daily Times.* With a clever metaphor, Wiggins (1999) described it this way: " . . . editors like Storey poured the foundation for the yellow journalism period, Pulitzer put up the frame while Hearst finished the roof" (p. 158).

Although Pulitzer engaged in sensationalism to sell newspapers, he also practiced ideals that characterize modern journalism. A famous exhortation to his staff was "Accuracy! Accuracy! Accuracy!" At the time of Pulitzer's death, his fiercest competitor had nothing but praise for the man. Hearst said in an obituary, as reported in W. A. Swanberg's 1967 book *Pulitzer*, "[A] mighty democratic force in the life of the nation and in the activity of the world has ceased; a great power uniformly exerted in behalf of popular rights and human progress is ended. Joseph Pulitzer is dead" (p. 412).

The Pulitzer Prize continues Joseph Pulitzer's legacy of journalism excellence. Under the terms of an agreement made between Pulitzer and Columbia University in 1903, and later made a part of his will, the Pulitzer Prize Fund derives from a gift of $2 million that Pulitzer bequeathed to Columbia. The gift also established Columbia's School of Journalism. The first awards were made in 1917, and they continue to be bestowed annually on the first Monday of May by the trustees of Columbia University, acting on the recommendations of the Pulitzer Prize Board of the university's Graduate School of Journalism. The board is guided by the principles that Pulitzer set forth in his will. In addition to fourteen award categories in journalism, various awards are given for books, drama, and music.

See also: BLY, NELLIE; HEARST, WILLIAM RANDOLPH; JOURNALISM, HISTORY OF; NEWSPAPER INDUSTRY, HISTORY OF.

Bibliography

Juergens, George. (1966). *Joseph Pulitzer and the New York World*. Princeton, NJ: Princeton University Press.

Swanberg, W. A. (1967). *Pulitzer*. New York: Scribner.

Wiggins, Gene. (1999). "Sensationally Yellow!" In *Three Centuries of American Media*, ed. Lloyd Chiasson, Jr. Englewood, CO: Morton Publishing.

Wilson, James, and Wilson, Stan Le Roy. (1998). *Mass Media/Mass Culture*. New York: McGraw-Hill.

Wood, Donald N. (1983). *Mass Media and the Individual*. St. Paul, MN: West Publishing.

CHARLES F. AUST

■ QUALITY OF AN ORGANIZATION

See: Organizational Quality and Performance Excellence

R

RADIO BROADCASTING

The radio broadcasting industry is the oldest form of electronic communication. At the beginning of the twentieth century, radio was purely an experimental medium, as innovators struggled with ways to transmit Morse code via the new wireless technology. Over time, the transmission of dots and dashes would give way to the broadcasting of voice and music. By the conclusion of the twentieth century, radio had developed into a multibillion-dollar entertainment and information industry used by individuals around the globe.

Radio is a business, linking advertisers with audiences attracted to a variety of programming formats. Radio has the ability to attract different demographic groups with its programming, making it an ideal medium for advertisers to target different messages. Programming is dominated by music on the FM (frequency modulation) band and by talk and information on the AM (amplitude modulation) band.

The radio industry consists of two distinct markets: the local market and the national market. Most listeners identify with the local market for radio programming, which consists of those stations licensed to a specific geographical area. The local market contains a mix of both AM and FM stations. Larger markets, such as New York, Los Angeles, and Chicago, each have more than sixty to seventy licensed stations. Smaller markets may only have three or four stations.

There are more than 10,300 commercial radio stations in operation in the United States. In addition, there are approximately 1,900 noncommercial radio stations, consisting of stations licensed to schools, colleges and universities, and religious/nonprofit organizations. Noncommercial stations operate on the FM band, assigned to the range of frequencies between 88.1 to 91.9 megahertz.

Stations in local markets attract different listeners by offering a variety of different music formats. There are numerous variations of radio formats across the country. The most popular formats are country, adult contemporary, news–talk–sports, religious, oldies, classic rock, and Spanish.

At the national level, radio networks provide syndicated programming to local stations in the form of talk shows (e.g., Rush Limbaugh, Art Bell) and news and specials (e.g., concerts, interview programs). Programming is also available twenty-four hours a day in a variety of satellite-delivered formats, each targeting different demographic groups with various types of music. There are also regional networks in radio, most of which are geared to the broadcasting of collegiate and professional sporting events.

Major Companies in the Radio Industry

In terms of ownership, the radio industry is best characterized as a two-tiered structure. On one tier are several large conglomerates that together own hundreds of radio stations. The major radio owners include Clear Channel Communications, CBS/Infinity, Entercom Communications, Cox, and ABC Radio (Disney). The other tier consists of numerous owners that perhaps

While many people think of radio broadcasting in terms of commercial stations, licenses are also granted for school stations, such as this high school station operated by students in Newport, Washington. (Bob Rowan; Progressive Image/Corbis)

own a single AM–FM combination or a small number of stations.

Prior to the passage of the Telecommunications Act of 1996, groups and individuals were limited to a certain number of stations that they could own in each class of stations. The 1996 act, however, removed all national ownership limits, instead placing caps on the number of stations that a single owner could control in a local market, depending on the total number of stations in the market. For example, in the largest radio markets (those with forty-five or more signals), the maximum number of stations that a single owner could own would be eight, with no more than five stations in a single class (i.e., AM or FM). Freed from ownership restrictions, the radio industry experienced rapid consolidation, especially in the financially lucrative major markets.

By 1998, more than seventy-five different companies had merged into one of four major group owners: AMFM Inc. (formerly Chancellor Media), CBS/Infinity, Clear Channel, and Jacor Communications. Clear Channel acquired both Jacor and AMFM in separate transactions in 1999, becoming the largest radio owner in the world with more than eight hundred stations in its portfolio. Industry consolidation, involving stations in medium and smaller markets, is expected to continue, but at a slower pace.

The Products of Radio

The radio industry is a dual-product industry, in that it offers distinct products to consumers in the form of entertainment and information, and access to audiences for radio advertisers. In terms of targeting consumers, stations provide entertainment and information in the form of different music formats that appeal to different demographic groups. Stations deliver music that is provided by the recording industry and geared to the format of the station. The recording industry uses the exposure provided by radio to help sell recordings along with music videos, publications, and other promotional vehicles (such as concert tours).

In terms of information, the radio industry offers talk, news, sports, and feature programming that is produced by a number of different sources. Information may be local in nature, such as news, sports, and features, or may be syndicated in the form of national news and talk programs. Talk programming became increasingly popular during the 1990s on AM stations, helping to rejuvenate the medium that, over the years, had lost audience share to FM stations. Sports-talk stations began to flourish as well, especially in large markets that were home to a mix of professional and collegiate teams.

Advertisers purchase radio time in order to reach audiences in cars, at home, or at work or school. Radio is an efficient medium for many advertisers, complementing the use of print and television to reach target audiences. Radio advertising is broken into three categories: local, national spot, and network. Local advertising is the most important area for the radio industry, reflecting the fact that radio is a locally driven medium. National spot refers to national advertising by major advertisers who buy radio time on stations in specific markets. National spot is primarily found in the top twenty-five radio markets. Network advertising, which consists of advertising that is sold for syndicated and network programs, represents the smallest category of advertising revenue.

Radio advertising experienced strong growth during the 1990s. According to the Radio Advertising Bureau, total radio advertising revenues totaled $8.8 billion in 1990, but by 1998, revenue topped $15 billion for the first time. From 1990 to 1998, the radio industry generated approximately 79 percent of its advertising revenue at the local level, with national spot advertising drawing about 15 percent, and network advertising drawing between 5 percent and 6 percent.

When it comes to audiences and advertisers, radio faces competition from a number of other media and an array of new audio-related technologies (e.g., Internet radio and digital satellite radio services). Economically, the radio industry has never been stronger, but the competitive challenges that face the industry are great. Aggressive marketing and branding remains the best strategy for radio to maintain its competitive edge and awareness among consumers and advertisers.

Industry Evolution

The radio industry showed remarkable resiliency during its first century of existence. As mentioned above, radio evolved as a result of a series of contributions by many different innovators, which led from being able to transmit dots and dashes to being able to broadcast voices and music. By the 1920s, radio had become an industry that was designed not to deliver programming but to sell radio receivers. Over time, radio became an important companion for Americans, a trusted friend during the Great Depression and World War II.

Radio historians refer to the 1930s and 1940s as the "golden age" of radio—a period when the popularity of the medium flourished. In a pre-television world, audiences tuned to radio for the latest news and entertainment programming, especially during the evening or prime-time hours. Amos and Andy, Bob Hope, and Bing Crosby were just as popular with listeners as were Edward R. Murrow, H. V. Kaltenborn, and President Franklin D. Roosevelt (with his fireside chats). Radio networks (e.g., NBC Red, NBC Blue, CBS, Mutual) distributed content on a national basis to affiliate stations around the country. Advertisers used radio to reach mass audiences with a single message, selling all types of products.

The 1950s forever changed the radio industry, as the advent of television in post-war America led to radio's loss of both entertainers and advertisers to the new visual medium. Networks de-emphasized their commitment to radio. Radio recast itself as a purely local medium, emphasizing different music formats to attract listeners. The FM medium began to emerge as an alternative to standard or AM broadcasting. FM provided a clearer signal, and during the 1960s, it would add the ability to transmit in stereo. FM growth was also fueled by the introduction of AM–FM radios in new automobiles in the mid-1960s.

The year 1973 marked the first time that more listeners tuned in to FM stations than to AM stations. FM radio became more suited for different types of music formats thanks to its higher fidelity and superior sound quality. As a result, AM radio began to lose audiences in significant numbers. An effort to revitalize AM radio with the introduction of AM stereo during the 1980s was a disaster. The Federal Communications Commission (FCC) refused to set a technical standard for AM stereo, which resulted in confusion among broadcasters and the public. Less than 10 percent of all AM stations adopted AM stereo.

During the 1980s, program consultants took on an increasing role in advising radio station owners how to program their stations. Formula radio was introduced and was quickly copied by other stations. "Formula radio" was a term to describe programming clusters of music separated by sets of commercials, leading to the perception of more music with fewer interruptions. Talk and information programming experienced a rebirth on AM stations, and shock radio, with personalities such as Don Imus, Howard Stern, and the Greaseman, both repelled and attracted audiences.

Most of the changes that the radio industry experienced during the 1990s involved revisions of ownership regulations. When the American economy suffered a recession in 1991–1992, many local radio stations experienced heavy losses as local advertising faced major cuts in their budgets. In 1991, three out of every four stations lost money. The FCC relaxed the duopoly rule in 1992, which previously limited ownership to only one AM–FM combination in a market. But it was the Telecommunications Act of 1996 that revolutionized radio ownership, eliminating all ownership restrictions at the national level and leading to the creation of several radio conglomerates. The strong revenue potential of radio, and the opportunity to cluster operations in many markets, led to increasing industry consolidation by the end of the 1990s.

Radio in the Twenty-First Century

Continuing evolution is expected to occur in the radio industry. A number of new technological innovations have the potential to affect the radio industry in both positive and negative ways. Digital audio radio services (DARS), such as Sirius and XM Satellite Radio, will offer high-quality subscription radio services to consumers. Because these services are subscription-based, their effect on terrestrial radio may be minimal in economic terms. However, they may help to siphon away radio audiences, especially among commuters using automobiles and public transportation. Digital audio broadcasting is now technically possible, but the expense to convert analog transmitters and millions of radio receivers to digital technology means digital audio will continue to be limited to technologies outside of radio.

The Internet has the potential to affect music listening habits. Hundreds of Internet-only radio stations have gone online, providing an alternative method of listening to music and information beyond a radio receiver. Internet-only stations face significant challenges in their ability to attract advertisers, but the costs to operate an Internet-only station are very modest compared to a traditional terrestrial station.

Another innovation in Internet-related broadcasting is the development of "personal" radio. The personal radio service uses digital music stored on a server. In a personal radio system, the user establishes a listener profile through an existing service. The user enters his or her music preferences, selecting a genre of music and, if preferred, individual artists. By adding a zip code, the listener can also access local weather. Eventually, access to other forms of local news and information will be possible.

Consumers can also build their own music collections by downloading MP3 audio files from the Internet and then record those files onto blank CD-ROM media. There are many issues, involving copyright and intellectual property, that are associated with MP3 technology. Recording companies are most affected by MP3, but radio stations could be affected as well if the recording industry adopts the Internet as the primary means to distribute music to consumers, thus bypassing radio. Furthermore, audience use of MP3 may mean less time spent with radio, which, over time, could have a cumulative effect on the ability of the industry to attract advertising.

The FCC established a new low-power FM (LPFM) service on January 20, 2000, to create new broadcasting opportunities for locally based organizations to serve their communities. LPFM stations will serve an area with a radius of approximately 3.5 miles, will have a maximum power of 100 watts, and will have noncommercial status. The commission began accepting applications for the new service in January 2001.

Conclusion

Although competition from new technologies is growing, traditional radio in the form of AM and FM broadcasting remains in a very strong economic condition. Furthermore, radio audiences remained stable throughout the 1990s, which in turn helped to increase radio advertising revenues.

Consolidation has helped to make radio a more competitive medium for local advertising dollars, outpacing both television and newspapers.

See also: BROADCASTING, GOVERNMENT REGULATION OF; FEDERAL COMMUNICATIONS COMMISSION; INTERNET AND THE WORLD WIDE WEB; RADIO BROADCASTING, CAREERS IN; RADIO BROADCASTING, HISTORY OF; RADIO BROADCASTING, STATION PROGRAMMING AND; RADIO BROADCASTING, TECHNOLOGY OF; RECORDING INDUSTRY; TELECOMMUNICATIONS ACT OF 1996.

Bibliography

Albarran, Alan B. (1996). *Media Economics: Understanding Markets, Industries and Concepts.* Ames: Iowa State University Press.

Albarran, Alan B., and Pitts, Gregory G. (2000). *The Radio Broadcasting Industry.* Needham, MA: Allyn & Bacon.

National Association of Broadcasters. (1999). "Did You Know . . . " <http://www.nab.org/radio/radfacts.asp>.

Radio Advertising Bureau. (1999). "Radio Marketing Guide and Fact Book for Advertisers." <http://www.rab.com/station/mgfb99/radfact.html>.

Shane, Ed. (1998). "The State of the Industry: Radio's Shifting Paradigm." *Journal of Radio Studies* 5(2):1–7.

Veronis Suhler & Associates. (1999). *Communications Industry Forecast.* New York: Veronis Suhler & Associates.

Weber. Thomas E. (1999) "Web Radio: No Antenna Required." *The Wall Street Journal*, July 28, pp. B1, B4.

ALAN B. ALBARRAN

■ RADIO BROADCASTING, CAREERS IN

Whether or not a person can find employment in the radio broadcasting industry depends on how well that individual's skills, professional background, and person interests fit with the requirements for on-air or off-air positions. When filling the high-profile on-air positions, employers are generally looking for individuals who have skills in vocal performance, a background in announcing or reporting, or an expertise with specific subjects such as sports or journalism. When filling the off-air positions, employers are looking for people who have sales, fundraising, organiza-

On-air personalities often answer telephone calls from listeners and respond to them as part of a live broadcast, as this senior reporter is doing for a Shanghai radio station. (AFP/Corbis)

tional, and management skills or are adept at working with engineering, electronics, and computer components. The opportunities for employment obviously depend on the size of the station. A small local radio station may employ a staff of fewer than ten people. A large regional station, however, will employ a correspondingly larger staff, which provides a broader range of possible careers.

On-Air Positions

The main on-air talent of a music-oriented station usually consists of a morning team of two announcers. One may be responsible for road traffic or news updates, while the other provides the flow of the program. Larger stations may have two people working together to provide the flow rather than just leaving it to one person. In any case, these prime positions are usually filled by the most appealing and experienced on-air personalities at the station. They have generally honed their skills by starting in the most basic entry-level jobs. Entry-level announcers are often assigned the overnight and weekend time slots at smaller professional or even college stations. This provides practice in on-air delivery and in handling the technical aspects of running a studio. When a person becomes proficient at the entry-level job, he or she may become the midday or evening disc jockey (deejay), eventually moving to the more prestigious morning or afternoon time slots, when audiences are large.

Other on-air positions include sports announcer, news reporter, or talk-show host. Entry into these jobs may require additional experience outside of radio broadcasting. For example, many sports announcers have had successful, high-level athletic careers (either amateur or professional). Others have worked their way up from announcing high school games to college games (with a very small number progressing on to the professional-level sports events). Many news reporters have a background in journalism and have already worked for newspapers before changing over to radio broadcasting. Others move directly into a news reporting position with a commercial radio station after serving an internship or gaining experience at a college radio station. Reporters at all-news stations generally specialize in weather, sports, business, or consumer affairs. Talk-show hosts, who often get their start as successful authors, politicians, doctors, clergy, or actors, require several assistants. Some assistants help to produce the show. Others screen calls or operate the control board while the host talks and interviews guests.

Off-Air Positions

The top off-air positions in radio broadcasting are station manager and general manager. These two positions, which involve overseeing the entire operation at a station or group of stations, are most likely to be held by people who have previously served as a sales manager. Therefore, someone who wants ultimately to become a station manager or a general manger should probably look for an entry-level position in the sales department. To be on a radio sales staff often requires some sales experience, although the experience does not necessarily have to be related to media industries. The most successful sales people will often be given the opportunity to move up into managerial roles within the sales department. Top stations break the managerial roles into those of local sales manager, who oversees all sales of time for local advertising, and national sales manager, who works with advertising agencies or national advertisers that are interested in buying time. These two managers report to the general sales manager. Some stations have research directors who read and interpret national audience surveys and conduct in-house studies to determine who listens to the station and why.

Managers do not come just from the sales staff; they can also come from the programming side of station operations. Sometimes, an on-air employee lacks the performance appeal that is necessary for him or her to reach the top and become a morning host. If, however, this person has strong organizational skills, he or she might decide to make the transition to off-air personnel and take on a position such as music director, which is responsible for choosing the songs and helping to design the rotation of the music that the station uses. A person in this position needs to understand research methods such as auditorium testing of songs to determine what the audience will like. The music director reports to the program director, who is responsible for overseeing the total station sound. In connection with this, the program director should keep up with all industry trends and monitor the programming at competing stations.

In addition to the music director, the program director must work closely with the news director, the promotions director, the production manager, and the traffic manager. The news director, who oversees all news operations, is often someone who was a highly motivated reporter but decided to make the change to the off-air side of the business. A promotions director heads up the a station's publicity campaigns, which can include giveaways, live remote broadcasts, station promos (i.e., promotional recordings), and general hype. This person must be extremely creative and have strong skills in the area of public relations. The production manager is in charge of scheduling, facilitating, and assisting in studio production work for commercials, promos, and programs at the station. The traffic manager schedules all commercial and promotional segments, as well as any program segments that occur during a given period. This person sometimes has a traffic assistant, who may also be assisting with the production and news operations.

On the technical side, engineers are important for installing and maintaining the equipment within the studio, building towers, hooking up transmitters to power the signal, and establishing satellite receivers and uplinks. The chief engineer may be a one-man department, or there may be an engineering staff, including a maintenance engineer who is responsible for general upkeep. Contract engineers may substitute for or supplement the chief engineer. The contract engineer usually serves several small stations that cannot afford a full-time employee in this area. A contract engineer may also be a person who provides a very specialized skill, such as transmitter tower construction or maintenance, to a large number of stations. The newest position in radio is probably the technical job of webmaster. The webmaster's duties may be more in line with promotions, sales, or production functions, depending on the station. Often, the webmaster must work with all three areas.

Other Industry-Related Opportunities

It is possible to have a career that is part of the radio broadcasting industry without being employed by a radio station. For example, there are companies that produce syndicated programs and newscasts that are sold to stations, while others companies provide stations with professional-quality recordings of station identifiers and teasers. These companies have many of the same personnel requirements that the stations have. The difference is that the final product is being sold to someone else to broadcast rather than being broadcast by the people who produced it.

Other opportunities for employment exist with companies that sell equipment, supplies, promotional materials, and the like that have been created specifically for radio stations. These companies are looking for sales professionals, engineers, and people who have promotion savvy.

Communication lawyers interpret government and judicial decisions and file complicated legal documents or defend the license of a station. A few law firms specialize in this area. Small stations would be more likely to contact these firms on a case-by-case basis. Larger station groups might have their own legal department to deal with these types of issues.

Finally, some Internet websites provide web-radio services. These operations may be run similar to an on-air station, but the signals are disseminated through streaming audio via computer. Thus, computer technicians are required in addition to many of the same personnel that are required for the operation of a standard radio station.

See also: RADIO BROADCASTING; RADIO BROADCASTING, HISTORY OF; RADIO BROADCASTING, STATION PROGRAMMING AND; RADIO BROADCASTING, TECHNOLOGY OF.

Bibliography

Brown, James A., and Quaal, Ward L. (1998). *Radio-Television-Cable Management,* 3rd edition. Boston: McGraw-Hill.

Fry, Ronald W., ed. (1991). *Radio & Television Career Directory.* Hawthorne, NJ: Career Press.

Mogel, Leonard. (1994). *Making It in Broadcasting: An Insider's Guide to Career Opportunities.* New York: Collier Books.

Smith, Leslie F. (1990). *Perspectives on Radio and Television.* Grand Rapids, MI: Harper & Row.

STEPHEN D. PERRY

■ RADIO BROADCASTING, HISTORY OF

No single person in the colorful history of radio can be credited with inventing radio. Radio's "inventors" almost all refined an idea put forth by someone else. Wireless communication became a theoretical proposition in 1864 when Scottish mathematician and physicist James Clerk Maxwell predicted the existence of invisible electromagnetic waves. More than twenty years later, German physicist Heinrich Hertz conducted experiments in 1887 to prove that Maxwell's theories were correct. The fundamental unit of electromagnetic wave frequency, the hertz (Hz), is named for him, though Hertz never promoted wireless communications.

Early Development of Technology

In the 1890s, four inventors simultaneously worked on wireless transmission and detection. French physicist Edouard Branly invented a signal detector called a "coherer" that consisted of a glass tube filled with metal filings that reacted when a signal was detected. English physicist Oliver Lodge worked on the principle of resonance tuning, which allowed the transmitter and receiver to operate on the same frequency. Russian Alexander Popoff developed a better coherer and a vertical-receiving antenna.

The fourth and best-known inventor–innovator was the twenty-year-old Italian Guglielmo Marconi, who began wireless experiments in 1894.

Lee De Forest holds one of his Audion vacuum tubes, which enabled live radio broadcasts. (Bettmann/Corbis)

Within two years, Marconi created a wireless system that was capable of sending and detecting a signal. When the Italian government showed no interest in wireless communication, Marconi's family contacts enabled him to meet investors in England. He founded British Marconi in 1897 and began marketing radio as a telegraph that required no wires to send Morse code dots and dashes. British Marconi and the U.S. subsidiary, American Marconi, dominated wireless communication for ship-to-shore and transatlantic communications until after World War I.

Canadian Reginald Fessenden created a wireless system that would transmit speech. On Christmas Eve in 1906, Fessenden broadcast programming from studios at Brant Rock, Massachusetts. An audience consisting of startled radio operators on ships at sea, newspaper reporters who had been alerted to his publicity-generating broadcast, and a small number of home experimenters heard Fessenden speak and play the violin.

After several failures and claims that he was a fraud, American Lee De Forest's radio company aired publicity-generating broadcasts, including one from the Eiffel Tower in Paris. In 1906, De Forest also took credit for creating one of the most important wireless components, the Audion—a triode vacuum tube that amplified signals and improved reception. Previously, receivers had dif-

ficulty detecting weak radio signals. Though De Forest held the patent for the Audion, historians contend that he did not fully understand what he had invented or how it worked.

Beginning in 1912, Edwin Armstrong studied the workings of the Audion and discovered the principle of regeneration. Regeneration enhanced the quality of signal amplification and produced an oscillating signal, or carrier wave, which became the founding principle behind modern radio transmitters.

Greed, the quest for glory, and, perhaps, simply the combination of many individuals focusing simultaneously on the same topic led to a series of patent lawsuits. The U.S. government halted these disputes after the United States entered World War I in 1917. During the war, as a security measure, the U.S. Navy took over the operation of all radio stations, even those owned by American Marconi, and closed most amateur and experimental stations. After the war, American Marconi attempted to return to business as usual, but opposition to a foreign company having a monopoly over wireless communications in the United States eventually led General Electric (GE) to buy a controlling interest in American Marconi in 1919. Along with co-owners Westinghouse and American Telephone & Telegraph (AT&T), GE transferred American Marconi's assets to the Radio Corporation of America (RCA), which would manufacture radio receiving sets. Probably the biggest single breakthrough in receiver design came from Armstrong, who developed a tuner with better amplification and sound quality. The superheterodyne receiver was licensed in 1920 by RCA and soon went into production.

The First Wireless Regulations

After wireless was credited with averting several maritime disasters, the U.S. Congress passed the Wireless Ship Act of 1910 to regulate broadcasting. The act required ocean-going vessels with fifty or more passengers and crewmembers to carry a wireless system operated by a skilled person.

The legislation was put to the test when the *Titanic* sank on April 14, 1912, during its maiden voyage. More than fifteen hundred passengers and crew died. The ship *Carpathia* responded to distress calls from the *Titanic* and ultimately saved approximately seven hundred people. A closer ship, the *California*, did not respond because that ship's sole radio operator, after many hours on duty, was asleep when the distress messages were being sent by the radio operator on the *Titanic*. The freighter *Lena* was closer but, because of its small crew and no regular passengers, the ship was not required to be equipped with a wireless.

The sinking of the *Titanic* led to newspaper and magazine editorials that called for federal government control over wireless operation and practices. Wireless regulation was viewed as a public good, equal in importance to previous social and antitrust regulation. Within four months, broadcast transmission in the United States was a privilege assigned by the U.S. government. The Radio Act of 1912 required all operators to be licensed, called for all stations to adhere to frequency allocations, made distress calls priority communications, and gave the U.S. Secretary of Commerce power to issue radio licenses and make other necessary radio regulations.

Public Embrace of Radio

The name for wireless evolved along with the technology. Known first as the "wireless telegraph," it transitioned to "radiotelegraphy" and "radiotelephony" (transmission of the human voice). The term was shortened to "radio" around 1912. The word "broadcast" was borrowed from agriculture and referred to the practice of planting seeds by scattering them across a field rather than in straight rows.

Until the invention of radio, it was impossible to transmit entertainment or information simultaneously to thousands of receivers. For the listener in 1920, 1930, or 1940, radio was the only way to learn about distant places and events. Radio programming was first developed as a means of encouraging people to buy receiving equipment. Radio networks were created to supply simultaneous, live, national programming to affiliate stations that encouraged receiver sales and then advertising sales.

Just as the public rushed to use the Internet in the 1990s, the public embraced radio in the 1920s. Middle-class Americans, intrigued with scientific applications and the potential for information and entertainment, purchased radio receiving sets at an astonishing rate. Sales of radio equipment totaled $60 million in 1922, $136 million in 1923, and $358 million in 1924. Individuals and families could enjoy the newly available information and entertainment from the comfort and privacy of their homes, where receiver sets fit in nicely because manufacturers built them to look like elegant furniture.

Regulation of Radio

Station and operator licensing was intended to provide monitored growth of radio, but the U.S. government failed to realize how quickly radio would grow. By the end of 1922, 690 licenses had been assigned to stations airing entertainment and information. These stations occupied one of two frequencies, 360 meters (833 kHz) or 400 meters (750 kHz). Because multiple stations were broadcasting on the same frequency, interference occurred and caused many station signals to become inaudible.

U.S. Secretary of Commerce Herbert Hoover began to establish a limited number of "superpower" radio stations and to limit the hours of operation for other stations. These actions were supported by the radio manufacturers, who believed that the entire country could be covered by a handful of high-power stations. Their plan was to encourage receiver sales but to limit operational and programming expenses.

Hoover's powers to regulate radio were challenged in 1925 by Zenith Radio Corporation, the owner of a station in Chicago that had been licensed to broadcast for only two hours a week. The related federal district court ruling denied the U.S. Secretary of Commerce the power to regulate radio.

The U.S. Congress passed the Radio Act of 1927 (to create new federal authority to regulate broadcasting) and established the Federal Radio Commission (FRC). The plan for the FRC, which had five commissioners to sort out the mess of the airwaves, was to reduce the number of radio stations and to favor the creation of high-power stations. The act revoked the licenses of all radio stations, including commercial stations, transoceanic stations, coastal stations, experimental stations, educational, religious, and training stations, and approximately 14,885 amateur stations—more than 18,000 transmitters in all—and started the licensing process anew.

Development of Radio Networks

AT&T started station WEAF in New York City in 1922 as part of a national "toll" broadcasting

The November 15, 1926, premiere broadcast of the National Broadcasting Company (NBC) featured a performance by the Million Dollar Quartet, which included (left to right) Lew Fields, Joe Weber, Frank Goldman, and Cesare Sodero. (Bettmann/Corbis)

service. AT&T was the first station owner to recognize the potential of advertising sales to pay for the operation of radio. The first reported radio advertisement, for an apartment complex in New York, aired on WEAF in 1922. It cost $100.

Antitrust concerns led AT&T to sell its radio stations in 1926 to RCA, which used the stations to form the National Broadcasting Company (NBC). The premiere broadcast of the network took place on November 15, 1926, when NBC aired a four-hour program from the Waldorf-Astoria Hotel in New York. The broadcast featured singers, orchestras, and comedy teams. It also included remote broadcasts from Chicago and Kansas City. As many as twelve million people were estimated to have heard the broadcast. In less than two months, NBC was operating two networks, the Red Network and the Blue Network.

The Columbia Phonograph Broadcasting System (named for partner Columbia Phonograph Record Company) was established in 1927 and later became the Columbia Broadcasting System (CBS). The Congress Cigar Company bought a controlling interest to promote its cigars. William Paley, son of the firm's founder, took over the network's operation and headed the network for more than half a century.

The Mutual Broadcasting System (MBS) began operation in 1934. The four founding stations—WGN in Chicago, WOR in New York, WLW in Cincinnati, and WXYZ in Detroit—remain on the air. The Mutual Broadcasting System ceased operation as an entity in 1999.

Much of the early network and local programming was musical. Concerts featured live and recorded classical compositions, popular dance music, jazz, and country. Radio drama developed as the complement to the musical programming. Network programming ranged from fortunetellers to gory thrillers. Commercials became more numerous and insistent in their pitch to listeners. Advertisers saw radio as an inexpensive and effective way to reach a national audience.

Golden Age of Radio Programming

Congress passed the Communications Act of 1934 to create the Federal Communications Commission (FCC) to supervise wired and wireless communication and to replace the FRC. By 1935, the U.S. Department of Commerce estimated that radio broadcasts served 18.5 million families, or more than 50 million people. Approximately 60 percent of all homes in the United States had radios. The radio sets in operation in the United States comprised 43.2 percent of the world total. For the public, radio offered comforting entertainment in the aftermath of the stock market crash of 1929. Radio receiver sets were not cheap, but once purchased, they supplied free programming. The only additional cost for the owner of a radio was the time spent listening to commercials.

Serial melodramas, called "soap operas" because they were sponsored by soap companies, ran during the daytime and drew a large audience of housewives. Radio news programming in 1933 carried four speeches by newly elected President Franklin D. Roosevelt. Called "fireside chats" because of Roosevelt's informal and relaxed tone as well as the perception that he was sharing his thoughts with the public, Roosevelt's addresses created good will among the public and enabled many of his New Deal reforms to be quickly passed by the U.S. Congress.

Newspaper owners briefly tried to limit radio networks to only two five-minute newscasts to protect newspaper circulation. Eventually, newspaper owners recognized the value of owning radio stations and the stranglehold on radio news ended. During World War II, CBS reporter Edward R. Murrow reported live from London during actual bombings by the Nazis. Battlefield reports brought home sounds of war that listeners had never before heard.

The U.S. government established the Voice of America (VOA) through the Office of War Information to counter international radio broadcasts coming from Germany, Japan, and Italy. By congressional mandate, all VOA programming was transmitted by shortwave for reception by listeners outside of the United States.

The Invention of FM Radio

The prospect of creating an additional radio service, using frequency modulation (FM), was barely an issue until the late 1930s. Prior to that point, all radio transmissions had been based on amplitude modulation (AM). FM service might have died for lack of support but for the dogged determination of Armstrong, who began work to eliminate static in 1923. A decade later, Armstrong received five patents for frequency modulation. He demonstrated his invention to David Sarnoff, who was at that point president of both RCA and NBC. While Sarnoff recognized the superior sound quality of an FM broadcast, he was unwilling to back the system because RCA was developing television. FM was seen as a competitor to AM radio; it would divert scientific and government attention from television.

Armstrong did not give up. He built an experimental FM station in Alpine, New Jersey, in 1939, supplied the financing to have FM receivers built, and petitioned the FCC to create FM stations. Although the service was authorized in 1940, fewer than 400,000 receivers were in the hands of the public by the start of World War II. In contrast, twenty-nine million households could listen to AM radio at that point. After World War II, FM service might have grown had the FCC not changed the assigned frequency range. When FM was moved from 42–50 MHz to 88–108 MHz, all of the receivers that had been produced before the frequency change suddenly became obsolete.

Local Radio Develops

More than fifty million AM receivers were manufactured between 1946 and 1948. As radio set prices dropped, the multiset household devel-oped. Radios spread from the living room to the kitchen and bedroom. The growth of television drew programming and audiences from radio, but radio survived by adopting the all-music format and shifting to a heavier emphasis on daytime listening. Radio became a local advertising medium.

One of the most popular all-music formats used by local radio stations in the 1950s was the Top 40 format. This format resulted from the independent work of four AM station owners, Todd Storz, Gordon McLendon, Gerald Bartell, and Harold Krelstein. In an attempt to develop a new approach to station programming, these four men all made substantial contributions to the development of the Top 40 format, which succeeded in creating a new identity for radio. One of the best explanations for a radio format built around forty songs came from Storz, who said he had observed people playing the same few songs over and over on the jukebox and concluded that listeners most wanted to hear hit songs over and over.

The Decline of AM Radio and the Rise of FM Radio

The Top 40 format helped reposition radio, but it also created a group of similar-sounding stations. AM stations aired similar music and jingles, played loud and lengthy sets of commercials, and generally had poor fidelity (i.e., sound quality). Attention thus shifted to FM radio during the 1960s. Besides the obvious availability of FM channels, operators began to recognize other FM benefits. FM provided day and night service, with uniform power levels and coverage areas. FM channel width meant superior audio, including stereo, and less interference.

If the Top 40 AM formula suggested playing no song longer than three minutes, the FM approach was to play an album cut that was ten-minutes long. Rock music, growing from the "flower children" and "make love not war" anti-Vietnam movements, provided much of the content for FM station programming. The music industry also encouraged the growth of FM radio. The playlists of Top 40 AM stations were tightly controlled, with few opportunities for new songs or new groups to gain on-air exposure. Many FM stations would play virtually anything, so record companies used FM radio to introduce new artists and styles of music. By 1971, nearly half of all radios sold included FM tuners. National FM listener share passed the AM listener share in the fall of 1978; 50.698 percent of the listeners were tuning to FM stations. FM radio subsequently became the *de facto* standard for most music-radio listeners, which caused many AM stations to shift to talk-radio formats in the 1980s.

In 1985, the FCC increased the limit on how many stations a person or company could own from seven stations to twelve stations. This number was increased to eighteen in 1992 and twenty in 1994. With the passage of the Telecommunications Act of 1996, broadcasters were allowed to own up to eight commercial stations in large markets and as many stations nationwide as they are able to purchase. As a result of these changes, many owners of smaller stations have sold their properties to corporate groups, who have built successful station groups that dominate not only station listening but also radio advertising sales in their markets.

Radio in 2000 and Beyond

By the year 2000, approximately 85 percent of all radio listeners were tuning to FM stations. The question, however, now may be whether AM radio and possibly FM radio are simply transitional delivery technologies. Already, broadcasters are investigating (and investing in) digital terrestrial broadcasting that could eventually replace the traditional AM and FM stations. At the same time, companies are streaming audio via the Internet and offering satellite-delivered audio services.

See also: ARMSTRONG, EDWIN HOWARD; BROADCAST-ING, GOVERNMENT REGULATION OF; COMMUNICA-TIONS ACT OF 1934; FEDERAL COMMUNICATIONS COMMISSION; MARCONI, GUGLIELMO; MORSE, SAMUEL F. B.; MURROW, EDWARD R.; PALEY, WILLIAM S.; RADIO BROADCASTING; RADIO BROADCASTING, CAREERS IN; RADIO BROADCAST-ING, STATION PROGRAMMING AND; RADIO BROAD-CASTING, TECHNOLOGY OF; SARNOFF, DAVID; TELECOMMUNICATIONS ACT OF 1996; TELEVI-SION, HISTORY OF.

Bibliography

Barnouw, Erik. (1966). *A Tower of Babel: A History of Broadcasting in the United States.* New York: Oxford University Press.
Barnouw, Erik. (1968). *The Golden Web.* New York: Oxford University Press.
Creech, Kenneth C. (1996). *Electronic Media Law and Regulation.* Boston: Focal Press.
Douglas, George. (1987). *The Early Days of Radio Broadcasting.* Jefferson, NC: McFarland.
Douglas, Susan J. (1987). *Inventing American Broadcasting, 1899–1922.* Baltimore, MD: Johns Hopkins University Press.
Duncan, James H., ed. (1987). *American Radio: Spring 1987.* Kalamazoo, MI: Duncan's American Radio.
Hettinger, Herman S., ed. (1935). "Foreword." *The Annals of the American Academy of Political and Social Science* 177:vii.
Lewis, Tom. (1991). *Empire of the Air: The Men Who Made Radio.* New York: HarperCollins.
MacFarland, David T. (1979). *The Development of the Top 40 Radio Format.* New York: Arno Press.
Smith, Sally B. (1990). *In All His Glory: The Life of William S. Paley.* New York: Simon & Schuster.
Sterling, Christopher, and Kittross, John M. (1990). *Stay Tuned: A Concise History of American Broadcasting.* Belmont, CA: Wadsworth.
Whetmore, Edward J. (1981). *The Magic Medium: An Introduction to Radio in America.* Belmont, CA: Wadsworth.
White, Llewellyn. (1947). *The American Radio: A Report on the Broadcasting Industry in the United States from The Commission on Freedom of the Press.* Chicago: University of Chicago Press.

GREG PITTS

▥ RADIO BROADCASTING, PUBLIC

See: Public Broadcasting; Public Service Media

▥ RADIO BROADCASTING, REGULATION OF

See: Broadcasting, Government Regulation of; Broadcasting, Self-Regulation of

▥ RADIO BROADCASTING, STATION PROGRAMMING AND

Susan Eastman and her colleagues (1997) state very clearly that the business of broadcasting is "the business of creating audiences that advertisers want to reach" (p. 8). This focus originated in the 1920s when WEAF, a radio station owned by the American Telephone and Telegraph Company (AT&T), began "toll broadcasting" (i.e., the exchange of money for airtime). This led to sponsorships of blocks of programs, such as the "Palmolive Hour" and the "Mercury Theater." It was not long before sponsorships progressed to shorter, more frequent announcements.

Radio advertising became even more attractive with the rise of networks. AT&T initiated this trend by linking its stations by using its existing telephone infrastructure. The telephone company soon left the broadcasting industry, selling its holdings to the Radio Corporation of America (RCA). As a result, RCA created a new company, the National Broadcasting Company (NBC), which operated radio stations under a "Blue" network that included former RCA, Westinghouse, and General Electric holdings and a "Red" network that included mostly former AT&T stations. These networks increased the audience for the network programming and thereby increased the advertising revenue. The "golden age" of radio, from around 1930 to 1948, saw the culmination of David Sarnoff's dream of radio being the center of entertainment in American households. Programming of this period included music, drama, and live variety. In addition, while advertisers were spending about $20 million on radio advertising by 1929, the figure had exploded to around $500 million by 1948. However, a new competitor was looming: television. The television industry used radio as a model for its programming and, as a result, many of radio's finest artists made the move to the new medium. Radio had to change in order to attract salable audiences for advertisers. In doing so, its programming went through a significant evolution.

Station Formats

According to Joseph Dominick and his colleagues (2000), radio advertising revenue dropped 58 percent between 1952 and 1958. In addition, the networks provided much less programming to local affiliates because of the loss of popular talent. As it turned out, radio was about to advance not on the backs of a national network but rather from creative ideas on the local level.

Top 40 Radio

Todd Storz, a radio station owner in Omaha, Nebraska, was in a bar one night when he noticed that people loved hearing the same hit songs over and over again. Storz decided to apply this strategy to radio programming, and the result was Top 40 radio. Another station owner, Gordon McLendon

of Dallas, Texas, took Top 40 and added the promotion of local on-air personalities called disc jockeys. This programming transition was also very timely. World War II had been over for a few years, and the United States was entering a period of economic prosperity. These economic freedoms trickled down to young people who had money to spend and were trying to distinguish themselves from their parent's generation. Listening to the newest hits and colorful disc jockeys of Top 40 radio gave this growing population a common rallying point. The Top 40 format was also very compatible with the rise of rock-and-roll music. Many of the early stars of rock (e.g., Elvis Presley, Jerry Lee Lewis, Little Richard) portrayed a rebellious image that teenagers admired. In addition, Top 40 helped to improve the relationship between the radio industry and the recording industry. The music industry found that the more the hits were played by radio stations, the more the records sold at stores.

As the number of radio stations grew in the mid-1950s, station owners were looking for other music formats that would target attractive audience groups. Middle-of-the-road, country and western, beautiful music, all-jazz, and album-oriented rock formats all grew out of this movement toward specialization. A programmer was also able to make changes to the station's sound as a response to the uniqueness of its market. This had not been possible when programming was fed via a national network.

FM Radio

A technological innovation also helped the development of music formats. From the early days, a radio station's signal was transmitted through amplitude modulation (AM). In simple terms, this process involves the transmission of radio information by the manipulation of the height of the electromagnetic waves. While this method served (and continues to serve) the industry well, it was not technically suited for the transmission of high-fidelity music. In 1933, Edwin Armstrong publicly demonstrated frequency modulation (FM), a mode of delivery that manipulated the distance between the electromagnetic waves. The technical differences resulted in a transmission system that had two key advantages over the existing AM method: an amazing reduction in static and the ability to reproduce high-quality music.

Howard Stern (center) is a well-known radio talk show host who has bridged the gap between radio and television by providing for a television broadcast of his radio broadcast. (Reuters NewMedia Inc./Corbis)

The advantage of FM was obvious, but the method was not adopted right away. FM broadcasting required a completely new system from transmitter to receiver. This meant that radio station owners would have to invest in expensive new equipment and that the public would have to replace their radios with new models. In the late 1930s, the radio industry was extremely strong, so major industry players, including RCA's Sarnoff, saw no reason to make this technological switch. In addition, RCA was investing at that time in a another developing technology: television.

It was not until the early 1960s that FM stereo broadcasting began to grow. The combination of excellent music reproduction and the proliferation of music formats helped with the expansion. FM received another boost when the Federal Communications Commission (FCC) passed the nonduplication rule. This regulation mandated that AM/FM combination stations must offer separate programming at least half the time. Original programming expanded on the FM stations, and by the late 1970s, listenership of FM stations exceeded that of AM stations. Music formats continue to flourish on FM progress into more even targeted genres (e.g., alternative, adult alternative, rock, active rock, adult contemporary, hot adult contemporary). However, just as the radio industry had adjusted to the introduction of television, AM radio was set to evolve once again.

Talk Radio

Talk radio had not attracted much attention in the early 1980s, but in 1988, when it was learned that Speaker of the House Jim Wright was about to push through a congressional pay raise without a vote, Ralph Nader turned to talk radio. He called *The Jerry Williams Show* in Boston and complained. At the same time, others called numerous talk radio hosts around the country to complain about Wright's action. After broadcasting Wright's fax number over the air, an enormous number of complaints filled his office. Needless to say, Wright's actions were halted, and the nation understood overnight the power of talk radio.

The years that followed marked a dramatic increase in the number of stations with either an all-talk format or a format that combined news and talk. In the early 1980s, there were only around two hundred stations that used these formats, but by 1994, that number had increased to more than eight hundred. This increase was fueled by the powerful personalities of talk radio. As had happened with the disc jockeys in the 1950s, these talk show hosts have become household names. The list includes such notables as Larry King, Howard Stern, Don Imus, Rush Limbaugh, Laura Schlessinger, and Jim Rome. By 1998, news/talk had become the most listened to format, attracting nearly 17 percent of the radio audience. As the popularity of confrontational talk grew on commercial radio, a similar growth was occurring on noncommercial radio.

The Pubic Broadcasting Act of 1967 created the Corporation for Public Broadcasting. This organization was designed to receive funds from the government and distribute it to public radio and television stations, as well as to television's Public Broadcasting Service (PBS) and National Public Radio (NPR). NPR produces much of its own programming, focusing mainly on national news. Jay Kernis, the creator of NPR's popular show *All Things Considered*, said that public radio should provide programming that "enriches and gives meaning to the human spirit" (Douglas, 1999, p. 286). The numbers speak volumes about the success of this approach. In 1971, 104 stations carried *All Things Considered*. By the mid-1990s, more than 520 stations carried the program, with a listener base of around 160 million.

The Era of Consolidation

The Telecommunications Act of 1996 loosened the longstanding radio ownership restrictions. After the national ownership cap was eliminated, group consolidation exploded. For example, Jacor Communications owned three radio stations in 1978, but by 1998, they owned more than two hundred. In 1999, Clear Channel Communications acquired both Jacor and AM/FM, Inc., creating a group of 959 stations and making Clear Channel Communications the largest group owner in the radio industry.

This boom in consolidation has received mixed reviews. The major group owners argue that the radio consolidation environment offers many advantages, including financial stability for the industry and improved programming for smaller markets through satellite delivered programs and formats. However, some critics say that consolidation is reducing the variety of voices in the public marketplace of ideas. While the jury is still out in this debate, both sides can offer support for their opinions. For example, the radio industry is on strong financial ground, despite the age of the Internet. Radio stocks saw 100 percent gains after the Telecommunications Act of 1996 was enacted, and radio's advertising revenue continues to grow. From the public advocate side, the FCC adopted rules in January 2000 that created a new low-power FM (LPFM) service for nonprofit organizations, churches, and community groups. By December 2000, the FCC had declared that more than 250 applicants were eligible for this new LPFM license. While technical interference issues remain paramount to broadcasters, the FCC believes that increasing the number of voices on the airwaves is of greater importance.

Contemporary Programming

While radio continues to be community based and primarily supported by local advertising dollars, that does not mean that all of the programming is locally originated. Many stations take advantage of satellite technology to acquire national network programming. Companies such as Premiere, Westwood One, the American Broadcasting Company (ABC), and the Cable News Network (CNN) provide choices for the local programmer that range from regularly scheduled news and high-profile talk shows to complete twenty-four-hour formats. These network programs provide a local station with a cost-effective alternative to the arduous task of recruiting and hiring quality local talent. Group-owned stations are also becoming more efficient with their programming practices by sharing their on-air talent. This practice, known as voice tracking, involves one station in a group programming three or more stations within the same ownership cluster. High-speed datalines, computer-controlled formats, and satellite technology all help to make this process sound seamless to the local listener. While this activity has certainly improved the bottom-line of radio group owners, some critics argue that voice tracking can never replace the "feel" and "personality" of live local talent.

However, despite the availability of excellent national programming, radio is still a local business. While national personalities such as Tom Joyner and Howard Stern attract a great deal of attention, the vast majority of morning shows around the country are hosted by local talent. Music programming is shaped by the idiosyncrasies of the local market and approximately 75 percent of total radio revenue comes from local advertising. In order to judge how they are performing in the local market, most radio stations depend on Arbitron, a national company.

Ratings

As explained above, broadcasters are in the business of attracting "desirable" audiences to hear the messages that are paid for by advertisers. It should come as no surprise that advertisers initiated the measurement of the radio audiences. It was a logical step in the sponsorship process; advertisers wanted evidence that their investment in radio advertising was reaching a significant audience. Archibald Crossley and his Crossley Inc. began an audience data service in 1930. The first competition for Crossley's company did not appear until 1934, when Claude Hooper and Montgomery Clark formed the firm of Clark-Hooper. Since that time, other companies have attempted a national radio service, including A. C. Nielsen and Birch Radio. However, Arbitron has emerged as the preeminent supplier of radio audience measurement statistics. Arbitron asks its participants to complete a diary over a seven-day period in order to document their use of radio, both in and out of the home. This data is compiled for subscribing stations (more often in large markets and less often in small markets) and sent to them in a summary report that is often referred to as "The Book." In general, the higher the ratings for a station, the more that station can charge for advertising time. Program directors design their schedules to maximize time that people spend listening, thereby increasing the chances that diary keepers will identify their particular stations during a ratings period. Stations' promotion department also takes advantage of the Arbitron methodology. Stations often run contests during "sweeps" periods in order to keep listeners tuned into their frequency. Call letters, slogans, and on-air imaging are all created to enhance a station's top-of-mind-awareness with listeners.

The Future

From a programming perspective, one could argue that radio's content has not changed a great deal from when the first radio broadcast was made. In that original 1906 broadcast, Reginald Fessenden played music on a violin, read passages from the Bible, and wished the listeners a merry Christmas—all of which, with slight stretches of the imagination, could be considered to fall into the music, news, and talk categories. While sweeping content innovations are rare, technological advancements continue to change the industry.

The Internet offers radio a tremendous opportunity and a challenge, both at the same time. Nearly half of all U.S. radio stations have an Internet website, and that figure is expected to grow. A website offers radio stations an additional opportunity to promote sponsors (creating a new revenue stream), receive feedback directly from the listeners, and provide up-to-date information for the local communities. In addition, more than eleven hundred U.S. radio stations are streaming their programming live over the web. While the Internet is growing by leaps and bounds, no one is predicting the death of over-the-air broadcasting. If history is any indicator, rather than disappearing, the radio industry can be expected to evolve while taking advantage of the online marketplace.

Another major advancement is digital radio. Digital audio broadcasting is a digital method of transmitting compact-disc-like quality audio signals to radio receivers, along with new data services such as station, song and artist identification, and news. The in-band, on-channel digital audio broadcasting (IBOC DAB) process accomplishes this goal. Basically, this allows broadcasters to transmit AM and FM analog signals simultaneously with the new digital feed. Just as with the television equivalent, digital radio offers great potential for expanded programming options. However, the established commercial model will most likely determine the direction of programming, which must continue to provide content that will attract a desirable audience for advertisers.

See also: ARMSTRONG, EDWIN HOWARD; INTERNET AND THE WORLD WIDE WEB; PUBLIC BROADCASTING; PUBLIC SERVICE MEDIA; RADIO BROADCASTING; RADIO BROADCASTING, HISTORY OF; RADIO BROADCASTING, TECHNOLOGY OF; SARNOFF,

DAVID; TELECOMMUNICATIONS ACT OF 1996; TELEVISION BROADCASTING, PROGRAMMING AND.

Bibliography

Alexander, Alison; Owers, James; and Carveth, Rodney, eds. (1998). *Media Economics: Theory and Practice*, 2nd edition. Mahwah, NJ: Lawrence Erlbaum.

Archer, Gleason L. (1971). *History of Radio to 1926*. New York: Arno Press.

Dominick, Joseph. (1999). *The Dynamics of Mass Communication*. Boston: McGraw-Hill.

Dominick, Joseph; Sherman, Barry; and Messere, Fritz. (2000). *Broadcasting, Cable, the Internet and Beyond: An Introduction to Modern Electronic Media*, 4th edition. New York: McGraw-Hill.

Douglas, Susan J. (1999). *Listening In: Radio and the American Imagination*. New York: Times Books.

Eastman, Susan Tyler; Ferguson, Douglas A.; and Klein, Robert A., eds. (1999). *Promotion and Marketing for Broadcasting and Cable*, 3rd edition. Boston: Focal Press.

Hillard, Robert L., and Keith, Michael. (1997). *The Broadcast Century: A Biography of American Broadcasting*. Boston: Focal Press.

Keith, Michael, and Krause, Joseph. (1993). *The Radio Station*. Boston: Focal Press.

MacFarland, David T. (1997). *Future Radio Programming Strategies: Cultivating Listenership in the Digital Age*. Mahwah, NJ: Lawrence Erlbaum.

Moore, Roy. (1999). *Mass Communication Law and Ethics*. Mahwah, NJ: Lawrence Erlbaum.

Vane, Edwin, and Gross, Lynne S. (1994). *Programming for TV, Radio, and Cable*. Newton, MA: Butterworth-Heinemann.

JOHN W. OWENS

RADIO BROADCASTING, TECHNOLOGY OF

Any discussion of the technology of radio broadcasting must, at the outset, acknowledge its rapidly changing nature. The almost exponentially increasing effect of computers is being felt in the domain of radio as it is in most other areas. Although computers have not replaced all of the tools in use in radio broadcasting by any means, they have greatly enhanced the effectiveness of most, if not all, of them.

Microphones

There are a number of tools used to introduce various signals into a broadcast system, and the microphone remains one of the most basic of these input tools in use in radio. The microphone is an instrument used to transduce, or convert, acoustic energy into electric energy. During this process, sound waves are changed into electricity that can then be sent through wires as variations in voltage. There are three types of microphones that are preferred by professionals: moving coil, ribbon, and condenser. These are also often referred to as dynamic, velocity, and capacitor microphones, respectively. Each produces the waveforms that are required for transmission in a different manner.

The moving-coil, or dynamic, microphone is the most widely used due primarily to its durable and rugged design and good frequency response to voices and most music. In this microphone, a flexible membrane, called the diaphragm, is suspended between two electromagnets and is connected to a conducting coil. When sound waves move the diaphragm, they move the coil through the magnetic field. This results in an electrical pattern in the wire that is analogous to the frequency of the sound wave.

The ribbon, or velocity, microphone replaces the moving voice coil and diaphragm with a thin, corrugated metal ribbon that is connected between two poles of a magnet to generate an electrical signal. The incoming sound vibrates the foil, thereby creating the effect. The long, vertical ribbon design of earlier ribbon microphones produced a very lush sound, especially with the human voice, but it was quite fragile and highly susceptible to wind damage. Newer designs use a smaller ribbon that is placed longitudinally between the pole pieces, making this type of microphone more durable and able to withstand louder sound-pressure levels. This microphone was quite common during the "golden age" of radio and is still frequently used in modern recording studios. The printed-ribbon microphone basically operates like the conventional ribbon microphone, but its more rugged design gives it some of the durability of the moving-coil microphone with the rich sound of the ribbon microphone.

Condenser, or capacitor, microphones operate on a different principle from that of the moving-coil and ribbon types. Condensers transduce energy by means of voltage variations instead of magnetic variations. They use a device that consists of two plates—a fixed backplate separated by a small space from a thin, metalized plastic diaphragm. Acoustic energy in the form of sound waves causes vibrations in the diaphragm, which creates voltage changes, varying the signal. These microphones require a power source, so they are usually equipped with internal batteries or with an outside "phantom" power supply. Advances in microelectronics make it possible to make condenser microphones small enough to clip onto a tie or lapel yet still produce a crisp sound. Because they are considered high-performance instruments, they are now the preferred microphones for news personnel.

Two important aspects of microphone technology are impedance and directional characteristics. Impedance is the electric flow resistance of a microphone, which is a factor in its performance. Lower impedance, or lower resistance to signal flow, usually means less interference from extraneous noise such as hum and static. Therefore, better performance can be expected from a microphone with low impedance. Directional characteristics are related to the fact that microphones are designed to pick up sound in varying ways. Lynne Schafer Gross (1986) identifies four basic pickup patterns: (1) unidirectional, which picks up sound mainly from one side; (2) bidirectional, which picks up sound mainly from two sides; (3) cardioid, which picks up sound in a heart-shaped pattern; and (4) omnidirectional, which picks up sound from all directions. The preference for a particular directional characteristic depends primarily on the use of the microphone. Unidirectional microphones are preferred when only one voice is to be picked up. Newscasters and sportscasters, for example, need background noises to be minimized by the single-direction pickup pattern. Bidirectional microphones, which are important for the production of radio dramas, allow actors to deliver their lines while facing each other. Cardioid microphones provide excellent results when two people are speaking side-by-side, such as during a talk show. The omnidirectional microphone is preferable when dealing with a large crowd, such as recording a play with a large cast or recording music that involves a large number of singers or instruments.

Music Sources

The turntable is an input tool that most radio stations no longer use. Those that do still use turntables mostly use them to access their "oldies" music files. Michael Keith (1990) lists the five primary elements of a turntable: (1) a heavy metal plate with a felt or rubber surface to protect the record and prevent slippage; (2) a power switch to control the motor; (3) a gear shift to act as a speed selector; (4) a drive mechanism that turns the plate; and (5) a tone arm or pickup arm that houses a cartridge and a stylus (i.e., a needle). The stylus picks up mechanical (analog) vibrations from the record grooves that the cartridge, acting as a transducer, then converts into an electrical signal. A phonograph preamplifier amplifies this small signal and then sends it to the console for further processing. Turntables were valuable in both production work and in on-air studios from the earliest days of radio broadcasting.

Compact disc (CD) players entered the radio production studio in the 1980s and quickly started to replace the turntable in many stations. Their almost instantaneous appeal was primarily due to superior sound reproduction. CD players offer far greater dynamic range than standard turntables, as well as a lower signal-to-noise ratio. Since the CD is "read" by a laser beam, physical contact is eliminated and distortion is virtually nonexistent. This superior sound performance derives from digital transduction instead of the analog system that is used for vinyl records; far less signal loss occurs. As a result, by 1987, the sale of CDs eclipsed the sale of records, and by 1996, vinyl records accounted for less than 2 percent of music sales. Both the buying public and the broadcast industry were opting for the better sound of digital. This CD dominance was to be of short duration, however; more changes were already on the way.

Just as the CD basically replaced the turntable in the radio station operation, computers have become the music source of preference for many broadcasters. Some stations transfer their music selections directly from CD to hard drive; others may skip the CD altogether and download directly from the music supplier. Another option for many stations is to eliminate in-house music completely. This may be especially applicable for stations that are part of multiple station operations. Music is received, usually by satellite, from outside sources. On-air personalities work from a list of preselected music that is downloaded before their show. That show may be done live, or the on-air

An employee monitors the control board at the radio station operated on the Hoopa Valley Indian Reservation in Humboldt County, California. (Bob Rowan; Progressive Image/Corbis)

personality might lay "voice tracks" (e.g., prerecorded song introductions and other remarks) between the songs in the computer and be at home asleep when the show is actually aired—and the listener will probably never know. The computer software perfectly times the introductions and segue remarks with the music "intro" and "outro" times to form a smooth, seamless programming flow.

Just as it took a while for CDs to replace records, it will be some time before computers completely replace CD players, especially in smaller stations. Economic factors are the primary reason for this delay; it costs more than many small-market stations can afford to completely make the switch. Still, the superior sound quality of digital reproduction will eventually bring about the change. As Joseph Dominick, Barry Sherman, and Gary Copeland (1996, p. 93) point out, " . . . unlike an analog signal, a digital wave is virtually constant—it is the identical shape on recording, on transmission, in the amplifier, and

out of the speakers." Listener demand for digital quality will force technological change, even in the smaller markets. In the long run, the economy of replacing live on-air personnel with computer automation will also reach smaller stations.

Tape Recorders

Another input tool that is still in use but far less than in previous years is the tape recorder. These devices rearrange iron oxide particles on magnetic tape in order to store sound impulses on the tape for playing back later. Stationary heads over which the tape is run do this particle rearrangement. There are usually three heads placed in order to erase, record, and play back. The three basic types of tape recorder used in broadcasting are open reel (often called reel-to-reel), cartridge, and cassette.

One important advantage of the open reel recorder is the accessibility of the tape for editing. Audio editing on this machine usually involves physically cutting the tape and then putting it back together with an adhesive tape. Open reel recorders are available in full-track monophonic (mono), stereo, and multitrack. The four-track is the most common multitrack recorder in radio stations. The advent of digital recording and editing is making the open reel machine only a memory in most radio stations.

Another item that is becoming obsolete at most radio stations is the cartridge machine. At one time, nearly every piece of short production intended for airplay was placed onto cartridge. The cartridge is a container with a loop of tape that varies in length from forty seconds to several minutes. There could be exceptions in length for specific purposes. A cue-tone was placed onto the tape when recording so as to stop it at the beginning of the recording. The machine itself might be a single player or a series linked together in a deck in varying numbers. Some radio stations recorded their music onto cartridges for convenience and to save damaging the vinyl records that were in use at the time.

The third type of tape recorder, the cassette, has more value for on-air play than for production purposes. Many stations still receive programs from outside sources on cassette. News personnel carry the small hand-held recorders to cover stories. Also, copies of advertisements are sent to sponsors on these tapes. Therefore, the cassette recorder may be the one recorder that is the most used by stations. Digital audiotape technology (DAT) has enhanced the usefulness of tape with a smaller cassette that holds more information yet allows a full 48-kilohertz frequency response. The digital signal processing also allows for fast-speed searching, quick cueing, and track programming, among other features.

The Audio Console

The place where all of the inputs meet is the audio console, or control board, as it is more often called. This is the piece of equipment through which all audio signals are processed. It can range in size from as few as five channels with two inputs each to dozens of channels with multiple inputs, looking as complicated as an airplane cockpit. The console has three basic functions: (1) allow the selection of one or more inputs, such as microphone, music, or tape, (2) amplify the sound, and (3) allow the operator to route the inputs to a number of outputs, such as monitors, transmitter, and so on.

A key, or toggle switch, allows an incoming signal to be routed to either an audition or program channel. Channels have volume controls called potentiometers, or pots or faders for short. These control the audio level, or gain, of each amplifier. Pots come in two forms: rotary and vertical slide, with the latter being more in vogue. In addition to individual pots for each channel, there is also a master gain that is usually set by the engineer, a monitor gain that controls the studio speakers, a cue gain, and a headset gain. The output signal is routed to the program amplifier, the final amplification stage before being distributed to a tape recorder or a transmitter.

Monitors, Audio Processors, and Transmitters

The signal is also sent to the volume unit (VU) meter, a device that measures the amount of sound that is being routed through the output of the console. Monitoring audio levels and keeping them consistent from one audio source to another are important in maintaining a consistent station sound. The modulation monitor indicates how the transmitter is performing and can reveal transmitter problems. A stereo monitor helps make sure that the left and right channels are not out of phase, since out-of-phase channels will cancel the majority of the signal in monophonic radio receivers.

Equalizers allow producers to correct problems by boosting and/or cutting frequency lows and highs. Equalizers help create parity between the different elements of production and are useful in creating special effects.

Compressors are used to enhance loudness and eliminate noise. Compression, which can remedy certain problems and get the listener to take greater notice of a piece of production, can make voices sound warmer, production tighter, and levels near perfect. Audio processors can be used to create a wide range of special effects, such as reverberation, echo, and so on.

When the transmitter receives the signal, usually by telephone line or microwave transmission, it is modulated, which means the electrical energy is superimposed onto the carrier wave that represents the frequency of the station. The modulated signal then travels to and through the antenna to, hopefully, many receivers.

Conclusion

As was stated earlier, radio is undergoing much technological change. Digital is thought to be the wave of the future and is already a powerful presence. Computers are replacing many of the input and storage devices in larger stations and will, doubtless, do so in all stations eventually. This is very important to the industry, but from the listeners' standpoint, the quality of what they hear is all that really matters.

See also: RADIO BROADCASTING; RADIO BROADCASTING, CAREERS IN; RADIO BROADCASTING, HISTORY OF; RADIO BROADCASTING, STATION PROGRAMMING AND; RECORDING INDUSTRY; RECORDING INDUSTRY, CAREERS IN; RECORDING INDUSTRY, HISTORY OF; RECORDING INDUSTRY, PRODUCTION PROCESS OF; RECORDING INDUSTRY, TECHNOLOGY OF.

Bibliography

Alten, Stanley R. (1994). *Audio in Media,* 4th edition. Belmont, CA: Wadsworth.

Dominick, Joseph R.; Sherman, Barry L.; and Copeland, Gary A. (1996). *Broadcasting/Cable and Beyond: An Introduction to Modern Electronic Media,* 3rd edition. New York: McGraw-Hill.

Gross, Lynne Schafer. (1986). *Telecommunications: An Introduction to Radio, Television, and Other Electronic Media,* 2nd edition. Dubuque, IA: Wm. C. Brown.

Keith, Michael C. (1990). *Radio Production: Art and Science.* Boston: Focal Press.

Montgomery, Ed. (1996–1997). "The Basics of AM Radio" (a twelve-part series that was originally published in *Radio World* beginning with the Oct. 16, 1996, issue). <http://www.rwonline.com/reference-room/EdMontgomery-BasicsofAMradio/1999/rr-am2a.html>.

Rathbun, Elizabeth A. (2000). "Radio Dreams of Digital." *Broadcasting and Cable* 30:68–70.

HAL HUGHES

⬛ RANGANATHAN, SHIYALI RAMAMRITA (1892–1972)

S. R. Ranganathan is considered by many to be the foremost theorist in the field of classification because of his contributions to the theory of facet analysis. In addition to being known as the "Father of Library Science" in India, his accomplishments include founding the Documentation Research and Training Centre in Bangalore, India; developing his *Five Laws of Library Science* (1931) and *Colon Classification* (1933); and authoring more than sixty books and two thousand articles.

Ranganathan was born in Shiyali in the Tanjavoor District of Tamil Nadu in southern India. His father, a learned and cultured man, was Ramamrita Ayyar, a landlord of a medium-sized rice-growing property. His mother was Seethalakshmi, a simple and very pious lady. Ranganathan attended school in his village and then went to Madras Christian College in 1909, where he earned B.S. and M.A. degrees in mathematics, studying with Edward B. Ross, who remained his favorite guru throughout his life.

As a teacher of mathematics at various institutions between 1917 and 1921, Ranganathan kept his students engaged and attentive by adopting the technique of assigning a new topic to students, having them gather data from books, and allowing them to learn from discussions among themselves and their teachers. From 1921 to 1923, he served as secretary of the Mathematics and Science Section of the Madras Teacher's Guild.

In January 1924, Ranganathan took the appointment as the first librarian of Madras University. In September of that same year, he left for England to spend nine months on a study–observation tour, during which he came into close contact with W. C. Berwick Sayers, Chief Librarian of Croydon Public Library and lecturer in the University School of Librarianship, London. Here Ranganathan discovered a social mission for the library profession and for himself. When he returned to Madras, he began to reorganize the university library in an attempt to attract more readers to the library and provide facilities for them. He took it upon himself to educate the public on the benefits of reading. Within the library he introduced the open shelf system and the active reference service. He designed a functional library building and developed principles of library management that expressed his philosophy of service. He shared his ideas with others by writing articles and books while active as a librarian and inspired them with his *Five Laws of Library Science*:

1. Books are for use.
2. Every reader, his book.
3. Every book, its reader.

4. Save the time of the reader (and the staff).

5. A library is a growing organism.

He helped form the Madras Library Association in 1928 and pushed the library movement to all corners of the Madras Presidency, which at that time covered almost two-thirds of South India. In 1929, Ranganathan initiated a school of library science (which is now at Madras University) and served as director for nearly fifteen years. In 1957, he donated his life's savings to endow a chair known as the Sarada Ranganathan Professorship in Library Science, to honor his second wife. Instead of retiring in 1945, he accepted an invitation to develop the library system of the Banaras Hindu University, where he single-handedly classified and cataloged 100,000 books between 1945 and 1947. He moved over to Delhi University in 1947 to teach and do research in library science, and from that time his international contacts began to grow. He served as chairman of the Classification Research Group of the International Federation for Documentation between 1950 and 1962.

While Ranganathan was in Delhi, he drafted a comprehensive thirty-year plan for the development of a library system for India as a whole, and he promoted the Madras Public Library Act. Earlier, he had delivered books to the prison where future leaders of an independent India were incarcerated. When they asked him what they should do about libraries in the new India, he had his plans ready.

In 1950, at age 58, Ranganathan visited the United States for the first time and wrote the book *Classification and Communication.* The second edition of his *Prolegomena to Library Classification* was published by The Library Association in London in 1957, and his lectures on classification in England were published in a book entitled *Elements of Library Classification,* which was edited by Bernard Palmer for The Library Association. The crowning achievement during the latter part of Ranganathan's life was the establishment of the Documentation Research and Training Centre in Bangalore, where young students and teachers from India and abroad could benefit from the atmosphere of academic excellence and simplicity that he created there. In 1965, Ranganathan was recognized by the Government of India, which made him the National Research Professor in Library Science. At that time, there were only four

other National Research Professors: in Physics (C. V. Raman and S. N. Bose); Law (P. V. Kane); and in Literature and Linguistics (S. K. Chatterjee).

Ranganathan is called the "Father of Library Science" in India because he catalyzed a human movement of endeavor that is witnessed even to this day in the libraries and information centers of India. Through his writings, he awakened librarians around the world to the underlying theories and principles that govern their work as catalogers and classifiers of knowledge and to the tenets of service that ensure that the Five Laws will be observed.

The words delivered by Ranganathan in his opening address at an international study conference on classification research at Elsinore, Denmark, in 1964 probably best express the significance of library science and his role in its development:

> Man has been reaching for one ideal for a long, long time—the ideal of "One World." Our discipline [of library science] brings us nearer to that much desired and much sought concept of "One World." In other contexts, that concept is very, very distant from the stage of realization. It is particularly so in the economic context. . . . In the political context, the resistance to "One World" idea is notorious. . . . In the technological context the profit motive obstructs us from a free sharing of ideas. . . . The whole idea of copyright itself is a barrier . . . [but] in our own subject, we come as near as possible to the idea of "One World." There is no secrecy. We know no cultural boundaries, no political boundaries, and no economic boundaries. We freely share ideas with one another. We believe that we find in everybody an identity. . . . The barriers melt away. We are prepared to think together without any reserve. . . . Our research can follow the relay method. That will lead to many technological achievements. [Our work] can lead to the elimination of all barriers except for the ego in man, the disturbance of which can be localized [Atherton, 1965, pp. 7–8].

See also: LIBRARIANS; LIBRARIES, FUNCTIONS AND TYPES OF.

Bibliography

Atherton, Pauline, ed. (1965). *Classification Research.* Copenhagen: Munksgaard.

Chan, Lois Mai. (1994). *Cataloging and Classification: An Introduction,* 2nd edition. New York: McGraw-Hill.

Gopinath, M. A., ed. (1994). *Memorabilia Ranganathan.* Bangalore, India: Sarada Ranganathan Endowment for Library Science.

Ranganathan, Shiyali R. (1957). *Five Laws of Library Science,* 2nd edition. Madras, India: Madras Library Association.

Ranganathan, Shiyali R. (1959). *Elements of Library Classification.* London, Eng.: The Library Association.

Ranganathan, Shiyali R. (1963). *Colon Classification,* 6th edition with amendments. New York: Asia Publishing House.

PAULINE ATHERTON COCHRANE

RATINGS FOR MOVIES

In the United States, most movies produced for theatrical distribution are rated by the Classification and Rating Administration (CARA), a division of the Motion Picture Association of America (MPAA). The rating system was first introduced in 1968, under the leadership of Jack Valenti, who was the MPAA president. This voluntary system was developed in the midst of increasing public pressure for censorship of movies.

The Rating Process

Under the MPAA system, producers or distributors submit their films to the Ratings Board for review. They pay a fee for this service. The board, by majority vote, determines a rating and provides a brief written rationale for the decision. CARA publishes the *Motion Picture Rating Directory* at quarterly intervals, with biweekly updates of the ratings decisions that have been made during the preceding two weeks. Producers or distributors who disagree with the rating their film receives have the option of editing their film and resubmitting it. If they are dissatisfied with the final ruling of the Ratings Board, they can submit their request to a separate Rating Appeals Board, whose membership is comprised of theater owners, producers, and distributors, with the president of the MPAA serving as chair. The decision of the Ratings Board may be overturned by a two-thirds vote

of the Rating Appeals Board. If they strongly object to the final decision, filmmakers can release a film without a rating, but strong economic concerns generally rule out this option.

There are no specific academic, professional, or occupational qualifications for serving on the CARA Ratings Board. All board members must be parents, however, and according to a description by the MPAA, members of the board must be "possessed of an intelligent maturity, and most of all, have the capacity to put themselves in the role of most American parents." With the exception of the board chair, the identities of the board members are kept secret from the public, although some information about family and occupational background is released, and the membership is diverse in terms of age, gender, race, and national origin.

The MPAA rating system has five levels that give general guidelines as to the age-appropriateness of a movie. The categories are as follows:

G: **General Audiences.** All ages are admitted. Film content does not include anything that most parents would consider offensive for even their youngest children.

PG: **Parental Guidance Suggested.** Some material may not be suitable for children. Parents are urged to give "parental guidance." Content may include some material that parents might not want their young children to see.

PG-13: **Parents Strongly Cautioned.** Some material may be inappropriate for children under thirteen years of age. Parents are urged to be cautious. Content may include some material that parents might find inappropriate for preteenagers.

R: **Restricted.** Admission of anyone who is under seventeen years of age requires him or her to be accompanied by a parent or adult guardian. The content includes some adult material. Parents are urged to learn more about the film before taking their young children to see it.

NC-17: **No One 17 and Under Admitted.** The content is patently adult. Children are not admitted.

CARA does not publish data on the percentage of movies that are given each rating. However, in an independent analysis of the more than 1,400

Ratings for movies are closely tied to the continuing controversy over portrayals of violence, which was the topic on which Chris McGurk (far left), Vice Chairman of MGM, testified during hearings that the U.S. Senate Commerce, Science, and Transportation Committee conducted in September 2000 to examine the motion picture industry's marketing of violence to children. (AFP/Corbis)

movies rated during 1995 and 1996, Joanne Cantor (1998b) and her associates reported that 66 percent were rated R, 16 percent were rated PG-13, 14 percent were rated PG, 3 percent were rated G, and 1 percent were rated NC-17.

The various rating levels have been modified over the years. For example, the rating of PG-13 was added in 1984, as a reaction to children's responses to intense scenes in the PG-rated movies *Gremlins* and *Indiana Jones and the Temple of Doom*. The "X" rating that was originally included in the system was abandoned because it had not been trademarked. That rating is sometimes self-imposed by filmmakers. However, this process is entirely independent of the MPAA system. The rating of NC-17 was introduced in the early 1990s.

Criticisms of the Ratings

The MPAA ratings have been criticized over the years for a variety of reasons. There have frequently been disagreements with the ratings of individual films. Some critics have charged that the Ratings Board is more likely to give restrictive ratings to films with sexual content than to those with violent content. Other critics have argued that the Ratings Board is not sufficiently independent of the movie industry that employs it. Spokespersons for CARA insist that the Ratings Board is immunized from attempts to influence its members.

In its defense, the MPAA has also pointed to the public opinion polls that it commissions each year. For example, its own poll conducted in 1995 reported that 76 percent of the American public found the rating system to be either "very useful" or "fairly useful." *A New York Times* survey conducted the same year reported more modest approval, with 53 percent of the parents surveyed saying they thought the movie rating system "does a good job in informing people about how much sex and violence to expect in a movie" and 46 percent responding that it does not do a good job.

Public health and child advocacy organizations have been critical of the MPAA rating system. For example, at its annual meeting in 1994, the national House of Delegates of the American Medical Association (AMA) adopted a policy statement concerning the way the entertainment industry labels its products. The AMA referred to the MPAA system as "fundamentally flawed" and called on the MPAA to adopt changes. Recommendations included adding child development experts to the Ratings Board and incorporating more sensitivity to age differences in young children. CARA has responded to such criticism by arguing that it is not the function of the Ratings Board to suggest what is harmful for children but rather to suggest what parents would consider offensive or inappropriate.

The failure of the ratings to indicate the content of movies has been a major area of criticism by the AMA and other public health and child advocacy groups. The MPAA's own polls have not asked parents about their desire for content information. However, several polls conducted during the time that ratings for television were being developed (1996–1997) indicated that parents overwhelmingly prefer content information (i.e., the level of sex, violence, or coarse language) over age recommendations when making viewing decisions for their children. Research has also shown that MPAA ratings are often not informative about the violent or sexual content of movies. A content analysis of the *Motion Picture Rating Directory*, for example, reported that 26 percent of movies rated PG during 1995 and 1996 were so classified as a function of coarse language only, and another 13 percent contained unspecified "thematic elements" (Cantor, 1998b).

Although the age-based television ratings, the "TV Parental Guidelines," were amended to include content indicators as well as age recommendations as a result of public pressure, the MPAA ratings have not integrated content information into the ratings. Since 1995, however, the MPAA has provided information related to the reasons for the rating of a movie when the rating is PG or higher. This information is available on the MPAA's website and in the *Motion Picture Rating Directory*. In 1999, the MPAA announced plans to include this content information in newspaper advertisements for movies as well. Therefore, many advertisements that are of suffi-

cient size include content information with the MPAA rating.

Effects of the Ratings

Another criticism of the MPAA ratings has come from those who perceive that providing a restrictive label to a movie, indicating that it is inappropriate for viewing by young people, may make the movie more attractive to children and thereby work to defeat the purpose of shielding children from inappropriate content.

A study was conducted in 1980 by Bruce Austin, who explored whether the ratings of G, PG, R, or X (the MPAA categories in place at the time of the study) would affect high school students' reported likelihood that they would go to a movie. Austin reported that the ratings of movies had no significant effect on the interest of students in the movies. More recent research, however, has shown that MPAA ratings do have effects on children's interest in movies.

In the first year of research for the National Television Violence Study (NTVS), children between the ages of five and fourteen years were given a programming guide and were instructed to select one of the three programs or movies described on each page. The findings revealed that among children between the ages of ten and fourteen, and especially among boys in this age group, the ratings of PG-13 and R made a movie more attractive and the rating of G reduced its attractiveness. The second year of the NTVS reported the same results. Moreover, it reported that more aggressive younger children were more interested in movies that had restrictive ratings. The research also showed that a variety of content-based rating systems did not increase children's interest in movies with higher violence levels. Research by Brad Bushman and Angela Stack (1996) has confirmed that, in general, restrictive warning labels make programming more attractive, whereas content information has less of a tendency to attract children's interest in programming with violent content.

MPAA ratings have an economic effect as well. In some cases, this is due directly to the responses of potential audiences. In other cases, the economic effect is due to the policies of members of the entertainment industry, such as television advertisers and owners of movie theaters and video stores.

Some producers and freedom of speech advocates argue that the MPAA's NC-17 rating, introduced to designate adult-only films, amounts to virtual censorship because many exhibitors refuse to show the films, many newspapers will not advertise them, and some leading video chains refuse to stock them. For example, Blockbuster Video, K-Mart, and Wal-Mart, which together account for more than half of the video sales in the United States, will not stock NC-17 videos. There is a commercial bias against unrated films as well. Few distributors will attempt to release a film without submitting it for a rating because 85 percent of theaters around the country will not accept an unrated film.

As a result of such commercial restrictions, the major studios, desiring releases of their larger-budget films in a thousand or more theaters, have usually chosen to cut films rather than face an NC-17 rating and thus be restricted to about three hundred theaters. Because of the commercial difficulties of an NC-17 rating, many directors are contractually obligated by the major studios to produce a film that is rated no more stringently than an R. As a result, films are often tailor-made to achieve a particular rating.

At the other end of the spectrum, however, there seems to be a desire on the part of moviemakers to avoid the rating of G except for movies that are explicitly designed for young children. As the research on the effect of MPAA ratings on children's interest in movies suggests, a G rating makes movies less attractive to youths as early as the preteen years. The economic implications of an unwanted G rating were acknowledged by former CARA president Richard P. Heffner in a 1999 television documentary aired on the Public Broadcasting System (PBS). He described the situation surrounding the 1981 Oscar-winning British film *Chariots of Fire*. According to Heffner, after CARA gave the film a G rating, the producer complained, asserting, "the G will kill us." When the Ratings Board refused to change the rating to a PG, the filmmakers forced CARA's hand by adding in one forbidden, off-color word. The film was then accorded the desired PG rating.

After the well-publicized school shootings in the late 1990s, many politicians called for greater scrutiny of the marketing of violence to children. One of the responses to these calls was an agreement by U.S. theater owners to check the identification cards of young people who were attempting to buy tickets for R-rated movies. The film rating system is likely to remain the subject of controversy as long as there is public concern regarding the effects of media content on audiences, especially on children.

See also: FILM INDUSTRY; FIRST AMENDMENT AND THE MEDIA; NATIONAL TELEVISION VIOLENCE STUDY; RATINGS FOR TELEVISION PROGRAMS; V-CHIP; VIOLENCE IN THE MEDIA, ATTRACTION TO; VIOLENCE IN THE MEDIA, HISTORY OF RESEARCH ON.

Bibliography

Austin, Bruce A. (1980). "The Influence of the MPAA's Film-Rating System on Motion Picture Attendance. A Pilot Study." *Journal of Psychology* 106:91–99.

Bushman, Brad J., and Stack, Angela D. (1996). "Forbidden Fruit Versus Tainted Fruit: Effects of Warning Labels on Attraction to Television Violence." *Journal of Experimental Psychology: Applied* 2:207–226.

Cantor, Joanne. (1998a). *"Mommy, I'm Scared": How TV and Movies Frighten Children and What We Can Do to Protect Them.* San Diego, CA: Harcourt Brace.

Cantor, Joanne. (1998b). "Ratings for Program Content: The Role of Research Findings." *Annals of the American Academy of Political and Social Science* 557:54–69.

Center for Communication and Social Policy. (1996–1998). *National Television Violence Study,* Vols. 1–3. Thousand Oaks, CA: Sage Publications.

Classification and Rating Administration. (2000). *Motion Picture Rating Directory.* Encino, CA: Classification and Rating Administration.

Classification and Rating Administration. (2000). "Questions and Answers: Everything You Always Wanted to Know About the Movie Rating System." <http://www.filmratings.com/questions.htm#q3>.

Federman, Joel. (1996). *Media Ratings: Design, Use, and Consequences.* Studio City, CA: Mediascope.

Mosk, Richard M. (1998). "Motion Picture Ratings in the United States." In *The V-Chip Debate: Content Filtering from Television to the Internet,* ed. Monroe E. Price. Mahwah, NJ: Lawrence Erlbaum.

Motion Picture Association of America. (2000). "Voluntary Movie Rating System." <http://www.mpaa.org/movieratings>.

Valenti, Jack. (1991). *The Voluntary Movie Rating System: How It Began, Its Purpose, The Public Reaction.* New York: Motion Picture Association of America.

JOEL FEDERMAN

JOANNE CANTOR

▮ RATINGS FOR TELEVISION PROGRAMS

The Telecommunications Act of 1996 contained a "Parental Choice in Television Programming" provision designed to permit parents greater control over the content seen on their home televisions. This provision passed in response to the accumulating evidence that television violence and other types of programming can have profound negative effects on the mental health of children, and in response to parental concerns about the increasingly violent and sexual content of television. The act mandated that within a specified time of its passage, new televisions be manufactured with a "V-chip," which would allow parents to block objectionable content on the basis of the rating of a program. It also recommended that the television industry develop a voluntary rating system that would be applied to television programs and be readable by the V-chip technology. Early in 1996, shortly after passage of the act, entertainment industry executives formed a Ratings Implementation Group and agreed to develop a rating system. The new system was released to the public on December 19, 1996, and began being implemented in January 1997.

The rating system is designed to be applied to all programming with the exception of news and sports programs. In addition to being read by the V-chip, the rating of a program (selected by that program's producers or distributors) is displayed visually in the upper left-hand corner of the television screen for the first few seconds of a program. Many newspaper programming guides and television schedules also publish the ratings in their listings.

The television rating system is referred to as the "TV Parental Guidelines," and in its initial form, it was based on the Motion Picture Association of America (MPAA) ratings for theatrical movies that have been in use since the late 1960s. The MPAA ratings contain four major levels based on the recommended age for viewing a movie: "G: General Audiences," "PG: Parental Guidance Suggested," "PG-13: Parents Strongly Cautioned," and "R: Restricted." The original TV Parental Guidelines had four levels similar to the MPAA ratings for programs not specifically directed to a child audience. They were "TV-G: General Audience," "TV-PG: Parental Guidance Suggested,"

"TV-14: Parents Strongly Cautioned," and "TV-MA: Mature Audiences Only." In addition, the system included two rating levels for programs designed for children: "TV-Y: All Children," and "TV-Y7: Directed to Older Children." Like the MPAA ratings, these ratings gave guidelines regarding the age of the child who should be permitted to see a program but did not provide specific information about its content.

The TV Parental Guidelines were controversial even before the official release of the system. Headed by MPAA President Jack Valenti, the Ratings Implementation Group had engaged in a public process of soliciting advice from child advocacy organizations such as the National Parent–Teacher Association (PTA), public health organizations such as the American Medical Association (AMA) and the American Psychological Association (APA), and academic researchers from a variety of universities. Most of the groups and individuals consulted advocated a program labeling system that indicates the content of a program rather than simply providing age recommendations. Many groups advocated modeling the television rating system after the system that is available on the premium cable channels HBO, Cinemax, and Showtime. The premium channel system indicates the level of sex, violence, and coarse language in a program with letters, such as, "MV: Mild Violence," "AL: Adult Language," and "SC: Strong Sexual Content."

Much of the controversy over the original television rating system was based on the findings of research regarding three issues: (1) the types of ratings that parents preferred, (2) the ability of different types of systems to communicate the content of programs, and (3) the effects of different types of rating systems on the interest of children in programs.

Research Relevant to the Television Ratings Controversy

The major disagreement between the Ratings Implementation Group and the majority of public health and child advocacy organizations related to whether the ratings should suggest the appropriate age for viewing a program (age-based ratings) or specify the type and level of content contained in the program (content-based ratings). Several national surveys conducted between August 1996 and March 1997 reported that parents overwhelm-

Experiments

Experiments are used when a researcher wants to observe effects under highly controlled conditions. For example, researchers for the National Television Violence Study (NTVS) conducted an experiment when they wanted to know whether adding a rating to a television program or movie would have an effect on the desire of children to see it. Rather than asking people their opinions regarding whether or not something would affect them, experimenters prefer to put people in a controlled situation, manipulate one thing while leaving everything else constant, and then observe whether what they manipulated made a difference.

In Year 2 of the NTVS, for example, researchers asked a group of 374 children between five and fifteen years of age to look at a booklet describing different programs and movies and to indicate how much they wanted to see each one. To increase the chances that they would give their sincere responses, children were told they would remain anonymous and they were led to believe that their opinions would count as votes influencing the program they would actually get to see. All the books contained the same program names and brief descriptions. However, unknown to the children, the same program was given different ratings in different booklets. For example, for one movie title and description, the effect of movie ratings was tested. In some booklets, at random, the plot description was followed by a rating of G; in others, it was followed by PG, PG-13, or R; and in some, there was no rating at all. All children indicated how much they wanted to see the movie on a scale ranging from "hate to see it" to "love to see it." Because everything was kept constant except the rating of the movie, the researchers could determine whether the rating, in and of itself, made a significant difference. In this case, the rating of a movie did have a strong effect, especially among the older children tested: Children wanted to see the movie significantly more when it was rated PG-13 or R than when it was rated G.

Experiments work best when the response being observed is short-term rather than of long duration. Moreover, it is often challenging to study controversial behaviors, such as violence, experimentally. One cannot ethically bring children into the laboratory to study the effects of media violence and encourage them to get into fights with each other. For this reason, experiments on media violence often use measures that do not look like violence, but are related to violence. For example, some violence studies ask children to fill out a questionnaire indicating how right or wrong it is to hit or kick another child, and the researchers compare children who have just witnessed violence on TV to those who have not. Others studies use "aggression machines," and children are led to believe that by pushing a button they are delivering painful stimulation to another person in another room. (This is actually not true). Others allow people to inflict a nonviolent negative outcome on another person, such as giving a negative evaluation with the expectation that it will affect that person's chances to get a job. The important things to remember in evaluating experimental procedures is whether the conditions are adequately controlled, whether participants are assigned to the different conditions at random, whether the situation created is plausible to the research participant, and whether the outcome measure is psychologically relevant to the attitude or behavior of interest.

ingly preferred content-based ratings for television over age-based ratings. Five out of six national surveys conducted during this period showed majorities ranging from 62 percent to 80 percent favoring content-based ratings. The one survey that showed a majority (54%) in favor of an age-based system was commissioned by the Ratings Implementation Group itself and was released on the day the rating system was introduced.

One reason that parents indicated a preference for a content-based system was that parents make distinctions between sex versus violence versus other types of content when they express concerns about the effect of television programs on their children. During the period in which the new rating system was being developed, researchers for the National Television Violence Study (NTVS), an independent monitoring project funded by the National Cable Television Association (NCTA), were exploring how the different MPAA ratings coincided with different forms of content in movies. Using a large, representative sample of television programming, the researchers investigated movies that were shown with both an MPAA rating and the premium channel content codes applied by the channel presenting the movie. For example, they explored the proportion of movies rated PG that contained different types of content. In their analysis for NTVS Year 1 (released in early 1996), 22 percent of the PG-rated movies had neither sex nor violence, but only adult language. Another 22 percent had adult language and sex, and 28 percent had adult language and violence. A separate study submitted to the Federal Communications Commission (FCC) in April 1997 as part of comments on the rating system of the industry, involved all movies rated by the MPAA during the years 1995 and 1996 according to the *Motion Picture Ratings Directory* of the MPAA. The findings indicated that more than one-fourth of movies rated PG were so classified as a function of coarse language only and another 18 percent had neither sex, nor violence, nor coarse language.

Extrapolating from these findings, critics argued that the content of a program rated TV-PG would be highly unpredictable—parents would not know whether it contained content they considered harmful and they thus would not be able to decide whether they should shield their child from it or not.

A third area of research relevant to the television ratings dealt with the effect of ratings on the desire of children to see programs. A major concern was whether parental advisories and ratings would have their intended effect or whether they would "boomerang," making the content seem more interesting and exciting and attract a larger child audience.

The first year of the NTVS research (released early in 1996) showed that the MPAA ratings of PG-13 and R increased interest in a movie, especially for boys and for young adolescents in general. The second year of the NTVS research (released in March 1997) subjected eight rating systems to the same test. Included in the systems tested were the MPAA ratings and three content-based systems: the violence codes used by the premium cable channels HBO, Showtime, and

Cinemax ("MV: Mild Violence," "V: Violence," and "GV: Graphic Violence"); the Recreational Software Advisory Council (RSAC) ratings used for video games ("Violence: Creatures Killed," "Violence: Humans Killed," "Violence: Humans Injured or Killed, Blood and Gore," and "Violence: Wanton and Gratuitous Violence"); and the violence ratings used in Canada in conjunction with early implementation of the V-chip ("Comedic Violence," "Mild Violence," "Brief Violence," "Violence," and "Graphic Violence").

The findings revealed that most of the rating and labeling systems did not significantly affect the interest of children. The only rating system to produce the so-called forbidden-fruit effect was the age-based MPAA system. For the older children (10 to 15 years of age) participating in the experiment, the more restrictive ratings of PG-13 and R increased the attractiveness of a program, and the lowest rating, G, decreased it. Moreover, children who were more aggressive and those who liked to watch television the most were the most likely to have their interest stimulated by the restrictive MPAA ratings.

Independently conducted research published in 1996 by Brad Bushman and his associates confirmed that restrictive warning labels make a program seem more enticing than labels that simply describe violent content. In three experiments, Bushman found that warning labels consistently increased the selection of violent programs and movies by both children and adults, but that violence labels did not.

In summary, the research findings reported around the time of the initial launch of the TV Parental Guidelines were uniformly unflattering to the new system: They showed that parents overwhelmingly preferred content-based labels over age guidelines; that age-based ratings are ambiguous as to the content contained in a program; and that restrictive, age-based ratings are more likely than content labels to entice children to violent programming.

Public Criticism and the Revised System

The critics of the TV Parental Guidelines were given several public forums in which to express their concerns. The U.S. Senate Subcommittee on Commerce, Science, and Transportation held a hearing on February 27, 1997, less than two months after the system began being applied. In addition to criticizing the rating system itself, several child advocates decried the fact that intense violence, crude sexual situations, and coarse language were quite common in prime-time programs that carried the TV-PG rating. The National Television Violence Study released its Year 2 report in March 1997, and press coverage of those findings publicized the possibility that the age-based ratings might be attracting more children than they were protecting. The FCC solicited comments on the acceptability of the system in April of that year, with most comments from the general public being critical of the new system. In May, the television industry held a town hall meeting in Peoria, Illinois, that was televised on C-SPAN. The participants in this forum were parents who were selected at random, and again the critics of the rating system remained more vocal and more numerous than the defenders. By this time, several members of Congress had begun threatening further legislation regarding television content if the television industry did not modify the system. By the beginning of the summer, the industry group had agreed to negotiate a compromise with representatives of the child advocacy organizations, and in July 1997, the groups released a compromise system, which added content indicators to the age-based guidelines.

In the revised system, the ratings of TV-PG, TV-14, and TV-MA could be supplemented by any or all of the following content indicators: V for violent content, L for coarse language, S for sexual content, and D for sexual dialogue or innuendo. In addition, for programs aimed at older children (designated with a TV-Y7), the supplemental indicator of FV for "fantasy violence" was added to indicate programs in which the violence may be "more intense or more combative." The industry group also agreed to add five nonindustry representatives from the advocacy community to the Oversight Monitoring Board for the guidelines. All but two networks agreed to use the revised system: NBC maintained the original TV Parental Guidelines without the addition of content letters, and Black Entertainment Television (BET), which had not adopted the original system, continued to refuse to rate its programs at all.

Research conducted after the revised TV Parental Guidelines were implemented showed that although parents liked the idea of television ratings, the revised system was poorly under- stood. For example, in a national survey of parents conducted by the Kaiser Family Foundation in April 1999, one and one-half years after the revised system was put in place, only 3 percent of parents knew that the content letters "FV" stood for "fantasy violence" and only 2 percent knew that "D" stood for "suggestive or sexual dialogue." Research also showed that although most networks were quick to adopt the initial TV Parental Guidelines, the revised system did not provide a consistent correspondence between the content letters and the presence of sex, violence, or coarse language in programs.

As the deadline of January 2000 was reached for all new televisions with a diagonal screen size of thirteen inches or larger to be produced with a V-chip, the FCC and child advocacy groups committed themselves to making greater efforts to publicize the V-chip and the revised rating system.

See also: NATIONAL TELEVISION VIOLENCE STUDY; RATINGS FOR MOVIES; RATINGS FOR VIDEO GAMES, SOFTWARE, AND THE INTERNET; SEX AND THE MEDIA; TELECOMMUNICATIONS ACT OF 1996; V-CHIP; VIOLENCE IN THE MEDIA, ATTRACTION TO; VIOLENCE IN THE MEDIA, HISTORY OF RESEARCH ON.

Bibliography

Bushman, Brad J., and Stack, Angela D. (1996). "Forbidden Fruit Versus Tainted Fruit: Effects of Warning Labels on Attraction to Television Violence." *Journal of Experimental Psychology: Applied* 2:207–226.

Cantor, Joanne. (1998). *"Mommy, I'm Scared": How TV and Movies Frighten Children and What We Can Do to Protect Them.* San Diego, CA: Harcourt Brace.

Cantor, Joanne. (1998). "Ratings for Program Content: The Role of Research Findings." *Annals of the American Academy of Political and Social Science* 557:54–69.

Center for Communication and Social Policy. (1996–1998). *National Television Violence Study*, Vols. 1–3. Thousand Oaks, CA: Sage.

Center for Communication and Social Policy. (1997–1998). *National Television Violence Study Executive Summary*, Vols. 2 and 3. Community and Organization Research Institute (CORI). Santa Barbara: University of California.

Federal Communications Commission. (2000). "V-Chip Homepage." <http://www.fcc.gov/vchip>.

Federman, Joel. (1996). *Media Ratings: Design, Use, and Consequences.* Studio City, CA: Mediascope.

Kaiser Family Foundation. (1999). *How Parents Feel (and What They Know) about TV, the V-Chip, and the TV Ratings System.* Menlo Park, CA: Henry J. Kaiser Family Foundation.

Kunkel, Dale; Farinola, Wendy J. M.; Cope, Kirstie M.; Donnerstein, Edward.; Biely, Erica; and Zwarun, Lara. (1998). *Rating the Ratings: One Year Out; An Assessment of the Television Industry's Use of V-Chip Ratings.* Menlo Park, CA: Henry J. Kaiser Family Foundation.

Motion Picture Rating Directory. (1997). Encino, CA: Classification and Rating Administration.

Price, Monroe E., ed. (1998). *The V-Chip Debate: Content Filtering from Television to the Internet.* Mahwah, NJ: Erlbaum.

JOANNE CANTOR

RATINGS FOR VIDEO GAMES, SOFTWARE, AND THE INTERNET

Ratings are labeling systems that index media content (e.g., films, television programs, interactive games, recorded music, websites) primarily to control young people's access to particular kinds of portrayals. The underlying assumption is that children and young adolescents are particularly vulnerable to message influences and therefore need to be shielded from certain types of content. The content most typically rated consists of portrayals of sexuality, violence, vulgar language, or adult themes, although this varies from country to country. For example, nudity, all but ignored in the Scandinavian countries, often earns more restrictive ratings in the United States; in Germany, violence and racist speech are of particular concern; Australia explicitly adds suicide to the list of problematic kinds of content.

The Ratings Controversy

Ratings have been controversial since their inception, and attempts to rate the content of new media have intensified the debate. As advances in communication technology increase the amount, accessibility, and vividness of media content that is available to ever-growing audiences, particularly young audiences, questions that first emerged in the early days of motion pictures are revisited. Is rating any different from censorship? Who should do the rating? What kinds of content require ratings? What criteria should be used? What form should the label or advisory take? How do ratings affect audiences, the profits, and the content producers?

Ratings have been characterized as representing a "middle ground," somewhere between doing nothing at all (i.e., allowing youths unfettered access to any and all content) and government censorship. It is not surprising that how close to the "middle" rating systems are perceived to be depends largely on who is looking. In the United States, for example, some parents and child advocates contend that ratings are inconsistent and often ineffective; they argue that more stringent controls are necessary. Most content producers and civil libertarians, on the other hand, view any attempt to rate or label content, even voluntary systems exercised by nongovernmental bodies, a threat to free speech. They contend that, at worst, ratings provide a means for full-blown government censorship and, at best, exert a chilling effect on whether and how "nonmainstream ideas" are expressed.

Typically, content ratings are developed in response to public and political pressures to "do something" about media content, pressures that arise when someone makes a case that particular kinds of media depictions threaten youths, if not society in general. This has certainly been the case with each of the new communication media. For example, in the early 1980s, when music videos first enabled parents to see violent, sexual, and misogynist images in a few music videos, public pressures to "do something" about popular music resulted in record industry self-labeling of recordings in order to head-off government intervention. Similarly, when in the early 1990s the U.S. Congress responded to public outcries about graphic violence in interactive games by threatening regulation, the video game and computer software industries developed parental advisory systems. In the mid-1990s, reports of children gaining easy access to pornographic materials on the World Wide Web fueled an intense debate about controlling children's access to information on the Internet. That debate ultimately led to passage of the Communications Decency Act (CDA), making the display or transmission of "indecent or patently offensive material" to minors a criminal offense. Legal challenges on First Amendment grounds led the U.S. Supreme Court to overturn the CDA in 1997, so controversy over whether and how to protect children on the Internet continues.

As part of a 1999 announcement about plans for the official examination of the marketing of violent media to children, President Bill Clinton presented video game advertisements featuring quotes such as "What kind of psycho drives a school bus into a war zone?" and "Get in touch with your gun-toting, cold-blooded-murdering side." (AFP/Corbis)

Descriptive Versus Evaluative Ratings

A fundamental issue in the debate over ratings concerns the difference between descriptive and evaluative ratings criteria (sometimes termed "rules based" and "standards based" criteria, respectively). Descriptive approaches attempt to classify content on the basis of concrete, objective criteria about which it is presumed very different individuals can agree (e.g., "Does a living creature suffer physical injury or death?"). Evaluative approaches attempt to be more sensitive to situational variations by allowing more subjective judgments (e.g., "Is the nudity artistic, erotic, or pornographic?"), but they risk disagreement over just what terms such as "artistic" and "erotic" mean to different people. Thus, a descriptive system would rule that any website displaying a bare female breast must be assigned the same rating, regardless of whether the was a painting by Amedeo Modigliani or Peter Paul Rubens, a *Playboy* centerfold, or an X-rated video. Under an evaluative system, on the other hand, these three websites could each be given different ratings, such as "artistic," "erotic," or "pornographic," with the ultimate ratings depending entirely on the judgment of the person doing the rating. Although evaluative approaches work relatively well within highly homogenous communities where values and definitions are closely shared, each successive step toward a more heterogeneous audience increases the likelihood of disagreement. Conversely, descriptive approaches increase the likelihood that different observers will agree with what is depicted but are less flexible in accounting for situational nuances. This issue becomes increasingly important as globalization makes the same content available to people in various locations that have widely different meaning and value systems. It has reached critical proportions with the development of the World Wide Web, a fundamental premise of which is that it reaches the most heterogeneous audience possible.

Age-Based Ratings

A closely related issue concerns whether and how to classify content on the basis of age. As the primary justification for ratings tends to be the protection of youths, it is not surprising that most systems around the world apply age-based advisories (e.g., "parental discretion advised") and/or restrictions (e.g., "no one under seventeen admitted"). In most cases, however, determination of which age restriction to employ is almost totally subjective. Different cultures, indeed individual parents, often disagree about what is or is not appropriate both for thirteen-year-olds in general and for particular thirteen-year-olds. Some of the most convincing testimony to the subjectivity of indexing by age is provided by the sheer number of different ages that various rating systems employ as markers. Depending on which medium and rating system is examined, advisories or restrictions can be found for ages six, seven, thirteen, fourteen, seventeen, eighteen, and twenty-one in the United States alone. Similarly, a survey of ratings in thirty different countries shows that every year between three and twenty-one (with the exception of nine and twenty) is used to mark some kind of content.

The alternative to indexing by age is simply to provide descriptive labels or icons, leaving it up to individual caretakers to decide whether to restrict a particular child's access. For example, the International Content Rating Association (ICRA), a global consortium of representatives from the public sector and the Internet industry, describes website content (e.g., "explicit sexual acts," "passionate kissing," "innocent kissing"), but it leaves judgments about what is or is not appropriate for an individual child entirely up to the parents or caretakers. The ICRA system also provides extensive, relatively objective definitions of the terms used for each label, in an attempt to reduce uncertainty about the meaning of any particular label.

At issue, of course, is the amount of parental effort required by each approach versus the opportunity to tailor control of access to the needs and abilities of individual children. It is relatively easy for a parent to rely on some general statement indicating that a particular game or website is or is not appropriate for children under a specific age. It is relatively demanding for a parent to work through descriptions and definitions of all of the different kinds of rated content that might appear

in order to decide what is and is not suitable for a particular child. Moreover, the value of age-based rating is further complicated by evidence that labeling content on the basis of age serves more to attract than to deter some children—a kind of forbidden fruit effect. This phenomenon seems most pronounced among youths who are slightly under a specified age. That is, labeling content as being inappropriate for children under thirteen years increases the appeal of that content among eleven- and twelve-year-olds.

Who Does the Rating?

Still another point of controversy surrounding ratings concerns whether they should be administered by some independent third party or by individuals who are involved in producing or distributing the content. Here, the issue is one of trust. Can consumers trust ratings that game designers or webmasters assign to their own creations, or is this a case of "asking the fox to guard the hen house"? This question increases in importance as the sheer volume of content increases. For example, it is feasible for an independent rating board such as the one employed by the Motion Picture Association of America to view and classify several hundred motion pictures each year. However, the hundreds of hours of television programming that most U.S. households receive daily makes such third-party ratings problematic, contributing to the broadcast television industry's decision to adopt a system that allows producers or broadcasters to rate their own material.

These two approaches (i.e., independent ratings and producer ratings) resulted in the two systems that were initially developed to rate interactive games. In this case, the problem was not so much the number of titles developed each year but the sheer amount of time that it takes to move through all aspects of an individual game (often several hundred hours). The Interactive Digital Software Association opted to create the Entertainment Software Rating Board (ESRB), a third-party group, to review videotapes (submitted by game developers) of selected sections of the video games and assign one of five, age-indexed ratings categories. The ESRB categories and their descriptors are as follows:

EC: early childhood, ages three-plus; should contain no material that parents would find inappropriate,

E: everyone, ages six-plus; may contain minimal violence or some crude language,

T: teen, thirteen-plus; may contain violence, strong language, or suggestive themes,

M: mature, seventeen-plus; may contain intense violence or mature sexual themes, and

A: adult, eighteen-plus; may include graphic depictions of sex or violence.

In contrast to the ESRB, the now defunct Recreational Software Advisory Council (RSAC) developed a self-rating system that enabled software developers to attach descriptive labels, icons, and intensity ratings to computer games. Because computer games are often translated for video game platforms, which are almost impossible to market without an ESRB rating, over time most interactive games opted to use the ESRB system, effectively eliminating the RSAC system. Ironically, both systems ran the risk of public distrust—the RSAC system because it employed self-rating, the ESRB system because it depended on whatever videotape excerpts game designers chose to submit for examination. In both cases, the solution was to provide means for public scrutiny and comment, coupled with sanctions for misrepresentation. If the experience of consumers contradicted the rating assigned by either system, it was a simple process to check the product fully and institute sanctions, including denying a rating to any game that had been misrepresented. To the extent that lack of a rating reduces or closes off distribution channels, the economic threat is presumed to motivate game designers and producers to make accurate content disclosures.

The Internet further complicates many of these rating issues. The vast reservoir of global and continually changing information on the World Wide Web renders third-party rating of all accessible material problematic. Although third-party ratings can identify a limited array of websites that are judged to be inappropriate or appropriate for children, sheer volume implies that tens of thousands of websites must go unrated. Self-rating systems for the web face a different problem—how to convince content producers to rate their websites voluntarily, as well as to rate them accurately. Since a fundamental attribute of the Internet is the provision of a free distribution channel, many content producers may see few incentives to rate their websites, and there are even fewer sanctions for misrepresentation or failure to rate. If one does not care whether or not children can access a website, why bother to rate it? A counterbalance to this, of course, would be the development of an Internet-filtering system that allows only rated websites to be accessed, strong motivation for content producers who want to reach children.

Many Voices, Many Values

The multitude of voices, values, and meaning systems inherent in a global communication system also leads to a proliferation of content that people want rated. In addition to advisories for sex, violence, nudity, and vulgar language, various international groups have called for indexing of racist, misogynist, or antireligious content, as well as content that involves other forms of "hate speech," portrayals of drugs or other "taboo" substances, or suicide. As more kinds of content are included on the web, there comes a point at which ratings become too burdensome to use.

Finally, because the web makes little or no distinction between news, education, art, entertainment, casual conversation, or any other kind of informational context, arguments about whether and how to differentiate content depending on context have become particularly thorny. Should graphic violence in a news report be exempt from rating? Should human genitalia displayed on a health-related website be rated differently from those displayed on an entertainment website? Should these things be rated at all?

On the plus side, the Internet industry has developed the Platform for Internet Content Selection (PICS), a system that enables easy design of content rating systems and makes it possible for parents to specify the kinds of content their children will be able to access on the household computer. Moreover, PICS can simultaneously host both self-rating and third-party systems, making it possible for consumers to combine these approaches.

The ICRA is developing a voluntary, descriptive self-rating system to operate at the heart of a PICS-based system. The ICRA system provides parents the option of (1) examining a list of descriptive labels and definitions developed to index each kind of content and then setting the browser to filter as they choose, (2) accepting the judgment of whatever third-party organization wishes to share the system, or (3) both. Thus, one parent might rely on the third-party judgment of a religious organization, another on a group of educators, and a third might make individual judgments based entirely on a personal assessment of what kinds of information are appropriate to his or her own child.

Such a system depends on there being a critical mass of content websites that have either self-rated or have been indexed by some third party, as well as the option for parents to block websites that have not been rated. Even given such a system, the complexities of developing ratings that fit the needs and desires of parents from around the world make it unlikely that a "perfect" system will ever emerge. What is clear is that the extent to which any rating system is effective depends on thoughtful, active participation of parents who care about the kinds of content to which their children have access.

See also: COMMUNICATIONS DECENCY ACT OF 1996; FIRST AMENDMENT AND THE MEDIA; INTERNET AND THE WORLD WIDE WEB; PORNOGRAPHY; PORNOGRAPHY, LEGAL ASPECTS OF; RATINGS FOR TELEVISION PROGRAMS; RATINGS FOR MOVIES; SEX AND THE MEDIA; V-CHIP; VIOLENCE IN THE MEDIA, ATTRACTION TO; VIOLENCE IN THE MEDIA, HISTORY OF RESEARCH ON.

Bibliography

Federman, Joel. (1996). *Media Ratings: Design, Use, and Consequences.* Studio City, CA: Mediascope, Inc.
Price, Monroe E., ed. (1998). *The V-Chip Debate: Content Filtering from Television to the Internet.* Mahwah, NJ: Lawrence Erlbaum.

DONALD F. ROBERTS

▌ READING
See: Literacy

▌ RECORDING INDUSTRY

The recording industry is dominated by five major companies that control about 85 percent of the marketplace for recorded music worldwide. The "Big Five" are Bertelsman Music Group (BMG), Electrical and Musical Industries (EMI), Sony Music, Universal Music Group (UMG), and Warner Music Group.

The Big Five

BMG is part of the German corporation Bertelsman, A.G., a large electronic media and publishing company. BMG acquired Arista in 1979 and the RCA Victor labels in 1986.

EMI, a British company, began with the merger of three labels in 1930. They were the Gramophone Company, Columbia Graphophone, and Parlophone. The company acquired U.S.-based Capitol records in 1956 and the Decca U.K. catalog in 1974. They also acquired Chrysalis records in 1989, and the Virgin Music Group in 1992. The company merged with the electronics company Thorn in 1979, creating Thorn-EMI, but they de-merged in 1996. The EMI Music Group now operates more than sixty record labels, a music publishing company, and the HMV stores (a retail division).

Sony Music is a unit of the Japanese electronics giant, Sony Corporation. It built its music interests (part of what is collectively referred to as its "software" interests) primarily through the acquisition of the CBS records group for $2 billion in 1988. This gave them the Columbia and Epic labels and their subsidiaries, as well as contracted artists such as Bruce Springsteen and Michael Jackson. Sony owns numerous other entertainment software businesses, including film studios, television production companies, compact disc (CD) and tape manufacturing facilities, and half of the Columbia House record club.

UMG is owned by the French corporation Vivendi, who purchased it as part of the acquisition of The Seagram Company of Canada in 2000. Its holdings consist of labels acquired from Matsushita Corporation of Japan in 1995, which had previously purchased the MCA Corporation in 1990. Seagram also acquired Polygram Records from Dutch electronics giant Philips in 1998. Labels now owned by UMG include, but are not limited to, MCA, Geffen, Uni, Mercury, Polydor, Motown, DefJam, A&M, Island, and Decca.

The Warner Music Group is part of U.S.-based Time Warner Entertainment Company, which is being acquired by America Online (AOL), for stock, in the largest merger in corporate history. Warner Music Group began as Warner Brothers Records in the 1920s. This company grew its music business by acquiring Atlantic Records in 1967. The parent company was purchased by the 7 Arts company and then sold to the Kinney

Corporation, which renamed it Warner Communications Inc. in 1969. The company acquired Elektra Records in 1970, organizing itself as the WEA Group and creating the WEA Distribution company. Warner Music Group labels include Atco, Atlantic, Elektra/Asylum, Reprise, and Warner Brothers. The gradual evolution of the mainstream record labels from entrepreneurial "independents" to members of corporate "groups" that in turn are owned by major transnational conglomerates has greatly increased concentration of ownership. The industry is moving toward conditions of tight oligopoly, where four or fewer firms hold 60 percent of the market. The movement of record companies into corporate business structures has led to increased emphasis on quarterly numbers and decreased focus on musical content, because parent companies depend on the cash flow generated by their music groups.

Corporate Versus Independent

Corporate music groups typically include record labels and music publishing companies, but they may also include CD and tape manufacturing companies, a distribution company, and record retail outlets. This vertical integration provides the parent company with the opportunity to profit from the creation, manufacture, distribution, and sale of music products. They are also horizontally integrated—by owning electronics hardware manufacturing companies, film studios, and television producers and networks, which can make use of their music products as content in other media. Some of the major labels have created smaller, subsidiary, "boutique" labels that operate with a degree of creative independence to serve specific musical genres (e.g., Americana, hardcore rap, and so on) or other niche markets. These labels usually maintain smaller artist rosters (allowing them to give more individualized attention to those who are under contract) and are often built around a key executive who has unique credentials and credibility in that area of the marketplace.

Independent labels, however, are those not owned in whole or part by the Big Five, although many of them do have distribution deals with the majors corporations to assure their product reaches all markets effectively. Throughout the twentieth century, smaller labels showed themselves to be better attuned to changes in popular music forms and evolutions in popular taste. When major labels would not sign artists in genres such as blues, jazz, rhythm and blues, rock-n-roll, and hip hop, the independents did. Around the 1950s, this shifted the balance of power in the industry away from established mainstream companies aligned with Tin Pan Alley commercial pop-song publishers. As the upstart independents gained sales momentum and the forms of music they championed proved to be more than fads, they were acquired by the larger companies. Decades of these acquisitions led to the concentration of ownership and marketplace domination described above. This has not completely undermined the marketplace for independent labels. They still serve as a development area for the Big Five, speculating on recording artists who have yet to find a mass audience.

In the mid-1990s, independent labels accounted for about 21 percent of record sales in the United States, releasing 66 percent of the titles. Most of these releases sell less than five thousand copies, and many of them sell far less. The scale of these companies' operations permits low-cost production, marketing, and distribution, allowing some to make a profit even at these comparatively low sales levels. With contemporary technology, professional quality recordings can be made without booking huge blocks of time in expensive studios, and tapes and CDs can be produced economically in shorter runs. When a recording artist on an independent label begins selling tens or hundreds of thousands of copies, the profits can be enormous, which often arouses interest from the major labels. When artists' contracts with independents expire, they can negotiate new contracts with larger labels from positions of relative strength. This pattern repeated itself, largely intact, for much of the twentieth century.

Despite the concentration of ownership, the vertical and horizontal integration of the Big Five, and their dominant market share of sales, the recording industry must be understood as an open system. None of these companies can infallibly predict or control consumer tastes and purchases. The industry takes the creative inputs of songwriters, musicians, and producers, transforms them into the final product (a packaged recording), and brings it to market. This involves making copies available to radio stations for airplay, producing videos for television outlets, advertising in trade and consumer media, making sure the product is in stores by the targeted release date, and creating promotional opportunities as the artist travels the country for concert appearances. In the production process, record label executives exert influence on the recording artists and repertoire executives who signed them to their contracts, as well as on the producers who work with them in the studio. Still, the executives for the label can only work from their existing assumptions about what sounds get radio airplay and are purchased for the collections of consumers. After shaping the final product to the best of its instincts and abilities, the industry then depends on the exposures it is able to create in hopes of actually finding a receptive audience who will purchase the product.

The greatest marketplace advantage the major labels have enjoyed is their distribution system. Their established relationships with retailers worldwide, warehouses, and shipping channels would be expensive to duplicate. Distribution costs have presented the highest barriers to entry into the recording industry for newcomers. Professional-quality recording equipment is available to consumers, and tape and CD duplication facilities can be found in most major cities. However, getting retailers to give up limited shelf space to untried artists on unknown labels is a nearly insurmountable challenge, especially with chain stores. Without a powerful distribution partner to place a product in the stores, independents must find alternate means of reaching consumers. Many independents have used a combination of ads in specialty magazines and direct mail to reach consumers. Free catalogs and low-priced sampler CDs are made available to introduce music buyers to the offerings of the label. Setting up display and sales spaces at music festivals featuring their artists and genres of music have also been successful. Still, the advent of the Internet is creating new, lower cost means of distribution.

Technology and the Internet

Digital data compression technology has made it possible to move sound files easily by computer. By putting up a company site on the World Wide Web, even garage- and bedroom-based independent labels can provide worldwide access to their offerings. Sample songs can be archived on a website for listening through realtime "streaming" technologies or by download. All of the other advertising and promotional activity of the independent labels can direct consumers to this site,

MP3 technology has become an important part of the recording industry. To fill that need, Japan's Casio Computer released in May 2000 the Wrist Audioplayer MPV-1V, which enables the owner to play a maximum thirty-three minutes of digital music downloaded from the Internet. (AFP/Corbis)

providing more immediate access to the company and its products. It then becomes possible to sell the digitized music electronically via download to the customers' computers or by taking credit card information and shipping product directly to the consumer. In the 1990s, the Motion Picture Experts Group created a data compression technology that could reduce the size of sound files tenfold, while retaining near-CD quality. What had been a 40-megabyte (Mb) file could now be 4 Mb. This technology, called MPEG-1, layer 3 (or MP3 for short) quickly became widely available on the Internet.

Ambitious musical artists quickly began putting their work onto the Internet via the web to raise their profiles. Fans began digitizing bootleg recordings and legitimate label releases to make them more broadly accessible to online taste groups. Even some big-name groups made digital copies of their latest songs available as MP3 files before their official release dates. The Beastie Boys, Public Enemy, Prince, and Tom Petty and the Heartbreakers were all asked by their labels to take such files down. The advance Tom Petty single was downloaded 150,000 times in the forty-eight hours that it was available. To the labels, unauthorized digitization of the music that they release is piracy. Several individuals have already been sued for copyright infringement, and many more have been threatened. Often, sites with unauthorized MP3 files on them are maintained by technology-savvy college students, part of the vanguard group of users. When their host institutions are advised of the illegal status of some of this content, the offending websites are usually taken down quickly. What is happening with the dissemination of MP3 technology is a revolution in the distribution of sound recordings.

The industry has weathered technological revolutions before, not the least of which was the evolution from mechanical to electronic means of production. There have been revolutionary changes in the means of distribution as well. When radio arrived in the 1920s, the industry feared and resisted it, expecting that free access to music would slow consumer purchases. While that may have been true in the short term, exposure to more musical artists and styles led to more purchases by consumers who had disposable income. The widespread distribution of jukeboxes in the 1930s almost single-handedly pulled the industry out of the Great Depression. By providing audiences, especially young people, with low-cost access to the music that they wanted to hear, sales of "hit" records were stimulated. The industry's initial response to digital music did seem to be one of fear, even panic, glossing over legitimate uses of MP3 technology with shrill cries about piracy. However, as the major corporations adapt to the new environment, they are finding ways to make the technology work for them. Announced in December 1998, the major labels are voluntarily participating in the Secure Digital Music Initiative (SDMI), which seeks to foster a broad voluntary agreement by major companies on digital security and compatibility of music. If this agreement was not voluntary, some might see it as a potential restraint of trade.

SDMI is working on the development of digital data compression technologies that are more advanced than MP3 and will protect the partici-

pating companies' proprietary interests in the content. In March 1999, Leonardo Chiariglione, who was instrumental in the original development of MPEG, was hired to lead the project. MPEG-4 and MPEG-7 have already been announced. These upgrades offer greater compression, searchability, as well as copy protection and "watermarking" of digital music files. The greater compression will make it practical to send sound files by e-mail. Searchability makes favored selections in larger files more accessible. Copy protection will give labels a measure of control over the digital distribution of sound files, and watermarking embeds a record of how and when copies were made in the data, to facilitate tracing of unauthorized product. The aim of SDMI is to review existing technologies and recommend a standard to the industry that is acceptable to all participating companies. This would then lead to the promotion of a new consumer format for audio data files that would permit the industry to continue to realize revenue from the sale and distribution of such files. The sheer magnitude of the participating major companies will cause many consumers of digital music to embrace this standard, and hardware companies whose equipment becomes part of the standard will reap a windfall.

This does not mean that MP3 will be completely eclipsed. Small labels and niche artists will continue to use this technology, legally. Original compositions will continue to be made available for free download, or for a cost, without copy protection. Just as the scale of independents brought profitability at relatively low levels of product sales, so it is with downloads. Success through this new distribution channel can lead to subsequent contracts with larger industry companies, and thereby greater visibility and, in the best case, greater sales. The opportunities for direct promotion and distribution of digitized music by artists and small labels are profound. In addition to their own websites, there are search engines for MP3 files and centralized sites for digital music where artists can make their music available in partnership with the site owners. Portable units that make digital music files mobile are accelerating in sales. Technologies that make the swapping of MP3 files easier are appearing, and smaller labels that are not participating in SDMI are establishing partnerships with specialized firms that can make their catalogs available in this marketplace. The adaptation to the digital music revolution is ongoing, and there are many opportunities yet to come.

Conclusion

Many companies in the recording industry have attached themselves to this complex of new technologies in the name of profit—some more single-mindedly than others. Music, the primary content of recorded products, is an element of culture and, as such, cannot be fully contained or controlled by industry. Indigenous music is an acknowledged contribution that the United States has made to world culture, and it will likely continue to be. The mix of major labels, independents, and entrepreneurial artists allows for the simultaneous evolution and commercialization of American musical culture, which allows for both profit and artistic expression, neither fully excluding the other. Still, the profound influence that major companies possess because of their dominance over the music marketplace is weakening (perhaps only slightly and perhaps just for a short time), and this bodes well for music as artistic expression and for the ongoing health of the industry.

See also: INTERNET AND THE WORLD WIDE WEB; PIRATE MEDIA; RADIO BROADCASTING; RADIO BROADCASTING, STATION PROGRAMMING AND; RECORDING INDUSTRY, CAREERS IN; RECORDING INDUSTRY, HISTORY OF; RECORDING INDUSTRY, PRODUCTION PROCESS OF; RECORDING INDUSTRY, TECHNOLOGY OF.

Bibliography

Hull, Geoffrey. (1998). *The Recording Industry*. Boston: Allyn & Bacon.

Krasilovsky, M. William, and Shemel, Sidney. (1995). *This Business of Music*, 7th revised edition. New York: Watson-Guptill.

Sanjek, Russell, and Sanjek, David. (1991). *American Popular Music In the Twentieth Century*. New York: Oxford University Press.

PAUL D. FISCHER

■ RECORDING INDUSTRY, CAREERS IN

The recording industry is made up of small companies as well as transnational corporations. Many are concentrated in music centers, such as New York, Los Angeles, London, and Nashville, while others thrive in markets where corporate and private products involving sound are produced, such as Chicago, Philadelphia, and Miami. Companies in the recording industry employ clerical and administrative staffs, accountants, and lawyers, though only the larger companies have in-house accountants and lawyers.

The everyday, essential staff areas are often the easiest way to gain employment with industry companies, thereby facilitating access to positions that are more directly engaged with creative processes. In major markets, there are usually temporary staffing companies that specialize in serving recording industry companies. Temporary assignments often lead to full-time jobs. Once an individual is employed in the industry, it becomes easier to find out about and move toward jobs that satisfy established desires and use specific skills. To land an entry-level position, a college degree, especially one related to the industry, is valued. Although it is possible to find employment without a degree, an individual in that situation must be able to compensate with positive assets such as daily dependability and the ability to deliver more than the minimum work that is requested. These characteristics can also lead to promotions and access to more responsible jobs. Recording industry jobs are part of the larger entertainment industry, a desirable place to work, so there are almost always more applicants than positions. Because of the highly competitive job market, even at the entry level, whom one knows and whom one has impressed can be very important.

Many people harbor the dream of becoming famous as recording artists, performing their own music. Few succeed, and the bulk of the industry is based on the expectation that dues will be paid before power and monetary payoffs are realized. For every visible star, there are at least twenty people behind the scenes working to keep them there. This is where most job opportunities in the industry appear. The recording industry is nothing without something to record, so beyond singer–songwriters, the song is key. Songwriters work on an independent basis, using personal and professional contacts, or under a contract to music publishing companies that market ("pitch," or "plug") songs. Personal managers, producers, and artist and repertoire (A&R) executives at record labels who have the power to include people in projects that they are overseeing are on the receiving end of these pitches. Publishing companies typically have creative and administrative divisions. Publishers' creative divisions decide which songwriters to sign, which songs to make demonstration ("demo") recordings of, and to whom the songs should be pitched in hopes of getting a "cut" (a song included on a recording). The administrative division handles payroll, distributes royalty payments, and keeps the bills paid. Getting a contract as a songwriter depends on the strength of the material one brings to market. Song pluggers are often successful songwriters themselves, former label employees, and/or individuals who have good connections around the industry. It is a business of relationships.

Personal managers and record producers stand at the crossroads of creativity and commerce. Personal managers have earned the trust of musical artists, and they work toward getting recording contracts and booking agents for the artists in an attempt to maximize the artists' income. In return, they receive a percentage of the artists' income—typically 15 to 20 percent—for providing that guidance. They have creative input into the songs that are recorded and their style and sequencing, as well as the photographs, packaging, and marketing of the final products and the artists themselves. Sometimes, managers and producers must caution performers to rein in their artistic impulses to fit better with trends in chart success, radio airplay, and sales. Personal managers also serve as the artists' legal representatives when dealing with record companies, booking agents, public relations firms, and so on. Producers, in command in the studio sessions, have to balance the musicians' desires to express themselves and realize their artistic visions with delivering a product that the record label can energetically bring to market. Producers also choose the studios to work in, which affects engineers, backup singers, and session musicians. Business managers, employed by the most successful artists, should be mentioned here. Also working for a percentage of the artists' income—only 5 to 10 percent—these managers collect the artists' income (making certain that the artists are being paid fully and properly), pay their bills, provide them with living expenses, prepare their taxes, and often oversee their investments. The overseeing of

financial matters by business managers provides a check on the activities of personal managers and the excesses of the artists themselves.

A&R executives are the creatives at record labels, the ears of the companies who advocate for performers they like—to get them "signed" to recording contracts. After signing, A&R executives serve as liaisons to the artists' management regarding the label's vision for the performer and the marketing plans. Within a major company, the ideal A&R person remains an advocate for the artists that they sign, "selling" them to the sales, promotion, publicity, and advertising departments. Marketing is usually the largest of these divisions, responsible for getting the product to consumers by getting it into stores and the awareness of the consumers. Promotion involves getting the recorded product radio and video airplay, as well as arranging live appearances at retail and broadcast outlets when the artist is on tour. Publicity efforts try to get unpaid exposure (other than airplay) for recordings. Advertising involves taking out advertisements in trade and consumer publications to create awareness and to arrange cooperative advertisements with retailers to promote the key releases of the company. At smaller labels, many of these functions may be combined. Because of the complex business nature of the industry, many of the presidents of major recording labels are attorneys.

Many job niches exist in working directly for recording artists. Performers who have recording contracts are expected to tour, which creates a demand for bus and truck drivers, roadies who set up the equipment, and technicians who set up and tune instruments and provide onstage support during performances. Some artists employ singers or dancers to enhance the onstage presentation, wardrobe people to look after their stage clothes, as well as hairstylists and makeup artists who travel with them so they look their best onstage and at media appearances. Road managers travel with performers to keep the complex logistics of a traveling show straight—getting all the people and equipment to the right place at the right time and looking after payment upon delivery of the performers' services.

In the recording industry, getting the first job is usually the hardest. Established relationships, such as becoming a trusted friend, can make one a road manager or personal manager overnight. Landing jobs with major companies may require contacts, or a stint as an intern or temp, to get noticed. Maintaining one's reputation as a sharp, dependable, and discreet person will do the most toward maintaining career momentum. Making decisions that make employers money provides the best chance of upward advancement.

See also: PUBLIC RELATIONS, CAREERS IN; RADIO BROADCASTING, CAREERS IN; RADIO BROADCAST-ING, STATION PROGRAMMING AND; RECORDING INDUSTRY; RECORDING INDUSTRY, HISTORY OF; RECORDING INDUSTRY, PRODUCTION PROCESS OF; RECORDING INDUSTRY, TECHNOLOGY OF.

PAUL D. FISCHER

RECORDING INDUSTRY, HISTORY OF

Recording and playback of sound was first achieved by Thomas Edison in 1877. His first recording was the nursery rhyme "Mary Had a Lit-tle Lamb." (If Edison believed it was going to work, he might have said something more momentous.) Edison patented his "talking machine," or phonograph, in 1878. Nearly deaf, he noticed that each sound had a distinct vibra-tion, and by etching or indenting those vibrations in a physical material, they could be retraced and replayed. The first phonograph combined previ-ously existing technologies to record and play sound by mechanical means. He used a trumpet to gather sound and concentrate it, causing a taut membrane at its smaller end to vibrate like a drumhead (i.e., a diaphragm). A stylus attached to the diaphragm indented a hill-and-dale pattern (created by the sound vibrations) on a moving surface (initially a cylinder) of a malleable sub-stance (originally tin foil or wax), which was turned by a wheel that was attached to a feed screw. This resulted in a spiral-shaped groove that could then be retraced with a lighter stylus, caus-ing the same vibration in the diaphragm, sending sound back up the trumpet to be heard.

Edison believed the device would be most valuable as an office machine, a dictation device. He also listed talking books for the blind and the teaching of elocution ahead of reproduction of music on his initial list of potential uses. Last on his list was "connection to the telephone." Genius that he was, Edison envisioned the answering machine before the turn of the century. Early com-petitors with the phonograph were the grapho-phone, a remarkably similar device patented in 1885 and marketed by Alexander Graham Bell and his associates beginning in 1887, and Emile Berliner's gramophone that played flat, round discs rather than cylinders and was brought to market in 1891. The Berliner Gramophone Com-pany was based in Philadelphia, and its first disc-pressing plant was located in Hanover, Germany. The similarities between the phonograph and graphophone prompted Edison to sue for patent infringement, but sufficient improvements were found in the graphophone that both were permit-ted in the marketplace. The gramophone was a playback-only device, geared to the home enter-tainment market from the outset, necessitating the development of the record business to spark and maintain the interest of the consumers.

There were substantial differences in the com-mercial production of cylinder and disc record-ings. Cylinders depended on the technique of multiple simultaneous recording. Numerous "horns" (large trumpets) were arranged to cap-ture the live sound and direct it to numerous phonographs and/or graphophones. In essence, each cylinder was an original recording. Phono-graph discs were produced from a metal (zinc) master disc from the very beginning. Also, they used a lateral groove, rather than the hill-and-dale formation. The first consumer discs were made of vulcanite, a mixture of rubber and sulfur that hardened when heated. Unfortunately, this material did not provide quality or durability that was consistent enough for a commercial product. The successful substance, durinoid (so named because it was a product of the Durinoid Com-pany of Newark, New Jersey), was a plastic used in the manufacture of buttons. A combination of shellac, clay, cotton fibers, and lampblack, duri-noid became the industry standard until the introduction of vinyl in the 1940s. The gramo-phone also introduced motors into the playback function, using a hand-cranked, spring-wound device with a governor, assuring constant turntable speed. These motors were manufac-tured by Eldridge Johnson, an engineer who had previously manufactured motors for sewing machines. Johnson also developed a wax master-ing process for discs, which greatly improved their sound. Eventually, he became head of the

The Berliner Gramophone is shown with its various accessories. (Bettmann/Corbis)

Victor Talking Machine Company and the Victor Record Company. In 1906, the Victor Talking Machine Company introduced the "Victrola," which was designed to look more like furniture than a machine and won mainstream acceptance and massive sales. Edison continued to promote cylinders until 1913, when he finally began marketing discs and players under his name. His discs used a diamond-tipped stylus, had hill-and-dale grooves, and sounded great, but he never seriously threatened the dominance of Victor Records in the marketplace.

With methods of production stabilized, the business turned its attention to matters of content. Fred W. Gaisberg, working with Berliner, was sent to Europe in 1902 to record operatic arias. There he found tenor Enrico Caruso, who would become the first million-selling recording artist. Caruso was recorded in a Milan hotel suite, using

Johnson's wax mastering process. The ten selections that Caruso recorded were released on the Red Seal label of Victor Records. Despite the success of these recordings, and the dedication of several early labels to classical music, the biggest sales came from more popular genres. Brass bands, such as John Phillip Sousa's, did well—in part because their sounds reproduced clearly through the early processes. Songs made popular through Broadway and vaudeville shows found ready buyers, as did novelties such as gifted whistlers and players of saws and other offbeat instruments. The music business was still dominated by sheet music, sales of which peaked in 1910, driven by the Tin Pan Alley songwriters and publishers that were based in New York City.

Increasing sales of recordings in the 1910s and 1920s, with a peak of $121 million in sales in 1921, shifted the balance of power in the industry toward the recording companies. The explosion of in-home radio receivers in the 1920s brought recorded music to a new, and larger, audience. The first jazz hit was "Livery Stable Blues," recorded by the all-white Original Dixieland Jazz Band in 1917. Most of the bands that were featured live on radio programs were white. It was not until the 1920s that black musicians came to be recorded with market success, initially by smaller labels. Ralph Sylvester Peer, with Okeh Records, was instrumental in the first recordings of another indigenous American music, the blues. He recorded Mamie Smith singing Perry Bradford's "Crazy Blues," which became a hit. Throughout that decade, female artists such as Ma Rainey, Bessie Smith, Alberta Hunter, Sippie Wallace, and others found success with what came to be called the vaudeville blues, crossing this music over to an appreciative white audience. Peer coined a name for all the music recorded by blacks, "race music," which became a marketing category.

Peer also pioneered commercial recording of rural white musicians, performing what he called "hillbilly music," later known as country. In 1923, he recorded Fiddlin' John Carson in Atlanta, Georgia. The first hillbilly hit was "The Prisoner's Song," by Vernon Dalhart in 1924. Dalhart, himself anything but a hillbilly, was a formally trained operatic singer. Radio "barn dance" programs on Chicago's WLS, and later, Nashville's WSM, helped raise the national profile of the music. A set of 1927 recording sessions by Peer in Bristol, Tennessee, also advanced the music commercially, bringing The Carter Family and Jimmie Rodgers ("The Singing Brakeman") to national prominence. In the 1930s, singing cowboys in the movies, such as Gene Autry and Roy Rogers, advanced the popularity of country and western music even further.

The stock market crash of 1929 and America's Great Depression were devastating to the recording industry. Radio became the dominant entertainment medium and fewer people bought recordings for private use. "Big band" music was the most popular music on the radio, playing complex jazz arrangements popularly known as "swing" music. Clarinetist Benny Goodman led a popular band on radio, earning him the nickname "King of Swing." Other bands, including those led by Tommy and Jimmy Dorsey, Artie Shaw, Glenn Miller, and Woody Herman, enjoyed success on

radio. Black bandleaders, such as Duke Ellington, Count Basie, and Cab Calloway, succeeded mainly through club dates and tours. A new distribution channel for popular music came along in the 1930s that almost single-handedly pulled the industry out of the Great Depression: the jukebox. By the end of the decade, nearly 250,000 of the coin-in-the-slot record machines were in place around America, and fully 60 percent of the record industry's output in 1939 was purchased by jukebox operators.

Recorded music in the 1940s faced a new set of challenges, mainly brought on by World War II. In addition to wartime rationing of products such as rubber, gasoline, butter, sugar, and flour, there were shortages of industrial raw materials. Shellac, a key ingredient in records, was imported, mainly from India, and quickly came into short supply. By April 1942, the government had limited the recording industry's consumption of shellac to 30 percent of prewar levels, and production thus ground to a halt. There was also a musician's strike by the American Federation of Musicians that made arranging commercial sessions difficult. Recording artists, however, began donating their services for inclusion in V-Discs ("V" for "Victory"), made by the War Department for distribution to Armed Forces Radio and servicemen worldwide. Many of the popular artists during the period, such as Bing Crosby, Frank Sinatra, and the big bands, made their only war-era recordings as part of the V-Disc effort.

The war years also helped lead to the death of the big bands. With many of the best players in the service and tires and gasoline rationed, it became uneconomical and somewhat unpatriotic to keep large performing units on the road. This gave rise to smaller combinations (or "combos") playing hard jazz (or "bebop") and "jump blues." The former, typified by the works of Dizzy Gillespie, John Coltrane, and Charlie Parker, went largely unrecorded, and the latter, epitomized by Louis Jordan's Tympani Five, sparked new commercial trends. Electric blues, featuring electric guitar leads by Muddy Waters and the like, also surfaced at this time, but this category did not reach a mainstream audience. During the war, the Union Carbide Company developed vinylite, a petroleum-based substance that was suitable for making discs. Soundwise, they offered substantial improvements over shellac-based discs—includ-

One of the key turning points in the history of rock-n-roll was the appearance of Elvis Presley on The Ed Sullivan Show *in 1956. (Bettmann/Corbis)*

ing less surface noise, hissing, and popping. The 1940s also saw the introduction of replacements for the 78-rpm (revolutions per minute) records that had generally become the standard for the industry. Columbia Records introduced their 12-inch, 33 1/3-rpm, long-playing record, and RCA introduced their 7-in, 45-rpm record. The long-playing records offered up to twenty minutes of playing time per side, a boon to jazz and classical fans. As other classical labels adopted the long-playing format, even RCA was forced to go along. By 1950, the 78-rpm record was a thing of the past, but the 45-rpm record offered inexpensive consumer access to the most popular songs, a key to the teen-driven music market of the period.

The late 1940s saw more black music being played on the radio, notably by 50,000-watt, clear-channel WLAC-AM in Nashville, Tennessee, which crossed jazz and rhythm and blues (R&B) sounds over to a large white audience. However, the major labels resisted recording black artists, which created an opportunity for new, independent labels. As more radio stations began playing jump blues, electric blues, and rhythm and blues, the records began selling in larger quantities. In 1951, WJW-AM disc jockey Alan Freed called this music "rock and roll," to lessen its racial connotations to his white teen audience, paving the way for a new wave of success for the industry. The major labels resisted signing R&B and rock-n-roll artists, believing either that the music was just a fad and/or that it was too raw and crude for corporate association. This created opportunities for songwriters, publishers, and independent record labels to get in on the ground floor. One of the biggest success stories in this era was Atlantic Records, founded by Ahmet Ertegun and Herb Abramson, with the early addition of Jerry Wexler. Recording artists such as Ray Charles and Ruth Brown rode the crest of the R&B wave into the rock-n-roll era to great success.

Elvis Presley was instrumental in making permanent the crossover of these types of music to white teenagers. He brought the style and substance of R&B to television in 1956 on the Milton Berle, Steve Allen, and Ed Sullivan shows, and his fusion of country, gospel elements, R&B music, and performance styles brought rock-n-roll closer to the American mainstream. Radio still did not play much music by black artists, which led to the regular creation of "cover versions," in which white vocalists and groups rendered faithful copies of songs that were successful on the R&B charts. Pat Boone enjoyed extensive chart success with songs that were originated by Fats Domino, Little Richard, and others. The beginning of the 1960s looked much like the decade that preceded it, but before it was half over, things had changed drastically. In 1964, the "British Invasion" began, with The Beatles. Appearing on Ed Sullivan' show in February of that year, their first U.S. long-playing record, *Meet The Beatles*, went on to sell 3.6 million copies, the first album to outsell its hit single. Their early records included covers of Chuck Berry and Little Richard songs, as well as original songs. Their sales momentum caused the major labels to take notice and opened the doors of the industry to many British pop groups, including The Dave Clark Five, Herman's Hermits, and Peter and Gordon.

The success of this first wave led to a second British wave, of more blues- and R&B-influenced

bands such as The Yardbirds, The Rolling Stones, and The Animals, who covered hits by Muddy Waters, John Lee Hooker, Howlin' Wolf, and other American bluesmen. In effect, these developments brought these powerful American types of music to white teenagers for the first time and provided a new foundation for the evolution of popular music with a blues base. Also, in the mid-1960s, Bob Dylan electrified his music, bringing the social conscience, lyrical complexity, and social commentary of folk into the rock mainstream. This provided a base for introspective singer–songwriters to share their personal insights about life, love, politics, the environment, and the world with millions of fans and propel the industry into the 1970s. By the end of the 1960s, even the largest record companies were recording rock artists and/or moving to acquire and distribute companies that did.

The 1970s was the decade when rock music and the recording industry really became big business. Top artists such as The Eagles, Elton John, Fleetwood Mac, and Peter Frampton could be counted on to sell more than ten million copies of each release. The more than seventy million "baby boomers" (born between 1946 and 1964) were a massive market, hungry for the musical input of their peers. Mid-decade, two types of music came in from the fringes to reenergize the complacent mainstream: disco and punk. Disco came out of the dance clubs, with fast beats, reintroducing the effect that rock-n-roll originally had of getting young people dancing. Punk took social commentary to a new extreme, criticizing many aspects of modern industrial society, even the companies that brought their sounds to the audience. For a time, both genres sold well and very expensive studios were built, including the first using digital recording technology. The 1980s saw the introduction of the "compact disc" (CD), the first digital playback format for consumers, and vinyl discs were quickly eclipsed at retail.

The massive cash flows generated by record companies in the 1970s made them attractive takeover targets, even with their countercultural cachet. The 1980s saw an accelerating concentration of ownership in the recording industry. By the end of the decade six major corporations, Columbia Broadcasting System (CBS), Radio Corporation Of America (RCA), Warner-Elektra-Atlantic (WEA), Britain's Electric and Musical Industries Ltd. (EMI), the Music Corporation of America (MCA), and Polygram, dominated the business. For a brief time these companies controlled more than 90 percent of the recorded music business worldwide. That percentage has since declined to somewhere in the mid to upper eighties, but even greater concentration has taken place. CBS was sold to Sony Corporation of Japan, RCA sold its labels to the Bertelsman Company of Germany, WEA became part of Time-Warner, EMI became part of the Thorn-EMI conglomerate, and MCA was sold three times—first to Matsushita of Japan and then to the Seagram Company Ltd. of Canada, which in turn bought out Polygram before being sold to the French environmental services and media giant Vivendi. These companies have tried to maintain their dominance in the marketplace by developing secure standards for the digital distribution of music over the Internet—yet another revolution in the distribution of music.

See also: MUSIC, POPULAR; RADIO BROADCASTING; RADIO BROADCASTING, HISTORY OF; RADIO BROADCASTING, STATION PROGRAMMING AND; RECORDING INDUSTRY; RECORDING INDUSTRY, CAREERS IN; RECORDING INDUSTRY, PRODUCTION PROCESS OF; RECORDING INDUSTRY, TECHNOLOGY OF.

Bibliography

Butterworth, W. E. (1977). *Hi-Fi: From Edison's Phonograph to Quad Sound*. New York: Four Winds Press.

Marco, Guy, ed. (1993). *Encyclopedia of Recorded Sound in the United States*. New York: Garland.

Read, Oliver, and Welch, Walter. (1959). *From Tinfol to Stereo: Evolution of the Phonograph*. New York: Bobbs-Merrill.

PAUL D. FISCHER

RECORDING INDUSTRY, PRODUCTION PROCESS OF

The process that allows a song, from its inception as a creative seed in the mind of a songwriter, to blossom into a compact disc, cassette, or data file downloaded from a website is a complicated one that includes a wide range of specialized vocations. In general, the recording production process can be broken down into three phases: preproduction, production, and postproduction. Although each genre of music, such as pop, urban, modern rock, or country, has some idiosyncrasies, all typically share similar procedures in the production chain.

In addition to the three production phases a song goes through, the completed work must be manufactured, promoted, and distributed to the public. Although these business functions are not part of the production process, they have a pervasive effect on most production decisions. Therefore, people who work in creative vocations such as songwriter, producer, audio engineer, and performer must understand them.

Preproduction

A song is born, from a legal standpoint, the moment that it is put into some fixed form. The most common fixed form is an audio recording—cassettetape or digital audiotape—which is the rough song demo. Once a song is fixed in this manner, it is protected by federal copyright laws. However, most songwriters go one step further and register their songs with the U.S. Library of Congress. By merely completing and mailing the appropriate copyright registration application (form PA), including a copy of the song demo and a nominal fee, the song becomes registered with the Library of Congress Office of Copyright. That simple procedure activates statutory protection and provides an accurate date of ownership.

An active songwriter, trying to earn a living from creating marketable songs, usually enlists the help of a publisher. The publisher will, for a percentage of future royalties, endeavor to get the song recorded and distributed. A songwriter generally agrees to a 50/50 split of all royalties derived from use of the song. One of the first things that a publisher does with a new song is record a more fully produced demo of the song to present to potential users.

Song pluggers from the publishing company pitch the song to people who are looking for songs for upcoming albums. The people who influence the decision regarding what songs will be included on a recording are the producer, record company staff members, the artist, and the artist's manager. Songs go through several levels of screening before even being seriously considered for the album. However, when the producer asks the publisher to "put the song on hold," it is not pitched to other producers.

The responsibility for signing new artists to a record label falls on the artist and repertoire (A&R) department. After an act is signed to a label, the A&R director works with the artist and the artist's management to select a producer for the album. Once a producer has agreed to take on the project, the A&R administrator and album producer develop a production budget. Odd as it may seem, the production costs are paid by the artist. A label will normally give the artist an advance against future royalties to pay for producing the album. The advance is, however, usually in the form of a production budget that is under the control of the producer.

The producer is responsible for developing the creative concept for each song that is included on the album. The producer might also enlist the assistance of specialized arrangers on one or more songs. A vocal arranger specializes in creating background vocals; a "horn section" arranger orchestrates arrangements for brass and woodwind instruments; and a string section arranger creates orchestrations for violins, violas, and cellos.

A critical part of preproduction is the selection of a recording studio in which to work. A studio not only provides the obvious recording equipment necessary to capture music on tape, it also offers an ambiance to support long and tedious recording sessions. Studios generally offer the option of analog or digital tape recorders. The mix console—or board—is an important factor in the producer's choice of studios.

The last set of choices the producer makes during preproduction concerns personnel who will be hired on an hourly basis. Even if the act being produced is a band, additional instrumentalists and vocalists are hired for the recording sessions. Recordings that are distributed by major labels typically use union performers. Singers fall under the jurisdiction of the American Federation of Television and Radio Artists (AFTRA), and instrumentalists are most often members of the American Federation of Musicians (AF of M).

Because much of the recording process is dependent on the skills of the audio engineer, a producer often has a preferred engineer (i.e., the first engineer) to work with in studio situations. In turn, first engineers characteristically work with a second engineer of choice. A team that consists of producer and first and second engineers is somewhat common in the industry.

Production

The production phase of a recording normally begins with the in-studio recording of the master recording. A master recording is created using either an analog or a digital tape recorder. The newest generation of recording media, hard-disk recorders, will likely replace magnetic tape in the future. All recording devices that are used for master recordings have one thing in common: multitrack capability.

Multitrack recording evolved as technological advances permitted. The early monophonic (1-track) recording format gradually evolved into the stereophonic (2-track) format. Then the number of tracks available to producers began to increase every few years: 4-track, 8-track, 16-track, and 24-track. Using tape recorders that are locked together offers a producer the option of 48 or more tracks for isolating sound inputs.

The first sounds to get recorded come from the rhythm section: keyboards, rhythm guitar, electric bass, and drum kit. These basic rhythm tracks are recorded using a vocalist to sing the melody and lyrics. This rough vocal track is referred to as a "scratch track" or "guide vocal" because it will, in all likelihood, be replaced with "keeper vocals" at a later time. This phase (i.e., tracking or cutting rhythm tracks) is laborious but critical. If these basic tracks are recorded without correct pitch, tempo, and rhythmic continuity, the entire album will be in jeopardy. The old adage "We'll fix it in the mix" is pure fiction.

In order to lock-in tempos, the producer usually records a click track onto one track of the multitrack tape. The click track acts like a metronome and helps ensure that each new layer of sound retains the rhythmic integrity. A click track is also very helpful in the editing stage, where precise location of the rhythmic pulse is essential. A more sophisticated variation on a click track is a musical instrument digital interface (MIDI) track. A MIDI track is created with the aid of synthesizers, drum machines, and computers.

Each instrument in the rhythm section is recorded in isolation from the other instruments. That way, if the bass player makes a mistake, the bass part can be fixed in isolation; the other parts will not need to be fixed. This is accomplished by using soundproof isolation booths or movable sound-absorbent baffles (i.e., gobos). In addition, each instrument—especially the drum kit—has the option of multiple input devices.

Input devices include microphones and direct boxes. A direct box routes an electronic signal from its source—guitar, electric bass, or keyboard—directly into the console. This eliminates the possibility of any sound from other instruments bleeding into the instrument's signal. Microphones, on the other hand, are placed near the sound source and are susceptible to other studio sounds bleeding into the sound of another instrument or voice being recorded.

It is possible to have the guitar played through an amplifier and speaker cabinet in the studio and then place a microphone in front of the cabinet. In addition, one could also simultaneously take the same guitar signal through a direct box. This range of options—the selection of microphones and/or direct boxes by the engineer—is somewhat like a painter choosing from a pallet of colors.

After basic tracks are recorded, subsequent sessions are used to layer more sounds (i.e., overdubs) onto the existing tracks. The first in a series of overdub sessions replaces scratch vocals with more precise lead vocals. Often, the lead vocal is recorded several times on different tracks to offer numerous versions from which to choose. This process (i.e., comping or compiling), gives the producer and engineer the ability to piece together selectively the best sections from different vocal tracks.

Because each instrument and voice is isolated on a separate track (or several tracks), "punching in" can be used to fix small mistakes by replacing them without disturbing other sounds. The singer or instrumentalist plays along with the recorded track, and the engineer punches the record button on the tape recorder just prior to the mistake. When done well, a punch-in is imperceptible to most listeners. The use of punch-ins and comping gives the illusion that studio recordings are nearly perfect performances.

After lead vocals are completed, guitar solos and harmony vocals are added to the existing tracks during overdub sessions. The last overdubs are horns and strings, if they are included in the arrangement.

Postproduction

The multitrack master contains many tracks that must now be manipulated and mixed down to a delivery format that might be 2-channel stereo or one of the newer multichannel formats such as 4- or 5.1-channel surround. This process (i.e., mixdown) is done by an audio engineer with input from the producer. It is not uncommon for the mixdown engineer to be different from the tracking engineer.

Each track on the multitrack tape can be electronically processed as it is blended with other tracks in the mixdown process. The most obvious type of signal processing that occurs during mixdown modifies the volume of each signal going to the tape. Slide faders on the console allow the engineer to change the volume of each track, either gradually or quickly. If a console is equipped with memory automation, all changes in volume throughout the recording are stored in memory and replicated during mixdown.

Dynamic range, something related to volume, can also be manipulated through signal processing of each track. If one thinks of dynamics, or volume, on a scale of 1 to 10, an engineer might want to keep certain sounds between 2 and 8. Still others might be electronically limited to between 4 and 6. Electronically limiting or compressing sounds is an important, but often abused, part of mixing tracks.

Another form of signal processing that is used during mixdown is equalization of the tonal quality of a sound. Most of the control knobs or sliders on a recording console are for adjusting the equalization of signals that are going to the tape. The equalization on a console is like a more precise version of the treble and bass controls on a home stereo.

The third type of signal processing manipulates the time domain of recorded sounds. Because recording studios are often nonreverberant by design, the mix engineer must add some type of reverberance (i.e., reverb) and echo to each sound. Echo, the discrete return of a sound after the initial articulation, gives music what some engineers call a third dimension. Reverb, a continuing nondiscrete return of the original sound, adds a sense of space to music. Different types of reverb are sometimes referred to with terms such as "big room," "cathedral," or "concert hall"— named after the types of acoustic space that they are intended to emulate.

Signal processing technology has reached a point where it is now possible to correct the pitch of vocals or instruments automatically or selectively. Some purists find this type of modification to be disturbing. However, the technology exists to correct out-of-tune singers, and many producers use it.

Mixdown of one song might take eight hours or more when the producer and engineer seek perfection. As sounds are blended from the numerous tracks of the multitrack master to the 2-track stereo version, the magic of the recording studio emerges; it sounds as if the singers and instrumentalists simply sat down and performed the song while someone recorded it. In reality, the process may have involved six separate recording sessions over a period of two months. In fact, some of the performers may have never met.

The last step before manufacturing is mastering. This type of mastering, not to be confused with the multitrack master production, is done by a mastering engineer. The mastering engineer puts the songs into the correct sequential order, makes any edits that are needed, and does a macro-mix to balance the overall recording. Mastering prepares the recording to be manufactured into compact discs, cassette tapes, vinyl records, or other configurations.

Variations in the Production Process

Although most commercially released recordings are created in a studio environment, occasionally albums are recorded live during a concert. The rationale is that some performers have an energy when they are interacting with a live audience that cannot be duplicated in the studio. The trade-off is, obviously, accepting the occasional imperfection that is inherent in a concert performance.

In order to record live shows with the same technology of a studio, remote audio recording trucks arrive at the performance venue with what is essentially a studio on wheels. The inside of the truck contains the mobile equivalent of a control room for the producer and engineer. The stage replaces the studio floor, with microphone and direct-box lines split three ways: one set to the on-stage monitors, another set to the audience public address system, and the third set running out to the production truck.

Because mobile production trucks can provide the same multitrack tape formats as found in a studio, it is possible to record the act live to multitrack and later fix mistakes or add overdubs in the studio. This gives the best of both worlds: audience interaction and multitrack isolation of sound inputs.

Another variation on studio multitrack recording is a process of recording directly to the 2-track format. This simple setup has the advantage of being quite portable. It is, therefore, a cost-effective alternative to multitrack remote recordings of live performances. In addition to its simple setup, direct to 2-track leaves more control of the recording in the hands of the performers. Direct to 2-track is more amenable to acoustic ensembles, such as classical and jazz, that do not characteristically depend on the mixdown process for dynamic balance of each instrument.

The development of synthesizers and computer interface software created the new concept of using MIDI in music production. MIDI technology allows a producer to assemble portions of the recording prior to any in-studio performances. It is not uncommon, especially in urban and pop genres, for a producer to employ a "drum programmer" to create the drum sounds in MIDI format. The drum sounds are transferred to the multitrack tape prior to or during the rhythm section sessions.

As the capacity of digital storage media increased since the advent of hard drives on personal computers, the viability of hard-disk recording has emerged. Hard-disk recording systems depend on the same storage media that computers do. Instead of storing audio information on magnetic tape, this new format converts analog sounds to digital information and stores the data on a hard drive or hard disk much like a computer. Therefore, in all likelihood, the cost associated with hard-disk systems will decrease in the future and the technology will become more sophisticated.

A major advantage of digital recording technology is the economy of space that is associated with it. For example, a digital console, MIDI system, and hard-disk recorder might fit neatly into less than one-third of the space that an analog console and tape recorder would require. The low costs that are associated with this type of studio, plus the small amount of space required, make it possible for more producers to have professional home studios. An additional advantage of these types of systems is that the recording process remains totally in the digital domain. No longer does one need to worry about the degradation of audio quality as tracks are mixed or transferred. The world of recorded music is clearly moving in the direction of digital technology.

TABLE 1.

Sales of Recordings by Genre of Music	
Proportion of Total Units Sold	**Genre**
25.2%	Rock
10.8%	Country
10.8%	Rap
10.5%	R&B
10.3%	Pop
5.1%	Religious
3.5%	Classical
3.0%	Jazz
0.8%	Soundtracks
0.7%	Oldies
0.5%	New Age
0.4%	Children's
9.1%	Other*

*"Other" includes ethnic, standards, big band, swing, Latin, electronic, instrumental, comedy, humor, spoken word, exercise, language, folk, and holiday music.

SOURCE: Recording Industry Association of America (1999).

The Business Environment of Recordings

Even before a song is written, one must consider certain facts of life that will ultimately decide the fate of any recording released to the public. Most music that is produced in a recorded format is intended to be heard by an audience. The audience may hear it broadcast on radio, played on a personal listening device, or in a myriad of other environments. However, the efforts that go into recording a musical work must be matched by equally masterful forms of promotion and distribution, or the production will exist in a vacuum.

Music that is created for aesthetic reasons, as opposed to music that is created to generate income, is most often appreciated during live performances in concert halls rather than in recorded form. On the other hand, most modern genres are created to be broadcast and sold to the general public in the form of compact discs and cassettes. Music producers depend on the sales of these recordings to make a living, so they pay close attention to statistics that indicate which genres of music sell more than the others.

The Recording Industry Association of America (RIAA) is a trade association that represents the interests of record companies in the United States. It monitors sales of recordings in the United States and presents annual summaries (see Table 1).

In addition to identifying the genres of music that are being sold, record companies (i.e., record labels) also get valuable information about the configurations on which music is recorded for distribution to consumers. As new configurations become more popular, and as others go out of vogue, producers of music must adjust to accommodate the newer technologies. For example, as the digital compact disc configuration began to replace analog recordings such as vinyl records and cassette tapes, producers were able to extend the range of dynamics. One marketing strategy of record labels in the early days of compact discs was to offer recordings with exaggerated dynamic range in order to dramatize their advantage over analog recordings. This is just one example of how people who are involved with the creation of recorded music have had to adjust to innovations in technology.

Record Promotion

The manner in which a recording will be promoted has a significant effect on production decisions. The primary medium for promoting recordings is radio, and a recording must meet certain criteria in order to be broadcast by radio stations. The most obvious, but nonetheless controversial, criterion is the lyric content of the song. Rap and rock music producers occasionally create two or more versions of a song in the studio. One is the "clean" version, also known as the "radio version," which is free of profanity or other lyrics that would prohibit stations from airing it. The other version, complete with explicit lyrics, is created for compact disc and cassette releases. A third mix (i.e., the dance mix or "remix) is a longer version that has strong bass and kick drum.

Another restriction that is placed on music by radio is the length of the completed production. Radio programmers prefer songs that are between 2.5 and 3 minutes in length. Again, producers often create a single version for release to radio and an album version and dance mix that are longer versions. The different lengths of a song are often created in the editing process.

No matter how great a recording is, the public needs to hear it before they can decide whether or not to buy it. In other words, the recording must get airplay on mass media in order to generate potential buyers. Although music videos and reviews in print media help create an awareness for a new record release, radio remains the primary means for promoting recordings.

All major record labels fights tooth-and-nail to obtain radio airplay for their artists. Each broadcast on radio, or "spin" in promotional jargon, ordinarily results in sales of recordings. The process of getting radio stations to play a record is one of the most controversial aspects of record-label operations.

The radio promotion department of a label uses several techniques to get airplay. First, they send information about the artist, along with a copy of a "single" from the album, to radio station program directors and music directors across the country. A single is merely the song that the label wants the radio stations to play first. The next step is the art of promotion—calling the station to persuade them to play the record and play it often.

Occasionally, a label will also enlist the help—for a pretty stiff fee—of an independent record promoter. Some independent promoters have been accused of going beyond legal means to get radio airplay. One illegal technique is the bribing of radio station employees to play the record. This nefarious tactic (i.e., payola) can get both the radio station employee and the promoter in big trouble with the law. Payola is, therefore, not something in which legitimate promoters ever engage.

Assuming that the record starts getting airplay on radio stations throughout the nation, it will appear in trade publications (i.e., the charts). A chart lists the top albums and singles in various radio formats, such as urban, adult contemporary, or country. Some well-known charts are *Billboard*, *Cashbox*, *The Gavin Report*, *Monday Morning Quarterback*, and *Radio and Records*.

The information that is used to create the various record charts has become somewhat more scientific than it was in the past. Airplay is monitored by a broadcast detection system operated by the Broadcast Data Systems (BDS) company. When a single is manufactured by a label, an electronic detection code is imbedded in the recording. This detection fingerprint is inaudible to human ears, but it is detected by BDS reception towers located throughout the country. Each detection indicates the code number for the single, what station broadcast it, and the time and date of the broadcast. All detections are transmitted to a central computer, and summaries of airplay are updated daily.

The other criterion for getting a record charted—sales—is also monitored electronically.

Bar-coded information that is scanned at the cash register of a record store is transmitted to Sound-Scan, a company that is somewhat like BDS. Sound-Scan captures sales data on all configurations that are sold at cooperating retail outlets and the cumulative data is maintained in their database. Anyone who wishes to access those data files can do so by subscribing to SoundScan and paying an annual fee.

Both labels and chart publishers watch BDS and SoundScan results on a daily basis. Some charts also include data from key radio stations in various markets. These stations (i.e., reporting stations) offer information on newly added singles and album cuts plus how often they are being played in program rotation.

Record Distribution

If a promotion staff has been successful in gaining airplay for a single, the next stage is distribution of the product. As fans hear a new single on the radio, many go to a retail store or website to purchase the album from which the single came. The path from the factory where a compact disc is replicated or cassette tape is duplicated to the retail outlet is not as simple as one might think. The channels of distribution, from label to consumer, have evolved into a strange labyrinth of subdistributors.

Although there are hundreds of record labels in the United States, there are relatively few distribution organizations. As major labels began buying independent labels in the consolidation era that began in the 1980s, each created a separate affiliated distribution entity. There are only five major distribution companies and several independent distributors. Oligopoly, which describes the situation where a few companies dominate an industry, is nowhere more apparent than in record distribution. The five major distribution companies account for about 80 percent all of records sold worldwide.

After a recording is manufactured, its marketing plan is created under the watchful eye of the label's product manager. The product manager, somewhat like a traffic cop, directs the recorded product through the distribution network. Working with the label's in-house sales staff and distribution arm, the product manager constantly works to get the product on the streets.

Orders are filled through a system of branch distribution offices. Branch offices, generally located in several large cities around the country, have the difficult balancing act of having adequate inventory in the warehouse but not overstocking any one release. Their goal is to process orders and returns in a timely manner.

Two types of subdistributors have emerged to serve special types of accounts. One such subdistributor, the "one-stop," acquires recordings through major- and independent-label branch offices and sells them to retail accounts. It is appropriately named, because it allows small independent retail stores the opportunity to purchase product from all major labels and many independent labels with only one stop.

A second type of subdistributor is a "rack jobber." A rack jobber supplies a full range of recordings, from all viable labels, to department stores, mass-marketing retail chains, and other retail stores that do not specialize in music. The largest rack jobber in the United States, The Handleman Company, essentially manages the recording sections of chains such as K-Mart and Wal-Mart. Because Handleman services more than twenty thousand retail locations, it is an extremely important account for a major label.

It is important to reiterate that the producers of music for commercial distribution must be cognizant of the preferences—and restrictions—of the marketing system. If a recording does not meet the demands of mass retailers, such as K-Mart or Wal-Mart, it simply will not be made available in their record bins. If a recording does not meet parameters dictated by radio broadcasters, it will not receive the necessary airplay to sell significant numbers to the public. Therefore, people who are involved with the creation of the artistic product must be aware of the business system in addition to the technical and artistic elements.

See also: COPYRIGHT; RADIO BROADCASTING; RADIO INDUSTRY, STATION PROGRAMMING AND; RECORDING INDUSTRY; RECORDING INDUSTRY, CAREERS IN; RECORDING INDUSTRY, HISTORY OF; RECORDING INDUSTRY, TECHNOLOGY OF.

Bibliography

Association for Independent Music. (2001). "AFIM." <http://www.afim.org>.
Audio Engineering Society. (2001). "Audio Engineering Society." <http://www.aes.org>.
Hall, Charles W., and Taylor, Frederic J. (1996). *Marketing In the Music Industry*. Needham Heights, MA: Simon & Schuster.

Hull, Geoffrey P. (1998). *The Recording Industry*. Needham Heights, MA: Allyn & Bacon.

Keating, Carolyn, and Anderton, Craig, eds. (1998). *Digital Home Recording: Tips, Techniques, and Tools for Home Studio Production*. San Francisco: Miller Freeman Books.

Moylan, William. (1992). *The Art of Recording*. New York: Van Nostrand Reinhold.

National Association of Recording Merchandisers. (2001). "National Association of Recording Merchandisers." <http://www.narm.com>.

Rapaport, Diane Sward. (1999). *How to Make and Sell Your Own Recording*. Upper Saddle River, NJ: Prentice-Hall.

Recording Industry Association of American. (1999). "Consumer Profile." <http://www.riaa.com/PDF/MD-10yr_ consumer_profile.pdf>.

Society of Professional Audio RecordIng Services. (2001). "Spars." <http://www.spars.com>.

United States Copyright Office. (2001). "United States Copyright Office, The Library of Congress." <http://www.loc.gov/copyright>.

Wilkinson, Scott; Oppenheimer, Steve; and Isham, Mark. (1998). *Anatomy of a Home Studio: How Everything Really Works from Microphones to MIDI*. Emeryville, CA: Mix Bookshelf/Mix Books.

RICHARD D. BARNET

RECORDING INDUSTRY, TECHNOLOGY OF

Thomas Edison never envisioned that the phonograph that he invented would ever be used for entertainment. He saw it as a business dictation machine or as a telephone answering machine, not as a music player. However, when he made the first acoustic music recordings on wax cylinders in 1877, Edison unwittingly unleashed the entertainment potential of prerecorded music. The possibility of a library of music recordings being available for personal use sparked a frenzy of recording that has continued unabated.

Many of the early electrical recording studios were essentially radio station facilities. The equipment that was so vital to the broadcasting industry was quickly adopted by the entertainment industry to record music as well as soundtracks for motion pictures. Whether broadcasting or making a record, the sequence of events was the same—performers and musicians created sounds that were gathered by microphones and transformed into electrical signals. These signals were sent to an audio mixer, where they were amplified and combined. Engineers monitored the signals, adjusted their levels, and mixed them into a single-channel output. This output was either recorded on a storage medium or broadcast live. An acetate disc was the preferred recording medium until magnetic tape was developed in the late 1940s.

The technical evolution of the music recording studio was slow, however, compared to the film industry. When Walt Disney's film *Fantasia* premiered in 1940, the soundtrack had been recorded on nine separate channels that were mixed down to four channels for theatrical presentation. Multiple-channel recording in the audio studio, however, would not be adopted until stereophonic (two-channel) sound was introduced to the public in the 1950s. Regardless of the format, the components in any recording studio signal chain were, and still are, microphones, audio consoles, recording equipment, and monitor loudspeakers. Peripheral equipment used to modify the audio signal includes equalizers, compressors, limiters, and reverberation chambers.

Microphones and Loudspeakers

Mechanical transducers, such as microphones and loudspeakers, are often considered to be the most critical links in the recording chain. They must accurately convert acoustical sound waves into electrical signals and vice versa. When sound waves strike the diaphragm of a microphone, small electrical currents are created that are proportional to the amount of diaphragm movement. This current, or signal, must be amplified for use. There are literally dozens of microphone types with varying electrical and physical characteristics, ranging from a rather large studio condenser microphone to a subminiature lavalier microphone that is the size of a pencil eraser.

Several characteristics that describe microphones include the type of diaphragm element, the directional pattern of sensitivity, and the frequency response. The element types for most professional applications are dynamic, ribbon, and condenser. Dynamic microphones come in all sizes and shapes, and they are very rugged and utilitarian. Ribbon microphones are more fragile, are more sensitive to low-level sounds, and have a better frequency response than do dynamic microphones. Condenser microphones generally have the widest frequency response, and they are preferred for studio use. They have built-in amplifiers that require external or internal power supplies to operate.

Microphones are sensitive to sounds coming from different directions. Directional sensitivity patterns in the shape of a heart (one direction), a figure-eight (two directions), and a circle (all directions) correspond to the pattern names of unidirectional, bidirectional, and omnidirectional, respectively. Some microphones have variable patterns, and a switch can be used to change the directional characteristics.

The human hearing range or audio spectrum is generally considered to go from 20 Hz (hertz, a unit of frequency) to 20,000 Hz. Although the best microphones should have a comparable frequency response, many sonic variations are acceptable and may even be desirable. Microphones with increased treble response can add brightness in some applications, while those with an increased bass response can enhance vocal performances.

Monitor loudspeakers should be able to reproduce the same audio spectrum but at volumes approaching rock concert level. Sonic variations are not desirable; they can actually overemphasize or mask portions of the musical material, making accurate audio evaluations in the control room somewhat difficult. Many speaker enclosures contain three or more loudspeakers called tweeters, midranges, and woofers. Each is designed to reproduce only a portion of the spectrum: high, middle, or low frequencies, respectively. Some loudspeaker systems use separate amplifiers for high and low frequencies, as well as multiple speakers for each frequency range to ensure the most accurate sound reproduction possible.

The Audio Console

The complexity of an audio recording console may initially be overwhelming, but its basic operations are relatively simple. Regardless of the console size or layout design, there are provisions for assigning inputs to outputs, adjusting the input and output levels, watching the levels on meters, and listening to the entire process on control room loudspeakers. A typical 1960s audio production console contained 24 input modules—each identical to the other—feeding 16 outputs. There were literally hundreds of knobs, switches, meters, and dials spread all over the seven-foot-long control board. Contemporary consoles can contain as many as 96 input modules feeding 48 outputs.

During recording, the signal from a microphone goes to an input/output (I/O) module or channel strip, and its volume and equalization are adjusted. The signal is then assigned to an output bus, or a pan control sends the signal to two output buses to create a stereo effect. Each I/O module includes auxiliary outputs (sends) either for external effects such as echo or for monitoring requirements such as headphone mixes for performers. A special patch point on each I/O module, called an insert jack, permits connection of external signal-processing devices. Compressors or limiters can control input signal dynamics by reducing sudden, extremely loud sounds to more manageable audio levels. Effects processors can create reverberation or delays, or modify virtually any aspect of an audio signal, while different types of equalizers increase or decrease portions of the audio signal. Stanley Alten (1999) separates processors into four categories: spectrum processors that affect the overall tonal balance, time processors that affect the time interval between a signal and its repetition, amplitude processors that affect a signal's dynamic range, and noise processors that reduce tape noise. A VU (volume unit) meter monitors the signal level of each input module, as well as the output buses. Each output bus is connected to a multitrack audio recorder.

After recording, the multitrack master is played back through the same console so the engineer can mix down or combine all the channels into a new master recording. The same signal processing that is available during recording can be used during the mixdown process as well. Trying to get the precise balance, equalization, effects, and stereo panning when mixing down 24 or 48 channels requires hundreds of level and control changes during a short recording. Prior to the development of console automation, recording engineers typically kept detailed logs of all the settings, and numerous rehearsals were required to get the right mix. With automation, a computer captures and stores each console setting change automatically, which greatly simplifies the mixdown process.

The Magnetic Tape Recorder

When Elvis Presley recorded his first demonstration tapes in 1954, an old six-input radio mixer

Country singer Garth Brooks leans on an audio mixing console as he listens to a playback in a recording studio in Nashville, Tennessee. (Nubar Alexanian/Corbis)

and two single-track recorders were all that was needed to launch the career of the "King of Rock-n-Roll." The Beatles recorded their first songs on a two-track tape recorder in 1962, putting all of the instrumentals on one track and the vocals on the second track. As artists demanded more creative flexibility, 16- and 24-track audio recorders using two-inch tape were developed, and by the 1970s, 32-track recorders were common.

Regardless of the number of tracks, all magnetic tape recorders operate on the same principles. A spool of iron-particle recording tape passes across three heads that are aligned in a tape transport. The tape is drawn at a precise speed by the drive mechanism. Each head contains a coil of wire wrapped around layers of steel, called poles. A very narrow gap between the poles focuses a magnetic field on a portion of the recording tape. The first head erases a track on the tape, the second head records a new audio signal on the track that has just been erased, and the third head plays back the recorded track.

A typical professional magnetic recorder can handle 70 dB (decibels, a unit of loudness) of dynamic range. Because the dynamic range of some music—measured as the difference between the loudest passages and no sound—can exceed 120 dB, the quietest passages can be lost in electronic noise. Each time a tape is played back and copied or re-recorded, the level of noise increases relative to the signal. The first noise reduction system, named Dolby after its inventor (Ray Dolby), improved a recorder's signal-to-noise ratio by as much as 20 dB, permitting more extensive re-recording or overdubbing.

Digital Conversion

Analog audio signals consist of continuously changing information with two characteristics: duration (or time) and volume (or amplitude). For example, a musical score visually represents notes of various frequencies that are played over time. The performer determines the appropriate amplitude. This musical information must be converted to digital data for processing and storage. The musical characteristics of time and amplitude correspond to the digital audio characteristics of sampling and quantization in the analog-to-digital (A/D) conversion process.

Sampling takes a snapshot of a musical moment in time, while quantization assigns numerical values to the snapshot information. The sampling rate must be able to capture successfully the highest frequency in the audio spectrum while avoiding sampling errors, so sampling rates have been standardized at 32, 44.1, and 48 kHz (kilohertz) for different digital audio applications.

Quantization uses binary numbers—ones and zeros—to measure the amplitude of an audio signal. These numbers are formed into words, or bits. The bit length determines the accuracy of a measurement. It actually takes a 16-bit word of 65,536 steps to quantize most audio signals. More accurate quantization calls for 20- or 24-bit words (more than 16 million steps). Reverberation devices, equalizers, and dynamics processors often use a 32-bit system to ensure the highest fidelity audio processing.

Along with multiple standards for sampling and quantization to convert analog audio to digital information, there are also standards for communication among digital devices. Signals sent from one machine to another can remain as digital data, rather than having to be converted to analog audio signals for transmission. There are two transmission standards or protocols: professional equipment uses AES/EBU (Audio Engineering Society/European Broadcast Union), while consumer equipment uses S/PDIF (Sony/Philips Digital Interface) for machine-to-machine communication. With one of these protocols, digital signals can be distributed to a number of devices without any degradation or digital-to-analog (D/A) conversion.

Digital Consoles

Digital audio consoles follow the form and function of analog audio consoles, although the inputs are converted directly into digital data before any channel assignment or signal processing occurs. Many consoles feature built-in signal dynamics and effects processing in each channel, rather than having to patch external devices into the desired channels. Full remote control is possi-

ble via the musical instrument digital interface (MIDI) protocol, working with a MIDI controller, sequencer, or computer. The output signals are in the AES/EBU format that can be connected directly to a digital audio recorder, although they must be converted to analog signals for monitoring purposes.

Innovative designs of the latest digital consoles permit I/O module cluster swapping from one console to another, enlarging a 48-channel console to 96 channels or more for a particular recording session. Some digital consoles offer an expansion capability of 200 channels or more. All the controls of any I/O module can be replicated on a central control module, so the recording engineer does not have to move constantly from one end of a ten-foot-long console to the other while making adjustments. Sampling frequencies are as high as 96 kHz to ensure the utmost fidelity.

Digital Recorders

Some digital audiotape machines are based on analog open-reel tape recorder transports that use fixed audio heads (the digital audio stationary head, or DASH, format). Others are based on videotape transports that use rotating heads and cassette tapes. A third group of digital recorders does not use tape at all; these record directly to computer hard drives or other portable storage media such as ZIP disks or magneto-optical (MO) disks.

The DASH machines appear similar to analog machines, and they retain many analog tape machine functions, including editing electronically or by the traditional cut-and-splice method. Either 24 or 48 tracks can be recorded on half-inch tape at 30 ips (inches per second).

The rotary-digital-audiotape (R-DAT or DAT) system has become one of the more popular formats. The miniature size of the DAT tape—about half the size of a standard audiocassette—belies the capabilities of the recording system. The DAT features two record tracks, digital inputs and outputs, high-speed search and cueing, and the capability to record time code for video production. Portable recorders with many of these features can be as small as a paperback book.

Multitrack digital tape recorders, also called modular digital multitrack (MDM) recorders, use two manufacturers' incompatible standards:

ADAT that records on standard S-VHS videotape and DTRS that records on Hi-8-mm videotape. Both types of MDMs feature 8 tracks of recording, external synchronization for videotape editing, and the ability to link several machines together to create a virtual 128-track digital audio recorder (the modular aspect of the name).

Newer machines record directly to a removable computer hard disk, thereby eliminating tape altogether. Some hard-disk recorders feature up to 24 tracks while retaining many of the MDM features. The more advanced hard-disk recorders are capable of 48 tracks, using 24-bit resolution and 96 kHz sampling. Still another type of digital recording format uses various-sized MO disks as the storage media. Personal mixer/recorders use the 2.5-inch MiniDisc to mix and record either 2 tracks or 8 tracks, while the professional MiniDisc recorders have replaced the venerable endless-loop tape cartridges for many broadcast applications. Consumer MiniDisc recorders and players are replacing analog cassette machines as the preferred portable personal format.

Digital Workstations

The digital audio workstation (DAW) is a computer-based audio recording and editing system that replicates every function of an entire recording studio—from the audio console, equalizers, compressors, and effects units to the multitrack recorders and editing controllers. Some systems are designed as computer software programs with plug-in boards for computers (host-based), while others feature custom control surfaces and function as stand-alone units. Various storage media are used with the DAW. These can be MO, ZIP, or internal hard disks, or they can be external MDMs. Because the DAW is a totally integrated system that includes recording, editing, and signal routing and processing, speed of operation and flexibility are superior to similar analog equipment. Control of external tape machines or video recorders, as well as MIDI control of electronic music devices, is often included.

Conclusion

Because the ultimate goal of any studio is to capture an artist's performance with the greatest fidelity and to provide the technical and creative tools that are necessary to produce the final mix, acquiring the right assemblage of analog hardware and digital software can be a never-ending quest. The tools can be a multimillion-dollar studio complex, an inexpensive, personal portable mixer/recorder, or a computer. When producer George Martin worked with the Beatles to create the *Sgt. Pepper's Lonely Hearts Club Band* album in 1967, more than seven hundred hours were spent recording, mixing, and editing on 4-track analog tape recorders to finish the project. Using modern digital equipment, Martin could have significantly reduced the amount of time spent producing that classic recording.

See also: DISNEY, WALT; EDISON, THOMAS ALVA; FILM INDUSTRY, TECHNOLOGY OF; RADIO BROADCASTING, TECHNOLOGY OF; RECORDING INDUSTRY; RECORDING INDUSTRY, HISTORY OF; RECORDING INDUSTRY, PRODUCTION PROCESSES OF.

Bibliography

Alldrin, Loren. (1997). *The Home Studio Guide to Microphones.* Emeryville, CA: MixBooks.

Alten, Stanley R. (1999). *Audio in Media,* 5th edition. Belmont, CA: Wadsworth.

Eargle, John. (1992). *Handbook of Recording Engineering,* 2nd edition. New York: Van Nostrand Reinhold.

Gelatt, Roland. (1977). *The Fabulous Phonograph: 1877–1977,* 2nd edition (revised). New York: Macmillan.

Millard, Andre. (1995). *America on Record.* Cambridge, Eng.: Cambridge University Press.

Pohlman, Ken H. (1998). *Principles of Digital Audio,* 3rd edition. New York: McGraw-Hill.

Read, Oliver, and Welch, Walter L. (1959). *From Tinfoil to Stereo.* Indianapolis, IN: H. W. Sams.

Runstein, Robert E. (1974). *Modern Recording Techniques.* Indianapolis, IN: H. W. Sams.

Runstein, Robert E., and Huber, David M. (1997). *Modern Recording Techniques,* 4th edition. Boston: Focal Press.

Schoenherr, Stephen. (2000). "Recording Technology History." <http://history.acusd.edu/gen/recording/notes.html>.

Woram, John M. (1989). *Sound Recording Handbook.* Indianapolis, IN: H. W. Sams.

JOHN M. HOERNER, JR.

■ RECORDS MANAGEMENT

See: Archives, Public Records, and Records Management

REFERENCE SERVICES AND INFORMATION ACCESS

The term "reference service" is defined simply as personal assistance provided to library users seeking information. Individuals who hold a master's degree in the field of library and information sciences or information studies typically provide the service. Reference librarians are variously referred to as "mediators between the user and the information" and "navigators of the information superhighway." Reference service traditionally has been offered in person at a designated desk within the library building, over the telephone, and through correspondence. More recently, libraries have expanded to offer reference service electronically via the World Wide Web, e-mail, and even two-way videoconferencing. Another form of reference service is classroom and one-on-one instruction in the use of print and electronic resources. Regardless of the delivery method, the value of reference service remains the same: to provide quality information through personalized service to library users at the time of need. Reference service is characterized by human interaction.

The Foundations of Modern Reference Service

The history of reference service is neither as long nor as illustrious as the history of libraries. Samuel Rothstein (1961) noted "May I remind you that in the United States of less than a century ago the library still took no responsibility whatsoever for the provision of personal assistance to its users." Samuel Swett Green, librarian at Worcester Public Library in Massachusetts, is credited with the "founding" of reference. In a paper read at a meeting of the American Library Association and published in *Library Journal* in 1876, Green provided numerous specific examples of questions that required the assistance of a librarian. He used the illustrations to "show that readers in popular libraries need a great deal of assistance." In this way, Green laid the foundation for reference service as it has been practiced ever since. His article noted that although catalogs and indexes are valuable, most users require instruction in their use. Users also must be guided in selecting the books that best meet their information needs. Green highlighted the importance of human interaction in the personal assistance process—librarians must be "easy to get at and pleasant to talk with"

(i.e., approachable), and librarians must mingle freely with users and help them in every way. Green further emphasized that "certain mental qualities are requisite or desirable in library officers who mingle with readers. Prominent among these is a courteous disposition which will disclose itself in agreeable manners. Sympathy, cheerfulness, and patience are needful." He concluded that "a librarian should be as unwilling to allow an inquirer to leave the library with his question unanswered as a shop-keeper is to have a customer go out of his store without making a purchase." This was the beginning of user-centered service. Green based his views on his experience at the Worcester Library, where he observed that the reference room was seldom used. His implementation of the practice of providing personal assistance to library users resulted in an increase in the use of the reference room.

The idea of personal service to users caught on slowly, particularly in academic libraries where it was thought that it was the faculty's role to provide research guidance to the students. The debate raged for years regarding the value of such service. At the heart of the matter was economics—this was just one more service competing for funds. By 1893, a government report identified "personal assistance" as one of the five library primary practices; the other four practices were book selection, classification, cataloging, and planning the building.

The period between World War I and World War II evidenced the growth and specialization of reference services. Beyond face-to-face interaction within a building, questions were handled by telephone and correspondence. Larger libraries installed separate information desks to help users with basic directional and information needs, hired librarians with subject expertise, and established reader advisory services.

Textbooks for students in librarianship programs began to appear by 1902. In 1930, the American Library Association published James I. Wyer's *Reference Work: A Textbook for Students of Library Work and Librarians*. As Green did in 1876, Wyer focused on the humanistic aspects of reference work. He wrote, "[H]ere is a service which defies and transcends machinery. It still is, and always will be, imperative to provide human beings as intermediaries between the reader and the right book. The utmost use of great libraries never can be attained by mechanics." The words continue to be echoed in the writings of modern thinkers on the reference process. *Buildings, Books, and Bytes: Libraries and Communities in the Digital Age* (1996), a report prepared by the Benton Foundation, recommends a high touch, high technology role for librarians, and it encourages greater publicity for the librarian as information navigator with the human touch.

Philosophies of Reference Service

The goal of the reference librarian is to meet the individual need of the user to the fullest extent possible. How and to what extent this is done varies from library to library and depends on the type of library. Academic libraries focus on teaching users how to find information, special libraries primarily find information and package it for their users, and public libraries practice some of both approaches. Special libraries (e.g., for governments, corporations, museums, and newspapers) developed after World War I and emphasized locating information over building and maintaining extensive collections. These were the first type of libraries to make use of online databases to identify appropriate resources. Limits of staffing, subject expertise, and resources prohibit most public and academic libraries from providing similar in-depth service.

In his textbook, Wyer (1930) identified three concepts of reference work. The conservative philosophy instructs users in how to find the information on their own. The liberal philosophy holds that the reference librarian should locate the information for the user and provide it in the form needed. The moderate philosophy recognizes that maximum assistance will be offered based on a combination of library staffing, resources, time factors, and user need. The latter approach balances the instructional function with the full-service mode. Debates on these issues raged in the 1960s and 1970s, but they have abated as reference librarians have determined that a balanced approach takes into account the needs of the user at a particular time.

The Reference Interview

At the center of the interaction between user and librarian is the reference interview, sometimes referred to as "question negotiation." The ability to draw from and work with the users to determine their precise information needs is an art and a science. Entire books have been written on the subject, and reference textbooks generally devote considerable space to this important facet of reference work. The reference interview is the process by which the librarian helps the user to state the information need—listening carefully to the user's responses, asking questions of clarification as necessary, and communicating clearly to move the discussion forward. Important features of the interview include the ability to be objective and nonjudgmental. The librarian must also be sensitive to nonverbal behaviors, as well as alert to signs of frustration that may indicate the need for a change in direction. Flexibility is critical, since what works with one user may not work at all with another. Too many questions from the librarian can lead to user self-doubt and withdrawal—and ultimately to failure in filling the information need. Wyer (1930) said that "there must be in evidence the reassuring psychology of a sympathetic manner, personally and more than casually intent upon and interested in the matter in hand." Wyer also stressed the importance of reading the user's mind: "The aim of library mind-reading, then, is to know how to give people what they do not know they want!"

The Practice of Reference

Reference service has traditionally been offered by librarians at a reference desk. Depending on the library, desks are generally staffed for many hours on all of the days on which the library is open. This structure, although considered by some administrators to be inefficient, has had the advantage of providing service to users at the time of need. In this face-to-face environment, the approachability of the reference librarian is of utmost importance. All of the knowledge in the world will be of little use if the librarian has an unwelcoming demeanor. The librarian's behavior toward the user sets the stage for the success of the interaction. Wyer devoted a chapter of his 1930 textbook to handling reference questions and "meeting the public." His simple list of appropriate behaviors is as applicable today as it was then: "Never appear annoyed or indifferent. Never look or seem too busy to be interrupted. Meet all comers more than half way. Meet the public as you would like to be met in a strange library. Never be patronizing or openly amused. Laugh with a person, but not at him. Never say 'Never heard of such a thing' in a way that might offend." Since the 1930s, many libraries have developed guidelines for service. The Reference and User Services Association (RUSA) of the American Library Association has been a leader in formulating standards for reference services. Two of their major documents are *Guidelines for Information Services* (2000) and *Guidelines for Behavioral Performance of Reference and Information Services Professionals* (1996). The latter set of guidelines addresses approachability, interest, listening/inquiring, searching, and follow-up. In all interactions, the user should be made to feel a partner in the transaction.

Once the librarian and the user have agreed on the nature of the question, the librarian begins the search process. If the question is factual, such as biographical or geographical, the librarian will determine which source might provide the best answer in the quickest manner. That source may be printed or electronic, or it may entail a telephone call or e-mail to another librarian, library, or agency. If it is an open-ended inquiry, as are most questions by those people who are undertaking research on a subject, the librarian will work with the user on a search strategy, suggesting resources and instructing in their use. The librarian will often provide guidance to the user in deciding which books, articles, or Internet sources provide the most relevant information given the scope of the topic and the level of information that is required. Research questions generally involve far more instruction than factual questions.

The telephone was the first electronic device to be used in reference services. Librarians quickly adopted it for use in providing service, but they have always had mixed feelings about its place. Most libraries locate their telephone reference service at the reference desk, so the librarian must juggle the in-person inquiries with those coming via telephone. Libraries often have a policy that the on-site person receives assistance before the caller, so the telephone goes unanswered. A number of public libraries operate their telephone reference service separately from the desk, advertising it as an "answer line" or "quick reference." Callers who need research assistance are generally asked to come to the library. Librarian interaction with the telephone user is more challenging than in-person communication. Cues must be obtained from voice level and intonation. The librarian needs to determine quickly the information need, determine whether or not to put the caller on hold or call back, and decide when a call should be referred.

Reference by correspondence is another form of reference service, but it has never enjoyed the same popularity as on-site or telephone reference. Much of the correspondence that is received by libraries entails questions that are related to genealogy or special collections. Much of this mail correspondence has been replaced by e-mail inquiries. Most libraries provide e-mail reference service, with policies following those that were already established for telephone and correspondence service. Reference librarians have found the reference interview to be problematic in the e-mail environment, since the interaction is asynchronous and it may take several days to elicit all of the information that is needed to respond satisfactorily to the inquiry.

In many academic institutions, reference librarians offer consultation services by appointment. This provides yet another option to users who need more time with a librarian than is generally available at the reference desk. In addition, the librarian has an opportunity to prepare for the session in advance.

Technology has had a major effect on reference services. Although the growing number of printed indexes made it possible to identify journal articles in many subject areas, the user had to wade through each year's index separately and search by prescribed subject headings or by the name of the author. Card catalogs allowed searching by title, author, and subject, but again, the subject headings were prescribed and users often had to seek the assistance of a librarian to identify the correct heading. In the 1960s, online databases were available only in the science areas, and they were used primarily in corporate libraries. Their use in academic and public libraries did not become common until the 1970s, when selected staff was trained. By the 1980s, the increase in the number of requests for online searching and the growth in the number of databases required that most reference librarians receive training. The searching was not performed by the user, and often, a fee was charged. Librarians began to experiment with the notion of end-user searching, but that did not occur until databases became available on CD-ROM. By the late 1990s, many libraries moved from CD-ROM to providing databases through the Internet. These databases encompass several years of indexing and offer a variety of searching options. Many also include the full text of the article, making searching by keyword rather than prescribed subject heading a powerful tool. The conversion of card catalogs to online catalogs has enabled librarians and users to find books by keyword as well. Modern reference librarians provide a strong link between the highly technological information environment and the user, advising on search strategies that help the user to focus the topic better and evaluate the information even as the user is able to access library catalogs and databases from home, office, and school.

Readers' Advisory Services

Of the many aspects of human mediated information services, recommending books to library users has long been a function of library services, primarily in public libraries. In the 1920s, libraries in Chicago, Cincinnati, Cleveland, Detroit, Indianapolis, Milwaukee, Portland (Oregon), and New York established what is known as readers' advisory services. Librarians interviewed readers to determine their interests, and the readers were also judged on their reading ability. Following the interview, a list of readings was prepared and mailed to the reader. Readers' advisory services expanded from 1936 to 1940. A number of articles written during this time exhibited a moralistic tone, assuming that reading recommendations would result in the improvement of readers. After 1949, the readers' advisory function declined, but it is enjoying a resurgence in the early 2000s. The focus is centered on the reader and emphasizes the personal relationship between librarian and reader. The service is less didactic, with librarians viewing themselves as the link between readers and their recreational reading interests. Forms of readers' advisory services are also offered in other venues, such as Amazon.com and Oprah Winfrey's book club. The former retains data about customers' reading interests to alert them to related books. Storing information about users' preferences jeopardizes their privacy, however, making it difficult for libraries to compete with commercial services.

User Education

User education, variously called "bibliographic instruction" or "library instruction," has in the past been the purview of academic libraries, but it

has since been encompassed by public libraries. The service, which is generally a part of the reference librarians' responsibilities, is considered to be complementary to desk service.

Lizabeth A. Wilson (1995) identifies four periods in the development of user education services. The first, between 1850 to 1920, saw slow growth as the focus of librarians was on building collections, not on service. An early pioneer in user education was Azariah Root, who ran a program at Oberlin College between 1899 and 1927 in order to introduce students to library systems, resources, and the history of the printed word. Public and academic libraries experimented with instruction through lectures and at the reference desk. The second period identified by Wilson, between 1920 and the 1970s, laid the foundation for instructional services. Notable during this time was the Monteith College Library Experiment at Wayne State University, which provided discipline-specific library instruction as an integrated part of the university's curriculum. One of the most significant developments in the 1970s was the shift from tool-based to concept-based instruction, as librarians realized that students needed a systematic way to develop, use, and evaluate a search strategy. This was also a period during which librarians drew upon learning theories and explored and debated a number of instruction techniques. The third period identified by Wilson occurred in the 1980s, when instruction became an accepted part of public services in libraries. By the fourth period, the post-1980s period, instruction had established itself as a field with its own literature, organizations, theories, and history. Librarians who are involved in instruction regularly draw upon current learning theory and instructional techniques. The term "information literacy" is widely used to refer to the entire scope of user education. In 1988, the American Association of School Librarians developed *Information Power*, which outlines standards and guidelines for user education programs in school library media centers. The 1999 edition includes information literacy standards for student learning. In 2000, the Association of College and Research Libraries issued "Information Literacy Competency Standards for Higher Education." Public libraries have increased their user education programs as well. Sessions are offered in those subject areas that are most heavily used by the public (e.g., genealogy and business resources) and in general areas (e.g., learning how to search the World Wide Web and evaluate the results). The teaching role of the reference librarian is very important, since it encourages users to use creativity in their searches and to evaluate the results from a critical perspective. User education can also serve to heighten user awareness of the library.

Models of Reference Service

Despite the advances wrought by technology, the structure and organization of reference service has changed little since its inception. Services continue to be tied to the physical desk, requiring that users come into the building for assistance. In 1992, a new model was proposed by Virginia Massey-Burzio of Brandeis University. She experimented with tiered reference service within the building, staffing a service desk with graduate students who were to refer complex questions to a librarian who was available in a consultation office. In 1993, Anne Lipow offered institutes devoted to "rethinking reference services," at which a number of speakers challenged reference librarians to examine whether or not their current structures best met the needs of users. Tiered models often failed, not because they were without merit or because they were inefficient, but because they were contrary to the deeply ingrained reference librarian value of providing quality service when users need it without barriers and because they required significant training of staff to ensure that inquiries were answered correctly.

Jerry Campbell, the then director of libraries at Duke University, outlined a new role for reference librarians in a controversial article published in the *Reference Services Review* in 1992. Campbell observed that reference service is essentially without a conceptual framework, lacks a clear mission statement, and is cost ineffective. He observed that the model of reference focused on a physical desk could not survive the information age. Campbell noted that users' expectations of service were changing and that the demand for rapid delivery of information in electronic form was growing. He challenged reference librarians to create a service that is "increasingly electronic and nonbuilding-centered." Although much of what he envisioned has occurred, the reference desk remains in the center of reference services.

In an article published in 2000, Chris Ferguson calls for the integration of reference and computing support services into a comprehensive information service for both on-site and remote users. The line between what is a pure technology question and what is an information question has blurred as they have become intertwined and interdependent. The concept of tiered service needs to be refined, making intermediate-level service available twenty-four hours a day. Ferguson emphasizes the need in this convergence to retain the values of equity of access, personal service, and services tailored to the individual in ways that are humane and scalable. He calls for reengineering libraries "in ways that bring librarians and technologists together within a common service environment" to meet users' needs in a more effective manner.

Reference Referral Centers and Networks

Some states and regional library networks offer tiered reference services, which allow reference librarians to refer questions to another level when they do not have the resources to respond to their users' needs. California is a good example of a state that has a strong referral system. Formal reference referral in California began in 1967, with the founding of the Bay Area Reference Center (BARC), which was funded by a Library Services and Construction Act grant to the San Francisco Public Library. Public libraries in the Bay Area could refer questions they were unable to answer to BARC, which drew on the collections of the San Francisco Public Library, as well as numerous sources beyond those walls. In 1969, the Southern California Answering Network (SCAN) was born, serving all of Southern California. By the mid-1970s, public libraries were organized into fifteen systems under the provisions of the California Library Services Act. As part of the act, each of the fifteen systems established a System Reference Center. Considered to be second-level reference, Centers were designed to work with the public libraries in their systems to ensure that the needs of users could be met regardless of physical location and to facilitate document delivery through the member libraries. The Centers provided training to local librarians, focusing on basic services and on those reference tools that are typically held in small public libraries. They became a primary conduit for questions to the third-level centers, BARC and SCAN. Although BARC and SCAN no longer exist, second-level reference service is still operating, and the involved reference centers collaborate in answering inquiries.

Many of the referral centers serve all types of libraries. They may be funded through state funds, through membership fees, or a combination of the two. The advantages of referral are many, with the strongest being the ability to answer even the most difficult questions received from users. Reference service at referral centers is characterized by creativity and the use of a wide range of resources and methods that are not generally employed in traditional reference settings. Personal contacts, organizations, associations, and businesses are often called on to provide answers that are not easily found in printed books or even on the Internet. Referral center librarians seldom work directly with users; they instead expect that the local librarian has done a thorough reference interview. Referral centers take advantage of the combined strengths of libraries and reference librarians. Resource sharing, collaboration, and cooperation among libraries of all types create a whole that is greater than the sum of its parts.

Fee-Based Reference Services

Users who have no time to devote to large research projects have the option of turning to a fee-based reference service. Although not widespread, some large public and academic libraries offer such a service. This is considered a value-added service that provides the research requested by the user, along with delivery of the cited documents. Users generally pay an hourly fee, in addition to charges for photocopying and mailing the resulting materials. The primary users of fee-based services are corporations and law firms that do not have their own libraries. They view information as a commodity and consider it worthwhile to pay for the service. Individuals often use fee-based services on a one-time basis for a special project, such as tracking down genealogy material, researching job opportunities, or seeking funding for college.

The Future of Reference Services

The advent of e-mail, the World Wide Web, and other new technologies has had a major effect on the provision of reference services. In the late 1990s, reports indicated that the number of in-person and telephone reference transactions had sharply decreased. The ability of many library users to access information via the web contributed to this decline, as did the growth of commercial services that offer to answer questions on almost any subject without charge. Many of these services do not employ librarians and rely solely on web resources to provide information. Questions are often taken at face value, with little or no follow-up communication with the inquirer to discover the real information need. Lacking the financial resources of commercial entities and working within the often bureaucratic structures of libraries, reference librarians nevertheless have moved rapidly and tirelessly to offer a variety of information service options to their users.

The combination of users connected to the Internet and a growing emphasis on distance learning places a demand on reference services to expand aggressively beyond the walls of the library. Although a number of Internet companies exist to provide answers to questions, they are not equipped to provide in-depth advice, access to sometimes costly databases that are restricted by licensing agreements, or assistance with complex search strategies. Reference librarians can play a unique role in this area, developing methods with online technologies to assist users with difficult questions, to offer guidance on research strategies, to instruct users in evaluation techniques, and to provide services customized to the users' needs. Digital reference removes the barriers of time and place, and it masks the internal operations of the library to which users are exposed in an on-site visit.

Reference librarians in the early 2000s are experimenting with a variety of new technologies designed to respond to user inquiries. Reference via e-mail has been practiced since the early 1990s and has expanded to include web forms that guide the user through the inquiry. Software that enables the librarian to work collaboratively with the user and to guide the web browser in providing searching assistance is being applied in some library settings. Susan McGlamery and Steve Coffman (2000) write that although it is too early to determine the effectiveness of such web contact center software, it may be readily adaptable to the new reference environment, which uses a number of web resources to answer inquiries. In an article published in 2001, Coffman notes that a combination of web contact center software and Voice over Internet Protocol (VoIP) shows promise for reference services. The application would allow the reference librarian to guide the user through web searches and hold a voice conversation through the same web connection, as though they were talking over the telephone. This technology would also solve some of the challenges that the digital environment presents in conducting an effective reference interview.

Joseph Janes (1998), a faculty member in the School of Information at the University of Washington, was one of the first to be involved in digital reference service. In 1995, Janes taught at the University of Michigan and wanted to provide his students with a laboratory for learning and doing reference and at the same time merge the strengths of the traditional, physical library with the virtual and timeless features of the World Wide Web. Thus was born the Internet Public Library (IPL). Janes specializes in researching the use, integration, and effect of digital reference services.

A number of other library-based and commercial digital reference services were established beginning in the early 1990s. David Lankes (1998), a pioneer in the field of electronic reference services, defines digital reference as Internet-based question and answer services that connect users with individuals who possess specialized subject or skill expertise. Digital reference services are often called "AskA services" because of the names of services such as Ask A Scientist. Many of these services cater to kindergarten through high school students. One example of such a service is KidsConnect, a project of the American Association of School Librarians.

On a large scale, the Library of Congress, in cooperation with a number of reference service providers, is experimenting internationally with a cooperative web-based reference service called the Collaborative Digital Reference Service. The goal of the project is to provide a service that is available seven days a week and twenty-four hours a day to users around the world. Libraries in North America, Australia, Europe, and Asia are part of the pilot program. The service combines the strengths of local library collections and staff with those of librarians around the world.

Stuart Sutton, in a 1996 article discussing the future roles of reference librarians, comments that "a library's principle goal is the creation of a context that increases the probability that the user will find the information he or she needs," regardless of whether this is through face-to-face service or through technological means. Reference librarians provide the value and context to information, helping users to ferret out what they need, providing instruction to guide the work, and teaching evaluation skills.

Electronic reference is the future, and reference librarians need to be actively involved in the development of systems that ensure quality and retain the human element. Technology affords reference librarians the opportunity to work internationally to provide timely, accurate, and expert reference services to all users. A major challenge facing reference librarians is the ability to retain the value of performing reference work as a highly personalized service in a largely digital environment.

See also: CATALOGING AND KNOWLEDGE ORGANIZATION; INTERNET AND THE WORLD WIDE WEB; KNOWLEDGE MANAGEMENT; LIBRARIANS; LIBRARIES, FUNCTIONS AND TYPES OF; LIBRARIES, DIGITAL; LIBRARIES, HISTORY OF; LIBRARIES, NATIONAL; LIBRARY ASSOCIATIONS AND CONSORTIA; LIBRARY AUTOMATION; RETRIEVAL OF INFORMATION.

Bibliography

American Association of School Librarians. (1988). *Information Power: Guidelines for School Library Media Programs.* Chicago: American Library Association.

American Association of School Librarians. (1998). *Information Power: Building Partnerships for Learning.* Chicago: American Library Association.

Association of College and Research Libraries. (2000). "Information Literacy Competency Standards for Higher Education." <http://www.ala.org/acrl/ilcomstan. html>.

Benton Foundation. (1996). *Buildings, Books, and Bytes: Libraries and Communities in the Digital Age.* Washington, DC: Benton Foundation.

Bunge, Charles. (1980). "Reference Services." In *ALA World Encyclopedia of Library and Information Services,* ed. Robert Wedgeworth. Chicago: American Library Association.

Campbell, Jerry D. (1992). "Shaking the Conceptual Foundations of Reference: A Perspective." *Reference Services Review* 20:29–36.

Coffman, Steve. (2001). "Distance Education and Virtual Reference: Where Are We Headed?" *Computers in Libraries* 21:21–25.

Ferguson, Chris. (2000). "Shaking the Conceptual Foundations, Too: Integrating Research and Technology Support for the Next Generation of Information Service." *College and Research Libraries* 61:300–311.

Ferguson, Chris, and Bunge, Charles. (1997). "The Shape of Services to Come: Values-Based Reference Service for the Largely Digital Library." *College and Research Libraries* 58:252–265.

Green, Samuel Swett. (1876). "Personal Relations Between Librarians and Readers." *American Library Journal* 1:74–81.

Internet Public Library. (2001). "The Internet Public Library." <http://www.ipl.org/>.

Janes, Joseph. (1998). "The Internet Public Library: An Intellectual History." *Library Hi Tech* 16:55–68.

Lankes, R. David. (1998). *AskA Starter Kit: How to Build and Maintain Digital Reference Services*. Syracuse: ERIC Clearinghouse on Information and Technology.

Library of Congress. (2001). "Collaborative Digital Reference Services." <http://www.loc.gov/rr/digiref/>.

Lipow, Anne Grodzins, ed. (1993). *Rethinking Reference in Academic Libraries*. Berkeley, CA: Library Solutions Press.

Massey-Burzio, Virginia. (1992). "Reference Encounters of a Different Kind: A Symposium." *Journal of Academic Librarianship* 18:276–286.

McGlamery, Susan, and Coffman, Steve. (2000). "Moving Reference to the Web." *Reference and User Services Quarterly*. 39:380–386.

Reference and User Services Association. (1996). "Guidelines for Behavioral Performance of Reference and Information Services Professionals." <http://www.ala.org/rusa/stnd_behavior.html>.

Reference and User Services Association. (2000). "Guidelines for Information Services." <http://www.ala.org/rusa/stnd_consumer.html>.

Rothstein, Samuel. (1961). "Reference Services: The New Dimension in Librarianship." *College and Research Libraries* 22:11–18.

Saricks, Joyce G., and Brown, Nancy. (1997). *Readers' Advisory Service in the Public Library*, 2nd edition. Chicago: American Library Association.

Sutton, Stuart A. (1996). "Future Service Models and the Convergence of Functions: The Reference Librarian as Technician, Author, and Consultant." *Reference Librarian* 54:125–143.

Wilson, Lizabeth A. (1995). "Instruction as a Reference Service." In *Reference and Information Services: An Introduction*, ed. Richard E. Bopp and Linda C. Smith. Englewood, CO: Libraries Unlimited.

Wyer, James I. (1930). *Reference Work: A Textbook for Students of Library Work and Librarians*. Chicago: American Library Association.

NANCY HULING

REGULATION

See: Broadcasting, Government Regulation of; Broadcasting, Self-Regulation of; Cable Television, Regulation of; Telephone Industry, Regulation of

■ RELATIONSHIPS, STAGES OF

William B. Gudykunst and his colleagues (1995) have argued that a stage model of relationship development is built on the assumption that relationships are characterized by patterns and regularities that are relatively consistent across relationships. This type of model helps to explain the general patterns that are involved in developing intimacy with others.

The model presented by Mark Knapp and Anita Vangelisti (2000) has gained wide acceptance in the field of communication. This model of relationship development consists of five stages of "coming together" (initiating, experimenting, intensifying, integrating, and bonding) and five stages of "coming apart" (differentiating, circumscribing, stagnating, avoiding, and terminating) and can be applied to both friendships and romantic relationships. It is important to remember that this model is descriptive, not prescriptive. In other words, this model does not describe what should happen in a relationship; it merely describes what researchers have observed in numerous studies of interpersonal relationships. Some relationships skip stages, while others move back and forth between two or more stages. Thus, this stage model of relationship development focuses on the consistent overall pattern that tends to occur as interpersonal relationships develop and potentially deteriorate over time.

Coming Together

The coming together stages usually begin with initiating, in which the participants in a potential relationship first meet and interact with each other. Most people tend to follow the "scripts" they have learned for meeting people at this stage. This is the "hello, how are you, it's nice to meet you" stage in which the participants make initial judgments about each other, such as "he seems friendly" or "she seems interesting."

In the experimenting stage, the participants try to reduce their uncertainty about each other. Small talk is the predominant form of communication, and a wide variety of topics may be covered in a superficial way. Knapp and Vangelisti consider small talk to be an "audition for friendship" in which the participants identify topics of mutual interest that they feel comfortable talking about. These topics help people identify areas of similarity that can form the basis for a developing relationship.

During the intensifying stage, the participants increase the information they disclose to each other. This step may make the participants feel more vulnerable because their disclosure can potentially be rejected by the other person. For example, one person may be ready to say "I think I'm falling in love with you," but the other person may not have reached this level of feeling, yet. Forms of address become more informal at this point, and generally affectionate terms may be used.

The intensifying stage is followed by the integrating stage, in which the participants begin to arrange their daily lives around each other and become involved in each other's social networks. The relationship begins to become visible to others. Interaction increases in frequency (e.g., daily telephone calls instead of weekly ones), and references to past conversations increase ("Remember when we . . . ").

Finally, the bonding stage involves a public ritual that signifies a formal commitment to the relationship. This involves actions such as getting engaged, moving in together, or getting married.

Coming Apart

Although many relationships remain at the bonding stage, some relationships do come apart. The coming apart stages begin with differentiating, in which the partners begin to recognize their differences and are unhappy with the realization. Fighting or conflict may occur as the partners begin to feel a growing interpersonal distance.

Constricted communication occurs during the circumscribing stage. Partners restrict their communication to "safe areas" in which they know they can agree. Controversial topics are avoided, and there is little depth to the conversations. The partners may exchange little personal information during their interactions with each other, but they are still able to maintain the public facade of a healthy relationship.

Stagnating occurs when the expectation of unpleasant conversations begins to emerge, along with the feeling that there is little to say to the other person. The partners avoid talking about the relationship at this point because they believe there is nothing to gain by further discussion.

In the avoiding stage, partners reorganize their lives so that they can minimize interaction with each other. Sometimes the partners try to avoid each other, or they directly state their desires, such as "I don't want to talk to you anymore."

Finally, the terminating stage involves physically and psychologically leaving the relationship. This stage may occur very quickly, or it may take a number of years for it to be accomplished. One partner may decide to move out, or both people may agree to stop contacting each other. Messages at this stage of a relationship are designed to create distance between people ("Please don't call me.") or to prepare for life without the other person (saying "I" or "me" instead of "we" when talking about certain topics with others).

Movement Between Stages

Knapp and Vangelisti argue that movement through the stages of relationship development tends to be systematic and sequential. That is, coming together or coming apart occurs in the order in which these stages are described above. Nevertheless, participants can skip stages in either coming together or coming apart.

In addition, movement through the stages may be either forward toward greater intimacy or backward toward less intimacy. Movement forward or backward may also increase in speed if both participants in the relationship want it to change. In other words, if both participants want to become more intimate, the relationship will change faster than if one participant is unsure of his or her feelings.

Conclusion

Understanding the ways in which relationships develop and potentially disintegrate is extremely important for people who live in a world that is based on interpersonal relationships. Individuals spend a significant amount of their time thinking about, being involved in, and attempting to maintain their relationships with others. Understanding how these relationships develop helps clarify ways in which relationships can be improved or terminated if necessary. In addition, it is important to realize the patterned nature of relationships so individuals may understand the commonalities among their relationships and those of others.

Terminating relationships is often a painful task but a common occurrence in the world of interpersonal communication. Understanding that others have gone through this experience in similar ways may help individuals cope with this distressing event. In addition, individuals who are contemplating ending a relationship may derive help by knowing what to expect as a relationship enters its terminating stages.

Understanding interpersonal communication, and especially the stages of interpersonal relationships, is a complex task, but one that may result in more fulfilling interpersonal relationships.

See also: INTERPERSONAL COMMUNICATION; INTERPERSONAL COMMUNICATION, CONVERSATION AND; RELATIONSHIPS, TYPES OF.

Bibliography

Conville, Richard L., and Rogers, L. Edna, eds. (1998). *The Meaning of "Relationship" in Interpersonal Communication.* Westport, CT: Praeger.

Gudykunst, William B.; Ting-Toomey, Stella; Sudweeks, Sandra; and Stewart, Lea P. (1995). *Building Bridges: Interpersonal Skills for a Changing World.* Boston: Houghton Mifflin.

Knapp, Mark L., and Vangelisti, Anita L. (2000). *Interpersonal Communication and Human Relationships,* 4th ed. Boston: Allyn & Bacon.

Montgomery, Barbara M., and Baxter, Leslie A., eds. (1998). *Dialectical Approaches to Studying Personal Relationships.* Mahwah, NJ: Lawrence Erlbaum.

Nussbaum, Jon F. (2000). *Communication and Aging,* 2nd ed. Mahwah, NJ: Lawrence Erlbaum.

LEA P. STEWART

▣ RELATIONSHIPS, TYPES OF

In general, researchers in communication define close or intimate interpersonal relationships as "friendships," "romantic relationships," "marital relationships," and "family relationships." These types of relationships are often characterized by interdependence (i.e., doing things together and feeling like part of a relationship) and mutual definition (e.g., introducing someone as "my friend").

Friendships

Friendships are social relationships in which the participants feel comfortable engaging in activities together and generally define their participation on an equal basis. Friendships are based on self-disclosure in which the participants feel free to share their thoughts and feelings about a variety of issues. Self-disclosure in friendships is particularly significant for women. For men, however, friendships may revolve around mutual activities such as sports or game playing.

In general, people assume that their friends will "be there" for them in a crisis or at other times when they need social support. Since friendship is voluntary, people are able to choose their friends and to decide when the friendship is no longer worth maintaining. People can maintain friendships over long distances through mediated contact such as telephone calls. Long-distance friendship is made even easier through electronic forms of communication such as e-mail.

William Rawlins (1992) has developed a dialectical theory of friendships that helps to explain how people can remain individuals while still being part of a friendship and loyal to the other person in the relationship. He believes that friendships involve tensions between competing responsibilities. For example, teenagers in certain situations may feel a conflict between remaining an individual and being a good friend. If a teenager's friend engages in a behavior that is not supported by the teenager, a tension may arise between loyalty to oneself as an individual and loyalty to the friendship. He also notes that friendships change as people grow older.

Romantic Relationships

Simply put, romantic relationships involve love. Romantic relationships are intimate (i.e., individuals feel connected to each other) and exhibit shared values (i.e., individuals agree on a number of important issues).

The individuals in this type of relationship may feel that they are getting more from the relationship than they are contributing. For example, the popular phrase "you complete me" may characterize the feelings of an individual in a romantic relationship. Dating has become more egalitarian over the years as it has become increasingly acceptability for women to ask men for a date and to pay at least their share of the dating expenses.

Leslie Baxter and William Wilmot (1984) have identified several "secret tests" that people in romantic relationships may use to test their partners. These tests include indirect suggestion (e.g., flirting to see if the partner responds), public presentation (e.g., introducing the other person as "my boy/girlfriend" to see how the person reacts), separation (e.g., spending time apart to test the strength of the relationship), and third-party questioning (e.g., asking a friend to find out the other person's feelings).

Romantic relationships may become institutionalized through marriage, dissolve, or remain as an intense connection between people.

Marital Relationships

Mary Ann Fitzpatrick (1988) has conducted extensive research on communication in marriage and divides marital relationships into three types: traditional marriages, independent marriages, and separate marriages.

Traditional marriages involve individuals who hold traditional views about the roles of men and women in relationships. The participants are highly interdependent and believe in concepts such as the man as breadwinner and woman as caretaker of the children. Companionship is important to traditional couples, and they tend to follow regular daily schedules that contribute to consistency in the relationship (e.g., the wife cooks dinner at approximately the same time each night).

Independent marriages are characterized by more nontraditional values in which the participants maintain a high degree of autonomy. Although there is an emphasis on companionship, the spouses may maintain independent spaces and not follow regular daily schedules. There is a great deal of negotiation in this type of relationship as the spouses continually negotiate their roles (e.g., whose turn it is to cook dinner on a given night).

Separate marriages are composed of individuals who may have a fairly traditional view of marriage but are not particularly interdependent. There is less sharing and companionship in separate marriages than in either traditional or independent marriages. The spouses in a separate marriage may try to persuade each other to do something, but they drop the idea if it looks like further attempts at persuasion will lead to conflict.

According to Fitzpatrick, 60 percent of married couples fit into one of these three categories. This means that both people in the relationship share the same characteristics. If the individuals in the relationship have different orientations, their union is categorized as a mixed-type marriage, such as separate–traditional, independent–separate, or traditional–independent. It should be kept in mind that the purpose of this scheme is to categorize couple types, not to determine the likelihood of marital happiness. Fitzpatrick maintains that no one type of marital relationship is more satisfactory than another type and that she has found satisfied individuals in all types of relationships.

Family Relationships

Family relationships are those relationships created among parents and children by birth, adoption, marriage, or life partnering. This means that unlike the other relationships discussed in this entry, family relationships, from a child's perspective, are not voluntary.

Many communication theorists have contended that the communication patterns people learn from their families are maintained throughout their lives. These families, according to Kathleen Galvin and Bernard Brommel (1999), are systems that need communication in order to adapt to their environments, including the communities in which they live, the educational systems they may be a part of, and the political and legal systems in which they exist. Because of the systemic nature of families, individuals in families adapt to their family, and the family, in turn, is influenced by their behavior. Galvin and Brommel contend that most families have sets of "rules" about behavior. These rules govern, among other things, what can and cannot be discussed (e.g., it is not appropriate to discuss a family member's tendency to abuse alcohol), how various topics are discussed (e.g., it is more important to tell the truth than to worry about hurting someone's feelings), and who can be told what (e.g., children should not be involved in discussions of their parents' health problems).

Because the rules can vary from one family to the next, conflict or other difficulties may occur when people from families with very different sets of rules get married and try to establish their own family.

Conclusion

This discussion has focused on the types of relationships that are typical of North American cultures. Although these types of relationships can be found in most other cultures, the specific norms and rules for conducting these relationships may vary—particularly in terms of appropriate communication behavior within a particular relationship type.

Understanding the types of relationships that characterize human experience is important to all people given the relational nature of human existence. It would be impossible to function in the world without these types of relationships. Most children are born into a family structure and are significantly affected by it throughout their lives. Friendships play a major role in the social activities of many individuals. Romantic relationships are important sources of interpersonal satisfaction throughout the life course. Knowing some of the sources of tension in these relationships, as well as the commonalities across relationship types, will foster individual growth and satisfaction.

See also: INTERPERSONAL COMMUNICATION; RELATIONSHIPS, STAGES OF.

Bibliography

Baxter, Leslie A., and Wilmot, William W. (1984). "'Secret Tests': Social Strategies for Acquiring Information about the State of Relationship." *Human Communication Research* 11:171–201.

Fitzpatrick, Mary Ann. (1988). *Between Husbands and Wives: Communication in Marriage.* Newbury Park, CA: Sage Publications.

Galvin, Kathleen M. and Brommel, Bernard J. (1999). *Family Communication: Cohesion and Change*, 5th ed. Reading, MA: Addison-Wesley.

Rawlins, William K. (1992). *Friendship Matters: Communication, Dialectics, and the Life Course.* New York: Aldine de Gruyter.

LEA P. STEWART

■ RELIGION AND THE MEDIA

Religious freedom is as integral a part of American cultural heritage as is freedom of speech. It is, therefore, not surprising that religious content can be traced to the onset of every form of mass communication technology and has evolved as American media has evolved. As popular media became distinctly evangelistic in their business practices, hoping to convert consumers to their respective medium to maximize ratings or increase readership, religious content turned entrepreneurial. As entertainment formats proved increasingly effective in capturing audiences, religious expression mimicked the methods of secular media, becoming increasingly high profile and, in turn, controversial.

Since the birth of mass communication, religious institutions have believed in the power of modern technology and in technology's ability to communicate the importance of faith. One of the first printed texts produced upon the introduction of movable type to the Western world in the 1400s was the Gutenberg Bible. Today, religious book publishing is a billion-dollar business, producing more than 175 million texts a year. Consumer magazines such as the *Christian Herald* and newspapers such as the *Boston Recorder* helped shape the developing American press in the 1800s. Today there are approximately 111,000 periodicals around the world, one-tenth of which are published in the United States, and one-tenth of those published in the United States—including *Christianity Today*—are religious in nature. With the advent of radio, religious expression found a voice of unparalleled reach. Religious broadcasting became even more powerful with the popularization of television and development of cable.

The Electronic Church

Religious broadcasting began as an experiment. On Christmas Eve 1909, voice transmission pioneer Reginald Fessenden demonstrated the practical utility of radiotelegraphy by reading passages of the Bible to ships at sea. The first radio church service was broadcast just two months after KDKA in Pittsburgh became the nation's first licensed radio station in 1921. Of the six hundred stations in operation by 1925, more than sixty were licensed to religious organizations. Many religious groups regarded radio as a means of promoting and enhancing local ministries; others debated the suitability of electronic media for religious expression. However, according to religious media scholar Quentin Schultze (1990, p. 25), the evangelical church was interested in radio as the best means to "catechize its youth, evangelize the unsaved, defend the faith, and organize religious institutions." The evangelicals—an umbrella term for Protestants who stress a conservative doctrine and literal interpretation of the Bible—regarded technology as God's gift for their work in spreading the gospel.

Finding it necessary to take control over an increasingly chaotic radio industry, the government issued the Radio Act of 1927 and assigned frequencies and licenses "as public convenience, interest, and necessity requires." According to policy, religious stations did not serve the public interest as well as their commercial counterparts, so, by 1928, many religious stations were reassigned low-powered frequencies or they had ceased operation. It is interesting to note that the airing of religious programming on commercial stations met public interest requirements for broadcast licenses. Thus, while fewer than thirty religious stations remained on the air by 1933, more than 8 percent of all programming was still religious in nature thanks to the free, or sustaining, airtime offered to mainstream Protestant, Jewish, and Catholic organizations and to the airtime sold to evangelical groups and others.

The result was an odd blend of religious fare. In order to appease the commercial stations and their networks, local houses of worship accepted free airtime in exchange for poor time slots and a lack of creative freedom. Programmers for paid time, however, experimented with various fundraising strategies to pay for airtime and a variety of programming formats to attract audiences. By the early 1940s, several innovative paid-time programs became nationwide successes. Charles E. Fuller's *Old Fashioned Revival Hour*, for example, was carried on 456 stations, 60 percent of all the licensed stations in the country. Walter Maier's *The Lutheran Hour* was regularly heard by approximately twelve million people.

Televangelism

As with radio, the television networks agreed to give free airtime to the three major faiths through centralized organizations and to allow others to purchase airtime. Long-running and award-winning programs such as *Lamp Unto My Feet* (CBS) began production in the early 1950s. However, in 1960, the Federal Communications Commission ruled that stations did not have to give away airtime to meet public interest requirements. This declaration was followed by a precipitous drop in the proportion of religious programming that was sustaining time, from 47 percent in 1959 to only 8 percent in 1977.

Many mainstream religious organizations chose not to pay for airtime that was once free,

resulting in a corresponding growth in the number of evangelical programs. As a means to facilitate more cost-effective program distribution, some evangelical ministries created their own networks by acquiring failing and relatively inexpensive UHF television stations. Others hooked up with cable, which offered increased market opportunities and better quality reception for their programs. The first religious cable network was the Christian Broadcasting Network (CBN) which, in the early 1980s, reached thirty million cable subscribers, making it not only the largest Christian cable operation at that time but the fifth largest cable operation of any kind. The structural changes in and sudden growth of religious broadcasting had a profound effect on the nature of religious fare in many ways.

Prime Time Preachers

The power of personality-driven religious programming was best demonstrated by Roman Catholic Bishop Fulton J. Sheen. His *Life is Worth Living* (Dumont) and *Mission to the World* (ABC) programs in the early- and mid-1950s were among the few religious shows ever aired during prime time. The success of these programs, along with the entrepreneurial individualism embraced by evangelicalism, led to the development of large media organizations headed by identifiable, charismatic individuals. By the early 1970s, the perceived truth of the gospels of media ministries was often associated with the personality and achievements of the individual ministry leader. According to religious television scholars Jeffrey Hadden and Charles Swann (1981, p. 19), evangelicals realized full well that they were not only in hot competition with secular and a few mainline religious programs, but with each other as well: "[T]hey realized that the sophistication and slickness of their production—in effect, their Hollywood quotient—can determine their success or failure." This led some critics, such as Janice Peck (1993) and Mark Pinsky (1989), to question whether the power of the message was overshadowed or undermined by the personality of the messenger.

The Electronic Church and State

As the prevalence and popularity of religious television programs increased in the 1980s, so too did the debate regarding the exercise of social and political power by nationally televised preachers and the new "religious right" they embraced. On

September 15, 1980, televangelist Jerry Falwell and his organization, the Moral Majority, were the subject of the cover story in *Newsweek* and "Preachers and Politics" was the feature story in *U.S. News & World Report*. "The idea that religion and politics don't mix," asserted Falwell (as cited in Lear, 1988, p. ix), "was invented by the devil to keep Christians from running their own country."

According to scholar Peter Horsfield (1984), the growth of evangelical broadcasting represented a massive takeover by the political and moral right and, for some observers, a plot to establish a religious republic with evangelical and fundamentalist broadcasters as the major spokespersons. Evangelicals accounted for roughly 20 percent of the votes received by Ronald Reagan in the 1984 presidential election, and this percentage was obtained largely through his close affiliation with religious broadcasters. Research by Robert Abelman and Gary Pettey (1988) examining viewers of religious television programming reported that Pat Robertson's national exposure as a televangelist on CBN and the politically peppered telecasts of his *The 700 Club* program launched and fueled his campaign for the Republican nomination in the 1988 presidential election.

Prosperity Gospel

Fund-raising became a critical task for religious broadcasters in order to pay for airtime, purchase radio and television stations, or maintain their presence on cable. In the early 1980s, the top-rated televangelists typically spent between 15 to 40 percent of their airtime on fundraising, which according to Razelle Frankl (1987) exposed the average viewer to approximately $31,000 in explicit requests per year. It appeared as if the business of religious broadcasting evolved into a "fiscal Catch 22" situation: the logic of the evangelical success formula demanded reaching as many people as possible, but in order to pay for the increased production and airtime costs of reaching larger audiences, one needed an even larger audience. This made it hard to tell whether televangelists were raising money to stay on television or whether they were staying on television to raise money.

Some critics have accused religious broadcasters of selling salvation. Joe Barnhart (1990), for example, suggested that fundraising has led to the transformation of the Gospel of Luke 6:38 ("Give, and it will be given to you")—which suggests the spiritual rewards of stewardship—into the Gospel of Prosperity, where spiritual gain is subordinated by material blessings and financial success. Similarly, Theologian Carl F. H. Henry (1988) found that these programs were transforming a motivation for giving into a motivation of getting.

Money and Sex Scandals

At their peak of popularity in the mid-1980s, the top four religious television programs received more than one-quarter of a billion dollars through on-air solicitations. The quest for financial gain led to controversial practices by some ministries. In March 1987, Oral Roberts, renowned tent show revivalist and head of Oral Roberts University, announced on the 165 television stations carrying *Oral Roberts and You* that God would claim his life if he could not raise $4.5 million by the end of the month. Although Roberts met his goal, many contributors became highly skeptical of televangelism as a result. Skepticism turned to dismay when viewers learned through the popular press that Jim and Tammy Faye Bakker, co-hosts of the religious talk show *PTL Club* and heads of the Praise The Lord ministry, had misappropriated PTL funds by amassing vast real estate holdings, an expensive home, and $1.9 million in combined salaries and bonuses.

That same month, Jim Bakker announced his resignation as head of his $129 million-a-year PTL empire because of a sexual encounter with a ministry secretary. Shortly thereafter, Jimmy Swaggart, a fiery preacher from Baton Rouge, Louisiana, with a syndicated television ministry on 222 stations, admitted to numerous encounters with prostitutes and a long-standing obsession with pornography. According to Robert Abelman and Stewart Hoover (1990), Swaggart reported a $1.5–1.8 million-per-month decline in contributions. Other televangelists were found guilty by association, and their revenue also diminished. Robert Schuller, whose *Hour of Power* was carried by 172 stations at that time, showed a 3 percent dip in donations. In a seven-month period, CBN revenues fell 32.5 percent. Collectively, these scandals rocked the very foundation of personality-driven televangelism, contributing to Pat Robertson's inability to obtain the Republican nomination and marking the end of the era of religious television programming's unprecedented popularity and prevalence.

Several electronic ministries survived the scandals. The Eternal Word Television Network and

Before the PTL (Praise the Lord) scandal occurred, Jim Bakker (right) and his wife Tammy hosted the program People that Love as part of their televangelism; this particular episode aired on April 28, 1986, and featured Edwin Louis Cole as the guest. (Bettmann/Corbis)

the Inspirational Network still had 41 million and 11.6 million subscribers, respectively, by the mid-1990s. Despite criticism of its own fundraising efforts, the Trinity Broadcasting Network could still be seen in 35 million homes through more than eight thousand broadcast and cable affiliates. It is interesting that in the aftermath of the scandals, many viewers turned to a most unlikely source for religious programming—the commercial television networks.

Faith-Friendly Secular Content

Network news has long been identified as slighting or ignoring religious issues. A recent study by the Media Research Center, a conservative media watchdog, revealed that only 14 percent of all nightly news stories broadcast by ABC, CBS, CNN, NBC, and PBS throughout the 1990s concerned religion, and most of the ones that did merely reported the activities of religious leaders rather than matters of faith or spirituality (Gahr, 1997). Similarly, the Center for Media and Public Affairs, a nonpartisan research organization,

reported that the majority of network news stories related to religion between 1969 and 1998 provided accounts of church politics and wrongdoings by prominent religious figures (Lichter, Lichter, and Anderson, 2000).

The depiction of people of faith on prime-time entertainment programming has been even more distorted. Michael Suman (1997) notes that commercial television has traditionally underrepresented people for whom religion is a strong force in their lives and tended to marginalize and often denigrate religious expression. According to social observer Steven Stark (1997), commercial television is ruthlessly secular and orthodox religion is antithetical to television's very notion of itself—that is, unless it can generate a sizable audience.

With the new millennium approaching and baby boomers beginning to confront their mortality, CBS was in search of light entertainment programming to reach this audience. In 1994, the network offered a drama, *Touched by an Angel*, in which an angel is dispatched from on high to inspire change. The program quickly reached the Top-10 in the Nielsen ratings. In response to this success, a significant body of prime-time programming surfaced that had religious or spiritual themes and featured angels or ministers (e.g., *Second Noah* (ABC), *Promised Land* (CBS), *7th Heaven* (WB), *The Visitor* (Fox)). In fact, the Parents Television Council, the entertainment-monitoring arm of the Media Research Center, reported an increase in the number of religious depictions on secular television, from 287 in 1995 to 436 in 1996 and a fourfold increase since 1993 (Rice, 1997). In addition, the majority of clergy and people of faith depicted in prime-time programming during the mid- to late-1990s were increasingly portrayed in a positive light.

Conclusion

Although televangelism is no longer the prominent method of religious expression it was in the 1970s and 1980s, the spirituality on broadcast television and conservative Christianity on cable are still flourishing. With 61 percent of television viewers in a 1997 *TV Guide* poll wanting "references to God, churchgoing, and other religious observances in prime-time" (Gahr, 1997, p. 58), religion in media will likely have a continuing presence on television.

See also: FEDERAL COMMUNICATIONS COMMISSION; CABLE TELEVISION, PROGRAMMING OF; RADIO BROADCASTING, STATION PROGRAMMING AND; TELEVISION BROADCASTING, PROGRAMMING OF.

Bibliography

Abelman, Robert, and Hoover, Stewart M., eds. (1990). *Religious Television: Controversy and Conclusions.* Norwood, NJ: Ablex Publishing.

Abelman, Robert, and Pettey, Gary. (1988). "How Political is Religious Television Programming?" *Journalism Quarterly* 65(2):313–318.

Barnhart, Joe E. (1990). "Prosperity Gospel: A New Folk Theology." In *Religious Television: Controversy and Conclusions*, eds. Robert Abelman and Stewart M. Hoover. Norwood, NJ: Ablex Publishing.

Frankl, Razelle. (1987). *Televangelism: The Marketing of Popular Religion.* Carbondale: Southern Illinois University Press.

Gahr, Evan. (1997). "Religion on TV Doesn't Have a Prayer." *American Enterprise* 8(5):58–59.

Hadden, Jeffrey K., and Swann, Charles E. (1981). *Prime Time Preachers: The Rising Power of Televangelism.* Reading, MA: Addison-Wesley.

Henry, Carl F. H. (1988). "Heresies in Evangelical Fundraising." *Fund Raising Management* 19(9):1–5.

Horsfield, Peter G. (1984). *Religious Television: The American Experience.* New York: Longman.

Lear, Norman. (1988). "Forward." *In A Plea For Common Sense: Resolving the Clash Between Religion and Politics*, ed. Joseph Castelli. New York: Harper & Row.

Lichter, S. Robert; Lichter, Linda; and Anderson, Daniel R. (2000). *Media Coverage: Religion in America.* Washington, DC: Center for Media and Public Affairs.

Peck, Janice. (1993). *The Gods of Televangelism: The Crisis of Meaning and the Appeal of Religious Television.* Creskill, NJ: Hampton Press.

Pinsky, Mark, I. (1989). "Crouch: Theologians Critical of Prayer." *Los Angeles Times*, February 16, pp. 1, 10.

Rice, Lynette. (1997). "Religion is on Rise in Prime Time," *Broadcasting & Cable* 127(13):35.

Schultze, Quentin J., ed. (1990). *American Evangelicals and the Mass Media.* Grand Rapids, MI: Academie Books.

Stark, Steven. (1997). *Glued to the Set.* New York: Free Press.

Suman, Michael. (1997). *Religion and Prime Time Television.* Westport, CT: Praeger Publishers.

ROBERT ABELMAN

▮ RESEARCH

See: Audience Researchers; Marketing Research, Careers in; Psychological Media Research, Ethics of; Researchers for Educational Television Programs; Research Methods in Information Studies; Violence in the Media, History of Research on

▮ RESEARCHERS FOR EDUCATIONAL TELEVISION PROGRAMS

Among the various production companies responsible for educational television programs, there is a vast range in the degree to which research plays a role in these productions. Many producers rely on little or no research input, limited, perhaps, to occasional consulting by educational advisers or a test of the appeal of a pilot episode. By contrast, a smaller number of producers use research more extensively. As Gerald Lesser (1974) has recounted, the latter approach was originated in the late 1960s by the Children's Television Workshop (CTW), the producer of numerous, highly respected educational television series such as *Sesame Street, The Electric Company, Square One TV, Ghostwriter,* and *Dragon Tales.*

Under the model of production that has come to be known as the "CTW Model," television producers, educational content specialists, and researchers collaborate closely throughout the life of a television series, from the creation of the original idea through the delivery of the finished program. Production staff (i.e., producers, writers, actors, and so on) are responsible for the physical production of the series. Educational content specialists devise the educational curriculum that sets goals for the series (e.g., to encourage literacy, positive attitudes toward science, or social development among viewers) and help to ensure that the material being produced is educationally sound. Researchers test material hands-on with the target audience (e.g., children of a certain age) to help ensure that the program will be appealing and comprehensible to that audience.

The testing that researchers conduct in support of educational television production falls into two broad categories. "Formative research" is conducted while material is being produced—or even before production begins—to investigate questions that arise out of the production process. These questions include such diverse issues as: Will a particular part of the program be comprehensible and appealing to its target audience? Where on the screen should text be placed to catch the attention of viewers and encourage reading as they watch? Which of several potential designs for the "look" of a character will be most appealing to viewers? What do viewers already know about a particular topic and where do their misconceptions lie, so that subsequent scripts can address these misconceptions directly? The results of these research studies inform subsequent production decisions and revisions of the material being produced. In this way, the voice of the target audience itself becomes a vital part of the production process.

The other type of research that is used is called "summative research." Summative research is conducted after the production of a television series is complete, and is intended to assess the impact of the series on its viewers. The kinds of questions addressed by summative research might include: Are viewers better able (or more motivated) to read and write after watching a television series about literacy? Do viewers become more interested in mathematics or science after watching series about these topics? Are preschool children more likely to cooperate with their peers after watching a television series designed to promote social development? The results of these studies provide a gauge of the success of a series in achieving its educational goals.

A book edited by Shalom Fisch and Rosemarie Truglio (2000) provides many examples of formative and summative research studies conducted to inform the production of *Sesame Street* over the past thirty years. These kinds of applied research studies bear numerous similarities to the kinds of research that might be conducted in an academic setting on the topic of the interaction of viewers with television. Yet, these two types of research are also very different. One of the chief differences between academic research and applied research in this area lies in their ultimate purposes. For example, the ultimate purpose of academic research on children and television is generally to inform our understanding of children's processing of, interactions with, and reactions to television— as exemplified by a review of the literature by Aletha Huston and John Wright (1997). Although such concerns are also important in applied research on children and television, they are not the end goal of the research; rather, the ultimate purpose in this case is to use that information to inform the design of television programs that will be comprehensible, appealing, and age-appropriate for their target audience. In other words, the implications of the academic research focus on children; the implications of the applied research focus on the television program.

Researchers in the field of applied television research typically come from backgrounds in education, psychology (particularly developmental psychology, in the case of educational programs for children), communications, anthropology, and related areas. Entry-level researchers generally come to their positions with bachelor's or master's degrees. Higher-level staff (e.g., research directors, content directors) generally hold doctorates, although some have master's degrees and extensive prior experience. Unpaid internships are often available in these types of research departments, and can provide valuable experience for those interested in the field.

See also: CHILDREN'S COMPREHENSION OF TELEVISION; SESAME STREET; TELEVISION, EDUCATIONAL.

Bibliography

Fisch, Shalom M., and Truglio, Rosemarie T., eds. (2000). *"G" Is for Growing: Thirty Years of Research on Sesame Street.* Mahwah, NJ: Lawrence Erlbaum Associates.

Huston, Aletha C., and Wright, John C. (1997). "Mass Media and Children's Development." In *Handbook of Child Psychology*, Vol. 4, eds. William Damon, Irving Sigel, and K. Ann Renninger. New York: John Wiley & Sons.

Lesser, Gerald S. (1974). *Children and Television: Lessons from Sesame Street.* New York: Vintage Books/Random House.

SHALOM M. FISCH

RESEARCH METHODS IN INFORMATION STUDIES

Researchers in the field of information studies investigate information systems and services to understand how people use them and to discover better designs for those systems and services. The research questions addressed are wide-ranging, and they evolve as information systems and services change. To meet the challenge of these many research questions, investigators have borrowed and adapted techniques from many other fields of science. These methods, each with its own advantages and disadvantages, offer a range of insights into information systems and services, the people who use them, and the intellectual and cultural content that they preserve. Research in information studies can be divided into three categories: (1) research into information interactions, using methods drawn from the social sciences, (2) research into cultural history, using methods from the humanities, and (3) information technology research and development, using methods from science and engineering.

Information Interaction

Information systems are developed for people who interact with them to search for, evaluate, and employ information. The interactions of users with information systems, and the factors that influence those interactions, are important focuses of information studies research.

Researchers ask a variety of questions about information interactions, and they base these questions in a variety of perspectives drawn from the social sciences.

Researchers with backgrounds in psychology might ask the following questions: What mental characteristics of users lead them to search for information in specific ways? How do personality, mental abilities, or learning styles affect how people interact with information systems? Researchers with backgrounds in sociology, anthropology, or business administration might ask the following questions: How does membership in a group such as a profession, or an economic class, lead people to use information systems in distinctive ways? How do people in organizations such as firms and non-profit associations understand information technology, and how do such organizations establish norms for information-related behavior? How do ethnic or organizational cultures construct their own understandings of information and of information technologies and services? Researchers with backgrounds in political science might ask the following questions: How does information influence policymaking by legislatures and government agencies? How does information influence voting patterns in the electorate? What effect do information policies have on society as a whole? Researchers with backgrounds in economics might ask the following questions: What value does information have for people? How much are people willing to pay for information?

To study information interactions, researchers sometimes use public opinion surveys to ask users about their perceptions of information systems. For example, investigators have surveyed engineers to determine the kind of information that they need and how frequently they consult various information resources. From these kinds of surveys, researchers have found that many professionals prefer to ask people for needed information, rather than to consult books or databases. Knowing these preferences can help in the design of information systems and services. Researchers also use surveys to investigate why consumers select specific information services, as well as the value that is attributed to the retrieved information. They then compare the perceived value of information services with the costs that are incurred in providing the services. The result is a cost-benefit analysis of information services that can influence how information systems and services are implemented and funded.

Surveys distributed by mail, telephone, or e-mail provide a quick and reasonably easy way to gauge user opinions about information systems. However, surveys typically collect only a limited amount of detail. In addition, survey responses tend to relate to perceptions rather than to actual behaviors. For example, a respondent may truly believe that he or she uses a particular information source several times a week. However, that perception may be mistaken, and only direct observations of user behavior can verify its accuracy.

When surveys fail to provide sufficient depth of detail to allow researchers to understand users' behaviors, qualitative research can provide a more complete understanding. Qualitative methods, which include observation and in-depth interviews, provide a great deal of personal detail about information users. For example, researchers have observed users in their workplaces to find out how people select information resources. Results have emphasized the importance of internally generated information (e.g., company policies and memos) over information that is derived from external resources such as books and databases. Similarly, researchers have interviewed users in depth to discover their opinions about information systems and their motivations in searching for and using information. Using detailed analysis and interpretation of interview responses, researchers have developed interpretations of the factors that influence how users interact with information systems. Another approach to qualitative research asks questions about culture and uses ethnographic methods to answer those questions. Such methods have been used to investigate how the organizational culture of corporations influences the employees' use of information systems, or how people in specific occupations or socioeconomic classes seek and use information. Market research provides another pattern for investigating how users interact with information systems. In order to study whether members of target markets are likely to use specific information systems, researchers have used focus groups to elicit the opinions of typical systems users.

Experiments give researchers the ability to investigate information interactions in much detail. For example, experimenters have randomly assigned individuals to several different information systems and then asked them to complete an information search. When researchers compared the results of the searches statistically, it was possible to assess the effect of different information system designs on search success. Other experimenters have used more complex experiments to assess how different users interact with information systems. Such experiments have shown the effect of cognitive abilities, cognitive styles, learning styles, and problem-solving styles on user interactions with information systems. The results of such experiments allow systems designers to tailor information systems to suit the cognitive abilities or learning preferences of different users.

One final method of investigating information interactions deserves mention. Researchers have analyzed patterns of information use to provide detailed analyses of the structure of intellectual communities. For example, investigators have examined how scientists refer to previous research when they report their findings. They have found that there are groups of scientists who focus on the same topic, read each other's work, and communicate with each other. This type of research, called citation analysis, has been used to chart the development of specialized areas of research and publication and to visualize the structure of scientific communities.

Cultural History

Information systems and services are part of a group's intellectual and cultural history. Consequently, approaches to scholarship that have been developed in the humanities can also be applied to information studies research.

From a historical perspective, research questions focus on the history of ideas, technologies, and institutions. Researchers study the development and evolution of scientific schools of thought, the history of the development of new types of communication media, and the influence that these new media have on communication patterns. The history of libraries and similar information agencies and institutions is also a component of this type of research in information studies.

Historical methods employ a wide-ranging search for evidence about the past. Scholars find primary evidence in the contemporary accounts of people who participated in past events. These accounts are typically preserved in letters and similar archival materials. Other documents may preserve the social and political context in which particular historical events or trends occurred. By combining primary evidence with secondary evidence (i.e., interpretations of events by individuals who were not participants, such as later critics), historians develop interpretations of historical events and trends. Historical research has been applied to both information systems (such as the development of computerized information retrieval systems) and to information services (such as the history of information services provided by public health agencies). As with most history, the idea behind this kind of research is to document approaches that have been taken and decisions that have been made, so future information systems and services can be founded on previous work.

Scholars use other types of primary evidence in studies of the history of ideas. For example, researchers have examined records showing the sales and circulation of books or the patterns of scholarly citations over time to investigate the evolution of ideas and their transfer by communications media. Sometimes these studies are controversial because it is not always easy to associate patterns of information transfer with social and historical trends. Researchers have tried to interpret the effect of certain information (e.g., specific books) or certain information technologies (e.g., printing) on events. For example, there is little consensus among scholars about the effect of Enlightenment publishing on the American and French revolutions. However, detailed studies of patterns of publishing and reading have revealed how some ideas may have influenced the ways in which people perceived their societies, thus setting the stage for revolution.

From a philosophical perspective, research questions focus on the theoretical foundations of knowledge and on the ethics of information services. Philosophical research methods are hard to define. In many cases, investigators read extensively the ideas of other scholars and then try to fit ideas together into new interpretations of information and information services. For example, interpretations of ontology and epistemology can influence how information systems and services are created. If information is considered to have external reality with fixed attributes such as "aboutness," it is possible to treat information as

objects and to develop systems to manage, categorize, and handle those objects. However, if a different philosophical view about the reality of information is maintained, the approach to information systems may be quite different. For example, if designers think that information is the process of becoming informed, then information systems must be created to facilitate the user-centered process rather than simply to manage information objects. Through the exposition of different philosophical approaches, scholars in information studies explore new ways of viewing information systems and services. In the area of information ethics, investigators have studied how people apply general principles to specific actions. These studies permit researchers to track the evolution of norms of behavior and to understand how these norms govern both professional practice and the actions of users.

Technology Research and Development

Information systems occur in the natural world, and they can be investigated just like any other natural phenomena. Aspects of information systems can be counted, measured, and documented. Here, the research questions are similar to those that are encountered in the natural sciences. Investigators might focus on patterns of authorship or on the use and obsolescence of materials. They would then describe these patterns mathematically and try to account for the influences that cause information patterns to vary.

This type of research is informetrics, and it includes more specific areas of study, such as bibliometrics and scientometrics. Informetrics involves measuring information phenomena and noting their distribution. For example, researchers have observed author productivity, the frequency of coauthorship, and the scatter of journal articles on a topic across a set of journals. Having observed the ways in which information phenomena are distributed, informetrics researchers create mathematical models that reflect these distributions. The mathematical models can then be used to predict how information phenomena behave in general and to compare how a variety of factors influence the distribution of information phenomena. A brief example will help to clarify this type of research. In any field of study, there are a few authors who produce a lot of the literature. These prolific authors write a lot of books and journal articles. There are more authors who are somewhat less prolific, writing fewer publications. There are also many authors who are not very prolific at all, writing only a few items. This relationship between author productivity and the number of authors can be described mathematically with a formula (i.e., Lotka's Law). Starting with this mathematical relationship, researchers have been able to compare different scientific fields to determine which fields tend to produce a greater concentration of prolific authors. Then, moving beyond pure science to applied science, researchers have been able to use Lotka's Law to optimize author indexes in databases of scientific literature.

Some informetrics studies relate to information services rather than information systems. For example, researchers have examined closely the patterns of book circulation from libraries. From these observations, the relationship between the age of materials and the probability that they will circulate has been quantified. Researchers have used this model of obsolescence of literature to decide how long certain materials should be maintained in active collections. The same models can help to predict numbers of hits on websites or the obsolescence of materials in digital libraries.

One of the most important goals of information studies research is to enable the design of new and improved information systems. Research that is patterned on that conducted in engineering helps researchers to achieve this goal. In general terms, these investigations involve building new or experimental information systems and then evaluating those systems in a variety of ways. One simple way of evaluating experimental systems is the information retrieval experiment. Here, researchers create a set of typical queries and a set of documents that may be relevant to those queries. They use these standard queries and documents in a series of different information retrieval systems. Using standardized measures of search quality, researchers can then assess which of the system designs produces the best search results.

Information retrieval experiments are, of course, very much more complex than this simple description would imply. Increasingly, researchers have moved toward evaluating new information system technologies in realistic settings. Rather than using small sets of documents, information retrieval experiments have begun to use very large databases. Similarly, instead of using a small set of "typical" queries, evaluations have begun to use real users with real information needs to test innovative technologies. This new approach to information retrieval experiments has introduced a new set of problems. In simple information retrieval experiments, researchers assumed that a document was either relevant or nonrelevant to a particular query. Once real users started to participate in information retrieval experiments, it became clear that users do not always have a clear assessment of document relevance. For example, the user might consider a document to be partially relevant. The user might also consider a document to be relevant but not particularly useful or important. Consequently, the crucial variables that allow information systems to be evaluated and compared have become considerably more complex.

The variety of technological innovations in information systems adds to the complexity of information retrieval experiments. The advent of information systems that handle images, video clips, and sounds has multiplied the number of retrieval capabilities to be assessed. To compare the many full-text retrieval engines that are being invented in laboratories has required a substantial, multiyear, international effort with funding from a number of public and private sources. Similarly, to develop and test the first generation of digital libraries has taken large efforts supported by substantial infusions of public funds in several countries.

Usability testing is another technique that has been derived from engineering research. In usability testing, the focus is not on the effectiveness or efficiency of the information systems; the focus is placed instead on how easy information systems are to use. Researchers typically give users the opportunity to work with experimental information systems and to assess their ease of use. Although this sounds like a relatively simple process, there are many factors to be considered. For example, any user group will include individuals who have different cognitive abilities, learning styles, or problem-solving preferences. Different ethnic and cultural groups in the user population may bring unique approaches to information seeking and use. In addition, there is usually a series of tradeoffs between ease of use and the capabilities of the information systems.

Finally, users frequently will find a familiar-looking system easier to use than a system that has greater capabilities and ease of use but looks "new" or "difficult." Balancing all of these user characteristics to come up with a meaningful assessment of usability requires rigorous investigation techniques.

Some usability testing uses a combination of experts and real users to test the features of new information systems. Experts in information system design can frequently judge certain aspects of the system designs more efficiently and effectively than the users themselves can. Experts can, for example, determine whether information systems provide users with adequate knowledge of the techniques that they need to use to conduct a successful search. Once experts have tested the design of the systems, users can test their functionality and ease of use.

Conclusion

Research in information studies addresses a large number of research questions. Because information systems and services are constantly evolving, there are always new questions about the best ways in which to meet the information needs of users. As a result, new avenues of research in information studies appear on a constant basis. Researchers in information studies have used techniques from a wide range of other scientific disciplines. Social science perspectives and methods predominate, but the humanities, natural sciences, and engineering have contributed to the variety of information studies research. Because of the use of multiple perspectives and varied research methods, information studies research is interdisciplinary and eclectic in nature. However, the many perspectives and methods that researchers bring to information systems and services have the potential to provide a rich understanding of information interactions, intellectual and cultural history, and information systems design and development.

See also: ARCHIVES, PUBLIC RECORDS, AND RECORDS MANAGEMENT; CHIEF INFORMATION OFFICERS; CULTURE AND COMMUNICATION; ETHICS AND INFORMATION; INFORMATION INDUSTRY; INFORMATION SOCIETY, DESCRIPTION OF; LIBRARIES, DIGITAL; LIBRARIES, HISTORY OF; MANAGEMENT INFORMATION SYSTEMS; OPINION POLLING, CAREERS IN; PRICE, DEREK JOHN DE SOLLA; PRINTING, HISTORY AND METHODS OF; RETRIEVAL OF INFORMATION; SYSTEMS DESIGNERS; TECHNOLOGY, PHILOSOPHY OF.

Bibliography

Boyce, Bert R.; Meadow, Charles T.; and Kraft, Donald H. (1994). *Measurement in Information Science.* San Diego: Academic Press.

Egghe, Leo, and Rousseau, Ronald. (1990). *Introduction to Informetrics: Quantitative Methods in Library, Documentation, and Information Science.* Amsterdam: Elsevier.

Gorman, Gary E.; Clayton, Peter; and Rice-Lively, Mary Lynn. (1997). *Qualitative Research for the Information Professional: A Practical Handbook.* London: Library Association.

Hernon, Peter. (1989). *Statistics for Library Decision-Making: A Handbook.* Norwood, NJ: Ablex.

Kraft, Donald H., and Boyce, Bert R. (1991). *Operations Research for Libraries and Information Agencies.* San Diego: Academic Press.

Powell, Ronald R. (1997). *Basic Research Methods for Librarians.* Norwood, NJ: Ablex.

Rubin, Jeffrey. (1994). *Handbook of Usability Testing: How to Plan, Design, and Conduct Effective Tests.* New York: Wiley.

Sparck-Jones, Karen. (1981). *Information Retrieval Experiment.* London: Butterworths.

Tague-Sutcliffe, Jean. (1995). *Measuring Information: An Information Services Perspective.* San Diego: Academic Press.

BRYCE ALLEN

■ RETRIEVAL OF INFORMATION

Information Retrieval (IR), has been part of the world, in some form or other, since the advent of written communications more than five thousand years ago. IR has as its domain the collection, representation, indexing, storage, location, and retrieval of information-bearing objects. Traditionally these objects have been text-based documents such as articles, reports, and books; however, as multimedia computing has progressed, the list of information-bearing objects has grown to include such things as images, videos, maps, sound, and music recordings. In the modern sense of the term, IR has its roots in the scientific information explosion that accompanied, and followed, World War II. Predating the computer, early modern IR systems used ingenious manual mechanisms to deal with the millions of scientific and technological research papers that were being written as part of the war against tyranny.

The remarkable growth in computerization has lead to a "chicken-or-the-egg" scenario with regard to the growth in IR research and design. As computers become more powerful, more information is generated. As more information is generated, the need for bigger, better, and faster IR systems increases. This need in turn spurs the need for bigger, better, and faster computers, and so on, *ad infinitum*. Until the mid-1990s, interest in IR was limited to a handful of highly trained researchers, librarians, information scientists, computer scientists, and engineers. With the growing use of the Internet, however, information retrieval through the use of search engines has become an activity that is engaged in by a large portion of the general public. This newfound popularity is making IR research and development one of the hottest growth areas in the new digital "e-economy."

General Model of Information Retrieval

An IR system begins with a person who has some need for information. A student may need to find information for a class project on IR, for example. If there were just a little information available, then a purely manual approach might work. If the student knows that all of the needed information is available in a specific book or encyclopedia, and the student knows where that resource is, then he or she can just go get it. There is no need for any retrieval system beyond the rather remarkable one in the student's head. What happens, however, when the student does not know where to get the information? Perhaps an appropriate book exists in the library. Perhaps more is available in an online database or on a CD-ROM. Finally, perhaps some useful information may even be available on the World Wide Web. The problem is that in all of these cases the student cannot just wander around, hoping to find the needed information. These information collections are all much too large for that. Fortunately, for hundreds or thousands of years, people have been making retrieval tools to help with this task. Since the 1960s, many of these tools have involved computer applications. The following discussion will focus on these computer-based systems, with occasional reference to the earlier manual systems.

FIGURE 1. *Information retrieval model.*

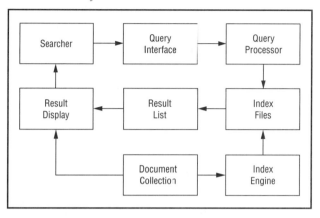

A general IR system has the following eight components (each with a particular function): (1) a query interface, (2) a query processor, (3) an index, (4) an index engine, (5) one or more collections of information, (6) a result list, (7) a result display, and, most important, (8) a user or "searcher" of the system. The basic relationships among these elements of an IR system are shown in Figure 1.

Query Interface

The student, who might more generally be called the "user," interacts directly with the query interface and the result display. Users tell the IR system what they need through the query interface. A query is the string of words that users input to tell the computer what they need. The retrieval system interface provides a place for users to write the request. It would be easiest if users could speak a request in their native language. Unfortunately, this would require a special kind of artificial intelligence that has not yet been developed for computers. Users must tell the information system what they need in a language that the computer can understand. Usually, this is a language composed of the words that the user thinks will be in the documents that they are trying to find. In some systems, these words can just be presented in a list. Other systems fake natural language queries by allowing users to enter natural language word strings from which the system strips out all but the nouns. Most systems, however, require that the user connect the words together with the words "and," "or," or "not." This is called Boolean logic. So, the student searcher might look for information on the topic of "information retrieval" by typing "((information OR data) AND retrieval)."

Query Processor

While this language is simple, the computer still needs to figure out what to do with the string of words. The part of the system that does this is the query processor. The query processor breaks the query, (information OR data) AND retrieval, into a set of simple operations. The processor searches for "retrieval" in the collection first. If no documents are found with this word, the search may stop, since the query states that the document that the person is looking for must contain the word "retrieval" plus something else. If it cannot find "retrieval," then there is no point in looking for anything else. If documents are found that contain the word "retrieval," then the system will search to see if those documents also contain either the word "information" or the word "data." Those documents (if any) that do contain one of those words in addition to the word "retrieval" then become part of the retrieved set.

Index Files

How does the system know which documents contain a word and which do not? While computers are fast, they are not fast enough to read all of the documents in a collection to see of a word is there every time a person asks. For example, if the World Wide Web were searched this way, the computer would need to read through millions of documents on millions of computers for each query. A better approach is to create an index file.

In full-text retrieval systems, an index file is an organized list of words. Each entry in the list contains a word and points to all of the documents that contain that word. It is something like a set of thousands of index cards. If they are unsorted, it would take a long time to find any one card, but if they are sorted into alphabetical order, then the search is much quicker. Once the correct entry is found in an index, it is relatively simple to read off the list of names of documents that contain the word.

There is a set of important issues related to the words that go into the index. This includes word selection and normalization. Indexing can be accomplished manually or by the computer. Computer indexing is generally faster but less precise, while manual indexing takes a long time, is generally of high quality, but is still fraught with problems such as inconsistency between indexers' choice of words. Vocabulary chosen by the indexers may not match that used by the individual searchers who are looking for information. Users must guess what terms are in the index, unless there is a term thesaurus.

Index Engine

An indexing engine is software that creates index files. It does this by processing the documents in the collection one by one. It takes each word from the document and tests to see if it should be included in the index. Some words are used so frequently in texts that they are not of much use for indexing. Words like "the" appear many times in all documents, so there is no point in including them in the index. The group of words that are to be ignored during indexing is called the "stop list." Sometimes the index engine performs additional processing on the words for the index. For example, the index engine may stem the words. Stemming is the process of removing endings from words that might otherwise tend to hide the similarity between words. For example, a person might be searching for "computing" but would be happy to match words such as "computer," "computers" and "computed." Stemming would reduce them all to "comput*." The indexing engine may perform other operations as well, such as converting all words to lowercase. After all of this processing, the index engine will make an entry in the index file for each word that it encounters in the documents and create a pointer back to the documents where the words occur.

Result Lists and Result Display

When a computer system combines all of the result lists of documents that match each of the search terms in the query, it displays a list of the names of the documents, or some sort of document surrogate, such as a brief description of the document. In traditional displays, the system will present a list that contains the document title, author, name of the publication, where the document came from, and in some systems, an abstract. This list must be presented in some order that is convenient for the user. Short lists can be presented in alphabetical order. Many result lists, however, particularly on the World Wide Web, tend to be very long, sometimes containing hundreds or even thousands of document names. Since only ten to twenty records at a time can appear on a computer screen, because of screen size limitations, this list may require the user to look though many screens to find a desired document.

Since the length of these lists makes alphabetical listings less than useful, it is typical in IR systems to present the list in an order that reflects how well the particular document matches the query. One simple way to do this is to count the number of words in the query that match the document. In the example, "((information OR data) AND retrieval)," some documents may match all three words while others may match only two words. Another ordering technique is to count the number of times the query words occur in the documents. For the sample query, if one document contains the word "retrieval" once and another contains the word "retrieval" three times, the document containing the word three times might be considered a better match and would be put closer to the front of the list.

Collections

An IR system searches for information in a collection of documents. These documents can take many forms. They might be individual articles from a scientific journal, newspaper stories, e-mail messages, poems, or encyclopedia entries. What all of these collections have in common is that they are composed of text.

The first and most important step in retrieving information is for the searcher to decide on what collection to search for the information. Collections are put together for different purposes. There are collections of news stories, collections for branches of science, collections of poems, and collections of web-pages. In short, there are collections for nearly every possible topic. No one index covers all of the topics. Collections may also exist in a variety of formats. Some collections are of music, sound, photography or video. The query example used above was based on a text-based collection. Usually, collections of sound or pictures are indexed using words that have been added to the documents to describe them. Alternatively, music can be indexed by its notes, sound by its dominant frequencies, images by their dominant colors or color layout, and video by the key images extracted from the motion. All of these indexing techniques are content-based methods. This contrasts with concept-based methods that are usually provided by humans and are more closely tied to the actual meaning of the document. In content-based methods, automatic computer programs are used to extract not the meaning but just some patterns from the documents. So, for example, a program must find the distribution of the most common colors in a photograph. These colors would be used to index the image. This, of course, changes the way in which a searcher must specify a query. It is difficult to type in a list of words that describes a photograph's distribution of color. Instead, some of these systems allow a person to search by drawing, by painting, or by selecting examples that are like the one that they want.

Display

After the IR system selects a set of documents, the selections are displayed to the user. The format of the display varies according to what part of a document is displayed, which documents are given prominent positions, and how the full text is displayed if it is available. The common form of display is a list of matching document identifiers. In a magazine, journal, or newspaper collection, the document identifiers might be the author, article title, name of the publication, and the date of publication. Only a small number of document identifiers, usually about ten, can be displayed on a computer screen at one time. If there are more then ten items in the retrieval set, then there is usually a button or command that will display the next group of ten items. If the collection contains the full text for an item, the computer interface usually provides a way to bring the full text onto the computer screen or to print it.

Frequently, a user's first search does not produce the information that the user wanted, there is not enough information, or the list of results is too long. In each of these cases, the user may choose to reformulate the query, perhaps by using some new knowledge that was gained by looking at the results of the earlier search. This search and retrieval cycle continues until the user either finds the desired information or gives up. All too often, people do not find the information that they want. Even worse, they sometimes believe that they have found all of the relevant information when they have not. Many new systems are being developed with advanced features that will help remedy this situation.

Advanced Search Features

Each of the components of the IR system as discussed above can be improved, particularly the query interface, the query processor, the index, the collections, and the result display.

Natural language query systems allow people to use everyday language, rather than Boolean logic, to state what they are interested in finding. The Boolean query "(information OR data) AND retrieval" could be written as "give me all records about information or data retrieval." While this may look like a good alternative to Boolean queries, some caution is warranted. Computers have limited ways of processing human languages, so it is easy to be misled about what a computer will do with a statement like the one given above. The computer is likely to select only the nouns from the sentence, remove words like "record" and "document," and then "OR" the nouns together into "information OR data OR retrieval." A cleverly written program might figure out the correct use of the "and" and the "or" in this situation, but such proficiency is the exception rather than the rule for most computer-based IR systems.

Vocabulary aids can improve retrieval. It is sometimes difficult for users to guess what words were used by the author or the indexer to describe the topic that is of interested. Consider what would happen in the above example if the author used the words "database retrieval" and not "data retrieval." Neither the Boolean query processor nor a natural language search would be able to find the record if the searcher used the term "data retrieval" instead of the term "database retrieval." To help with this problem, some systems provide either a term thesaurus or a controlled vocabulary. A term thesaurus can be provided in a separate printed book, or it can be built into the retrieval system. A term thesaurus lists what words can be used in place of other words in a query. This type of thesaurus has entries such as "DATA STORAGE use DATABASE" to tell the searcher, in this case, to use the word "database" rather than "data" when performing a search. The thesaurus may also suggest broader and narrower words. For example, "DATABASE broader term is DATA MANAGEMENT" or "DATABASE narrower term is RELATIONAL DATABASE MANAGEMENT SYSTEM (RDBM)". A thesaurus may also be used for automatic query expansion. For example, when a person searches for "data," the system might automatically add the word "database" to the query without asking the person.

Another feature that is available in more advanced systems is relevance feedback, which allows users to incorporate previously retrieved documents into a query. Users mark the documents as "relevant" (i.e., similar to what they are wanting) or "irrelevant" (i.e., not at all what they are wanting). The query processor uses this information to form a new search for the user. The query processor might do this by adding keywords from the relevant documents to the query and adding "not" to the keywords from irrelevant documents.

When most information retrieval systems return a list of retrieved documents, the only way to indicate potentially "good" documents is to put them at the top of the list. Using computer graphics, some systems can give the person doing the search more information about why a particular document was returned. One such system is called WebVIBE. In this system, queries may be broken into parts at the "or" in Boolean queries. For example, one query might be "information AND retrieval," and at the same time, the user can search for "data AND retrieval." Each query is represented as a "magnet" on a different part of the screen. The documents that match the queries are represented on the computer screen as icons, such as small images of pieces of paper. The magnets attract icons that represent documents that match the query. If a document icon matches only one of the queries, the icon for that document will fall directly on the magnet. The more interesting case is when a document matches both queries. In that case, the magnets that represent the queries have a "tug-of-war" over the document icon, and it will end up on the computer screen somewhere between the two magnets. The searcher can see which parts of a query best match a document by the position of the icons on the computer screen. Contrast this with the standard result list format, which simply lists relevance-sorted matches to the query "(information OR data) AND retrieval." In this case, the user cannot tell if a document was returned because it matched "information," "data," or both "information" and "data."

Evaluation of Information Retrieval Systems

Information scientists are continually arriving at new ways to improve IR, requiring the evaluation of IR systems to become an important component of IR research and development. In order that the comparisons be as consistent as possible, IR researchers have developed the "Cranfield Model" of evaluation. The Cranfield Model is named after a series of experimental IR evaluations performed by Cyril Cleverdon and his colleagues in Cranfield, England, during the 1960s. The second of the Cranfield studies (Cranfield II) has been called "the exemplar for experimental evaluation of information retrieval systems" (Harter and Hert, 1997). Thus, the Cranfield experiments are considered by most IR researchers to be the progenitor of the discipline of IR evaluation. The Cranfield Model can be described as

1. a test collection of documents,
2. a set of queries, and
3. a set of relevance judgements (i.e., lists, for each query, of all of the relevant documents in the collection).

For a given query and act of retrieval, the following document sets and associated numbers are known:

1. relevant and retrieved documents (RelRet),
2. nonrelevant and retrieved documents (NRelRet),
3. relevant and nonretrieved documents (RelNret), and
4. nonrelevant and nonretrieved documents (NrelNret).

Ideally, for any given query, an IR system should find for the user all relevant, and only relevant, documents. To determine how close to this ideal an IR system is working, a collection of IR evaluation measures, or metrics, have been developed. Two metrics, recall and precision, are the most commonly used measures. Recall evaluates, for any given query, how close an IR system comes to retrieving all the relevant documents in its database. Precision evaluates, for any given query, how close an IR system comes to presenting to the user only relevant documents. Recall and precision are both expressed either as a number from 0 to 1, or as a percentage. A score of 0 (0%) represents complete failure, while a score of 1 (100%) represents perfection. An ideal system would, therefore, have a recall score of 1 (100%) and a precision score of 1 (100%) for each and every query submitted. The recall and precision metrics can be expressed as easy-to-calculate equations:

Recall= RelRet/(Relret + RelNret)= A/(A+C)

Precision= RelRet/(RelRet + NrelRet)= A/(A+B)

Imagine that a test collection contains 100 documents that are relevant to the query "What is information retrieval?" Further imagine that when this query is submitted to the system, 25 documents are retrieved. After examining all 25 retrieved items, it is determine that 20 of them are relevant to the original query. In this case, the recall for the search is 0.2 (20%) and the precision is 0.8 (80%). These scores were calculated:

Recall= RelRet/(RelRet + RelNret)= 20/100= 0.2= 20%

Precision= RelRet/(Relret + NrelRet)+ A/(A+B) = 20/25= 80%

The spirit of the Cranfield evaluations lives on in the form of the Text REtrieval Conferences (TREC), which started in 1992 as a joint IR evaluation project between the National Institute of Standards and Technology (NIST) and the Defense Advanced Research Projects Agency (DARPA). The TREC evaluations are famous for the depth and breadth of the assigned retrieval tasks on which the entered IR systems are evaluated.

The evaluation of IR system performance is more of an art than a true science. The accurate calculation of recall scores is just one of the many problems that IR evaluators must overcome in their quest to be scientific. Note how the calculation of recall is predicated on knowing exactly how many relevant documents there are in the database for each query. When evaluators use a test collection, this is not a problem because previous researchers have examined every document in the collection to determine whether a given document is relevant to a given query. In real-world IR systems (e.g., AltaVista), systems with millions of documents, the examination of each document to determine its relevance to a query is impossible. Various techniques have been used to estimate the number of relevant documents that are present in a collection. For example, in their evaluation of a real-world legal collection, David Blair and M. E. Maron (1985) used a method of iterative searching to uncover potentially relevant documents that had initially been missed by a set of legal researchers. Using this technique, they revealed two important facts. First, users consistently overestimate the recall scores of their initial searches. Second, recall scores, in general, were shockingly low. Because the Blair and Maron approach is time-consuming and labor-intensive, other researchers have attempted to estimate the number of relevant documents by randomly sampling unretrieved documents. Still others have compared results of a series of similar searches and used the documents that were found to be in common as the basis for their estimates. Notwithstanding the estimation technique that is employed, it is important to stress that these methods provide only rough estimates of the actual number of relevant documents in a collection. Because real-world recall scores are based on such estimates, they too are considered mere estimations.

Since IR systems are developed by, and used by, humans, all of the problems associated with measuring the myriad variety of human behaviors also apply to IR evaluation. Questions of experimental validity are often raised. Are evaluators really measuring system performance, or are they measuring the IR skills of the users? Human users come to a system with a wide range of skills and abilities that must be accounted for if one is to determine whether the observed retrieval scores are the result of system performance or user skill. Experimental reliability is another problem. How well does the experimental evaluation of a system predict its behavior in the "real world"? It is one thing to claim that a system works well under laboratory conditions, but it is quite another to claim that it will work just as well once an IR system has been released to the public for general use.

A classic example of the reliability issue is the "recall-precision tradeoff" problem. Some users, such as doctors, lawyers, and graduate students, often need to conduct exhaustive searches (e.g., "I need all legal decisions handed down concerning malpractice lawsuits."). Exhaustive searches are those where each and every relevant document must be retrieved and then examined to ensure that no important information has been overlooked. Obviously, an IR system would need to have perfect recall to satisfy such users. Other users (even doctors, lawyers, and graduate students) occasionally need to conduct question-answering searches (e.g., "What year was *Roe v. Wade* decided?"). Specific searches, as this type of quest is sometimes called, require only that a small set of documents be retrieved. So long as one or more of the documents contains the desired answer, the size of the retrieved set is immaterial because once an answer-bearing document is retrieved and the answer is found, the remaining documents are no longer needed. Under this scenario, users with question-answering searches would be best served by an IR system with high precision. In a perfect world, the ideal IR system would be able to satisfy both types of uses simultaneously. Research has consistently shown that when users of IR systems aim for high recall, precision suffers significantly; similarly, when precision is the goal, recall performance suffers. This inverse relationship between recall and precision is the recall-precision tradeoff.

Since system evaluators cannot know all the different types of queries that an IR system might be called on to address, some researchers have questioned the meaningfulness of recall and precision scores as measures of true IR system performance. For example, how meaningful is a low recall score when a user only needs one document to answer a query? To overcome the problems posed by the recall-precision tradeoff, some IR researchers have proposed the adoption of special metrics that combine aspects of both recall and precision simultaneously.

Another difficulty that plagues the scientific examination of IR systems is what is meant by the term "relevance." Most researchers agree that relevant documents are those that somehow "satisfy" the query that is presented by a user. The debate hinges on the idea of "satisfaction." For some, the question is black and white—either the documents in question answer the query, or they do not. For others, satisfaction comes in shades of gray, with some documents being more relevant than others. Into this contentious mix is often thrown the notion of "pertinence," or the usefulness of the documents irrespective of relevance. Pertinent documents are those that a user finds useful. Pertinence and relevance are closely related, but they are not necessarily the same. Think of pertinence, like beauty, as being in the eye of the beholder. For example, a document retrieved about astrophysics might be relevant in response to a student's query about solar eclipses; however, the same document might also be nonpertinent to the student because the complex mathematical formulas that are presented within the document make the text incomprehensible. This debate over the nature of relevance might appear esoteric to an outsider, but it is important to IR researchers. Note the central role played by the counting of relevant documents in the calculation of both recall and precision. If one researcher decides to calculate precision by using the black-and-white interpretation of relevance and another decides to use pertinence, two very different sets of information will be generated. Since these two sets of results purport to evaluate the same thing, it is obvious how the relevance problem can lead to considerable confusion and uncertainty.

In reaction to the many problems that are associated with the accurate measurement of recall and precision, a new group of researchers has emerged, and they are called the "user-centered" school. User-centered IR evaluators believe that the Cranfield style of evaluation, along with its reliance on recall and precision, is fundamentally flawed because it is too "system centered" and thus does not capture the most important aspect of the interaction between users and IR systems, namely the successful informing of the users. Under the user-centered theory, an IR system is only successful if it assists users in moving forward with their lives by quickly, and with minimum of effort, fulfilling their broadly defined information needs. User-centered researchers perform qualitative assessments of achievement using a mixture of personal interviews, focus groups, surveys, and observations, and they eschew the quantitative measures of recall and precision.

Multimedia Information Retrieval

If one thinks of the development of modern computerized IR systems as forming a family tree, then in some sense the early online public access catalogues (OPACs) that are found in libraries would be the grandparents to all subsequent systems. Their children, nicely matured, would be the text-based search engines that are now found just about everywhere, including the World Wide Web, CD-ROM workstations, and palmtop personal digital assistants (PDAs). The teenaged grandchildren, full of promise but not quite ready to leave home, would be the visual information retrieval (VIR) systems that are designed to provide access to image and video information. To complete this family tree, the youngest grandchildren, just barely toddlers, would be the music information retrieval (MIR) systems and their cousins, the auditory information retrieval (AIR) systems. MIR provides an illustrative example of the challenges that are faced by multimedia information retrieval (MMIR) as it grows to maturity.

Interest in MMIR is growing rapidly. The advent of powerful multimedia-capable home computers and the point-and-click ease of the Internet have combined to create a huge demand for nontext information, including pictures, maps, speech, video, and music recordings. For example, according to WordSpot (2000), an Internet consulting company that tracks queries submitted to Internet search engines, the search for music—specifically, the now-popular MP3 format—has surpassed the traditional search for sex-related materials as the most popular search engine request.

Why is the obvious demand for music and other multimedia information not being met by IR research and development? Why are the "MP3 search engines" merely indexing the textual labels supplied by the creators of the files and not the music itself? MMIR is fraught with difficult problems that must be overcome before the technology can mature. First, multimedia information objects (e.g., images and music recordings) tend to be large. A single minute of CD-quality music takes up about 10 MB. These large sizes make multimedia information difficult to transmit, process, and store. Second, and more problematic, multimedia information is multifaceted (i.e., it has many different components that together make up the information). Music information can be said to comprise a complex array of pitch (e.g., notes), temporal (e.g., rhythm, meter), harmonic (e.g., chords), timbral (e.g., tone color), editorial (e.g., performance instructions), textual (e.g., lyrics), and bibliographic (e.g., composer, publisher) information, which together all form a coherent whole. The fact that the facets themselves have many different ways of being represented compounds this complexity to dizzying heights. For example, the pitch facet can be represented by note name (e.g., e-flat, g-sharp), interval (i.e., distance between notes), solfège (e.g., do, re, mi, fa, sol, la, ti), and sonic frequency, to name but a few options. MIR and other MMIR researchers must find comprehensive methods of dealing with this awe-inspiring complexity before MMIR systems can achieve the success of their text-based ancestors.

The goal of every MMIR system is to provide the user with the ability to search for and then retrieve multimedia objects using the medium of the desired objects. Thus, in the case of music information, MIR systems are being designed so music queries can be posed musically. Music-specific query methods that are being developed and refined include singing, humming, notation (i.e., traditional note and staff), pitch names, intervals, melodic contour (i.e., the overall shape of a melody), music keyboard, and so on. Each of these methods has its strengths and weaknesses. For example, contour queries are forgiving of user errors because they only have to remember the general shape of a melody, rather than the exact pitches. This approach, however, can result in retrieval of many unwanted songs (i.e., high recall but low precision). Using a music keyboard to input the exact pitches does offer the user the opportunity to achieve more precise results, but many users are not trained to play a music keyboard, so the chance for error is greatly enhanced. It is interesting to note that the recall-precision tradeoff of traditional text-based IR appears to have been handed down in full measure to its MMIR descendants.

See also: ARTIFICIAL INTELLIGENCE; COMPUTER SOFTWARE; COMPUTING; DATABASES, ELECTRONIC; INTERNET AND THE WORLD WIDE WEB; MANAGEMENT INFORMATION SYSTEMS; USE OF INFORMATION.

Bibliography

Blair, David C., and Maron, M. E. (1985). "An Evaluation of Retrieval Effectiveness for a Full-Text Document-Retrieval System." *Communications of the ACM* 28(3):289–299.

Harter, Stephen P., and Hert, Carol A. (1997). "Evaluation of Information Retrieval Systems: Approaches, Issues, and Methods." *Annual Review of Information Science and Technology* 32:3–91.

Korfhage, Robert. R. (1997). *Information Storage and Retrieval*. New York: Wiley.

National Institute of Standards and Technology. (2000). "Text REtrieval Conference (TREC)." <http:// trec. nist.gov/>.

Pollit, A. S. (1989). *Information Storage and Retrieval Systems: Origin, Development, and Applications*. New York: Wiley.

Salton, Gerry, and McGill, Mike J. (1983). *Introduction to Modern Information Retrieval*. New York: McGraw-Hill.

WordSpot. (2000). "Top 500 Custom Pick Report Example: MP3." <http://www.wordspot.com/ samplecustom.html>.

P. BRYAN HEIDORN
J. STEPHEN DOWNIE

■ RHETORIC

Although it is frequently understood to refer to the art of effective discourse, the term "rhetoric" refers variously to the study or analysis of discourse, to the ability to create and deliver messages effectively, and to the study of the theoretical issues that underlie the relationship that exists between knowledge and language. It refers to both the study and application of communicative practices. Traditionally associated with the art of persuasion, especially in the oral tradition, rhetoric has at times been viewed as encompassing the study of virtually all communication interactions on the grounds that all communication can be viewed as intentional. Rhetoric is the foundational discipline on which contemporary concerns for subjects as diverse as audience research, media criticism, marketing, public speaking, semiotics, communication ethics, nonverbal communication, and the philosophy of language are based. The term also has a long history of pejorative use as a label for dishonest or empty discourse, such as when a politician characterizes the speech of his or her opponent as "mere rhetoric," suggesting that its claims are unsubstantiated or that its beautiful phrases are actually meaningless. One reason for the complexity of meanings in the term is simply that rhetoric is an ancient art, the practices of which are closely linked to political systems and cultural norms. As cultures have risen and fallen since ancient times, the significance, meaning, and practice of rhetoric has gone through a variety of transformations.

Rhetoric Emerges as a Discipline

The first formal discussions of the art of rhetoric in the Western tradition emerged in the fifth century B.C.E. in Greece, though more ancient texts of Chinese and Jewish origin as well the works of Homer indicate that there was an even earlier interest in speech making. The growing use of the courts to adjudicate disputes, such as those concerning property ownership, prompted by political changes in Sicily, led to the increasing use of oral public argument that was aimed to produce a decision that was favorable to an advocate. Some individuals began to observe that there were standard practices or lines of argument that were successful. Recognizing that people would pay to learn these strategies, these individuals began to teach the strategies that they had observed or used. News of these prescriptions for successful arguments was soon carried to Athens, where the emergence of increasingly democratic forms of government offered fertile ground for the development of the art of public oratory beyond the courtroom. The teaching of the art of rhetoric flourished in this environment.

From these early days, the teachers of rhetoric, who were often philosophers in a group that was known as the Sophists, faced opposition. Plato, a major spokesperson for this opposition, was concerned that rhetoric, at best, was no art but simply a knack, and, at worst, that it was a morally bankrupt endeavor. Rhetoric, he argued, was not concerned with discovering truth or reality; it was only concerned with appearances. Rhetoric was not considered to be a science, as it led to no certain knowledge, and it was not a respectable art such as dialectic (the use of strict deductive logic to test and defend claims when scientific demonstration was impossible). The Sophists defended their position on philosophical and practical grounds. Truth is rarely attainable and often what one imagines to be the truth of an issue will not be considered true elsewhere. "Man is the measure of all things," argued Protagoras in his contemporary-sounding expression of cultural relativism. For the Sophists, rhetoric was a necessary art, useful to discover and reach agreement about truths, as well as to decide on courses of action when no truth about an issue could be known.

In the most influential work on rhetoric from the Greek period, Aristotle's *Rhetoric* (circa 335 B.C.E.), an effort is made to transcend this debate. Defining rhetoric as "the faculty of observing in any given case the available means of persuasion," Aristotle offered a scientific examination of rhetoric to counter the almost mystical powers that the Sophists sometimes attributed to it. Aristotle saw rhetoric as a morally neutral art—a habit of mind and a systematic practice that could be of help to anyone who was engaged in persuasive practice in any situation. He agreed with the Sophists that rhetoric was necessary to answer questions about contingent matters—issues of discussion where "Truth" could not be known. He also identified three areas where rhetorical activity took place. These were the courtroom, where, in response to the presentations of advocates, judges rendered decisions about disputed past facts (e.g., Did they commit the offence? What offence was it?); the senate, where, in response to public arguments, judges rendered decisions about future actions (e.g., Should we go to war with Sparta? Should we spend public money for this building?); and the realm of what might be called public opinion, where the listeners in the audience rendered a decision about present attitudes toward a person who was attacked or praised in a speech or even about the speaker himself. For example, in his speech "On Helen" (circa 414 B.C.E.), Gorgias, a prominent teacher of rhetoric, beautifully exonerated the historical figure Helen of Troy—whom popular culture accused of causing the Trojan War. Aristotle also systematically addressed lines of argument, the psychological characteristics of audience members, cultural values and norms on which one could build an argument, and even how to use language successfully. Aristotle was most interested in the effectiveness of discourse because speakers functioned as advocates who were trying to persuade judges or audiences to decide in their favor. Perhaps his most long-standing contribution is his discussion of the three basic modes of proof. Aristotle identified (and modern textbooks on public speaking echo) three basic ways in which people come to be persuaded: *logos*, or appeals that are grounded in rationality or logical argument; *ethos*, or appeals that are grounded in the credibility of the speaker; and *pathos*, or appeals that are grounded in emotions or are aimed to arouse emotions in such a way that a listener is placed in the right frame of mind to render appropriate judgment.

Rhetoric as a Practical Skill and Master Art

Ancient Rome (from 200 B.C.E.) was deeply influenced by Greek thought about rhetoric and adopted rhetorical training into its emerging educational system. The Romans produced a clear course of study for the training and development of orators. Textbooks such as the *Rhetorica ad Herennium* (which appeared around 84 B.C.E.) set forth the five elements that students were expected to master. These are referred to as the "rhetorical canon," and they continue to influence how public speaking is taught. The first canon, *inventio*, or invention, referred to the creation or discovery of the content of the speech. This is the issue to which Aristotle had devoted most of his energies. Modern public speaking textbooks treat issues related to invention when they advise students about selecting and narrowing speech topics, conducting research, and developing supporting materials and arguments for their speeches. The second canon, *dispositio,* or disposition, referred to the selection and arrangement of this content to create the speech. Modern teachers of public speaking continue to advise students about appropriate patterns of organization and ways to connect one idea to another in an oral presentation. *Elocutio,* or style, constituted the third rhetorical canon, focusing on the creation of the right wording to express ideas and on the use of stylistic devices to enliven discourse. Modern courses in public speaking still discuss the use of strategies such as clarity, metaphor, antithesis, and parallel structure as ways to increase the effectiveness of a public speech. The fourth canon was called *memoria,* or memory. Ancient orators were trained to commit even lengthy addresses to memory. Special mnemonic strategies were developed to aid in this process. Contemporary public speakers are trained to use key-word outlines, TelePrompTers, and computer-generated visual aids to assist them in recalling the main points and details of their presentations. The fifth canon was training in *pronunciatio,* or delivery. To be effective, a speech must be delivered with the voice and body used in a way that enhances the ability of the audience to understand and/or be moved by the message.

The rhetorical canon and its institutional status in Greco-Roman culture, as well as its place as a pillar of the Seven Liberal Arts, demonstrates that from its earliest days, rhetoric has been linked to pedagogy; it has been recognized as a necessary skill of an educated person. However, there has always been a competing history that viewed rhetoric as more than a skill. The Sophists saw it as a way to generate truth. Cicero, regarded as the greatest of the Roman rhetoricians, saw rhetoric as a master art that was linked to the development of the person of public affairs. Cicero's eloquence in speaking in defense of the Roman Republic as it tottered toward monarchy in the first century B.C.E. demonstrates his powerful fusion of rhetorical theory with rhetorical practice. In the first century C.E., Quintilian's *Institutes of Oratory* set forth an exhaustive system for the education of young men, where rhetoric was no longer the neutral art of Aristotle but was deeply linked to ethics. Although written in Imperial Rome when the political structure constrained civic discourse and

Cicero's vision of the rhetorician as a man of public affairs had become unviable, Quintilian's writings nevertheless held up the ideal of "the good man speaking well." Modern communication scholars continue to be concerned with the place of discourse in a democratic community as well as with the ethical dimensions of discourse.

The Persistence and Expansion of Rhetoric

From the Medieval period through the Enlightenment, the study of rhetoric passed through a series of highs and lows as the economic, religious, scholarly, and political conditions changed. Instruction in at least part of the rhetorical canon continued alongside studies of grammar and logic, but in some writings during the period, rhetoric was reduced to a focus on the single canon of style or expression, while logic (or dialectic) was elevated in importance. In the early Renaissance, manuals on the art of letter writing and on poetry were linked to classical treatments of rhetoric, but the oral tradition faded while the connection of rhetoric with style in writing was strengthened. Other handbooks on courtly etiquette and preaching kept alive some interest in other aspects of the rhetorical canon. These works clearly express human interest in developing rhetorical sensitivity; they underscore the belief that there is a strategy or art concerning how people know what to say and how they express themselves in language, whether written or oral. The rediscovery of key classical texts during the fourteenth and fifteenth centuries renewed interest in rhetoric, and rhetorical training continued as a regular part of Western educational systems well into the nineteenth century. The Ciceronian ideal of the public orator experienced a renaissance in the nineteenth-century American oratorical tradition, but in schools, rhetorical training was typically limited to elements of composition and, in some quarters, practice at declamation (reciting speech excerpts) or elocution (developing skills of memorization and delivery).

The renewed interest in rhetorical studies in the mid-twentieth century grew out of several causes. Internationalism, wartime propaganda, new media, and the growth of advertising all increased attention to the creation and analysis of persuasive messages. Academic interest in argumentation, a maturing sense of the complexities of audience analysis, and a renewed interest in the relationships that exist among knowledge, language, and power have supported a burgeoning field of study that reaches across disciplinary boundaries. Practitioners such as motivational speakers, marketers, and politicians are interested in how to discover information about their audiences and, once they have that information, how to create appeals that will be successful.

One way to learn how to create more effective messages is to study past rhetorical efforts. From this theory emerged the discipline of rhetorical criticism. When discourse intends to have an effect on an audience, the questions that are used to analyze it should concern rhetorical rather than simply literary features. In the 1940s and 1950s, Kenneth Burke argued that "identification" rather than "persuasion" is the key rhetorical concept, and he encouraged critics to investigate both the conscious and unconscious ways in which symbol users attempt to get an audience to share their beliefs and values. Rhetorical scholars have investigated a wide range of public discourse, examining everything from the arguments and appeals of the abolition movement of the nineteenth century to the rhetorical power of public memorials to the influence of media coverage of war.

Rhetorical studies is influencing and being influenced by many disciplines. Feminist rhetorical critics have added new perspectives by asking a new set of questions. A contemporary rhetorical study, for example, may investigate how many times women are cited as experts in hard news versus soft news stories and may hypothesize about what that data means as a reflection of the value system of a culture. Influenced by European thinkers such as Michel Foucault and Jacques Derrida, rhetorical critics have explored the hidden assumptions that are revealed by the choices that are made in the production of discourse. Even the discourse of the sciences has been examined to expose the rhetorical conventions that are common to the disciplines and to reveal the belief and value systems as well as the power structures that constrain and shape research questions, processes of investigation, and the reporting of results. The study of semiotics and the relationship among words, meanings, and reality offers further richness for analytical study that produces both practical and theoretic insight.

Although rhetoric as a discipline continues to offer opportunities to reflect on theoretical questions that concern the nature of knowledge and language, for the contemporary student, rhetorical study often remains focused on the effective use of discourse. Students of composition develop the skills that are necessary to improve the clarity and effectiveness of their writing. Students of public speaking practice analyzing the particular demands of a speaking situation and audience, creating materials for a speech, and then organizing, wording, and delivering it. Rhetoric instruction leads students to consider how their choices of content, structure, language, and/or delivery strategy will have a rhetorical effect. Students learn that their choices will influence how the audience receives the message; indeed, they will influence the very meaning of the message for that audience. By developing this consciousness, as well as by underscoring the potential power of discourse in shaping and maintaining culture, the study of rhetoric persists at being central to the mission of higher education.

See also: DEMOCRACY AND THE MEDIA; ETHICS AND INFORMATION; LANGUAGE AND COMMUNICATION; LANGUAGE STRUCTURE; NONVERBAL COMMUNICATION; PROPAGANDA; PUBLIC SPEAKING; SEMIOTICS.

Bibliography

Aristotle. (1954). *Rhetoric,* tr. Rhys Roberts. New York: Random House.

Bizzell, Patricia, and Herzberg, Bruce. (2001). *The Rhetorical Tradition: Readings from Classical Times to the Present,* 2nd edition. Boston: Bedford/St. Martin's Press.

Burke, Kenneth. (1945). *A Grammar of Motives.* New York: Prentice-Hall.

Burke, Kenneth. (1950). *A Rhetoric of Motives.* New York: Prentice-Hall.

Brummett, Barry. (1994). *Rhetoric in Popular Culture.* New York: St. Martin's Press.

Cicero. (1979). *De Oratore,* 3 vols., trs. E. W. Sutton and H. Rackham. Cambridge, MA: Harvard University Press.

Conley, Thomas. (1990). *Rhetoric in the European Tradition.* New York: Longman.

Covino, William A., and Jolliffe, David. A. (1995). *Rhetoric: Concepts, Definitions, Boundaries.* Boston: Allyn & Bacon.

Foss, Sonja K.; Foss, Karen A.; and Trapp, Robert. (1991). *Contemporary Perspectives on Rhetoric,* 2nd edition. Prospect Heights, IL: Waveland Press.

Kennedy, George. (1980). *Classical Rhetoric and its Secular Tradition from Ancient to Modern Times.* Chapel Hill: University of North Carolina Press.

Medhurst, Martin J. (1993). *Landmark Essays on American Public Address.* Davis, CA: Hermagoras Press.

Medhurst, Martin J., and Benson, Thomas W., eds. (1991). *Rhetorical Dimensions in Media: A Critical Casebook,* 2nd edition. Dubuque, IA: Kendall/Hunt.

Schiappa, Edward. (1994). *Landmark Essays on Classical Greek Rhetoric.* Davis, CA: Hermagoras Press.

Amy R. Slagell

■ ROLES AND RESPONSIBILITIES IN GROUP COMMUNICATION

See: Group Communication, Roles and Responsibilities in

S

SARNOFF, DAVID (1891–1971)

David Sarnoff was born in Minsk, Russia. Sarnoff's serious adult demeanor evolved from a childhood of poverty and hardship. His family suffered through Cossack raids and repression that characterized life for millions of Jewish people in Russia. From the time he was four years of age, Sarnoff was drilled on the Torah and the Talmud because his parents hoped that he would become a rabbi. The family emigrated to the United States in 1900, first settling in Albany, New York, and then moving to New York City. After he arrived in the United States, however, Sarnoff's life took on the characteristics of a Horatio Alger story. His father's poor health meant young Sarnoff became head of the family. He began selling Yiddish newspapers, taking English lessons, and delivering telegraph messages.

After being fired from a telegraph delivery job because he requested time off from work for a religious holiday, Sarnoff was hired as an office boy at American Marconi, the struggling U.S. subsidiary of British Marconi. A chance opportunity allowed Sarnoff, at age fifteen, to introduce himself to Guglielmo Marconi, and the relationship that developed between the two of them enabled Sarnoff to pursue additional career opportunities with the company and to further his education.

His employment as a wireless operator for American Marconi, served as the basis for one of Sarnoff's feats of self-promotion. According to stories that he told later in life, Sarnoff monitored the first distress messages from the *Titanic* when it was sinking on April 14, 1912. According to Sarnoff's accounts, he did not leave his post for seventy-two hours because he was the lone wireless operator who was responsible for monitoring the wireless dispatches. In fact, Sarnoff was one of several dozen operators who may have heard transmissions from or about the *Titanic*. Tom Lewis (1991) notes that Sarnoff's wireless equipment was located atop the Wanamaker Department Store in New York City and that the store was closed on Sunday night, April 14, 1912. Therefore, Sarnoff probably did not have access to his equipment until the next day. Furthermore, because of his location in relation to the sinking ship, any reports he did hear would have probably been retransmissions of information received from ships at sea.

Some histories report that Sarnoff envisioned the use of radio as a source of personal entertainment during radio's infancy. The so-called radio music box plan was reported to have been written by Sarnoff to his boss at American Marconi in 1915. Neither the document nor the reply from his boss exists, nor do any other confirming documents from the time. Louise M. Benjamin (1993) notes that there is record of a 1920 memo from Sarnoff to Owen D. Young, who was the chief executive officer of the Radio Corporation of America (RCA) and General Electric at that time. The memo, which is twenty-eight pages long, discusses a number of possibilities for the development of radio broadcasting and was written at a time when a number of ventures were already underway to experiment with radio broadcasting for public consumption. Furthermore, a 1920

As part of the first television broadcast, David Sarnoff speaks at the dedication ceremony for the RCA Building at the 1939 World's Fair in New York City. (Bettmann/Corbis)

"prediction" lacks the foresight that is sometimes falsely attributed to Sarnoff, and the 1920 document illustrates the awareness Sarnoff's superiors already had regarding the future possibilities of radio broadcasting.

These historic myths, however, should not deprive Sarnoff of proper recognition for his role in the development of broadcasting. Sarnoff, who became general manager of RCA in 1921, helped push RCA beyond the business of selling radios and into the field of network radio broadcasting. The National Broadcasting Company (NBC), a wholly-owned subsidiary of RCA, began network service on November 15, 1926. As many as twelve million people were estimated to have heard the premiere broadcast. Soon thereafter, Sarnoff was operating two networks, NBC Red and NBC Blue. Sarnoff faced competition from William Paley and the Columbia Broadcasting System (CBS) network. Paley reportedly admired Sarnoff's propensity for empire building and his Horatio Alger adeptness in creating an industry. Although Paley

lacked Sarnoff's intellect and technological vision, his personal magnetism would create a strong rival for Sarnoff. Sarnoff sought to identify technology that would be useful to the development of both RCA and NBC. He purchased rights to mass-produce Edwin Armstrong's superheterodyne tuner in June 1922 and secured first refusal rights for all other Armstrong inventions. Sarnoff invested in television research in 1929 by hiring Vladimir Zworykin to develop an electronic television system. The RCA television system was publicly demonstrated at the New York World's Fair in 1939. Although inventor Philo Farnsworth successfully demonstrated electronic television in his laboratory in 1927 and in extensive public demonstrations in Philadelphia in 1935 and 1936—and won television patent infringement suits against RCA in 1940—history often reports Sarnoff and RCA as the inventors of television.

Sarnoff's plans for television were almost halted by Armstrong's invention of FM (frequency modulation) radio. While Sarnoff recognized the superior audio quality of the FM signal, he was unwilling to back the system because RCA was developing television. FM radio was seen as a competitor to the success of AM radio, and it would have diverted scientific and government attention away from television. FM service was first authorized in 1940 on the frequency range of 42–50 MHz. After World War II, Sarnoff was able to lobby the Federal Communications Commission (FCC) to move FM service to the frequency range of 88–108 MHz. Because this made all existing FM radio sets obsolete, the change effectively halted the development of FM radio, and Sarnoff moved ahead with his plans for television.

When CBS, in 1945, introduced a color television system that would have made all black-and-white receivers obsolete, Sarnoff used the resources of RCA to develop a color system that was compatible with the existing black-and-white system. Ultimately, the FCC adopted a color system patterned after the RCA system in 1953, giving Sarnoff his greatest company victory by maintaining RCA's dominance in set production and NBC's leadership in color broadcasting.

Sarnoff's service during World War II included planning the radio stations that would broadcast news and information during the D-Day invasion. He was promoted to the rank of brigadier general. After the war, Sarnoff instructed staff members to call him "General Sarnoff."

Sarnoff's RCA and NBC companies were, for him, the start of a dynasty. He retired as chairman of the board in 1970 and died a year later. Including his years with American Marconi, Sarnoff spent more than sixty years with RCA/NBC. Sarnoff's son Robert became president and later chief executive officer but was fired four years after his father's death. After that, Sarnoff's dynasty drifted, lacking a company vision and the necessary leadership. General Electric purchased RCA/NBC in 1985 and promptly sold the RCA assets, including the RCA name.

See also: ARMSTRONG, EDWIN HOWARD; FARNSWORTH, PHILO TAYLOR; FEDERAL COMMUNICATIONS COMMISSION; MARCONI, GUGLIELMO; PALEY, WILLIAM S.; RADIO BROADCASTING, HISTORY OF; RADIO BROADCASTING, TECHNOLOGY OF; TELEVISION BROADCASTING, HISTORY OF; TELEVISION BROADCASTING, TECHNOLOGY OF.

Bibliography

Barnouw, Erik. (1966). *A Tower of Babel: A History of Broadcasting in the United States.* New York: Oxford University Press.

Barnouw, Erik. (1968). *The Golden Web.* New York: Oxford University Press.

Benjamin, Louise M. (1993). "In Search of the Sarnoff 'Radio Music Box' Memo." *Journal of Broadcasting & Electronic Media* 37:325–335.

Bilby, Kenneth. (1986). *The General: David Sarnoff and the Rise of the Communications Industry.* New York: Harper & Row.

Douglas, George. (1987). *The Early Days of Radio Broadcasting.* Jefferson, NC: McFarland.

Lewis, Tom. (1991). *Empire of the Air: The Men Who Made Radio.* New York: HarperCollins.

Lyons, Eugene. (1966). *David Sarnoff, A Biography.* New York: Harper & Row.

Smith, Sally B. (1990). *In All His Glory: The Life of William S. Paley.* New York: Simon & Schuster.

Sterling, Christopher, and Kittross, John M. (1990). *Stay Tuned: A Concise History of American Broadcasting.* Belmont, CA: Wadsworth.

GREG PITTS

▪ SATELLITES, COMMUNICATION

In the most basic terms, the communications satellite industry is made up of those who use satellite transponder time and those who provide or broker satellite time. Satellites are used to transmit all types of video and other data. Uses include news feeds and other occasional services, special events transmission for broadcast and cable outlets, transmission of syndicated programming, video conferencing for business and other applications, distance learning, satellite media tours, distribution of video news releases (VNRs) and commercials, direct-to-home delivery of television programs and events, as well as telephone, data, and Internet applications. Local television and radio stations, or even broadcast networks or major corporations, would find it very costly to launch and maintain their own satellites. Therefore, most outlets lease time on existing satellites if they are going to send satellite news and programming feeds or other types of data.

Major Satellite Service Providers

Some in the industry credit General Electric (GE) with playing a major role in the beginnings

An artist's rendition shows the 7,600-pound DirecTV 1-R satellite, which was launched in October 1999 and made possible the delivery of local broadcast network channels to DirecTV customers. (AFP/Corbis)

of satellite newsgathering (SNG). GE Americom, one of the largest satellite brokerage firms in the United States, operates a fleet of twelve satellites that serves the United States and Canada. Additional satellites serve Latin America, Europe, and Asia. The company operates four tracking, telemetry, and control Earth stations in the continental United States, along with other global facilities.

GE Americom introduced "hybrid" satellites that contain both C-band and Ku-band transponders. GE's subsidiary, NBC, was the first commercial network to have programming delivered by satellite, via Americom satellites and facilities. Americom was also the first provider to make it possible for newsgathering operations to maintain voice communications with home bases while transmitting video.

Loral Skynet is another major supplier of satellite space and services. Loral Skynet came into being when the satellite manufacturer Loral Space & Communications purchased Skynet from AT&T

in 1997. Loral Skynet operates eight satellites in the Telstar fleet and has acquired or partnered with ventures in France, Mexico, and Brazil to expand its reach to most of the world's population.

Vyvx is another of the primary suppliers of satellite time to users in the United States. In addition to its fiber-optic services, Vyvx operates both analog and digital satellites that use both C-band and Ku-band frequencies. Like most providers, Vyvx allows its customers to book time in increments that are as short as fifteen minutes for transmission of news items and short programming segments.

Smaller companies often serve as intermediaries between the users and the providers. These companies, such as Centrex, specialize in acquiring satellite time during peak demand periods. Other providers with more of an international focus include PanAmSat, Intelsat, and ComSat. ComSat is headquartered in Clarksburg, Maryland, and began operation in the 1970s. ComSat is a major investor in New Skies (the commercial component of Intelsat), which was introduced as part of the organization's move toward privatization. Intelsat was formed in 1964 and is an international satellite consortium of more than 140 member countries. Intelsat operates seventeen geostationary satellites, bringing global access to more than two hundred territories and countries worldwide.

PanAmSat is the youngest of the three major international providers. PanAmSat serves major companies such as ESPN and Associated Press Television News (APTV, which is the international television arm of the Associated Press). PanAmSat is also a primary provider of satellite services for transmission of special events, such as the 1996, 1998, and 2000 Olympic Games. When PanAmSat merged with the satellite operations division of Hughes Electronics in 1997, its fleet and support systems grew dramatically. PanAmSat operates twenty-one satellites, with plans to increase its fleet to twenty-five. PanAmSat operates seven technical ground facilities and each month beams approximately ten thousand hours of news, sports, and special events transmissions to audiences around the world.

Independent and Network News Feed Services

The primary users of satellite time for news distribution are local stations, networks, and feed services. A local station can book time unilaterally through one of the major providers, but often stations acquire transponder time through the satellite feed arm of their networks or through satellite newsgathering cooperatives. One of the first of these cooperatives was Florida News Network. The news managers of the involved stations agreed to share video via satellite, allowing each of them to increase coverage of other parts of the state. CONUS (derived from "continental United States") works on the same principle, but on a much broader scale.

CONUS is the world's largest satellite newsgathering cooperative (though not the largest feed service). The company is based in Minneapolis–St. Paul, Minnesota, with offices in New York, Washington, D.C., and London. CONUS offers a number of daily news feeds, custom live reports, and other video services to more than one hundred domestic partners. The company operates eight regional news hubs and transmits more than five hundred news stories each week. CONUS also sells and brokers satellite time via its full-time transponders on SBS-6 and operates All News Channel. In addition to working with news users, CONUS offers its services for a wide range of transmissions for educational and business applications.

The cooperative specializes in customized, live remote coverage using Ku-band satellite technology. CONUS and its members point to a strong regional presence as its biggest strength. Using the satellite trucks of its members and a few that are owned by the company itself, CONUS sends crews to remote sites to cover breaking news such as tornadoes, hurricanes, train wrecks, and other disasters. In this way, they provide a live presence to any station that wishes to include the reports in its newscasts. Stations that are owned by the same parent company often work together through their own satellite cooperatives, outfitting news crews to cover events and issues for the group stations.

CNN NewSource is not strictly a cooperative in the sense that CONUS is. NewSource is the news feed arm of the cable network CNN, which was originally founded on the idea of getting worldwide news to consumers using an extensive network of satellites. NewSource operates on a nonexclusive basis, meaning that more than one station in a market can be affiliated with CNN. In many cases, every station in a market works with CNN, and though some in the business suggest

that NewSource is used to supplement rather than supplant network-run news services, it remains the dominant force in the news feed business with more than five hundred commercial news clients in the United States. Because NewSource has multiple affiliates within markets, it is able to offer its stations a choice of video shot by each of the stations in a particular market when news breaks in that area. The only restriction is that the stations in that market cannot use each other's video. This is referred to as a market embargo.

Other feed services have more of a specific focus, such as Bloomberg, which primarily feeds items about the stock market and business in general, and international news providers, such as *Reuters* and APTV. APTV bought World Television News (WTN) in 1998, leaving only two major suppliers of world news. ABC owned a substantial portion of WTN, and as part of the deal, APTV provides material to ABC and its affiliate news service.

As is the case with other feed services, New-Source offers franchise pieces and features on its twelve regular weekday feeds. It also works with visiting affiliates that want to do live coverage of events in Washington or in other cities in which CNN operates bureaus. NewSource is also available to university and high school news operations at no cost. Through this program, CNN occasionally receives material from its student partners and, perhaps more important, builds name recognition among those who will be making newsroom decisions in the future. In addition to NewSource, CNN also runs NewsBeam, a satellite booking service for its affiliates.

Each of the over-the-air networks offers a feed and satellite booking service for its affiliates as well. NBC News Channel is the only such operation not located in New York City. News Channel is headquartered in Charlotte, North Carolina. Its personnel believe being located somewhere other than New York gives News Channel and the NBC affiliates an edge when it comes to getting the affiliates the video and live-shot capabilities that they need. This is because although News Channel is part of the network, it operates as more of a surrogate for the affiliates than it could as part of the large New York operation. Similar to its counterparts at the other networks, News Channel provides as much as six to eight hours of rolling video per day, sending up to 250 stories in twenty-two different feeds. Approximately 185 NBC affiliates do local news, and News Channel employees estimate that they provide some six hundred live reports per month to the local news operations. Some practitioners say that local stations fill between 10 and 15 percent of their news time with material from satellite feeds. To help feed this appetite for video, News Channel and its counterparts offer business and sports reports, regional coverage, and technical assistance for affiliates that want a live presence at the major national stories.

ABC's feed service is known as NewsOne. As with other services, it has correspondents who do reports that are specifically intended for the local affiliates that use the service. These correspondents travel extensively, covering big, breaking stories and doing custom and/or generic live reports for the affiliates. NewsOne personnel estimate that the service provides some ten thousand custom live reports per year. There are approximately two hundred ABC affiliates that use NewsOne, and those affiliates receive hundreds of stories per day (including medical, consumer, and entertainment reports) for possible inclusion in their newscasts.

The CBS feed service is Newspath, which provides some three hundred to four hundred stories per day to approximately two hundred affiliates through thirteen regional offices. As is the case at the other networks, CBS Newspath works to provide its affiliates with news material for all of their daily newscasts, from predawn to late night. To meet the demand for material, Newspath feeds video every hour, twenty-four hours a day. Newspath also offers its service to college and high school television news operations, the only network feed service to do so. Newspath also provides special sports feeds that allow affiliates to use material to preview NFL games that the network will televise. In addition, Newspath coordinates satellite time for nearly two hundred satellite trucks worldwide.

Fox NewsEdge supplies video to more than one hundred Fox affiliates that offer local news. Compared to the other news feed services, NewsEdge does not have as many affiliates that can contribute material. Therefore, NewsEdge tries to tailor some of its stories to make them specific to Fox affiliates and their viewers. These stories include material such as behind-the-scenes looks at popular Fox programs. As the more established feed services do, NewsEdge strives to make live shots from the sites of breaking news possible for its affiliates. NewsEdge assists affiliates with their regional news needs and provides coverage from cities, such as Washington, D.C., that generate a lot of national news.

Benefits and Costs of Satellite Services

It is common for local television stations to affiliate with more than one video feed/satellite booking service. This generally occurs because station news managers desperately want to avoid "getting beat" on a story. It would be disastrous for stations to see compelling video of a major news event that happened elsewhere in the country appear on the competitor's newscast but not on their own. Having more than one source also makes it possible for news managers to choose the best available video, which allows them to achieve two goals: (1) get material and (2) get better material than the competition.

Belonging to multiple services can be expensive, though all services charge according to market size. The networks would like to see their affiliates sever ties to other feed services, but it is important to the local stations to make sure that they can get material and set up live shots at any time they need. If that means paying for more than one service, news managers appear willing to accept that cost. However, as in any competitive environment, the degree to which a particular service is used, and, ultimately, whether contracts are renewed, depends on which outlet provides the best service at competitive rates.

The biggest benefit satellites provide to any news organization, business, or educational institution is the ability to get video and/or program material to multiple sites simultaneously. For example, well into the 1990s, advertising agencies that placed commercials on television stations in markets across the country had the expense of duplicating and shipping analog (nondigital) videotapes to each station. Being able to transmit digital signals via satellite solves that problem for advertising agencies and any other organization that is interested in top-quality video arriving on the other end of a satellite transmission. Of course, video and programming signals had been sent via satellite for years before digital technology became available, but signal breakup was always a possibility. With digital technology, the receiver gets either a crystal-clear signal or no signal at all.

Satellites, Compression, and Digital Technology

Every company that uses satellites on a regular basis is involved in the move to digital transmission, which goes hand-in-hand with signal compression, video on demand, and media convergence. Digital transmissions make it possible for those who are sending information via satellite to put more material on existing satellite transponders. With geostationary orbit already as crowded as a Los Angeles freeway, satellite users are finding ways to put more signals on existing space. Being able to compress up to six signals on a single transponder allows communications organizations to make better use of resources without having to purchase lots of transponder time from outside vendors.

Digital technology also makes news-on-demand possible. Video feed services are able to make stories available on central data servers as soon as the stories are received. News stations that wish to use the stories do not have to wait until a scheduled feed time, nor is failing to record feeds a problem with news-on-demand. Rather than rolling a videotape at a specified time and waiting until the desired item appears (or forgetting to record the feed), producers can call up a story from a central server on desktop workstations, view the story there, read the accompanying script, and download the story if they choose to use it. Some in the industry say the move to digital news-on-demand is as important as the move from film to videotape. Stories are available as soon as they are stored in a server, and they remain available indefinitely, with none of the quality loss that comes with making analog copies.

Conclusion

Satellites have and will continue to play a key role as media continue to converge. All media have information delivery in common, and satellites are an effective and efficient way to deliver a lot of material to a number of sites at once. Satellite businesses already deliver the Internet to fifty countries, and as print, broadcast, and online operations come together, satellites are likely to remain a mainstay in the delivery of information to audiences worldwide. Satellite providers realize that satellites are the medium that they use, not the business that they are in; they are in the business of information delivery.

See also: CABLE TELEVISION, PROGRAMMING OF; CABLE TELEVISION, SYSTEM TECHNOLOGY OF; DIGITAL COMMUNICATION; RADIO BROADCASTING, TECHNOLOGY OF; SATELLITES, HISTORY OF; SATELLITES, TECHNOLOGY OF; TELECOMMUNICATIONS, WIRELESS; TELEPHONE INDUSTRY, TECHNOLOGY OF; TELEVISION BROADCASTING, PROGRAMMING AND; TELEVISION BROADCASTING, TECHNOLOGY OF.

Bibliography

Anderson, Karen. (1999). "PanAmSat to Deliver Digitally." *Broadcasting & Cable* 129(44):74.

CONUS Communications Company. (2001). "CONUS Communications." <http://www.conus.com>.

Cremer, Charles; Keirstead, Phillip; and Yoakam, Richard. (1996). *ENG: Television News.* NewYork: McGraw-Hill.

Dickson, Glen. (1996). "NBC Adopts Digital SNG Technology." *Broadcasting & Cable* 126(44):55.

Dickson, Glen. (1999). "'News on Demand' for NBC Affils." *Broadcasting & Cable* 129(15):50–51.

GE Americom. (2001). "Newsroom." <http://www.geamericom.com>.

Intelsat. (2001). "Welcome to Intelsat." <http://www.intelstat.com>.

Kerschbaumer, Ken. (1999). "NBC Newschannel Feeds the Future with VNI." *Digital Television* 2(9):1.

Lockheed Martin. (2001). "Global Telecommunications." <http://www.comsat.com>.

Loral Space & Communications. (2001). "Loral Overview." <http://www.loral.com/overview/overview.html>.

McAvoy, Kim. (1998). "Battling for Global News Supremacy." *Broadcasting & Cable* 128(33):34–35.

McAvoy, Kim. (1998). "Fox's News Edge Comes into Its Own." *Broadcasting & Cable* 128(33):29.

McAvoy, Kim. (1998). "Net Expands to Fill News Hole." *Broadcasting & Cable* 128(33):24–28.

PanAmSat. (2001). "Welcome to the Future." <http://www.panamsat.com>.

Silverstein, Sam. (1999). "New CEO's Expertise Reflects PanAmSat Focus on Internet." *Space News* 10(11):16.

Williams Communications. (2001). "Vyvx Services." <http://www.williamscommunications.com/>.

C. A. TUGGLE

SATELLITES, HISTORY OF

A history of communication satellites must begin with the first satellite, though it was not used for communication. On October 4, 1957, the former Soviet Union launched *Sputnik I*, making the Soviet Union the first space power and starting the space race between the United States and the Soviet Union. The United States was the second country to reach space. Four months after *Sputnik I* achieved orbit, the United States launched *Explorer I*.

The idea of using satellites for communication predates both *Explorer* and *Sputnik*. In 1945, Arthur C. Clarke first suggested that satellites in geosynchronous orbit could be used for communication purposes. The belt that circles the Equator more than 22,000 miles in space is often called Clarke orbit, in his honor.

In 1960, the National Aeronautics and Space Administration (NASA) and Skynet joined forces to launch an experimental aluminum-coated balloon. *Echo I* was used to reflect microwave radio signals between Holmdel, New Jersey, and Goldstone, California. What engineers learned from *Echo I* formed the basis of all future satellite transmission engineering calculations. In 1962, *Telstar I*, another joint venture of NASA and Skynet, became the world's first active communication satellite. The founding of the Communications Satellite Corporation (ComSat) in 1963 marked the beginning of deployment and operation of satellites on a commercial basis.

Early Satellites

The International Telecommunications Satellite Organization (Intelsat) was created in 1964. Intelsat is a consortium of countries that bonded together to form a cooperative to operate communication satellites. In August of that year, NASA's *Syncom 3* became the first geostationary communication satellite. A few months later, in April 1965, Intelsat began operations with *Early Bird*, which provided 240 telephone circuits and a single, fuzzy black-and-white television link between Europe and the United States.

Once Intelsat had launched additional satellites, it was able to establish the first global communication satellite system in 1969. On July 20, 1969, Intelsat provided television coverage of the historic lunar landing of the U.S. spacecraft

Apollo 11. The first words spoken by a human on the moon (Neil Armstrong's "That's one small step for man, one giant leap for mankind") were heard by millions of people around the world because of one giant leap in communication technology, which continued to improve. In 1978, approximately one billion people in forty-two countries were able to watch World Cup soccer matches that were beamed around the globe by Intelsat.

Westar I, which was the first U.S. domestic communication satellite, was launched on April 13, 1974. By the end of 1976, there were 120 transponders available over the United States. Each transponder could provide fifteen hundred telephone channels and one television channel. The Public Broadcasting System (PBS) was the first network to send programming to its affiliates via satellite. On February 1, 1978, twenty-four stations in the southeastern United States began receiving programming through a single C-band transponder on *Westar I*. For a month, PBS continued to use telephone company lines as a backup to the satellite. It took nearly one year to get all PBS affiliates across the nation on the system. By then, PBS was using three transponders to provide time-delay feeds to stations in different time zones.

Lyndon Johnson watches the first television transmission from France via the Telstar satellite, which was put into orbit by the United States in July 1962. (Bettmann/Corbis)

The Satellite Boom

In the early 1980s, the Intelsat V and VI spacecraft series made it possible, for the first time, for broadcasters to transmit news feeds using relatively small, portable Earth stations. Prior to that time, broadcasters used the land lines of a single company, AT&T, to transmit news feeds, and indeed, until the late 1970s, all network programming was fed to affiliates via land lines. A failure of AT&T's lines meant no television for viewers in the affected area. The networks first began to use C-band satellites as a backup to the telephone company lines, and generally, the satellite transmissions proved to be more dependable. However, C-band dishes are quite large and not very portable, and all transmissions on those frequencies require clearance by the Federal Communications Commission (FCC) to minimize interference problems with other communication devices (such as terrestrial microwave) that operate on the same frequency band. All of those factors made it almost impossible to use C-band to transmit news feeds, except of the most important, preplanned events. When CNN went on the air on June 1, 1980, the cable network fed its programming using C-band.

At about the same time, Ku-band became more of a possibility. There was only one class of primary users for Ku-band, and the higher frequency meant that the wavelength was shorter, hence, the size of the dish was about one-third that needed for C-band. The size, mobility, and lack of interference on Ku-band opened up a world of possibilities for news operations.

One date in the early 1980s stands out in the minds of many as the day that satellites made a lasting change in the way in which local stations covered news. On the same day that Ronald Reagan was sworn in as president of the United States, January 20, 1981, Iran released fifty-two American hostages who had been held for more than one year. News operations from markets across the United States had crews in place to cover the inauguration and in place to cover the return of hostages to the soil of a friendly country and, eventually, back to the United States. Many local stations devoted extensive coverage to the return of "home-town" people among the hostages.

Satellites gave news operations a whole new array of news sources, and they changed the very definition of local news. Prior to the early 1980s, local news included only what stations could cover in the surrounding area. After satellites became a part of a local station's coverage options, local news expanded to include anything that would be of interest to local viewers, regardless of where the event occurred. News managers could send crews to cover interesting cultural events in other parts of the state, events of the day from the state legislature, and even events that took place in other parts of the world.

The mid-1980s saw an explosion of live reporting via satellite, as news outlets and programmers realized that properly sizing Ku-band dishes would eliminate most of the concern about weather interference with Ku-band signals. Technological advances also made the equipment smaller, lighter, and, perhaps most important, less expensive. Various satellite cooperatives arose at that time, including CONUS (derived from "continental United States"), which was formed in 1984 by Hubbard Broadcasting and a group of limited-partner television stations. CONUS built its product with the needs of local news operations in mind, and uplink-equipped trucks became the satellite equivalent of electronic newsgathering (ENG) field units. CONUS began feeding video on half transponders as early as 1985. Because the dishes had to be larger to send narrower bandwidth signals (to take up only half a transponder), Earth stations were more expensive, but news operations and satellite vendors were able to recoup those expenses by spending less on satellite time. Being able to get more than one signal on a transponder became increasingly important during peak news hours as more and more stations started to do live reporting.

Video Feed Services

CNN started its video feed service, NewSource, in October 1987, and it and CONUS became viable ways for local stations to get video from other stations across the country. The success that NewSource and CONUS had in attracting local stations to use their services caused news executives at the major networks to rethink their commitment to their affiliates, and all three networks soon revamped their own feed services. For example, NBC helped many of its affiliates to purchase Ku-band satellite trucks and was a leader in the switch to Ku-band feeds. Many industry observers say satellites changed the relationship between networks and their affiliates forever, as the networks turned more and more to the affiliates to get news material for network programs and became more responsive to the affiliates' needs for video from other markets.

Soon, local stations and networks were sending and receiving video so frequently that what some have called a "river of video" developed in space. Through the 1980s, more stations acquired satellite newsgathering equipment and more channels developed, requiring the distribution of programming to cable headends (distribution points) throughout the United States and beyond. The explosion of cable channels would have been impossible without satellite distribution of material. Likewise, local news operations began to expand from sixty or ninety minutes of news per day to as much as three or four hours per day. In many cases, this was done with little or no additional staff. Much of the material that was used to fill the extra news time came from regional and national feed services and consortia.

About that time, Hubcom developed fly-away packs. All of the hardware that was needed to send satellite signals could be put into cases that were small enough to fit into the cargo area of airliners. With an engineer to operate the system, a news crew could be on-site and sending signals from some of the most remote places on Earth within a few hours of landing.

International Uses

The international market for satellite distribution continued to expand as well. However, one man felt that the Hispanic market was being ignored by the only international carrier at the time, Intelsat. Rene Anselmo was head of what has since become the Spanish-language network, Univision. In the late 1980s, he lobbied the Reagan administration for permission to launch his own satellite. He hoped to use the satellite to link the United States and Latin America. *PAS-1* was launched in 1988. It was the world's first privately owned international satellite, and it cost Anselmo most of his personal fortune to put it in the sky. Still, the company that he founded—PanAmSat— soon came to rival Intelsat as an international provider of satellite services.

Compression

The early 1990s saw the beginning of signal compression as more and more users tried to fit more and more material on a limited number of communication satellites. Because there is only so much room in geostationary orbit, the satellite industry had to figure out a way to get more signals onto existing satellites. PanAmSat was an early leader in this arena. The idea is simple. If more than one signal can be squeezed (compressed) so that they fit on a single transponder, feed capacity can double, triple, or even quadruple without the launch of a single new satellite. The only other option was to reduce the spacing of satellites in Clarke orbit from two degrees to one degree, but that would have made it necessary to double the size of Earth-based uplink antennas. That would have limited the number of places where ground stations could go, and it would have been costly as well.

Satellite companies continue to launch new spacecraft that occupy the few remaining orbital slots and expand the number of transponders that are available. In July 1997, *Telstar V* ushered in the digital age, giving users the opportunity to use full transponders or to channelize (compress) signals to get more capacity out of existing hardware with no loss of quality. On January 24, 2000, PanAmSat deployed a powerful hybrid satellite (having both C- and Ku-band transponders).

See also: CABLE TELEVISION, SYSTEM TECHNOLOGY OF; DIGITAL COMMUNICATION; SATELLITES, COMMUNICATION; SATELLITES, TECHNOLOGY OF; TELECOMMUNICATIONS, WIRELESS; TELEPHONE INDUSTRY, TECHNOLOGY OF; TELEVISION BROADCASTING, TECHNOLOGY OF.

Bibliography

Cremer, Charles; Keirstead, Phillip; and Yoakam, Richard. (1996). *ENG: Television News.* NewYork: McGraw-Hill.

McAvoy, Kim. (1998). "Net Expands to Fill News Hole." *Broadcasting & Cable* 128(33):24–28.

Paxman, Andrew. (1999). "Steel Beams." *Variety* 374(6):58.

C. A. TUGGLE

■ SATELLITES, TECHNOLOGY OF

As with radio or television itself, it is not necessary to understand thoroughly the electronics and physics of satellites in order to understand how they work. Operating a satellite system is a bit more complicated than turning on a television and changing the channel, but the concepts are not difficult to grasp.

Satellites are Earth-orbiting spacecraft that are used to relay radio frequency signals. They are normally powered by batteries and/or solar cells. Satellites operate on various frequency bands, and they carry voice, data, fax, audio, and video information. The focus of this entry will be on television news uses of satellites, so it will be more concerned with audio and video than with other types of transmissions.

The Uplink

All satellite transmissions (i.e., feeds) begin with an uplink, which is the Earth-based transmission station that sends a signal to the satellite. The word "uplink" is also used as a verb; to uplink is to send a signal to a satellite. Two of the most common frequency bands that are used for audio and video transmissions that originate in the United States are Ku-band and C-band. C-band is the part of the electromagnetic spectrum between 3.7 and 4.2 gigahertz, and the range for Ku-band is 11.7 to 12.7 gigahertz. Ku-band is the more portable of the two, but it is not as powerful as C-band. Because C-band is very powerful and because some frequencies in the range are also used for other types of transmissions, each C-band transmission that originates in the United States requires clearance from the Federal Communications Commission (FCC).

The dishes that are used for C-band transmissions are so large it takes tractor-trailer rigs to get them into place. Ku-band satellite dishes are small enough to fit on the roofs of medium-size trucks, and transmissions on those frequencies do not require prior clearance. Hence, the portability and speed that are afforded by Ku-band transmissions make it the choice for most news uses. However, because Ku-band signals can be affected by adverse weather, C-band transmissions are commonly used for lengthy, planned events, such as sports contests or political conventions.

Hardware and "Windows"

In order to make a satellite feed, a television or radio station needs hardware and satellite time. The hardware includes the uplink. Uplinks can either be fixed or portable. Fixed satellite uplinks are those that would be mounted on the roofs of television stations or elsewhere. Portable uplinks (PUPS) would be mounted on the roofs of large vans or medium-size trucks, and it is those types of uplinks that are used to send signals from remote sites. The technology has become sophisticated and small enough that all of the necessary hardware for a satellite transmission can fit into a case that is the size of a large suitcase. These fly-away packs allow news crews to access sites to which they could not drive even a medium-size satellite truck.

Most satellite trucks include the following elements:

- controls to raise and position the dish,
- monitors to check that signals are meeting technical requirements and are going to the desired satellite and transponder,
- a complete communication package, including land-line phones, cell phones, and a way to communicate via audio subcarrier on the satellite in places that have no regular or cell phone service,
- a means to access electrical power and a generator for use in remote locations,
- videotape playback units, and
- inputs for one or more live cameras.

Many trucks also come equipped with redundant transmission systems, which means they contain two of every component that is needed to send a signal. Some also include editing equipment for on-site compilation of stories.

Some large-market television stations or networks might own one or more uplinks, but most do not own satellites; instead, they lease space. A coordinator merely calls one of the many providers of satellite time and books a window. The "window" is the time that is reserved by that news operation for that particular satellite feed. Windows are set up in military-style time (meaning, for example, that they are scheduled for "18:10" instead of "6:10 P.M."), and they can be booked in intervals that can last for as little as five minutes. Satellite feeds run the allotted time and no more. Should a station book a window from 18:10 to 18:15, someone in the news operation must ensure that the feed ends by 18:15 because the computer that times the window will "pull the plug" at 18:15.00, even if the reporter who is live on the scene needs only a few more seconds to finish the story.

Once the window is purchased and "opens" (at 18:10 in the above example), an uplink operator directs the signal to a specific transponder on a satellite. Most communication satellites carry a minimum of twenty-four transponders, which are the specific parts of the satellite that accept the signal, process it, and direct it back to Earth. Some satellites carry as many as seventy-two transponders, thirty-six C-band and thirty-six Ku-band. Each transponder operates on a specified frequency, and all communication satellites are in the same relative orbit at all times, so by merely consulting a chart of satellite positions and "dialing in" the signal, the uplink operator can locate the desired satellite. This does require some precision. Because there are more than two hundred communication satellites in geostationary orbit above the Equator, they are so close to each other as to be positioned only two degrees apart. (If satellites are aimed at different landmasses or operate on different frequency bands, they can be even closer than two degrees apart.) If a satellite suddenly stopped in its orbit for some unexplained reason, there would be a space pile-up of major proportions. The International Telecommunications Union (ITU) and the FCC help maintain order in the satellite industry by assigning orbital slots to spacecraft. Because of the closeness of one satellite to another, technicians must be careful not to "light up" the wrong satellite. However, once the proper satellite has been identified, it is merely a matter of punching in the frequency of the particular transponder on which the news or programming operation has booked time and then sending the signal.

Geosynchronous Orbit

Communication satellites are always in the same relative orbit because they are programmed to match the speed of Earth's rotation. This puts them in geosynchronous (or geostationary) orbit. What this means is that the satellite appears to be stationary relative to a given point on Earth. In the early days of satellite communication, before the use of geosynchronous orbit, Earth-based transmission units had to track the satellite as it passed overhead, and because of that, the satellite was available to accept signals only a few minutes out of each hour. Modern satellites, until they fall out of geostationary orbit, are available around the clock and never change their relative locations.

The Downlink

The transponder accepts the signal, processes it, and sends it back to Earth on a different frequency. Many satellite dishes are equipped both to send and receive, so the dish on top of a building or atop a satellite newsgathering (SNG) truck is capable of sending a signal on one frequency and receiving the return signal on a different frequency. If two different dishes were required, it would be a much more costly and difficult process to do satellite feeds. Although the signal from the uplink to the satellite is very directed, the signal that comes back to Earth from the satellite covers a wide area that is referred to as the "footprint." Any receiver (downlink) that is within the footprint can receive the downlink signal if the receiver is tuned to the correct frequency. As with the term "uplink," "downlink" can refer to the hardware or the process.

Any given satellite can have a footprint that covers land area that is equivalent to the size of the continental United States. Beyond that, Earth's curvature becomes a problem. So, for example, in order to broadcast portions of the 2000 Summer Olympics live back to the United States from Sydney, Australia, NBC had to use satellite "hops." This entails sending the signal up to a satellite, back to a downlink, back up to another satellite, and so on until the signal reaches the intended receiving point on the other side of the globe.

Often, a satellite feed actually involves two feeds: the distribution feed and the backhaul. The backhaul is the feed that goes to the distribution point for refeed. For example, a news feed service brings in a number of stories from various sources and compiles those stories to be sent out as part of a regularly scheduled feed. Another example is sports. A game might be beamed back to a central point for insertion of commercials, graphics, or other material before it is beamed back out for distribution. Therefore, a game telecast might occupy two transponders for hours. The same is true of coverage of political conventions and the like.

Because of the large area that is covered by the footprint, stations are able to share audio and/or video with each other quickly and efficiently. In the "dark ages" of television news, if several sta-

The large number of television satellite trucks that were parked next to the State Capitol in Tallahassee, Florida, in the period shortly after the 2000 election testify to how pervasive satellites have become for the transmission of news material. (AFP/Corbis)

tions in various markets requested a story from a sister station in another city, it would involve reshooting film for each of the requesting stations and putting it on a bus or driving it to the other city. Even when video came into use, stations had to make a copy of the story for each of their requesting partners and ship the tapes somehow. With satellite technology, however, the originating station merely sends its version of the story via satellite to all of the requesting stations at once. To take advantage of the technology, groups of stations have banded together to share video from market to market. These cooperatives are called consortia.

All geostationary communication satellites are positioned 22,300 miles above the Equator. It is at this precise distance that a satellite can maintain an orbit that perfectly matches the period of rotation of the earth: twenty-four hours. Although satellites are so far out in space, they are not necessarily directly overhead, and a line-of-sight is required between the uplink and the satellite. For example, if a particular satellite is low on the eastern horizon and the satellite truck is positioned on the west side of a high-rise building, it will be impossible to hit the satellite with the signal, and the news operation will have to move the truck or use a different satellite.

Mix-Minus

It takes about half a second for a signal to hit the satellite and bounce back to Earth. Because of that delay, a reporter can be caught off-guard and be confused if he or she starts hearing what was just said as he or she is trying to say something different. It is necessary for a reporter on a remote site to hear any questions that a news anchor might ask, so to deal with the problem of voice delay, an audio operator feeds "mix-minus" into the earpiece of the reporter. Mix-minus is the audio mix that is going out from the station to the viewers, minus the reporter's own voice. The station's program audio is fed to the reporter on-scene through an interruptible fold back (IFB) system. This is the same system through which a producer in the control room communicates with the news anchors in the studio.

Consortia

At times, a reporter will be doing a story live and will do the same live report for sister stations in rapid succession. However, if the story is big enough to be the top story on a number of stations in a state or region, the personnel at station B will not want to postpone airing the story for the three to five minutes that it might take station A to complete its report. In these instances, news managers will arrange for the story to appear simultaneously on the reporter's station and on other stations within a consortium. These are referred to as "hit-time" or "hard-start" live shots. Each station in the consortium must arrange to "hit the window" at a precise time. At each station, an anchor will say something like "John Smith joins us from the scene." Since the reporter can hear only his or her own station's anchor, timing is critical, because the reporter will start talking as soon as the anchor tosses to him or her. Therefore, a hard-start live shot with a hit time of 6:01:00 means exactly that. Each station must be ready to have the reporter start talking at exactly 6:01:00.

In most cases, the reporter would have fed the taped portion of the report via satellite earlier, and each station will have a copy. When the reporter reaches a predetermined roll cue (i.e., the final few words that will be said before the tape is to begin), each station will play its copy of the tape. When the tape reaches its conclusion, each station will switch back to the reporter live on the scene. He or she will then wrap up the story and end it with a generic line such as "and now back to you in the studio." All stations that are using the hit-time live report can move on to other stories, and the anchors at the reporter's own station can continue to talk to him or her if the newscast producer has decided to have the anchors do so. By doing shared live shots this way, all the stations that are within the consortium have the advantage of having a reporter live on the scene, even though, except for one station, it was someone else's reporter and equipment that generated the story.

Conclusion

It is no exaggeration to say that satellite technology has changed many things about television and radio news. In fact, the technology has changed the very definition of local news. No longer does a local newscast on television or radio contain only stories that occurred within a half-hour drive of the station; it can include anything of interest to the local audience, from anywhere in the nation or the world. Whereas it once took a crew of technicians the better part of a day to set up a live television remote, now one person can set up a satellite truck and be sending pictures to any number of stations within about fifteen minutes of having arrived on the scene. This has led to concerns that technology now drives journalism, particularly in television news. It has also led to calls for news managers to use the technology to advance stories rather than as an end in itself.

See also: CABLE TELEVISION, PROGRAMMING OF; CABLE TELEVISION, SYSTEM TECHNOLOGY OF; DIGITAL COMMUNICATION; RADIO BROADCASTING, TECHNOLOGY OF; SATELLITES, COMMUNICATION; SATELLITES, HISTORY OF; TELECOMMUNICATIONS, WIRELESS; TELEPHONE INDUSTRY, TECHNOLOGY OF; TELEVISION BROADCASTING, PROGRAMMING AND; TELEVISION BROADCASTING, TECHNOLOGY OF.

Bibliography

Cremer, Charles; Keirstead, Phillip; and Yoakam, Richard. (1996). *ENG: Television News.* New York: McGraw-Hill.

McAvoy, Kim. (1998). "Net Expands to Fill News Hole." *Broadcasting & Cable* 128(33):24–28.

C. A. TUGGLE

■ SCHRAMM, WILBUR (1907–1987)

Wilbur Schramm established the field of communication study by founding the first doctoral-granting programs and the first university-based communication research institutes and by writing the first textbooks for the field. For several decades, he had great influence in shaping the directions of communication research. The academic field has since grown to approximately two thousand university departments that award about fifty thousand bachelor-level degrees per year—5 percent of all the degrees awarded by U.S. universities. In addition, communication study is widely taught in Latin American, European, and

Asian universities, where far more students are enrolled than in the United States.

Schramm grew up in the town of Marietta, Ohio, and received his bachelor's degree from Marietta College in 1928. He then earned his master's degree in American civilization at Harvard University in 1930 and his doctoral degree in English literature at the University of Iowa in 1932. After two years as a postdoctoral fellow in experimental psychology, Schramm became a faculty member at the University of Iowa, where he also founded and directed the Iowa Writers' Workshop, a famed graduate-level fiction-writing program. Here, from 1934 to 1941, he worked out the pedagogical principles for the doctoral programs in communication that he was to establish later at the University of Iowa, the University of Illinois, and Stanford University. His approach involved the careful selection of graduate students, small-sized classes and seminars, and a supportive and participatory learning environment.

The turning point in Schramm's career, leading to his founding the new field of communication study, occurred when the United States entered World War II. A patriot, Schramm immediately volunteered for government duty in Washington, D.C., where he directed programs for the Office of Facts and Figures and its follow-on agency, the Office of War Information (which became the U.S. Information Agency). From 1941 to 1943, he worked with the sociologist Paul F. Lazarsfeld, the political scientist Harold Lasswell, the social psychologists Kurt Lewin and Carl Hovland, and other American social scientists who were involved in various wartime duties in Washington. They met regularly to plan communication activities to promote the war effort (such as national campaigns to grow Victory Gardens; conserve gasoline, tires, and certain foods; buy War Bonds; and participate in scrap iron and scrap rubber drives). Schramm and his network of fellow scholars shared an interest in communication research and sought to apply this new scholarly perspective in evaluating military training films, in analyzing Allied and Axis propaganda, and in designing public communication campaigns aimed at the American people. Schramm's vision for the scholarly field of communication study grew out of the multidisciplinary network to which he belonged in Washington. He possessed the can-do spirit needed to launch this vision in the university setting.

In 1943, Schramm left Washington to return to the University of Iowa, where he was appointed director of the School of Journalism. He promptly established the Bureau of Communication Research and offered a doctoral degree in communication. His model for the research institute at Iowa was Paul Lazarsfeld's Office of Radio Research at Columbia University, which Schramm saw as an opportunity to found the new academic field of communication within existing university structures. There were other movements in launching doctoral programs in journalism and mass communication at the University of Wisconsin and at the University of Minnesota at about this same time, championed by Willard Bleyer, a professor of journalism at Wisconsin, and his former students, but Schramm's vision was to have a greater eventual influence.

From 1947 to 1953, Schramm was to implement his vision for communication study on a grander scale at the University of Illinois at Urbana. Here he served as director of the Institute of Communications Research, a research and doctorate-granting unit, and became dean of the newly formed College of Communication. He also was editor of the University of Illinois Press, and in this capacity he published Claude E. Shannon's important book, *The Mathematical Theory of Communication* (1949). Schramm's University of Illinois Press also published his edited book, *The Process and Effects of Mass Communication* (1954), a textbook that helped define the new field. Administrative support for Schramm's innovative academic activities at Illinois ended when the university president was fired. Schramm began to look for other opportunities.

In 1953, Schramm went to Stanford University, where he was to spend the next twenty years as director of the Institute for Communication Research, which became the most respected and influential center for communication study. Schramm was also the Janet M. Peck Professor of International Communication, a title that reflected his growing interest in international communication and in the role of communication in the development of the nations of Latin American, Africa, and Asia (his 1959 and 1964 books, respectively, defined these new applications of communication theory and research). Schramm was also influential in directing communication study to the effects of television violence on children (this in his 1961 book with Jack Lyle and Edwin Parker). At Stanford, Schramm trained a cadre of outstanding scholars in communication research and theory.

These new doctorates in communication from Schramm's research institute joined the faculty of existing schools of journalism and departments of speech, gradually converting these units to a dominant concern with communication science. This change, reflected in the increasingly widespread use of the term "communication" in their names, largely occurred in the 1970s and 1980s.

In 1973, Schramm retired from Stanford University and then wound down his career at the East-West Communication Institute at the University of Hawaii at Manoa. During this final stage of his career, Schramm served as the Ah Boon Haw Professor of Communication at the Chinese University of Hong Kong in 1977. More generally, during his fourteen years in Hawaii, Schramm assisted the growth of communication study in Asia. He died in 1987, leaving unfinished a book of his memoirs about the beginnings of communication study. This volume was finally published in 1997.

Unlike such forefathers of the field of communication as Lasswell, Lazarsfeld, Lewin, and Hovland, who pioneered in conducting research on propaganda, mass communication effects, small-group communication, and persuasion, respectively, Schramm left his original academic field of English literature. He was the first scholar in the world to carry the title of professor of communication. He founded communication research institutes, departments of communication, and a college of communication, and thus his students earned degrees in communication. Then they spread out like scholarly missionaries to implement his vision at various universities in the United States and abroad. His quality as a visionary, institution builder, and trainer of early communication scholars distinguished Schramm from the four forefathers of the field. For this reason, Wilbur Schramm is the founder of the academic field of communication.

See also: LAZARSFELD, PAUL F.; MODELS OF COMMUNICATION.

Bibliography

Rogers, Everett M. (1994). *A History of Communication Study: A Biographical Approach.* New York: Free Press.

Schramm, Wilbur, ed. (1954). *The Process and Effects of Mass Communication.* Urbana: University of Illinois Press.

Schramm, Wilbur. (1959). *One Day in the World's Press.* Stanford, CA: Stanford University Press.

Schramm, Wilbur. (1964). *Mass Media and National Development.* Stanford, CA: Stanford University Press.

Schramm, Wilbur. (1997). *The Beginnings of Communication Study in America: A Personal Memoir.* Newbury Park, CA: Sage Publications.

Schramm, Wilbur; Lyle, Jack; and Parker, Edwin B. (1961). *Television in the Lives of Our Children.* Stanford, CA: Stanford University Press.

EVERETT M. ROGERS

■ SEMIOTICS

What do words, visual ads, art performances, make-up, uniforms, and pictures have in common? They all are signs—"something which stands to somebody for something in some respect or capacity," to use the words of Charles Sanders Peirce. They all mean something to someone; for example, the word "house" may stand for "a building that serves as living quarters for one or more families," uniforms may represent certain occupations, and so on. What signs mean, how meaning is generated and interpreted, and how signs are used are all issues that are studied in the field of "semiotics" (from the Greek word *semeion*, or "sign"). Sometimes, the study of signs is referred to as "semiology," but the term "semiotics" is much more common.

Origin of Semiotics

People have been interested in signs for many centuries. In fact, the first definition of "sign" was given by Hippocrates (460–377 B.C.E.), who treated it as a medical symptom (e.g., sore throat standing for a cold). After that, signs have been studied through the ages by such thinkers as Plato, Aristotle, St. Augustine, John Locke, and Immanuel Kant. However, it was only toward the end of the nineteenth century that semiotics was developed as a separate field, thanks to the works of Peirce, an American philosopher, and Ferdinand de Saussure, a Swiss linguist.

Conceptual Framework of Semiotics

The range of semiotics is very broad, but there are a number of concepts that are central to the field, including sign, code, medium, types of signs, and dimensions of signs.

There are two main conceptions of sign: dyadic, developed by de Saussure, and triadic, developed by Peirce. In the dyadic conception, sign is an arbitrary relationship between signifier and signified. Signifier is an image of the world that people experience through the senses; signified is the concept people connect with their experiences. For example, an advertisement (sign) combines the signifier (acoustic or visual image) and the signified (corresponding concept). In the triadic conception, sign combines representatum that stands for its object and generates interpretant (its meaning). It is important to note that, in both conceptions, signs have meanings only because the experience and the concept are connected by people (i.e., signs generate meanings only within sociocultural frameworks).

Signs are organized into codes, or coding systems, for example, spoken/written language, dance, clothing, dating rituals, body language, and Morse code. Codes are normative since they present a set of rules of how (not) to act; in this sense, codes can be broken deliberately or through incompetence (e.g., offending someone by using inappropriate gestures that one knows will cause offense or offending someone by using inappropriate gestures without knowing they will cause offense). Codes are used for designing and interpreting messages.

One and the same message can be designed in more than one medium, that is, involve different senses (e.g., visual, auditory, tactile, etc.). The medium presupposes the use of certain code/s (e.g., the phonemic code presupposes the auditory medium). Each medium has its own sense ratio, depending on how much information can be processed during a certain time interval. For example, in most situations the visual medium is more dominant. In all cases, the medium is not something separate from information. In that respect, signs do not simply transmit meanings; they constitute a medium in which meanings are constructed. To use the famous expression of Marshall McLuhan, "The medium is the message."

The most well-known classification of signs is the one developed by Peirce, who identified three types of signs, based on how they represent the objects of the world. Icons signify the world through resemblance so that people can recognize the object (e.g., a photograph visually looks like its object; the word "cock-a-doodle-do" resembles the sounds made by a rooster). Indexes signify the world through indication so that people can figure out this causal relationship (e.g., smoke indicating fire; pointing finger indicating where an object is located in space). Symbols signify the world through convention so that people must learn the relationship between the sign and its object (e.g., most verbal signs). Signs are considered genuine, that is, generating most meanings, if the connection between the representatum and the object is conventional.

According to Charles Morris, a famous American semiotician, all signs have three main dimensions: syntactic (signs in relation to other signs within the same system), semantic (signs in relation to the objects they represent), and pragmatic (signs in relation to their users, i.e., people who produce and interpret signs). For example, syntactically, the sign "cow" is made up of three letters in a certain order; semantically, the sign denotes "mature female of cattle"; and, pragmatically, this sign may generate different responses (e.g., in India a cow is viewed as a sacred animal).

Scope of Semiotics

The scope of semiotic studies is very broad. Among the objects of semiotic analysis are literary works, clothing, advertisements, music, architecture, urban planning, human–computer interaction, sports and games, law, and so on. All these objects are regarded as "texts." When people interpret these semiotic objects, they gain an access to the world and make it meaningful. They always try to capture the most immediate (the most "real") meanings; however, these meanings are presented in an indirect way (i.e., mediated). Thus, signs as texts are forms of mediation; in this sense, different communication situations are characterized by different degrees of mediation (e.g., theatrical performance is less mediated than television). With the development of new information technologies, the line between the natural world taken for granted and the constructed world becomes more and more blurred. This could have certain advantages (e.g., the use of "virtual reality" for educational purposes) and possible disadvantages (e.g., increase of violence, especially among youths, due to the influence of mass media).

Semiotics is applied to the study of both the structural organization of texts ("structural semiotics") and the different social meanings these texts may generate ("social semiotics"). Thus, semiotics moves from language to all modes of representation employed in production and interpretation of texts. Semiotics can reveal the signifying practices behind ideology, power, gender, and so on. Semiotics emphasizes the role of signs in the construction of reality and demonstrates how the "real world" can be challenged and changed. Ultimately, semiotics can help people to understand how they construct their identities, that is, make sense of themselves.

See also: ADVERTISING EFFECTS; HUMAN-COMPUTER INTERACTION; LANGUAGE ACQUISITION; LANGUAGE AND COMMUNICATION; LANGUAGE STRUCTURE; McLUHAN, HERBERT MARSHALL; PEIRCE, CHARLES SANDERS.

Bibliography

Berger, Arthur. (1999). *Signs in Contemporary Culture: An Introduction to Semiotics.* Salem, MA: Sheffield Publishing.
Colapietro, Vincent. (1993). *Glossary of Semiotics.* New York: Paragon House.
Danesi, Marcello. (1999). *Of Cigarettes, High Heels, and Other Interesting Things: An Introduction to Semiotics.* New York: St. Martin's Press.
Eco, Umberto. (1979). *A Theory of Semiotics.* Bloomington: Indiana University Press.
Hartshorne, Charles; Weiss, Paul; and Burks, Arthur, eds. (1931–1935, 1958). *The Collected Papers of Charles Sanders Peirce,* 8 vols. Cambridge, MA: Belknap Press of Harvard University Press.
Jensen, Klaus. (1995). *The Social Semiotics of Mass Communication.* Thousand Oaks, CA: Sage Publications.
Merrell, Floyd. (1995). *Semiosis in the Postmodern Age.* West Lafayette, IN: Purdue University Press.
Nöth, Winfred. (1995). *Handbook of Semiotics.* Bloomington: Indiana University Press.

IGOR E. KLYUKANOV

■ SESAME STREET

Sesame Street, produced by Sesame Workshop (formerly known as the Children's Television Workshop), premiered on November 10, 1969. What began as an experiment to use television to help prepare preschool children for school, particularly those children from minority and low-income families, has grown into a cultural icon. *Sesame Street* has won more Emmy awards than any other series in the history of television. It is watched each weekday by one million children in the United States who are between two and five years of age, and it has been viewed in more than 140 countries, including twenty co-productions.

History

Sesame Street was a revolutionary departure from the existing state of children's television in the late 1960s. While some television series conveyed positive messages to children, none attempted to address a set of specified educational goals—to teach a holistic curriculum that encompasses traditional academic subjects (e.g., number and literacy skills) and interpersonal skills to foster self-confidence and getting along with others. In 1966, Joan Ganz Cooney, a producer at Channel 13 (a New York affiliate of the Public Broadcasting Service (PBS)), developed the original vision of using television to educate preschoolers, an idea she discussed with Lloyd Morrisett, Vice President of the Carnegie Corporation of New York. With funding from the Carnegie Corporation, the Ford Foundation, and the U.S. Office of Education, Cooney formally launched planning for *Sesame Street.*

In the context of adorable, warm, and zany muppets, nurturing adults, and lots of humor, *Sesame Street* is designed to foster intellectual, social, and cultural development. Reaching far beyond letters and numbers, *Sesame Street* introduces children to a broad range of ideas, information, and experiences about diverse topics such as death, cultural pride, race relations, people with disabilities, marriage, pregnancy, and even space exploration. For many children, *Sesame Street* may be the first place they see a ballet or see someone who resembles them on television. Moreover, it may be the only place they see a ballet performed by a girl in a wheelchair.

Research and Production

Sesame Street was the first series to employ research as an integral part of its production. From the beginning, the *Sesame Street* team realized it would need substantial and ongoing involvement by experts in education and early childhood development to develop curriculum

Formative and Summative Research

Formative research is conducted while the story or a segment is being produced, or at times before production begins, to investigate questions such as the appeal and comprehension of the messages among the target audience. Research results then inform subsequent production decisions and revisions.

In 1983, *Sesame Street* dealt with the death of its longtime storekeeper, Mr. Hooper. Will Lee, the actor who had played this character since it was created in 1969, died in 1982, and the producers decided to deal with his death on the show rather than replace him with another actor. This single episode was kept simple, conveying the following messages: Mr. Hooper is dead; Mr. Hooper will not be coming back; and Mr. Hooper will be missed by all.

Prior to broadcast, the *Sesame Street* Research Department conducted a series of formative studies to answer the following questions for the production staff: (1) will children understand the three key messages about Mr. Hooper's death; (2) how attentive will children be to the story line; (3) how will parents respond to the treatment of such a sensitive topic; and most important of all, (4) will children be disturbed by this story either immediately after viewing or during the following week?

Research revealed that the majority of four- and five-year-olds understood that Mr. Hooper was not coming back and that Big Bird and the adult characters felt sad. The second study revealed that on average, the majority of the children were attentive during the show. Reception of the show by parents was overwhelmingly positive, with parents using words such as "well done," "compassionate," "helpful," "honest," and "age-appropriate" to describe the episode. Approximately one-half of the twenty-one parents who were interviewed stated that they discussed death with their children after viewing the show, and none of the parents reported any negative immediate or delayed reactions in their child.

Summative research is conducted after the production of a television series is complete, and it is intended to assess the effect of the series on its viewers. Although most of the summative research is conducted by independent researchers, the following is an example of a summative study conducted internally by the *Sesame Street* Research Department.

For the twenty-ninth season, the producers of *Sesame Street* decided to revisit the science curriculum. The objective of the "Science of Discovery" curriculum was to link the natural curiosity of preschoolers with their love of exploration by illustrating both science content and scientific processes. The topic of space was included in the science curriculum because the production department decided to develop an eighteen-week story line featuring Slimey, Oscar the Grouch's pet worm, as he participates in the very first "wormed" moon mission for the Worm Air and Space Agency (WASA).

A longitudinal study was designed to assess (1) children's understanding of space, the moon, astronauts, and space travel and (2) the degree to which their understanding of such concepts changed as a result of exposure to the "Slimey to the Moon" story. Baseline results revealed that preschoolers from a middle-income center had significantly greater knowledge of space and space exploration than did preschoolers from a low-income center. After viewing the programs, children from the low-income center demonstrated the greatest gains in comprehension. These children gained knowledge about what to call someone who travels to the moon, what astronauts do and how they travel to the moon, what astronauts wear on the moon, and that the planet they live on is called "Earth." Although preschoolers from the middle-income center already had a good understanding about space, they also showed some significant increases in their knowledge of how long it takes to get to the moon and what astronauts wear on the moon. Overall, children enjoyed the space shows, remained interested in the story, and most important, they acquired more specific knowledge about astronauts and space travel over a period of time.

goals and to work with the producers and writers to create appealing and educational stories and segments. The *Sesame Street* Research Department, with guidance from educational advisors, develops the *Sesame Street* curriculum and evaluates it annually to incorporate current changes in knowledge and understanding of children's growth, development, and learning; innovative educational methods; and changes in society. The research department also conducts formative research studies with preschoolers to inform the production team about the appeal and comprehension of the content of the program. In addition, the research department contracts independent researchers to evaluate the effect of the series through summative research.

This unique, ongoing integration of curriculum development, formative research, and summative research into the process of production is known as the Sesame Workshop model. This interdisciplinary approach to television production brings together television producers, educational content experts, and educational researchers to work hand-in-hand at every stage of production. Many media professionals and educators predicted that this operating model would never succeed because of the very different backgrounds and values of the three groups. However, the model was effective and this "marriage" between these three groups of individuals continues today as the cornerstone of the long-term success of *Sesame Street.*

Educational Effectiveness

Sesame Street is the most researched series in the history of television, with more than one thousand studies examining its educational effectiveness in areas such as literacy, numeracy, and prosocial behavior, as well as investigating the use of production features to enhance children's attention and comprehension. The following is an overview of the key studies on the educational effectiveness the series has had in the area of school readiness, academic achievement, and social behavior.

Before any production began, the Educational Testing Service was contracted to design and conduct an evaluation of the educational effectiveness that *Sesame Street* had on a variety of cognitive skills during its premiere season. Both before and after the broadcast of the first season, children who were three to five years of age (predominantly from disadvantaged backgrounds) and were from geographically and ethnically diverse backgrounds were tested extensively on a range of content areas including knowledge of the alphabet, numbers, relational terms, names of body parts, recognition of forms, and sorting and classification skills.

The results of the study indicated that exposure to *Sesame Street* had the desired educational effects across content areas. Children who watched the most showed the greatest gains between pretest and posttest, and the topics getting more screen time on the show (e.g., letters) were learned better than were topics receiving less screen time. The gains occurred for children across the ages (although three-year-olds showed the greatest gains, presumably because they knew the least before viewing), for both boys and girls, and for children from different geographic and ethnic backgrounds. The study also showed that these results were not influenced by whether the children watched at home or in school.

The results of the second-year evaluation confirmed earlier findings, demonstrating significant gains in many of the same content areas and in new areas, which were added in the second season. Moreover, viewers who watched *Sesame Street* on a frequent basis were rated by their teachers as being better prepared for school (e.g., verbal and quantitative readiness, attitude toward school, relationships with peers) than were their classmates who watched infrequently or not at all.

With success comes questions and criticisms. Some question whether television is a suitable medium for teaching intellectual and academic skills, particularly those that depend on language, because its salient visual qualities interfere with children's processing of language. Others criticize the rapid pace and entertaining qualities of *Sesame Street* that leave children with little or no time to process information at more than a superficial level (i.e., learning information by rote rather than acquiring skills at a deeper or more conceptual level). For both criticisms, there is little or no supporting evidence.

In fact, several studies assessing the long-term effects of viewing *Sesame Street* echoed the earlier research on the positive educational benefits of the program. Researchers at the Center for Research on the Influences of Television on Children (CRITC) found that preschoolers who watched *Sesame Street* spent more time reading and engaged in educational activities, and performed significantly better than their peers on age-appropriate standardized achievement tests of letter-word knowledge, mathematical skills, and vocabulary development. Results from a national survey conducted for the U.S. Department of Edu-

The early members of the Sesame Street *cast of characters included (left to right) Big Bird, Mr. Hooper, Oscar the Grouch, Gordon, Bob, and Susan, as well as (in the windows) Cookie Monster, Grover, Ernie, and Bert. (Bettmann/Corbis)*

cation revealed significant associations between viewing *Sesame Street* and the ability of preschoolers to recognize letters of the alphabet and tell connected stories when pretending to read. In addition, when they subsequently entered first and second grade, children who viewed *Sesame Street* as preschoolers were also more likely to read story books on their own and were less likely to require remedial reading instruction.

Perhaps most notably, a "recontact" study by researchers from CRITC and the University of Massachusetts at Amherst employed a sample of high school students whose television viewing as preschoolers had been tracked ten to fifteen years earlier. The results showed that adolescents who viewed *Sesame Street* on a frequent basis as preschoolers (compared to those who rarely watch the program) had significantly better grades in high school English, science, and mathematics; read more books for pleasure; perceived themselves to be more competent in school; placed higher value on achievement in math and science;

and elected to take more advanced mathematics courses.

Clearly, the curriculum goals included in the *Sesame Street* segments cannot directly improve high school grades. Rather, it is more likely that a related series of processes can be initiated by watching educational programs. Children who watch *Sesame Street* enter school not only with good academic skills but with a positive attitude toward education. Perhaps as a result, teachers consider them bright and ready for school, expect high levels of achievement, place them in advanced groups, and give them positive feedback. Early school success, in turn, fosters better learning and greater enthusiasm about school, leading to a trajectory of long-term achievement.

Influence on Social Behavior

Sesame Street can have a significant effect on children's social behavior, but the research evidence is not as strong as it is with cognitive effects, nor are there as many studies in the literature. One of the earliest studies to examine the effect of *Sesame Street* on social behavior focused on cooperation. Levels of cooperation among children from disadvantaged, inner-city backgrounds were tested before and after viewing the third season of *Sesame Street*. Results indicated that viewers cooperated more than nonviewers when tested in situations similar to those presented on the program. Also, viewers were more likely than the nonviewers to recognize examples of cooperation presented in the show, to judge the cooperative solutions as "best," and to use the word "cooperation" in an appropriate manner.

These results were consistent with other studies conducted in the 1970s that found exposure to prosocial segments on *Sesame Street* was associated with positive social behavior only when the measures closely resembled the behaviors modeled in the program. However, results of a small-scale field observational study showed that viewing prosocial segments on *Sesame Street* reduced aggressive behavior (physical and verbal aggression) in free-play sessions conducted later on the same day.

More generalized effects of viewing *Sesame Street* episodes that had prosocial content were found in a quasi-experimental study conducted in eight daycare centers. Across eight days, children watched either prosocial or cognitive show segments and engaged in follow-up activities that were either cooperative or individualistic. Observations were made during the activities and during free play, with an eye toward several types of prosocial behavior: positive interaction, cooperation, helping, giving, sharing, turn taking, comforting, and affection. Viewers of the prosocial segments exhibited the highest level of prosocial behavior during the planned activities. Furthermore, viewers of prosocial segments who also participated in cooperative follow-up activities were lowest in antisocial behavior during free-play.

Over the years, *Sesame Street* has dealt with many social issues relevant to preschoolers (e.g., childbirth, marriage, death). Since its inception, *Sesame Street* has been a celebration of diversity, and race relations is a core curriculum area. In 1989, as a result of rising racial unrest in the United States, a four-year race relations curriculum initiative was launched to be more explicit about physical and cultural differences and to encourage friendship among people of different races and cultures. In collaboration with the production staff and with consultation from content experts, the *Sesame Street* Research Department developed curriculum goals to promote positive interactions among five cultural groups: African Americans, American Indians, Latinos, Asian Americans, and white Americans. Emphasis was placed on the similarities that make individuals all human and on fostering an appreciation of racial and cultural differences. Through these curriculum goals, preschoolers were encouraged to perceive people who look different from themselves as possible friends and to bring a child who has been rejected because of physical and/or cultural differences into the group.

Initial results from a series of formative research studies produced striking results, indicating that it was clear that preschoolers were not only aware of racial differences, but the topic was both appropriate and timely. For example, although the majority of African-American, Crow-Indian, Chinese-American, Puerto Rican, and white children tested said that they would want to be friends with children from other groups, less than half reported that their mothers would be positive about them having a friend from another race. Moreover, when given the opportunity to create a neighborhood using paper dolls, white preschoolers, in particular five-year-olds, were significantly more likely than African-American children to segregate cut-out dolls of African-American and white children in homes, schools, playgrounds, churches, and stores.

To achieve a better understanding of the children's nonverbal responses, small groups of white preschoolers were told a story about a group of white children who separated white and African-American children in each of the neighborhood structures. The children were then asked to explain why the children responded as they did. The majority of the white children agreed that the African-American and white children should be separated and gave the following reasons to explain the segregation: physical differences, economics, conflict, existing separate housing, and the opinions of others. However, they also said that the separation would lead to sadness for both white and African-American children.

Based on these results, segments were produced with the intention to counteract some of these beliefs. For example, in direct response to the segregation that was noted in the formative research, two segments were created: "Visiting Ieshia" and "Play Date." In "Visiting Ieshia," a white girl visits an African-American girl in her home. "Play Date" shows a similar family visit with a white boy visiting an African-American friend in his home. Formative research revealed that the majority of the children, regardless of race or sex, found the segments appealing and stated that the visiting white child felt positive about being at the other child's home.

Conclusion

While *Sesame Street* has varied its formats and approaches over the years to remain innovative, one thing remains constant—its desire to entertain and educate children. By addressing children on their own level, by employing appealing characters and authentic depictions of the children's own worlds, and by continually demonstrating the fun of learning, *Sesame Street* strives to help all preschool children reach their greatest potential.

See also: CHILDREN'S COMPREHENSION OF TELEVISION; CHILDREN'S CREATIVITY AND TELEVISION USE; CHILDREN'S PREFERENCES FOR MEDIA CONTENT; MINORITIES AND THE MEDIA; PUBLIC BROADCASTING; RESEARCHERS FOR EDUCATIONAL TELEVISION PROGRAMS; TELEVISION, EDUCATIONAL.

Bibliography

Anderson, Daniel, R. (1998). "Educational Television Is Not an Oxymoron." *Annals of the American Academy of Political and Social Sciences* 557:24–38.

Fisch, Shalom M., and Truglio, Rosemarie T., eds. (2001). *"G" is for Growing: Thirty Years of Research on Sesame Street.* Mahwah, NJ: Lawrence Erlbaum.

Fisch, Shalom M.; Truglio, Rosemarie T.; and Cole, Charlotte F. (1998). "The Impact of *Sesame Street* on Preschool Children: A Review and Synthesis of 30 Years' Research." *Media Psychology* 1:165–190.

Lovelace, Valeria; Scheiner, Susan; Dollberg, Susan; Segui, Ivelissse; and Black, Tracey. (1994). "Making a Neighborhood the *Sesame Street* Way: Developing a Methodology to Evaluate Children's Understanding of Race." *Journal of Educational Television* 20(2):69–78.

Truglio, Rosemarie T.; Scheiner, Susan; Segui, Ivelisse; and Chen, Lisa. (1999). "*Sesame Street's* Science of Discovery." Poster presented at the biennial meeting of the Society for Research in Development, Albuquerque, New Mexico.

Wright, John, C.; and Huston, Aletha C. (1995). *Effects of Educational TV Viewing of Lower Income Preschoolers on Academic Skills, School Readiness, and School Adjustment One to Three Years Later: A Report to the Children's Television Workshop.* Austin, TX: Center for Research on the Influences of Children, University of Texas.

Zielinska, Ida. E., and Chambers, Bette. (1995). "Using Group Viewing of Television to Teach Preschool Children Social Skills." *Journal of Educational Television* 21:85–99.

Zill, Nicholas; Davies, Elizabeth; and Daly, Margaret. (1994). *Viewing of Sesame Street by Preschool Children and Its Relationship to School Readiness: Report Prepared for the Children's Television Workshop.* Rockville, MD: Westat.

ROSEMARIE T. TRUGLIO

■ SEX AND THE MEDIA

Most young people are in contact with some kind of media during most of their waking hours. Much of the media content they are exposed to contains messages, images, and ideas about sex and sexuality. This content is especially salient for adolescents and young adults who are developing their own sexual beliefs and behaviors.

The Media As Sex Educators

Research suggests that adolescents do learn about sexuality from the media, and some young people deliberately turn to the media for information that is difficult to obtain elsewhere. Mike Sutton, Jane Brown, Karen Wilson, and Jon Klein (2001) analyzed a national sample of high school students and found that more than half of the respondents said they had learned about birth control, contraception, or preventing pregnancy from magazines or television. School health classes, parents, and friends were the only other sources that were cited more frequently. However, parents often broach sexual topics awkwardly, if at all, and schools tend to address sexuality in clinical terms rather than in the context of relationships, emotions, and desire. Television, movies, music, music videos, magazines, and websites, in contrast, capitalize on topics that are considered taboo in other social situations, thus often making sexual media fare especially attractive for younger consumers.

TABLE 1.

Sexual Media Content and Attitudes, Beliefs, and Behaviors

Medium	Sexual Content	Effects
Television	• Women are most likely to be young and thin. • Sexual talk is frequent; sexual behavior less frequent but common. • Negative consequences of sex are infrequently shown. • Contraception and planning for sex are also rare.	• Ideal body image programming and commercials affect the perceptions that girls have of their own bodies. • Gender-role stereotypes are accepted by some viewers. • Heavy viewers are more likely to believe that single mothers have an easy life. • Intercourse is initiated earlier by heavy viewers.
Magazines	• One-third of the articles concern dating; one-third focus on appearance. • One to six articles per issue focus on sexual health. • Women's magazines encourage females to put men's interests before their own.	• Exposure to thin models in magazines can produce depression, stress, shame, and body dissatisfaction. • Girls report that images in women's magazines make them feel bad about themselves.
Movies	• Romantic and sexual relations are present in almost all top-grossing movies. • More sexual talk than behavior is represented. • Women are more likely than men to talk about romantic relationships. • Women are the only characters seen "promising" sex. • Sexual relations tend to occur with little reference to characters' attraction for each other or relationship expectations. • Older people rarely are shown expressing tenderness or love for each other.	
Music and Music Videos	• Videos emphasize physical appearance of women musicians over musical ability. • Frequent references are made to relationships and sexual behavior. • Less gender-role stereotyping occurs in videos than earlier, but females are still more often affectionate, nurturing, and sexually pursued than males.	• Exposure to music videos results in more permissive attitudes about premarital sex. • Exposure to stereotypical images of gender and sexuality in videos has been linked to greater acceptance of interpersonal violence.

Sexual Content

The perceived sensitivity of sex as a research topic and a focus on television to the exclusion of other media has restricted the kind of research that has been done. Much of the work has been analyses of content, rather than assessments of effects on audiences. However, the few studies that go beyond content to address how audiences respond to and incorporate sexual content in their lives suggest that the media may indeed play a role in the sexual lives of young people. (See Table 1 for a summary.)

Television

Television has received the bulk of attention from researchers who are interested in portrayals of sexuality and the effects of these portrayals. After all, according to a national study conducted by the Kaiser Family Foundation (1999), the television is turned on about seven hours per day in the average home, and children spend about three to four hours per day watching television.

Content analyses of various television dayparts and genres reveal that sexuality, broadly defined, is a frequent ingredient across the television landscape. In a study by Dale Kunkel and his associates (2001), more than two-thirds of 1,114 television programs on 10 popular broadcast and cable television channels contained sexual content (either talk or behavior). Prime-time television shows (8:00 P.M. TO 11:00 P.M. eastern standard time) were full of talk about and depictions of sexual activity.

Kirstie Cope and Kunkel (2001) analyzed forty-five episodes of the prime-time television shows that teenagers watched most frequently in 1996 (including *Friends, Seinfeld,* and *Married with Children*) and found that the primarily late teenage and young adult characters talked about sex and engaged in sexual behavior in two-thirds of the shows. However, most of the sexual content on television still is *talk*—characters discussing their own or others' current or future sexual activity.

Sexual *behaviors* on prime-time television, although frequent, are relatively modest—mostly flirting and kissing. Sexual intercourse rarely is depicted on these shows, but it is sometimes implied (e.g., the scene fades as a couple is kissing in a bed and the next scene shows the couple waking up in each other's arms). In the forty-five episodes of top shows viewed by teenagers, Cope and Kunkel found that sexual intercourse was depicted once (although no genitals were displayed) and implied five times.

Talk shows that frequently feature dysfunctional couples publicly disclosing their troubles and infidelities are another favorite television genre of older children and teenagers. These shows also talk about, rather than explicitly depict, sexual behavior, but the discussions often are detailed and racy. Some studies have found that parent–child relations, marital relations and infidelity, other sexual relations, and sexual orientation are common topics. Sexual themes are more frequent on the shows that teenagers most prefer (e.g., *Geraldo Rivera*, *Jenny Jones*, *Rolonda Watts*, and *Jerry Springer*) rather than on others that attract older audiences (e.g., *Oprah Winfrey*). Bradley Greenberg and Sandi Smith (2001) found that a number of talk shows include professional therapists who are supposed to comment on how the problems might be solved, but these "experts" get less airtime than anyone else on the set, including the audience.

Frank discussions about sex—ranging from Dr. Joy Browne's on-air psychological counseling to the sexual banter of disc jockeys such as Howard Stern who were hired to capture the teenager/young adult audiences as they drive to school or work—are common on radio as well.

Soap operas, another popular genre, also have a prominent focus on sex. Katherine Heintz-Knowles (1996) analyzed one hundred hours of daytime soap operas and found that they depict more sexual talk than sexual behaviors, although sexual behaviors (ranging from kissing to sexual intercourse) are not infrequent. Although planning for sexual activity (e.g., visiting a health clinic, purchasing contraceptives) as well as negative consequences of sexual activity (e.g., the transmission of a sexually transmitted disease, an unplanned pregnancy) are shown more frequently than in the past, such precautions and consequences still are rarely portrayed.

Despite their prolific portrayal of sexuality, most television programs do not provide realistic depictions of the risks that accompany sexual activity. Indeed, the American Academy of Pediatrics concluded in 1995 that only 165 of the nearly 14,000 sexual references, innuendoes, and jokes that the

average teenager views on television per year deal with topics such as birth control, self-control, abstinence, or sexually transmitted diseases.

Across all television depictions, most sexual intercourse takes place between adults, but although more than half of the couples are in established relationships, a majority are not married to each other, and about one in ten have only just met. Kunkel and his colleagues (2001) found that in almost two-thirds of the programs in which characters have sex, no clear consequences are shown. When consequences are portrayed, they are almost four times more likely to be positive than negative. Only about one-tenth of programs include anything to do with sexual patience, sexual precaution, and/or the depiction of risks and negative consequences of unprotected sex.

Monique Ward (1995) found that one in four of the speaking interactions between characters of the top shows for children and adolescents (1992–1993 broadcast year) contained some sort of sexual message. The most frequently occurring types of messages equated masculinity with being sexual or commented on women as sexual objects. The picture of sexuality presented was one of sex as recreation, where competition and game playing are anticipated and the prize is a physically attractive person.

Women on television, as in most other media, are unnaturally physically attractive and slim. The standard of attractiveness on television and in magazines is slimmer for women than for men, and the standard is slimmer than it was in the past.

Studies of media content can tell only so much, however. The big question remains: How do viewers apply what they see about sex on television to their own sexual lives? Only a few studies have investigated the link between exposure to sexual media content and sexual attitudes and behaviors. These few studies suggest that television depictions of sexuality do have an influence on beliefs, which may in turn influence behavior.

Surveys have found relationships between viewing daytime soap operas and beliefs about single parenthood. In a study by Mary Larson (1996), junior and senior high school students who frequently viewed daytime soap operas were more likely than those who watched less often to believe that single mothers have relatively easy lives, have good jobs, and do not live in poverty.

The soap viewers also thought that the babies of single mothers would be as healthy as most babies and would get love and attention from adult men who are friends of the mothers.

The perception that frequent viewers of television have about marriage is not as pleasant as the perception of single motherhood. Nancy Signorielli (1991) found that college students who watched large amounts of television were more likely than viewers who watched less frequently to be ambivalent about the possibility that marriage is a happy way of life.

Two studies suggest that more frequent exposure to sexual content on television is related to earlier initiation of sexual intercourse. In surveys of high school students, Jane D. Brown and Susan Newcomer (1991) and James Peterson, Kristin Moore, and Frank Furstenberg (1991) found that those students who watched more "sexy" television shows were more likely than those who watched fewer such shows to have had sexual intercourse. However, because neither study assessed television viewing and sexual behavior at more than one time, it is not possible to say whether the television viewing or the sexual behavior came first. It may be that sexually experienced youths seek out sexually relevant media content because it is now salient in their lives. It may also be that sexual content encourages youths to engage in sexual behavior sooner than they might otherwise, but studies that follow young people over time are needed to sort out the causal sequence.

Magazines

Sexuality portrayed in magazines is especially salient for teenage girls. Kate Peirce (1995) analyzed magazines directed at teenage girls and concluded that these magazines are designed primarily to tell girls that their most important function in life is to become sexually attractive enough to catch a desirable male. The message (e.g., "What's your lovemaking profile?" "Perfect pickup lines: Never again let a guy get away because you can't think of anything to say") is repeated even more explicitly in women's magazines, such as *Cosmopolitan, Glamour,* and *Mademoiselle,* which many adolescents read.

Kim Walsh-Childers, Alyse Gotthoffer, and Carolyn Lepre (2001) found that magazines for girls and magazines for women have both increased their coverage of sexual topics since the mid-1980s. Magazines for teenage girls may be doing a better job than the magazines for women in educating their readers about such sexual health topics as contraception, pregnancy, abortion, emergency contraception, and sexually transmitted diseases.

These magazines are the standard bearers of unattainable beauty ideals. A study by Children Now (1997) found that 33 percent of the articles in leading magazines for teenage girls include a focus on appearance, and 50 percent of the advertisements appeal to beauty to sell their products. Approximately 33 percent of the articles focused on dating, compared to only 12 percent that discussed either school or careers.

Ana Garner, Helen Sterk, and Shawn Adams (1998) analyzed 175 articles and columns about health, sex, and relationships appearing in *Glamour, Seventeen, Teen, Mademoiselle,* and *YM* magazines during the 1970s, 1980s, and 1990s. Garner and her colleagues argued that the magazines were urging girls to be enthusiastic consumers in pursuit of perfection—perfect hair, perfect complexions, and perfect wardrobes. They concluded that the magazines were serving as "field guides" for sexual indulgence.

Movies

Teenagers are one of the primary audiences for Hollywood movies in theaters or at home on television or videocassettes. More than two-thirds of the movies produced and rated each year in the United States are R-rated movies, frequently because of the sexual content. Although, technically, only people older than sixteen are allowed to see R-rated movies unless they are accompanied by an adult, most children see R-rated movies much earlier than that age.

Bradley Greenberg and his colleagues (1993) conducted an analysis of the R-rated movies that were popular with teenagers in the early 1980s. They found an average of 17.5 sexual portrayals per movie. Carol Pardun (2001) found that in the top-grossing movies of 1995, romantic and sexual relationships were present even in action-adventure movies such as *Apollo 13*. In these 1995 movies, there was more talk than action, and women tended to talk about sex more than men.

Although more thorough character and story development might be expected in movies than on television, sexual relations tend to occur in movies with little reference to why the characters are attracted to each other or what they might expect from each other in the future. Older people in long-term relationships are rarely shown expressing tenderness or love for each other, and precautions against unwanted outcomes are as rare in movies as they are on television.

Music and Music Videos

Even before the gyrating hips of Elvis were censored on *The Ed Sullivan Show* in 1956, popular music had been linked with sex. Especially appealing to young people, popular music and music videos contain frequent references to relationships, romance, and sexual behavior.

Music videos may be especially influential sources of sexual information for adolescents because they combine visuals of adolescents' favorite musicians with the music, and many of the visual elements are sexual. Although adolescent girls watch videos as frequently as their male peers, popular music videos underrepresent women, with men outnumbering women in lead roles by almost a five to one margin. Joe Gow (1996) found that when women do appear in music videos, their physical appearance rather than musical ability is emphasized. Steven Seidman (1999) documented that the women in music videos are more affectionate and nurturing, wear the most revealing clothing, and are more often sexually pursued than the males in the videos.

Music lyrics have drawn criticism from groups such as the Parents Music Resource Center, leading to some voluntary labeling of recorded music. For some teenagers, however, such warnings may represent a stamp of approval rather than a deterrent to buying the recording. Keith Roe (1995) proposed a theory of "media delinquency" that suggests that some teenagers may gravitate toward socially devalued or outlawed media content because it reflects their anger or estrangement and helps signal to others that they are not a part of the mainstream culture.

Some variants of rap music (e.g., gangsta rap) are particularly explicit about both sex and violence. Although some observers are critical of the sometimes misogynistic and violent imagery and lyrics, Imani Perry (1995) argues that the explicit "sexual speak" of black women rappers follows in the liberating tradition of the "blues," which gave voice to black women's sexual and cultural politics during the black migration to northern states in the early twentieth century. This striving for empowerment may explain why some rap musicians have responded to concerns about unsafe sex and sexually related behavior and have included alternative messages in their songs. Some rap music includes talk of "jimmy hats," or condoms. An album by the female rap group Salt 'n' Peppa, for example, was about the responsibilities as well as pleasures of sex.

Only a few studies have investigated how exposure to the sexual content of music and music videos is related to the sexual beliefs and behaviors of adolescents. An experiment by Larry Greeson and Rose Ann Williams (1986) found that adolescents who were exposed to a few music videos had more permissive attitudes about sex than did those who were not exposed. Another experiment by Linda Kalof (1999) found that exposure to the stereotypical images of gender and sexuality in music videos had an influence on college women's sexual beliefs, especially greater acceptance of interpersonal violence.

Conclusion

In short, it is clear that the media are an important part of how young people learn about sexual norms and expectations in the culture. From music to magazines, to television and movies, sex is a staple of young people's media diets. Although relatively little is known about how this ubiquitous sexual content is used by and affects children and adolescents, existing research suggests that such media content can have powerful effects, especially when other sources of information are difficult to access or are less compelling. Most of the media that young people attend to provide alluring and relatively risk-free opportunities to learn more about sex than their parents, teachers, or even friends are willing to provide. These portrayals rarely, however, include accurate depictions of the emotional and physical risks that may be involved in sexual activity. In the media world, women still are engaged primarily in seducing men, but the costs of doing so regardless of love, commitment, or protection against pregnancy or disease are rarely addressed.

See also: ADVERTISING EFFECTS; BODY IMAGE,
   MEDIA EFFECT ON; GAYS AND LESBIANS IN THE

Bibliography

American Academy of Pediatrics. (1995). "Sexuality, Contraception, and the Media (RE9505)." *Policy Statement* 95(2):298–300.

Brown, Jane D., and Newcomer, Susan. (1991). "Television Viewing and Adolescents' Sexual Behavior." *Journal of Homosexuality* 21(1/2):77–91.

Children Now. (1997). *Reflections of Girls in the Media.* Los Angeles: Children Now and the Kaiser Family Foundation.

Cope, Kirstie, and Kunkel, Dale. (2001). "Sexual Messages in Teens' Favorite Prime-Time TV Programs." In *Sexual Teens, Sexual Media,* eds. Jane D. Brown, Jeanne R. Steele, and Kim Walsh-Childers. Hillsdale, NJ: Lawrence Erlbaum.

Davis, Donald M. (1990). "Portrayals of Women in Prime-Time Network Television: Some Demographic Characteristics." *Sex Roles* 23(5-6):325–332.

Field, Alison; Cheung, Lilian; Herzog, David; Gortmaker, Steven; and Colditz, Graham. (1999). "Exposure to the Mass Media and Weight Concerns Among Girls." *Pediatrics* 103(3):361–365.

Garner, Ana; Sterk, Helen; and Adams, Shawn. (1998). "Narrative Analysis of Sexual Etiquette in Teenage Magazines." *Journal of Communication* 48(4):59–78.

Gow, Joe. (1996). "Reconsidering Gender Roles on MTV: Depictions in the Most Popular Music Videos of the Early 1990s." *Communication Reports* 9(2):151–161.

Greenberg, Bradley; Siemicki, Michelle; Dorfman, Sandra; Heeter, Carrie; Stanley, Cynthia; Soderman, Anne; and Linsangan, Renato. (1993). "Sex Content in R-rated Films Viewed by Adolescents." In *Media, Sex and the Adolescent,* eds. Bradley Greenberg, Jane D. Brown, and Nancy L. Buerkel-Rothfuss. Creskill, NJ: Hampton Press.

Greenberg, Bradley, and Smith, Sandi. (2001). "Talk Shows: Up Close and in Your Face." In *Sexual Teens, Sexual Media,* eds. Jane D. Brown, Jeanne R. Steele, and Kim Walsh-Childers. Hillsdale, NJ: Lawrence Erlbaum.

Greeson, Larry, and Williams, Rose Ann. (1986). "Social Implications of Music Videos for Youth: An Analysis of the Content and Effects of MTV." *Youth & Society* 18(2):177–189.

Heintz-Knowles, Katherine. (1996). *Sexual Activity on Daytime Soap Operas: A Content Analysis of Five Weeks of Television Programming.* Menlo Park, CA: Kaiser Family Foundation.

Hofschire, Linda, and Greenberg, Bradley. (2000). "Media's Impact on Adolescents' Body Dissatisfaction." In *Sexual Teens, Sexual Media,* eds. Jane D. Brown, Jeanne R. Steele, and Kim Walsh-Childers. Hillsdale, NJ: Lawrence Erlbaum.

Kaiser Family Foundation. (1999). *Kids & Media @ the New Millenium: A Comprehensive National Analysis of Children's Media Use.* Menlo Park, CA: Kaiser Family Foundation.

Kalof, Linda. (1999). "The Effects of Gender and Music Video Imagery on Sexual Attitudes." *Journal of Social Psychology* 139(3):378–385.

Kunkel, Dale; Cope-Farrar, Kirstie; Biely, Erica; Farinola, Wendy Jo; and Donnerstein, Edward. (2001). *Sex on TV: A Biennial Report to the Kaiser Family Foundation.* Menlo Park, CA: Kaiser Family Foundation.

Larson, Mary. (1996). "Sex Roles and Soap Operas: What Adolescents Learn About Single Motherhood." *Sex Roles* 35(1/2):97–121.

Morgan, Michael. (1982). "Television and Adolescents' Sex-Role Stereotypes: A Longitudinal Study." *Journal of Personality and Social Psychology* 43(5):947–955.

Myers, Phillip, and Biocca, Frank. (1992) "The Elastic Body Image: The Effect of Television Advertising and Programming on Body Image Distortions in Young Women." *Journal of Communication* 42(3):108–133.

Pardun, Carol. (2001). "Romancing the Script: Identifying the Romantic Agenda in Top-Grossing Movies." In *Sexual Teens, Sexual Media,* eds. Jane D. Brown, Jeanne R. Steele, and Kim Walsh-Childers. Hillsdale, NJ: Lawrence Erlbaum.

Peirce, Kate. (1995). "Socialization Messages in Seventeen and Teen magazines." In *Women and Media: Content, Careers, and Criticism,* ed. Cynthia Lont. Belmont, CA: Wadsworth.

Perry, Imani. (1995). "It's My Thang and I'll Swing It the Way I Feel!" In *Gender, Race and Class in Media: A Test-Reader,* eds. Gail Dines and Jean Humez. Thousand Oaks, CA: Sage Publications.

Peterson, James; Moore, Kristin; and Furstenberg, Frank. (1991). "Television Viewing and Early Initiation of Sexual Intercourse. Is There a Link?" *Journal of Homosexuality* 21(1/2):93–118.

Roe, Keith. (1995). "Adolescents' Use of Socially Disvalued Media: Towards a Theory of Media Delinquency." *Journal of Youth and Adolescence* 24(5):617–632.

Seid, Roberta. (1989). *Never Too Thin: Why Women Are at War With Their Bodies.* New York: Prentice-Hall.

Seidman, Steven. (1999). "Revisiting Sex-Role Stereotyping in MTV Videos." *International Journal of Instructional Media* 26(1):11–25.

Shaw, J. (1995). "Effects of Fashion Magazines on Body Dissatisfaction and Eating Psychopathology in Adolescent and Adult Females." *European Eating Disorders Review* 3(1):15–23.

Signorielli, Nancy. (1991). "Adolescents and Ambivalence Toward Marriage: A Cultivation Analysis." *Youth and Society* 23:121–149.

Silverstein, Brett, Purdue, Lauren, Peterson, Barbara, and Kelly, Eileen. (1986). "The Role of the Mass Media in Promoting a Thin Standard of Bodily Attractiveness for Women." *Sex Roles* 14(9/10):519–532.

Stice, Eric, and Shaw, Heather. (1994). "Adverse Effects of the Media Portrayed Thin-Ideal on Women and Linkages to Bulimic Symptomatology." *Journal of Social and Clinical Psychology* 13(3):288–308.

Sutton, Michael; Brown, Jane D.; Wilson, Karen; and Klein, Jonathon. (2001). "Shaking the Tree of Knowledge for Forbidden Fruit: Where Adolescents Learn About Sexuality and Contraception." In *Sexual Teens, Sexual Media*, eds. Jane D. Brown, Jeanne R. Steele, and Kim Walsh-Childers. Hillsdale, NJ: Lawrence Erlbaum.

Walsh-Childers, Kim; Gotthoffer, Alyse; and Lepre, Carolyn. (2001). "From 'Just the Facts' to 'Downright Salacious': Teens' and Women's Magazines Coverage of Sex and Sexual Health." In *Sexual Teens, Sexual Media*, eds. Jane D. Brown, Jeanne R. Steele, and Kim Walsh-Childers. Hillsdale, NJ: Lawrence Erlbaum.

Ward, L. Monique. (1995). "Talking About Sex: Common Themes about Sexuality in the Prime-Time Television Programs Children and Adolescents View Most." *Journal of Youth and Adolescence* 24:595–615.

JANE D. BROWN
SUSANNAH R. STERN

SOAP OPERAS

Daytime serials, or soap operas as they are better known, have a form and structure that separates them from other television genres. Rather than beginning and ending within the space of thirty to sixty minutes, soap operas never really begin or end. The stories continually unfold year after year at a slower pace than other genres and without episodic resolution. Soap operas leave unanswered questions at commercial breaks, they include flashbacks and repetition as a device to clue viewers in on elements they may have missed and to prompt further contemplation, and there are no reruns. In other words, a soap opera is a never-ending story that does not abide by traditional television rules.

One of the biggest nighttime soap operas in the early 1980s was Dynasty, *which dramatized events surrounding the wealthy Carrington family and featured the actors (left to right) Kathleen Beller, Pamela Sue Martin, Joan Collins, Linda Evans, and John Forsythe.* (Bettmann/Corbis)

Soap operas began on the radio in the 1930s as a device to sell soap products to women. Sponsors created programming to air between their product commercials. In 1940, there were sixty-four soap operas on the radio that ran fifteen minutes each. *Guiding Light,* which debuted on the radio in 1937 and on television in 1952, was the only soap opera to make the change from radio to television.

By the 1980s, each of the three major networks had more airtime dedicated to daytime serials (210 to 240 minutes) than to prime-time programming (180 minutes). Indeed, prime-time programming included a number of its own serials such as *Dallas, Dynasty, Falcon Crest,* and *Knots Landing.* Although audiences eventually declined and several soap operas were canceled, including NBC's *Another World* (which aired for thirty-five years), by the end of the 1990s, eleven serials were broadcast daily.

One reason for the apparent decline in viewers was the introduction of videocassette recorders (VCRs), which allowed viewers to decide when to watch. Although nearly 12 percent of the U.S. population reported videotaping soap operas in 1996, VCR viewers have not generally been included in audience ratings because advertisers assume the viewers do not watch the commercials. In response to the viewers' need for alternative viewing times coupled with the advertisers' need to show commercials, a new cable network was launched on January 24, 2000, in Los Angeles and New York. SoapNet runs current ABC soap operas three times a day along with reruns of older soap operas that are no longer on the air. By June 2000, SoapNet was available in select cities across the United States and through DirecTV. New technology continues to affect soap operas. The introduction of the Internet brought more of a sense of community among soap opera fans who discuss the serials online.

The audience for soap operas has always been mostly women. However, in the United States, the percentage of male viewers increased to about 25 percent in the 1990s. The percentage of teenage viewers also increased over time. African Americans represent nearly 27 percent of the viewers for some soap operas, although they comprise only 12.8 percent of the total U.S. population.

Other than the occasional content analysis, academics paid little attention to soap operas until the early 1980s, when feminists began to defend the decidedly female genre. Feminists challenged academics to examine what made soap operas so popular with women. Tania Modleski (1983) argued that women were attracted to soap operas because they followed a feminine rather than a masculine narrative. She defined the feminine narrative of soap operas as stories that are (1) nonlinear, which means they have no clear beginning, middle, and end, (2) based on dialogue rather than action, (3) contain numerous interruptions, and (4) disperse the attention and loyalties of the viewers. Modleski also argued that unlike masculine narrative, in which the climax is resolution, the ultimate resolution is constantly yet to come in soap operas. Pleasure comes from anticipation rather than resolution.

Content is another defining element of soap operas, in which the elements of conflict and family are central. The ratio of male characters to female characters is approximately equal, similar to that of the United States, whereas in prime-time television male characters have outnumbered female characters as much as three to one. Although the number of African-American characters on soap operas has increased, research has found that those characters are less likely to have intimate contact than white characters. In the late 1960s and early 1970s, serial writers and producers introduced more social issues, such as interracial romance, mental illness, homosexuality, AIDS, abortion, and alcohol and drug addiction. Health issues have long been a part of soap operas, particularly women's health issues, such as breast cancer and systemic lupus erythematosus.

Sexual content has been a controversial mainstay of soap operas since the 1970s. The frequency of sexual behaviors on daytime serials is greater than that on prime-time television. According to a 1996 content analysis by Bradley Greenberg and Rick Busselle, sexual portrayals substantially increased during the 1980s, slightly decreased by the early 1990s, and increased again in the mid-1990s. As Katherine Heintz-Knowles reported in a 1996 Kaiser Family Foundation study, until the mid-1990s, talk about sex was more prevalent than actual depictions of sexual behavior. Although early studies found that consequences for sexual behavior were rarely shown, discussions about planning for and the consequences of sexual behavior increased in the 1990s. Yet, even with the increase, those discussions remain infrequent. Some studies have found that a majority of the portrayals of sexual behaviors are socially responsible because they are in the context of a healthy, committed relationship. Other studies have found that messages about sex are contradictory.

A 1983 book by Muriel Cantor and Suzanne Pingree reported that in the early 1980s, violence on soap operas was less frequent than in prime time. In addition, it was mainly verbal, between men and women, and between family members or lovers. In contrast, in prime time it was mostly between men who were strangers, and it was physical. Soap opera depictions of rape that start off as socially responsible and then send mixed messages when the rapist is redeemed, have drawn a lot of fire from critics. Extreme physical aggression that is rewarded in relationships has also been criticized, although aggressive sexual contact has decreased, according to research.

Although soap operas are shown all over the world, the content is not necessarily all the same. Soap operas in North America focus more on the rich, whereas soap operas in Great Britain focus more on the working class. Soap operas in Latin American (where they are called "telenovelas") are used as educational tools for issues such as family planning. The introduction of soap operas from North America and Latin America prompted several countries around the world to produce their own serials. These serials, however, are not simply copies; they reflect more of their own cultural values and social norms. Content is not the only difference in soap operas produced around the world. In Latin America, Japan, and China, the serials are often finite, even though they run for long periods of time.

Robert Allen (1995) claims that content analyses of soap operas are meaningless because any potential implication of daytime serials must be derived from the entirety of the serial (something that cannot occur until a show is cancelled) rather than in small chunks. Allen and others have also argued that the structural characteristics that make soap operas "open" allow viewers to make multiple interpretations of story content. According to this reasoning, in order to understand how viewers might be affected by soap operas, it is necessary to understand the interpretations that they make. Research from this perspective has proposed that women are empowered by watching soap operas. Moreover, it has found that how viewers identify with and perceive characters has an influence on how they are affected by those characters and their actions. Finally, it concludes that some viewers are affected by the more obvious message of the content, whereas others negotiate their own meanings for the content and are therefore affected differently.

Traditional research about the effect of soap operas on viewers usually looks at the amount of time that viewers spend watching soap operas in relation to how viewers might be affected by soap opera content. This research has found that viewers who watch a large amount of soap operas overestimate the number of divorces, illegitimate children, pregnancies, extramarital affairs, and cases of sexually transmitted diseases in the real world, as well as the amount of crime. Other research has found that women who are depressed spend more time watching soap operas than others; viewers who watch a large amount of soap operas believe single mothers live a much better life than they really do; and soap operas can effectively promote health concerns and practices when tied to a public-service announcement.

See also: ATTACHMENT TO MEDIA CHARACTERS; DEPENDENCE ON MEDIA; GENDER AND THE MEDIA; HEALTH COMMUNICATION; SEX AND THE MEDIA; VIOLENCE IN THE MEDIA, ATTRACTION TO; VIOLENCE IN THE MEDIA, HISTORY OF RESEARCH ON.

Bibliography

Allen, Robert C., ed. (1995). *To Be Continued: Soap Operas Around the World.* London: Routledge.

Brown, Mary Ellen. (1994). *Soap Opera and Women's Talk: The Pleasure of Resistance.* Thousand Oaks, CA: Sage Publications.

Cantor, Muriel, and Pingree, Suzanne. (1983). *The Soap Opera.* Beverly Hills, CA: Sage Publications.

Cassata, Mary, and Skill, Thomas. (1983). *Life on Daytime Television.* Norwood, NJ: Ablex.

Frentz, Suzanne, ed. (1992). *Staying Tuned: Contemporary Soap Opera Criticism.* Bowling Green, OH: Bowling Green State University Popular Press.

Greenberg, Bradley S., and Busselle, Rick W. (1996). "Soap Operas and Sexual Activity: A Decade Later." *Journal of Communication* 46:153–160.

Heintz-Knowles, Katherine. (1996). *Sexual Activity on Daytime Soap Operas: A Content Analysis of Five Weeks of Television Programming.* Menlo Park, CA: Kaiser Family Foundation.

Klingle, Renee Storm, and Aune, Krystyna Strzyzewski. (1994). "Effects of a Daytime Serial and a Public Service Announcement in Promoting Cognitions, Attitudes, and Behaviors Related to Bone-Marrow Testing." *Health Communication* 6(3):225–245.

Larson, Mary Strom. (1996). "Sex Roles and Soap Operas: What Adolescents Learn About Single Motherhood." *Sex Roles* 35:97–110.

Larson, Stephanie Greco. (1991). "Television's Mixed Messages: Sexual Content on *All My Children*." *Communication Quarterly* 39(2):156–163.

Lowry, Dennis T., and Towles, David E. (1989). "Soap Opera Portrayals of Sex, Contraception, and Sexually Transmitted Diseases." *Journal of Communication* 39(2):76–83.

Modleski, Tania. (1983). "The Rhythms of Reception: Daytime Television and Women's Work." In *Regarding Television: Critical Approaches*, ed. E. Ann Kaplan. Fredrick, MD: University Publications of America.

Museum of Television and Radio. (1997). *Worlds Without End: The Art and History of the Soap Opera.* New York: Harry N. Abrams.

RENÉE A. BOTTA

SOCIAL CHANGE AND THE MEDIA

The influence of the media on society has for a long time preoccupied researchers in the field of communication. Various normative, social scientific, and critical communication theories have addressed how media influence social change.

Early media effects theories assumed a direct and unmitigated influence of media on individuals and society. Later research questioned the assumption of all-powerful media effects, launching what became known as the limited-effects tradition. From those early days of communication research, there has been a constant ebb and flow of theories and empirical research attempting to understand the real effect of media on social change.

Numerous theories have also attempted to understand the effect of the media on social change from a variety of perspectives and for different objectives. These include theories of media and democratization, theories of development communication and social learning, and theories in health communication, social marketing, and participatory communication. Also, a variety of areas of inquiry in mass communication dealt with social change. These include research on alternative and pirate media, public service and educational broadcasting, public opinion and political communication, and research on propaganda.

Development Communication

In the 1950s and 1960s, the wave of decolonization in the developing world created a need for nation-building and social, political, and economic development. It is in that context that development communication emerged as a strategy to use the mass media to foster positive social change, which, in turn, was believed to enhance the socioeconomic development of a country. Among the pioneers in development communication were Daniel Lerner and Wilbur Schramm. Lerner's *The Passing of Traditional Society* (1958) and Schramm's *Mass Media and National Development* (1964) were founding texts of development communication, and they have had a defining influence on the paradigm since their publication. Their basic principle was that desirable social change could be produced by scientifically designed and executed communication campaigns.

Until the late 1970s, development communication theory, research, and practice was grounded in what Everett Rogers (1978) termed a "dominant paradigm." This dominant paradigm, according to Rogers, was a consequence of a specifically Western legacy. That legacy includes the Industrial Revolution in North America and Western Europe, colonialism in the developing world—from Latin America to the Middle East, and from Africa to East Asia—the quantitative tradition of American social science, and capitalism. These historical, geopolitical, economic, epistemological, and ideological factors molded the dominant paradigm on the role of the mass media in development and social change.

That perspective led to shortsighted theories and applications. For example, Rogers (1978) wrote that the dominant paradigm wrongly relied on the introduction of technology to solve the social problems of the developing world. In addition, the strong dependence on quantitative information inherited from American social science reduced standards of living to mere numbers, which often failed to reflect actual social situations in the developing world. More relevant to this discussion was the gradual realization by development researchers and practitioners that the role of the mass media was indirect and more limited than it was previously assumed. Advocating a shift in the general orientation of development communication, Rogers (1978, p. 68) gave a new definition of development that he called "a widely participatory process of social change in a society, intended to bring about both social and material advancement . . . for the majority of the people."

Two years after Rogers thus declared the passing of the dominant paradigm, Robert Hornik (1980) published an article in the *Journal of Communication* in which he reviewed and summarized evaluations of a cluster of development projects spanning several continents. This evaluation was done as part of a review of Agency for International Development communication policy, which Hornik undertook with several colleagues. Hornik articulated his article around three central questions. The first question was concerned with the role that communication plays in processes of development. The second question focused on the conditions that make a particular development communication project a success or a failure. Hornik's third question concerned knowledge about specific applications in development communication.

In addressing these questions, Hornik drew examples from development projects in El Salvador and Nicaragua (in Latin America), Tanzania and Senegal (in Africa), and India, China, and Korea (in Asia). The geographical diversity of these examples made Hornik's piece an excellent review of how development projects work or do not work in different sociocultural environments.

At the end of his article, Hornik reached the following conclusions. First, he found communication to be a useful complement to development because communication functioned as a catalyst, organizer, maintainer, equalizer, and legitimator–motivator for social change. Second, Hornik concluded that development communication is effective only as a complementary strategy to changes in resources and environments. Finally, Hornik states that the relationship between communication and development was more complex than previous research tended to assume. In conclusion, Hornik's wide-ranging review indicated that communication is necessary, but not sufficient, for meaningful development to take place.

Social Learning Theory

Social learning theories are based on the simple but powerful assumption that people learn from observation. This assumption has been held for generations as conventional wisdom, and it has been applied in areas such as education and training. Applied to the mass media, this assumption becomes more problematic and more difficult to prove, since media scholars cannot reach a strong agreement on what behaviors people learn from the media, to what degree, and under what conditions. There are rare examples in which viewers, especially younger ones, imitate a scene from a television program or a movie in close detail. Copycat crime is one of the worrisome examples of imitation. Most people, however, will imitate images and behaviors they see on television screens in discriminate, selective, and, often, indirect ways.

In his book *Psychological Modeling: Conflicting Theories* (1971), social psychologist Albert Bandura has argued for an indirect and complex understanding of how people model their behavior on images that they obtain from society. Bandura's social learning theory maintains that humans acquire symbolic images of actions and behaviors, which they adapt and then use to inspire their own behavior. According to Bandura, social learning from the media is achieved in one or a combination of observational learning, inhibitory effects, and disinhibitory effects.

Observational learning is the most direct way in which social learning operates. It is based on the fact that by observing a behavior, people can learn how to perform it themselves. In vocational training, for example, apprenticeship developed as a more or less lengthy process of initiation primarily based on learning by observation. By observing the master at work, the apprentice was to learn the trade. Inhibitory effects operate on the assumption that if someone observes a person being sanctioned for behaving in a certain way, then the observer will learn not to behave in that way. In other words, inhibitory effects produce an avoidance of a behavior that the observer associates with sanctions. The opposite occurs with disinhibitory effects. If a person is rewarded for destructive behavior, it is probable that an observer would imitate the behavior. This is why some television critics have been especially disturbed by programming that glorifies violence and leaves it unpunished. Social learning theory has had a lasting effect on efforts to induce social change using the mass media because it recognized that social learning is not a rote process of direct imitation, but one in which several forces affect both observation and behavior.

Social Marketing Theory

In 1971, the same year that Bandura published *Psychological Modeling*, Philip Kotler and Gerald Zaltman published an article in the *Journal of Marketing* in which they proposed and coined the term "social marketing theory." Reprinted in 1997 in the specialized journal *Social Marketing Quarterly*, the Kotler and Zaltman article is considered to be one of the leading pioneering publications in the field of social marketing. The authors advocated the application of consumer marketing techniques to social problems, and they laid the conceptual foundations for their approach.

Social marketing is based on one basic premise. Since marketing has been largely successful in making people chose to buy some products as opposed to competing products, then the same techniques should be effective in encouraging people to adopt certain behaviors that would lead to better physical and mental health, and eventually to wide-scale social change. As a hybrid theory that proposed to induce positive social change, social marketing borrowed concepts from psychology, sociology, communication, and preventive medicine. Similar to communication theory and research, social marketing theory is an interdisciplinary venture that requires collaborative research between scholars in several traditional disciplines.

Social marketing campaigns are simultaneously directed at two audiences. First, because social problems have behavioral causes, social marketing campaigns target the individuals and groups who would benefit from a behavior change. Second, since social problems have socioeconomic causes as well, social marketing campaigns are aimed at policymakers who have the power to make policy changes that would enhance the chances of success of social marketing campaigns.

Social marketing campaigns are organized around three principles. First, in order to be successful, a campaign has to have a consumer orientation. This means that the target group is treated as an active audience whose members participate in the process of social change. Second, the campaign should be premised on a social exchange of values and ideas between campaign organizers and the target group. This exchange is based on the important idea in social marketing that behavior is voluntary and not coerced. Third, campaigns should have a long-term plan that goes beyond immediate or short-term measures of success. This should include mechanisms of monitoring, feedback, and evaluation. Social marketing has been criticized for fostering a consumer approach to social change, with its underlying capitalist premise. Still, social marketing has become a preferred approach to creating and sustaining positive social change.

Convergence, Critique, and Conclusion

Development communication and social marketing theory share several assumptions and methodologies. In fact, they share the most basic of assumptions: that social change can be achieved by using carefully conceptualized and operationalized persuasion campaigns. Since the dominant channels of persuasion are radio, television, popular music, and the Internet, these mass media are highly significant and hold considerable potential for positive social change.

However, the motives of media campaigns for social change have been scrutinized by critics who believe that development communication is a neo-colonialist paradigm that maintains a relationship of dependency between the rich industrialized countries and the developing world. Peter Golding (1974) was one of the early critics of the role of the media in national development. He criticized development communication as an ethnocentric

theory that constructed and maintained Western European and North American social and economic standards as "goal-states from which calibrated indices of underdevelopment can be constructed" (p. 39). In the same vein, development was criticized for being a self-serving, even colonial, Western project that is designed to open markets in the developing world for commodities produced in the wealthy countries of North America and Western Europe. Both development communication and social marketing theory do have elements that are grounded in assumptions about the relationship of consumption to social change. Development communication, starting from Schramm's early work, has tended to focus more on economic issues than on social and cultural issues. Social marketing theory, after all, is derived from concepts developed in marketing and advertising, two areas that focus on making individuals good consumers. As a result, social marketing theory runs the risk of regarding individuals as consumers to be persuaded to buy a commodity, rather than citizens to be informed about issues.

The line between regarding individuals as either consumers or citizens in campaigns focusing on promoting positive social change is understandably difficult to draw. Theories of media and social change have tremendous potential, but they also have serious limitations. Research has attempted to move beyond previous models of social change and has advocated more interactivity, transparency, and sensitivity to context in using media for social change. Even if the influence of the mass media is indirect and difficult to monitor, measure, and understand, the media are an important instrument to be used in continuous efforts to improve people's quality of life.

See also: DEMOCRACY AND THE MEDIA; PIRATE MEDIA; PROPAGANDA; PUBLIC BROADCASTING; PUBLIC HEALTH CAMPAIGNS; PUBLIC SERVICE MEDIA; SOCIAL COGNITIVE THEORY AND MEDIA EFFECTS; SOCIAL GOALS AND THE MEDIA; SOCIETY AND THE MEDIA; TELEVISION, EDUCATIONAL.

Bibliography

Andreasen, Alan R. (1995). *Marketing Social Change: Changing Behaviour to Promote Health, Social Development and the Environment*. San Francisco: Jossey-Bass.

Bandura, Albert. (1971). *Psychological Modeling: Conflicting Theories*. Chicago: Aldine Atherton.

Centre for Social Marketing, University of Strathclyde. (2001). "Welcome to the Centre for Social Marketing." <http://www.csm.strath.ac.uk>.

Gillespie, Marie. (1995). *Television, Ethnicity and Cultural Change.* London: Routledge.

Golding, Peter. (1974). "Media Role in National Development: Critique of a Theoretical Orthodoxy." *Journal of Communication* 24(3):39–53.

Goldsmith, Edward. (1996). "Development as Colonialism." In *The Case Against the Global Economy,* eds. Jerry Mander and Edward Goldsmith. San Francisco: Sierra Club Books.

Gonzalez, Hernando. (1989). "Interactivity and Feedback in Third World Development Campaigns." *Critical Studies in Mass Communication* 6:295–314.

Hornik, Robert. (1980). "Communication as Complement in Development." *Journal of Communication* 30(2):10–24.

Kotler, Philip, and Zaltman, Gerald. (1997). "Social Marketing: An Approach to Planned Social Change." *Social Marketing Quarterly* 3:7–20.

Lefebvre, R. C. (1996). "25 Years of Social Marketing: Looking Back to the Future." *Social Marketing Quarterly* 3:51–58.

Lerner, Daniel. (1958). *The Passing of Traditional Society: Modernizing the Middle East.* Glencoe, IL: Free Press.

Rogers, Everett M. (1978). "The Rise and Fall of the Dominant Paradigm." *Journal of Communication* 28(Winter):64–69.

Schramm, Wilbur. (1964). *Mass Media and National Development: The Role of Information in the Developing Countries.* Stanford, CA: Stanford University Press.

Servaes, Jan. (1990). "Rethinking Development Communication: One World, Many Cultures." *Journal of Development Communication* 1:35–45.

Shah, Hemant. (1996). "Modernization, Marginalization, and Emancipation: Toward a Normative Model of Journalism and National Development." *Communication Theory* 6(2):143–166.

Singhal, Arvind, and Svenkerud, Peer J. (1994). "Pro-Socially Shareable Entertainment Television Programmes: A Programming Alternative in Developing Countries?" *Journal of Development Communication* 5(2):17–30.

Tehranian, Majid. (1999). *Global Communication and World Politics: Domination, Development, and Discourse.* Boulder, CO: Lynne Rienner.

MARWAN M. KRAIDY

SOCIAL COGNITIVE THEORY AND MEDIA EFFECTS

Learning would be exceedingly laborious, not to mention hazardous, if people had to rely solely on direct experience to tell them what to do. Direct experience is a toilsome, tough teacher. Fortunately, humans have evolved an advanced capacity for observational learning that enables them to expand their knowledge and competencies through the power of social modeling.

Much human learning relies on the models in one's immediate environment. However, a vast amount of knowledge about styles of thinking and behaving and the mores and structures of social systems is gained from the extensive modeling in the symbolic environment of the electronic mass media. A major significance of symbolic modeling lies in its tremendous reach, speed, and multiplicative power. Unlike learning by doing, which requires shaping the actions of each individual laboriously through repeated consequences, in observational learning a single model can transmit new ways of thinking and behaving simultaneously to countless people in widely dispersed locales. Electronic delivery systems feeding off telecommunications satellites are now rapidly diffusing new ideas, values, and styles of conduct worldwide.

Symbolic modeling can have diverse psychosocial effects. Such influences can serve as tutors, motivators, inhibitors, disinhibitors, social promoters, emotion arousers, and shapers of the public consciousness. The determinants and mechanisms governing these many effects are addressed in some detail by Albert Bandura in *Social Foundations of Thought and Action* (1986) and by Ted Rosenthal in "Observational Learning Effects" (1984).

Observational learning of behavioral and cognitive competencies is governed by four component subfunctions. Attentional processes determine what people observe in the profusion of modeling influences and what information they extract from what they notice. A second subfunction involves an active process of transforming the information conveyed by modeled events into rules and conceptions for memory representation. In the third subfunction, symbolic conceptions are translated into appropriate courses of action. The fourth subfunction concerns motivational processes that determine whether people put into practice what they have learned.

Modeling is not simply a process of response mimicry as commonly misbelieved. Observers extract the rules underlying the modeled style of

News images of injured people being carried away from Tiananmen Square after clashes between students and Chinese soldiers in 1989 shocked the world and had a chilling effect on further pro-democracy protests. (AFP/Corbis)

thinking and behaving, and those extracted rules enable the observers to generate new behaviors in that style that go beyond what they have seen or heard.

Much of the research on media effects has centered on the effect of televised violence. Exposure to televised violence has at least three distinct effects. It teaches aggressive styles of conduct. It also reduces restraints over aggressive conduct. This occurs because violence is portrayed as a preferred solution to conflict that is often successful, and relatively clean. Superheroes are doing most of the killing. When good triumphs over evil by violent means, such portrayals legitimize and glamorize violence. In addition, heavy exposure to televised violence desensitizes and habituates people to human cruelty.

With live global broadcasts of societal conflicts, televised modeling is becoming an influential vehicle for political and social change. In his analytic article "A Sociology of Modeling and the Politics of Empowerment" (1994), John Braithwaite provides evidence that the speed with which Eastern European rulers and regimes were toppled by collective action was greatly accelerated by televised modeling. The tactic of mass action modeled successfully by East Germans was immediately adopted by those living under

oppressive rule. Televised modeling of civic strife is a double-edged sword, however. Modeling of punitive countermeasures can also curb social change, as when the Chinese watched on Cable News Network (CNN) as the army broke down doors and arrested student activists following the 1989 Tiananmen Square massacre.

The actions of others can also serve as social prompts in activating, channeling, and supporting previously learned styles of behavior that are unencumbered by restraints. By social exemplification one can get people to behave altruistically, to volunteer their services, to delay or seek gratification, to show affection, to select certain foods and drinks, to choose certain kinds of apparel, to converse on particular topics, to be inquisitive or passive, to think creatively or conventionally, or to engage in other permissible courses of action. Thus, the types of models that prevail in a social setting partly determine which human qualities, from among many alternatives, are selectively activated. The fashion and taste industries rely heavily on the social prompting power of modeling. The actions of models acquire the power to activate and channel behavior when they are good predictors for observers that positive results can be gained by similar conduct.

In her article "Fright Reactions to Mass Media," Joanne Cantor (1994) reviews the literature on fear arousal and the acquisition of fearful dispositions through exposure to modeled threats. The world of television is heavily populated with unsavory and villainous characters. Consequently, people who watch a large amount of violent fare have a greater fear of being criminally victimized and are more distrustful of others than are viewers who watch only a limited amount of violent fare.

Fears and intractable phobias can be eradicated by modeling influences that convey information about effective coping strategies. In *Self-Efficacy: The Exercise of Control*, Bandura and his colleagues (1997) have shown that modeling influences exert their effects partly by altering viewers beliefs in their personal efficacy to exercise control over events that affect their lives. The stronger the instilled perceived coping efficacy, the bolder the behavior. Values can similarly be developed and altered vicariously by repeated exposure to modeled preferences.

During the course of their daily lives, people have direct contact with only a small sector of the physical and social environment. In their everyday routines, they travel the same routes, visit the same familiar places, and see the same group of friends and associates. As a result, their conceptions of the wider social reality are greatly influenced by symbolic representations of society, mainly by the mass media. George Gerbner and his associates (1994) provide a comprehensive analysis of this cultivation effect through symbolic modeling in their work "Living With Television: The Dynamics of the Cultivation Process." To a large extent, people act on their images of reality. The more their conceptions of the world around them depend on portrayals in the media's symbolic environment, the greater is the media's social effect.

See Also: ADVERTISING EFFECTS; CULTIVATION THEORY AND MEDIA EFFECTS; DESENSITIZATION AND MEDIA EFFECTS; FEAR AND THE MEDIA; NATIONAL TELEVISION VIOLENCE STUDY; VIOLENCE IN THE MEDIA, ATTRACTION TO; VIOLENCE IN THE MEDIA, HISTORY OF RESEARCH ON.

Bibliography

Bandura, Albert. (1986). *Social Foundations of Thought and Action: A Social Cognitive Theory.* Englewood Cliffs, NJ: Prentice-Hall.

Bandura, Albert. (1997). *Self-Efficacy: The Exercise of Control.* New York: Freeman.

Braithwaite, John. (1994). "A Sociology of Modeling and the Politics of Empowerment." *British Journal of Sociology,* 45:445–479.

Cantor, Joanne. (1994). "Fright Reactions to Mass Media." In *Media Effects,* eds. Jennings Bryant and Dolf Zillman. Hillsdale, NJ: Lawrence Erlbaum.

Gerbner, George; Gross, Larry; Morgan, Michael; and Signorielli, Nancy. (1994). "Living With Television: The Dynamics of the Cultivation Process." *Media Effects,* eds. Jennings Bryant and Dolf Zillman. Hillsdale, NJ: Lawrence Erlbaum.

Rosenthal, Ted. (1984). "Observational Learning Effects." In *Personality and the Behavioral Disorders,* 2nd edition, eds. Norman Endler and J. McVicker Hunt. New York: Wiley.

ALBERT BANDURA

▌▇ SOCIAL GOALS AND THE MEDIA

Media effects researchers have tended to focus on negative rather than positive effects of watching television. However, given that the same processes of observation, learning, and imitation should be at work for both types of effects, it is plausible that there should be prosocial as well as antisocial outcomes of television exposure.

Prosocial Content on Television

During the 1970s, prosocial behaviors were reported to appear quite frequently on television. However, these behaviors typically occurred in a context of violence and hostility. As Bradley Greenberg and his associates reported in 1980, the favorite programs of a sample of grade-school children contained equal numbers of prosocial and antisocial acts. Marsha Liss and Lauri Reinhard (1980) found that even those cartoons that were considered by the researchers to have moral messages contained high levels of violence—the same amount as in standard cartoons that had no such moral lessons. Moreover, only some types of prosocial behaviors were shown. Rita Poulos, Eli Rubinstein, and Robert Liebert reported in 1975 that although there were an average of eleven altruistic acts and six sympathetic acts per hour, there were very few depictions of self-control (e.g., controlling aggressive impulses or resisting temptation).

Content analyses of prosocial behavior on television were scarce throughout the 1980s, but prosocial content received more attention again in the 1990s with the introduction of legislation aimed at improving the quality of television programming for children. The Federal Communications Commission (FCC) enacted a processing guideline known as the "three-hour rule" that went into effect in 1997. Under the three-hour rule, broadcasters that wish to have their license renewals expedited are required to air a minimum of three hours a week of educational and informational (E/I) television that meets the "cognitive/intellectual or social/emotional" needs of children. The E/I programs must be specifically designed for children who are sixteen years of age or under and must air between the hours of 7:00 A.M. AND 10:00 P.M. Broadcasters are required to place an on-air symbol at the beginning of E/I programs to indicate to the public that they are educational. This information must also be provided to listing services, such as the local newspaper and *TV Guide.*

In the late 1990s, the Annenberg Public Policy Center conducted a series of content analyses of all children's programs that were aired over the course of a composite week in Philadelphia, a large urban media market. Emory Woodard (1999) examined the frequency with which programs contained social lessons about how to live with oneself (i.e., intrapersonal skills such as understanding emotions, maintaining self-esteem, and overcoming fears) and how to live with others (i.e., interpersonal skills such as acceptance of diversity, altruism, and cooperation). In Woodard's sample, 50 percent of all children's shows contained at least one social lesson. These were mostly concentrated in programming for preschool children; 77 percent of preschool children's programming contained a social lesson. Public Broadcasting Service (PBS) programming had the highest overall rate with 72 percent of the children's programming containing social lessons. This was followed by premium cable channels, such as The Disney Channel and Home Box Office (HBO), with 59 percent of the children's programs containing social lessons. PBS also had the highest level of programs with traditionally academic lessons (i.e., reading, writing, and arithmetic), since 89 percent of the programs fell into this category.

Using the same sample of programs, Kelly Schmitt (1999) reported that of the subset of children's programs that had been designated as meeting the "educational and/or informational needs of children," 75 percent of those offered by the commercial broadcast networks were prosocial in nature. In this case, "prosocial" was broadly defined as promoting "learning to live with oneself and others." That is, broadcasters appeared to be meeting the three-hour rule by focusing on general prosocial messages rather than conveying traditionally academic information.

Although these content analyses suggest that children's television is full of material that has the broad social goal of teaching life skills, children may actually see relatively little of this potentially positive content. Woodard (1999) examined the content of the twenty shows in the sample that received the highest Nielsen ratings among children between two and seventeen years of age. Only four of the twenty contained social lessons in the episodes that were analyzed. Of those four, only two contained content that was related to specific prosocial outcomes such as positive social interactions, stereotype reduction, or altruism. Of these two, only one was designed explicitly for children. These findings highlight the fact that it is relatively rare for children to watch the prosocial programming that is designed for them.

Evidence of Prosocial Effects?

Marie-Louise Mares and Woodard (2000) conducted a meta-analysis to summarize the results of thirty-nine studies of prosocial effects of television. Meta-analysis involves averaging statistical information across studies on a particular topic, in order to estimate the overall consistency and strength of effects. Mares and Woodard reported that prosocial content had an overall weak to moderate effect. Effects were strongest for studies of altruism, largely because such studies were more likely to model behaviors that were identical to the behaviors that were subsequently observed in the children. Efforts to promote other prosocial behaviors such as positive interaction, aggression reduction, and stereotype reduction were less likely to use identical treatment and outcome measures. Effect sizes for these treatments were smaller and remarkably similar to each other.

How do these effect sizes compare with the effects of violent content? Hae-Jung Paik and George Comstock (1994) looked at studies of the effects of television violence on viewer aggression. They reported an overall moderate negative effect of violent television content. Therefore, it is reasonable to suggest at this point that the effects of violent and prosocial content are reasonably close in magnitude.

Investigating Prosocial Effects

Research strategies for investigating television effects have evolved over the years, which is true of research on prosocial effects as well as in other areas. Early studies of prosocial effects were often simple one-shot experimental tests of modeling. These simple tests of modeling generally found quite strong, positive effects when comparing a group that watched explicit depictions of prosocial actions with a group that did not see the content.

A second strategy was to conduct a field experiment that typically involved repeated exposure to real television content in relatively uncontrolled environments. The major field experiments in this area looked at the effect of using a particular prosocial program such as *Sesame Street*, *Mister Rogers' Neighborhood*, or *Barney & Friends* as part of the school or preschool experience. Children generally watched whole episodes every week for a number of weeks and were then evaluated, often by observation over several days or weeks, rather than by assessing their performance on a single task. These studies often found that prosocial content could be effective, but chiefly when the content was combined with other forms of teacher intervention.

A third strategy was to conduct a survey to find out how much of an effect could be observed when children simply self-selected to watch prosocial programming at home. That is, these studies examined the effects of everyday viewing rather than special interventions. The results of such correlational studies are more easily and reliably applied to general audiences than are the other types of studies. However, as in all correlational studies, the question of whether prosocial programming causes prosocial outcomes is plagued by issues of causal direction and spuriousness. Maybe children who are already tolerant, friendly, caring people are attracted to prosocial programming. Maybe prosocial behavior and prosocial viewing are both caused by other variables such as parental style, gender, and so on. Overall, once these possible third variables are statistically controlled, most correlational studies find very weak effects of prosocial viewing.

Effects on Positive Social Interactions

In one example of a field experiment, Lynette Friedrich-Cofer and her associates (1979) focused on the effects of *Mister Rogers' Neighborhood* on "urban poor children." They had children who were in Headstart programs watch twenty episodes of the program over a period of eight weeks. Comparisons were then made between children from four different groups: (1) those who simply watched *Mister Rogers' Neighborhood* at the Headstart center without any additional prosocial materials, (2) those who watched it and had access to prosocial books, games, and so on, (3) those who watched it, had access to the prosocial materials, and had follow-up activities such as verbal labeling of the prosocial behaviors and role playing, and (4) those who were part of a control group that simply saw neutral films.

Friedrich-Cofer and her associates found that *Mister Rogers' Neighborhood* alone produced relatively few behavioral changes. Children who watched the program and had access to the proso-

cial materials became more active overall—they had a greater number of positive interactions, but they also had more aggressive interactions. The most successful group, in terms of prosocial behavior, was the one that watched the program and received training in role playing and verbal labeling. That group showed significant increases in positive social interactions without any increases in aggression.

Jerome and Dorothy Singer (1998) examined the effects of repeated exposure to *Barney & Friends* in preschool and daycare settings, and they found similar results. There were minimal effects of exposure when children simply watched the program without further adult elaboration of the content, but there were significant positive effects when viewing was combined with adult commentary and related activities.

Maurice Elias (1983) examined whether videos could be used as one component of treatment for boys who had serious emotional and educational disturbances. The ten videos, which were shown twice a week for five weeks, portrayed realistic scenarios of common problematic situations such as teasing and bullying, dealing with peer pressure, learning how to express feelings, and coping with new social situations. After watching each video, the boys were encouraged to discuss what they had seen and how they felt about it. The boys were measured (both for three months before and two months after the video series) on a variety of behavioral and emotional responses that were related to interactions. Compared to control children who did not see the videos, participants in the experiment were rated by their counselors as being less emotionally detached and less isolated, as having improved in their ability to delay gratification, and as having decreased in overall personality problems. These effects were still evident two months after the intervention.

Despite these encouraging results, researchers generally find much weaker outcomes when they use surveys to look at the effects of normal, everyday viewing. Joyce Sprafkin and Eli Rubinstein (1979) studied children who were seven, eight, and nine years of age and lived in middle-class communities. The children reported how often they watched each of fifty-five television series that were then rated for levels of prosocial and antisocial content. The children's prosocial behavior was measured by teacher and classroom peer reports.

Sprafkin and Rubinstein found that the strongest predictors of prosocial behavior were background variables. Children who were high academic achievers or whose parents were well educated received more reports of prosocial behavior. Girls were also rated as being more prosocial than boys. Compared to these effects, television viewing was only weakly related to prosocial behavior. The partial correlation between prosocial viewing and behavior (controlling for background variables) reflects very minimal differences between heavy viewers of prosocial content and light viewers of prosocial content.

Oene Wiegman, Margot Kuttschreuter, and Ben Baarda (1992) studied second- and third-grade children in The Netherlands for three years (until the children were in fifth and sixth grade). Children were measured once a year on a number of variables, including exposure to prosocial television content and levels of prosocial behavior. As in the Sprafkin and Rubinstein (1979) study, prosocial and antisocial exposure were measured by the frequency of viewing specific programs, and prosocial behavior was assessed by peer nominations. Wiegman and his colleagues found no relationship between prosocial viewing and prosocial behavior, despite the considerable power granted by their large sample size (i.e., 466 children). If anything, the relationship tended to be very weakly negative, rather than positive. Why was this the case? The researchers noted that watching prosocial content was very highly correlated with watching antisocial content—children who saw the most prosocial content were simply heavy television viewers who were exposed to numerous antisocial models as well.

Effects on Altruism

In a well-known study of altruism (i.e., generosity), Poulos, Rubinstein, and Liebert (1975) randomly assigned first-grade children to one of three viewing conditions: (1) a prosocial episode of *Lassie,* in which the protagonist, Jeff, risked his life to save a puppy, (2) a neutral episode of *Lassie,* or (3) a neutral episode of *The Brady Bunch.* After viewing the episode, the children were told how to play a "game" in which they could accrue points by pressing a button. The more points they earned, the larger the prize they would win. At the same time, they were asked to listen to puppies in a distant kennel and to push a help button to call the researcher if the puppies seemed distressed. As children played the game, the recorded puppy sounds grew increasingly loud and intense. The researchers compared the average number of seconds children spent pushing the help button (and thereby sacrificing points in the game) in each of the conditions. Children who saw the prosocial episode pushed the help button nearly twice as long as children in the other two conditions.

In a more typical study of altruism, conducted by James Bryan and Nancy Walbek (1970), children were brought into the laboratory and told that they would learn how to play a new game by watching a video. The children watched one of several versions of the video, in which the model played the game, was rewarded by tokens that could be used to win a prize, and then immediately behaved either altruistically (giving some of the tokens to charity or to another child) or selfishly (cashing in all the tokens for a big prize). The children then played the game, won a fixed number of tokens, and were given the opportunity to donate some tokens. Children who saw the altruistic model donated more tokens than those who had seen the selfish model. As in this example, studies of altruism have generally involved explicit modeling of very specific behaviors immediately after observing the model.

Effects on Tolerance and Stereotype Reduction

In one of the largest and most impressive studies of stereotype reduction, Jerome Johnston and James Ettema (1982) conducted a field experiment that involved more than seven thousand children. Fourth- to sixth-grade classrooms in seven sites across the United States were randomly assigned to watch twenty-six episodes of *Freestyle,* a public television program that was designed to reduce stereotypes about gender roles. Children were assigned (1) to watch the program at school and to engage in teacher-led discussions about the material, (2) to watch the program at school without any such discussions, or (3) to watch the program at home. The students completed extensive questionnaires before seeing any episodes and again after the exposure period. Compared to a control group that had not viewed the program, there were significant positive changes in the students' perceptions of personal ability and their interest in various types of jobs, and there were reductions in the stereotypes that students had about gender roles in employment. These effects were strongest when the program was viewed in the classroom and accompanied by teacher-led discussions. Much smaller effects were observed among students who simply watched the program in school or at home.

Two studies of attempts to counteract gender stereotypes suggest that the same content may have positive effects on some groups but cause a backlash in other groups. Suzanne Pingree (1978) showed commercials to children who were in the third and eighth grades. The commercials featured women in either traditional or nontraditional roles, and Pingree found that, among most children, stereotyping was reduced when the children viewed the commercials that showed the nontraditional behaviors. This result was particularly strong when children were told that the advertisements depicted real people. However, among eighth-grade boys, there appeared to be something of a contrary reaction because stereotyping was significantly higher for this group when commercials featured the nontraditional condition than when they featured the traditional condition.

Shirley O'Bryant and Charles Corder-Bolz (1978), over a period of one month, showed nine half-hour cartoons to children who were between five to ten years of age. Embedded in each cartoon were commercials for a fruit-juice drink. In the traditional condition, the commercials featured a female telephone operator, fashion model, file clerk, and manicurist. In the nontraditional condition, the commercials featured a female pharmacist, welder, butcher, and laborer. Over the course of the month, children saw many repetitions of the commercials. Comparisons between pre- and post-test scores for occupational stereotyping found that children who were exposed to the nontraditional commercials were significantly more likely to say that a traditionally male job was also appropriate for a woman. Moreover, girls who viewed the nontraditional condition gave higher ratings to traditionally male jobs when asked how much they would like to have that job in the future. Boys' ratings of future interest in traditionally male jobs were lower for those who had viewed the nontraditional condition—apparently seeing women in those roles was a deterrent. This effect is consistent with the finding by Pingree (1978) of a "backlash" among boys, and it under-lines the point that seemingly prosocial content can have unintended effects on certain subgroups.

Gerald Gorn, Marvin Goldberg, and Rabindra Kanungo (1976) assessed the effects of *Sesame Street* on children's tolerance for playmates of different ethnic and racial backgrounds. They assigned white, English-Canadian children who were 3.5 to 5.5 years of age to see twelve minutes of *Sesame Street* programming—either with multicultural inserts or without the inserts. The children were then shown two sets of four photographs that were taken from the inserts. One set featured Caucasian children, and the other set featured children from other ethnic and racial backgrounds. The participants in the study then chose which of the photographed children should be brought to the nursery school the next day. The control group that did not see the inserts showed a marked preference for playing with the Caucasian children (67%). Among children who saw the multiracial inserts, this was reversed, with a marked preference for the non-Caucasian playmates (71%) over the Caucasian playmates (29%). However, in one of the very few prosocial projects that involved delayed testing, Goldberg and Gorn (1979) expanded their earlier study and found that children who were tested a day after viewing the multicultural inserts were no longer significantly more willing to play with non-Caucasian playmates than those who had not seen the inserts.

Early studies of *Sesame Street* confirmed that the message of tolerance in *Sesame Street* took time to extract. Gerry Ann Bogatz and Samuel Ball (1971) conducted longitudinal studies of children who were exposed to *Sesame Street*. They reported that viewing *Sesame Street* was positively related to tolerant racial attitudes, but only after two years of exposure. Measures at the end of the first year had found no such relationship.

Mixing Prosocial and Antisocial Content

A final point worth noting is the particularly harmful effect of combining prosocial and antisocial content. As Wiegman, Kuttschreuter, and Baarda (1992) pointed out, not only do heavy prosocial viewers also tend to be heavy viewers of violence, but many of the prosocial acts shown on television are actually presented in the context of violence, as when a "good" group of people fights a "bad" group. When Mares and Woodard (2000) conducted their meta-analysis, they found stronger negative effects of aggressive-prosocial content than of aggressive content that was unadulterated by any prosocial themes. Perhaps having antisocial acts within the context of positive behaviors actually lends legitimacy to the antisocial acts.

The research suggests that prosocial content can have positive effects that are as strong as the negative effects of antisocial content. However, prosocial content may require repetition as well as related adult commentary and activities for long-term positive effects to occur. Moreover, prosocial content may have different effects on different populations, occasionally causing a backlash among groups that feel threatened by themes such as gender equality.

See also: ADVERTISING EFFECTS; AROUSAL PROCESSES AND MEDIA EFFECTS; CHILDREN AND ADVERTISING; CHILDREN'S ATTENTION TO TELEVISION; CHILDREN'S COMPREHENSION OF TELEVISION; CHILDREN'S PREFERENCES FOR MEDIA CONTENT; GENDER AND THE MEDIA; INTERPERSONAL COMMUNICATION; PARENTAL MEDIATION OF MEDIA EFFECTS; PUBLIC BROADCASTING; PUBLIC HEALTH CAMPAIGNS; SESAME STREET; SOCIAL CHANGE AND THE MEDIA; SOCIETY AND THE MEDIA; TELEVISION, EDUCATIONAL; VIOLENCE IN THE MEDIA, ATTRACTION TO; VIOLENCE IN THE MEDIA, HISTORY OF RESEARCH ON.

Bibliography

Bogatz, Gerry Ann, and Ball, Samuel. (1971). *The Second Year of Sesame Street: A Continuing Evaluation*. Princeton, NJ: Educational Testing Service.

Bryan, James H., and Walbek, Nancy H. (1970). "The Impact of Words and Deeds Concerning Altruism Upon Children." *Child Development* 41:488–500.

Elias, Maurice J. (1983). "Improving Coping Skills of Emotionally Disturbed Boys Through Television-Based Social Problem Solving." *American Journal of Orthopsychiatry* 53:61–72.

Friedrich-Cofer, Lynette K.; Huston-Stein, Aletha; Kipnis, Dorothy M.; Susman, Elizabeth J.; and Clewett, Ann S. (1979). "Environmental Enhancement of Prosocial Television Content: Effect on Interpersonal Behavior, Imaginative Play, and Self-Regulation in a Natural Setting." *Developmental Psychology* 15:637–646.

Goldberg, Marvin E., and Gorn, Gerald J. (1979). "Television's Impact on Preferences of Non-White Playmates: Canadian 'Sesame Street' Inserts." *Journal of Broadcasting* 23:27–32.

Gorn, Gerald J.; Goldberg, Marvin E.; and Kanungo, Rabindra N. (1976). "The Role of Educational Television in Changing the Intergroup Attitudes of Children." *Child Development* 42:277–280.

Greenberg, Bradley; Atkin, Charles K.; Edison, Nadyne G.; and Korzenny, Felipe. (1980). "Antisocial and Prosocial Behaviors on Television." In *Life on Television: Content Analysis of U.S. TV Drama*, ed. Bradley S. Greenberg. Norwood, NJ: Ablex.

Johnston, Jerome, and Ettema, James S. (1982). *Positive Images: Breaking Stereotypes with Children's Television*. Beverly Hills, CA: Sage Publications.

Liss, Marsha B., and Reinhardt, Lauri C. (1980). "Aggression on Prosocial Television Programs." *Psychological Reports* 46:1065–1066.

Mares, Marie-Louise, and Woodard, Emory H. (2000). "Prosocial Effects on Children's Social Interactions." In *Handbook of Children and the Media*, eds. Dorothy G. Singer and Jerome L. Singer. Thousand Oaks, CA: Sage Publications.

O'Bryant, Shirley L., and Corder-Bolz, Charles R. (1978). "The Effects of Television on Children's Stereotyping of Women's Work Roles." *Journal of Vocational Behavior* 12:233–244.

Paik, Hae-Jung, and Comstock, George. (1994). "The Effects of Television Violence on Antisocial Behavior: A Meta-Analysis." *Communication Research* 21:516–546.

Pingree, Suzanne. (1978). "The Effects of Nonsexist Television Commercials and Perceptions of Reality on Children's Attitudes about Women." *Psychology of Women Quarterly* 2:262–277.

Poulos, Rita W.; Rubinstein, Eli A.; and Liebert, Robert M. (1975). "Positive Social Learning." *Journal of Communication* 25:90–97.

Schmitt, Kelly L. (1999). *The Three Hour Rule: Is it Living up to Expectations?* (Report No. 30). Philadelphia: Annenberg Public Policy Center, University of Pennsylvania.

Singer, Jerome L., and Singer, Dorothy G. (1998). "*Barney & Friends* as Entertainment and Education." In *Research Paradigms, Television, and Social Behavior*, eds. Joy Keiko Asamen and Gordon L. Berry. Thousand Oaks, CA: Sage Publications.

Sprafkin, Joyce N.; Liebert, Robert M.; and Poulos, Rita W. (1975). "Effects of a Prosocial Televised Example on Children's Helping." *Journal of Experimental Child Psychology* 20:119–126.

Sprafkin, Joyce N., and Rubinstein, Eli A. (1979). "Children's Television Viewing Habits and Prosocial Behavior: A Field Correlational Study." *Journal of Broadcasting* 23:265–276.

Wiegman, Oene; Kuttschreuter, Margot; and Baarda, Ben. (1992). "A Longitudinal Study of the Effects of Television Viewing on Aggressive and Prosocial Behaviors." *British Journal of Social Psychology* 31:147–164.

Woodard, Emory H. (1999). *The 1999 State of Children's Television Report: Programming for Children Over Broadcast and Cable Television.* Report No. 28. Philadelphia: Annenberg Public Policy Center, University of Pennsylvania.

MARIE-LOUISE MARES

■ SOCIETY, INFORMATION

See: Information Society, Description of

■ SOCIETY AND THE MEDIA

The relationship between society and the mass media in the United States has been at the center of attention for media theorists and researchers ever since the end of the nineteenth century and the first decades of the twentieth. Several forms of new media—mass circulation newspapers and magazines, movies, sound films, and radio—came on the scene at the same time that industrialization and urbanization, great population shifts within the country, and heavy immigration wrought profound change in the nature of U.S. society. The traditional rural character of America was slipping further into history, replaced by a boiling brew of new and different people with strange and different habits crowded into rapidly growing cities. Crime rose. Social and political unrest spread. Workers agitated for greater rights, safety, and security. Magazine muckrakers used their popular publications to challenge the abuses of business and the privileged.

Many cultural, political, educational, and religious leaders saw a connection between the new forms of communication and the social upheaval that threatened their positions in the status quo. Events overseas offered additional proof of the media's might, as powerful European nation-states made effective use of propaganda to mobilize their people for World War I. The elites recognized the need to understand better the effect of the media on society, and they recognized the necessity to control it.

The result was a macroscopic theory (it presumed to explain society-wide effects of the media) that came to be called mass society theory. Mass society theory viewed the media as corrupting influences that undermined the social order. The media wielded this pernicious power simply because "average" people (that is, those who did not share the supposed superior tastes and values of the elites) were psychologically, socially, and morally defenseless against their corrupting influence. Mass society theory was often expressed as the hypodermic needle or magic bullet theory. That is, the media are a dangerous drug or a killing force that directly and immediately penetrated a person's system.

Despite the worst fears of the threatened elites, not all "average" people were defenselessly influenced by the corrupting mass media. People selected, consumed, and interpreted media content, often in personally important and interesting ways. The media did have effects, but these were beneficial as well as problematic. Since mass society theory could not explain this variety of media use and effects, it eventually collapsed under its own weight.

The Limited Effects of the Media

Paradigm shifts (movement from one overarching theoretical perspective to another) usually occur slowly, and this is true of the move away from mass society theory. However, media researchers traditionally mark the beginning of the end for this perspective as Halloween Eve 1938, when actor and director Orson Welles broadcast a dramatized version of H. G. Wells's science fiction classic *The War of the Worlds* on the CBS radio network. This realistically presented radio play, in which the Earth came under deadly Martian attack, frightened thousands of people who fled their homes in panic.

Elite media critics argued that this event was proof of mass society theory. However, researchers from Princeton University demonstrated that, yes, one million people had been frightened enough by the broadcast to take some action, but the other five million people who heard the show had not, despite what might have been predicted by mass society theory. More important, these scientists discovered that there were different factors that led some people to be influenced and others not.

If not all "average" people were helplessly influenced by the mass media, new media theories were needed to explain the media and society relationship, theories that could identify those individual and social characteristics that did or did not lead to effects. What emerged was the view that the influence of the media was limited by individual differences (e.g., intelligence and education), social categories (e.g., religious and political affiliation), and personal relationships (e.g., the influence of friends and family). The theories that were developed were the first systematic and scientific study of media effects. Taken together they are called limited effects theory. This paradigm shift represented more than a move from mass society to limited effects theory. There was also a shift from interest in macroscopic theory to microscopic theory, that is, theory that focuses on the media–individual relationship rather than the media–society, relationship. This was in part the natural product of the research methods that were then being developed and applied to media studies, because empirically based, objective research methods such as surveys and experiments focus on media use by individuals and the effect of the media on individuals.

Typical of ideas that gained support under the limited effects rubric is two-step flow theory of mass media and personal influence. Research on the 1940 presidential election in the United States indicated that the influence of the media on the voting behavior of people was limited by opinion leaders—people who initially consumed media content on topics of particular interest to them, interpreted it in light of their own values and beliefs, and then passed it on to opinion followers.

During and after World War II, the limited effects paradigm and several theories that it supported became entrenched, dominating research and thinking about the media until well into the 1960s. It was the war itself that was crucial to the development of mass communication theory during this era.

At the beginning of World War II, media theorists were challenged by important barriers as they sought to develop public information campaigns. Memories of World War I were still very much alive, and many Americans were unenthused about entering another distant world conflict. Those who joined or were drafted into the armed forces knew little about their comrades-in-arms from different regions of the country and from different backgrounds. The Office of War Information (OWI), therefore, set out to change public opinion about the wisdom of entering the war and to educate military people about their fellow soldiers and sailors. Speeches, lectures, and pamphlets failed. The OWI then turned to filmmakers

such as Frank Capra and radio personalities such as Kate Smith for their audience appeal and looked to social scientists to measure the effectiveness of these new media campaigns.

The U.S. Army established the Experimental Section inside its Information and Education Division, staffing it with psychologists who were expert in issues of attitude change. Led by Carl Hovland, this group of researchers tested the effectiveness of the government's media campaigns. Continuing its work at Yale University after the war, it produced some of the most influential communication research of the twentieth century, which led to the development of attitude change theory, explaining how people's attitudes are formed, shaped, and changed through communication, and how those attitudes influence behavior.

Among the most important attitude change theories are the related ideas of dissonance and selective processes. Dissonance theory argues that, when confronted by new information, people experience a mental discomfort, a dissonance. As a result, they consciously and subconsciously work to limit or reduce that discomfort through three interrelated processes that help them "select" what information they consume, remember, and interpret in personally important and idiosyncratic ways. Selective exposure is the process by which people expose themselves to or attend to only those messages that are consistent with their preexisting attitudes and beliefs. Selective retention assumes that people remember best and longest those messages that are consistent with their preexisting attitudes and beliefs. Selective perception predicts that people will interpret messages in a manner consistent with their preexisting attitudes and beliefs.

Because limited effects theory was the dominant paradigm at the time of the development of dissonance theory, the selective processes were seen as limiting the effect of the media because content is selectively filtered to produce as little attitude change as possible. More important, however, the selective processes formed the core of the influential book *The Effects of Mass Communication* (1960). In it, Joseph Klapper, an eminent scientist and the head of social research for CBS broadcasting, articulated firmly and clearly the core of the limited effects paradigm:

1. Mass communication ordinarily does not serve as a necessary and sufficient cause of audience effects, but rather functions among and through a nexus (a web) of mediating factors and influences.

2. These mediating factors are such that they typically render mass communication as a contributory agent, but not the sole cause, in the process of reinforcing existing conditions [p. 8].

Klapper's theory, based on social science evidence developed prior to 1960, is often called reinforcement theory. It was very persuasive at a time when the nation's social fabric had yet to feel the full effect of the change brought about by the war. In addition, the public, flush with enthusiasm and optimism for the technology and science that had helped the United States defeat the Axis powers, could see little but good coming from the media technologies, and they trusted the work of Klapper and other scientists. If the media had little effect other than reinforcement on individuals, they could have little effect on society as a whole.

The Paradigm Begins to Shift

In retrospect, the value of reinforcement theory may have passed with its 1960 publication date. With rapid postwar urbanization, industrialization, and the entry of women into the workplace, Klapper's "nexus of mediating factors and influences"—church, family, and school—began to lose its traditional socializing role for many people. During the 1960s, a decade of profound social and cultural change, it became increasingly difficult to ignore the effect of the media. Most important, however, the research that Klapper studied in preparation for his book had been conducted before 1960, the year in which it is generally accepted that television became a mass medium. Almost none of the science that he examined in developing his reinforcement theory examined television.

During the era of limited effects, a number of important ideas were developed that began to question the assumption of limited media influence on people and cultures. They are still respected and examined. Among the most influential is agenda setting, a theory that argues that the media may not tell people what to think, but through specific journalistic practices, they tell

people what to think about. The agenda-setting power of the media resides not only in factors such as the amount of space or time devoted to a story and its placement in the broadcast or on the page. Also lending strength to the agenda-setting power of the media is the fact that there is great consistency between media sources across all media in the choice and type of coverage they give an issue or event. This consistency and repetition signal to people the importance of an issue or event.

In their 1975 book *Theories of Mass Communication*, Melvin DeFleur and Sandra Ball-Rokeach offered another view of potentially powerful mass media, tying that power to the dependency of audience members on the media and their content. This media systems dependency theory is composed of several assertions:

- The basis of the influence of the media resides in the "relationship between the larger social system, the media's role in that system, and audience relationships to the media."

- The degree of people's dependence on the media and their content is the "key variable in understanding when and why media messages alter audience beliefs, feelings, or behavior."

- In the modern industrial society, people are increasingly dependent on the media (a) to understand the social world, (b) to act meaningfully and effectively in society, and (c) to find fantasy and escape or diversion.

- People's level of dependency is related to (a) "the number and centrality (importance) of the specific information-delivery functions served by a medium" and (b) the degree of change and conflict present in society.

It is clear that limited effects theory is being left behind here. Dependency theory argues that, especially in a complex and changing society, people become increasingly dependent on the media and media content to understand what is going on around them, to learn how to behave meaningfully, and to escape.

At the same time that some media researchers were challenging the limited effects paradigm with ideas such as agenda setting and dependency theory, psychologists were expanding on their social cognitive theory—the idea that people learn through observation—and applying it to mass media, especially television.

Social cognitive theory argues that people model (copy) the behaviors they see and that modeling happens in two ways. The first is imitation, the direct replication of an observed behavior. For example, a child might see a cartoon cat hit a cartoon mouse with a stick and then hit his sister with a stick. The second form of modeling is identification, a special form of imitation in which observers do not copy exactly what they see but make a more generalized, still-related response. For example, the child might still be aggressive to his sister, but dump water on her head rather than hit her.

The idea of identification was of particular value to mass communication theorists. Obviously, people can imitate what they see on television, but not all do. When imitation does occur in dramatic instances—for example, when someone hijacks a plane after seeing it done on television—it is so outrageous that it is considered an aberration. Identification however, although harder to see and study, is the more likely way that television influences behavior.

Return to Macroscopic Theory

Some of the obvious and observable effects that television has on society include increased sophistication of the media industries and media consumers, entrenched social problems such as racial strife, the apparent cheapening of the political process, and the emergence of calls for controls on new technologies such as cable, satellites, and computer networks. These are only a few of the many factors that forced mass communication theorists to rethink the influence of media—and to attempt once again to understand the media–society relationship in macroscopic terms.

The theories that have gained the most support among media researchers and theorists are those that accept the potential for powerful media effects, a potential that is either enhanced or thwarted by the involvement of audience members in the mass communication process. One such theory is symbolic interaction. This is the idea that the meaning of symbols is learned through interaction and then mediates that interaction. In other words, people give things meaning, and that meaning controls their behavior. The American flag is an example. Americans have decided that an array of red, white, and blue cloth, assembled in a particular way, represents not only the nation but its values and beliefs. The flag has

meaning because Americans have given it meaning, and now that meaning governs certain behavior. For example, Americans are not free to remain seated when a color guard carries the flag into a room. Symbolic interaction is frequently used when studying the influence of advertising, because advertisers often succeed by encouraging consumers to perceive products as symbols that have meaning beyond their actual function. This is called product positioning.

Another macroscopic view of the societal role of the media is social construction of reality, developed by sociologists Peter Berger and Thomas Luckmann. Their 1966 book, *The Social Construction of Reality*, although never mentioning mass communication, offered an explanation of how, using signs and symbols, societies construct and maintain the realities that allow them to function.

Social construction of reality theory argues that people who live in a society share "an ongoing correspondence" of meaning. Things generally mean the same to all members. A stop sign, for example, has just about the same meaning for everyone. Things that have "objective" meaning are symbols—people routinely interpret them in the usual way. However, there are other things in the environment to which people assign "subjective" meaning. These things are signs. In social construction of reality, then, a car is a symbol of mobility, but a Cadillac is a sign of wealth or success. In either case, the meaning is negotiated, but for signs the negotiation is a bit more complex.

Through interaction in and with the culture of a given society over time, people bring together what they have learned about their society's signs and symbols to form typification schemes—collections of meanings assigned to some phenomenon or situation. These typification schemes form a natural backdrop for people's interpretation of—and therefore the way they behave in—"the major routines of everyday life, not only the typification of others . . . but typifications of all sorts of events and experiences" (Berger and Luckmann, 1966, p. 43). When people enter a room, they automatically recall the meaning they have given to its elements—desks in rows, chalkboard, and lectern. They recognize this as a classroom and automatically impose their "classroom typification scheme." They know automatically how to behave—to address the person standing at the front of the room with courtesy, to raise their hands when asking a question, to talk to neighbors in whispers. These "rules of behavior" are not published on the classroom door.

Social construction of reality is widely applied to the study of how the media, especially news, shape people's political realities. Crime offers one example. What do politicians mean when they say they are "tough on crime"? What is their (and people's) reality of crime? It is likely that "crime" signifies (is a sign for) gangs, drugs, and violence. The statistical, rather than the socially constructed, reality of crime is that there is ten times more white-collar crime in the United States than there is violent crime. Social construction theorists argue that the "building blocks" for the construction of this "reality" come primarily from the mass media.

Symbolic interaction and social construction of reality provide a strong foundation for another macroscopic theory of the relationship between society and the media. Cultivation analysis says that television "cultivates" or constructs a reality of the world that, although possibly inaccurate, becomes the accepted reality simply because people believe it to be true. They then base their judgments about and their actions in the world on this television-cultivated reality.

Although cultivation analysis was developed by George Gerbner out of concern over the effects of television violence, it has been applied to countless other television-cultivated realities, such as beauty, sex roles, religion, the judicial and political processes, and marriage. In all cases, its assumptions are the same—television cultivates its own realities, especially for heavy viewers.

Cultivation analysis is based on five assumptions:

1. Television is essentially and fundamentally different from the other mass media. Unlike books, newspapers, and magazines, viewing requires no reading ability. Unlike the movies, it requires no mobility or money; it is in the home and it is free. Unlike radio, it combines pictures and sound. It is the first and only medium that can be consumed from people's very earliest to their last years of life.

2. Television is the "central cultural arm" of U.S. society. Gerbner and his colleagues (1978, p. 178)) wrote that television, as culture's primary storyteller, is "the chief creator of synthetic cultural patterns (entertainment and information) for the most heterogeneous mass publics in history, including large groups that have never shared in any common public message systems." The product of this sharing of messages is the mainstreaming of reality, moving people toward a shared, television-created understanding of how things are.

3. The realities cultivated by television are not necessarily specific attitudes and opinions but rather more basic assumptions about the "facts" of life. By the choices the producers make, television news and entertainment programs present a broad picture of "reality" with little regard for how their "reality" matches that of their audiences.

4. The major cultural function of television is to stabilize social patterns, that is, maintain the existing power relationships of the society. Because the media industries have a stake in the political, social, and economic structures as they exist, their stories rarely challenge the system that has enriched them.

5. The observable, measurable, independent contributions of television to the culture are relatively small. This is not a restatement of limited effect theory. Instead, Gerbner explained its meaning with his Ice-Age analogy, arguing that just as a change in temperature of just a few degrees over centuries brought about the Ice Age, a relatively small but pervasive degree of media influence can produce important social change. In other words, the size of the media's influence on society is not as important as its steady direction.

Critical Cultural Theory

A major influence on contemporary understanding of the relationship between the media and society comes from European scholarship on media effects. Critical cultural theory—the idea that the media operate primarily to justify and support the status quo at the expense of ordinary people—is rooted in neo-Marxism. Traditional Marxists believed that people were oppressed by those who owned the means of production—the base—that is, the factories and the land. Modern neo-Marxist theorists believe that people are oppressed by those who control the culture—the superstructure—in other words, the mass media.

Modern critical cultural theory encompasses a number of different conceptions of the relationship between the media and society, but all share a number of identifying characteristics. They are macroscopic in scope. They are openly and specifically political. Based in neo-Marxism, their orientation is from the political left. Their goal is at the least to instigate change in the media policies of governments; at the most, their goal is to effect wholesale change in the media and societal systems. Critical cultural theories assume that the superstructure, which favors those in power, must be altered. Finally, they investigate and explain how elites use the media to maintain their positions of privilege and power. Issues such as media ownership, government–media relations, and corporate media representations of labor and disenfranchised groups are typical topics of study for critical cultural theory.

The critical cultural perspective arrived in the United States during the 1930s, when media scholars Max Horkheimer and Theodor Adorno of the University of Frankfurt escaped Adolf Hitler's Germany. Their approach valued serious art—literature, symphonic music, theater—and saw its consumption as a means to elevate people toward a better life. Typical media fare—popular music, slapstick radio and movie comedies, newspapers full of soft-news—pacified ordinary people while assisting in their repression.

The influence of Horkheimer and Adorno on U.S. media theory was minimal during their lifetimes. The limited effects paradigm was about to blossom, neo-Marxism was not well received in the United States, and their ideas echoed claims by the mass society theory of a debasing popular media. More recently, though, the Frankfurt School has been "rediscovered," and its influence can be seen, for example, in the British cultural theory.

There was significant class tension in England after World War II. During the 1950s and 1960s, working-class people who had fought for their country were unwilling to return to England's traditional notions of nobility and privilege. Many saw the British media supporting long-standing class distinctions and divisions. This environment of class conflict produced theorists such as Stuart Hall, who first developed the idea of the media as a public forum where various forces fight to shape perceptions of everyday reality. Hall trusted that the media could serve all people, but that the forum was dominated by the reigning elite because of factors such as ownership patterns, the commercial orientation of the media, and sympathetic government policies toward the media. In other words, the loudest voice in the cultural forum's give-and-take belonged to those who were already well entrenched in the power structure. British cultural studies theory provides a home for much feminist research, as well as on popular culture both in Europe and in the United States.

Contemporary Theories

Modern theories of the relationship between the media and society have to contend with a mass-mediated world, which was not a factor in the creation of the perspectives discussed above. Digitalization, especially in the form of the Internet and the World Wide Web, poses a significant challenge to much of what is known and understood about the relationship between the media and society. For example, many theorists go as far as to reject the term "mass communication," preferring instead the term "mediated communication." They do this because not only are the "traditional" media prospering by serving smaller fragments of what was once a mass audience, but the Internet can make a single individual a mass communicator or allow a giant media company to reach individuals one person at a time. Clearly, new conceptions of how the media and society interact will be called for. Communication science and the media literacy movement are two such examples.

Many empirical media researchers concluded that the constant debate about competing ideas and research methods was impeding the development of a meaningful understanding of how the media and society interact. They proposed communication science, a perspective that integrates approaches grounded in quantitative, empirical, behavioral research methods. It unites limited effects research with some of the beliefs of culture theory in a potentially active audience, and with research on interpersonal communication. Communication science is as an effort to rebuild the empirical media research tradition by breaking its association with limited effects and broadening it to address a larger range of research questions and issues. It is an effort to be inclusive rather than exclusive, to reject many of the outdated assumptions of the limited effects paradigm while retaining the strong empirical focus of that approach—to unify under a single banner empirical researchers working in all areas of communication. In this way, communication scientists hope their microscopic research can lead to macroscopic theories about the relationship between the media and society.

Cultural and critical cultural theories, because of their assertion that meaning and, therefore, reality are mutually created by the participants in a culture or society, provide the impetus for the media literacy movement. The arguments are straightforward. If a society debates and defines itself in a forum provided by the mass media, the society (and the democracy that supports and sustains it) will benefit from greater numbers of people being able to function appropriately and effectively in that forum. If a society knows itself through the stories it tells about itself, people who understand how those stories are created, who can interpret them in personally important and relevant ways, or even who can create those stories themselves can best know and participate in that society. Media literacy, then, is the ability to use mass communication effectively and efficiently.

See also: ADVERTISING EFFECTS; AROUSAL PROCESSES AND MEDIA EFFECTS; BROADCASTING, GOVERNMENT REGULATION OF; CABLE TELEVISION, REGULATION OF; CATHARSIS THEORY AND MEDIA EFFECTS; CULTIVATION THEORY AND MEDIA EFFECTS; CULTURAL STUDIES; CULTURE AND COMMUNICATION; CULTURE INDUSTRIES, MEDIA AS; CUMULATIVE MEDIA EFFECTS; DESENSITIZATION AND MEDIA EFFECTS; ELECTION CAMPAIGNS AND MEDIA EFFECTS; INTERNET AND THE WORLD WIDE WEB; MEAD, GEORGE HERBERT; NEWS EFFECTS; NEWS PRODUCTION THEORIES; PARENTAL MEDIATION OF MEDIA EFFECTS; POLITICAL ECONOMY; PROPAGANDA; SCHRAMM, WILBUR; SOCIAL CHANGE AND THE MEDIA; SOCIAL COGNITIVE THEORY AND MEDIA EFFECTS; SOCIAL GOALS AND THE MEDIA; SYMBOLS; WELLES, ORSON.

Bibliography

Baran, Stanley, and Davis, Dennis. (2000). *Mass Communication Theory: Foundations, Ferment, and Future.* Belmont, CA: Wadsworth.

Bennett, W. Lance. (1988). *News: The Politics of Illusion,* 2nd edition. New York: Longman.

Berger, Peter L., and Luckmann, Thomas. (1966). *The Social Construction of Reality: A Treatise in the Sociology of Knowledge.* Garden City, NY: Doubleday.

DeFleur, Melvin L., and Ball-Rokeach, Sandra. (1975). *Theories of Mass Communication,* 3rd edition. New York: David McKay.

Gerbner, George; Gross, Lawrence; Jackson-Beeck, Marilyn; Jeffries-Fox, Susan; and Signorielli, Nancy. (1978). "Cultural Indicators: Violence Profile No. 9." *Journal of Communication* 28:176–206.

Horkheimer, Max, and Adorno, Theodor W. (1972). *Dialectic of Enlightenment.* New York: Herder and Herder.

Klapper, Joseph T. (1960). *The Effects of Mass Communication.* New York: Free Press.

Lowery, Shearon A., and DeFleur, Melvin L. (1995). *Milestones in Mass Communication Research.* White Plains, NY: Longman.

McCombs, Maxwell E., and Shaw, Donald L. (1972). "The Agenda-Setting Function of Mass Media." *Public Opinion Quarterly* 36:176–187.

Potter, W. James. (1998). *Media Literacy.* Thousand Oaks, CA: Sage Publications.

STANLEY J. BARAN

■ SOCIOLINGUISTICS

Sociolinguistics is the study of the relationships between language use and social structure. It investigates the correlation between linguistic (i.e., phonological, lexical, and grammatical) variables and social (i.e., gender, age, status, and ethnicity) variables. Since sociolinguistics is concerned with both linguistic and social aspects of language, researchers identify two main distinctions in sociolinguistic inquiry. Micro-sociolinguistics focuses on the social aspects of language, while macro-sociolinguistics examines how linguistic features can provide explanations for certain social phenomena. In other words, micro-sociolinguistics investigates how society influences the way people communicate, while macro-sociolinguistics studies society in relation to language.

Sociolinguistics is a relatively new branch of linguistics. Despite a long tradition of dialect research dating back to the nineteenth century, it was not until the 1960s that sociolinguistics became a recognized area of language research. This came about as a result of the projects that were carried out by William Labov (1966, 1972) in the United States and Peter Trudgill (1983) in the United Kingdom. Labov, in his studies in New York and Martha's Vineyard, investigated linguistic change and variation as social phenomena. For example, he found that in New York, people who were less secure about their social status were more likely to pronounce the "r" in words such as "car" and "fourth." He found that such pronunciation was treated as newer and more prestigious. Trudgill, in his study of Norwich, England, found that women used more "correct" and prestigious forms of language than did men. He attributed this difference to the differences in the roles and expectations that society placed on men and women. In society, it is "normal" for women to speak "better" than men. Both Labov and Trudgill found evidence of the interconnectedness of language and society and demonstrated that it is possible to find social explanations for linguistic structure and change.

Sociolinguists do not seek to find and prescribe the "correct" or "standard" variant of a language. Rather, they aim to describe the variety in language against a systematic correlation between linguistic and social variables. Labov, for example, in his influential study of black English, argued that African-American Vernacular English (AAVE) is not a poor or illogical way of talking but a rich variant of English that is governed by specific rules.

Unlike theoretical linguists (e.g., Noam Chomsky), who disregard "real-life" conversations and instead study language in terms of ideal speakers who are situated in a homogeneous community, sociolinguists find it difficult and artificial to separate language from the rest of society. Thus, sociolinguistics, without necessarily rejecting the main premises of theoretical linguistics, looks beyond prescribed phonological and grammatical rules at language that is produced by real speakers in a real world.

Regional Dialects

A native speaker of a language in many instances can identify where his or her conversational partner grew up or is currently living. Such identification is based on pronunciation, grammar, and vocabulary. A variation of language spoken in a specific geographical area is a dialect; more specifically, it is a regional dialect. A dialect should not be confused with an accent, which is usually associated with the speech of a nonnative speaker whose native language phonetics penetrates into the target language.

Mutual intelligibility is often used as a criterion to distinguish between a language and a dialect. For example, if a person who is speaking Spanish cannot understand a person who is speaking French, they are said to speak different languages. However, if a person from the southern part of the United States can understand a person from the northern part of the United States, they are said to speak different dialects of the same language. The distinction between language and dialect is not always so clear-cut. For example, Danes and Norwegians understand each other well, but Danish and Norwegian are considered to be two different languages. At the same time, a speaker of Cantonese would not understand a speaker of Mandarin, but Cantonese and Mandarin are both recognized as being dialects of Chinese. Thus, the distinction between a language and a dialect does not lie in mere intelligibility. The distinction is also related to political, historical, social, and cultural factors. Furthermore, Richard Hudson (1998) argues that mutual intelligibility is not between linguistic varieties but between people who are either motivated or not motivated to understand each other. Motivation can be said to be the speakers' attempt to minimize cultural differences and stress similarities.

Social Dialects, Style, and Register

Dialect varieties are not limited to geography; they are also related to the age, social class, and gender of the speakers. All play a significant role in the way people speak. The term "social dialect" is used to describe a speech variety that is associated with a certain social group. For example, Standard American English is a social dialect that is associated with the educated middle- and upper-class population, so it is, therefore, considered to be more prestigious. A nonstandard or vernacular language is usually ascribed less societal prestige. For example, the form "getting" (which is associated with the standard variant) is generally considered to be more prestigious than "gettin'" (which is associated with the nonstandard variant). However, "lower-class" speech, especially that of men, has what Labov called "covert prestige," which is different from the standard or "overt prestige" and is associated with group solidarity. Trudgill (1983), in his study of Norwich, found that women are more status conscious and concerned with overt prestige, while men are more concerned with acquiring covert prestige.

Language variety plays an important role in conveying information about a speaker. A person's identity is created, to a large extent, in and by conversation. Identity, however, is not fixed and static; it is fluid and dynamic. Its fluidity depends on the context in which communication is taking place and the social relations between the communicants. For example, the same person can demonstrate different linguistic styles as well as extralinguistic behavior when speaking to a subordinate, a boss, a relative, or a neighbor. Thus, a person can express approximately the same meaning using different language styles that depend on the relationship between the communicants and the level of formality of the situation. Consider the phrases "I have purchased some refreshments" and "I got something to drink." In both cases, the meaning is more or less the same, while the level of formality is different. Where the first is formal and appropriate for official conversation, the second is informal and appropriate for a conversation among friends.

Charles Ferguson (1994, p. 20) states that groups of people who share common interests or jobs develop "similar vocabularies, similar features of intonation, and characteristic bits of syntax and phonology that they use in these situations." This shared language variant is a register. While some researchers do not distinguish between register and style, others see the difference as being essential when examining the language of a particular group of people who are united by interest or occupation. Style, register, and dialect are not mutually exclusive. For example, a person can speak as a doctor to another doctor in informal style and with pronunciation characteristic of her or his dialect. Moreover, a given person can use a variety of registers, such as being a carpenter and a musician. With all of the complexity that is created by dialect, style, and register, it is amazing that people are still so skillful at using speech to identify other people's status, profession, class, and so on.

Multilingualism, Bilingualism, and Diglossia

A person who has the ability to use more than two languages is a multilingual; a person who can use two languages is a bilingual; and a person who uses only one language is a monolingual. The number of bilinguals and multilinguals in a given country depends on many factors, such as proximity to other countries, the language policy in the country, and patterns of immigration. However, it has been estimated that half of the population in the world is bilingual.

People who are bilingual or multilingual do not necessarily have equal linguistic ability in all of the languages that they use; however, people whose competence in two or more languages is approximately equal are balanced bilinguals or multilinguals. As the result of the limited use of a language or languages for an extended period of time, some people may become dormant bilinguals or multilinguals; that is their linguistic competence in that language or languages "gets rusty." (Dormant bilinguals or multilinguals usually can restore their linguistic competence by placing themselves in an environment where their subordinate language or languages are used constantly.)

Another interesting aspect of bilingualism and multilingualism is code-switching. A language or its variant is often called a "code"; thus, code-switching refers to the situation when a person switches from one language or dialect to another in the same utterance or conversation. For example, a professor from France delivers a lecture in English at one of the universities in the United States; however, during the informal meeting after the lecture this professor may switch back and forth from English to French in conversations with French-speaking colleagues and students. Bilinguals or monolinguals turn to code-switching to establish solidarity and rapport with their conversational partners; moreover, code-switching helps them to maximize their linguistic expressiveness. In code-switching, bilinguals and multilinguals preserve the rules of all of the languages that are being used. In code-mixing, a person uses elements of one language in a conversation that is being carried on for the most part in another language. Nancy Bonvillain (1993) has identified examples of code-mixing in Kannada, a Dravidian language in South India. For example, some speakers incorporate English words in conversations in Kannada by adding the Kannada suffixes to English words, such as "educated-*u*," "control-*ma*," and "sacred occasion-*nalli*." Bonvillain states that such code-mixing has a social function. People who make use of English words in Kannada try to associate themselves with a more prestigious group of the population because, in India, English is perceived as being the language of those who are more educated and refined than the general population.

Another situation where people use different linguistic codes in different social contexts is diglossia. The term "diglossia" was introduced in 1959 by Charles Ferguson to indicate situations where two varieties of the same language exist in the society and are employed in different sets of social circumstances. Moreover, one of the two varieties is a more prestigious "high" variety (H), while the other is a less prestigious "low" variety (L). For example, Classical Arabic (H) is used in delivering official speeches, while colloquial Arabic (L) is used in everyday communication. Joshua Fishman (1970) extended the concept of diglossia to include not only two varieties of the same language but bilingual and multilingual situations as well. The linguistic situation in Paraguay, where diglossia exists between Spanish (H) and Guaraní (L), can serve as an illustration. In most of the situations, high form (H) is appropriated through formal education and in public domains, while low form (L) is acquired before formal education and is practiced in private domains. Ronald Wardhaugh (1998) suggests that in contrast to code-switching, which reduces differences, diglossia reinforces them. He explains that code-switching often happens on the subconscious level (when a person is unaware of a switch), while diglossia involves speakers who are aware of the switches that are being made from one variant to the other. Overall, choosing a code is not a matter of linguistic preference per se; rather, it is a social act because the code that is chosen creates and re-creates one's social identity.

Lingua Franca, Pidgins, and Creoles

When people who speak different languages have to communicate with each other, they must find a language that they all know, a *lingua franca*. Any language can become a *lingua franca*. For example, in the former Soviet Union, Russian was used as a *lingua franca* in the interactions between non-Russian speakers of the country. In East Africa, Swahili helps people from different tribes to trade with each other; thus, it is "a trade language" between people who do not otherwise share a common language. Due to globalization, and to globalization of the media in particular,

English has become an international language—a *lingua franca* for much of the world.

People from different cultures and with different native languages, when they are in contact with each other over an extended period of time, often develop some common, often simplified code that they use as a medium of communication. This code is a pidgin, or a "reduced" language. Therefore, a pidgin is a contact language. Trade and colonization are considered main reasons for the development of pidgin languages. Thus, many pidgins are based on the languages of people who were involved in travel and trade (e.g., English, French, Dutch, Spanish, Portuguese) and are influenced by the languages of people with whom they came into contact. For example, there are more than sixty varieties of English-based pidgin languages; Tok Pisin, a pidgin English spoken in Papua New Guinea, is among them. It should be noted that pidgins are not "bad" or "inferior" languages. Though simplified or "reduced," they are not languages without structure; they are rule governed.

When a pidgin is widely used by the community and serves as a native language for second and future generations, it becomes a creole. Thus, while a pidgin has no native speakers, a creole is the mother tongue—the first language that is acquired by the community of speakers. For example, French creoles are spoken by people in the Caribbean and in some parts of Louisiana. It is estimated that from seven million to seventeen million people in the world speak creole languages. Pidgins and creoles have certain typical characteristics, such as multifunctionality of words, semantic broadening, little or no inflectional morphology, and polysemy.

Researchers of pidgins and creoles do not have a unified theory of the origin of pidgins and creoles. The fact that pidgins and creoles demonstrate certain similarities among them is explained differently by two main theories. Monogenesis (one origin) theory argues that the source of the similarities lies in the development of pidgins and creoles from a single source. Polygenesis theory, or relexification, views these similarities as the result of similar circumstances of their origin. There are, however, theories that explain the development of pidgins and creoles by the inability of non-Europeans to acquire European languages. Extensive studies of pidgins and creoles indicate that they are not deviations from other languages caused by inferiority of their speakers; they are languages with their own rules and systems. According to Suzanne Romaine (1988), many countries experience the phenomenon of recreolization, which is the conscious effort of teenagers who spoke standard English in childhood to speak creole and to listen to songs in creole.

Language and Culture

One of the areas of sociolinguistic research is concerned with the relationship between language and culture. The word "culture" in this context does not mean art, music, or literature of a particular time or society; rather, it is used to describe "any of the customs, world views, language, kinship system, social organization, and other taken-for-granted day-to-day practices of a people which set that group apart as a distinctive group" (Scollon and Scollon, 1996, p. 126). There is no agreement, however, among researchers about whether language determines or at least influences the way in which people experience the surrounding world, or if language merely reflects people's experiences.

The claim that language and its structure influence the way in which people who use it view the world goes back to the beginning of the twentieth century, to the work that Edward Sapir and Benjamin Whorf did in relation to Native American languages. This influence of language on perceptions of the world is known as the Sapir–Whorf hypothesis. It should be noted that similar ideas were expressed by William Humbolt, a prominent linguist of the nineteenth century. The Sapir–Whorf hypothesis is also called the principle of cultural relativity. That is to say, people are influenced by their native languages in the process of perception of the surrounding world. Sapir (1949a, p. 162) states, "human beings do not live in the objective world alone, not alone in the world of social activity as ordinarily understood, but are very much at the mercy of the particular language which has become the medium of expression for their society."

Sapir, in his study of the language of Paiute (in Arizona, Nevada, and Utah), noticed that for some geographical terms the English language does not have comparable words, so a descriptive translation is required. For example, English does not have words that directly correspond to "canyon without water, plain valley surrounded by moun-

tains, rolling country intersected by several small hillridges" (Sapir, 1949b). Whorf's studies of Hopi, the language of Native American people in Arizona, demonstrate that the notion of time in Hopi does not correspond to the notion of time in English and any other Standard Average European (SAE) language. Thus, while in English, time is a three-tiered division of past, present, and future, in Hopi, time is more indicative of the manner in which the events occur. The focus is on the events in the world as a continuous process where fixed distinctions between tenses are minimized (Whorf, 1956). Though the ideas put forward by Sapir and Whorf have been criticized for their deterministic view on language, their studies have inspired extensive research on the interrelationship between language and culture.

Different kinship systems and color terminology are just a few fascinating areas of research on language and culture. Every language has ways of expressing kinship relationships; however, some kinship systems are more detailed than others. For example, in English, the word "mother-in-law" is used by both wife and husband to identify the mother of the spouse, while in Russian, the husband calls his wife's mother *tjoshcha* and the wife calls her husband's mother *svekrov'*. Some languages have separate linguistic terms for older and younger siblings, for maternal and paternal relatives, and so on. Kinship systems reflect social relations within the family. In general, the more extensive the social contact is between the family members, the more detailed is the related kinship terminology.

According to Brent Berlin and Paul Kay (1969), who put forward a universal principle of color classification, most but not all languages have a term for each of the following colors: white, black, red, green, yellow, blue, brown, purple, pink, and gray. Berlin and Kay noted that there are no languages with only one color term. However, they also pointed out that the more cultural and technological changes that a society undergoes, the more detailed the color terminology tends to become. For example, Jale (New Guinea) has two terms (black and white); Tarascan (Mexico) has five (white, black, red, yellow, green); and Javanese has seven (white, black, red, yellow, green, blue, brown). Thus, if a language uses only two terms to identify colors, they are white and black; other colors are added systematically. This finding supports the view of many sociolinguists that color naming in all languages and cultures is a systematic, rule-governed process.

Power and Solidarity

Every language has a system of expressing power and solidarity relations between people. When people speak, they make choices among different linguistic markers to signal their social distance or closeness with their communicants. Social distance may indicate a difference is status, rank, education, or age. While distance often establishes power relations between the speakers, closeness tends to establish solidarity. Address forms are among the most distinct linguistic choices that reflect power or solidarity relations. When someone is addressed by his or her first name, the addresser usually signals solidarity. The use of titles such as "Mr.," "Ms.," and "Dr." demonstrates that the addresser recognizes the addressee as deserving more respect. An important element in the choice of an address form is the level of formality of a given situation. For example, students in many U.S. colleges can often call their professor by his or her first name during class discussion, but most of those same students would likely address the professor with a formal title during an official ceremony.

Languages differ in their familiar versus polite distinctions. Many languages differentiate between "familiar you" (T) and "polite you" (V). In English, for example, a person who wants to get somebody's attention can say, "Excuse me, *you* forgot your book," while many languages with familiar versus polite (T/V) distinction are less flexible. Unlike English, which has no T/V distinction, *Tu/Vous* in French, *Ty/Vy* in Russian, and *Du/Ni* in Swedish make a speaker choose the form that is appropriate for the addressee and the situation. The T form is usually reserved for symmetrical relations and indicates solidarity, while the V form usually signals asymmetry and power. However, the relationship between symmetrical/asymmetrical and power/solidarity cannot be reduced to a simple formula where asymmetry indicates power and symmetry indicates solidarity. Power and solidarity are often expressed by the same form; that is, people who are close can address each other using the V form, including their titles, as an indication of solidarity. For example, two professors who happen to be friends might

address each other using "professor" and the V form during a conference. However, when an employer addresses an employee by first name and the T form while the employee uses "Mr." or "Ms." and the V form in return, it is a signal of power imbalance and asymmetry. Therefore, the reciprocity is one of the most important markers of solidarity.

The choice of an address form and/or T/V form is influenced by sociocultural norms. For example, after the October Revolution in Russia, people addressed each other as "comrade" to indicate solidarity. However, even before the collapse of the former Soviet Union, the address form "comrade" ceased to exist, which was as an indication of changes in society. Thus, different address forms and the T/V form are not a static category; rather, they change in accordance with social changes.

Politeness

While social closeness and distance are factors in people's choices of formal or informal forms of address, politeness is the decisive factor in degree of friendliness and amount of imposition in communication. Social psychologist Erving Goffman (1956, 1967) and linguists Penelope Brown and Stephen Levinson (1987) worked extensively on the phenomena of politeness. Goffman introduced the notion of "face," an image that is produced by a person in social contacts with other people. Goffman differentiated between a "positive face" (i.e., the need to be appreciated) and a "negative face" (i.e., the need to be not disturbed). Brown and Levinson identified positive and negative politeness, where "positive politeness" is a warm friendly behavior toward others and "negative politeness" is the avoidance of imposition. Both negative and positive politeness, thus, can be understood as consideration for another person's face.

Any demand, request, and even advice can be seen as a face-threatening act (FTA), which threatens a person's public image, or face. For example, if a speaker issues a direct command to the listener, "Send this letter immediately," this directive might threaten the listener's face. Politeness repairs the damage that is inflicted by FTAs. Polite people try to avoid FTAs or minimize their effect. For example, they soften commands by making them less direct, "Could you send this letter immediately"; they use compliments and stress solidarity between them and their listeners, "I really appreciate your work." Thus, politeness explains the indirectness of human communication as people's desire to save their communicants' and their own face in interactions; moreover, politeness helps to understand presequencing, or the preparation to a request, question, and so on. For example, some speakers, instead of directly requesting something from a listener, start with a prerequest:

Prerequest by A: Do you have a minute?

"Go ahead" signal by B: Sure.

Request by A: Could you send this itinerary to Green?

Accept by B: Okay.

In the interchange above, the prerequest by A is a face-saving maneuver for both A and B. If B indicates that she or he is busy, it eliminates the request and accept stages, and A does not receive a refusal to the main request, which would have caused A to lose face. Speakers use similar strategies in preannouncing ("You will never guess what happened today") or preinvitations ("Are you busy this weekend?"). Politeness is analyzed in a greater detail in pragmatics, the study of the relationship between language and its users. Pragmatics is concerned with how meaning is communicated by the speaker and is interpreted by the listener.

Language and Gender

While the term "sex" refers to the biological differences of women and men, the term "gender" indicates the psychological and sociocultural significance that is attached to those differences. Since ancient times, scientists from different fields of human research have been interested in determining if men and women think, act, and speak differently or alike. It has been reported that only male and female Carib Indians from the West Indies speak different languages, whereas in other parts of the world, women and men are reported to speak the same languages with some differences, mainly in vocabulary. It should be noted that research on gender and language is not limited to male–female interactions; it also studies gay, lesbian, and other gender communication.

Robin Lakoff (1973) noted that it is more typical of women to use such color words as mauve, beige, and lavender and more emphatic expressions such as adorable, lovely, and divine. Lakoff

also claimed that in word pairs (gentleman–lady, bachelor–spinster, master–mistress), female parts acquire a more negative meaning. Research on language and gender has contributed to uncovering sexism in language. For example, as recently as the early 1970s, it was normal in English to use the pronoun "he" and words such as "chairman," "policeman," and "mankind" in a generic manner or to address women as "Miss" or "Mrs.," but these have all subsequently come to be known as elements of sexist language. Researchers have also found differences in covert and overt prestige in language use between women and men. Gerhard Leitner (1997) has discussed the dynamic role of media in creating awareness of gender-specific language. According to Leitner, the ABC network's pioneering ruling in 1984 on the avoidance of gender-specific (sexist) language was unfavorably met by both the audience and the media, but ABC adhered to its new policy.

The main division of the study of gender can be classified as either culture/difference or power/dominance theories. According to the first approach, the clear-cut division of labor and, consequently, same-sex socializing promoted the development of different communicative strategies and, more broadly, different cultures. To achieve understanding, women and men have to learn and respect the cultures of each other. The second, focuses more on the power imbalance in society. According to this critical feminist approach, the language in a male-dominated society is created by and for men. In general, these researchers view power imbalance as the key impediment that prevents women and men from successful communication both at work and in private relationships.

Ethnography of Communication

Because of their common interest in human communication, the ethnography of communication unites linguistic and anthropological studies. This framework stresses the mutual responsibility of the speaker and the listener for successful communication. Dell Hymes (1974), the founder of this approach, proposed the acronym SPEAKING, where each letter stands for an important component of communication:

S = Setting or Scene

P = Participants

E = Ends

A = Act Sequence

K = Key

I = Instrumentalities

N = Norms of Interaction and Interpretation

G = Genre.

"Setting" refers to the physical circumstances (time and place of the event), while "scene" refers to the subjective definition of the event (psychological or cultural). "Participants" refers to the speaker–sender–addresser and hearer–receiver–audience–addressee. "Ends" refers to the outcome (both conventional and personal). "Act sequence" refers to the form and content of the message (i.e., what is said and how in relationship to the actual topic). "Key" refers to the tone and manner (e.g., serious, light-hearted) of the delivery. "Instrumentalities" refers to the channel (e.g., oral, written, telegraphic, and so on). "Norms of interaction and interpretation" refers to the specific behavior and properties that are attached to speaking (e.g., formal, casual). "Genre" refers to the types of texts (e.g., poems, prayers, lectures, editorials, and so on).

Each component of SPEAKING is important in communication. To be a competent communicant, a person must know when and in what setting it is appropriate to speak and when to be silent, how to issue a request and accept an apology, and how to address a person of the same or different status and age. The ethnography of communication is closely connected with social and cultural norms and rules, which are different in different societies. Thus, to prevent the failure of cross-cultural communication, a person should not limit himself or herself to the rules of his or her society but instead should take into consideration the rules of the society of his or her communicant.

Language and Media

According to Allan Bell (1991), media are dominating presenters of language in society. Advertisers use language to persuade people, and news organizations attempt to influence the attitudes of people. Thus, the media use language as a tool in shaping and reflecting people's values and people's perceptions of themselves and others. In presenting information, the media target the audience, their tastes, and beliefs. Bell argued that

instead of targeting the individual, media cater to a social group—specifically, to a stereotypical social group. This means that the language of presentation reflects linguistic features that are stereotypically associated with a certain social group. For example, a program that targets women would use a "typical" female linguistic variant to establish rapport with its audience. Traditionally, the relationship between media and audience is presented as unidirectional, where media send messages to the target audience. Joshua Fishman (1974, p. 1644) stated that the standard language is the most appropriate variant for the media, government, legal, and educational networks because this variety is "the 'safest' for those communications in which the speaker cannot know his diversified and numerous listeners." However, with the development of new interactive media such as the Internet, the diversity of the target audience cannot be disregarded.

Bell (1991) indicated that research on the linguistic styles of several British newspapers showed that upmarket papers (e.g., *The Times*, *Financial Times*, *Guardian*) operate on distance and negative politeness, while the downmarket papers (e.g., *Daily Mirror*, *Star*, *Sun*) dwell on solidarity and positive politeness. In other words, linguistic choices reflect social stratification of society, as well as its values and beliefs.

Advertisers use a multilingual approach to present the quality of their products. For example, stereotypically, French has been associated with elegance and refinement. Therefore, numerous cosmetics and fashion-goods commercials employ French and/or French-accented messages. Torben Vestergaard and Kim Schroder (1985) found that in many commercials, the advertisers avoid using the word "buy" in the imperative clause to avoid direct imposition; instead, they call on the audience to act with the words "try," "ask," "get," "take," "use," "call," "make," and so on. Advertisers rely on more indirect ways of attracting the attention of prospective buyers because telling the audience what to do is considered to be a face-threatening strategy.

In media, every linguistic element, from the headline and structure of the lead paragraph to the choice of words in indirect speech, is important in creating information that is aimed at the target audience. Thus, research on media language uncovers the techniques of creating the information for the target audience. It provides insights on language, media, and society in general.

Conclusion

From a new subdiscipline within linguistics, sociolinguistics has developed into an elaborated area of interdisciplinary research on the dynamic relationship that exists between language and society. As the study of language in relation to society, sociolinguistics is closely connected with other areas of human research, such as anthropology, sociology, psychology, education, and media studies. Sociolinguistics not only incorporates the insights from these disciplines into its research but also feeds back to these other disciplines, thereby promoting knowledge and awareness of certain linguistic varieties that are spoken by different groups in relation to the value systems and social structures of society.

See also: CULTURE AND COMMUNICATION; CULTURE INDUSTRIES, MEDIA AS; GENDER AND THE MEDIA; GLOBALIZATION OF CULTURE THROUGH THE MEDIA; INTERCULTURAL COMMUNICATION, ADAPTATION AND; INTERPERSONAL COMMUNICATION; LANGUAGE ACQUISITION; LANGUAGE AND COMMUNICATION; LANGUAGE STRUCTURE; SOCIETY AND THE MEDIA.

Bibliography

Bell, Allan. (1991). *The Language of News Media*. Cambridge, MA: Blackwell.

Berlin, Brent, and Kay, Paul. (1969). *Basic Color Terms: Their Universality and Evolution*. Berkeley: University of California Press.

Bonvillain, Nancy. (1993). *Language, Culture, and Communication. The Meaning of Messages*. Upper Saddle River, NJ: Prentice-Hall.

Brown, Penelope, and Levinson, Stephen. (1987). *Politeness: Some Universals in Language Usage*. Cambridge, Eng.: Cambridge University Press.

Ferguson, Charles A. (1994). "Dialect, Register, and Genre: Working Assumptions about Conventionalization." In *Sociolinguistic Perspectives on Register*, eds. Douglas Biber and Edward Finegan. Oxford, Eng.: Oxford University Press.

Fishman, Joshua. (1970). *Sociolinguistics: A Brief Introduction*. Rowley, MA: Newbury House.

Fishman, Joshua. (1974). "The Sociology of Language: An Interdisciplinary Social Science Approach to Language in Society." In *Current Trends in Linguistics*, Vol. 12, ed. Thomas Sebeok. The Hague: Mouton.

Goffman, Erving. (1956). *The Presentation of Self in Every Day Life*. Edinburgh: University of Edinburgh Press.

Goffman, Erving. (1967). "On Face-Work: An Analysis of Ritual Elements in Social Interaction." In *Interaction Ritual. Essays in Face-to-Face Behavior*, ed. Erving Goffman. Chicago: Aldine.

Hudson, Richard A. (1998). *Sociolinguistics*. Cambridge, Eng.: Cambridge University Press.

Hymes, Dell. (1974). *Foundations in Sociolinguistics: An Ethnographic Approach*. Philadelphia: University of Pennsylvania Press.

Labov, William. (1966). *The Social Stratification of English in New York City*. Washington, DC: Center for Applied Linguistics.

Labov, William. (1972). *Sociolinguistic Patterns*. Philadelphia: University of Pennsylvania Press.

Lakoff, Robin. (1973). *Language and Woman's Place*. New York: Harper & Row.

Leitner, Gerhard. (1997). "The Sociolinguistics of Communication Media." In *The Handbook of Sociolinguistics*, ed. Florian Coulmas. Cambridge, MA: Blackwell.

Levinson, Stephen. (1997). *Pragmatics*. New York: Cambridge University Press.

Malmkjaer, Kristin, and Anderson, James M., eds. (1996). *The Linguistics Encyclopedia*. New York: Routledge.

Romaine, Suzanne. (1988). *Pidgin and Creole Languages*. London: Longman.

Sapir, Edward. (1949a). "The Status of Linguistics as a Science." In *Selected Writings of Edward Sapir*, ed. David G. Mandelbaum. Berkeley: University of California Press.

Sapir, Edward. (1949b). "Language and Environment." In *Selected Writings of Edward Sapir*, ed. David G. Mandelbaum. Berkeley: University of California Press.

Scollon, Ron, and Scollon, Suzanne Wong. (1996). *Intercultural Communication: A Discourse Approach*. Cambridge, MA: Blackwell.

Trudgill, Peter. (1983). *Sociolinguistics: An Introduction to Language and Society*. Harmondsworth, Eng.: Penguin.

Vestergaard, Torben, and Schroder, Kim. (1985). *The Language of Advertising*. Oxford, Eng.: Basil Blackwell.

Wardhaugh, Ronald. (1998). *An Introduction to Sociolinguistics*. Oxford, Eng.: Blackwell Publishers.

Whorf, Benjamin. (1956). "The Relation of Habitual Thought and Behavior to Language." In *Language, Thought, and Reality*, ed. John B. Carrol. Cambridge, MA: MIT Press.

ALLA V. YELYSEIEVA

SOFTWARE

See: Computer Software; Computer Software, Educational; Computing

SPORTS AND MEDIA EFFECTS

Since the dawn of civilization, people have enjoyed viewing sports. From the time that there was gladiatorial combat in Rome and frenetic ball games in the land of the Aztecs, there have been avid sport spectators (for an excellent review of the history of sport spectators, see Guttman, 1986). A sport spectator is defined herein as someone who regularly watches, listens to, or reads about sporting events. Spectators can be further subdivided into two classifications: direct sport consumers and indirect sport consumers (Wann, 1997). Direct sport consumers are individuals who are actually in attendance at the sporting event. Indirect sport consumers are individuals who view the event on television, listen to it on the radio, or read about it in the newspaper or on the Internet. This entry focuses primarily on the reasons why indirect sport consumership is so ubiquitous and discusses the effects that sport fanship has on people.

The prevalence of sport spectatorship in Western society is undeniable. Consider that in 1986, American viewers reported a preference for watching televised sports over watching newscasts, documentaries, sitcoms, and every other category of televised entertainment except movies (Guttmann, 1986). Major events such as the Super Bowl regularly top 100 million viewers, while the World Cup is reported to have drawn more than 2 billion viewers internationally. There are more than half a dozen cable channels in the United States devoted exclusively to sports programming, and numerous other sports-related subscription packages are available from cable providers, so the sport spectator has greater access to sporting events than ever before. But what is it that draws so many people to watch sports?

To begin to answer this question, it is important to note the unique features involved in watching sporting events compared to watching other forms of entertainment. Lawrence Wenner and Walter Gantz (1989, p. 242) outline these fundamental differences:

Most nonsport entertainment programs are prerecorded, scripted stories with actors playing roles. Plot outcomes are rarely in doubt, protagonists tend to survive, and actors "bloodied" in action show no scars off the set. Most televised sport is live and unrehearsed, and "bloodied" athletes carry scars off the field. Athletes' careers hinge on their performances, and outcomes are uncertain.

Thus, it appears that the inherent uncertainty of sporting events is firmly linked to the enjoyment of viewing them. Indeed, Dolf Zillmann, Jennings Bryant, and Barry Sapolsky (1989) point out that the uncommon, unexpected, and surprising events "hold greater promise for being appreciated" due to their novelty. The unthinkable upset can happen (e.g., the victory of the U.S. Hockey Team over the heavily favored Soviet National Team in the 1980 Winter Olympics) and thus an individual has the chance to see something never seen before (e.g., fantastic finishes, amazingly acrobatic defensive plays, dominating performances).

Motives of Indirect Sport Spectators

Several motives of both direct and indirect sport spectators have been theorized or identified by researchers. These motives include, but are not limited to, catharsis, stimulation seeking, social needs, escapism, entertainment needs, aesthetics, and self-esteem management. Although each of these motives will be discussed in turn, it is important to point out that these different motives are in no way mutually exclusive; it is likely that for many individuals, sport spectating serves a number of different motives. A consideration of the range of different motivations provides a fuller picture of the widespread appeal of sport spectatorship in Western society.

Catharsis

The first of the motives, catharsis, is a theory invoked by Sigmund Freud in 1920 and which later gained popularity through the work of Konrad Lorenz (1966). The theory of catharsis is based on Freud's belief that aggressiveness and hostility are unavoidably inherited traits or predispositions, rather than characteristics gained through learning or experience. Freud (1955) believed that an inherent need to act aggressively was evolutionarily adaptive and served people well until laws and societies were formed wherein aggressive behavior was frowned upon. In such a society, other outlets would be necessary to vent the natural predisposition toward aggressiveness. Hence, the theory of catharsis, wherein individuals seek to view aggressive acts as a vicarious way of satisfying their need to act aggressively (Bryant and Zillmann, 1983). This theory has been used to explain the popularity of many of the kinds of violent sports. It is proposed that by watching others engage in brutal and violent actions, one can vicariously release pent-up aggressive impulses and feelings.

This "hydraulic" model of aggression has been widely accepted in contemporary society, and many people subscribe to the view that participating in or watching violent sports or movies is an effective way to reduce aggressive inclinations. Although it makes intuitive sense that an individual might achieve some sort of "release" through watching violent or highly competitive sports, this theory has not been substantiated by research. In fact, the findings of almost all related studies show that the aggressiveness and hostility levels of spectators actually increase as they watch a competitive or aggressive sporting event (Goldstein and Arms, 1971). The work of social psychologist Leonard Berkowitz (1969) and others have shown that exposure to violence and aggression "primes" people to think, feel, and act more aggressively. Social-learning theorists such as Albert Bandura (1971) have demonstrated that people exposed to others who are rewarded for acting violently are more likely to display violent behavior in their own behavior. Both of these findings have been used to explain the increase in fan violence often observed during and after the viewing of sporting events. Thus, there seems to be little evidence for the cathartic effect of sports; instead, watching violent sports seems to fuel aggressiveness in spectators.

Stimulation Seeking

The second motive, stimulation seeking, is almost the exact reverse of catharsis theory. Researchers Jennings Bryant and Dolf Zillmann propose that individuals, whether consciously or not, seek out stimulation to achieve an increased level of arousal or excitation (Guttmann, 1998; Bryant and Zillmann, 1983). This view stems from the perspective that humans, similar to other organisms, seek stimulation and novelty in their environment. Participating in or watching sports is one avenue toward alleviating boredom and achieving an optimal level of arousal. This line of research has shown that subjects tend to rate more

violent and aggressive plays in football and other sports as more fun to watch. Anecdotally, it is known that many individuals enjoy the fights in hockey games or the crashes at auto races, presumably because these events add to the excitement of the contest. In their fittingly titled 1970 essay "The Quest for Excitement in Unexciting Societies," Norbert Elias and Eric Dunning propose a direct relationship between decreasing opportunities for overt excitement and thrill in society, and an increase in the prevalence of violent sports (Guttmann, 1998). Thus, there seems to be converging evidence that people find the vicarious experience of violence and aggression to be stimulating and enjoyable.

It should be borne in mind that catharsis and stimulation-seeking motives can serve as explanations only for the spectating of violent sports. Wenner and Gantz (1989) found that stimulation-seeking motives applied most strongly to spectators of fast-paced and contact sports. Because not all sports are violent, it is clear that other motives must underlie the attraction for spectating nonviolent as well as violent sports.

Social Needs

The third motive for sport spectating, social needs, applies to nonviolent and violent sports alike. This motive is based on a proposed desire of spectators to spend time with their family or others that they socialize with, such as friends or coworkers. The work of Wenner and Gantz (1989) has shown that spectators will often cite social involvement and companionship as motives for their spectating of sports on television. Zillmann, Bryant, and Sapolsky (1989) discuss the possibility that indirect spectatorship of sports with others should create bonds between people who affiliate themselves with the same teams. Spectators who root for teams together share the joys of victory with each other, as well as the humiliation or anguish of defeat. Though intuition suggests that the sharing of such experiences surely creates a lasting bond between people, these researchers are quick to point out that the actual social effects of spectatorship have received little empirical examination.

Roy Baumeister and Mark Leary (1995) have discussed the "need to belong" as a fundamental human motivation. This belongingness need is satisfied when individuals feel strong, stable social attachments to others. These social attachments

Participation in group viewing of a sports event can fulfill some of the social needs of the individuals, especially when they are cheering for a local hero, which is what these people in Austin, Texas, were doing when they watched Lance Armstrong win his second consecutive Tour de France on July 23, 2000. (Reuters NewMedia Inc./Corbis)

may be derived through connections with family or friends, but they can also be satisfied by the groups to which individuals belong. Bonds formed by individuals sharing a common allegiance (to a hometown team, for example), like the bonds between members of a church or other social group, serve the important purpose of satisfying the belongingness need and helping an individual to feel a part of a community. Indeed, in many communities and social circles, following the local sports team is part of the cultural norm; those who do not follow the team are considered social outcasts. Moreover, in the company of fellow spectators, an individual is able to feel accepted and can share his or her feelings, thoughts, and emotions freely. Thus, fundamental affiliative and emotional needs can be satisfied through watching and following sports with fellow spectators.

However, given that there are many other ways that people can satisfy basic belongingness needs, there is still a question as to why so many choose

sports. In Western society, sport has some unique features that make it a particularly desirable and attractive avenue to achieve a sense of belonging. Sports are an extremely popular conversational topic, and many people often spend hours talking about past, present, or future sporting events with friends and acquaintances. Sports events can also be conversational topics that help establish social contacts with others; people can promote good relations with colleagues and coworkers by discussing last-night's game and can initiate conversations with strangers on buses and planes by "talking sports" with them. Zillmann, Bryant, and Sapolsky (1989) theorize that this popularity is due in no small part to the low risk of sports topics in conversation. They postulate that, while most opinions on music, movies, and politics are extremely open to argument, great performances in sports are rarely refutable. One person may think a movie actor is fantastic while another considers him terrible, but few people would disagree with the opinion that Michael Jordan was a great basketball player, that Mark McGwire is a great power hitter, or that the U.S. Women's National Soccer Team had a great season in winning the 1999 World Cup. Thus, watching and following sports may be one of the easiest and most societally acceptable ways to create social bonds with others and satisfy basic social needs.

Escapism

The fourth motive, escapism, applies quite broadly to many varieties of entertainment. People will often go to a movie or watch a television drama to escape momentarily their everyday humdrum. Sport spectating, however, seems to be an extraordinarily effective escape as evidenced by the following examples. During World War II, President Franklin D. Roosevelt made a decision to let the professional baseball seasons continue. In spite of the burden on the teams, players, and families, he hoped that it would provide Americans with an escape from their trying times (Wann, 1997). This, combined with the creation of the All-American Girls Professional Baseball League in 1943 (immortalized in the 1988 film *A League of Their Own*), at a time when a large number of male ballplayers were drafted for military service, points to the particular salience of sport spectatorship as an effective route for escape from worries.

Entertainment

The fifth motive, entertainment, is relatively self-explanatory. Spectators seek to be entertained by watching or listening to sporting events. According to sport psychologist Daniel Wann (1997), this motive may play heavily into the spectating of pseudosports. Pseudosports are athletic contests that are scripted and staged; for example, roller derby or professional wrestling. Sport researcher George P. Stone found in 1971 that although there is no surprise in the rigged outcome of these events—which is one of the factors that differentiates sports from other entertainment—spectators were still attracted to them for their sheer entertainment value.

The seemingly paradoxical enjoyment of even these highly predictable sporting events may be due in part to the two basic tenets of disposition theory in sport fanship. These are laid out simply by Zillmann, Bryant, and Sapolsky (1989) as follows: (1) positive feelings for a party (i.e., a team or player) will increase the enjoyment of witnessing the victory of that party and (2) negative feelings toward a party will increase the enjoyment of witnessing the defeat of that party. These simple propositions are easy to apply to a sport where the victory of the proverbial "good guy" over the "bad guy" is doubtlessly written into the script. However, such a view would also predict that the entertainment value should be magnified when the outcome is uncertain, making victory sweeter and defeat more devastating. Indeed, Zillmann, Bryant, and Sapolsky (1989) reported that factors that accentuate the human drama of sports (e.g., announcers that present the players as embittered rivals or the fierce competitive spirit of the participants in a contest) enhance the enjoyment of the sporting event.

Aesthetics

The sixth motive for sport spectatorship, and one closely related to entertainment, is aesthetics. By the motive of aesthetics, it is meant that spectators are drawn to certain types of sports for the qualities of beauty, grace, and skill inherent in them. Sports such as figure skating, synchronized swimming, or gymnastics lend themselves for obvious reasons to aesthetic appreciation. American football, baseball, and hockey might not seem such likely candidates for this motive, but one need only talk with a devotee of hockey or pay notice to the title of Robert Mayer's 1984 book *The Grace of Shortstops* to realize that this is not necessarily the case. People marvel at the athletic ability of these skilled individuals who make difficult, unbelievable plays. In fact, the cable sports network ESPN has begun to give out awards known as ESPYs to plays that are recognized as the most outstanding ones of the year.

Although relatively little research has been devoted to investigating the particular role of aesthetics in sport spectatorship, there is some evidence that people appreciate and enjoy more complicated and difficult plays. However, it is often hard to separate the effects of the riskiness of a play from the success of the play. Risky or difficult plays that are successful lead to greater enjoyment ("great call"), but unsuccessful risky plays often result in the greatest disappointment. Nonetheless, there is sufficient evidence to this point that spectators derive enjoyment from an aesthetic appreciation of the skill and agility, as well as the competitiveness and intensity, of the players.

Self-Esteem Management

The last motive that will be discussed in this entry, self-esteem management, is one of the more thoroughly researched and complex motives of sport spectators. Several researchers have found that sport spectators derive self-esteem enhancement from identifying with a successful team. Robert Cialdini and his colleagues (1976) denoted a phenomenon known as "basking-in-reflected-glory" (or BIRGing), which refers to the tendency for individuals to proclaim their association with a successful other. For example, Cialdini and his colleagues found that fans of a university's college football team were more likely to wear school-identifying apparel on the Mondays following team victories than on Mondays following team defeats. Moreover, in describing the outcome of team games, university students used the pronoun "we" to describe team victories (e.g., "We won that game, 20–17") but used the pronoun "they" to describe team losses (e.g., "They lost, 38–14"). This research demonstrated that sports fans are more likely to illustrate their connection with a team when that team is successful. Conversely, sports fans tend to distance themselves from a team when that team is unsuccessful, a phenomenon that has been labeled "cutting-off-reflected-failure" (or CORFing). Cialdini and his colleagues argued that by BIRGing, an individual can derive positive esteem from their association with a successful other. Indeed, people often state their association (e.g., from the same hometown, attended the same school) with a famous celebrity or personality. Similarly, identifying with a successful sports team can be a way to derive self-esteem from the success of the team. Team success becomes a personal success, and one can take pride in the accomplishment of one's team.

But do people really feel greater self-esteem when a team is successful? Cialdini and Kenneth Richardson (1980) found that people whose self-esteem had previously been threatened (by failure on a social-skills task) were more likely to bask in the success of their school's teams (as well as its other assets). Moreover, these same individuals experiencing a self-esteem threat were most likely to blast their school's rival. Thus, it appears that self-esteem needs are indeed involved in the BIRGing phenomenon. Furthermore, Edward Hirt and his colleagues (1992) directly measured the self-esteem of fans after team victories and defeats and found that fans showed some elevation in mood and self-esteem after team wins, but reported lower mood and self-esteem following team losses. Indeed, in one study (Hirt et al., 1992; study 2), the reactions of fans to team success and failure were compared to a personal success and failure (i.e., doing well or poorly on a test of general intellectual ability). The results indicated that the mood and self-esteem of fans were as high after team success as after personal success, and as low after team failure as after personal failure.

These data strongly suggest that fans ally themselves so closely to their team that they view team success as a personal success and team failure as a personal failure. Moreover, the outcome of a team had profound effects on the predictions by fans of their own future performance. Hirt and his colleagues (1992) had fans predict how well they would do at a series of tasks following the game. It was found that after wins, fans were much more optimistic about their performance at these different tasks than they were after losses. After wins, fans viewed themselves as winners and predicted that they would be more successful in their future endeavors; after losses, they viewed themselves as losers and were much more pessimistic about the future. The most interesting implication of these findings is that, at least for highly allegiant fans, following their team is a precarious proposition. Fans can derive greater self-esteem when their team is successful but suffer self-esteem decrements when their team is unsuccessful.

It is important to note that not all sport spectators are highly allegiant fans. Many spectators may have little or no allegiance to the teams playing or may be best characterized as "fair weather fans" who jump on the bandwagon of teams who are successful and can bask in their reflected glory (BIRG). When these teams are no longer successful, these spectators lose interest in the team and can cut off reflected failure (CORF). However, for fans who strongly identify with a team, they maintain their allegiance to the team through thick and thin. They suffer through the poor seasons and hard times, but relish the successful seasons and good times. The sense of loyalty that these individuals feel to their team becomes a critical part of their identity and they steadfastly maintain their allegiance to the team (case in point, the long-suffering Chicago Cubs fans).

An intriguing aspect of the BIRGing phenomenon is that the spectators feel justified in taking some credit for the success of the team. While many people acknowledge the "home-field advantage" in sports and view this advantage as at least partially due to the support and cheering of the fans in the audience during home games, it is more difficult to imagine how spectators watching the game on television can believe that they had a causal effect on the game. However irrational this belief may appear to be, psychological research has shown that individuals merely associated with positive or desirable events are liked, whereas individuals associated with negative or undesirable events are disliked (cf. Zajonc, 1980). Thus, associating with a winner or a team of winners will elevate the esteem of an individual in the eyes of others and is an avenue for improving an individual's self-evaluation.

Research has attempted to understand other bases for the desire of fans to affiliate themselves with sports teams. Mark Dechesne, Jeff Greenberg, and their colleagues (2000) argued that one source may be a fear of death. In their research, they compared the reactions of people who are first asked to consider their own death (a mortality salient condition) to a control condition wherein people are not asked to ponder their own mortality. They found that fans who were reminded of their own death showed stronger affiliation and identification with their team, suggesting that allegiance to a successful team may help individuals cope with and transcend mortality concerns. These conclusions also fit in nicely with the notion that identifying with sports teams serves social needs for belongingness: individuals who feel connected to and identify with a successful other or group may feel better about themselves and the meaningfulness of their existence.

Dispositional Approaches

As has been discussed, there are a variety of different theories about what motivates people to be sport spectators. It is likely that, for many individuals, multiple goals and motives are being satisfied while watching sports. Sport spectating may serve as a source of highly stimulating and captivating entertainment, while simultaneously satisfying social and self-esteem needs. Indeed, the pervasiveness of sport spectatorship in Western society almost requires that this is so, since its appeal extends to so many different types of people.

This is not to say that there are not individual differences in the kinds of people who are the most avid sport spectators. A good deal of research has attempted to identify a personality profile of the sports fan. The word "fan," short for "fanatic," implies an individual with an undying devotion to their team. Indeed, the behavior of these highly devoted fans (whose rituals before and during games are legendary) is often bewildering to those individuals who are not fans. A dispositional approach to sport fanship has yielded some interesting findings, but its greatest contribution appears to be demonstrating how individual differences moderate the strength of the various motives underlying sport spectatorship. For example, individuals differ in their degree of sensation seeking (Zuckerman, 1979). High-sensation seekers crave excitement and are easily bored; these individuals tend to prefer high-risk sports and activities. Low-sensation seekers, on the other hand, tend to prefer the safety and predictability of routine. Thus, the extent to which stimulation motives underlie sport fanship should be greater for high-sensation-seeking individuals. Similarly, individuals with low self-esteem have been shown to be likely to engage in indirect forms of self-enhancement, such as basking in reflected glory (Brown, Collins, and Schmidt, 1988). Individuals with high self-esteem prefer to derive their esteem from their own accomplishments as opposed to the accomplishments of others with whom they are associated. As a result, the self-esteem management function of sport fanship is likely to play a greater role for individuals with low self-esteem. These results underscore the value in considering that certain types of individuals may be more prone to be attracted to sports and to become sport spectators precisely because salient motives in their lives can be satisfied through sport fanship.

Conclusions and Future Directions

It is clear at the beginning of the twentieth century that sport spectatorship is growing to unprecedented proportions. Further research is needed in order to understand the bases for this phenomenon. Although the theories and research reviewed in this entry have provided some insights to the reasons and motives that may be associated with sport spectatorship, the work has been generally descriptive in nature and has not fully elaborated the factors underlying these motives or the ways in which watching sports satisfies these fundamental needs and motives. One potential fruitful avenue for future research is an examination of the biological bases for these motives. Indeed, some of the work on individual differences has focused on the biological differences between individuals who are high or low in sensation seeking. People who have a high level of sensation seeking have a lower baseline level of arousal than people who have a low level of sensation seeking—which may account for their greater need to seek arousing stimuli in their environment. Work by Paul Bernhardt, James Dabbs, and their colleagues (1998) has found changes in the testosterone levels of fans in response to the winning and losing of their sports teams, changes that seem to parallel the psychological changes to winning and losing that were documented earlier in this entry. Increases in testosterone levels were associated with watching winning performances, implying that physiological changes may underscore psychological phenomena such as basking in reflected glory. Furthermore, changes in testosterone levels have been shown to be associated with expressions of dominance and aggressive behavior, which may provide some links to understanding achievement-seeking motives in sport spectating as well as the increases in violent behavior often associated with sport spectating. When combined with the solid foundation in research and theory outlined in this article, results such as these provide some exciting future directions for the study and understanding of sport spectatorship and all its many facets.

See also: AROUSAL PROCESSES AND MEDIA EFFECTS; CATHARSIS THEORY AND MEDIA EFFECTS; SOCIAL COGNITIVE THEORY AND MEDIA EFFECTS.

Bibliography

Bandura, Albert. (1971). *Social Learning Theory.* Morristown, NJ: General Learning Press.

Baumeister, Roy, and Leary, Mark. (1995). "The Need to Belong: Desire for Interpersonal Attachments as Fundamental Human Motivation." *Psychological Bulletin* 117:497–529.

Berkowitz, Leonard. (1969). "The Frustration-Aggression Hypothesis." In *Roots of Aggression,* ed. Leonard Berkowitz. New York: Atherton.

Bernhardt, Paul C.; Dabbs, James M., Jr.; Fielden, Julie A.; and Lutter, Candice. (1998). "Changes in Testosterone Levels During Vicarious Experiences of Winning and Losing Among Fans at Sporting Events." *Physiology and Behavior* 65:59–62.

Brown, Jonathon; Collins, Rebecca; and Schmidt, Greg. (1988). "Self-Esteem and Direct and Indirect Forms of Self-Enhancement." *Journal of Personality and Social Psychology* 55:445–453.

Bryant, Jennings, and Zillmann, Dolf. (1983). "Sports Violence and the Media." In *Sports Violence,* ed. Jeffrey Goldstein. New York: Springer-Verlag.

Cialdini, Robert; Borden, Richard; Thorne, Avril; Walker, Marcus; Freeman, Stephen; and Sloan, Lloyd. (1976). "Basking in Reflected Glory: Three (Football) Field Studies." *Journal of Personality and Social Psychology* 34:366–375.

Cialdini, Robert, and Richardson, Kenneth. (1980). "Two Indirect Tactics of Image Management: Basking and Blasting." *Journal of Personality and Social Psychology* 39:406–415.

Dechesne, Mark; Greenberg, Jeff; Arndt, Jamie; and Schimel, Jeff. (2000). "Terror Management and the Vicissitudes of Sports Fan Affiliation: The Effects of Mortality Salience on Optimism and Fan Identification." *European Journal of Social Psychology* 30:813–835

Edwards, John, and Archambault, Denise. (1989). "The Home-Field Advantage." In *Sports, Games, and Play: Social and Psychological Viewpoints,* 2nd edition, ed. Jeffrey Goldstein. Hillsdale, NJ: Lawrence Erlbaum.

Freud, Sigmund. (1955). "Beyond the Pleasure Principle and Civilization and Its Discontents." In *The Standard Edition of the Complete Works of Sigmund Freud,* Vols. 18 and 21, ed. James Strachey. London: Hogarth.

Goldstein, Jeffrey, and Arms, Robert. (1971). "Effects of Observing Athletic Contests on Hostility." *Sociometry* 34:83–90.

Guttmann, Allen. (1986). *Sport Spectators.* New York: Columbia University Press.

Guttmann, Allen. (1998). "The Appeal of Violent Sports." In *Why We Watch: The Attractions of Violent Entertainment,* ed. Jeffrey Goldstein. New York: Oxford University Press.

Hirt, Edward; Zillmann, Dolf; Erickson, Grant; and Kennedy, Chris. (1992). "Costs and Benefits of Allegiance: Changes in Fans' Self-Ascribed Competencies After Team Victory Versus Defeat." *Journal of Personality and Social Psychology* 63:724–738.

Lorenz, Konrad. (1966). *On Aggression.* New York: Harcourt, Brace, & World.

Sloan, Lloyd. (1989). "The Motives of Sports Fans." In *Sports, Games, and Play: Social and Psychological Viewpoints,* 2nd edition, ed. Jeffrey Goldstein. Hillsdale, NJ: Lawrence Erlbaum.

Stone, George P. (1971). "Wrestling: The Great American Passion Play." In *Sport: Readings from a Sociological Perspective,* ed. Eric Dunning. Toronto: University of Toronto Press.

Wann, Daniel. (1997). *Sport Psychology.* Upper Saddle River, NJ: Prentice-Hall.

Wenner, Lawrence, and Gantz, Walter. (1989). "The Audience Experience with Sports on Television." In *Media, Sports, & Society,* ed. Lawrence Wenner. Newbury Park, CA: Sage Publications.

Zajonc, Robert. (1980). "Feeling and Thinking: Preferences Need No Inferences." *American Psychologist* 35:151–175.

Zillmann, Dolf; Bryant, Jennings; and Sapolsky, Barry. (1989). "Enjoyment from Sports Spectatorship." In *Sports, Games, and Play: Social and Psychological Viewpoints,* 2nd edition, ed. Jeffrey Goldstein. Hillsdale, NJ: Lawrence Erlbaum.

Zuckerman, Marvin. (1979). *Sensation Seeking: Beyond the Optimal Level of Arousal.* Hillsdale. NJ: Lawrence Erlbaum.

EDWARD R. HIRT
NATHAN L. STEELE

STANDARDS AND INFORMATION

It is a tribute to the power and effectiveness of information processing standards that people benefit from so many of them without noticing. Standards allow computers and computer programs to share information, even when the hardware or software has been designed by different individuals or companies. When a new expansion card or peripheral works in a computer without any problems, it is because the device has been designed to conform to standards. When software is able to read a data file sent to a user by a friend, it is because the data is written and read according to a standard format. Information processing is only one of many areas of daily life in which standards are important. For example, automobile parts and the voltage of household electrical current are standardized, and money is a standard medium of exchange.

When a person refers to an information or data processing "standard," he or she may mean any of the following:

1. A method, protocol, or system for accomplishing a particular task, such as encoding information in a file or sharing it over a network.

2. Hardware or software that employs or executes that method or protocol (e.g., a word-processing program).

3. A document that specifies the method or protocol in very detailed, precise technical language.

4. An agreement that such a document represents among organizations or individuals.

For the purposes of this entry, an adequate definition of "information processing standards" is that they are precisely documented agreements about methods or protocols for information processing that are realized in the operation of computer hardware and software.

Standards as Solutions

The impetus for the creation of any standard is to address a particular problem. As indicated by Martin Libicki (1995), the goal of standardization is almost always to make a process more efficient or reliable, or to define a single consistent interface that allows unlike systems or applications to interoperate.

Consider the problem of representing the content of documents in computer files. The most basic problem is how to represent individual text characters as sequences of binary digits (ones and zeros). Solutions to this problem in the 1960s eventually culminated in one of the most successful and widely used data interchange standards: ASCII (the American National Standard Code for Information Interchange). For many computer users, the term "ASCII" is synonymous with "plain text," but all computer files consist of binary data, and an ASCII file is simply a binary file with contents that are meaningful when interpreted according to the ASCII standard. An application that represents text using the ASCII code can exchange information with other programs that read and write ASCII files.

ASCII is very limited as a solution to the problem of representing document content. The code consists of only 128 characters, each represented by a sequence of seven bits. That is not even enough for every European alphabet, let alone the many alphabets and other forms of writing in the world. A number of extended, ASCII-based character sets have been proposed for the representation of non-Roman alphabets such as the Arabic and Hebrew alphabets. Some have become standards, like the eight-bit ISO 8859 family of character sets (approved by the International Organization for Standardization). The Unicode standard (created by the Unicode Consortium) uses a sixteen-bit encoding system and aims to include every major script in the world and every technical symbol in common use.

Another limitation of ASCII and other plain-text formats is that documents contain forms of information other than alphanumeric characters, punctuation, and blank space. The software industry has produced many technologies for the representation of images, multimedia data, specifications for presentation and formatting, and hypertext links. Some of these technologies have also become standards.

Standards as Documents

Standards documents are notoriously difficult to read. This reputation is deserved, but largely due to factors that are unavoidable. Almost all standards emerge from the work and consensus of many people, and they therefore represent solutions that are general enough to address a variety of problems. For example, the Standard Generalized Markup Language, or SGML (ISO 8879), is a successful and influential standard that enables the structure of a document to be encoded separately from its presentation. Invented by Charles Goldfarb in the 1970s, SGML would be much easier for novices to understand if it defined a single character set (such as ASCII or Unicode) for all conforming documents. But SGML is flexible enough to accept any number of different character sets, and for that reason, SGML syntax must be described at more than one level of abstraction. This is only one example of how the generality and flexibility of standards makes them difficult documents to read. On the other hand, adopting a general solution to a problem often forces one to think more broadly and deeply about an application. That can help avoid additional work and expense in the long run.

There are other reasons why standards documents can be problematic for newcomers. As the adoption of a standard becomes more widespread and formalized, the same solution (or nearly the same) may be published by different organizations under different names. For example, the original ASCII standard was published in 1968 by the American National Standards Institute as ANSI X3.4. When ASCII was adopted as an international standard, the same encoding was published by the International Organization for Standardization as ISO 646. Each of the eight-bit character sets in the ISO 8859 family subsumes ASCII and is in turn subsumed within Unicode. Finally, Unicode is nearly identical with the ISO 10646 standard.

Standards as Agreements

There are various criteria for what counts as a standard, and the same person may use different criteria depending on the context in which they are writing or speaking. When a person refers to a particular technology as "standard," the term is usually used in one of three senses:

1. A *de facto* standard is a solution that has become widely adopted and is considered standard by virtue of its popularity.

2. A *de jure* standard has been reviewed and formally approved by a standards developing organization such as the International Organization for Standardization or one of its member organizations (e.g., the American National Standards Institute in the United States).

3. There are public specifications that are similar to *de jure* standards but are authorized by industry consortia. These consortia operate according to somewhat different rules than standards developing organizations.

Each of the three kinds of standards can be understood in how they vary along four key dimensions: acceptance, openness, stability, and consensus.

Acceptance is the key to the success of any standard, and some technologies are deemed standards solely by virtue of their wide acceptance and popularity. Native file formats for popular word-processing software are examples of these *de facto* standards. If a person receives such a file on diskette or as an attachment to an e-mail message, the ability to read the file requires that the recipient have access to the word processor that reads and writes that format. Problems of compatibility and interoperability are avoided if most people adopt exactly the same solution (i.e., use the same software).

A *de facto* information processing standard need not be a commercial product, nor must its popularity extend to the general community of computer users. For example, the file format for the (nonproprietary) TeX typesetting system, designed by Donald Knuth in the late 1970s, has been widely adopted for mathematics and engineering documents, but it is not popular for office documents.

The hallmark of any *de jure* standard or public specification is its openness. Formal information processing standards are designed and documented with the aim of making every detail public. They are written with the expectation that engineers will develop hardware and software to implement the solutions that the standard represents. For that reason they are documented in exhaustive detail.

Specifications for *de facto* information standards vary in their degrees of openness. An organization controlling a *de facto* standard may publish a reference manual in paper and/or electronic form. For example, Adobe Systems Incorporated publishes both digital and paper references for their PostScript and Portable Document Format technologies. Knuth's published documentation for the TeX typesetting system includes both a reference and the complete annotated source code for TeX itself. In contrast, the publishers of popular office and productivity software (such as word processors) keep their source code secret in the interests of protecting their copyright. The native file formats and communications protocols used by such programs may be proprietary, and their full specifications unpublished.

Potential adopters of a standard may perceive a tug-of-war between the stability of strict adherence and the freedom to innovate. If a developer limits his or her application to those functions covered by a standard, then users of the technology enjoy stability in its interoperability with other systems. However, standards are slow to change and may not accommodate new functions and capabilities that could improve a system. For that reason, developers may introduce nonstandard extensions to a method, protocol, or format. Such extensions come at the cost of stability, since deploying them involves making changes to the format or protocol.

Finally, standards differ in the type of consensus they represent. *De facto* information standards represent a consensus among users that an existing application or protocol is worth adopting because it meets particular needs, is judged better than competing technologies, or simply because so many other people have already adopted it. However, *de jure* standards are designed from the beginning to address as wide a range of needs as possible. Standards developing organizations such as the International Organization for Standardization and its member organizations represent many different stakeholders and interested parties in coordinating the development of a standard. Industry consortia need not be as inclusive, but they often are inclusive in practice. For example, the Unicode Consortium includes churches, libraries, and individual specialists among its members, in addition to corporations. Closer cooperation between consortia and standards developing organizations (as exists between the International Organization for Standardization and the Unicode Consortium) bodes well for the future role of standards in improving information management and information processing.

See also: ALPHABETS AND WRITING; COMPUTER SOFTWARE; COMPUTING; DIGITAL COMMUNICATION.

Bibliography

Adobe Systems Incorporated. (1993). *Portable Document Format Reference Manual*. Reading, MA: Addison-Wesley.

Adobe Systems Incorporated. (1999). *PostScript Language Reference*. Reading, MA: Addison-Wesley.

American National Standards Institute. (1986). *Information Systems—Coded Character Sets—7-Bit American National Standard Code for Information Interchange (ANSI X3.4-1986)*. New York: American National Standards Institute.

Cargill, Carl F. (1997). *Open Systems Standardization: A Business Approach*. Upper Saddle River, NJ: Prentice-Hall.

Goldfarb, Charles F. (1990). *The SGML Handbook*. Oxford, Eng.: Oxford University Press.

International Organization for Standardization. (1993). *Information Technology—Universal Multiple-Octet Coded Character Set (UCS)—Part 1: Architecture and Basic Multilingual Plane (ISO/IEC 10646-1:1993)*. Geneva, Switzerland: International Organization for Standardization.

International Organization for Standardization. (1998). *Information Technology—8-Bit Single-Byte Coded Graphic Character Sets—Part 1: Latin Alphabet No. 1 (ISO/IEC 8859-1:1998)*. Geneva, Switzerland: International Organization for Standardization.

Knuth, Donald E. (1986). *TeX: The Program*. Reading, MA: Addison-Wesley.

Knuth, Donald E. (1990). *The TeXbook*. Reading, MA: Addison-Wesley.

Libicki, Martin. (1995). *Standards: The Rough Road to the Common Byte*. Washington, DC: Center for Advanced Concepts and Technology, Institute for National Strategic Studies, National Defense University.

Unicode Consortium. (2000). *The Unicode Standard, Version 3.0*. Reading, MA: Addison-Wesley.

DAVID S. DUBIN

▌■ STATION OPERATION

See: Radio Broadcasting, Station Programming and; Television Broadcasting, Station Operations and

▌■ STORYTELLERS

Storytellers are a significant voice of culture, and their storytelling takes myriad forms, from anecdote to ballad, film, and novel. The focus of this entry is on the storyteller as oral narrator and on the unique practice of oral craft. Unlike the processes of writing and image-making, which result in tangible or virtual formats that are saleable as products in commercial/professional venues, the greatest work of a storyteller often seems to evaporate into the ether of oral tradition. The words of storytellers may permeate the minds and hearts of listeners—or, through repetition, entire cultures—without leaving physical traces. Yet the intellectual and emotional impact of effective storytellers is undeniable, whether they perform at home, on stage, in classrooms, libraries, corporate boardrooms, or in a broad range of other locales. Some people make a living as professional storytellers; many more use storytelling, consciously or unconsciously, to enhance other activities. The stories of a teacher, for instance, can make a point more effectively than long, less interesting explanations and may be the only thing a student remembers from the lecture. Good stories are by nature memorable—therefore told, remembered, and retold. Making the best of a good story is up to the teller, who improves through experience with word choice, pace, tonal variation, physical expression, and interaction with listeners.

Although most tellers have spun their stories informally as a respected but unpaid part of domestic and community activities, the profession of storyteller is an old one with many names: minstrel, troubadour, jongleur, trouvère, minnesinger, scald, scop, skaziteli, seanachie, pinkerrd, and griot, to name a few. Before common usage of the printing press, storytellers were a primary means of circulating news and preserving historical, cultural, and literary records, which required feats of memory. Homeric poet/singers had a store of 25,000 epic formula. Irish bards had to learn a minimum of 178 historical tales during their training, with 1,000 at the highest level. So great was their power to sway people that Edward I of England ordered all Irish bards to be killed in 1284 lest they foment a revolt against his rule.

Even as oral modes were replaced by a print tradition, storytellers continued to adapt their tales to new settings. A good example is the U.S. public library movement, where, at the beginning of the twentieth century, librarians specializing in children's literature established story hours as an important part of the early learning experience of children, especially among immigrant youths struggling to bridge different languages and folk traditions. Marie Shedlock, Sara Cone Bryant, Gúdrun Thorne-Thompsen, Anna Cogswell Tyler, Mary Gould Davis, Eileen Colwell, Ruth Tooze, Augusta Baker, and others were not only great storytellers in their own right, but also influential in shaping children's librarianship to include the training of children's librarians as storytellers and the establishment of story hour programs.

A U.S. storytelling revival in the 1970s centered on the annual festival at Jonesborough, Tennessee, which soon spawned other regional festivals. The National Association for the Perpetuation and Preservation of Storytelling, founded in 1973–1974 and now known as The National Storytelling Association, serves to represent many interests of contemporary U.S. storytellers, but storytellers thrive outside such organizations as well. Although some folklorists are good storytellers, a degree in folklore grounds one in the scholarship rather than the practice of storytelling. As in the case of creative writers, the best preparation for a storyteller is experience: immersion in stories by listening, reading, and telling. Some storytellers specialize in folktales, others in personal narrative or original stories. The ethics of adaptation and appropriation from other cultures or tellers have been controversial, especially where commercial interests such as recording and publishing are involved. The prevailing code is for storytellers to cite the source of a story they have incorporated from any other source, oral or print, into their own repertoire. Aside from the question of ownership, it is in the best interests of a storyteller to research the background of an unfamiliar tale for purposes of deeper understanding. Exploring folktale variants, for instance, can greatly enhance one's grasp of structural elements that have defied change across time, despite differences in detail.

Some storytellers use props, puppets, costumes, and other accoutrements to enhance their presentations, but these can be distracting if the storyteller does not possess the central power of personality required to project a story or does not have faith in the story alone to hold attention. Most storytellers learn by absorbing rather than memorizing a tale. A story truly absorbed and honed through repeated retellings survives stage fright. Though storytelling in the oral tradition is different from dramatic performance, it nevertheless requires confidence and preparation. The tools of a storyteller are selection, visualization, practice, concentration, projection, and invention. Every storyteller must find the kind of story that individual is suited to tell. Finding the right story is where the good storyteller begins. The next stage is visualizing the story as if one were walking through it until each step of the way is familiar, and then relating one's journey aloud. Just as a good writer must show rather than tell, a good storyteller provides not a description but an experience. Telling the story to others requires great concentration to the exclusion of concern with one's image, effects, interruptions, or anything else besides the story itself and the bond it forms with listeners. Indeed, the interchange between teller and listeners—whether vocal or communicated through eye contact, facial expression, or physical gesture—creates an intense sense of community that is greater than the separate elements of story, teller, and audience. Participation in this alternative world is perhaps the greatest reward for the storyteller.

Like musicians, artists, writers, and actors, few professional storytellers can make a living without supplementary income from other employment. Training and experience in storytelling may begin through education for professions such as librarianship, teaching, or ministry; through academic programs in folklore and anthropology; or simply through independent observation and practice. Certainly, no degree is necessary to become a storyteller. Selection of a good story, skill in telling it, and sense of audience are the only three requirements for success. Anyone who has experienced the successful merging of these three elements is in danger of becoming a storyteller.

See also: BAKER, AUGUSTA; STORYTELLING; WRITERS.

Bibliography

MacDonald, Margaret. (1993). *The Story-Teller's Start-Up Book: Finding, Learning, Performing and Using Folktales.* Little Rock, AR: August House Publishers.

Sawyer, Ruth. (1977). *The Way of the Storyteller,* 2nd edition. New York: Viking Penguin Books.

Schimmel, Nancy. (1992). *Just Enough to Make a Story,* 3rd edition. Berkeley: Sisters' Choice Press.

Sierra, Judy. (1996). *Storytellers' Research Guide.* Eugene, OR: Folkprint.

Sobol, Joseph. (1999). *The Storytellers' Journey: An American Revival.* Urbana: University of Illinois Press.

Zipes, Jack. (1995). *Creative Storytelling: Building Community, Changing Lives.* New York: Routledge.

BETSY HEARNE

STORYTELLING

Storytelling is a universal human activity that involves kaleidoscopic variations across time, culture, form, and personality. From prehistoric pictograms to current computer networks, people have cast their stories in countless ways: as verbal narrative in the oral, print, and electronic traditions; as music, dance, and graphic image; and as film, television, and theater productions. Stories that one absorbs as a child imprint patterns of language, literature, and social values; stories that one chooses to remember and pass on reflect the elements most important in a lifetime. Stories shape both individuals and groups. This significance makes storytelling a subject of study in numerous fields, including folklore, anthropology, sociology, psychology, speech/communication, library and information science, education, religion, literature, and theater. Each of these domains emphasizes different aspects, but almost any exploration of storytelling involves an interdisciplinary approach in dealing with the complexities of story and society, the interaction of text and context.

The Nature of Storytelling

Most courses in storytelling emphasize the oral tradition, past and present. Students work with selection, absorption, and narration of folklore for a broad range of age groups, from cumulative tales for preschool children to oral history among the elderly. Fieldwork and practical experience in col-

A group of young Native American children gather around a storyteller on the Barona Indian Reservation in Lakeside, California, to participate in the continuation of an oral tradition of passing on cultural values through stories. (Bob Rowan; Progressive Image/Corbis)

lecting and swapping stories leads to a deeper theoretical understanding of the nature of story and its place in society. Background in folklore and its dissemination, awareness of ongoing controversies about the meaning and interpretation of narratives, and practice in oral interpretation and planning programs are all essential. Most important is an appreciation of the enormous range and depth of story—from myth, epic, ballad, legend, folktale, literary tale, and family narrative to personal anecdote—and the confidence that each person is already a storyteller with the potential to become a better one. The stage for storytelling "performances" can include homes, schools, workplaces, and all kinds of social and recreational situations. Listening to stories acculturates individuals, while telling stories reveals who they are.

Although storytelling is an activity for all ages, children are often considered a natural audience because stories are a memorable way to communicate knowledge. Storytelling in educational settings increases concentration span, expands vocabulary, enriches cultural literacy, transmits patterns of language and narrative, and bonds children with literature. Folktales make an especially valuable story foundation for young listeners because characters fall into archetypes such as hero, villain, trickster, helper; plots often assume the form of a journey or quest with a clear beginning, middle, and end; style is clean and simple; and settings and details are spare and symbolic. Experts disagree on the meaning and effects of such tales. Bruno Bettelheim, for instance, argues from a Freudian perspective in *The Uses of Enchantment* (1976) that fairy tales represent crucial stages of psychological development. Many folklorists, however, see Bettelheim as universalizing from a few specific European sources, and Jack Zipes in *Breaking the Magic Spell* (1979) argues from a Marxist–feminist position that Bettelheim neglects the sociopolitical implications of fairy tales. Folklorist Max Lüthi in *The Fairytale as Art Form and Portrait of Man* (1984) interprets the aesthetic characteristics of folktale. Robert

Darnton asserts, from the viewpoint of a cultural anthropologist in *The Great Cat Massacre* (1984), that many fairy tales depict actual conditions during historical periods of common child abuse and abandonment.

Since many folktales fall into patterns that seem to repeat themselves in various times and cultures, folklorists have categorized and numbered them by tale type. *Cinderella,* for instance, is classified as Tale Type 510A and has hundreds of variants, each with a similar structure but different details. Another classification system involves motifs, or story elements that appear in different tale types. These are useful in studying stories but have come under fire as oversimplifying stories and taking them out of context. While structuralists find common characteristics of stories to reveal global patterns, contextualists maintain that the real meaning of a story depends on the values and belief systems of its particular culture. Joseph Campbell, famous for his identification of a universal myth pattern in *The Hero With a Thousand Faces* (1949), has been accused of reducing all stories to one ur-tale or "model" in a way that uproots their meaning in different social contexts.

Other controversies center on the ownership of stories. Does a European American, for instance, have the right to adapt a Native American story, make changes, and tell or publish it without tribal consent? Does copyright law favor an outsider's private authorship of materials that were in fact generated over a long period of time by a group of people who have no control over or share in profits from their cultural heritage? Equally problematic is the clash of values in a multicultural society exposed to stories that potentially offend conflicting segments of a community. Storytellers have been challenged in schools and libraries for introducing tales that some parents consider violent, sexist, or otherwise offensive. Mass media storytelling, too, has raised issues of selection and adaptation; Disney's films have been both celebrated and censured for representing changes in classic fairy tales.

Nineteenth-century folklore collections reflected a concurrent rise of nationalism. Jacob and Wilhelm Grimm are by far the most famous collectors of German tales; Peter Asbjornsen and Jorgen Moe, of Scandinavian; Aleksandr Afanas'ef, of Russian; and Joseph Jacobs, of British. Charles Perrault is famous for his earlier (1698) collection of French fairy tales. In the United States, collectors have often concentrated on regions or genres, with Richard Chase, for example, collecting and retelling Appalachian tales, and Jan Harold Brunvand specializing in urban legends. As definitions of folklore have expanded to include storytelling in factories, corporations, therapy groups, nursing homes, urban gangs, and other contemporary settings, informal storytelling has become a common subject for ethnographers analyzing organizations of all kinds. Stories about the founding partner of a law firm, for instance, may be the truest indicators of the culture of that firm. Similarly, the stories passed around a class of students in a long-distance education program can reflect the value system of an electronic community as well as the legendary aspects of the effects of computer technology on the individual, for better or for worse. Long before people become adults, however, stories permeate their lives.

The Storied Life

Humans are immersed in stories even before birth. A fetus floats in a dark, warm world of its own. It cannot see, but it can sense the beat of a heart. Whatever else intrudes on its senses, that beat is basic, rhythmic, and sure, organizing the baby's sensibilities into a predictable pattern. Heartbeat is the first storyteller. The baby also hears, in its underwater world, bumps and thumps from far away and one other sound, steady, up and down, silent, and steady again. The voice of the baby's mother moves in patterns even as the baby's brain is formed. With the rhythm of those patterns is born the baby's story self: its sense of emphasis, continuity, and—above all—the rise and fall of sounds that lead to expected patterns. Patterns elicit order from disorder; stories, which are patterns of sound and narrative, also elicit order from disorder. Even submerged, the baby is exposed to the very elements of story. After it is born, the child's story self develops with the acquisition of language, interacts with stories that it hears informally, extends into literacy, intertwines with literature, and embraces social culture. From lullabies to nursery rhymes to finger games to folktales to fairy tales to family lore, children absorb patterns of language and narrative from hearing stories.

From hearing stories, children learn to tell stories, progressing from unformed efforts at description to clearly articulated realistic accounts to expressive flights of imagination. There are many theories about this development. Arthur Applebee, in his book *The Child's Concept of Story: Ages Two to Seventeen* (1978), says that children organize stories in increasingly sophisticated arrangements, beginning with a first primitive level called "heaps," or stories containing no obvious means of organization, and progressing through a second level he identifies as "sequences," or stories with a particular idea that associates their elements. The third level is "primitive narrative," in which elements are associated by complementary relations, with the consequences of certain actions becoming important. The fourth level consists of "unfocused chains" organized into chunks that bear some relation to each other; the fifth level involves "focused chains," with one central character maintained throughout; and the last is "narrative," in which events are organized to form a coherent whole. A study by developmental psychologist Peggy Miller has shown adults and children narrating or co-narrating from four to thirteen personal stories every hour among families of African-American, Anglo-American, and Chinese backgrounds.

As an effective form of socialization and acculturation, storytelling helps integrate the old and the new. One tells old stories to new children to help integrate them into society. One tells old stories about new events to enlist the wisdom of those who have gone before. Even new stories reveal old patterns, because stories symbolize human experience. This balance of the old with the new is something everyone seeks, on both an individual and an international level. Every nation, industrialized or developing, has a common need to balance the preservation of unique traditions with the incorporation of global changes. Every community struggles to maintain self-identity while merging with an increasingly diffuse world community.

Storytelling allows people to strike this balance: While vastly different cultures share common motifs and tale types, each tale carries its own cultural flavor. When people share traditional stories, they are not only passing along their own cultural values, but also sharing a universal tradition. As the world has moved from oral to printed to electronic modes of communication, the interpersonal sometimes seems lost to the impersonal, but storytelling is an irrepressible activity. The Internet carries a frequent exchange of urban legends, which are often variants of older rural legends making themselves at home in the city. Traditional stories travel well, but, paradoxically, they also root easily.

Most people are familiar with a variant of the persecuted heroine, often called Cinderella, and can identify with the child abandoned in a wilderness. This is one of the most common motifs in folklore precisely because abandonment is the child's—and many an adult's—deepest fear. From Ishmael or Moses, to Aladdin, to Hansel and Gretel, to Babar the Elephant, to E.T., the generations recast this fear and resolve it in story form. Each community shapes the problem according to its own landscape: Ishmael survives a desert; Moses, a river; Aladdin, a cave; Hansel and Gretel, a forest; Babar, a journey to the city; and E.T., an odyssey among modern scientific earthlings. In "The Story of Two Jealous Sisters" from *The Arabian Nights*, all three of the sultan's children—Bahman, Perviz, and Parizade—are abandoned to a river before they win their rightful place. Anyone can identify with those children, especially with Parizade, who combines courage, virtue, and quick wit to save her brothers and fulfill her fate.

The same baby who was described earlier as being imprinted with the patterns of her mother's voice before the first breath was taken will move with bated breath through the patterns of "The Story of Two Jealous Sisters" and learn from it the value of courage, virtue, and quick wit. Stories teach the art of survival, and they offer hope for the small, the vulnerable, and the powerless. Humans of all ages have within them the elements of hero and of villain. Stories help to distinguish one element from the other and to make decisions about which role to choose. By communicating social experience through archetypal characters and symbolic conflict, traditional stories help pattern people's lives in a socially thoughtful way. The more confused and threatening a situation becomes, the more need there is to understand stories that have cast light on the pathways of the past. The generations living at the beginning of the twenty-first century, who must formulate peaceful alternatives to nuclear extinction, can find inspiration in the epic of Gilgamesh, where the wild man Enkido leads a king to be more humane, offering friendship to end their battle for supremacy.

Each community and nation abounds in story. Paradoxically, the poorest communities are sometimes the richest in story wealth. It is of national and, ultimately, of global importance that each community glean its stories and preserve them by passing them on. Old people, who are often the unsung heroes of tradition in a modern world that undervalues traditional wisdom, can add their store of the traditional stories they heard as children, along with the personal stories that have patterned and made sense of their lives. In the nineteenth century, Scandinavian folklorists established an invaluable archive in Ireland and organized the collection of Irish tales just in time to preserve a tradition changing almost too fast to record. Increasingly, however, collection within a community by members of the community is emphasized when anthropologists view their informants as collaborators rather than subjects. Through storytelling, people can heighten their own awareness, increase support for the collection and preservation of their cultural heritage, and reach out to others. The exchange, comparison, and contrast of people's separate stories can only underscore their common humanity.

Why sing lullabies to a baby? Why say nursery rhymes? Why chant along with the games played on a toddler's fingers and toes? Why tell children stories of what happened to grownups in their own youth? Why pass on tales of the African trickster Anansi or the Greek trickster Odysseus in a library story hour? Why read poetry aloud in a classroom? Why lead students to read literature or view art at all? Why spin extraordinary tales of ordinary events during coffee break? Why encourage the elderly to exchange stories about their lives? The answer to the first question is the answer to them all, for they are inextricably connected. Storytelling offers to a listener patterns that give comfort through rhythm and repetition, patterns that identify shapes of human behavior, patterns that lead to understanding a random world, and, ultimately, patterns that lead to understanding oneself. At a time when miraculous technologies often convey words devoid of deep meaning, people can renew themselves with old patterns of story.

Folklorist Howard Norman (1985) quotes the Cree Indians of North America as saying that stories wander through the world looking for a person, inhabit that person for a while, and then are told back out into the world again. A symbiotic relationship exists: If people nourish a story properly, it tells them useful things about life. Humans need to nourish their stories, collect them, and release them back into the world for the sake of the future.

See also: COPYRIGHT; STORYTELLERS; WRITERS.

Bibliography

Bauman, Richard, ed. (1991). *Folklore, Cultural Performances, and Popular Entertainments: A Communications-Centered Handbook.* New York: Oxford University Press.

Birch, Carol, and Heckler, Melissa, eds. (1996). *"Who Says?" Essays on Pivotal Issues in Contemporary Storytelling.* Little Rock, AR: August House.

Brunvand, Jan Harold. (1981). *The Vanishing Hitchhiker: American Urban Legends and Their Meanings.* New York: W. W. Norton.

Greene, Ellin. (1996). *Storytelling: Art and Technique,* 3rd edition. New Providence, NJ: Bowker.

Norman, Howard. (1985). "Crow Ducks and Other Wandering Talk." In *The Language of the Birds: Tales, Texts, and Poems of Interspecies Communication,* ed. David M. Guss. San Francisco: North Point.

Leeming, David A., ed. (1997). *Storytelling Encyclopedia: Historical, Cultural, and Multiethnic Approaches to Oral Traditions Around the World.* Phoenix, AZ: Oryx Press.

MacDonald, Margaret. (1982). *The Storyteller's Sourcebook: A Subject, Title, and Motif Index to Folklore Collections for Children.* Detroit, MI: Neal Schuman.

Miller, Peggy J.; Potts, Randolph; Fung, Heidi; Hoogstra, Lisa; and Mintz, Judy. (1990). "Narrative Practices and the Social Construction of Self in Childhood." *American Ethnologist* 17:292–311.

Mullen, Patrick B. (1992). *Listening to Old Voices: Folklore in the Lives of Nine Elderly People.* Urbana: University of Illinois Press.

Paley, Vivian. (1990). *The Boy Who Would Be a Helicopter: The Uses of Storytelling in the Classroom.* Cambridge, MA: Harvard University Press.

Pellowski, Anne. (1990). *The World of Storytelling.* New York: Wilson.

Stone, Elizabeth. (1988). *Black Sheep & Kissing Cousins: How Our Family Stories Shape Us.* New York: Random House/Times Books.

Stone, Kay. (1998). *Burning Brightly: New Light on Old Tales Told Today.* Peterborough, Ontario: Broadview Press.

Thompson, Stith. (1977). *The Folktale.* Berkeley: University of California Press.

Warner, Marina. (1994). *From the Beast to the Blonde: On Fairy Tales and Their Tellers.* New York: Farrar, Straus and Giroux.

BETSY HEARNE

■ SUBLIMINAL ADVERTISING

See: Advertising, Subliminal

■ SUBSTANCE ABUSE

See: Alcohol Abuse and College Students; Alcohol in the Media

■ SYMBOLS

Symbols are characters, letters, numbers, icons, objects, people, actions, or places that stand for or represent something other than themselves. In the most general sense, a symbolic language (or system) is a set of symbols combined with the rules for their use in relation to one another. Human language is the most familiar and important symbol system. Beginning in childhood, individuals are taught how to use oral and written symbols (e.g., letters, numbers, words) and how to use these symbols to create messages that make human communication possible.

Systems of Symbols

Typically, a speaker or writer selects and uses specific symbols to create a message that will bring about a particular response among listeners or readers. Consider a simple communicative situation, such as when one person says, "Pass the sugar." Here, the letters "p," "a," "s," and "s," as well as the other letters in the phrase, are selected and combined with the goal of conveying a particular meaning and accomplishing a specific task. The letters—which are symbols—have been grouped together to form words, which are also symbols. Effective communication depends on the extent to which the listener and the speaker attach more or less the same meaning to the symbols. If the listener does not speak English, for example, or if the listener is unfamiliar with the symbols "pass" or "sugar," effective communication is unlikely.

While spoken and written languages are the most familiar examples of a symbol system, computer languages, Morse code, Braille, and the genetic code are also symbol systems. Money is another fundamental symbol system. Little conscious attention is given to how this symbol system operates, but as Brent Ruben and Lea Stewart (1998, pp. 93–94) describe, the process is very much a communication event that involves symbolic language:

We think little about the communication process that occurs when we go into a store, pick out an item priced at $15, go to the cashier, hand over a ten- and a five-dollar bill, and leave the store with a "thank you" and the item in a bag. . . . When we give the clerk a ten- and a five-dollar bill, in effect, we are only handing over two pieces of high-quality paper. They have no inherent value, other than the expense of the paper and ink. They are symbols.

Besides alphanumeric language and money, there are many, many other symbols that play an essential role in human communication. The green–yellow–red light at a street intersection is a symbol, as are the White House, a Mercedes automobile, an "A" on an exam, a handshake, and a wedding ring.

People live, quite literally, in an environment that is filled with symbols, thus requiring the use of symbolic language. Symbolic language allows individuals to code and transmit messages from one point—in space or time—to another point using one or more communication modes. Oral and other acoustically coded languages make use of the auditory mode. Written or light-based languages use the visual channel.

Most human symbols have the potential for portability and permanence. Communication technology and mass media allow symbols to be copied, stored, duplicated, amplified, and transmitted. For example, spoken words can be stored in recorded form before being broadcast across space and preserved across time. Similarly, something that originates as personal correspondence can be captured on paper, stored on a computer, printed in a book, posted online, archived in a library, and transmitted across time and space.

Meaning

Humans create symbols, and they also create the meanings of those symbols. There is no necessary or natural connection between a symbol and the idea or object to which it refers. For example, there is no particular reason why the color red must mean "stop," or why the symbol "5" should be equivalent to "1" + "1" + "1" + "1" + "1." Each of these symbols has a meaning that is arbitrary and invented by humans. As another example, consider a word such as "encyclopedia." "Encyclopedia" has no inherent, intrinsic meaning or significance. When spoken, the word is nothing more than a particular pattern of auditory vibrations that an individual creates through the manipulation of the vocal cords, lips, tongue, and mouth. In its written form, "encyclopedia" is nothing more than a particular configuration of ink on paper.

While humans invent the meanings of symbols, this invention process is not a solitary activity. Rather, it is a collective and ongoing activity of humanity, and it is the essence of social communication. In order for symbols to function as communication, all parties involved must associate more or less the same meaning with the symbols. For example, if most drivers and pedestrians (and police officers) did not attach more or less the same meaning to "red" lights at street intersections, the variations in interpretation would have dire consequences. Perhaps less dire, but no less frustrating, are the consequences of communication efforts where there are language, cultural, or interpretive differences between the interactants. It is important to remember that even among those people who have similar cultural backgrounds and linguistic competencies, variations in meaning are frequent. For example, the symbol "love" means many things to many different people, and this variation on such a "simple" symbol can cause a great deal of complication within relationships.

Humans do not inherit their knowledge of what particular symbols mean. They learn these meanings through interaction—through communication—with others. Beyond certain basic message-responding tendencies (i.e., reflexive responses) with which humans are born, most of the meanings that people need in order to function as humans have to be learned through social interaction. Reflexive responses, such as the reaction to the sensation of being burned by a flame, can be thought of as first-order information processing events. They consist of natural and automatic responses to nonsymbolic signals. The majority of human responses are connected to symbols, and these responses represent what may be thought of as second-order information processing events (Ruben and Stewart, 1998). Second-order information processing involves symbolic communication. From family, friends, and peers, individuals become literate and able to use written and spoken language, monetary sym-

bols, and the other symbols systems that will be necessary in order to function as adults.

The learning process and the social shaping of symbols and their meanings are imperfect, as has been noted above. Individuals do not all learn the same things in the same ways, which helps to explain the variation and complexity of human communication. This imperfection is a major factor in explaining the complexity and challenges of human communication. On the one hand, interpretative variation of symbols is the source of frustration, misunderstanding, and anxiety in human communication. On the other hand, it is the basis for creativity, personal change, and social change.

Nonetheless, the effectiveness of symbols and people's proficiency in their use are quite remarkable. Whether one thinks of verbal exchanges, the Internet, intimate interactions with loved ones, a casual walk through a street intersection, or shopping at the store, communication works. None of this social interaction or predictability would be possible were it not for the existence of symbols and the human capacity for teaching and learning how to use them.

See also: ANIMAL COMMUNICATION; CULTURE AND COMMUNICATION; INTERCULTURAL COMMUNICATION, ADAPTATION AND; INTERPERSONAL COMMUNICATION; LANGUAGE ACQUISITION; LANGUAGE AND COMMUNICATION; LANGUAGE STRUCTURE; NONVERBAL COMMUNICATION.

Bibliography

Bates, Elizabeth; Bretherton, Inge; and Snyder, Lynn S. (1988). *From First Words to Grammar.* Cambridge, Eng.: Cambridge University Press.

Blumer, Herbert. (1969). *Symbolic Interactionism.* Englewood Cliffs, NJ: Prentice-Hall.

Duncan, Hugh D. (1968). *Symbols in Society.* Oxford, Eng.: Oxford University Press.

Ruben, Brent D., and Stewart, Lea P. (1998). *Communication and Human Behavior,* 4th edition. Needham Heights, MA: Allyn & Bacon.

BRENT D. RUBEN

■ SYSTEMS DESIGNERS

Systems designers are the people who are responsible for the analysis and design of information systems that are involved in the operation of organizations. They study business, scientific, or engineering data-processing problems, use their knowledge and skills to solve problems, design new solutions, and enable computer technology to meet the individual needs of the organizations. Systems designers may design entirely new information systems, including both hardware and software, or they may add a single new software application to an existing system.

Roles

Systems designers have to assume a variety of roles throughout the design process. Among these roles are (1) analyst in order to study the existing system in detail, paying meticulous attention to understanding and distinguishing between users' problems and users' viewpoints, (2) designer in order to propose new procedures for information flow, reporting, and computer processing, (3) technical writer in order to document the results of the design effort, (4) consultant in order to provide advice on options that are available to users and indicate the implications that each of these options has for the performance of the system, (5) team member in order to be able to work with other computer specialists and user representatives toward achieving a common goal, and (6) behavioral scientist in order to design an interface between the system's users and the computer so that the design itself and its method of implementation result in users being satisfied with the final result.

Problem Solving

Most systems designers use some variation of a system problem-solving approach called a "systems development life cycle" to build information systems. A systems development life cycle consists of a set of iterative activities and usually incorporates the following general problem-solving steps: planning, analysis, design, creation, test, implementation, and maintenance. The planning step involves identifying the problem, determining the cause, scope, and boundary of the problem, and planning the development strategy and goals. The analysis step involves studying and analyzing the problems, causes, and effects and then identifying and analyzing the requirements that must be fulfilled by any successful solution. Typically, the logical elements of a system are defined during analysis. The design step involves determining how the problem will be solved. The designer's focus shifts from the logical to the physical. Processes are converted to manual procedures or computer programs. Data elements are grouped to form physical data structures, screens, reports, files, and databases. The hardware components that support the programs and the data are defined. The creation step involves coding, debugging, documenting, and testing programs, selecting and ordering new hardware, writing and testing procedures, preparing end-user documentation, initializing databases, and training users. The test step involves ensuring that the system does what it was designed to do. The implementation step involves implementing the physical system into the normal business operation. The maintenance step involves keeping the system functioning at an acceptable level, analyzing the implemented system, refining the design, and implementing improvements to the system. Different support situations can thread back into the previous steps.

The problem-solving steps for design can be simplified to three phases: analysis, design, and development. The systems analysis phase focuses on what the system is required to do. These specifications are then converted to a hierarchy of increasingly detailed components. These components define the data that are required and decompose the processes to be carried out on data to a level at which they can be expressed as instructions for a computer program. The systems development phase consists of writing and testing computer software and of developing data input and output forms and conventions.

Requirements

Modern information systems are increasingly used by individuals who have little or no previous experience with information technology but who possess a perception about what this technology should accomplish in their professional and personal environments. Systems designers must correctly understand the information needs, the tasks and activities accomplished in meeting the needs, the requirements preferences, and information-use patterns of their end users.

Successful systems designers must possess a wide range of talents. They may work in many different environments or functional units (e.g., finance, marketing) of various organizations, including management and systems consulting firms. Any description of their work is destined to fall short in some way; but there are qualities that most systems designers seem to display.

Above all, designers are problem solvers They must be able to take a large organizational problem, break down that problem into its component parts, analyze the various aspects of the problem, and then assemble an improved system to solve the problem through skillful application of tools, techniques, and experience.

Systems designers must be experts in the area of information systems and technology. They must have a working knowledge of database management systems, telecommunications and networking, client/server and distributed computing architecture, object technology, rapid application development technology, graphical user interfaces, the Internet, and programming, including operating systems and utilities and application development tools.

Systems designers must be adaptable. No two systems development projects encountered by a system designer are identical, and many organizations have standards that dictate specific approaches, tools, and techniques that must be adhered to when developing a system. Systems designers must be able to communicate, both orally and in writing, and they must relate well to other people over extended periods of time.

Systems designers must also be self-disciplined and self-motivated as individuals. They must also be able to manage and coordinate innumerable project resources, including other people. Systems analysis and design is demanding, but the compensation is that it is an ever-changing and always challenging occupation.

There is no universally accepted way to prepare for a job as a systems designer because the preferences of employers depend on the work to be done. A bachelor's degree in computer science, electrical engineering, or information science is virtually a prerequisite for most employers. For some of the more complex jobs, people who have graduate degrees are preferred. Relevant work experience is also very important. People who are looking for entry-level positions may enhance their employment opportunities by participating in internship or co-op programs offered through their schools.

See also: COMMUNITY NETWORKS; COMPUTER SOFTWARE; COMPUTING; DATABASE DESIGN; INTERNET AND THE WORLD WIDE WEB.

Bibliography

Davis, William S., and Yen, David C. (1998). *Information Systems Consultant's Handbook: Systems Analysis and Design.* Boca Raton, FL: CRC Press.

Modell, Martin E. (1996). *A Professionals Guide to Systems Analysis.* New York: McGraw-Hill.

Whitten, Jeffrey L., and Bentley, Lonnie D. (1998). *Systems Analysis and Design Methods.* Boston: Irwin/McGraw-Hill.

HONG XU

■ TALK SHOWS ON TELEVISION

The number of daytime television talk shows increased rapidly during the 1990s. In the late 1980s, there were only three national daytime talk show personalities (Phil Donahue, Oprah Winfrey, and Sally Jessy Raphael). By 1995, there were almost twenty daytime syndicated talk shows watched by an estimated ten million viewers each day.

Controversies over Talk Shows

As talk shows proliferated, so did criticism by politicians such as U.S. Senator Joseph Lieberman (D-CT) and U.S. Department of Health and Human Services Secretary Donna Shalala, who refer to these programs as "trash TV." Part of the concern arises from reports that children and adolescents often watch these programs. In a national survey conducted by the Annenberg Public Policy Center in 1996, children were more likely than their parents to say they watched shows such as *Ricki Lake, Jenny Jones, Montel Williams,* or *Geraldo.* According to this survey, 39 percent of the parents, more than 50 percent of the twelve- to seventeen-year-olds, and nearly 30 percent of the ten- and eleven-year-olds reported watching those talk shows.

A number of distinct criticisms have been put forward, mostly focusing on the probability that the viewers' perceptions of reality become distorted as a result of watching talk shows. One such criticism is that talk shows give viewers a warped sense of reality in which dysfunctional relationships and bizarre problems seem typical of life in the United States. As the viewers' percep-

tions of society change, those people become more tolerant of deviant behaviors and possibly more willing to try such behaviors themselves. A second criticism is that viewers who watch talk shows on a regular basis become desensitized to the graphic discussions and emotional outbursts of the participants and subsequently develop a callous attitude toward misfortune even outside the realm of talk shows. A third criticism is that talk shows, by using personal exemplars and by offering simplistic advice such as "love conquers all" or "race shouldn't matter" as solutions to problems, cause viewers to trivialize complex social issues. Finally, talk shows have been charged by authors such as Elaine Showalter (1997) and Jeanne Heaton and Nona Wilson (1998) with contributing to hysteria and misinformation on issues such as repressed memory, satanic ritual abuse, and alien abduction.

In contrast, a number of advocates such as Patricia Priest (1996) and Joshua Gamson (1998) have argued that talk shows provide a valuable source of celebrity and self-esteem for the marginalized individuals who appear as guests. In addition, Gamson has suggested that talk shows give much needed, high-impact public visibility to outgroups such as sexual nonconformists, moving previously taboo topics into public awareness and changing the norms of what can be presented on television. Patricia Priest and Joseph Dominick (1994) reported that informants who had appeared on *Phil Donahue* to discuss sensitive topics viewed talk shows as a pragmatic way to reach both the mainstream public and members of their own outgroup.

Oprah Winfrey, who spoke with Al Gore on her talk show on September 11, 2000, has transformed her talk show success into a media empire that includes publishing a magazine, producing movies, and continuing her talk show. (Reuters NewMedia Inc./Corbis)

The Content of Talk Shows

What evidence is there for this set of criticisms in the content of talk shows? Bradley Greenberg, Sandi Smith, and their associates analyzed ten episodes of each of the eleven most highly rated daytime television talk shows of 1994 (see Greenberg and Smith, 2000). They reported that, contrary to public perception, talk shows most frequently focused on parenting and marriage problems, as well as dating. Sexual issues, such as frequency of intercourse, cheating, and sexual orientation, were raised in this context, but they were not the only focus. Other common topics included victims and perpetrators of criminal activities, physical health problems, and physical appearance. Despite the image of talk shows as a hotbed of verbal and physical conflict, yelling and shouting occurred no more often than laughing among the guests, and the positive affect suggested by hugging or holding hands was found twice as often as the negative affect suggested by shouting. Verbal statements of denial, rejection,

shame, and anger were common, but so were statements of affection.

Greenberg and Smith (2000) reported that, in the majority of cases, they could identify a clear theme for the program that reflected rather conservative perspectives (e.g., "pornography is not ok," "transsexuality is not acceptable," "people should not have multiple sex partners"). In other cases, the theme of the program reflected basic societal standards (e.g., "adults should not rape minors").

Greenberg and Smith also coded the first two reactions of a talk show host to a guest's disclosure. Typically, these were simple requests for further information or noncommittal sounds that encouraged further communication. However, 11 percent of the first two reactions by hosts were moralizing questions (e.g., "You knew that was wrong, didn't you?"), and 10 percent were questions or statements emphasizing the severity of the event (e.g., "He hit you with a baseball bat?"). The reactions of others on the show (other guests or the studio audience) included character attacks and name-calling. Overall, almost one-quarter of the time, studio audiences and hosts reacted with disapproval to the guests' disclosures. In summary, when talk shows cover behaviors that can be considered dangerous or inappropriate, they are often met with disapproval rather than presented as normal or desirable.

What about the argument that talk shows oversimplify complex issues? Greenberg and Smith were able to identify a clear, simplistic theme such as "prostitution should not be done" in the majority of episodes that were coded. The host of the show often stated a theme or title of the show for that day and then repeated it after returning from a commercial break. On some programs, such as *Ricki Lake*, the theme of the show was often printed on the screen as advice from one guest to another (e.g., "Dump that guy before I dump you."). In addition, the focus of each program is clearly on the individuals rather than the implications of issues for society as a whole.

Research on the Effects of Talk Shows

Do talk shows alter the viewers' perceptions of reality and subsequently affect their behaviors and policy judgments? John Hill and Dolf Zillmann (1999) focused on arguments that *Oprah Winfrey* increases sympathy for perpetrators rather than victims of crime as a result of the emphasis on the nearly irresistible forces (e.g., childhood trauma) that drive people to commit violent and illegal acts. Undergraduate students who watched segments of *Oprah Winfrey* with such mitigating information present gave lighter prison sentences to criminals depicted in the segments than did those who saw the segments without the mitigating information. Those who viewed the mitigating information also gave lighter sentences in a seemingly unrelated exercise in which they were asked to give sentences for six violent and nonviolent crimes that were not depicted in the segments.

As a test of some of the other popular criticisms of talk shows, Stacy Davis and Marie-Louise Mares (1998) surveyed 292 high school students in North Carolina. Consistent with the hypothesis that talk shows alter perceptions of what is typical, subjects who were heavy viewers of talk shows gave significantly higher estimates of the frequency of behaviors depicted on talk shows (e.g., bringing guns to school) than did subjects who were light viewers of talk shows. This was still true even after statistically controlling for overall television viewing and background demographic variables such as parental education. However, when subjects who were heavy viewers of talk shows were asked to rate the harm done to victims in a series of scenarios, their responses showed no sign that they were becoming desensitized to the sufferings of others. Finally, there was no evidence that talk shows led viewers to believe that serious issues such as drug abuse or teen pregnancy were trivial. In fact, talk show viewing was positively related, among people between fifteen and eighteen years of age, to perceived importance of social issues.

Conclusion

Talk shows have been a focus of considerable controversy. The little evidence that is available suggests that talk shows may be less sensational and less harmful than is often suggested.

See also: SEX AND THE MEDIA; TELEVISION INDUSTRY; VIOLENCE IN THE MEDIA, ATTRACTION TO.

Bibliography

Davis, Stacy, and Mares, Marie-Louise. (1998). "Effects of Talk Show Viewing on Adolescents." *Journal of Communication* 48(3):69–86.

Gamson, Joshua. (1998). *Freaks Talk Back: Tabloid Talk Shows and Sexual Nonconformity.* Chicago: University of Chicago Press.

Greenberg, Bradley S.; Sherry, John L.; Busselle, Rick W.; Hnilo, Lynn; and Smith, Sandi W. (1997). "Daytime Television Talk Shows: Guests, Content and Interactions." *Journal of Broadcasting and Electronic Media* 41(3):412–426.

Greenberg, Bradley S., and Smith, Sandi W. (1995). *The Content of Television Talk Shows: Topics, Guests and Interactions.* Report prepared for the Kaiser Family Foundation

Greenberg, Bradley S., and Smith, Sandi W. (2000). "Talk Shows: Up Close and in Your Face." In *Sexual Teens, Sexual Media*, eds. Jane D. Brown, Jeanne R. Steele, and Kim Walsh-Childers. Hillsdale, NJ: Lawrence Erlbaum.

Heaton, Jeanne, A., and Wilson, Nona, L. (1998). "Memory, Media, and the Creation of Mass Confusion." In *Truth in Memory*, eds. Steven Lynn and Kevin McConkey. New York: Guilford Press.

Hill, John R., and Zillmann, Dolf. (1999). "The Oprahization of America: Sympathetic Crime Talk and Leniency." *Journal of Broadcasting and Electronic Media* 43(1):67–82.

Priest, Patricia. (1996). "Gilt by Association: Talk Show Participants' Televisually Enhanced Status and Self-Esteem." In *Constructing the Self in a Mediated World*, eds. Debra Grodin and Thomas R. Lindlof. Thousand Oaks, CA: Sage Publications.

Priest, Patricia, and Dominick, Joseph R. (1994). "Pulp Pulpits: Self-Disclosure on 'Donahue.'" *Journal of Communication* 44(4):74–97.

Showalter, Elaine. (1997). *Hystories: Hysterical Epidemics and Modern Culture*. New York: Columbia University Press.

MARIE-LOUISE MARES

TECHNOLOGY

See: Cable Television, System Technology of; Film Industry, Technology of; Radio Broadcasting, Technology of; Recording Industry, Technology of; Satellites, Technology of; Technology, Adoption and Diffusion of; Technology, Philosophy of; Telephone Industry, Technology of; Television Broadcasting, Technology of

TECHNOLOGY, ADOPTION AND DIFFUSION OF

Although not originally designed as such, diffusion of innovations has proven to be an important theory for explaining the dynamics of communication. Diffusion of innovations is a theory originally designed to explain how change agents influence social processes. It has become a theory used to address how a technology or technological artifact becomes adopted, what forces affect the adoption process, and how proponents of a given technology or artifact may better influence the adoption process. The theory addresses how new ideas and technologies are communicated, evaluated, adopted, and reevaluated.

Foundations of Diffusion Theory

Diffusion of innovations is important to the study of communication because of its focus on process and what factors influence the process of communication. Specifically, diffusion is conceptualized as the process by which an innovation is communicated through channels over time among the members of a particular audience. Innovations are ideas, practices, or objects perceived as new by members of that particular audience. Thus, the theory addresses how knowledge is strategically managed to create specific effects on particular audiences.

While not using the terms of the theory as they are known today, Gabriel de Tarde (a French sociologist and legal scholar of the late nineteenth and early twentieth centuries) has been credited with the initial conceptualization of diffusion of innovations. Tarde (1903) observed many of the key factors of the theory, including the influence of public-opinion leaders as change agents upon social systems, the role of socioeconomic status as a factor affecting interpersonal diffusion, and the basic S-shaped model of innovation adoption over time. Anthropologists recognized the significance of this model and began to use it in attempts to explain processes of social change.

The Iowa hybrid seed corn study conducted by Bryce Ryan and Neal Gross (1943), however, is considered to be the event that clarified the practicality of diffusion of innovations for explaining the process of large-scale social influence. The initial Ryan and Gross study was designed to explain why hybrid seed corn was readily adopted by some farmers while many others were much slower to adopt the product. The foundation of diffusion of innovations as it is presently known is a by-product of this study, and the theory retains the basic components of that foundation in modern, diverse applications.

Preindustrial society in the United States was very slow to change. As people moved to cities from rural America and as diverse international populations immigrated to the United States, pockets of innovative ideas began to emerge. Modern industrial society provided technological advantages in production that aided in the establishment of an infrastructure for further technological development. Technological advancements became very evident in agriculture, particularly in the United States, during the period preceding World War II. Technological growth coupled with the concerns of an economic depression encouraged the development of a hybrid of corn that was particularly resistant to the harsh agricultural climate of the 1930s. While resistant to drought and disease, however, the hybrid corn did have a drawback; it could not reproduce. Therefore, farmers would have to buy new seed for each planting season. Why, then, would farmers invest in what many perceived to be such a risky venture when the stakes were already so high during the Great Depression?

Why and how the innovative seed was adopted was the concern of agricultural researchers who were supported by the government and backed by land grants. Did farmers respond to the pitches of company salespeople, the brochures produced by early cooperative extension agents, information provided in print and radio broadcasts, or their neighbors? As it turns out, farmers responded to all of these channels. Although initial information tended to be provided by individual seed company salespeople, most influence tended to come from within the farming community. In other words, in the early stages of hybrid seed corn (innovation) adoption, many attempts to influence the adoption process affected only a few farmers. As a few farmers became successful and endorsed the use of the hybrid seed corn, they became opinion leaders who influenced even larger numbers of their neighbors in the adoption process (diffusion). Mass communicated messages proved effective in influencing the early stages of adoption, but interpersonally communicated messages proved more effective during the widest range of diffusion. Thus, what was learned from the Ryan and Gross study is that the mass media helped to draw attention to the innovation, create a deeper awareness of the potential of the seed corn, and define the product as important to particular opinion leaders who would act as change agents for their communities. Diffusion of the hybrid seed corn would not work, however, without an ordered structure of social and media contacts that work together in establishing clear patterns of interaction among salespersons and neighbors.

What has been learned as a result of the Iowa hybrid seed corn study and subsequent research into diffusion of innovations is that those innovations that are actually adopted tend to follow a very distinctive pattern as their use in society increases. That pattern of adoption develops as an S-shaped curve. The shape of the curve represents the tendency of a few individuals within society to adopt the innovation initially. These individuals have a low threshold of resistance to the potential innovation. In other words, those people who are involved in the earliest stages of the process require little persuasion to consider adoption of a potential innovation. The mass media and inter-

personal contacts may make relevant important information concerning the potential innovation for these earliest adopters. Therefore, under the assumptions of diffusion of innovations, awareness of the product or idea does not occur incidentally. The innovation is intentionally brought before an audience for consideration. If the product or idea maintains the interest of these individuals, they then must evaluate it for its potential usefulness. Adoption increases rapidly as those who adopt early are successful in persuading others to do so. The rapid rise of adoption begins to decline as the adoption process reaches a "critical mass," or a point when the diffusion process becomes self-regulating.

A second basic curve consistently appears in the diffusion process. According to researcher Everett Rogers (1995), those who play a role in the adoption process fall relatively neatly into a normally distributed bell-shaped curve. True "innovators" are those who make up approximately 2.5 percent of the population of adopters, and they fall beyond the earliest second standard deviation of the curve. Those who may be considered "early adopters" comprise about 13.5 percent of the population, and they fall between the second and first standard deviation of the curve. The widest range of those who take part in the diffusion of an innovation fall within the first standard of deviation above and below the mean or average phase of adoption; these are the "early majority" and "late majority" of adopters. This segment is approximately 68 percent of the population of adopters. All remaining participants in the adoption process, about 16 percent of the population, are the "laggards."

Application of Diffusion Theory

Rural sociologists maintained an interest in the application of the diffusion of innovations for explaining why and how agricultural innovations are adopted. Those interested in communication research, however, not only apply this theoretical framework to the adoption of the technology itself; they also are interested in the diffusion process as a form of communication independent of the types of innovations that may be adopted. The three general areas of interest include (1) the innovation-decision process, or first knowledge of and confirmation of the innovation, (2) innovativeness, or the degree to which an individual is relatively early as an adopter of a potential innovation, and (3) the actual rate of adoption by early adopters as compared with other members of a social system. The diffusion process is considered to be defined by communication among similar individuals because diffusion is conceptualized as depending on a social system. Thus, many are interested in the types of people who adopt at different times along the diffusion process. Furthermore, diffusion occurs at different rates due to the interests of different social systems in a potential innovation. Because different innovations are adopted at different rates, unique groups or families of S-curves representing the rate of adoption have emerged. For example, the rate at which the telephone initially was adopted was much slower than the rate at which present-day personal telecommunication devices are adopted.

Another key assumption of diffusion of innovations is that it is not the actual innovativeness of an idea, product, or process that is important, but it is the perception of innovativeness that matters for members of the social system. Even perceived innovativeness may be insufficient to encourage adoption and diffusion. The trial stage in which the potential innovation is actually used is very important to the diffusion process. The diffusion process will end at this stage if the benefits of the innovation do not outweigh the costs. As noted previously, the adoption process must reach the stage of critical mass for many technologies to prove successful for all adopters. If initial adopters do not perceive the utility of the innovation for both the self and for the wider social system, the practicality of the innovation may be called into question and the adoption process will be terminated. Beta personal video products were not as successfully marketed in the United States as were VHS products; thus, VHS established the critical mass necessary to encourage diffusion via the movie rental market. While Apple computers were marketed successfully to U.S. school systems, and thus began to establish a critical mass of individuals who would grow up using and buying Apple computers, Microsoft has been much more successful in establishing the critical mass of software users worldwide to control much of the computing innovations market. The potential for telecommunications via the personal computer has further justified the diffusion of computing innovations. The commercial utility of the Internet, a relatively old technological process in relation to present-day telecommunications, has created the need for the establishment of a critical mass for various new social systems for the diffusion of new communication products and processes. Just as with the initial adoption of the telephone, the practical utility of communication technologies is nonexistent without the acceptance of a wider audience of adopters. Thus, social systems are persuaded to accept social change and encouraged to adopt potential innovations for the benefit of those who have perceived that making the initial investments in a given technology are worth the risks.

The nature of merging technologies, and thus merging social systems, confounds simple assessment of the diffusion of innovations. Early research indicated that social systems concentrated in cities were more likely to rely on mass media in the diffusion process than those who lived in rural areas, who would rely more on interpersonally communicated information in deciding to accept an innovation. The capabilities of modern telecommunications have blurred the lines of geography, as well as the lines separating mass-mediated and interpersonally communicated information; therefore, identifying specific social systems becomes much more problematic. Furthermore, the layering of the utility of technologies within technologies confounds the ability to determine the rate of adoption for communication systems. Nevertheless, the diffusion of innovations has become an important and useful theoretical perspective for analyzing the effect of communication technologies.

Broad Scope and Appeal of Diffusion Theory

Diffusion of innovations research continues to be a diverse endeavor. Recognizing that diffusion theory is used primarily to explain what has already occurred, some researchers have attempted to create modifications of the theory that would allow its use as a tool for predicting the process of innovation adoption. Thus, diffusion of innovations may provide predictive as well as descriptive analyses of communication events.

Evidence of the effect of diffusion of innovations may be found in a variety of research contexts and disciplines. Diffusion of innovations is a theoretical perspective that has been widely accepted in marketing research. For example, some have noted that marketing research may be ignoring the difference in the adoption of "continuous" innovations versus the adoption of "discontinuous" products. Other contexts where diffusion of innovations theory is represented in research literature include the adoption of health and social services.

In general, the major effect of diffusion of innovations is due to its focus on process. Diffusion of innovations allows communication scholars to focus on the effect of specific channels of communication. The effect of channels influences the process of diffusion and subsequent degrees of adoption of an innovation.

Three important characteristics of the theory appear evident. First, diffusion of innovations truly is a multidisciplinary theory. Second, the theory is pragmatic by definition. In other words, the theory responds well to different research contexts. In fact, the theory, in addition to adapting well to context, depends on context—which is the third characteristic in the contextual nature of the theory. These characteristics may be at once benefits and deficiencies for communication scholars. Diffusion of innovations, as a theoretical perspective, does not belong to communication researchers. The identity of the theory necessarily is diffused into a myriad of specialties. Yet while diffusion of innovations enjoys great popularity beyond the realm of communication research, those interested in the study of communication should find the application of this theoretical perspective practical for the analysis of mass-mediated and interpersonally oriented social systems.

See also: DIFFUSION OF INNOVATIONS AND COMMUNICATION; INTERNET AND THE WORLD WIDE WEB; MARKETING RESEARCH, CAREERS IN; PUBLIC HEALTH CAMPAIGNS; SOCIAL CHANGE AND THE MEDIA.

Bibliography

Allen, David. (1988). "New Telecommunication Services: Network Externalities and Critical Mass." *Telecommunication Policy* 12:257–271.

Backer, Thomas E., and Rogers, Everett M. (1998). "Diffusion of Innovations Theory and Work-Site Aids Programs." *Journal of Health Communication* 3:17–28.

Dearing, James W., and Meyer, Gary. (1994). "An Exploratory Tool for Predicting Adoption Decisions." *Science Communication* 16:43–57.

Lowery, Shearon A., and DeFleur, Melvin L. (1995). *Milestones in Mass Communication Research: Media Effects*, 3rd edition. New York: Longman.

Markus, M. Lynn. (1987). "Toward a 'Critical Mass' Theory of Intensive Media: Universal Access, Interdependence, and Diffusion." *Communication Research* 14:491–511.

Meyer, Marcy; Johnson, David J.: and Ethington, Caroline. (1997). "Contrasting Attributes of Preventive Health Innovations." *Journal of Communication* 47:112–131.

Rogers, Everett M. (1962). *Diffusion of Innovations,* 1st edition. New York: Free Press.

Rogers, Everett M. (1995). *Diffusion of Innovations,* 4th edition. New York: Free Press.

Rogers, Everett M., and Kincaid, D. Lawrence. (1981). *Communication Networks: A New Paradigm for Research.* New York: Free Press.

Rogers, Everett M., and Singhal, Arvind. (1996). "Diffusion of Innovations." In *An Integrated Approach to Communication Theory and Research,* eds. Michael B. Salwen and Don W. Stacks. Mahwah, NJ: LEA.

Ryan, Bryce, and Gross, Neal C. (1943). "The Diffusion of Hybrid Seed Corn in Two Iowa Communities." *Rural Sociology* 8:15–24.

Tarde, Gabriel de. (1903). *The Laws of Imitation.* tr. Elsie Clews Parsons. New York: Holt.

Valente, Thomas W. (1995). *Network Models of the Diffusion of Innovations.* Creskill, NJ: Hampton Press.

MARTIN L. HATTON

■ TECHNOLOGY, PHILOSOPHY OF

As communication technology is invented and adopted, inventors and users alike ponder its meaning and value. Communication technology is very useful but its effect can also trigger both questions and problems. Philosophy provides tools to explore those questions and to solve those problems. Gary Percesepe, in *Philosophy: An Introduction to the Labor of Reason* (1991), states that the tasks of philosophy are to identify, clarify, classify and analyze problems that seem to resist common sense or scientific resolution.

Communication technology is an appropriate area for philosophical exploration. Some philosophers have pondered and even warned of the dangers of scientific and technological developments that ignore or fail to consider human values and the human spirit. Others have pondered the enhancements to the human spirit brought about by science and technology. This entry will apply the four branches of philosophy—logic, epistemology, metaphysics, and axiology—to concerns about communication technology.

Logic

Logic is concerned with thought itself. As a discipline, logic scrutinizes and classifies thought and establishes rules of correct thinking. According to Percesepe, it is indispensable where truth and conceptual clarity are sought. It is an abstract science that people use to think correctly and evaluate their thinking. It is essential to the pursuit of a philosophy of communication technology. Whether the concern is, for example, about the meaning of film editing sequences or gathering evidence about the credibility of a news source, logic and the philosophical questions it invites are relevant to these and many other communication activities. Communication technology must wrestle with the challenges that are involved in assembling content in logical form and then appropriately and logically conveying to audiences the meanings that are contained within that content.

Epistemology

Epistemology examines the nature of knowledge, where knowledge comes from, and the validity and limits of knowledge. This branch of philosophy can be used to explore many aspects of communication technology. For example, computer technology provides the means for generating and collecting knowledge, sending and receiving knowledge, interpreting and applying knowledge, sorting and storing knowledge, and judging whether to save or delete it. A philosophy of communication technology invites many epistemological questions. The techno-skeptic thrives in this realm of exploration. For example, communication technology makes possible the generating of vast amounts of prose and data of all kinds. However, when critical thinking of a philosophical nature is applied by the techno-skeptic to this ever-growing volume of electronically generated information, some of it is considered to have value only as one person's individual expression and is otherwise useless, while other computer-generated information may be of value not just to its creator but to other people as well.

Metaphysics

Metaphysics addresses the nature of reality. Metaphysics can be divided into the philosophy of being (ontology), the philosophy of mind (philosophical anthropology) and the philosophy of religion. One of the questions that metaphysics deals with is the nature of the human person. A philosophy of communication technology could explore such a question since communication and its technical use are unavoidable features of human experience. In addition to the many benefits of communication technology, some undesirable effects can also occur. For example, technology can threaten financial security, eliminate jobs, undermine the skill and dignity of work and the worker, and isolate workers from each other so that it is more difficult to exert collective pressure on employers to improve pay and working conditions. Communication technology can make possible the use of a temporary work force that has little job security and few if any fringe benefits.

Another metaphysical issue is the contrast between freedom and determinism. Marshall McLuhan's "technological determinism" is a prominent example of metaphysical exploration about communication technology. Inventions change culture, he asserted. He pondered the communication inventions of the alphabet, movable type, the telegraph, television, and computers. Changes in communication technology shape human experience, McLuhan asserted through his famous statement, "We shape our tools and they in turn shape us." He believed that people's experience of life is largely a function of how they process information. His perspective included another famous phrase, "the medium is the message." Instead of pondering only the content of a medium, McLuhan challenged individuals to consider the effect of the medium itself. His thinking was that content is influential, but so is the technology that distributes that content.

In the historical aspects of his philosophy, McLuhan's "tribal age" consisted of oral cultures, in which hearing was the dominant reception mode of communication. In his "literate age" the phonetic alphabet changed communication to a more visual experience and made it more linear than holistic, because printed text occurs line by line and the eye follows the text in a straight line across the page. This ear-to-eye switch detaches the person from the tribe/community, yet that person can still participate in a flow of information, a visual flow. Printed communication brought about a shift from collective tribal involvement to private detachment. McLuhan argued that literacy also fostered independent thinking and revolutions, among them the Protestant Reformation and political upheaval in colonial Africa.

McLuhan also posed questions about relationships. He argued that the mass production of books fragmented society and fostered the isolation of readers from one another. Electronic communication, he predicted, would return humankind to a pre-alphabetic oral tradition in which sound and touch dominate in the communication process and foster community. McLuhan envisioned a "global village" of instantaneous electronic connections between people. According to McLuhan devotees, the Internet brings his vision to reality. The Internet can connect individuals with one another, but critics point out that it also can fragment and isolate. The metaphysical debate is just beginning about the changes that the Internet causes in human experience.

Axiology

Axiology pertains to values. Its traditional subdivisions within philosophy are ethics, social and political philosophy, and aesthetics. Ethics is the philosophical discipline that explores the rational grounds for making normative statements (i.e., evaluative judgments of right and wrong). Many questions about the effects of mass media technologies, for example, revolve around ethical questions of good or bad, right or wrong, and healthy or unhealthy.

Social and political philosophy concerns value judgments that are relevant to the relation between the individual and the state. It examines questions such as what justifies the restricting of personal liberties and the difference between moral and legal justice. Communication technologies play a role here as well and generate controversy. For example, a frequently debated philosophical theme is the tension between freedom of expression and attempts at restriction of that expression. The communication technology of the Internet often generates such concerns.

Aesthetics asks questions about beauty and art. Judgments of beauty and art reveal aesthetic values. Aesthetics explores the underlying criteria that inform the normative claims of art as being good or bad or that deem all art to be a relative matter of judgment independent of criteria. Aesthetics also examines the activity of making judgments about art and the role of artists in society. This is relevant to a philosophy of communication technology because communication media are used to produce art, alter it, deliver it, and evaluate it.

Uses of communication technology are not value free. Therefore, a philosophy of technology can help in the exploration of the values on which these technological capabilities are based. Explorations might be in the form of questions such as "Are individuals in the society communally responsible for the good or evil effects of such technology?" or "If technological inventions are the work of powerful elites, then how can a society determine which technological advances to embrace and which paths to follow?"

Another example of philosophical exploration of communication technology comes from the social and political philosopher Jacques Ellul. In pondering the phenomenon of propaganda, Ellul, in *The Technological Society* (1973), examines the role of "psychoanalytic mass techniques" as instruments in the "suppression of the critical faculty, the formation of a good social conscience and the creation of a sphere of the sacred" (p. 370). Propaganda's social effects indicate that a collective experience, a mass experience, is occurring and that "a unifying psychism has come into being" (p. 370). In other words, Ellul contended that many people are persuaded, through a sort of mind control by communication technology, to think the same way about someone or something.

Using both logic and axiology, Ellul's writing offers a critique of advertising. His social and political philosophy offers an ethical judgment and a warning. He considered advertising to be a part of the manifestation of "mass man" and its creation of psychological collectivization that is designed not for "man's welfare" but "just as well for his exploitation" (p. 409). "When psychological techniques, in close cooperation with material techniques, have at last succeeded in creating unity, all possible diversity will have disappeared and the human race will have become a bloc of complete and irrational solidarity" (p. 410).

Conclusion

When communication technologies are introduced and become a part of human experience, they pose many questions and problems that need to be pondered. When people seek understanding about such matters, they are philosophizing.

Philosophy can help when a standard or obvious answer does not seem readily available. Communication technologies pose challenging and novel questions that are not easily answered. The four branches of philosophy—logic, epistemology, metaphysics, and axiology—provide tools with which inventors and users alike can explore the benefits, detriments, consequences, and implications of communication technologies that have become vital and inextricably woven into the human condition. Greater understanding of this ubiquitous and influential facet of daily life is in order in the message-saturated world, and the methods of philosophy contribute to that understanding.

See also: ALPHABETS AND WRITING; DIFFUSION OF INNOVATIONS AND COMMUNICATION; INTERNET AND THE WORLD WIDE WEB; LITERACY; MCLUHAN, HERBERT MARSHALL; PRINTING, HISTORY AND METHODS OF; PROPAGANDA; TECHNOLOGY, ADOPTION AND DIFFUSION OF.

Bibliography

Cross, Gary, and Szostak, Rick. (1995). *Technology and American Society: A History*. Englewood Cliffs, NJ: Prentice-Hall.

Ellul, Jacques. (1973). *The Technological Society*. New York: Knopf.

McLuhan, Marshall. (1964). *Understanding Media*. New York: McGraw-Hill.

McLuhan, Marshall, and Fiore, Quentin. (1967). *The Medium is the Massage: An Inventory of Effects*. New York: Random House.

Percesepe, Gary. (1991). *Philosophy: An Introduction to the Labor of Reason*. New York: Macmillan.

CHARLES F. AUST

■ TELECOMMUNICATIONS, WIRELESS

The explosion of digital technology in the late 1990s began what came to be known as the information age. An important change that was made possible by digital technology was the switching of many kinds of communication from wired devices to wireless devices. Two types of wireless devices have come to the forefront during the digital age: radio-frequency (RF) devices and infrared-emitting (IR) devices.

IR devices are used mainly for indoor applications. In order for an IR device to work, both the transmitter and receiver must "see" each other. The television remote controls that most Americans have in their homes are IR devices. Several companies developed IR devices that do more than change the channel of the television. IR devices can transport video, audio, and data, and they can control functions at amazing speeds.

The infrared light that IR devices use to transport data is long-wavelength light that is beyond the range of human vision. These devices work by sending the digital data, the 1s and 0s, via flashes of light. A flash within a digital word is "on" or "yes," whereas no flash within the same word is "off" or "no." By counting the flashes and non-flashes within a prescribed amount of time, the 8-, 16-, or 24-bit "word" (i.e., byte) can be created. The microprocessor within the receiving device sets the clock speed and decodes the flashes to determine what the user wishes to happen. Computer keyboards, computer mice, digital cameras, and other input devices can use IR to accomplish their mission.

Using RF allows one to travel outside the confines of the home or office. RF signals pass through most walls, work while in motion, deliver more bits per second than IR, and are available almost worldwide. RF can be delivered through transmission towers, satellites, portable transmitter–receivers, and even through the leakage from cable television wires. As more and more ways are thought of to transport information, and the importance of people continuously moving from place to place is acknowledged, RF devices will become more prevalent—while IR will supplement other devices.

Traditionally, these services (e.g., audio, video, data, and control functions) were contained in the wired universe. Coaxial cable was the wire of choice for transporting video (e.g., cable television). Twisted-pair copper wire carried voice traffic and fax traffic over the traditional telephone system. Serial cable carried instructions between computers and their peripheral devices. "Fire-wire" came into being in the late 1990s; this hybrid of coaxial and serial cable allows faster transfer of data than either coaxial or serial. Designed for Apple computers, the PC clone computers soon became able to use Fire-wire to operate. Fire-wire found its first niche in the profes-

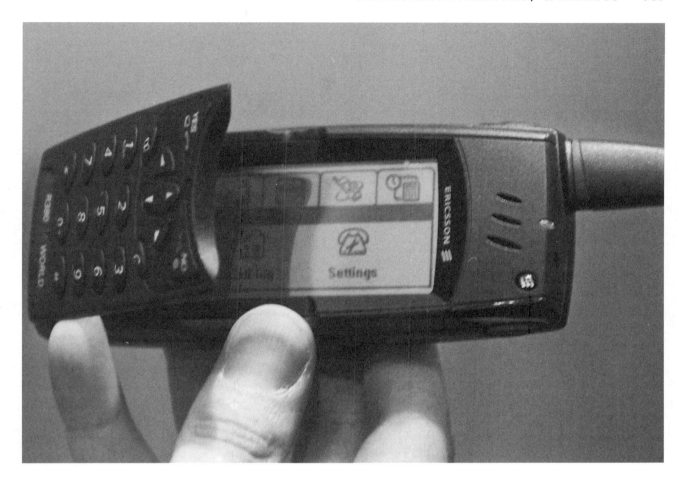

To accommodate the need for an increasing variety of wireless telecommunications devices, Ericsson produced in November 2000 a cell telephone (R380) that can also be used as a personal digital assistant (PDA) to send e-mail and SMS (short message service) messages when the number pad is opened to reveal a touch screen. (Reuters NewMedia Inc./Corbis)

sional audio–video industry. Fire-wire allowed those that edited music and video on their desktops to speed up the transfer from the hard drive to the final storage medium.

Soon thereafter, web-streaming electronics and programs allowed those creative artists to send their creations to others via the World Wide Web. Compression increased the speed of the process and provided a whole new way for listeners and viewers to find their favorite music and video. Just point and click, download, and save, and an individuals could have their favorite music or movie right there on the computer hard drive. One never had to leave home again to purchase entertainment. It was all there, just a mouse-click away.

The computer went wireless too. Wireless modems let web surfers take their laptops with them where they roamed. No more did they have to be connected to a telephone line. All they had to do was power up their modems, dial the number, and they were on the Internet.

The wireless computer uses the same technology as the cell telephone. The cell telephone uses spread-spectrum technology to switch from cell to cell while simultaneously transmitting and receiving.

"Spread-spectrum technology" means that the same device can operate on more than one frequency at the same time. This technology came into being in the 1940s as a way to prevent enemies from jamming the homing mechanisms on U.S. Navy torpedoes. Because the homing device used more than one radio frequency to find its target, the enemy could not confuse the torpedo by flooding one frequency with RF. In order to stop a torpedo, the enemy would have to know all of the frequencies that were being used by the torpedo, in what order the torpedo used those frequencies, and how long the torpedo used each frequency. This was next to impossible.

Cell telephones used the same idea—not to jam enemy torpedoes but to allow a user to travel from one cell to another without losing the telephone call. A cell is just the geographical area that a particular cell tower covers with its three-watt signal. As the user moves beyond the range of one tower, the tower "hands off" the call to the next tower in line that has the strongest signal from the cell telephone. The cells can be thought of as giant invisible circles. If a person stands in one circle, then one tower is used. If the person moves beyond the edge of the circle and enters another circle, then the second tower is used.

The personal communications system (PCS) uses the same technology, only instead of using towers, PCS uses cable television wires and shorter, less powerful one-watt towers to carry a telephone conversation. Digital cable television systems allow many telephone calls to be carried with digital television within the spectrum that is not used by the cable company to carry television. At the cable company office, the call is switched to the traditional telephone company's wires to complete the call.

Satellite telephones work like cell telephones in that they use spread-spectrum technology. Instead of handing off to another tower, the satellite telephone hands off to another satellite. Satellite telephones use low-Earth-orbiting satellites to give the user a dial tone anywhere on the planet. Both the user and the satellites move. As a satellite passes over the horizon, out of "sight" of the telephone, the call is handed off to the next satellite in line. If no satellite is available, then the call is routed through the nearest available cell network. The downside to satellite telephones, at least in the beginning, was the high cost of satellite time. It is expensive to launch and maintain satellites, and this cost was passed on to the user. However, satellite telephones allow one to make calls or to log on to the Internet anytime and anywhere.

All of these devices that had formerly been restricted to wire carriers were liberated by the use of the radio spectrum. However, since the spectrum is used for other purposes, there is less available spectrum for new services. Nicholas Negroponte addressed this new problem with what he called the "Negroponte switch."

The Negroponte switch is the change from wired technology to wireless technology and vice versa. Traditional wired services found their way onto the RF spectrum and RF devices went to wires. The Negroponte switch works on one basic

principle: "bits are bits." The computer or television or telephone or any other device does not care, nor does it know, what the bits are meant to represent. Any device that can pass digital bits and bytes can pass them along. Only at the final destination do the bits get turned into what they are supposed to be. The most important bits, according to Negroponte, are the "header bits." These are bits about bits. These bits tell the output device what they are supposed to be.

The Negroponte switch deals with voice and data, as well as with the way in which people interface with their devices. "Intellisense" is the word that Negroponte created to describe how all household, workplace, and personal devices will communicate with each other to better serve the needs of people. For example, say that an individual wants to get up thirty minutes later than usual. All that person would have to do is set his or her alarm clock. Intellisense would then tell the coffeemaker, the computer, the water heater, the furnace or air-conditioner, the car, and the telephone that the person will be sleeping for an additional thirty minutes. Once this is done, the telephone will not ring during the additional thirty minutes, the coffeemaker will make coffee thirty minutes later than usual, the computer will download any important information that the person might have missed by sleeping late, and the hot water and room temperature will be at their optimum level thirty minutes later than usual. All of this saves the person both trouble and money. A person does not need a warm house or hot water until he or she is ready to get up and shower. If the person is low on milk, the refrigerator will tell the car to remind the person to get some milk on the way home. Or, if the refrigerator is in need of service, it will call the repair service before it breaks down.

When the person goes to work, Intellisense will know where to route incoming telephone calls and e-mail messages. Instruction manuals will be obsolete. Intellisense will tell people how to operate devices. A person will tell the computer/television (according to Negroponte, there will soon be no difference) what news is important, and the device will "filter" the content to suit the viewer's tastes. People will no longer have to remember to program the video recorder or read the television listings to know when to watch a favorite program. People will be able to watch anything, anytime.

When the Negroponte switch becomes the norm, extremely targeted advertising will come directly to individuals through the program content, but they will not know it is advertising; it will be seamless with the program. An individual will become part of the machine. Electronics will be woven into people's clothing. Dick Tracy's two-way wrist television will become reality. A person's belt will contain the batteries to operate all of his or her gear. An individual will be able to access the telephone, the Internet, e-mail, call home, and program home devices from a distance. The only question is how will those signals be passed along to the chosen destination.

Because bits are bits, all of this is possible. The Negroponte switch will allow those media that were once sent over wires (e.g., the telephone) to be sent over the air. Those media that used to be sent through the air (e.g., radio and television) will soon be sent over wires, similar to cable television.

The problem will show itself soon after the switch begins—there is only so much open spectrum that is available to use for all these devices. One day, the usable spectrum will be exhausted. What then? Negroponte suggests that those things that can use wires should continue to do so and that those things that can only use the spectrum should go wireless.

Spectrum saturation was a problem with early cell telephones, which were analog devices that operated in the 800-megahertz (MHz) range. People who had programmable scanners regularly listened in on conversations that took place over cell telephones. The cell telephone industry went to the U.S. Congress to get laws passed to make it illegal to intercept and eavesdrop on cell telephone conversations. That did not do much for those who already had scanners, nor did it stop others from listening to conversations. In the mid-1990s, the cell telephone industry came out with digital cell telephones. These telephones, which sounded clearer than their analog cousins did, were also harder to intercept. Digital cell telephones use header bits to tell the cell telephone tower who the telephone belongs to, who they are calling, and what is going to be traveling over the signal. Voice, data, or other media can be sent over digital cell telephones with a greater degree of privacy than is available with analog cell telephones because the potential interceptor has to be able to know what "channel" and tower the digital cell

Nicholas Negroponte, creator of the Negroponte Switch, spoke with reporters during a press conference in Singapore on November 13, 2000, and said that developing nations are likely to become the dominant players on the Internet as they are pushed by necessity to leap the economic divide. (AFP/Corbis)

telephone is on, along with what the header code is when the conversation is started. Without that information, the scanner is useless. All the listener hears is the digital bits traveling back and forth, not what those bits represent.

Negroponte has stated that as the limited spectrum is taken up by cell telephones, satellite telephones, wireless computers, wireless body wear, and other peripherals, some of these devices will go back to using wires to communicate with each other. Already, the spectrum for pagers and two-way communication (e.g., police, fire, and emergency services radio) is getting squeezed by commercial digital broadcasting and the other users of RF energy. Soon, society will have to find ways to go back to the wired world for those devices that do not need to travel.

These wireless devices give users the freedom to travel about without worrying about missing an important call or message. As with all freedom, a price comes with it. That price is the overflowing river that is the RF spectrum. With the Negroponte switch, all wired services will become wireless and vice versa. The television and the computer will be intertwined into one box. Those individuals who need to be in communication with others all the time will have that opportunity, and they will still be able to roam about outside the home or office. While the "modern" devices will quickly become obsolete, the new ways to communicate and stay in the know have not been thought of yet. One's house and office will know whether one is at home or at work. The building will know where an individual is, where the nearest telephone is located, and what calls an individual must receive. People will program these devices with their voices. The content does not matter. Bits are bits. Only how those bits are moved will change. From an economic standpoint, only those devices that are cheap and easy to operate will survive in this new information age. Consumers will not tolerate anything that is merely an improvement over preexisting technology. Merely redesigning a graphic interface without making it easier or more efficient to operate will not be enough.

Digital devices that bring people information have to be inexpensive, easy to operate, and, ultimately, useful if their creators want to survive in the world of business. Until then, people will use pencil and paper because it is easy. In general, people will watch a fuzzy television and listen to a radio that is full of static because they are more inexpensive than high-definition television and compact disc players. Until the above conditions for digital devices are met, the Negroponte switch will not become a reality.

See also: CABLE TELEVISION, SYSTEM TECHNOLOGY OF; DIGITAL COMMUNICATION; DIGITAL MEDIA SYSTEMS; INTERNET AND THE WORLD WIDE WEB; RADIO BROADCASTING, TECHNOLOGY OF; SATELLITES, COMMUNICATION; SATELLITES, TECHNOLOGY OF; TELEPHONE INDUSTRY, TECHNOLOGY OF; TELEVISION BROADCASTING, TECHNOLOGY OF.

Bibliography

Dertouzos, Michael L. (1997). *What Will Be: How the New World of Information Will Change Our Lives.* New York: Harper.

Gershenfeld, Neil A. (1999). *When Things Start to Think.* New York: Henry Holt.

Negroponte, Nicholas. (1995). *Being Digital.* New York: Knopf.

Papert, Seymour A. (1996). *The Connected Family: Bridging the Digital Generation Gap*, with forward by Nicholas Negroponte. Atlanta, GA: Longstreet Press.

ERIC E. HARLAN

■ TELECOMMUNICATIONS ACT OF 1996

The Communications Act of 1934 brought the telephone, telegraph, and the then-fledgling broadcasting industry under the control of the newly created Federal Communications Commission (FCC). The U.S. Congress reasoned that because the radio spectrum was a permanent resource, owned by the citizens of the United States, representatives of the federal government should regulate those that sought to exploit this resource for profit. The 1934 act governed the licensing, operation, and conduct of the broadcast industry for more than sixty-two years.

History

The FCC and its predecessor, the Federal Radio Commission, designed and enforced a system of frequency allocation and transmission regulation to assure the maximum availability of radio service to Americans. When the 1934 act was passed, AM (amplitude modulation) radio was king. Over the years, various amendments were added to the 1934 act as Congress tried to keep up with newly discovered radio spectrum, new transmitting and receiving devices, and the tastes of the American people. For example, when FM (frequency modulation) radio came into being in the 1940s, the FCC attempted to regulate the new service in a manner that would be in the public interest.

Beginning in 1947, the television industry slowly usurped radio's dominance of the American public's in-home entertainment. To make sure that all Americans could have equal access to television signals, the FCC asked Congress to amend the 1934 act to create a broadcast standard for television, and, later, for color television. When color television became the norm, the FCC required stations to continue to broadcast a "compatible" signal that could be viewed on a monochrome (black-and-white) television—a rule that is still in effect.

The 1960s and 1970s saw the FCC move into the Equal Employment Opportunity Act arena with its regulation of broadcast stations. The commission's equal employment opportunity rules said that the workforce of a television or radio station had to reflect the percentage of minorities located within the city of license. At least 50 percent of the full-time workers and 25 percent of the part-time staff had to reflect this ethnic diversity.

The Communications Act of 1934 also delved into the programming area, with limited regulations that dealt with the content of broadcasts. Obscene and indecent material was banned from the airwaves at times when children could be viewing or listening. A "safe-harbor" was created during the late-night and early-morning hours, when children were less likely to be viewing or listening, so that stations could broadcast their more adult-oriented programs.

In the early 1990s, it became clear to Congress and the FCC that the 1934 act was inadequate to regulate the new technologies that were changing the role of broadcasting and other media. There were wireless devices (e.g., cell phones), cable television, satellite television, the Internet, and other new digital ways to communicate that were not even in the realm of science-fiction in 1934. Thus, the FCC, with the help of Congress, drafted the Telecommunications Act of 1996. This act is supposed to work with the newly emerging technologies in the same way that the Communications Act of 1934 worked with the early radio and television technologies.

Regulations and Deregulations

The Telecommunications Act of 1996, which amends the Communications Act of 1934 to reflect technological change, is an omnibus law that regulates most of the electronic communication technologies that are in existence, as well as others that are still in development. The following is a list of new regulations and deregulations that are present in the act as it was formulated by the FCC and by Congress and as it pertains to the broadcasting industry. They are presented in the order in which the FCC implemented the key portions of the act.

Access by People with Disabilities

As mandated by the Americans with Disabilities Act, the FCC becomes the sole arbitrator of disputes that deal with disabled people and their access to telecommunications. Broadcast stations are required to give access to disabled people, making any required physical changes to their facilities to allow disabled people to use the facilities. The act created the Architectural and Transportation Board to mediate disputes of this nature.

Market Entry Barriers

The FCC is required under the act to identify and eliminate barriers that prevent entrepreneurs and other small businesses from participating in the ownership of telecommunications services and information services or the provision of parts of those services. Every three years, the FCC is required to report to Congress on the outcome of their review of regulations that are to eliminate barriers, and they must recommend statutory remedies for those barriers.

Broadcast Spectrum Flexibility

The biggest news in television broadcasting is the change from the National Television Standards Committee (NTSC) television standard to digital television. The 1996 act gives existing television stations a timetable in which to convert their broadcast facilities to digital, and this timetable depends on the market size. The act also gives television stations another channel for their digital broadcasts until a certain percentage of their market purchases digital television receiving equipment. After that threshold is reached, the stations must give back their old analog channel. The old channel will then be used for other services, such as two-way communication and wireless phones.

One of the advantages of digital broadcasting for broadcasters is the ability to operate more than one service within the new channel. If the television station does not broadcast in high-definition television (HDTV), then that leaves spectrum for other, or ancillary, services. These ancillary services can take the form of other television programs, Internet access, or subscription services. The 1996 act allows stations to use these ancillary services; however, if they choose to use them, the act states that the stations must pay a user fee to the FCC for the use of the public spectrum for profitable services other than advertisements. This fee can amount to what the FCC could have collected had the agency charged a licensure fee for those services in the first place. This provision is being challenged by the broadcasting industry.

Broadcast Ownership

Depending on the size of the market that a broadcast group serves, the number of radio stations one group can own has greatly increased. Before, to ensure a "diversity of voices," broadcasters were severely limited in the number of stations that they could own. Under the 1996 act, this has changed. In large markets, an entity can own up to eight stations, so long as no more than five are of the same service (AM or FM). In medium markets, up to seven stations can be owned so long as no more than four are of the same service. In small markets, five stations can be owned so long as no more than three are of the same service. However, no entity can own more than 50 percent of the stations in any given market. In addition, the FCC may permit an entity to maintain interest in a broadcast station, so long as the station will increase the number of radio stations in operation in a market (as long as the new stations have the room in the spectrum to broadcast without interfering with an existing broadcaster). In other words, if an entity is in danger of exceeding the limits, it is in the entity's best interest to encourage another station to enter the market—if there is room in the spectrum.

Television Ownership Limitation

An entity can own as many television stations as it wants, so long as the total audience served does not exceed 35 percent of the national audience. Still to be resolved is whether or not the same entity can own more than one television station in a single market that is not among the top fifty markets. The one-to-a-market rule has been waived in the top fifty markets. The prohibition of cross-ownership of a television station and a cable system that serve the same market has been dropped.

Over-the-Air Reception Devices

The FCC has preempted local zoning regulations of satellite Earth stations. That means that local governments can no longer prohibit residents from putting up satellite dishes in their yards or on their houses.

Cable Reform

The act established so-called uniform rate structures that apply to cable systems that are not subject to competition from other cable, or wireless cable, systems. However, this structure does not apply to pay-per-view or subscription channels. It makes the FCC the arbitrator of complaints that deal with rate structure, declaring "predatory pricing" illegal. Predatory pricing is the offering of discounts on some aspects of cable service to entice potential customers from a competing cable company and then raising the rates after the customer has switched cable services. In franchise areas of fifty thousand subscribers or less, the basic service pricing rules do not apply. The act's cable reform also requires that cable equipment be compatible with televisions and video recorders that are owned by the consumer. Also, the equipment that makes the televisions and video recorders compatible should not interfere with features of other electronic equipment. One other aspect of the cable reform portion of the act permits cable franchises to pass aggregation of equipment costs along to subscribers to help pay for upgrades to the cable system—so long as people who subscribe to only the "basic tier" service are not charged for the equipment used to view that service. The cable box that is used by the viewer to navigate the cable channels can be purchased at vendors that are not affiliated with the cable company, so long as such devices have not been altered to allow the home viewer to watch subscription services without paying for that service.

The 1996 act also requires broadcasters and cable channels to include closed captioning for hearing-impaired viewers. The FCC will eventually require a separate video description channel, within the digital channels, for those viewers who are blind.

The most publicized television portion of the Telecommunications Act of 1996 deals with the "V-chip" requirements for manufacturers and broadcasters. The first part of the act required broadcasters and cable casters to place a rating in the upper left-hand corner of the television screen to alert the viewer about the content of each program. The V-chip, or violence chip, is to be included in the electronics of the set. Broadcasters and cable casters are required to send an encoded, invisible, and inaudible signal with the beginning of each program. This signal communicates with the V-chip and tells it what the program rating is. Parents can then program the television set to not display programs that have ratings beyond a preselected threshold. That way, absent parents can control what their children watch without being in the room. The V-chip is to be included in all sets that have a measurement of thirteen inches or larger.

Beyond broadcasting, the act gives the FCC exclusive jurisdiction to regulate the direct-to-home satellite industry. The FCC has given the direct-to-home satellite industry permission to rebroadcast local stations into television markets where before they were forbidden. The act also contains numerous changes in the regulation of the telephone industry. These changes are designed to allow greater competition among local telephone services, long-distance services, and cable services in providing their customers with Internet access and new kinds of digital voice and video transmission.

Conclusion

As with the Communications Act of 1934, the Telecommunications Act of 1996 was intended to be flexible, so that the FCC and other regulatory agencies can keep up with communications technology that changes every day. The Telecommunications Act of 1996 will allow consumers the freedom to choose the source of their entertainment and information, and it ensures that the broadcasting, cable, and satellite industries will remain viable and competitive well into the twenty-first century.

See also: BROADCASTING, GOVERNMENT REGULATION OF; COMMUNICATIONS ACT OF 1934; FEDERAL COMMUNICATIONS COMMISSION; RATINGS FOR TELEVISION PROGRAMS; TELECOMMUNICATIONS, WIRELESS; V-CHIP.

Bibliography

Aufderheide, Patricia. (1999). *Communications Policy and the Public Interest: The Telecommunications Act of 1996*. New York: Guilford.

Emeritz, Bob, ed. (1996). *The Telecommunications Act of 1996: Law and Legislative History*. Bethesda, MD: Pike & Fischer.

National League of Cities. (1996). *The Telecommunications Act of 1996: What It Means to Local Governments*. Washington, DC: National League of Cities.

Reams, Bernard D., and Manz, William H., eds. (1997). *Federal Telecommunications Law: A Legislative History of the Telecommunications Act of 1996*, 21 vols. Buffalo, NY: William S. Hein.

ERIC E. HARLAN

▌■ TELEPHONE INDUSTRY

From 1877 to 1984, the public switched telephone network (PSTN) in the United States was operated as a virtual monopoly by American Telephone & Telegraph (AT&T). Since 1984, the industry has experienced tremendous change as technology and government policy have combined to introduce competition and to expand the scope of the industry beyond the provision of local and long-distance telephone service. During its second century, the telephone industry will continue to evolve into a full-service information utility, capable of delivering telephone, data, and interactive video among other services—part of what David Goff (2000, p. 242) characterizes as "a massive transformation of global information and communication facilities."

The First Telephone Century

Alexander Graham Bell launched the first Bell Telephone Company in 1877, and the firm quickly established local telephone exchanges on the East Coast from Washington, D.C., northward. In order to connect the growing number of local exchanges, a system of "long lines" was established under a subsidiary called the American Telephone & Telegraph Company. Throughout most of the twentieth century, the Bell System built the national telephone network by creating a system of local-exchange carriers operated by twenty-two Bell operating companies and interconnected by AT&T's long-distance service. At first, independent (non-AT&T) local telephone operations were denied access to AT&T's long lines, and the company used its powerful position to acquire attractive independents to become new regional Bell operating companies. David Atkin (1998) notes that the U.S. Department of Justice threatened antitrust action against AT&T in 1913, resulting in the Kingsberry Commitment (named for the company vice-president who drafted it), whereby AT&T pledged to interconnect independent telephone companies.

The 1920s saw the emergence of radio broadcasting, and AT&T entered this new communications industry for a time. However, a series of legal disputes with other broadcasting firms distracted AT&T from its core business and once again attracted unwanted government scrutiny. As a result, AT&T sold its broadcasting properties, but continued to serve the new industry profitably by providing leased lines from the Long Lines Division for networking. The Communications Act of 1934 placed regulation of the common-carrier telephone industry and broadcasting under the same agency, the Federal Communications Commission (FCC). The administration of President Franklin D. Roosevelt set the goal of providing universal telephone service in the United States and promised AT&T immunity from antitrust action in order to achieve this goal.

AT&T was able to provide near-universal telephone service through a system of cross-subsidies. Business and long-distance customers were charged at a rate higher than the cost of service, while residential customers were generally charged at rates lower than the cost of service. In addition, urban customers were overcharged for their service, while rural customers were undercharged. Government seemed to view these cross-subsidies as a fair exchange for universal service and considered AT&T to be a "natural monopoly." Nonetheless, the U.S. Department of Justice sought to break up the company in the 1940s, but the effort was ended with a negotiated final judgment in 1956. AT&T aggressively resisted the attachment to its network of any device not approved (manufactured) by AT&T. Between 1956 and 1969, AT&T lost several legal battles against firms with new or competing technologies, including a 1969 case that gave upstart long-distance service MCI the authority to connect to the AT&T network.

The Breakup of AT&T

By the mid-1970s, AT&T, the largest company in the world, was increasingly regarded as inefficient and anticompetitive, and its once-protected monopoly status was seen as a detriment to the future of the telephone network. In 1974, the U.S. Department of Justice determined to break apart this corporate giant. In 1982, AT&T and the Department of Justice reached a negotiated settlement, technically a modification of final judgment (MFJ) from the 1956 proceeding.

Under the terms of the MFJ, the twenty-two Bell operating companies were reorganized into seven regional Bell operating companies (RBOCs): Bell Atlantic, NYNEX, BellSouth, Ameritech, US West, Pacific Telesis, and Southwestern Bell. These RBOCs, or "Baby Bells," were authorized to operate local-exchange carriers, but they could not provide long-distance service beyond the markets within each firm's territory. In addition, the RBOCs were prohibited from offering video (cable) or information services. AT&T retained its long-dis-

tance franchise, subject to competition, and was forbidden to enter the local services market.

In the aftermath of the AT&T divestiture, the cost of long-distance service has declined, initially due to the ending of cross-subsidies, and later due to aggressive competition in this sector. Generally, the cost of local service increased immediately after the divestiture, with the largest increases experienced by rural customers. Competition in local telephone service remains limited.

Convergence, the Internet, and the Telecommunications Act of 1996

By the 1990s, a shift from analog to digital communication technologies was well under way within the telephone industry. With digital technology, all information takes the same form, a code composed of bits or binary digits (0 or 1). Nicolas Negroponte (1995, p. 18) describes this phenomenon elegantly with the phrase "bits are bits." Any technology that can process or transfer digital data can handle digital representations of text, graphics, sounds, video, or other computer data. "Convergence" is the term used to describe the digital-era erosion of the technical boundaries that used to define and separate communications and media technologies and industries.

Digital signals are considered to be technically superior because they are less subject to electrical interference and signal loss than the analog variety. Both AT&T and the Baby Bells developed and employed digital technology from the 1950s onward. However, the legacy that PSTN built during AT&T's first century remains a substantially analog network designed to optimize voice traffic. In the digital era, the telephone industry has found it both necessary and profitable to adapt its vast national and global infrastructure to carry both digital data and analog voice signals. This process of change is both a cause and effect of a large-scale restructuring of the telephone industry.

The euphoric vision of an "information superhighway" emerged in the United States in the early 1990s as politicians and others began to consider the potential of digital information technologies. The emergence and growth of the public Internet after 1994 gave substance to the vision. The desire of government to enable the development of advanced information technologies and the skill of corporate and industry lobbyists combined to create the Telecommunications Act of

1996. As Wilson Dizard (1997, p. 132) describes it, "the law drastically reduced, and in many cases eliminated, the regulatory barriers between telephony, cable TV, satellites, and broadcasting in ways that permitted open competition among all digitally based services." For the telephone industry, the net effect of convergence, the Internet, and the Telecommunications Act of 1996 has been a major transformation, as firms attempt to become full-service information utilities and as new competitors enter the fray.

In the aftermath of the AT&T divestiture and the Telecommunications Act of 1996, wireline telephone services are currently provided by firms from two sectors of the telephone industry: the incumbent local-exchange carriers (ILECs) and the competitive local-exchange carriers (CLECs).

The Telephone Industry Transformed

In *Trends in Telephone Service*, the Federal Communications Commission (1999) reported $246 billion in U.S. telephone industry revenue for 1998. Local service generated $104.6 billion plus another $10.6 billion for toll (long-distance) calls handled within local-service areas. Long-distance services generated $94 billion, and wireless had grown to $36.8 billion. In the United States, 104.8 million households (94%) subscribe to telephone service, with each household spending an average of $809 annually (in 1997).

The ILECs, generally the RBOCs, remain a dominant force in the telephone industry. Atkin (1998) reports that the Baby Bells control 98 percent of local telephone service in the United States. A hands-off regulatory approach by the government since 1996 allowed mergers and acquisitions to reduce the number of RBOCs to four: Bell Atlantic, SBC Communications, BellSouth, and US West. In 1999, Bell Atlantic acquired the largest non-Bell local carrier, GTE, and renamed the company Verizon. US West was acquired by Qwest Communications in 2000. Despite the intent of the Telecommunications Act of 1996 to open all telephone markets to competition, the ILECs have maintained control over their core businesses, creating what both competitors and regulators call "the last mile bottleneck."

Within their local strongholds, the ILECs operate with a mixture of digital and analog technology. The consolidation that reduced the number of major ILECs has contributed to economies

of scale and scope that facilitate the rebuilding of networks with optical fiber and other advanced technologies that these firms will require to become full-service information utilities, offering telephone, Internet, business data services, and video to subscribers. Sequential digital improvements in the local loop have generated new revenues for local-service providers from such services as caller ID, call waiting, three-way calling, call return, and repeat dialing. However, much of the local loop is composed of twisted-pair copper wire, an analog transmission medium that dates back to the beginning of the industry.

Prior to the 1990s, the incumbents were the only option available to businesses needing data networking services. The ILECs initiated integrated services digital network (ISDN) service for smaller businesses, and faster (and more expensive) T-1 lines to meet the needs of larger institutions. However, the data needs of businesses grew exponentially during the 1990s, and the emergence and growth of the Internet meant that a growing number of residential and small-business subscribers would need digital data connections as well. Goff (2000) reports that the existing network of the ILECs represents a $250 billion investment. Rebuilding this infrastructure to digital standards will take years. As a result, a new, second-generation type of telephone company, the CLEC, has emerged.

While most indeed offer local (and long-distance) telephone services, CLECs emerged in the digital era to provide modern data services at competitive prices. As Goff (2000, p. 248) describes them, "CLECs are free to pursue markets opportunistically and typically target businesses (the traditional cash cows of the ILECs) in high-tech markets and larger cities where faster return on investment can be found." Firms such as WorldCom, Nextlink, Qwest, Williams, and ICG are building new, broadband, high-speed, packet-switched fiber networks, the "fat pipes" that are capable of carrying the growing volume of data traffic generated by businesses. These firms are also developing and operating the fiber backbone networks that speed huge volumes of digital data (including Internet data) between domestic and international business capitals.

Because the business market is so lucrative, the large-data CLECs have shown very little interest in residential telephone services. However, the tight

In November 1999, MCI/Worldcom President and CEO Bernard Ebbers (left) and Sprint Chairman and CEO William Esery testified before the Senate Judiciary Committee because U.S. lawmakers who were examining a proposed merger between the companies expressed strong fears that the proposed combination would harm consumers by reducing long-distance telephone competition. (Reuters NewMedia Inc./Corbis)

control of the residential market by the ILECs is being challenged by competing technologies.

The cable television industry has strong potential to develop competitive telephone services and to play a role as a CLEC. Cable systems are wired with coaxial cable, a transmission medium with a large signal-carrying capacity, and cable "passes" 97 percent of U.S. households. However, cable systems were built to send signals in only one direction, and like the ILECs, the cable industry must replace analog technology with digital. Still, the per-household cost of rebuilding cable systems to function as full-service information utilities is substantially less than the cost of rebuilding the PSTN to an equivalent level of technology. Many of the leading cable firms (including Cox Communications, MediaOne, and Time-Warner) offer telephone services in selected markets. AT&T, the nation's largest long-distance company, purchased Tele-Communications Inc., the nation's largest cable multiple system owner, in 1998. This acquisition will enable AT&T

to offer local telephone service in many parts of the United States and reduce its payment of access fees to local telephone companies for their role in completing long-distance calls.

The greatest challenge to the dominance of local wireline telephone service is posed by the wireless telephone industry. This new service began as (analog) cellular telephone service in 1984. Initially, two cellular franchises were awarded in each market area with one reserved for the local wireline company. Digital wireless service was initiated in 1994 with the introduction of personal communications services (PCS), a higher frequency variant of cellular technology. By late 1999, there were eighty-three million wireless subscribers in the United States, and wireless revenue was near the $50 billion level.

Portability helped this technology catch on quickly in the business community, particularly among business people on the move. Many also recognized the value of a wireless telephone as an emergency link from the car, briefcase, purse, or backpack. As the price of wireless service declined and wireless telephones became smaller, they began to appear everywhere. Despite the rapid growth of wireless services in United States, America still lags behind European countries in the percentage of wireless users. One major reason is that in the United States, wireless subscribers pay to both send and receive calls, whereas in Europe the cost of a wireless call is borne by the sender. In addition, roaming charges, additional fees that are assessed when wireless subscribers venture outside of their service provider's territory, represent a cost that is not incurred with wireline service.

In many U.S. markets, wireless telephony is very competitive, with two cellular and as many as six PCS firms vying for market share. Some of the nation's largest wireless operators, major long-distance services (e.g., AT&T, Sprint, Nextel), offer flat-rate pricing plans for local and long-distance service without roaming fees. In this way, wireless services escape franchise territories and become national in scope. In the competitive wireless market, flat-rate pricing and the elimination of roaming charges are practices that are expected to spread.

The introduction of digital PCS technology had a positive effect on the older, analog cellular services. Rather than fading away, the cellular systems converted to digital technology and developed the ability to offer basically the same range of services as digital PCS, including advanced telephone services, paging, fax, and data (even Internet) services. Increasingly, additional devices such as laptop computers and personal digital assistants (PDAs) are being interfaced with wireless technology. As the range of wireless services continues to improve and the cost continues to become more competitive with wireline rates, it is expected that a growing number of telephone users will disconnect from wireline systems and use wireless to meet all of their telephone service needs.

As the twenty-first century began, the often-chaotic transformation of the telephone industry was continuing. Several trends were clear, however. First, the packet-switching technology of the Internet will increasingly become the preferred switching technology of the industry. The CLECs have exploited this technology, and the ILECs must continue to integrate packet switching within networks designed for a different approach (circuit switching). Second, an increasing share of telephone-related services will migrate to wireless technologies and wireless will challenge wireline businesses for market share. Residential consumers should have more choices of both technologies and providers. The predicted information utility, a single two-way connection carrying telephone, video, and data, will become a reality, but the likely provider is yet to be determined, with telephone companies, cable firms, wireless providers, satellite systems, and even electric utilities competing in this sector.

See also: BELL, ALEXANDER GRAHAM; CABLE TELEVISION; COMMUNICATIONS ACT OF 1934; DIGITAL COMMUNICATION; FEDERAL COMMUNICATIONS COMMISSION; INTERNET AND THE WORLD WIDE WEB; TELECOMMUNICATIONS, WIRELESS; TELECOMMUNICATIONS ACT OF 1996; TELEPHONE INDUSTRY, HISTORY OF; TELEPHONE INDUSTRY, REGULATION OF; TELEPHONE INDUSTRY, TECHNOLOGY OF.

Bibliography

Atkin, David. (1998) "Local and Long Distance Telephony." In *Communication Technology Update,* 6th edition, eds. August E. Grant and Jennifer H. Meadows. Boston: Focal Press.

Baldwin, Thomas F.; McVoy, D. Stevens; and Steinfeld, Charles. (1996). *Convergence: Integrating Media, Information & Communication.* Thousand Oaks, CA: Sage Publications.

Bittner, John R. (1991). *Broadcasting and Telecommunication: An Introduction,* 3rd edition. Englewood Cliffs, NJ: Prentice-Hall.

Dizard, Wilson P., Jr. (1989). *The Coming Information Age: An Overview of Technology, Economics, and Politics,* 3rd edition. New York: Longman.

Dizard, Wilson P., Jr. (1997). *Meganet: How the Global Communications Network Will Connect Everyone on Earth.* Boulder, CO: Westview Press.

Federal Communications Commission. (1999). *Trends in Telephone Service.* Washington, DC: U.S. Government Printing Office.

Goff, David H. (2000). "Issues of Internet Infrastructure." In *Understanding the Web: Social, Political, and Economic Dimensions of the Internet,* eds. Alan B. Albarran and David H. Goff. Ames: Iowa State University Press.

Negroponte, Nicholas. (1995). *Being Digital.* New York: Vintage Books.

DAVID H. GOFF

TELEPHONE INDUSTRY, HISTORY OF

One of the greatest factors in shaping the modern age may well have been the evolution of the telephone industry. The roots of the communication age are found in the history of that evolution, primarily in the United States, and particularly in developments created by one company: American Telephone & Telegraph (AT&T).

Early Organization

The telephone industry was not the first to use electricity as the fundamental basis of a communication medium. Telegraphy had been firmly established in the United States and much of the industrialized world before efforts began in the late 1870s to develop telephony as the primary telecommunications industry in the United States. Furthermore, Alexander Graham Bell's technical innovations and U.S. patents in telephony should not overshadow the fact that others deserve as much or more credit for invention of the telephone. Although Europe was slow to adopt the telephone, Germany deserves more credit for its invention than the United States, due to Philip Reis's efforts in 1861. Nevertheless, most subsequent technological innovations that have led to the modern state of the telecommunications industry have been the by-product of Bell's vision and organization. While technological developments and regulatory processes have been key influences in the evolution of the telephone industry, the pivotal force motivating this history has always been economics.

AT&T's history, which has provided the context for all other developments in the telecommunications industry, can easily be divided into two distinct periods. The first period extends from the founding of Bell's company in 1877 to its legally mandated divestiture in 1982 (in spite of its claims to be a natural monopoly). The second period involves the post-1982 history of the company.

The first period in the history of the Bell System may be divided further into three separate periods leading to the establishment of the AT&T monopoly. The first is the period from 1877 to 1900, which may be best identified in terms of the Bell System's effort to control all aspects of the telephone product. The second is the period from 1900 to 1925, which involves the evolution of AT&T, the company's focus on an expanding infrastructure, and the original meaning of universal service. The third period, from 1925 to 1982, is related to the events that eventually challenged the company's identity as a natural monopoly.

The origin of the telephone industry is best explained through the Bell System's progression throughout North America via control of product development. Bell received four of his U.S. patents between 1875 and 1877. One of Bell's original financial supporters for development of the telephone was Gardiner Hubbard, who eventually became Bell's father-in-law and was one of the founding members and the first trustee of the Bell System. The original Bell System was designed to protect Bell's telephone patents and to control the use of all patented equipment. The first commercial organization of the Bell System was an agreement signed by Bell, Hubbard, and George Sanders on February 27, 1875, called the "Bell Patent Association." Hubbard's business experience influenced the concept of the Bell organization. Before he became associated with Bell, Hubbard had worked as an attorney for the Gordon-McKay Shoe Machinery Company. Hubbard applied the shoe company's practice of leasing equipment and receiving royalties for products created by that equipment to the business strategy of the Bell Telephone Company (formally established on August 4, 1877). In other words, each telephone service provider in a local market would pay fees to the company for use of the Bell telephone patents. Telephone customers would buy only service from providers. Bell essentially owned and controlled the hardware. Thus, the first phase in the establishment of a Bell telephone monopoly through vertical integration had begun.

The need to continue product innovation was recognized during this early phase of organization. Thomas Watson, essential to Bell for product development during the original patent applications, had been brought into the organization exclusively for product development. Yet Bell's greatest rival for patent rights and the evolving telephone industry, Western Union Telegraph Company, had strong ties to the Western Electric Manufacturing Company, the largest producer of electronic products in the United States. It was through Western Electric that Western Union chal-

Alexander Graham Bell obtained a patent for his telephone transmitter and receiver in 1876. (Underwood & Underwood/Corbis)

lenged Bell's patents and exclusive rights to the telephone. Elisha Gray, who applied for a caveat as a precursor to a telephone patent on the same day as Bell's patent was filed, was an employee of Western Electric. Western Union formed the American Speaking Telephone Company on December 6, 1877, using the associated talents of innovators such as Gray and Thomas Edison and the production capabilities of Western Electric.

The eventual confrontation between Bell and Western Union concerning exclusive rights to telephone licensing and production led to an out-of-court settlement in 1879. Bell had opened the first U.S. commercial exchange in New Haven, Connecticut, in 1878, and by 1879, he had established several more local exchanges throughout the United States and Canada. The Bell System reorganized under the name American Bell Telephone on March 20, 1880. The company barely had survived with little working capital during its first years of operation, yet the philosophy of competition through product development and control remained firmly rooted in the Bell business strategy. American Bell began to recognize the value in interexchange, or "long distance," telephony during the 1880s, and it formed a subsidiary company on February 28, 1885, the American

Telephone & Telegraph Company, to develop long-distance service. The acquisition of Western Electric from Western Union, however, gave the Bell System the foundation it needed to maintain control over product innovation. On November 26, 1881, the newly named Western Electric Company took over the research and product manufacturing unit of the Bell System under the supervision of Watson. Most essential technological developments leading to the modern telecommunications infrastructure have their origins in Bell System's acquisition of Western Electric. Subsequently, Bell System's research and development helped to establish the financial base that the company would need for further expansion.

The financial benefits of owning its own product development unit allowed the Bell System to focus on widening its market influence in one other way. Western Union had given the Bell System a part of its customer base in the 1879 settlement. The Bell System was based on the control of several exchanges throughout the North American continent. Bell attempted to gain European control for his company, but Edison beat Bell by establishing the Edison Telephone Company of Great Britain, Ltd., in 1878. Furthermore, Western Union controlled most of the wired infrastructure throughout the United States, essentially isolating the local exchanges that were controlled by the Bell System. Ironically, while Bell's vision for the telephone was the point-to-point use by the average customer, Edison and others thought that the device would be too expensive and complicated for an international, or even a national, telephone system to evolve. As in Europe, many in the United States thought that the telegraph would remain the only true communication network. Hubbard actually refused to finance much of Bell's early development of the telephone, believing instead that telegraphy would remain more profitable. Nevertheless, from 1880 to 1884, the Bell System began establishing long-distance lines that connected major cities throughout the New England area. While intercity telephony grew relatively slowly throughout the 1880s, perhaps due to the initially slow expansion of urbanization, the apparent financial benefits of connecting local exchanges through "long lines" motivated another change in strategy and corporate restructuring of the Bell System.

The AT&T Monopoly and Technical Advances in Telephony

AT&T became the parent company and long distance became the focus of the Bell System in 1900 due to several factors, including public fears that the company practiced unfair business practices in the local exchange market, technological advances that allowed for greater interconnectivity, and the leadership of Theodore Vail. Vail, related to Samuel Morse's associate Alfred Vail, accepted the position of general manager of the Bell Telephone Company in 1878. Vail was put in charge of AT&T in 1885 but resigned as the company's president in 1887. Vail's return to AT&T in 1907 is considered the true origin of the modern telecommunications industry. While Vail's conception of universal service at affordable rates proved to be a great marketing strategy with the public, it also would continue to redefine the logical progression of the entire industry. AT&T's interests in Western Electric were reorganized, and that division was renamed Bell Telephone Laboratories in 1925. Also in 1925, Vail's vision for AT&T's complete control of a national infrastructure was generally accepted throughout the Bell System. Frequently challenged but essentially unchanged until 1982, the corporate structure of

AT&T was well established by 1925. AT&T led a corporate structure that included the original Bell operating companies and Bell Laboratories. AT&T became the world's largest business enterprise, a fact that led to the U.S. Department of Justice (DOJ) challenging its operation as a highly integrated corporate monopoly.

Many technological advances by AT&T and others improved the marketability and led to expansion of the telephone industry between 1925 and 1982. In 1951, Bell competitor General Telephone and Electronics Corporation (GTE) developed direct distance dialing (DDD), which gave telephone customers the ability to dial a long-distance number directly without the facilitation of a switchboard operator. However, direct-dialing technology was not widely accepted throughout the telephone industry until the late 1960s. Commercial international telephony between Europe and North America began in 1927 via radio telephony service established by the British Post Office and AT&T. The first intercontinental submarine telephone cable between Europe and North America was opened for service in 1956. In 1962, Arthur C. Clark's vision of the communication satellite was realized when *Telstar* became operational. *Telstar*, developed by Bell Laboratories, was nothing more than a microwave relay device. It is therefore ironic that microwave technology and the transistor, also developed by Bell Laboratories, indirectly put an end to AT&T's monopoly over the telephone industry. Other important technological firsts that were essential to the evolution of the telephone industry include *Intelsat 1*, which was a communication satellite that linked Europe with North America in 1965.

AT&T helped to establish almost all of the advances in telecommunications technology and used the strategy of monopoly to control the implementation of each innovation by the telephone infrastructure. Yet these technology-driven innovations pushed reconsideration of the industry's structure and viability as a natural monopoly. Competitive forces increased pressure to destroy the Bell System's control over the industry with each wave of technological advances. In 1949, the DOJ filed suit against AT&T for its dominance over product development. The suit was settled in 1956 with AT&T's agreement to stay out of new product developments and sales that included innovations such as computer technology. Also in

In Atlanta, Georgia, on April 20, 1983, American Telephone & Telegraph held its 98th and last annual meeting before the company's divestiture. (Bettmann/Corbis)

1965, the U.S. government, through the Federal Communications Commission (FCC), ordered AT&T to allow customers the right to attach non-AT&T electronic, devices to their telephones as long as these devices would not interfere with the telephone system. The FCC, which was established as the U.S. telecommunications regulatory agency through the enactment of the Communications Act of 1934, tended to approach telephone industry regulation based on a concept of universal service not necessarily intended by Vail in 1907. For the FCC, universal service meant universal access. In other words, instead of taking the perspective of AT&T's drive for expansion and total interconnectivity, the FCC tended to address universal service as the consumer's need for access to an essential facility for daily living.

By 1966, the U.S. government and the FCC began looking into possibilities of merging telecommunications and computer technology in the "Computer Inquiry I" review. While the benefits of merging the technologies became clear, the FCC realized that encouraging the unregulated development of computer-based services with regulated telecommunications services would be difficult. The FCC's 1968 Carterfone decision extended the 1965 ruling, allowing electronic equipment not produced by Bell Laboratories, including devices such as computers, answering machines, and facsimile (fax) machines, to be attached to AT&T lines. The Carterfone decision of 1968, which allowed non-AT&T electronic equipment to be attached to existing networks, relaxed U.S. federal regulations and was intended to encourage further technological innovation and competition.

Competition was again the central debate of the telephone industry in 1974. The DOJ, extending concerns originally raised in its 1949 suit, intervened in AT&T's monopoly once again in 1974. The DOJ attacked AT&T's right to maintain a highly integrated corporate structure, arguing that the control over local exchanges, long-distance services, and product development gave the company an unfair business advantage. The concern of the DOJ was that AT&T's corporate structure and massive capital base discouraged others from entering the telephone market, thus discouraging both competition and further technological innovation. Adding to the DOJ's complaint was the Execunet case concerning Microwave Communications, Inc. (MCI). In 1975, MCI petitioned for approval of Execunet, which was an interconnected, switched network. While the FCC did not originally support MCI's petition to use microwave technology to bypass AT&T lines, a federal court overturned the FCC decision in 1978. MCI's Execunet appeal, along with the DOJ's 1974 suit and its eventual out-of-court settlement in 1982 (in which AT&T agreed to divest its operating companies), have been the most important influences on the modern structure of the telecommunications industry.

After Divestiture

The Bell System completed the process of divestiture in 1984. AT&T became a long-distance services provider exclusively, and Bell's operating companies were divided among seven regional organizations that were commonly known as Regional Bell Operating Companies (RBOCs), or Baby Bells. The RBOCs were being considered for entry into interstate long-distance service almost immediately after divestiture. They, along with AT&T, had been banned from entry into new unregulated lines of business since 1956. While competition in the long-distance market did increase, the level of competition in the U.S. market had not reached industry expectations by 1996. Just three major long-distance carriers, AT&T, MCI, and Sprint, and the incumbent RBOCs, controlled most of the national market. The Telecommunications Act of 1996 was enacted partly to increase competition in the telecommunications industry by allowing the RBOCs to enter new markets. What the 1996 act has served to do, however, is to allow any company in the industry to enter any other telecommunications market. Thus, where previously there were clear lines of separation between industries such as telephone and cable, barriers to cross-ownership essentially were removed by the 1996 act.

Not only have diverse technologies been allowed to merge, but the individual corporations that own these technologies have also begun to merge. While the industry's organization has been manipulated in order to create competition, the capital bases of many of the competing companies grant each a particular advantage by blocking the entry of smaller competitors into the marketplace. The merging of corporations grants each more competitive power. International mergers provide corporate giants with the power to dominate the telecommunications industry on a global scale. While the 1996 act was designed to create competition in the United States, it may be facilitating the creation of new telecommunications monopolies reminiscent of the system that Bell envisioned and helped to create in the late 1880s. Thus, AT&T's legacy of marketplace control continues to influence the structure of the modern telecommunications industry.

See also: BELL, ALEXANDER GRAHAM; COMMUNICATIONS ACT OF 1934; MORSE, SAMUEL F. B.; TELECOMMUNICATIONS ACT OF 1996; TELEPHONE INDUSTRY; TELEPHONE INDUSTRY, REGULATION OF; TELEPHONE INDUSTRY, TECHNOLOGY OF.

Bibliography

Alleman, James H., and Emmerson, Richard D., eds. (1989). *Perspectives on the Telephone Industry: The Challenge for the Future.* New York: Harper & Row.

Bradley, Stephen P., and Hausman, Jerry A., eds. (1989). *Future Competition in Telecommunications.* Boston: Harvard Business School Press.

Brooks, John. (1976). *Telephone: The First Hundred Years.* New York: Harper & Row.

Gershon, Richard A. (1997). *The Transnational Media Corporation: Global Messages and Free Market Competition.* Mahwah, NJ: Lawrence Erlbaum.

Hugill, Peter J. (1999). *Global Communications since 1844: Geopolitics and Technology.* Baltimore, MD: Johns Hopkins University Press.

Hyman, Leonard S.; Toole, Richard C.; and Avellis, Rosemary M. (1987). *The New Telecommunications Industry: Evolution and Organization*, 2 vols. Arlington, VA: Public Utilities Reports.

Kellerman, Aharon. (1993). *Telecommunications and Geography.* London: Belhaven.

Langdon, William Chauncy. (1959). *The Early Corporate Development of the Telephone.* New York: American Telephone and Telegraph Company.

Lax, Stephen. (1997). *Beyond the Horizon: Communications Technologies: Past, Present, and Future.* Luton, Eng.: University of Luton Press.

Lighthill, M. J.; Eastwood, E.; May, C. A.; and Cattermole, K. W. (1978). *Telecommunications in the 1980s and After.* London: The Royal Society.

Oslin, George P. (1992). *The Story of Telecommunications.* Macon, GA: Mercer University Press.

Schlesinger, Leonard A.; Dyer, Davis; Clough, Thomas N.; and Landau, Diane. (1987). *Chronicles of Corporate Change: Management Lessons from AT&T and Its Offspring.* Lexington, MA: Lexington Books.

Singleton, Loy A. (1989). *Global Impact: The New Telecommunication Technologies.* New York: Harper & Row.

Smith, George David. (1985). *The Anatomy of a Business Strategy: Bell, Western Electric, and the Origins of the American Telephone Industry.* Baltimore, MD: Johns Hopkins University Press.

Spurge, Lorraine. (1998). *Failure Is Not an Option: How MCI Invented Competition in Telecommunications.* Encino, CA: Spurge Ink.

Thimm, Alfred L. (1992). *America's Stake in European Telecommunication Policies.* Westport, CT: Quorum Books.

Wasserman, Neil H. (1985). *From Invention to Innovation: Long-Distance Telephone Transmission at the Turn of the Century.* Baltimore, MD: Johns Hopkins University Press.

MARTIN L. HATTON

TELEPHONE INDUSTRY, REGULATION OF

Commercial telephone service began in the United States in 1877. Recognizing the advantage of monopolistic control over the industry, the fledgling Bell Telephone Company sought regulation as protection from "aggressive competition" during the period from 1877 to 1910. The U.S. Congress responded with the Mann–Elkins Act of 1910, which effectively brought interstate telecommunications traffic within the regulatory jurisdiction of the Interstate Commerce Commission (ICC). The ICC, however, maintained a focus on interstate rail traffic more than on interstate telecommunications. Nevertheless, the ICC, along with the U.S. Department of Justice (DOJ), became concerned with the rapid growth of Bell Telephone. The two agencies attempted, in 1913, to force Bell Telephone into the Kingsbury Commitment, which was a decision designed to limit monopolistic growth by requiring Bell Telephone to provide interconnection to independent telephone companies and to refrain from further acquisitions. The Willis–Graham Act, however, overturned the Kingsbury Commitment, so after 1921, the ICC was authorized to approve telecommunications consolidations, and the agency approved almost all of them.

The ICC regulated interstate telecommunications, but individual states controlled intrastate telecommunications. The distinction between interstate and intrastate communication, however, has been a vague one. Two cases, the *Shreveport Rate Case* (1914) and *Smith v. Illinois Bell Telephone Co.* (1930), broadened federal authority at the expense of state power due to the often unclear distinction between intrastate and interstate telephone service. This power, later transferred to the Federal Communications Commission (FCC), facilitated the breakup of the Bell System in the 1980s and allowed for the reentry of the individual Regional Bell Operating Companies (RBOCs) into interstate service in the 1990s.

The ICC actually did little to regulate consolidations and the monopolistic growth of Bell. While the commission was given this authority in 1921, the ICC was not powerful enough to regulate the growth of the industry. The Willis–Graham Act indicated that telecommunications regulation was an imperfect and inadequate adaptation of railroad regulation to the communication field; the ICC lacked significant broad statutory authority under such ambiguously applied policies. However, the ICC did prove to have the power to preempt state regulation. The stage was now set for the development of a new federal agency with broader statutory authority than the ICC and a mandate to encourage the development of a telecommunications infrastructure designed for adoption by all U.S. citizens.

By the early 1930s, 98 percent of all calls still did not cross state lines. Therefore, at some level, there remained a distinct geographic division in the regulation of state and federal telecommunication services. Furthermore, the potential of telephone services was not being exploited. The main objective of the Communications Act of 1934, then, was to make available to all U.S. citizens wire and radio communication service at reasonable charges in order to support the expansion of the communication infrastructure. The act addressed telecommunications services generally, but it specifically addressed in subchapter two the regulation of common carriers, or those entities whose services are open to public hire for handling interstate or international communications by electrical means.

The FCC was created by the Communications Act of 1934 as the primary regulatory agency of the telecommunications industry. Among other duties, the FCC was created to oversee common carriers. While the distinction between intrastate and interstate telecommunications services has always been a tenuous one, individual states were granted authority over most matters of intrastate services, terminal equipment, and intercity services. The FCC does, however, influence the economics of intrastate communication through local exchange carriers (LECs)—to the extent that it prescribes a uniform system of accounting to be followed by all providers, prescribes the depreciation practices to be followed by providers, and has the authority to set the value of communications property used in providing services.

Established as the primary regulatory authority over U.S. telecommunications services, the FCC carried the mandate to enforce the Communications Act of 1934. The FCC has relied on its serving of the public interest as the root of its power as a regulatory authority. As is obvious in section 201(a) of the 1934 act, public interest was implicitly defined by consumer access, traditionally referred to as universal service. Thus, while the industry faced little competition until the 1970s and sought regulation as a form of protection from competition, section 201(a) clearly establishes the requirement for interconnection with other companies and services if the FCC deems such interconnection necessary for the advancement of the public interest.

Competition, in service of the public interest, is the implicit guiding principle for regulation under Title II of the Communications Act of 1934. Therefore, since 1959, federal regulators began to view telephony less as a natural monopoly and adopted and implemented a consistent policy that encouraged competitive entry into the telecommunications market. Furthermore, beyond the shifting attitudes concerning competition and monopoly-based pricing, technology-driven changes began to affect the rules of entry for new companies and services.

Refusal to interconnect with new technology and face potential competition is what led to the eventual dissolution of the Bell telephone monopoly. The FCC made its "Above 890" decision in 1959, which allowed companies other than American Telephone & Telegraph (AT&T) to provide long-distance services using microwave frequencies. The FCC allowed Microwave Communica-

tions, Inc. (MCI) to enter the telecommunications market in 1969. This decision effectively destroyed Bell Telephone's monopoly and opened common-carrier services to competition. The aggressive defense taken by AT&T/Bell drew the attention of the DOJ, which brought a major antitrust suit against the company in 1974. This federal action against the Bell System was actually a carryover from an earlier 1956 consent decree between the DOJ and AT&T to settle a 1949 lawsuit. In 1949, the DOJ determined that AT&T had violated the Sherman Antitrust Act of 1890 by monopolizing manufacturing, distribution, sales, and installation of telephone equipment. The DOJ determined that the lack of competition in the telephony market inhibited the growth of universal service. The DOJ requested that AT&T relinquish Western Electric, which was the manufacturing unit of AT&T. AT&T signed a consent decree in 1956 that prohibited the company from engaging in any business other than common-carrier service.

The 1974 antitrust suit against AT&T was settled after several years in what has become known as the 1982 Consent Decree. AT&T agreed to divestiture of its operating companies under this agreement so long as it could enter other unregulated markets. The parent company became three distinct entities after completion of divestiture in 1984: (1) AT&T provided common-carrier service, (2) the company's products division eventually became Lucent Technologies, and (3) the company's LECs produced seven RBOCs. The Modified Final Judgment governing the process produced a change in how exchanges were conceptualized. Exchanges were no longer defined by state boundaries but were now defined by much larger local access and transport areas (LATAs). Thus, the RBOCs were not responsible for intrastate communication but intraLATA services; AT&T and the other interexchange carriers were now responsible for interLATA telecommunications.

This attempt to dissolve the power of a telecommunications monopoly seems, ironically, to have facilitated later attempts at reconsolidation of the industry. LATAs further blurred the distinction between intrastate controls over telecommunications and federal interstate controls. It is important to note that the Communications Act of 1934 did not specify the regulatory jurisdiction for any matter that did not divide neatly along intrastate and interstate boundaries. Also, by the time the Modified Final Judgment was implemented, technology, not the states, was driving policy. Technology-driven innovations further facilitated the evolution of the industry from monopoly to competition. The FCC is granted power by section 154(i) of Title 47 of the Communications Act of 1934 to expand its authority with changes in technology as long as such changes are necessary for performance of its functions. Under authority of the 1934 act, the FCC began in 1966 to look into the possibilities of merging telecommunications and computer technology. While the benefits of merging the technologies became clear, the FCC realized that encouraging the unregulated development of computer services with regulated telecommunications services would be difficult. The FCC made its Carterfone decision in 1968, allowing non-AT&T equipment to be attached to existing networks, thus relaxing regulations to encourage such technological innovation.

Because the Communications Act of 1934 encouraged increased public access, and because lower costs to the consumer encouraged wider adoption of telecommunication services, technological innovations were encouraged for furthering the expansion of the infrastructure. Federal regulators' allowance, after the 1982 Consent Decree, of AT&T and other common carriers into unregulated markets encouraged exploration into the potentials of merging telephony with other technologies, such as cable and computer technology. The use of unregulated technologies, such as fiber optics, have allowed telephone companies to bypass regulation altogether because alternative services fall outside the realm of "common carrier" as technically defined by the 1934 act.

The FCC had broad discretion in the enforcement of the 1934 act; section 401(a) gave federal district courts jurisdiction over FCC enforcement actions that failed to comply with any provision of the act. The U.S. Court of Appeals for the District of Columbia, in fact, did challenge a major FCC decision in 1978 concerning MCI. In 1975, MCI petitioned for approval of Execunet, which was an interconnected, switched network. The FCC determined that the network was not a private system and therefore was not allowable under the 1970 Specialized Common Carrier decision. While not disagreeing with the FCC, the court insisted that the commission had not presented

evidence illustrating that Execunet would harm the telecommunications infrastructure. The Execunet appeal was the major turning point in the FCC's stance on competition and was possibly as significant as the divestiture of AT&T for telecommunications deregulation.

Telecommunications regulation falls under the control of the individual states and under the FCC. Nevertheless, the U.S. telephone industry appears to have been shaped more by antitrust law than any aspect of federal or state regulation. While the FCC may address unfair business practices leading to potential monopolies, antitrust violations fall primarily under the jurisdiction of the DOJ. Antitrust policy typically is brought to bear upon perceived monopolies under the Sherman Antitrust Act, this being an act originally targeted at the U.S. rail system. One important doctrine of antitrust policy relates to the notion of "essential facilities." The principle behind this doctrine is that one firm may control a market, thus blocking competitors from entering or punishing those already in the system, through the control of facilities necessary for operation in that market. The doctrine does not mandate the absolute equality of access for all, but is often used to enforce a reasonable and feasible attempt at fair competition.

The FCC began to support antitrust-based regulation once its philosophy toward telephony evolved from that of natural monopoly to one of competition. In retrospect, it is evident that the period from the mid-1950s to the early 1970s would lead to an eventual confrontation between the key players in telephony, AT&T/Bell and the FCC. Furthermore, the FCC has always had individual states with which to contend in telecommunications regulation, since the 1934 act that established the commission also created the tenuous divide between state and federal lines of communication. With the major exception of *Louisiana Public Service Commission v. FCC* in 1986, the courts have traditionally held that the FCC has jurisdiction over all facilities except those that clearly belong to intrastate networks, and the U.S. Court of Appeals for the Fourth Circuit effectively established a presumption that all facilities are interstate facilities. Also important in the enforcement of telecommunications policy is the DOJ, which is the agency responsible for the enforcement of fair U.S. trade practices.

The RBOCs were being considered for entry into interstate long-distance service almost immediately after divestiture. In fact, the RBOCs requested waivers for entry into new unregulated lines of business from the point of their genesis in the 1982 Consent Decree. The basic policy debate at the time, of course, was between fears of rising anticompetitive behavior on the part of the RBOCs versus fears of lost competitive benefits by restricting their entry into markets beyond intraLATA telecommunications service. A particular antitrust concern that remains is the "bottleneck" dilemma. The concern has been that monopoly control over essential facilities, the LECs, was inevitably created by restricting the RBOCs to intraLATA telephony. Beyond this basic antitrust issue, the courts were also worried that the rush of the RBOCs to diversify just weeks after divestiture represented their lack of concern for universal service.

Nevertheless, the mood toward telecommunications in the United States after divestiture was one that supported competition. In a proposal that foreshadowed the Telecommunications Act of 1996, the Danforth Amendment (1986) attempted to define the primary objective of the FCC as the preservation of universal availability of affordable telephone service while maintaining a particular emphasis on competition rather than regulation for the future development of telecommunications services. If any one individual illustrated the competitive tone concerning telecommunications deregulation leading up the 1996 act, however, it was none other than the then-chairman of the FCC, Mark Fowler. From his appointment in 1981, Fowler's reconception of "public interest," the guiding principle of the FCC in most matters of telecommunications regulation including merger review, demonstrated his push for marketplace principles. Fowler considered marketplace principles to be the best means for access for the poorest segments of the U.S. population. Therefore, competition, not protection, was clearly established as being synonymous with the public interest.

One principle seems to have defined telecommunications policy in the mid-1980s: uncertainty. The principle regulatory authority was pushing for competition, not regulation. It was clear that, with the exception of the 1986 *Louisiana* decision, the states had little say in the future of regulation of telecommunications. Most would agree that technological advancement guided regulatory

decisions by the time the FCC proceeding known as the Third Computer Inquiry (Computer III) was settled in 1987. The deregulatory context leading into the 1990s indicated that there was a need for an updated policy with regard to regulating telecommunications. Furthermore, in retrospect, it appears evident that it would be only a matter of time before monopoly would once again dominate U.S. telecommunications. Many predicted that once the RBOCs were allowed to enter the long-distance market, bundled services and "one-stop shopping" would again be available. It seemed that almost everyone anticipated the marketplace approach to regulation as the means to serve the public interest the best. Fowler insisted that the local-exchange market would become competitive with the inclusion of services such as cable and cellular radio providers and called for a reexamination of the government's regulation of the U.S. telecommunications industry. Fowler, essentially, called for implementation of the Telecommunications Act of 1996.

See also: BELL, ALEXANDER GRAHAM; COMMUNICATIONS ACT OF 1934; TELECOMMUNICATIONS ACT OF 1996; TELEPHONE INDUSTRY; TELEPHONE INDUSTRY, HISTORY OF; TELEPHONE INDUSTRY, TECHNOLOGY OF.

Bibliography

Brenner, Daniel L. (1992). *Law and Regulation of Common Carriers in the Communications Industry.* Boulder, CO: Westview Press.

Cain, Rita M. (1987). "Constitutional Struggle over Telecommunications Regulation." *Hastings Communications and Entertainment Law Journal (Comm/Ent)* 10(1):1–31.

Corn-Revere, Robert, and Carveth, Rod. (1998). "Economics and Media Regulation." In *Media Economics: Theory and Practice,* 2nd edition, eds. Alison Alexander, James Owers, and Rod Carveth. Mahwah, NJ: Lawrence Erlbaum.

Demipsey, Paul Stephen. (1989). "Adam Smith Assaults Ma Bell with His Invisible Hands: Divestiture, Deregulation, and the Need for a New Telecommunications Policy." *Hastings Communications and Entertainment Law Journal (Comm/Ent)* 11(4):527–606.

Forrest, Herbert E., and Wiley, Richard E. (1986). *Telecommunications 1986: Competition and Deregulation After the AT&T Divestiture. No. 234. Patents, Coyprights, Trademarkes, and Literary Property.* Washington, DC: Practicing Law Institute.

Horwitz, Robert Britt. (1989). *The Irony of Regulatory Reform.* New York: Oxford University Press.

Kellogg, Michael K.; Thorne, John; and Huber, Peter W. (1992). *Federal Telecommunications Law.* Boston: Little, Brown.

Kellogg, Michael K.; Thorne, John; and Huber, Peter W. (1995). *Federal Telecommunications Law: 1995 Supplement.* Boston: Little, Brown.

Larson, Alexander C. (1995). "Reforming Telecommunications Policy in Response to Entry into Local Exchange Markets." *Hastings Communications and Entertainment Law Journal (Comm/Ent)* 18(1):1–50.

Teske, Paul Eric. (1990). *After Divestiture: The Political Economy of State Telecommunications Regulation.* New York: State University of New York Press.

MARTIN L. HATTON

▐▌ TELEPHONE INDUSTRY, TECHNOLOGY OF

The public switched telephone network (PSTN) in the United States operated as a virtual monopoly from 1877 until the government-sanctioned breakup of American Telephone & Telegraph (AT&T) in 1984. Since that time, deregulation and technological advances have given rise to an array of competing wired and wireless telephone technologies. The most significant factor driving these changes has been the shift from analog to digital technologies.

On a March evening in 1876, Alexander Graham Bell learned in his Boston laboratory that his idea for conveying sounds through a wire worked. Bell's crude system harnessed the acoustical energy of speech by using sound waves to vibrate a thin diaphragm attached to an electrically charged wire that was dipped into an acidic solution. As the vibrations caused the depth of the wire to vary, the electrical resistance of the wire varied in proportion to the wire's depth. At the other end of the wire, the process was reversed. The changing electrical current caused a diaphragm to vibrate, enabling the telephone receiver to replicate the sounds of human speech. Bell's words, "Mr. Watson, come here, I want you," were heard in another room by his assistant. In July 1877, the first Bell Telephone Company was formed, launching a new industry and a new communication technology. By the turn of the century (only twenty-three years later), the company had been renamed American Telephone & Telegraph

(AT&T), and almost every element that would be important during the first one hundred years of telephone technology had already been developed by AT&T's Bell System.

The Telephone Network

The basic telephone technology of the United States, despite many refinements, is still known by the acronym POTS (plain old telephone service). The telephone instrument combines a microphone, a speaker or earphone, a ringer, and a touch-tone keypad or rotary dial (on older devices). A call is initiated when the handset (combining the microphone and earphone) is lifted, thereby activating the circuit. The destination telephone number is "dialed" by pressing a sequence of numbers on the keypad, thereby generating distinct tones for each number pressed. The older rotary-dial device generated a series of electrical pulses that corresponded to each number that was dialed.

At the local level, telephone subscribers (residential and business) are served by a local-exchange carrier (LEC). Each telephone in "the local loop" is served by a separate line that is connected to the central office of the LEC, giving the local telephone network a star configuration. When a subscriber "dials" the number of another local customer, the signal travels from the originating location to the central office, where it is switched (connected) to the line that is serving the second customer. An electrical signal is sent through the line to activate the ringer at that location. The talking path is created when the called party answers. In the early days of telephone service, switching was done manually by plugging and unplugging wire connectors. By the 1920s, mechanical switches were in use, and by the 1950s, electromechanical switches were standard. Modern switching uses computer technology. Local exchanges are arranged by sets of telephone numbers that are designated by three-digit prefixes. Each exchange includes up to ten thousand separate lines, and a central office can handle the calls of several exchanges.

Calls to another community are routed from the local central office through a series of higher-order central offices. Technically, the central office that serves individual subscribers is known as a class 5 "end office." Class 5 offices are connected by high-capacity trunk lines to class 4 offices, and

A telephone operator works an early switchboard, which was necessary for connecting the various elements of the telephone networks. (Bettmann/Corbis)

most of the telephone traffic above the local class 5 end-office level is carried by long distance, or interexchange carriers (IXCs). Long-distance calls (initiated by dialing 0 or 1) are routed by the central office switch to the trunk line that is connected to the chosen IXC's point-of-presence (POP), from which the call is further routed to the central office that serves the receiving customer. The territory of each LEC is divided into local access and transport areas (LATAs) and includes a number of local-exchange central offices. Long-distance calls within the LATA (intra-LATA calls) may be carried by the LEC. However, an increasing percentage of intra-LATA traffic, and all inter-LATA calls, are carried by interexchange carriers.

The same computer technology that routes telephone calls also handles the complicated process of measuring the length (in time) of calls and determining both the charges to the customer and the amount of payment to the local and interexchange carriers that were involved in completing the call.

Transmission Technologies

According to the Federal Communications Commission (1999), 82 percent of telephone subscribers are still linked to the PSTN by a twisted-pair copper wire, the oldest form of wireline telephone interconnection. At one time, almost all telephone lines consisted of bundles of copper pairs, and the capacity of a circuit was limited to the number of pairs. As the telephone network and the amount of long-distance telephone traffic grew, Bell Labs perfected improved signal-carrying technologies. Coaxial cable, developed in the 1940s, is composed of a single strand of copper wire (which carries the signals) surrounded by foam insulation with a conductive outer shield that prevents signal leakage. The three concentric layers of the cable are wrapped in an insulating material. "Coax" enabled tremendous increases in the capacity of terrestrial and undersea cables. In 1947, AT&T began using microwave radio transmission technology to connect distant points in its network and operated a coast-to-coast microwave link by 1951.

By the 1960s, digital compression technologies enabled telephone engineers to multiplex (i.e., send) increasing numbers of calls over a single wired or wireless circuit. By 1970, geostationary satellites had become important elements of the telephone network infrastructure. The first generation of communications satellites could carry 240 separate telephone calls, but by 1998, capacity was 22,500 voice circuits that digital compression boosted to the equivalent of 112,500 circuits. Yet, as important as coaxial cable and satellites have been, the most significant transmission technology for the future appears to be optical fiber.

Optical fiber cable is composed of bundles of flexible hair-thin strands of glass. The signals in an optical fiber are light waves generated by laser light, which provides a transmission medium with incredible speed (the speed of light) and signal-carrying capacity. In addition, fiber is immune to electrical interference. The telephone network has been undergoing a steady conversion to optical fiber since the early 1980s. Debate continues with regard to the extension of optical fiber from trunk lines into the local loop. The cost of providing fiber to every home is considered to be prohibitive, and alternative approaches such as fiber-to-the-neighborhood or fiber-to-the-curb (with subscribers being connected by copper wire) are more likely.

The Digital Revolution

A shift from analog to digital technologies has been the strongest force behind changes in electronic communications. Analog audio signals vary continuously in frequency (pitch) and amplitude (loudness). For example, in Bell's first telephone, the electrical signal varied continuously in response to the movement of a wire attached to a diaphragm that was vibrated by sound waves. The sounds heard through the receiver were analogous to Bell's original speech. A digital signal processes sound discontinuously by sampling or measuring the source thousands of times per second. Each discrete measurement is in the form of binary code that can have only two values, 0 or 1, corresponding to the presence or absence of some quantity. Digital signals retain greater fidelity to the original sound because they are less subject to interference and other forms of signal degradation that are common to analog technologies. Starting with the development of electronic computers in the 1940s, all forms of information have become

digital. Furthermore, since all digital signals are alike, computer data, digital audio, and digital video signals exist in the same binary code. The superiority of digital technology over analog technology provided a strong incentive to convert the telephone network to digital. However, competitive forces unleashed by the breakup of the Bell System in 1984 and the Telecommunications Act of 1996 greatly accelerated the process.

By the 1970s, computer technology had diffused from large institutions to small businesses and even households, generating increasing volumes of computer data. With its vast network, the telephone industry was positioned to play a key role in the movement of data and began offering separate leased lines optimized to carry digital data at high speeds. As Wilson Dizard (1989) explains, telephone companies first provided integrated services digital network (ISDN) lines that combined voice, data, and other services within one circuit at 64 kbs. (A bit, or binary digit, is the smallest unit of digital data. A kilobit is 1,000 bits, and 64 kbs is a data rate of 64,000 bits per second.) Even faster and more expensive, leased T-1 lines could speed data at 1.5 Mbs (million bits per second).

The growth of the Internet after 1994 expanded the volume of data as small businesses and individuals went online in increasing numbers. By the late 1990s, data traffic was increasing faster than voice, and it began to exceed the volume of voice traffic on telecommunication networks. This trend posed both competitive and technological challenges to the PSTN that was built and optimized to carry a limited range of the frequencies of human speech, not data.

The most significant network technology to emerge in the digital era has been packet switching. The PSTN largely uses circuit switching, a technology that causes each call to use the full capacity of a telephone circuit for the entire duration of the call. Even during pauses, the full circuit is in use, although no information is being transferred. With packet switching, digital data is packaged into packets of data that also contain information identifying their destination, source, order, and size. At their intended destination, computer software extracts the data from the packets and reconverts it into the original form (sound, text, graphics, or even video). Packet switching uses networks more efficiently because data packets from many different sources can be sent through the same circuit at the same time, using the entire bandwidth (data capacity) of that circuit.

In the competitive environment of the 1990s, a new type of telephone company emerged. Competitive local-exchange carriers (CLECs) began to offer services to businesses using a combination of technologies. Initially, CLECs leased telephone lines from older telephone companies, now called incumbent local-exchange carriers (ILECs). According to Thomas Baldwin, D. Stevens McVoy, and Charles Steinfeld (1996), the ISDN service offered by ILECs was too slow for large businesses, and T-1 lines were too expensive for all but the biggest firms. CLECs were able to capitalize on the explosive growth in data traffic and build both new high-speed, high-capacity, packet-switched networks to meet the data needs of businesses and broadband data backbone services capable of speeds of 155 Mbs to 2.4 Gbs (billion bits per second).

Competition and technology, then, have added a public switched data network (PSDN) that now operates alongside the traditional public switched telephone network (PSTN). Data networks typically use packet-switching technology, but the technologies of the PSTN and PSDN do overlap.

Wireless cell telephones revolutionized the telephone industry, and the Matsushita Communication Industrial Co. Ltd. produced in January 2001 the P503i, which has installed JAVA script computer language that allows it to be used as a handy computer terminal as well as a telephone. (AFP/Corbis)

For example, asynchronous transfer mode (ATM), a high-performance switching and multiplexing technology, is used by both. ATM employs data packets of fixed length so that time-critical data (such as voice or video) is not delayed as large data packets are processed. The ILECs are attempting to retain a share of the data market by offering digital subscriber line (DSL) service. DSL technologies use copper wire, providing high-speed data services to residences and small businesses. However, the technology is limited to a three and one-half mile radius of the telephone company's central office.

The cable television industry is also developing CLEC status. Although cable technology was designed to carry one-way signals from a central location to a customer's residence, cable systems use coaxial cable, a connection with substantial signal-carrying capacity. Similar to telephone companies, cable franchises are rebuilding their networks with optical fiber in addition to coax, as they reengineer their systems to carry two-way signals in order to provide telephone service and Internet access in addition to traditional cable television.

Wireless Telephony

Wireless telephony uses low-power ultrahigh-frequency (UHF) radio signals within small areas (cells) that may be as small as a few city blocks or as large as a twenty-mile radius in rural areas. At the center of each cell is a base-station tower, which transmits/receives the signals of up to four hundred separate voice channels. As users of wireless telephones move from one cell to another, a central switching computer "hands off" the calls of roaming subscribers to the tower in the next cell. A key device in wireless telephony is the mobile telephone switching office (MTSO), which detects calls placed by subscribers, assigns each call to a voice channel, and facilitates the hand-off of calls between cells. In addition, the MTSO interconnects all of the towers in the service area and links the wireless system to the terrestrial PSTN.

Modern wireless telephone service began with analog cellular telephony in the early 1980s and experienced explosive growth in the 1990s, when digital PCS (personal communication services) emerged. Cellular services operate at 800 MHz, while digital PCS technology uses a frequency of 1.9 GHz. In the United States, policymakers mandated that each market would be served by two cellular franchises (with one awarded to the local wireline service) and up to six PCS franchises. Competition quickly reduced the prices of both telephones and service, and in many markets, the price of wireless service is comparable to that of wireline service

As Susan O'Keefe (1998) notes, after the introduction of digital PCS, most analog cellular systems converted to digital technology, enabling cellular firms to offer most of the services provided by PCS. Increasingly, all wireless services integrate voice and data (including Internet) services, in addition to providing voice mail, fax, encryption, and advanced paging and telephony services. A remaining technical issue for wireless telephony is to resolve the presence of four different technical standards in use by wireless firms around the world.

The desire to provide a global "anywhere, anytime" telecommunications service has led several entrepreneurs to offer mobile satellite services (MSS) using low Earth orbit (LEO), medium Earth orbit (MEO), and geostationary (GEO) communications satellites. LEOs and MEOs orbit faster than Earth rotates, necessitating a network of as many as 288 satellites distributed around the globe. The technology is somewhat like that of cellular telephony, except that for MSS services, the network grid moves instead of the subscriber. As the satellite handling a call begins to move out of range of the user's satellite telephone, the circuit is passed to another, closer satellite.

The Future

There will be continuing competition among telecommunication technologies in the twenty-first century. Sam Masud (1999) reports that telephone industry seers predict the eventual shift of most voice traffic to the newer data networks, as networks continue to develop increased bandwidth and speed. Future telecommunications networks will be broadband in nature, and they will carry voice, data, and video. Wireless services are also expected to develop broadband capabilities and become increasingly competitive in the full range of services that are offered by their terrestrial competitors.

See also: BELL, ALEXANDER GRAHAM; CABLE TELEVISION; DIGITAL COMMUNICATION; FEDERAL COMMUNICATIONS COMMISSION; INTERNET AND THE WORLD WIDE WEB; SATELLITES, COMMUNICATION; TELECOMMUNICATIONS, WIRELESS; TELECOMMUNICATIONS ACT OF 1996; TELEPHONE INDUSTRY; TELEPHONE INDUSTRY, HISTORY OF; TELEPHONE INDUSTRY, REGULATION OF.

Bibliography

Baldwin, Thomas F.; McVoy, D. Stevens; and Steinfeld, Charles. (1996). *Convergence: Integrating Media, Information & Communication.* Thousand Oaks, CA: Sage Publications.

Bittner, John R. (1991). *Broadcasting and Telecommunication: An Introduction,* 3rd edition. Englewood Cliffs, NJ: Prentice-Hall.

Dizard, Wilson P., Jr. (1989). *The Coming Information Age: An Overview of Technology, Economics, and Politics,* 3rd edition. New York: Longman.

Federal Communications Commission. (1999). *Trends in Telephone Service.* Washington, DC: U.S. Government Printing Office.

Goff, David H. (2000). "Issues of Internet Infrastructure." In *Understanding the Web: Social, Political, and Economic Dimensions of the Internet,* eds. Alan B. Albarran and David H. Goff. Ames: Iowa State University Press.

Grant, August E., and Meadows, Jennifer H., eds. (1998). *Communication Technology Update,* 6th edition. Boston: Focal Press.

Masud, Sam. (1999). "Transforming the PSTN." *Telecommunications* 33(7):22–27.

Moore, Geoffrey; Johnson, Paul; and Kippola, Tom. (1999). "The Next Network." *Forbes ASAP* 163(4):93.

National Research Council. (1996). *The Unpredictable Certainty: Information Infrastructure Through 2000.* Washington DC: National Academy Press.

O'Keefe, Susan. (1999). "Transforming the PSTN." *Telecommunications* 32(11):30–36.

DAVID H. GOFF

▐ TELEVISION, EDUCATIONAL

Since the beginnings of television, educators have endeavored to harness its power to educate a mass audience. This entry examines educational television programs with a particular focus on how to maximize their effectiveness. Much of the research reported here has also been summarized in Sandra Calvert's 1999 book *Children's Journeys through the Information Age.*

Researchers have generally defined educational television programs as those programs that focused on academic content areas that are taught in schools, such as reading, mathematics, science, and social studies. In contrast, prosocial television programs have been considered to be those that taught positive social interaction skills, self-control and achievement behaviors, and creative fantasy and imaginative play. Some researchers, however, have defined educational content broadly to include both educational and prosocial programs.

Research on Educational Television Programs

Early educational television typically consisted of instructional programs that were intended for classroom use. Lessons traditionally presented by a verbal lecture were simply moved to the audio-visual medium of television. These "talking heads" presentations were often directed at adult college students and focused on some kind of academic lesson. Presentations were most effective when concrete visual depictions emphasized the verbal message.

Sesame Street was the first academically oriented television program to enjoy wide success in attracting a young viewing audience while teaching important academic lessons. This program, which was created by the Children's Television Workshop (now known as Sesame Workshop), was initially organized around an academic curriculum. Much research has revealed the educational benefits of *Sesame Street*.

Comprehensible language was one key to the educational success of *Sesame Street*. According to the comprehensibility model advanced by Daniel Anderson, children pay attention to a program when they think they will understand its content. For example, Anderson and his colleagues (1981) have shown that children are more attentive to program vignettes when the language is concrete than when it is abstract. Moreover, manipulations that make the vignettes incomprehensible, such as speaking a foreign language, reduced children's attention.

The magazine format of *Sesame Street*—in which short vignettes repeatedly emphasize academic messages—was adapted to other educational television programs produced by the Children's Television Workshop. Although the programs directed to older viewing audiences were effective teaching tools, they were not as effective as *Sesame Street*. Researchers documented that pro-

grams such as *The Electric Company* and *Square One* were effective in teaching reading and math skills, respectively, but only when the children viewed it at school. Other programs, such as *3-2-1 Contact*, taught children science, but that particular program was not effective in maintaining a large enough viewing audience to sustain its production.

Nickelodeon, a cable television network, followed the lead of the Children's Television Workshop by carefully constructing and analyzing the effects of their educational television programs. Research showed that preschool children who viewed educational Nickelodeon programs such as *Gullah Gullah Island* and *Allegra's Window* improved in flexible thinking, problem solving, and prosocial behaviors, particularly when they were encouraged to view these programs. Similar cognitive benefits were found for preschoolers who viewed *Blue's Clues*, an educational program that promotes problem-solving skills through an interactive program format that repeats the same episode for five consecutive days.

At times, commercial broadcasters have also focused on teaching children academically oriented content. For example, *School House Rock*, which originally aired during the 1970s, was a series of three-minute vignettes that used songs to present lessons on English, science, mathematics, and history. According to research, repeatedly viewing the vignettes improved verbatim memory of the content. However, learning appears to have been superficial and rote rather than facilitating comprehension of important program messages. In other words, children and adults could recite program content well after viewing the series, but prose presentations of the same content were more effective in promoting viewers' understanding of the central program concepts.

Children can also benefit from prosocial television programs that are designed to promote positive social skills, achievement behaviors, and imagination and creativity. Research has shown that, when preschoolers viewed *Mister Rogers' Neighborhood*, there was an increase in task persistence, toleration of delays, and rule obedience, which are facets of achievement behaviors. Children who viewed *Mister Rogers' Neighborhood* also showed an increase in the display of prosocial interpersonal behaviors such as cooperation, nurturance, and verbalizing feelings. Although they

Bill Cosby was involved in many popular educational programs of the 1970s, including Sesame Street, The Electric Company (shown here), and Fat Albert and the Cosby Kids. (Bettmann/Corbis)

occurred for children from all income levels, these effects were most pronounced for children who came from low-income families.

During viewing, learning can be enhanced when programs include advance organizers that preview the important content that will be included, summaries that review important program themes, and replays of key program events. After viewing, prosocial outcomes are enhanced when rehearsal activities, such as verbal labeling of program themes and role playing of key program actions, take place in the children's viewing environments. Verbal labeling is especially useful for promoting children's learning of content, whereas role playing works best when behavioral performance is the objective.

Production techniques can be used selectively to improve children's learning of prosocial program content. A study by Calvert and her colleagues (1982) of Fat Albert and the Cosby Kids demonstrated the utility of using sound effects as

signals or markers of important content, thereby increasing children's attention to, and subsequent memory of, the contiguously presented, plot-relevant content. In addition, essential program content that was presented with both moderate action and child dialogue was well understood, in part because both visual and verbal modes were used to present content that children could then use to represent that information. Visual features such as action provide a developmentally appropriate mode that young children often use when thinking about content.

Longitudinal research demonstrates long-term benefits for children who view educational television programs. For example, in a study conducted by Aletha Huston and her colleagues (2001), adolescents who had viewed more educational television programs as children had better grades, better academic self-concepts, better values about academic success, higher levels of achievement, and higher levels of creativity when in high school than those who had viewed less educational television. The demonstrated contribution of educational television to children's academic success has led to a current Public Broadcasting System (PBS) initiative called "Ready to Learn," in which a block of educational programs teaches preschool-aged children the skills that they will need when they begin formal schooling.

Research has demonstrated that well-designed television programs that focus on academic or prosocial content can enhance children's learning and performance of academic and prosocial behaviors, respectively. Repetition of key program concepts, rehearsal activities in the actual viewing environment or embedded in the program, the use of comprehensible language, and the use of interesting production techniques have been shown to improve children's learning of targeted content.

Newer technologies are enhancing the effectiveness of educational television. The videocassette recorder allows children to view repeatedly the content that they do not understand. As television becomes a more interactive medium in the twenty-first century, it will be in a position to answer children's questions or provide new information that is contingent upon children's earlier responses.

Children's Television Act of 1990

Because of the well-documented beneficial effects of educational television on children's development, Congress passed the Children's Television Act of 1990. This law required commercial broadcasters to provide educational and informational television programs for the child audience as a condition for license renewal. In 1991, the Federal Communications Commission (FCC), the government agency charged with implementing that law, broadly defined educational television programs. An educational program simply had to meet any educational or informal need of children who were sixteen years of age or younger. Television programs addressing social and emotional needs, as well as cognitive and intellectual ones, were acceptable, by definition, for broadcaster license renewals.

The guidelines developed by the FCC initially left considerable flexibility in the types of programs broadcasters could count as educational and informational, in the times that such programs could be broadcast, and in the amount of programming that was required. Consequently, programs of questionable educational value, such

as *GI Joe* and *DuckTales*, were offered as evidence of compliance by some commercial broadcasters. A gap emerged between what commercial broadcasters labeled as educational and informational and what researchers considered educational and informational.

Based on the accumulating evidence of poor broadcaster compliance, the FCC implemented more stringent rules for the Children's Television Act in 1996. In order to receive an expedited license renewal, each broadcaster was required to present a minimum of three hours of educational and informational programs each week. This change was known as the three-hour rule. Another requirement involved broadcasting core educational programming. Core programs were defined as those that met the educational and informational needs of children aged sixteen and under, aired between 7 A.M. AND 10 P.M. (when children were likely to be in the viewing audience), were scheduled on a weekly basis, and lasted a minimum of thirty minutes.

Content analyses conducted by Amy Jordan and Emory Woodard (1998) revealed an increase in the number of commercially broadcast educational and informational television programs since the changes in these rules were made. Nonetheless, about one-fifth of such programs continue to be weak in educational quality. Most of the commercial programs also focused on social and emotional lessons rather than academic ones. PBS continues to broadcast the most programs that contain an academic lesson and are high in educational strength.

Conclusions

Educational television programs are designed to promote the cognitive and prosocial development of children. Research finds that children benefit from viewing well-designed programs in both of these areas. Children who frequently view academically oriented television programs are better prepared for school and are more successful through the high school years. Similarly, children who view prosocial television programs learn achievement behaviors and prosocial skills. Beneficial effects are enhanced by the use of specific production techniques, comprehensible language, previews and reviews, and by repetition, role playing, and verbal labeling of key program content. Social policy initiatives, such as the passage and implementation of the Children's Television Act of 1990, have increased the number of educational and informational programs on commercial stations. However, ongoing research is needed to measure the quality and the effectiveness of these programs.

See also: ACADEMIC ACHIEVEMENT AND CHILDREN'S TELEVISION USE; CHILDREN'S ATTENTION TO TELEVISION; CHILDREN'S COMPREHENSION OF TELEVISION; CHILDREN'S CREATIVITY AND TELEVISION USE; CHILDREN'S PREFERENCE FOR MEDIA CONTENT; EDUCATIONAL MEDIA PRODUCERS; FEDERAL COMMUNICATIONS COMMISSION; PUBLIC BROADCASTING; SESAME STREET; TELEVISION BROADCASTING, PROGRAMMING AND.

Bibliography

Anderson, Daniel; Lorch, Elizabeth; Field, Diane; and Sanders, Jeanne. (1981). "The Effects of TV Program Comprehensibility on Children's Visual Attention to Television." *Child Development* 52:151–157

Calvert, Sandra L. (1999). *Children's Journeys through the Information Age.* Boston: McGraw-Hill.

Calvert, Sandra L.; Huston, Aletha; Watkins, Bruce; and Wright, John. (1982). "The Relation between Selective Attention to Television Forms and Children's Comprehension of Content." *Child Development* 53:601–610.

Calvert, Sandra L., and Tart, Maureen. (1993). "Song Versus Prose for Students' Very Long-Term, Long-Term and Short-Term Verbatim Recall." *Journal of Applied Developmental Psychology* 14:245–260.

Center for Media Education and Institute for Public Representation, Georgetown University. (September 29, 1992). *A Report on Station Compliance with the Children's Television Act.* Washington, DC: Center for Media Education.

Federal Communications Commission. (1991). "Report and Order: In the Matter of Policies and Rules Concerning Children's Television Programming." *Federal Communications Commission Reports* 6:2111–2127.

Federal Communications Commission. (August 8, 1996). "FCC Adopts New Children's TV Rules (MM Docket 93-48)." *Federal Communications Commission News.* Report No. DC 96-81.

Friedrich, Lynette, and Stein, Aletha. (1975). "Prosocial Television and Young Children: The Effects of Verbal Labeling and Role Playing on Learning and Behavior." *Child Development* 46:27–38.

Huston, Aletha; Anderson, Daniel; Wright, John; Linebarger, Deborah; and Schmitt, Kelly. (2001). "*Sesame Street* Viewers as Adolescents: The Recontact Study." In "*G*" *Is for Growing: Thirty Years of Sesame Street*, eds. Sholly Fisch and Rosemarie Truglio. Mahwah, NJ: Lawrence Erlbaum.

Huston, Aletha, and Wright, John. (1998). "Mass Media and Children's Development." *Handbook of Child Psychology, Vol. 4: Child Psychology in Practice*, 5th ed., eds. William Damon, Irving Sigel, and K. Ann Renninger. New York: Wiley.

Jordan, Amy, and Woodard, Emory. (1998). "Growing Pains: Children's Television in the New Regulatory Environment." In *Children and Television: The Annals of the American Academy of Political and Social Science*, special volume eds. Amy Jordan and Kathleen Jamieson. Thousand Oaks, CA: Sage Publications.

SANDRA L. CALVERT

TELEVISION, FAMILIES AND

See: Families and Television

TELEVISION BROADCASTING

Almost everyone in the United States watches television. About 99 percent of homes have at least one television set, and, on average, the set stays on for slightly more than seven hours each day. Most viewers have favorite television programs, and they may even have favorite channels. What most viewers may not think about is how the channels and programs get to the set.

Television broadcasting is still the most prevalent form of television in the United States—compared to cable television, for example, which reaches around 70 percent of U.S. homes. Broadcasters also transmit the television programs that reach the largest audiences. Even though their share of the television audience has been decreasing since the 1980s, broadcasters still stand at the center of the television industry.

The Television Broadcasting System

About fifteen hundred television stations make up the core of the television broadcasting system. Each is licensed by the Federal Communications Commission (FCC), a U.S. government agency, to operate in a particular area. The FCC gives out licenses to operate on frequencies in one of two bands of the electromagnetic spectrum: the very-high frequency (VHF) band and the ultrahigh frequency (UHF) band. VHF stations are more valuable than UHF stations because they have a greater geographical reach and thus can be seen and heard by more people.

It is quite possible for a television station to scramble its signal so that only members of the public who pay the broadcaster for a descrambler will be able to view it. This way of getting revenue is not how television broadcasting developed in the United States. Anyone who owns a television set and lives within range of a broadcast transmitter can receive its signals without charge. As a result, stations must make money through other means.

Most stations make money by selling time on their airwaves to advertisers; these broadcasters are called "commercial" stations. "Noncommercial" stations receive support in other ways, such as viewer donations as well as donations from private foundations, government agencies, and commercial firms in return for mentions at the start and end of programs.

More than 80 percent of the local stations link up with television networks for at least part of their broadcast day. A television network is an organization that distributes programs, typically by satellite and microwave relay, to all of its linked stations so that the programs can be broadcast at the same time. The American Broadcasting Company (ABC), the Columbia Broadcasting System (CBS), the National Broadcasting Company (NBC), and Fox are the broadcast networks that regularly reach the largest number of people. Known as the "big four," they are advertiser-supported networks, as are three smaller networks, the Warner Brothers (WB) network, the United Paramount Network (UPN), and Paxnet. The Public Broadcasting Service (PBS) is the network for noncommercial stations.

The commercial networks, particularly the big four, are the giants of the broadcast television business, primarily because of their role in coordinating the distribution of shows to hundreds of local stations, which then transmit the shows to viewers' homes. However, ABC, CBS, Fox, and NBC, especially, are more than distributors. Each company is also involved in production of programs and their exhibition through broadcast stations. That is, the networks produce news, sports, situation comedies, dramas, and other types of programs for use on their networks. They also own stations (sometimes called "exhibition outlets") in the largest cities.

In the television industry, the local stations are called network O&Os (i.e., owned and operated). The federal government regulates the number of O&Os that a broadcast network can own. It does this primarily by prohibiting a network from owning stations that in total reach more than 35 percent of the U.S. population. The aim of the rule is to hinder networks from gaining too much power over the entire broadcast system. Federal rules also prohibit a company from owning more than one broadcast network. In 2000, executives from the newly merged Viacom-CBS were hoping to convince lawmakers to eliminate or modify this rule, because it would force them to sell UPN. NBC, which has a station management agreement with Paxnet, was also lobbying for the law's death. Both corporations argued that strong competition from cable and the weak state of UPN and Paxnet justified their ownership of two networks.

Local stations that are not owned by broadcast networks and yet transmit the network signals are called network affiliates. A network affiliate transmits the network's program feed on a daily basis. Traditionally, the network has agreed to return the favor by giving the affiliate a portion of the revenues that are received from advertisers that buy time on the network. Many affiliates are part of station groups, which are companies that own several local television stations. In the wealthiest of the groups, such as Allbritton Communications, each station is an affiliate of one of the major networks. A broadcast station that is not affiliated with one of the big four networks is called an independent. (Industry executives often consider WB, UPN, and Paxnet affiliates to be independent because they air relatively few hours of network programming per week.) Practically speaking, independents must find all (or almost all) of their programming themselves. Actually, even network affiliates and O&Os must look to sources other than ABC, CBS, Fox, and NBC for some programming because the big four do not distribute enough shows to fill a full period of twenty-four hours. Fortunately for the local stations, the broadcast industry has no shortage of companies that produce programming to sell to the independents, affiliates, and O&Os.

Advertisers are another set of key industry players. With the help of advertising agencies, advertisers pay for time between programs and segments of programs. In return, broadcasters allow advertisers to air commercials, which call attention to their products. A lot of money changes hands in this activity. In 1998, advertisers spent approximately $37 billion on television broadcast advertising.

Unlike cable or satellite television, viewers of broadcast television do not have to pay to receive the programming. As a result, there are few non-advertising revenue sources for television broadcasters. This situation suits local stations, because they are doing quite well with four sources of advertising money: their share of national network advertising, their sale of advertising time during their own programming (mostly local news), their sale of advertising time during programming that they purchase from nonnetwork sources (e.g., reruns of *Seinfeld* or new episodes of *Oprah Winfrey*), and their sale of local commercials during some pauses in network programming.

Broadcast networks have only one source of advertising revenue, national commercials. Although that source yields a lot of money—approximately $14 billion in 1998—the expenses of running a network are such that only one or two broadcast networks have typically been profitable. A major reason for this is that the cost of the programming exceeds the advertising money that the networks are able to get when they air the shows. In an important sense, then, broadcast networks have been "loss leaders" for their O&Os. That is, although they operate at a loss, they provide their company's O&Os with programming and shared advertising monies so that the stations (which do not pay for the network programming) can make huge profit margins from their four commercial revenue streams.

Network executives do not enjoy operating at a loss, however, and they have been searching for new sources of revenue. They have tried three major ways. One involves owning more of the programming that they distribute. A second involves trying to change the standard affiliate agreement, asking affiliates to share some of the network programming costs. The third involves branching into new distribution venues, most notably cable television and the Internet.

Production

From the standpoint of a broadcast executive, the word "production" actually has two meanings.

Perhaps the most obvious is the creation of individual programs. The other, equally important, meaning is the creation of a lineup of programs to be aired on a broadcast channel or network.

The task of producing a channel is huge. Imagine having twenty-four hours of air time to fill every day of the year. How can it be accomplished in a way that will make money for the owners of the channel? That is the challenge that confronts programmers, the people who are in charge of operations as different as WWOR (Channel 9) in New York, an independent station; Channel 4 in Los Angeles, an NBC O&O; and the NBC-TV network.

The most basic challenge that confronts a local or network programming executive is to choose programming that attracts the intended audience. In some cities, where the FCC added several UHF stations and increased audience competition, a few stations have decided to pursue Spanish-speaking viewers, or non-English-speaking viewers generally, to maximize their profits. Because they reach virtually everyone in their area, however, broadcast stations do not generally aim at the narrow audience slices that cable or satellite networks often try to attract. They typically try to create schedules that reach large population segments that interest advertisers—men and/or women who are between eighteen and forty-nine years of age—because they tend to have families and spend a lot of money.

In the television industry, audits of people's viewing behavior (i.e., ratings) help to determine where much of the advertising money goes. The size of a program's audience helps to determine the amount of money a station or network can charge an advertiser for time during that program. Ratings are consequently always on the minds of the programmers who produce schedules for their stations or networks. Many programmers break down their work into creating discrete schedules for different parts of the day. The most prominent of these dayparts is 8 P.M. to 11 P.M. eastern standard time, when the largest numbers of people are viewing. These are the prime-time hours when the major broadcast networks put on their most expensive programs and charge advertisers the most money for commercial time.

The building block of a television schedule is a series. A series is a set of programs that revolve around the same ideas or characters. Series are useful to programmers because they lend predictability to a schedule. Programmers can schedule a series in a particular time slot with the hope that it will solve the problem of attracting viewers to that slot on a regular basis.

Programmers generally aim to bring viewers to more than just one show on their station or network. Keeping people tuned to more than one series also means keeping them around for the commercials between the series. In television-industry lingo, the challenge is to maximize the audience flow across programs in the daypart. Over the decades, programmers have developed a number of tactics with which they try to do that.

The key to audience carryover involves finding shows that attract the desired audience in large numbers. Every spring, network programming executives meet with creators from several production companies. Based on these meetings, the executives choose a large number of program ideas that they like. These ideas are then submitted in polls to see which ones the "audiences" are most interested in seeing. Once an idea passes the polling stage, a pilot (or sample) program is created. All of the pilots are then shown to sample audiences to get reactions. The pilots that get the strongest reactions are given a place on the next season's schedule. Once this has happened, the network executives typically sign contracts with the respective production companies to create thirteen episodes of each series. The contract—called a "license"—give the network permission to air each episode a certain number of times.

One might think that with such a deal in hand, the executives of the production companies would be ecstatic, sure that the show will enrich the company. This is not necessarily the case. For one thing, the show may not last long because of low ratings. In addition, network licensing agreements typically do not agree to pay the full costs of each episode. A production company may find itself millions of dollars in debt as a result of producing thirteen episodes of a series.

Why would any company want to create shows while losing money? The answer is that production companies see network broadcasts as only the first step of a series of television domains in which they can make money from their series. They can make it from local stations, from cable networks, and from broadcasters outside the United States.

Distribution

As suggested earlier, not all television programs are distributed through networks. The reason is that not all broadcast television stations affiliate with networks, and these independents need to get their programming from somewhere. Another reason is that even network stations do not broadcast the network feed all of the time. Certain hours in the morning, afternoon, earlier evening, and late night (past 1:00 A.M.) belong to the stations. Therefore, they can take for themselves all the advertising revenue that they bring in during those periods. However, they must first find programs that attract an audience at a reasonable price.

Many nonnetwork distributors are very willing to help local stations find attractive shows. Their business, syndication, involves licensing programs to individual outlets on a market-by-market basis. One way to attract audiences "off network" is with programs that are newly created for syndication. Examples include the talk show *Oprah Winfrey,* the entertainment news program *Entertainment Tonight,* the game show *Wheel of Fortune,* and the action-adventure series *Xena, Warrior Princess.* Another major method through which stations get programming is off-network syndication. In off-network syndication, a distributor takes a program that has already been shown on network television and rents episodes to television stations for local airing. Off-network syndication enables the distributor to make back money that it lost when it delivered the program to the network at a deficit.

If producers fail to place their reruns on local stations, there are other venues. Cable and satellite networks have become voracious users of programs that have already been seen on broadcast networks. This interest results in part because such programs are less expensive than new shows and in part because they have shown (in their network run) that they can reliably attract certain categories of viewers. Foreign countries have also been useful markets for certain types of reruns. Broadcasters around the world purchase U.S.-made series as components for their schedules, though in most cases homegrown programming gets better ratings than the U.S. material.

Broadcast network executives, suffering from monetary losses even when the license fees they pay do not fully cover the costs of program production, have been looking at these postbroadcast network distribution venues with envy. From 1970 to 1996, federal law prohibited broadcast networks from owning or distributing most of the programming that they aired. Government regulators feared that allowing them to both own and distribute programming would give them too much power over the television system. With the rise of a new spectrum of program distribution routes beginning the 1980s—cable, satellite, videocassette recorders, and even the Internet—the broadcast networks were able to convince the U.S. Congress that the prohibition had outlived its usefulness.

The new right to own and syndicate the programs that they air has meant that broadcast network executives have placed great emphasis on trying to improve their bottom line by making money through more than advertising. By licensing their own made-for-broadcast series and their own made-for-television movies to local stations, cable networks, and foreign television firms, executives hope to make their broadcast networks more predictably profitable. Another part of their plan for increasing revenues goes beyond new sources of distribution to new ideas about exhibition.

Exhibition

Local stations act as exhibitors when they broadcast material directly to viewers. However, the broadcast television exhibition system is in the midst of a major upheaval. Local broadcasters, the bedrock of the medium since its commercial introduction in the late 1940s, face ever-escalating competition from cable, satellite, and even telephone businesses. Local stations still make money, but observers wonder how the situation will change in the twenty-first century, as hundreds of channels race into American homes.

For the near term, network executives would like Congress to change the rule that prevents them from reaching 35 percent of U.S. homes. They reason that more revenues from local stations would flow back to their companies, rather than to affiliates that they do not own, thus better justifying the expenses of program creation. At the same time, the broadcast affiliates that are not owned and operated by the networks have begun to worry that the networks may at times be acting against their interests. Local television executives are concerned about the strong, increasing participation that the networks have in the cable, satellite, and Internet worlds. Disney-owned ABC, for example, controls cable/satellite networks ESPN, ESPN2,

The Disney Channel, Lifetime, and A&E. NBC participates in MSNBC and CNBC, as well as other channels. Viacom-CBS runs MTV, Nickelodeon, Country Music Television, and The Nashville Network. Local broadcast affiliates worry that these channels chip away at the audiences that might otherwise be viewing their stations.

Some local station executives also worry that huge growth in the number of video channels in cable or broadband Internet will encourage the networks to send their feeds directly to homes, instead of, or in addition to, local stations. Or, even if they continue to send local stations the daily feed, the networks will give people the opportunity to view (for a small fee) previous network programming that they missed on their local stations. That might still lead substantial numbers of viewers away from local stations.

Another impending change in exhibition involves the conversion to digital television. This conversion essentially will give every network and broadcast station the capability of sending out either one high-definition television signal or a number of regular-definition signals. What will the stations broadcast on the extra channels if they choose to go the regular-definition route? Will some of the channels require a decoder to allow the local stations to tap into subscription as well as advertising revenue? What will be the relationship between local and network broadcasters in this environment? Only time will tell. What seems clear, though, is that the broadcast television system will change dramatically in the twenty-first century.

See also: BROADCASTING, GOVERNMENT REGULATION OF; BROADCASTING, SELF REGULATION OF; CABLE TELEVISION; DIGITAL COMMUNICATION; FEDERAL COMMUNICATIONS COMMISSION; PUBLIC BROADCASTING; SATELLITES, COMMUNICATION; TELEVISION, EDUCATIONAL; TELEVISION BROADCASTING, CAREERS IN; TELEVISION BROADCASTING, HISTORY OF; TELEVISION BROADCASTING, PRODUCTION OF; TELEVISION BROADCASTING, PROGRAMMING AND; TELEVISION BROADCASTING, STATION OPERATIONS AND; TELEVISION BROADCASTING, TECHNOLOGY OF.

Bibliography

Turow, Joseph. (1999). *Media Today: An Introduction to Mass Communication*. Boston: Houghton Mifflin.

Walker, James R., and Ferguson, Douglas A. (1998). *The Broadcast Television Industry*. Boston: Allyn & Bacon.

JOSEPH TUROW

▐■ TELEVISION BROADCASTING, CAREERS IN

Careers in television broadcasting range from studio production to newsgathering to administration and sales. Likewise, the necessary educational training and experience differ according to position, as well as according to the size of the market that a television station serves. Market size further influences the staff size, and, consequently, the breadth of positions that are available at a given station. However, several positions remain staples of the typical television station, including the general manager, the controller, the accountant, the general sales manager, the account executive, the program director, the master control operator, the chief engineer, and the news and production personnel.

The general manager, who holds the highest position in a local television unit, works long hours overseeing a station's financial management and budgeting, short-range and long-range planning, administration and morale, and compliance with Federal Communications Commission (FCC) regulations. The typical general manager usually has a bachelor's or master's degree in a field such as communication or business, although the overall college experience is generally well rounded. The typical career path for most general managers can usually be traced through television advertising sales, although a few general managers are appointed from managerial positions in programming, news, or production. In addition, most general managers are selected from inside a television company, although some are lured from management positions at different broadcasting stations or from other business arenas in sales or marketing.

The controller is in charge of administration, budgeting, accounting, and forecasting the financial future of a station. Duties include the management of accounting personnel, general administrative staff, administrative operations, and office equipment. Controllers typically hold a bachelor's degree in a business-related field and have prior experience in sales. Consequently, most controllers are promoted to their positions from the accounting department within a television station.

The accountants at a television station are responsible for the bookkeeping, billing, and other logging of financial transactions. Furthermore, the accountants keep records of unused facilities and equipment, FCC-related correspondence, insurance claims, and tax-related reports. The typical accountant holds a bachelor's degree in accounting and obtains accounting experience either from other fields or from a communications operation.

The general sales manager manages the advertising accounts that a station has with local businesses and supervises the practices of the account executives. The general sales manager also monitors the activities of local competitors and creates rate cards, an airtime pricing schedule by which the account executives will sell airtime. General sales managers usually hold degrees in business-related fields and are former television station account executives. Many also have previous experience in retail or door-to-door sales, which provides a good background for selling airtime.

Much of the account executive's long day is in dealing with local businesses or advertising agencies and negotiating the sale of airtime. At some stations, the account executive will also help create a client's advertisement or promotional spot. For these positions, the account executive needs production or writing experience as well as sales experience. However, most account executives have retail or door-to-door experience only and some also hold academic degrees in business.

The duties of the program director range from the acquisition and scheduling of programs to the supervision of locally produced programming and promotional spots. In addition, program directors in small stations may also be responsible for creating daily logs, which detail the day's programming minute-by-minute. Job requirements for the program director usually include academic training in a business-related or media-related field. Adequate job experience is also needed and is usually gained from previous employment as an assistant programming director, programming staff member, or, less frequently, as a syndicator or network employee.

Master control operators put the programs on the air according to the daily logs, monitor the transmission quality, and record incoming program feeds. Master control operators do not necessarily need prior experience or academic degrees. In fact, all operators receive on-the-job training. However, competitive positions do require prior experience or academic training in a technical field.

The chief engineer purchases, maintains, and repairs the transmission, master control, studio, and other station equipment. The chief engineer also ensures the compliance of a station with FCC rules and keeps abreast of technological developments in the industry. Beyond these duties, the chief engineer supervises the broadcast technicians and master control operators. Almost all chief engineers have a degree in engineering or technology. Most chief engineers also have prior engineering experience and hold a broadcast engineering certification. A few engineers have additional training in business administration or a related field.

The news director directs the news programs and supervises the various actions of the news personnel. Assignment editors assign stories to the various news reporters, who create news packages with the help of the photographers. The packages, edited by editors, are presented with other scripted stories by the news anchors. For news or other locally produced programs, the production manager will assign and monitor a production crew. The crew consists of camera operators, audio operators, videotape operators, technical directors or video switchers, floor managers, videotape editors, computer graphics operators, teleprompter operators, and editors. A crew will produce the local programs, and it may also create promotional spots or client commercials. Directorial, managerial, and news positions are usually won with prior experience and perseverance in job advancement. Academic training in a media-related field can be attractive in securing these positions. However, a résumé tape and references usually have more weight in this competitive area than does a degree without experience. Crew positions require moderate to no experience depending on the market size and competition, and all provide on-the-job training.

Outside of the local station, several employment possibilities exist. For example, national sales managers are needed to win advertising contracts from national or regional companies for local stations. These salespeople usually begin as account executives, local sales managers, or as advertising representatives. Another option is syn-

Most television news reporters must do location work, while the news anchors work mainly in the studio. (AFP/Corbis)

dication, in which programs are obtained from networks or production companies and are then contracted out to local stations. The obvious alternative providers of employment, however, are the networks, who have job opportunities that both encompass and expand the offerings of the local television station.

See also: CABLE TELEVISION; CABLE TELEVISION, CAREERS IN; TELEVISION BROADCASTING.

Bibliography

Brown, James A., and Quaal, Ward L. (1998). *Radio–Television–Cable Management,* 3rd edition. Boston: McGraw-Hill.

Sherman, Barry L. (1995). *Telecommunications Management: Broadcasting/Cable and the New Technologies,* 2nd edition. New York: McGraw-Hill.

FRANCESCA DILLMAN CARPENTIER

▌■ TELEVISION BROADCASTING, EDUCATIONAL

See: Educational Media Producers; Researchers for Educational Television Programs; Television, Educational

TELEVISION BROADCASTING, HISTORY OF

The first flickering shadows of television were already in the ether before radio was well established. In 1923, Vladimir K. Zworykin, an employee of Westinghouse, patented the iconoscope television picture tube. Four years later, at about the time when NBC was organizing its radio network, Philo Farnsworth improved the system and patented the dissector tube. While others had experimented with ways to broadcast an image, these two independent inventors share credit for the birth of all-electronic television transmission.

The Great Depression of the 1930s slowed down television development, but the 1939 World's Fair in New York gave Americans their first look at the medium that would dominate the second half of the twentieth century. The Radio Corporation of America (RCA), owner of the National Broadcasting Company (NBC) and its radio networks, sponsored a Hall of Television that gave fairgoers a glimpse of the future. Franklin D. Roosevelt became the first president to appear on television when NBC broadcast the opening of the fair. The only viewers were the lucky few who gathered around a handful of sets in the New York area. A few weeks later, the first sports event was telecast when a New York station showed the Princeton–Columbia baseball game.

These historic broadcasts were among the first regularly scheduled television broadcasts in the United States, but other countries had already been on the air for years. Germany began broadcasting its nonexperimental national television service in 1935, while England's British Broadcasting Corporation (BBC) began broadcasting the following year. The first U.S. commercial television licenses were issued in 1941, when WCBW (later WCBS-TV) and WNBT (later WNBC-TV) began broadcasting to the New York City market.

Before television became a firmly established medium, however, the United States entered World War II, and television set production halted. In 1946, television sets went on sale again, and network television began to provide programming, although there were only ten licensed television stations in the country. At the time, radio was the dominant broadcast medium, already in almost thirty-four million homes, but it would soon experience a mass exodus of its audience.

By 1948, only two years later, almost one million homes had televisions, and there were 108 licensed television stations. Later that year, the Federal Communications Commission (FCC) ordered a licensing freeze to address interference issues. With the Korean War taking much of the country's resources, the ban lasted until 1952. During this time, some cities had only one or two stations, and reception was often poor. Other cities, including Denver, Austin, and Little Rock, had no television. Dozens of areas established community antenna television (CATV) systems to receive and distribute distant television signals. These CATV systems would eventually develop into the extensive cable television business.

In the 1950s, the new medium of television was replacing the old medium of radio. Attendance dropped at movies and sporting events, and once-popular radio shows saw their ratings plummet. In 1950, movie attendance among adults dropped 72 percent. Radio use fell from 3 hours and 42 minutes each night to just 24 minutes. By the time President Dwight D. Eisenhower took office in 1953, about one-half of the homes in the United States had television sets, and American mass media was changing forever.

By 1965, 94 percent of American homes had television sets; by 1990, more than 98 percent had televisions, and more than one-half of all U.S. homes had more than one set. While professional sports, the movie industry, and radio have regained popularity, television continues to dominate home entertainment.

Programming

By 1952, television broadcasts were reaching 15 million television sets in 64 cities. the American Broadcasting Company (ABC), the Columbia Broadcasting System (CBS), NBC, and DuMont offered a wide variety of programming choices, though DuMont ceased operations in August 1956. Although programming was in its infancy, the 1950s were considered to be the "golden age" of television. Some of the earliest entertainment programming on television came directly from radio, including such popular programs as *Amos 'n' Andy, The Adventures of Superman, The Lone Ranger,* and a number of soap operas.

Original variety shows such as *Your Show of Shows* with Sid Caesar and Imogene Coca, *Texaco Star Theater* with Milton "Mr. Television" Berle,

The New York World's Fair was part of the first television broadcast, which took place in April 1939. (Bettmann/Corbis)

and *Toast of the Town* with Ed Sullivan (later *The Ed Sullivan Show*) were popular draws. Programming also included dramas and westerns, such as *Playhouse 90* and *Gunsmoke*, respectively. Situation comedies, led by the still popular *I Love Lucy*, and quiz shows, such as *The $64,000 Question*, attracted large audiences. Children watched *Kukla, Fran, and Ollie* and, later, *Captain Kangaroo* and *Howdy Doody*.

While many shows were broadcast live during the golden age, *I Love Lucy* was produced with a new technique. Three cameras caught the action, which reduced interruptions and retakes. The filmed episodes could then be rerun by the network and sold into syndication for extended profitable runs. This and other similar production techniques continue to be used.

In the 1960s and 1970s, as color televisions became more prominent, westerns declined in popularity, but medical dramas thrived and realistic police dramas such as *Police Story* found audiences. Even the science fiction and fantasy genre

carved out a niche audience with programs such as *Star Trek*. Feature films were popular, and by 1966, the networks were airing their own made-for-television movies. In the early 1970s, the networks also began producing "event" programming in the form of limited-run series. Following the success of *Roots* in 1977, the miniseries became a mainstay of prime-time ratings sweep weeks (the periods that are key to the determination of the amounts that can be charged for commercial time).

By the 1980s, the audience for network television was diminishing as cable networks and prerecorded home video began to lure viewers. In addition, a new television network, the Fox Broadcast Network (Fox), debuted in 1986 and found success in the 1990s by targeting young audiences with shows such as *Beverly Hills 90210* and *The Simpsons*.

The television programming landscape has changed much since the golden age. Variety shows, so prevalent in the early days of television, were all but extinct by the 1990s. Prime-time network programming maintained its sitcoms and dramas (including the seemingly ever-popular police and medical shows), but it also showcased a number of reality-based programs. ABC, CBS, and NBC increased their newsmagazine offerings by 1993 and with good economic reason—a news-magazine show is cheaper to produce than an hour-long drama, and the network does not have to share profits. By the end of the 1990s, quiz shows had even made a successful return to prime-time network schedules. The 1990s also saw increased competition from new broadcasters, as the United Paramount Network (UPN) and the Warner Bros. Network (WB) debuted in January 1995. Paxson Communications' PAX-TV debuted in 1998.

Television News

As television was coming of age, so was television news. Just as the first programs came from radio, so did the first newscasters. Edward R. Murrow, who gained his reputation as a "newsman's newsman" for his coverage of Europe on CBS Radio during World War II, took his talent, and many of his colleagues, to television in the 1950s. His *See It Now*, which started as a radio news special titled *Hear It Now*, was the forerunner of many of the magazine shows that appear on television. Murrow was the first television reporter to take on Joseph McCarthy, the Wisconsin senator who falsely accused many people of having Communist sympathies (giving rise to the expression "McCarthyism"). Many people credit Murrow with helping to expose McCarthy.

Murrow also hosted *Person to Person*, which featured celebrity interviews rather than hard news. Murrow, in a New York studio, would be linked with people in their homes for a casual conversation. Among the celebrities who appeared on this program were Elizabeth Taylor, Marilyn Monroe, and John F. Kennedy when he was the newly elected senator from Massachusetts.

Television newscasts were short and lacking in much film coverage in the early days. In September 1963, CBS expanded the network newscast from fifteen to thirty minutes, with Walter Cronkite as the anchor. NBC, with Chet Huntley and David Brinkley, followed one week later. ABC did not expand its newscast to thirty minutes until January 1967. The basic formula for the modern nightly network newscast is little changed from those days.

When President Kennedy was assassinated about two months after CBS and NBC went to a thirty-minute newscast, television devoted the next four days to live coverage of the nation in mourning. This brought television into a new age. People no longer relied on their newspapers; instead, they turned to television for information in a crisis. Television news would further mature during the Vietnam War, which some have dubbed "the living room war," since it brought the war home to Americans each night as they ate dinner and watched the news. Antiwar demonstrations and the civil rights movement also gained wide exposure on television. The nation again found itself glued to the television in the summer of 1969 as live pictures were beamed back from the surface of the moon.

In the 1970s, television broadcast the Watergate hearings. "What did the president know and when did he know it?" and "smoking gun" became household expressions. Americans watched as President Richard Nixon resigned and as Gerald Ford assumed the office, assuring Americans that "our long national nightmare is over." By the end of the 1970s, Americans were held hostage in Iran and a popular news program was born. ABC started out counterprogramming *The Tonight Show with Johnny Carson* on NBC and old movies on CBS with a twenty-minute nightly news special called *The Iran Crisis: America Held Hostage*. U.S. State Department correspondent Ted Koppel soon became anchor of the program. When Ronald Reagan defeated Jimmy Carter and assumed the presidency in January 1981, the fifty-two hostages were released, and the program became *Nightline*.

Satellite technology started to come into frequent use by the news networks in the 1980s, allowing live or same-day recorded broadcasts from remote parts of the country and the world. In 1986, the U.S. Senate joined the U.S. House of Representatives in allowing broadcast coverage of floor debate. By the 1990s, satellite technology allowed live coverage of missile attacks and fighting during the Gulf War. Portable satellite dishes allowed transmission from Kuwait before the first liberation troops arrived. In 1994, the nation and the world watched the slow-speed chase of O. J. Simpson on a Los Angeles freeway. The subsequent live coverage of the Simpson murder trial attracted large ratings and a loyal following.

Technology

Much of the immediacy of the modern broadcast news environment can be attributed to advances in videotape technology. The first magnetic videotape recorder (VTR) was demonstrated by Bing Crosby Productions in 1951. Five years later, Ampex introduced the first commercial VTR, a 900-pound machine that recorded black-and-white images on two-inch tape housed on fourteen-inch reels (at a cost of $75,000 per unit). As technology progressed, VTRs became more portable, videotape became smaller while providing better resolution, and equipment prices dropped sufficiently to make video a viable alternative to film.

Sony debuted its U-Matic videocassette recorder (VCR) in 1972. The new format used a 3/4-inch tape in a $1,600 deck and soon became the industry standard. It continues to be used by some broadcasters, though Sony's Betamax SP format dominates the news industry. More recent digital tape formats, including Sony's DVCAM and Panasonic's DVCPRO, are also being integrated into electronic newsgathering (ENG) and other video productions. The new tape formats provide portability.

Videotape also found a prominent place in U.S. homes. Though earlier attempts at home video had flopped, Sony introduced its Betamax "video time-shift machine" in 1976. VHS, a rival system from JVC, debuted the next year, boasting longer recording times at a lower price. Television set manufacturers were divided in their support of the two formats, but VHS dominated the market within a few years. By 1983, VHS had more than 80 percent of the market. Sony finally withdrew Betamax from the United States in 1986 and began selling VHS VCRs in 1988. Despite several home-video formats on the market, consumers have remained loyal to VHS. According to the Consumer Electronics Association (CEA), VCRs were in 91 percent of U.S. homes by June 1998, and 40 percent of all households have at least two VCRs.

Audio, often considered an afterthought of television broadcasting, has also been improved. Stations began stereo broadcasts in 1985. In the 1990s, as stereo television, stereo VCR, and home theater sound system sales continued to increase, stereo surround sound became common for network programming. CBS, for example, broadcast all of its college and professional football games in

The growing use of satellite coverage allows for much more diversity in the reporting of major news stories, such as the O. J. Simpson murder trial in Los Angeles in the mid-1990s. (Joseph Sohm; ChromoSohm Inc./Corbis)

stereo surround sound for the first time during the 1999–2000 season.

Television began as a black-and-white medium. Color television technology had been demonstrated in 1929, and equipment had been developed as early as the 1940s, but the legal battle over color television took several years. Originally, the FCC approved a CBS-sponsored system in 1950. The National Television Standards Committee (NTSC), which included many companies with a financial interest in the decision, then researched the system, and in mid-1953, the committee recommended that the CBS system should be rejected. In December 1953, the FCC reversed its decision and approved RCA's color system, which was supported by rival network NBC. This NTSC transmission standard, which broadcasters adopted in January 1954, remains in use, though color sets did not see extensive U.S. household penetration for more than a decade. By the 1990s, almost every home in the United States had at least one color television set.

Looking Ahead

The future of television broadcasting is already here. Digital television (DTV) is nothing less than a revolutionary new way to broadcast television, replacing the NTSC analog standard that has been in place since 1953. The FCC adopted the new system in 1996, following more than a decade of development. Dozens of stations across the country are already broadcasting digital signals (in addition to their regular NTSC signals) in accordance with the FCC mandate. The FCC, which mandated the move to DTV and set 2006 as the date for completion of the transition from NTSC to DTV broadcasting, does have the option of reviewing and changing the DTV timetable, if necessary.

DTV promises improved pictures and sound for viewers, as well as greater flexibility in signal distribution for broadcasters. Stations will have the option of broadcasting more than one programming feed over the same channel simultaneously through a process called multicasting. High-speed data services will also be possible. High-definition television (HDTV), which provides outstanding picture resolution and a wider aspect ratio (an HDTV screen is 16:9, compared to NTSC screen, which is 4:3), is another potential service. All four major networks, ABC, CBS, Fox, and NBC, have already committed to prime-time HD programming. On April 26, 1999, NBC became the first network to provide regularly scheduled HD programming when it began to simulcast *The Tonight Show with Jay Leno* in both NTSC and HDTV.

See also: CABLE TELEVISION, HISTORY OF; DIGITAL COMMUNICATION; FARNSWORTH, PHILO TAYLOR; FEDERAL COMMUNICATIONS COMMISSION; MURROW, EDWARD R.; RADIO BROADCASTING, HISTORY OF; SATELLITES, HISTORY OF; TELEVISION BROADCASTING; TELEVISION BROADCASTING, CAREERS IN; TELEVISION BROADCASTING, PRODUCTION OF; TELEVISION BROADCASTING, PROGRAMMING AND; TELEVISION BROADCASTING, STATION OPERATIONS AND; TELEVISION BROADCASTING, TECHNOLOGY OF.

Bibliography

Barnouw, Erik. (1966). *A Tower in Babel*. New York: Oxford University Press.

Barnouw, Erik. (1968). *The Golden Web*. New York: Oxford University Press.

Barnouw, Erik. (1970). *The Image Empire*. New York: Oxford University Press.

Black, Jay, and Bryant, Jennings. (1992). *Introduction to Mass Communication*, 3rd edition. Dubuque, IA: Wm. C. Brown.

Blanchard, Margaret A., ed. (1998). *A History of the Mass Media in the United States*. Chicago: Fitzroy Dearborn.

Bliss, Edward, Jr. (1991). *Now the News: The Story of Broadcast Journalism*. New York: Columbia University Press.

Caldwell, John. (1995). *Televisuality: Style, Crisis, and Authority in American Television*. New Brunswick, NJ: Rutgers University Press.

Consumer Electronics Manufacturers Association. (1997). *U.S. Consumer Electronics Industry Today*. Arlington, VA: Consumer Electronics Manufacturers Association.

Consumer Electronics Manufacturers Association. (1998). *U.S. Consumer Electronics Sales & Forecasts, 1994–1999*. Arlington, VA: Consumer Electronics Manufacturers Association.

Greenfield, Jeff. (1977). *Television: The First Fifty Years*. New York: Harry N. Abrams.

Jennings, Peter, and Brewster, Todd. (1998). *The Century*. New York: Doubleday.

Levy, Mark R., ed. (1989). *The VCR Age: Home Video and Mass Communication*. Newbury Park, CA: Sage Publications.

Pescatore, Mark J. (1999). "Broadcast Options for the Transition to Digital Television." *Feedback* 40(4):1–7.

Roman, James. (1996). *Love, Light, and a Dream: Television's Past, Present, and Future*. Westport, CT: Praeger.

Silbergleid, Michael, and Pescatore, Mark J., eds. (1999). *The Guide to Digital Television*, 2nd edition. New York: Miller Freeman.

Trundle, Eugene. (1996). *Guide to TV and Video Technology*, 2nd edition. Boston: Newnes.

RICHARD LANDESBERG
MARK J. PESCATORE

■ TELEVISION BROADCASTING, PRODUCTION OF

Television production, whether it is a sitcom episode, a feature-length movie, a corporate training video, an educational program, or a newscast, must complete four basic phases before it is realized. These phases are the conceptualization phase, the preproduction phase, the production phase, and the postproduction phase. Completion of these phases may take months or years depending on the type, length, and complexity of the production, and, in fact, some programs such as a daily newscast may only allow for a single day to follow these phases on a loose basis. However, a good, tight production will usually execute each these four phases to some degree.

Conceptualization

The conceptualization phase of production is where the bulk of the creative work is completed. This phase begins with the generation of ideas. These ideas can be brainstormed by one or more creators, or in the case of a corporate video or other production that must meet certain objectives, several different people may be assigned to a specific area for which they will generate a creative concept. If needed, research via computer databases, interviews, or other sources may be performed to supplement the concepts that will be brought to the table for organization.

The second major part of the conceptualization phase is the organization of ideas. While there are many ways in which to organize concepts, some successful methods are worth mentioning. These are outlines, word trees, and the similar word webs. However the production group attempts this organization, it is helpful to at least think of the ideas as weaving together into an executable production process.

From here, two roads can be taken to turn the organized ideas into a scriptable proposal. The first option is the content avenue, which focuses solely on the content irrespective of the medium, in this case, television. A chosen person selects from the organized ideas the concept that best fits the desired program content. This content is then massaged into a workable script that is given to a television producer, who tries to make this content as compatible with the medium as possible. This avenue, though perhaps more accurate to the artist's vision, may ultimately fail when trying to translate a concept to the restrictive television screen. Distortion, crowding, and other problems may arise, thus diminishing the desired effect on the target audience. Therefore, the second option may elicit a better product.

This second option is the effect avenue, which takes into account the desired audience effect and molds the chosen concept accordingly. First, a concept coordinator chooses a concept from the pool of organized ideas. Next, the coordinator defines a desired audience effect or viewer experience, such as an emotion or a given amount of learning. The coordinator then tests the concept against the desired effect to see if the couple is compatible. If the coordinator determines that the concept has a successful chance at delivering the desired effect through the chosen medium, then the production chain continues. If the concept does not appear to be able to deliver given the medium, then the coordinator must go back to the pool of ideas and test another concept.

After an organized concept is chosen, it is time to write a program proposal. This is where a production team solidifies in writing its chosen title, objective, target audience, treatment, medium, and proposed budget. The title, of course, must be "catchy," but it must also serve as a good identifier of the proposed production. The objective may be simply to tell a story, or in the case of a corporate or educational video, it may be to teach a given set of topics. The target audience may be fairly general. However, every production has an optimal audience as defined by specific demographics (i.e., age, economic status, and gender), and, at times, by specific psychographics (i.e., likes and dislikes). The treatment answers the "what" and the "how" of the production, meaning the plot, the genre, and other identifying features. This can be answered via a brief descriptive of the proposed program or an illustrated storyboard of the various events or scenes. The medium is generally a type of technology such as television, radio, or print. However, medium can also be further specified into broadcast television, cable, satellite, and so forth. Finally, a proposed budget must be formulated. This budget will include above-the-line costs, which include creative personnel such as writers, directors, and artistic designers. The other part of the budget will consist of below-the-line costs such as the production crew, production equipment and rentals, and any other tangibles needed to produce the program. Once the budget is estimated, the proposal can be submitted for acceptance. Acceptance begins the second production phase.

Preproduction

Preproduction, which encompasses everything from the writing of the script to the gathering of props and costumes, begins with the gathering of personnel. These personnel may include writers, script editors, directors, art designers, costume designers, makeup artists, actors, production assistants, musicians, camera operators, audio operators, lighting directors, videotape operators, character generator or computer graphics operators, videotape editors, and other crew and support depending on the scope of the project. In other words, the number of people who are involved in preproduction of a given program can range from a small handful of people to a small army. Once the personnel are hired and money has changed hands, a writer is given the chosen concept and the desired effect and begins to work on a script. This script, which may experience several revisions depending on feedback by the producers and clients (if applicable), will then be given to a director, who will block the script, translating each scene into a workable audiovisual image. An art director will then take the blocked script and create a storyboard that illustrates each image and suggests locations, sets, graphics, costumes, or other aesthetic elements that will complete the director's vision. Once again, the producers and other interested parties will review this material. Once the overall vision for the project has been finalized, each image will be planned using several criteria.

The first criterion asks whether the program would best serve as a live production or as a recorded production. This decision will most likely dictate the fate of the other criteria, in that live productions by definition will require all shots to be executed in sequence, whereas recorded programs have the luxury of being edited.

The second criterion involves location. If the image is to be shot in a studio, then studio equipment and facilities will need to be acquired. If the image is to be shot in the field, then the producer must choose whether a single-camcorder setup is sufficient, or if a more sophisticated remote studio setup is necessary.

The third criterion involves camerawork. If a single camera is desired, then production will need to be stopped for each change in camera angle. If the more expensive multicamera effect is wanted, then multiple camera angles and shots can be recorded and manipulated simultaneously. This decision is partially affected by the earlier choice of location. For example, it may be desirable to use two cameras in a studio setting, whereas it may be more feasible to shoot single-camera style in the field. However, both camera options require efficient planning and direction of each shot and shot sequence.

The final criterion involves sequencing. Depending on the previous choices, the director may want to record shots in-sequence or out-of-sequence. For example, single-camera work is executed best when shots are planned out-of-sequence and according to which images share the same or similar backdrops. This, consequently, will require considerable editing during postproduction. Conversely, studio work lends itself well to in-sequence shooting, which requires little to no editing upon completion of the shooting.

Once each image is planned, a production schedule must be made that maximizes the use of time and money. Shots, therefore, are organized according to location as well as according to the featured actors. Equipment, props, scenery, costumes, makeup, and other electrical and mechanical necessities are also identified for each shot and location. Finally, the schedule is approved and the project goes into production.

Production

The production phase is perhaps the most exciting and most exhausting phase for the entire crew. This phase begins with long rehearsals amidst the creation of the setting. Only when the producers and directors are satisfied, or when the production schedule demands it, rehearsals become shoots and each scene is recorded. During this time, the various shots are recorded, reviewed, revised, and/or re-recorded as the production crew try to capture a good product within the confines of the production schedule. Also during this time, each shot is carefully logged according to position on the videotape or film, date and time of recording, content of the footage, and any other necessary information that will enable the editors to locate and identify it during postproduction. Without this log, hundreds of hours may be wasted trying to find certain footage for key scenes or needed filler. Therefore, it is imperative that every shot be logged and every tape be labeled so that the postproduction phase can be efficiently executed.

Postproduction

Postproduction involves the actual constructing of the envisioned program. It is the culmination of the long hours spent conceptualizing, planning, and recording the various program elements. Unfortunately, unless the program is a live program, postproduction usually takes longer than expected and therefore may stretch the estimated budget to its limits.

The main component of postproduction is the editing. Editors use either old-fashioned linear editing or nonlinear computer editing programs to put shots together in their designated order. However, not only do the editors follow the script, but they also take creative license in selecting the best shots, adding filler sequences, and even changing the sequence of certain scripted shots if deemed necessary. This means that they use the logs to find the desired footage to realize their own envisioned effect.

Meanwhile, graphic artists create any graphics, credits, or other computer-generated content. This content, along with any special audio tracks, is delivered to the editors, who incorporate the additions into the rough-cut. A review and revision process follows until the program is satisfactorily completed. The production is almost ready for release.

Other components of postproduction include publicity. This may mean the creation of advertisements, flyers, or other notices that attract the target audience to the program. This may also mean entering the project into a contest, a circuit, or other venue in which the project will be publicized and shown. Client feedback, if applicable, is also necessary to determine if the client's goals were obtained as well as if the client may be open to a future production contract. A final component of postproduction is record keeping. A record of personnel, production schedules, footage, and final cuts are good for reference both in planning and hiring for new projects and for winning new production contracts. In addition to creating a memorable project, the ultimate goal of a production should include the creation of a memorable résumé.

Production Differences for News Programming

News programming differs fundamentally from other production processes in several ways. For example, news programming is usually produced under the umbrella of a television station, which means that on-staff personnel are available to gather and compile the day's content. However, the production schedule of a news program spans just a single day, and its content depends on available news stories. The environment surrounding the production of news, therefore, can be quite hurried and intense.

Several news employees contribute to the surveillance and research of the local, regional, national, and international landscapes in order to find potential news stories. However, the assignment editors ultimately select the specific stories for the various reporters to pursue. As evident in the local news, many stories are written and read by news anchors with or without accompanying footage or graphics. Other news stories allow for the creation of a news package, in which a reporter will go into the field with a videographer and record stand-ups or narratives, interviews, and other footage over which the reporter will further narrate the story. This footage will then be brought back to the station and will be edited together into a succinct package. Final stories and packages will then be timed and arranged in order to create a twenty-two-minute newscast that runs twenty-two minutes and has designated breaks for commercial. Scripts are entered into a TelePrompTer from which the news anchors will read, graphics are rendered that will be used for names and other visuals, and the news director readies the crew for live broadcast. The culmination of this production, which can be altered at any time during the broadcast, is realized at the production phase, where the program is disseminated to the television audience.

In television news, some aspects of postproduction occur before production. Editing, for example, occurs when videotape editors put together news packages, and publicity occurs throughout the day whenever the station advertises its newscasts. However, the four phases of production are still present.

Other Considerations

In a simple world, all the producer needs to think about is the idea and the realization of that idea. However, several legal considerations need to be kept in mind when producing a program. For example, copyright clearance needs to be obtained if proprietary music, reproductions of paintings, or content from books or other items are to be used in the set, the script, or some other part of the production. Related to this are the rights of unionized personnel. Many creative and

The time pressures involved in news production are crucial because reports, such as those issued by reporters in the middle of the Kosovar refugee crisis in 1999, must be filed on a daily basis under less-than-ideal circumstances. (Howard Davies/Corbis)

technical personnel, such as directors, actors, camera operators, and engineers, belong to unions or guilds that may dictate minimum salaries, fees, or working conditions in exchange for employment. Authorization may also be needed to hire nonunion personnel if the production is being originated from a unionized organization.

Regarding program content, there may be certain content requirements, depending on the categorization of the program. The Federal Communications Commission lists eight mutually exclusive groups of programs: agricultural (A); entertainment (E); instructional (I); news (N); public affairs (PA); religious (R); sports (S); and other (O). If a program is considered to be educational, it may have to comply with various children's programming regulations. Furthermore, a program originating from, created by, or in cooperation with a certain organization, such as an educational institution, may automatically fall under a certain category, such as education, despite the program content.

Finally, all program content must be suitable, both legally and socially, for its target audience. In the legal realm, matters such as libel or slander must be considered when profiling or commenting on the life of a real person. In addition, lawyers or other legal counsel may help tackle the murky issues of right of privacy, indecency, and obscenity in a media production. Social guidelines for acceptability, however, will change with time and culture. However, broadcast standards and practices departments, media professors, and other counseling sources are available to aid in the ultimate conception of the television production.

See also: CABLE TELEVISION, PROGRAMMING OF; FILM INDUSTRY, PRODUCTION PROCESSES OF; TELEVISION BROADCASTING; TELEVISION BROADCASTING, CAREERS IN; TELEVISION BROADCASTING, HISTORY OF; TELEVISION BROADCASTING, PROGRAMMING AND; TELEVISION BROADCASTING, STATION OPERATIONS AND; TELEVISION BROADCASTING, TECHNOLOGY OF.

Bibliography

Alten, Stanley R. (1994). *Audio in Media*, 4th edition. Belmont, CA: Wadsworth.

Browne, Steven E. (1993). *Videotape Editing: A Postproduction Primer*, 2nd edition. Boston: Focal Press.

Wurtzel, Alan. (1983). *Television Production*, 2nd edition. New York: McGraw-Hill.

Zettl, Herbert. (1990). *Sight, Sound, Motion: Applied Media Aesthetics*, 2nd edition. Belmont, CA: Wadsworth.

Zettl, Herbert. (1992). *Television Production Handbook*, 5th edition. Belmont, CA: Wadsworth.

FRANCESCA DILLMAN CARPENTIER

TELEVISION BROADCASTING, PROGRAMMING AND

While the television set and the radio receiver are considered to be "hardware," programming is the essential "software" that actually tempts people to use these devices. The primary function of the station or network is to provide programming content that will appeal to some segment of the audience. The ability of a station to reach its desired audience will determine its success. Its programming mission and strategy are critical to its viability. As such, programming is the most visible and most vital commodity of television.

Programming Sources

There are some basic programming strategies that are common to both radio and television. A station or network must analyze the audiences that is available during a given time of day, examine its own schedule as well as that of the competition, determine the budget and revenues that are available for that time, and—with its ultimate goals in mind—make programming decisions. The programming day is broken into several dayparts, which (in the eastern time zone) are early morning (6:00 A.M. to 9:00 A.M.); daytime (9:00 A.M. to 4:00 P.M.); early fringe (4:00 P.M. to 6:00 P.M.); early evening (6:00 P.M. to 7:00 P.M.); prime access (7:00 P.M. to 8:00 P.M.); prime time (8:00 P.M. to 11:00 P.M.); late fringe (11:00 P.M. to 11:35 P.M.); late night (11:35 P.M. to 2:05 A.M.); and overnight (2:05 A.M. to 6:00 A.M.). The general manager, program director, and/or sales manager must determine the best type of program that is available for a given daypart and determine the

source of the program. There are five primary sources for programming: network-fed, syndicator-delivered, independently produced, locally produced and in-house, and paid programming.

Network-Fed Programming

In the earliest days of radio broadcasting, each station produced all of its own content locally. However, the production effort and programming costs were too great for most stations to bear this. Between 1923 and 1928, stations banded together to receive programming from a single, originating station. This innovative practice of networking decreased the production effort and spread the programming costs over a number of stations. Stations that affiliated with the networks (e.g., NBC and CBS) had the option of carrying local programming or the network-fed shows. This basic model is still alive and well in the broadcast television industry.

Local television stations are generally affiliated with one of the broadcast networks. Broadcast networks include ABC, CBS, NBC, Fox, WB, UPN, Pax TV, Univision, and Telemundo. An affiliated station, or affiliate, can choose to carry the programming that is fed by its network. The affiliate's agreement to broadcast the network program is a clearance, and the affiliate's decision not to broadcast a program is a preemption.

Upon clearing the show, the station airs both the show and all commercials that are sold by the network. The local station makes money on the arrangement by selling local commercial time during breaks in the network feed. These breaks are referred to as "availabilities." Generally, broadcast networks do not feed programming twenty-four hours a day. When the local station has no network feed available or decides to preempt network programming, it relies on one of the remaining sources of programming. The most common source in this situation is program syndication.

Syndicator-Delivered Programming

A syndicator is a company that makes contractual arrangements to place programs or movies on television stations and cable networks. Syndicators make a wide variety of programming available to each broadcast market and/or to cable networks. The shows range from *Oprah Winfrey* to *The Flintstones* to individual college football games. Station and cable network executives are usually responsible for examining the syndicated programming options and for conducting negotiations to obtain the rights to the programs that are best suited to their needs. Some negotiations occur at the annual National Association of Television Programming Executives convention. It is a "shopping mall" of syndicated programming options, and it is attended by syndicators and television executives.

The three most common types of syndicated packages are referred to as "first run," "off network," and "feature film packages." Feature film packages are groups of movies that are put together by a syndicator and offered to a local station. The local station negotiates the number of runs it gets for each film title, the amount of money that it may have to pay for airing the movies, and the dates and/or daypart(s) in which the film may air. Feature film packages may come with a mixture of box office hits and critical misfires. The station must determine the best way to use the titles to meet its programming goals.

Off-network programming refers to episodes of series that have previously played on a broadcast or cable outlets. Local stations negotiate with syndicators for episodes of series ranging from *The Andy Griffith Show* to *Buffy, the Vampire Slayer.* For the majority of successful network sitcoms and dramas, syndication is their major source of revenue. This is not surprising when one considers that off-network contractual agreements are made at virtually every television station in the United States and in many international stations and networks as well. Some successful series such as *Cheers*, *Home Improvement*, and *Seinfeld* have each generated hundreds of millions of dollars in syndication sales.

First-run programs are those series that have had no previous network exposure. The majority of syndicated fare is considered first run. Included in the category of first-run series are talk shows such as *Oprah Winfrey* and *Jerry Springer,* court shows including *Judge Judy* and *Divorce Court,* game shows such as *Wheel of Fortune* and *Jeopardy!,* news/entertainment series including *Entertainment Tonight* and *Inside Edition*, and entertainment series including *Xena, Warrior Princess* and *Hercules, the Legendary Journeys.* Stations and cable networks contract with companies such as Paramount, King World, and Studios USA for the rights to syndicated series. Contractual negotiations for all syndicated programs fall into one of

the following three categories: barter, cash, and cash-plus-barter.

The contract in barter syndication is the simplest. A station contracts for the rights to air a series or special. The station pays nothing for the program but must run all of the commercials that are sold by the syndicator. A one-hour program may contain fourteen minutes of commercial time or "inventory." The syndicator makes its money by selling about half of the commercial inventory in the show. The station makes its money by selling the remaining minutes of commercial availabilities in the show. Although economical, the station sacrifices a great deal of commercial inventory time in such arrangements. Barter programs are usually scheduled by frugal stations and/or in the less desirable time slots of a channel.

The contract for off-network series and some new programming is handled on a cash basis. In such cases, the station receives the series, as well as the entire commercial inventory, for a stated length of time. It attempts to turn a profit on the contract by selling advertisements. Cash deals can either be long-term contracts to run older series or short-term contracts to cover newer series with fewer numbers of episodes.

The most lucrative arrangement for the syndicator is one in which it can sell commercial inventory within a series and receive further compensation from individual stations. Such contractual agreements are called cash-plus-barter, or cash-plus. The station or network pays a cash license fee and must air the commercials that are sold by the syndicator. Unlike the barter deal in which the station is generally left with just half of the commercial inventory, cash-plus contracts leave the station with the majority of the commercial inventory. The station must attempt to recoup its investment by selling the remaining commercial availabilities. Though the cash-plus appears to be the worst value for the buyer, almost every successful daily syndicated series is sold on a cash-plus basis. This includes *Oprah Winfrey*, *Wheel of Fortune*, and *Entertainment Tonight.*

Independently Produced Programming

An independently produced program is one in which a station or network makes an exclusive contract with an outside producer to deliver a series, telefilm, or special. Though rare in local television programming, it is a standard operating procedure for networks. Networks make series and film commitments to producers such as Steven Bochco (Steven Bochco Productions) and Marcy Carsey and Tom Werner (Carsey-Werner) for a portion of their prime-time programming. They agree to a set amount for a project and determine the number of episodes to be delivered. The networks attempt to make their investment back through commercial sales.

Locally Produced and In-House Programming

In the early days of television, locally produced television shows ranged from children's programs to sports to news programs. Since that time, however, local productions in television have largely been limited to newscasts that air in the early morning, early evening, and late fringe time periods. Local newscasts can be the most profitable programs of a station, and they are used to establish an identity in the station's local community. Because of the heavy reliance on network and syndicated fare, some stations are returning to the concept of regularly scheduled local programs in an attempt to regain the notion of localism. Despite their relative rarity, local productions can be the most important programs of a station because they connect the station to its core audience.

For the major television networks and many cable networks, in-house programming is commonplace. NBC produces the *Today Show*, the *Tonight Show*, and others on a daily basis. The cable network E! produces *Talk Soup*, *Mysteries & Scandals*, and many other series and specials. The networks can air these shows whenever they wish and can syndicate them for added revenues.

Paid Programming

Another source of material for television outlets is that of paid programming. There are three types of paid programming: program-length commercials (i.e., infomercials), paid religion, and program-length political advertisements. In each type, the station or network sells an entire block of time to an entity in exchange for a cash payment. Through paid programs, the station lowers its programming costs and does not have to concern itself with selling commercial time. Paid programs are economically sound, but they generally deliver poor ratings and can interrupt the station's regular flow of programming. The use of any program source, including paid programming, is largely dependent on the goals of a station.

Local news programming is the area in which local television stations are able to exert the most control over what specific content they air, including which people are the best subjects for in-depth interviews. (Reuters NewMedia Inc./Corbis)

Programming Goals

Every broadcaster—commercial or noncommercial—must fulfil at least one goal: to serve the "public interest" as mandated by the Federal Communications Commission (FCC). To stay viable, broadcast licensees and networks watch their profit and loss statements closely. However, not everyone's programming goal is to be number one in the ratings. For the majority of stations and networks, this is unrealistic. Each broadcaster must have a set of specifically worded goals to see if it is meeting the needs of the public and the owner. These programming goals may include one or more of the following concepts: reaching a stated target audience, conserving programming resources, creating a positioning statement, branding of programming, and integrating technology.

Reaching a Stated Target Audience

Targeting the "mass audience" and striving for the top spot in the market or nation may be the goal of a station or network. Given the dizzying array of program options, most stations prefer to focus on a subset of the television audience. Stations that are affiliated with Univision and Telemundo (the Spanish-language networks) attempt to reach a significant portion of the local Hispanic audience. Other stations, such as ESPN, work to become the top sports source in the market. With that goal in mind, the station will combine live sporting events and shows that cater to the sports-minded audience. The notion of targeting specific audiences has long been associated with the magazine industry, with local and national radio, and with cable television. Since the 1980s, as programming options have continued to grow, targeting audiences has been refined and expanded to become the norm for all forms of television.

Conserving Programming Resources

Some stations or networks will sacrifice ratings to avoid the risk that is associated with high programming costs. These outlets have conserved programming costs by accepting barter programs, airing reruns, and/or allowing paid programming instead of pursuing superior programming alternatives that would involve a higher cost. As the concept of reaching a "mass audience" becomes less probable other than for major events (e.g., the Super Bowl), stations and networks will continue to lower programming risks by being very choosy in the area of high-budget programs and by relying on modest- to low-budget programs, reruns, and local and in-house productions.

Creating a Positioning Statement

A positioning statement is a one- or two-sentence description that distinguishes one business from another. In broadcasting, radio broadcasters have used positioning to help audience members make a link between the statement and the programming that is carried by the station. A statement such as "All Oldies, All the Time" can explain one's programming goal in a memorable manner. In television, the increased number of cable networks has encouraged both local stations and cable networks to adopt positioning statements. In cable, Lifetime uses "The Network for Women." In local television, "Family First" stations may make programming decisions to limit on-screen violence and offensive language, while a "Watch and Win" station may use promotional contests to call attention to its program lineup. As was the case in the magazine and radio industries, increased television outlets will result in more stations adopting program-based positioning statements.

Branding of Programming

Branding is a concept in which a show or, moreover, a block of shows is given its own unique identity. ABC uses this concept with its "TGIF" Friday night of situation comedies. This concept allows a network to target a specific audience for a portion of the day and to focus attention on that group of shows.

Integrating Technology

Stations and networks often use technological innovations to call attention to their programming, especially news and weather on local stations. Stations that are the first to adopt and actively promote digital technology, high-definition transmission, active Internet programming, and interactive television options are promoting their programs through technology. High-definition Monday Night Football games, Internet communities that are devoted to popular television shows, and interactive play-at-home versions of television games are just some of the concepts that have been successful. The convergence of digital television, Internet applications, and interactivity will be the fastest-growing area of television in the early part of the twenty-first century.

Audience Measurement

The Nielsen television ratings measure the percentage of the television audience that is watching a particular program. Most of commercial television's best programming and first-run episodes of series are shown during the major ratings periods called the "sweeps." The sweeps months of November, February, May, and July, are the only months that Nielsen gathers audience data for the entire nation. Families are selected to take part in the ratings process and fill out diaries about each show that is watched in the household for a stated ratings period. Nielsen tabulates the results both for the local stations that buy the ratings information and for the national networks.

Ratings data is also collected on a daily basis. For the national ratings estimates, five thousand selected households are sampled every day, and the results are published the next day. This quantitative data, known in the industry as the "overnights," is made possible because of the "People Meter" technology. The meter attaches to the television and sends instantaneous viewership data. These meters are also used in most of the fifty largest U.S. television markets and provide stations with daily statistics. As a result of this instant ratings data, stations and networks can quickly assess which programs are living up to expectations and which ones should be moved to a different time period or eliminated from their schedules altogether. The ratings information has a direct effect on what programming the audience sees—or does not see—on its television set.

Though programming maneuvers are made based primarily on the ratings numbers, the programmer also uses qualitative information. Viewers have mounted successful write-in campaigns to save quality programs and to have offensive programming either changed or removed from the schedule. Overwhelming critical praise of shows can also sway a programmer toward keeping an underperforming show on the schedule. Research departments often obtain information from test audiences (i.e., focus groups) that screen or pre-screen television programs. A focus group may give the program producers critical insights concerning program elements that may need adjusting. Viewers, therefore, have a direct and indirect effect on the programming process from development to ultimate success or failure.

See also: AUDIENCE RESEARCHERS; BROADCASTING, GOVERNMENT REGULATION OF; BROADCASTING, SELF-REGULATION OF; CABLE TELEVISION, PROGRAMMING OF; RADIO BROADCASTING, STATION PROGRAMMING AND; RATINGS FOR TELEVISION PROGRAMS; RESEARCHERS FOR EDUCATIONAL TELEVISION PROGRAMS; SOAP OPERAS; TALK SHOWS ON TELEVISION; TELEVISION, EDUCATIONAL; TELEVISION BROADCASTING; TELEVISION BROADCASTING, CAREERS IN; TELEVISION BROADCASTING, HISTORY OF; TELEVISION BROADCASTING, PRODUCTION OF; TELEVISION BROADCASTING, STATION OPERATIONS AND; TELEVISION BROADCASTING, TECHNOLOGY OF.

Bibliography

Blumenthal, Howard J., and Goodenough, Oliver R. (1998). *The Business of Television*, 2nd edition. New York: Billboard Books.

Brooks, Tim, and Marsh, Earle. (1999). *The Complete Directory to Prime Time Network and Cable TV Shows: 1946–Present*, 7th edition. New York: Ballentine Books.

Cahners Business Information. (2001). "Broadcasting and Cable." <http://www.tvinsite.com/broadcastingcable/index.asp?layout=webzine>.

Cahners Business Information. (2001). "Variety." <http://www.variety.com/>.

Crain Communications. (2001). "Electronic Media." <http://www.emonline.com/>.

Eastman, Susan Tyler, and Ferguson, Douglas A. (1996). *Broadcast/Cable Programming: Strategies and Practices*, 5th edition. Belmont, CA: Wadsworth.

Nielsen Media Research. (2001). "Nielsen Media Research." <http://www.nielsenmedia.com/>.

Vane, Edwin T., and Gross, Lynne S. (1994). *Programming for TV, Radio, and Cable*. Boston: Focal Press.

VNU Business Media. (2001). "Hollywood Reporter." <http://www.hollywoodreporter.com/>.

DAVID SEDMAN

TELEVISION BROADCASTING, PUBLIC

See: Public Broadcasting; Public Service Media

TELEVISION BROADCASTING, RATINGS FOR

See: Ratings for Television Programs

TELEVISION BROADCASTING, REGULATION OF

See: Broadcasting, Government Regulation of; Broadcasting, Self-Regulation of; Cable Television, Regulation of

TELEVISION BROADCASTING, STATION OPERATIONS AND

The various operations of a television station revolve around the manufacturing and sale of a product, much like any industry; and like any industry, the various departments of the station work both independently and cooperatively to meet its production goals. In the case of the television station, however, that product is the programming airtime that is consumed by the public, and the sale of that product is advertising time. Therefore, the various departments of the television station can be categorized according to their tasks of creating the product, advertising the product, transmitting the product, selling the product, and managing the revenue from the product.

General Organization of a Television Station

The organization of a television station depends on the size of the market in which it operates and the type of ownership under which it exists. For example, small-market television stations may only retain skeleton crews for each department whereas large-market stations may have as many as fifty employees on the payroll for a given department. In addition, larger stations may necessitate the division of departments into smaller branches in order to increase efficiency. Regarding ownership, stations under multiple ownership often have a higher-level organizational pyramid consisting of a manager that oversees the operations of all owned stations, managers that oversee regions of stations, and so on. However, the typical television station will contain the following seven operations: general administration, sales, programming, production, news, advertising, and engineering.

General Administration

General administration operations manage and distribute the revenue received from station sales of advertising time. This includes the appropriation of available funds to each department as well as the billing of supplies and services both interdepartmentally and externally to clients and advertising agencies. In short, the general administrative function supports and maintains the operations of the entire station.

Under the general administration division are the general manager or station manager, the business manager, the accountants, the secretaries, and other administrative and office staff. These employees serve various duties such as the payment of wages and salaries, membership fees and subscriptions for industry information, license and other government-imposed fees, taxes, insurance, legal and auditing fees, and contributions to charitable organizations. In addition, maintenance of the building and of equipment, utilities, office supplies, computers, station automobiles, and other administrative services and supplies are also provided by the general administrative department. It is not surprising, then, that this department consumes one-third of the total operating expenses of a station, although only about 13 percent of the total staff may be in administration.

Sales

The sales department at a television station is responsible for generating the revenue for the station to survive. A general sales manager leads a team that is comprised of a national/regional sales manager, a local sales manager, account executives, and at times, a traffic manager. In most cases, the national/regional sales manager will be a liaison from an outside organization that wins advertising contracts from regional and national advertisers. The local sales manager, then, is charged with securing advertising accounts with local businesses and organizations. A staff of account executives helps the local sales manager sell advertising time to local businesses employing solicitation tactics similar to other sales businesses. However, the salespeople of television must negotiate advertising sales using a rate card, a definitive list of airtime costs during the various time periods and television programs. Furthermore, the television account executive can also offer to create the advertisement for a client if the client so chooses, in which case the sales department cooperates with the production and programming departments for this venture.

A linking figure between the sales department and the programming department is traffic, which has traditionally fallen under programming but is increasingly becoming an arm of sales. Traffic prepares the daily log, which details to the second every program, promotional spot, and commercial that will air each day. Responsibilities for this position include staying well informed of new advertising accounts, ensuring that all slated commercials are available to air, and monitoring proposed programming schedules for commercial placement. For example, the traffic manager may want to ensure that two commercials advertising a similar product are not placed back-to-back or that a single commercial is not run twice in the same commercial block. A final duty of the traffic department is to maintain a careful record of every commercial and promotional spot that has run so that the accounting and sales departments can cooperate in the proper billing of the client.

In order to market a station effectively, the sales department must be intimately familiar with the ratings, viewer numbers, and the types of viewers that are watching during various programming periods. Therefore, the department must subscribe to ratings services and perform market research. In addition, the sales personnel, who account for about 17 percent of the total staff, receive wages, salaries, or commissions for every contract won, as well as expense accounts and benefits. However, the total cost of this department with respect to the total operating budget of a station is around 9 percent, a small price to pay considering that sales generates more than 95 percent of the revenue of a station.

Programming

The programming department, in conjunction with the production and news departments, acquires and schedules the product that the audience consumes, which in turn allows the sales department to create revenue, which in turn allows the general administration department to facilitate station operations. The programming department is responsible for filling the entire broadcast day with programming and is therefore saddled with arguably the most challenging job in television. Consequently, this department also works closely with the traffic department in structuring the daily programming schedule.

Programming is second only to general administration in terms of operating expenses. The department, if its station is affiliated with a network, needs almost 25 percent of the total budget of the station to function. However, an independent station may give as much as half of its total operating budget to the acquisition of programs.

Programming may consist of a program director, a videotape librarian, a ratings researcher, an acquisitions staff, a continuity standards staff, and on-camera personalities for use in locally originated programs. The program director, helped by the acquisitions personnel, may obtain the majority of the programming of a station from syndicators and other program suppliers. If a station is affiliated with a major television network, then programming will have the luxury of choosing how much programming it will schedule from the network. In a larger market, viewership research may be conducted to help the program director select a programming plan that will attract a substantial audience. Community feedback also aids in planning decisions. However, all decisions concerning program acquisition are ultimately controlled by the amount of revenue gained from sales and the resulting budget allotted the programming division.

Another responsibility of programming besides program acquisition is program creation. Many stations produce public-affairs programming in order to meet their public-interest obligations. The programming department is usually given the job of preparing and producing these programs. Therefore, on-camera talent may be employed to create these public-affairs programs. In addition, the programming department may also be solicited to help the sales department create an advertisement for a client. In this situation, the continuity standards staff may write the advertising script, revise a script given to the station by a client or advertising agency, and/or review a script against government and station standards and policies. However, in any case where programming must produce a program, the production department is there to bring the program to its culmination.

Production

The production department works closely with the programming, news, engineering, and sales divisions. Its sole responsibility is to produce the various programs, be they news packages, newscasts, public-affairs programs, station promotional spots, client commercials, or other productions that a station may require. Because of its close relationship with the other departments, much of the production department's costs are absorbed into the other departments. As a result, it is difficult to say how much production really costs a station, although production in conjunction with programming takes approximately 31 percent of the total budget and production in conjunction with news takes approximately 12 percent.

Production usually consists of a production manager, producers, directors, and studio and remote crews. The studio crews operate the cameras, the audio board, the videotape recorders, the TelePrompTer, the video switcher, the computer or character generator, and any other equipment needed to complete the in-house production. In contrast, the remote crews operate the ENG (electronic newsgathering) or more sophisticated EFP (electronic field production) cameras and other equipment to produce programs or packages outside the television studio. Once footage is obtained, editors edit the programs together and insert any computer graphics and audio tracks until the product is satisfactorily completed. Then, the program may be given to the programming department to review and schedule, and then to the traffic manager to enter into a daily log. In the case of news, programs are prescheduled and the production is completed via live broadcast. In the case of any production, the engi-

The control board is the center of operations for in-house production and editing of television programs. (Shelley Gazin/Corbis)

neering crew monitors the equipment and, ultimately, the transmission of the program.

News

The news department is primarily responsible for creating news programming such as newscasts and news interview shows, although sometimes members of the news team will participate in the production of public-affairs programs. The news department is headed by the news director, who oversees all news operations and produces the final program. Assignment editors coordinate with the news director and assign stories to available reporters. Copy editors may also be employed to review and edit the written stories, and videotape editors may be employed to edit footage together. The remaining staff may consist of news anchors and reporters, sports anchors and reporters, and meteorologists.

Naturally, news must work closely with both the production and engineering departments. Production crews are needed to run the studio production of newscasts and other programming. In smaller stations, videographers (or photographers) from the production team will accompany reporters when gathering stories in the field, and the production department editors will put these packages together. Similarly, engineering will be present during studio recordings, live studio broadcasts, and, at times, field shoots to ensure that all equipment is calibrated correctly and that transmission of the signal is of broadcast quality.

Although not as costly as the average programming department, news can command as much as 20 percent of the budget of a station. In fact, news personnel in a medium-sized market may comprise almost one-fourth of the total staff of a station, as well as consume a generous amount of resources such as videotape, office materials, and power. For these reasons, perhaps, many independent stations choose not to produce many newscasts, which can cut this expenditure down to around 5 percent of the total budget. The irony of this situation, however, is that many television stations are able to sell more advertising because their stations produce news, making news a profit center for the station.

Advertising and Promotions

Advertising and promotions is where a station creates its own promotional spots and advertisements in an attempt to gain more viewership, and therefore more advertising dollars from local, regional, and national companies. This division is often combined into sales, although it may make an appearance in programming. This varying categorization of advertising and promotions makes it difficult to get an average number of staff or percentage of operating budget required. However, a fairly accurate estimation is that an average station may spend up to 5 percent of the budget on promotional and advertising activity.

Advertising and promotions works in close conjunction with the sales, production, and engineering departments. Often, it will also cooperate with the news department to create promotional spots for the various newscasts and news programming that the station produces. Other promotional spots may advertise specific shows that the station offers, or they may inform the audience of some community service or event that will be taking place in the near future. Usually, sales looks to the programming and promotions departments to increase the number of viewers that the sales department can then "sell" to an advertiser. Programming may then conduct audience research to determine the main attractions, or selling points, of a station. This information will then be synthesized into content that production will turn into a ten-, fifteen-, or thirty-second spot highlighting the chosen station asset. The ultimate goal is to advertise and promote the product in a way that maximizes the audience and revenues from advertising sales.

Engineering

The linchpin of a television station is the engineering department. It is the duty of this department to transmit the programming product of a station to its audience. An average of twenty employees may have the responsibility of ensuring that a station transmits properly. These employees include the chief engineer, who oversees all technical operations, the broadcast technicians, who help maintain the equipment, and the master control operators, who actually put the programming on air.

The two main areas of responsibility for engineering are master control and technical supervision. Master control plays and transmits the programs, commercials, and live broadcasts according to the daily log created by traffic. In addition, master control also monitors the video and audio signals being transmitted, records incoming satellite feeds, and airs emergency broadcast announcements when necessary.

Technical supervision encompasses everything from maintenance to surveillance of industry developments. Broadcast engineers, for example, are responsible for fixing a broken videotape machine, but they also monitor the signals coming from cameras, microphones, and other studio and field equipment to ensure the best possible quality. In addition, engineering must perform necessary equipment upgrades, both to maintain the competitive strength of a station and to ensure compliance with the technical requirements of the Federal Communications Commission. Engineering and its various acquisitions of parts, supplies, and equipment typically require only 6 percent of the total budget of a station. However, when new technologies evolve, stations find it necessary to allocate more funds to incorporate these technologies into their operation.

The Evolution of Station Operations

Two general and inevitable trends identified in television must be considered when evaluating the potential future of station operations. The first trend is that of the shrinking local market. Television traditionally enjoyed increases in audience reach and influence. However, individual stations must continually fight for a shrinking piece of the advertising pie. The development and adoption of new media offer consumers more choices, which splits the potential audience and reduces the potential advertising revenue that any one medium may capture. Therefore, sales departments are becoming more creative and other departments more efficient for stations to respond to the changes in their competitive environment.

The second trend is the development of new technologies. As analog television technology makes way for digital, competitive concerns as well as government mandates are compelling stations to upgrade their entire production and transmission equipment. This very expensive alteration is not new. Television went through a similar change when it adopted color, and doubtlessly, television will need to adjust to other technical changes in the future. Therefore, as new and competing technologies develop, and as industry and government implement standards to adopt new technologies, stations will continue to evolve to meet the challenge and expense.

See also: CABLE TELEVISION; CABLE TELEVISION, CAREERS IN; CABLE TELEVISION, PROGRAMMING OF; TELEVISION BROADCASTING; TELEVISION BROADCASTING, CAREERS IN; TELEVISION BROADCASTING, HISTORY OF; TELEVISION BROADCASTING, PRODUCTION OF; TELEVISION BROADCASTING, PROGRAMMING AND; TELEVISION BROADCASTING, TECHNOLOGY OF.

Bibliography

Brown, James A., and Quaal, Ward L. (1998). *Radio-Television-Cable Management*, 3rd edition. Boston: McGraw-Hill.

Sherman, Barry L. (1995). *Telecommunications Management: Broadcasting/Cable and the New Technologies*, 2nd edition. New York: McGraw-Hill.

FRANCESCA DILLMAN CARPENTIER

■ TELEVISION BROADCASTING, TECHNOLOGY OF

Television production and postproduction require an extensive array of equipment, but the most important element for television production is patience. Before any equipment has been turned on, before the lights have been focused, before the director has called his or her first shot, creative personnel must take the time to plan the production. Despite the best intentions of the production team, poor planning or a weak premise will only result in a feeble finished product.

Cameras and Accessories

Central to television is the use of cameras, which provide most of the visual elements that the audience sees. Basically, the camera is the visual acquisition tool that uses a lens to project an image (technically, the light reflected from the subject) onto the camera's pickup element, either an electron tube or a solid-state imager. The tube encodes the image into thousands of dots, and then an electron gun "reads" the dots and outputs the signal. Most cameras have replaced the tube system with a "chip" system (solid-state imager) that uses one or several charge-coupled devices (CCDs), which are smaller, more durable, and use less power than tubes.

Camera operators can control various elements of the image through lens selection and camera features. For example, electronic shutter speed can vary, video signals can be amplified through gain control, the aperture can be opened or closed to adjust for lighting conditions, and the field of view can be changed without physically moving the camera (provided that the camera is equipped with a zoom lens). Most professional cameras also have built-in white balance control, which compensates for light temperature and adjusts the picture to reflect optimal color rendition.

Generally, cameras are configured as either studio cameras or portable cameras. Portable cameras, often called handheld cameras, are often used for electronic newsgathering (ENG). Most professional portable cameras are designed to rest on the right shoulder of the operator, with camera controls within reach and the viewfinder resting in front of the operator's right eye. Handheld cameras are designed to run using battery power. Either the battery is attached to the rear of the camera or the camera is connected to a battery belt pack. Modern ENG cameras, often called camcorders, also have a built-in videotape recorder (VTR) and microphone, and they often sport a removable mini-light for better closeups.

In contrast, the studio camera does not have a built-in VTR or microphone. In addition, studio cameras use conventional power instead of batteries because they are in a studio environment. Studio cameras often feature more sophisticated lens systems (a box-type lens) than ENG cameras. Some high-end cameras feature swappable components, so they can be configured as a studio or remote camera.

The camera pedestal provides a large, stable mount with wheels for studio cameras. Pedestals allow camera operators to change easily the position of the camera on the studio floor, as well as the camera height and angle. They are also built to accommodate studio-configured camera controls, often called "configs." Rather than making adjustments directly on the camera, studio configs allow the camera operator to control focus and zoom from remote controls on rods that are attached to the pedestal. The operator can also view the picture on a monitor that is attached to the top of the camera, rather than through the ENG camera's

The technology for cameras is continually being refined to accommodate digital advancements, and one of the results was Sony's 2000 release of its professional-use digital video camcorder DSR-PD150, which features three 380,000-pixel CCDs (light-sensitive picture elements) on its image sensor, a 6.0-72.0 mm zoom lens, and a 200,000-pixel 2.5-inch color LCD (liquid crystal display) on its monitor. (AFP/Corbis)

smaller and less convenient viewfinder. Studio configs also incorporate a headset microphone, which allows the camera operator to communicate with the director in the control room.

For remote shoots, tripods are often the preferred camera-mounting equipment, due to their compact size and lighter weight. Tripods allow remote cameras to be configured like studio cameras and save operators from constant handheld shooting. Tripods support the camera on three legs but do not have wheels, so the camera is physically fixed in one position. Camera operators can attach wheels to the bottom of a tripod with a dolly, but movement is not as smooth and predictable as when a pedestal is used.

In special production circumstances, cameras are mounted in a fixed position, though camera operators can maintain camera control remotely. Network football game coverage, for example, routinely includes a camera mounted on the goal post, while cooking programs will often mount a

camera above the talent to provide a better view of the work area. Cameras can also be attached to counterweighted jib or crane arms or suspended on a wire for smooth, moving shots. Cameras can even be mounted to the body of the camera operator for more stable handheld shots.

Video Switcher

The technical director (TD) sits at the heart of the control room, the video switcher, which has rows of buttons that are used to select which video source will be recorded or broadcast. Each row is called a bus or bank. The program bus controls which image is recorded on a VTR or is broadcast. The preview (or preset) bus, which usually has its own monitor, provides the TD (who is sometimes referred to as the "switcher") the opportunity to check images that are not on-screen before switching to them on the live program bus. TDs can also "key" one source, such as graphics, over another source, such as a camera.

For example, if there are five cameras covering a football game, each camera will have its own button on the program bus and preview bus. When a camera is "hot," or on-the-air, the TD can use the preview bus to preview an effect. Other video sources, such as the graphics station and slow-motion replay, will have buttons on the switcher as well. If a reporter interviews a coach on the sideline, the TD can key the coach's name (using the character generator) over the camera image.

Using the switcher, the TD can switch between cameras and other video sources in a variety of ways. A cut, an instantaneous change, is the least obtrusive transition between images. A fade transitions gradually from a color (usually black) to another image or vice versa. Dissolves simultaneously fade-in one image while fading-out another, and they are often used to illustrate the passage of time. Finally, wipes and digital video effects (DVE), which can be created using external equipment, are the most noticeable transitions, as one image literally wipes across another to replace it, often in a dynamic pattern that attracts attention. Fades, wipes, and DVE moves are controlled manually with a fader bar, though some switchers offer preset controls as well.

All video switchers essentially do the same job, but not all video switchers are created equal. More advanced switchers can include a number of additional functions and effects. Some switchers can handle dozens of inputs and have multiple input buses, while others have limited sources and only preview and program buses. Other switchers have downstream keyers, which allow key inserts just before the program source leaves the switcher without using a switcher's mixing or effects systems. Some switchers even have chroma key, which inserts one image over another to create a composite image (often used for weather reports where meteorologists stand in front of live satellite footage).

Graphics

The graphics station is the home of the character generator (CG), often called the Chyron, based on the name of the dominant CG manufacturer. The graphics operator is responsible for providing pages of text and other graphic images that will be used during a production, from opening titles to the closing credits. Improvements in technology have made graphics more dominant on television

than ever, with more detailed and visually energetic images. Digital paint systems can create three-dimensional and animated images, while even simpler PC-based CG programs can manipulate and animate text efficiently.

Most graphics are built in preproduction so that access is simple during production. At a football game, for example, player names would be typed in before the game, and introductory graphic images, such as the starting lineups, would be ready for broadcast before kickoff. Game statistics, however, would be composed on the CG as the game progressed.

Audio

Different audio performances require different audio acquisition tools, some of which are visible to the audience. On-camera microphones include (1) the handheld microphone, which is used extensively for interviews, (2) the desk microphone, which remains in a fixed position on a small stand, (3) the stand microphone, which can be adjusted to match the height of the performer, (4) the headset microphone, which is used by sportscasters to keep the microphone close to the mouth and provide program audio and directions in a noisy environment, and (5) the lavalier microphone, which is an unobtrusive microphone that is clipped to the front of the talent's clothing.

When productions call for microphones that are not visible to the audience, highly directional boom microphones are positioned out-of-frame above or below the action, often using a collapsible aluminum pole (i.e., a fishpole). Comments from a roundtable of panelists can be recorded using a pressure-zone microphone (PZM), which captures sound from a variety of sources but equalizes the volume of all sounds (so shuffling papers sound as loud as a person speaking). Other types of microphones can be concealed throughout a set, though wires must also be hidden and talent must be positioned near the microphones for optimal effectiveness.

Microphones also vary in their audio pickup patterns, or the way in which they capture audio. The omnidirectional microphone, for example, provides equal audio pickup from all sides. It is useful for capturing crowd noise in a stadium during a football game. During that same game, however, a sideline commentator may want to interview a coach. The commentator will use a handheld unidirectional microphone, which features a much more narrow pickup pattern, to isolate the coach's comments from the noisy stadium around him. For isolating the sounds of football players on the field, an audio assistant will hold a microphone in a parabolic reflector, which resembles a shallow dish and increases microphone sensitivity and direction. Other audio pickup patterns include the cardioid, which maintains a heart-shaped pattern; the supercardioid, which features a more narrow, directional pattern with limited pickup behind the microphone; and the bidirectional, which picks up sound in front of and behind the microphone but is deaf to noise on the sides.

Production sound is coordinated through the audio board (though some remote shoots use smaller but less flexible portable audio mixers). Prerecorded music, videotape roll-ins, and live sound are all input into the audio board as electrical signals. Each audio source is given its own channel, and the operator sets the volume for each channel using rotating knobs called potentiometers (pots) or sliding bars (faders). Each signal can also be manipulated through equalizers to improve sound quality. The board operator monitors the intensity of the sound level using a volume unit (VU) meter, which indicates the volume in terms of decibels and percentage of modulation. Overmodulation, which occurs when the audio signal is stronger than the maximum percentage of 100 percent modulation, can lead to distortion, especially in digital audio situations. The master output from the audio board provides the audio mix for the program.

The audio board is not set once and forgotten for the rest of the shoot; it needs to be constantly monitored, or ridden. Also, audio levels vary during a telecast, so the board operator must "ride" the levels of the inputs. During a football game, for example, if a commentator gets excited and begins to shout, the board operator must be ready to bring down the volume of the signal or risk distortion. Also, the sideline commentator's microphone only needs to be open or "hot" during interviews. The board operator must be ready to close or "kill" the microphone when it is not in use to avoid broadcasting comments that are not supposed to be on the air.

Editing

For live programming, the show is usually over when the director declares the production a "wrap" and the crew strikes the set and equipment. However, most productions are followed with some kind of postproduction work. Even when a program is shot live-to-tape, so the production is recorded as it happens and without stopping, directors may want to insert video or graphics over bad shots, clean up or add sound effects, or add other special effects.

During production, when mistakes are made, the director often says, "We'll fix it in post." Postproduction usually corresponds with a trip to the editing suite. Editing is a process that is used to put shots in different chronological order, vary shot selection, alter the timing of shots to improve pacing, and add transitions between shots. Editing is a tool to help the director tell his or her story better, and different programs will use different editing strategies. A promotional video for a sports event, for example, may edit action shots together in a furious frenzy of short clips to create excitement. A music video for a romantic ballad, in contrast, may use slow dissolves and far fewer cuts so that a more relaxed mood is created.

Traditionally, video editing has been a linear process, where the editor works with videotape and other inputs to build a program in chronological order (assemble editing) or replace sections of video and/or audio in an existing project (insert editing). The main advantage to linear editing is speed; an experienced editor can literally cut together a news package or other short, basic projects in minutes. Advanced editing systems also can incorporate graphics and other digital video effects (DVE). However, there are several limitations. Editing with analog videotape results in loss of video quality with each generation; in other words, an edited package that contains video copied from original video will not look as good as the original footage. A copy or "dub" of that edited footage will look even worse. Some tape formats show minimal loss during the first few generations, but loss of video quality cannot be avoided entirely. Excessive use can also wear down videotape and equipment. Also, it is troublesome to return to a completed project and make changes, because then the rest of the project must either be re-edited to accommodate the change, or it must be dubbed to a new tape and attached to the changed footage, which results in a generation loss.

Nonlinear editing became an affordable alternative to linear editing in the 1990s. Footage is digitized, or fed into the computer and turned into data. Editors can then manipulate graphics, audio, video, and transitional effects in any order. The advantages of nonlinear editing are numerous. First, there is less tape and equipment wear; once footage is digitized, tape is not needed for the editing process. Because there is no tape, there is also no generation loss. Digitized video maintains its quality no matter how much or how little it is used, although compression can affect quality. Editors can also "jump around" in the nonlinear world; pieces can be edited and re-edited without concern for the timeline. This opens the door to much more creative experimentation and flexibility. The major drawback to nonlinear editing is digitizing time. Footage must be digitized in real time for most systems, so editing has to wait until the footage has been loaded into the computer. For projects with tight deadline constraints, this can be impractical.

See also: CABLE TELEVISION, SYSTEM TECHNOLOGY OF; DIGITAL COMMUNICATION; FILM INDUSTRY, TECHNOLOGY OF; TELEVISION BROADCASTING; TELEVISION BROADCASTING, CAREERS IN; TELEVISION BROADCASTING, HISTORY OF; TELEVISION BROADCASTING, PRODUCTION OF; TELEVISION BROADCASTING, STATION OPERATIONS AND.

Bibliography

Millerson, Gerald. (1988). *Video Production Handbook.* Boston: Focal Press.

Millerson, Gerald. (1993). *Effective TV Production,* 3rd edition. Boston: Focal Press.

Silbergleid, Michael, and Pescatore, Mark J., eds. (1999). *The Guide to Digital Television,* 2nd edition. New York: Miller Freeman.

Wurtzel, Alan, and Acker, Stephen R. (1989). *Television Production,* 3rd edition. New York: McGraw-Hill.

MARK J. PESCATORE
MICHAEL SILBERGLEID

■ TOBACCO AND MEDIA EFFECTS

Although cigarette smoking by adults has declined steadily since the 1960s, smoking by adolescents has risen sharply since 1992. In 1999, the Centers for Disease Control (CDC, 2000a) reported that teenage daily smoking increased 73 percent between 1988 and 1996. Coincidentally (or not), 1988 was the first full year, and 1996 the last, that R. J. Reynolds featured the "Joe Camel" cartoon-advertisement campaign (which had considerable appeal among children). The increase in adolescent smoking in the 1990s has been attributed to a variety of factors, including the targeting of youths by tobacco companies, teen emulation of media celebrities, and the ineffective health-based antismoking efforts of the 1980s and 1990s.

In light of the upsurge in teen smoking in the 1990s and the highly addictive nature of tobacco, smoking prevention is considered to be particularly important. The 1994 U.S. Surgeon General's report, "Preventing Tobacco Use Among Young People," estimated that more than three thousand adolescents begin smoking each day, with 12.5 years being the average age of smoking initiation. The report urged that, for preventative efforts to be successful, they must reach adolescents at or before the transition from elementary to secondary school. It is at this age that youths are most vulnerable to the positive images of smokers depicted in movies and in cigarette advertisements.

Research demonstrates that cigarette advertising is an important contributor to adolescent smoking. Nicola Evans and her colleagues (1995) found that exposure of youths to tobacco advertising was more predictive of smoking than being exposed to family and friends who smoked. Indeed, evidence suggests that adolescents are uniquely susceptible to cigarette advertisements. During the period when Camel, Marlboro, and Newport were the three most heavily advertised cigarette brands, the three brands captured 86 percent of the adolescent smoking market but only 35 percent of the adult market. Cornelia Pechmann and Irvine S. Ratneshwar (1994) reported that more youths than adults recognized that Joe Camel promoted cigarettes.

Since it was barred in 1971 from using broadcast advertisements, the tobacco industry depends exclusively on magazine advertisements to associate cigarettes with images of independence, adventure, and youthfulness. According to Simmons Market Research Bureau (1990), tobacco advertisements typically appear in magazines read by teenagers, such as *Sports Illustrated* and *Glamour* (twelve- to nineteen-year-olds make up 33 percent and 28 percent, respectively, of the readership of these magazines). The research described above suggests that cigarette advertisements significantly influence children's decisions to take up smoking. The Surgeon General's 1994 report argued that these advertisements work by influencing the perceptions that youths have of the images associated with smoking. According to research by Dee Burton and her colleagues (1989), the images that adolescents link to smoking, such as sophistication and independence, are similar to the images that are portrayed in cigarette advertising.

Critics have claimed that tobacco companies target youths in order to replace dying smokers with new customers. This accusation, in part, motivated the tobacco master settlement agreement (MSA) between a coalition of attorneys general in forty-six states and the tobacco industry. The MSA of 1996, among other things, banned the tobacco industry from targeting eleven- to seventeen-year-olds with cartoon characters, brand-name merchandise, free samples, and event sponsorship. The agreement also eliminated outdoor and transit advertising and paid product placement on television and in motion pictures. The intent was to reduce the exposure of adolescents to cigarette promotions.

Nonetheless, cigarettes are being promoted by new means. The incidence of smoking in movies that are popular with teenagers is on the rise, and the American Lung Association (1999) partially blames exposure to celebrity smokers for increased adolescent smoking. The association reviewed the fifty movies that had the top box-office sales in 1997 and found that 88 percent of the movies featured tobacco use and 74 percent showed the lead actors smoking. Furthermore, study sponsored by the Office of National Drug Control Policy (Roberts, Henriksen, and Christenson, 1999) found that tobacco was used in 79 percent of G- or PG-rated movies, with adverse consequences infrequently portrayed. In fact, Stanton Glantz (1997) claims that lead movie characters are three times more likely than the adult population to smoke. Similarly, Anna Hazan and her colleagues (1994) compared the incidence of smoking among high socioeconomic status movie characters and real people. They found that, whereas 57 percent of the movie characters smoke, only 19 percent of similarly situated real people smoke.

The prevalence of smoking in movies is considered problematic because, according to the Motion Picture Association of America (1999), 49 percent of twelve- to seventeen-year-olds are frequent

Joe Camel, the R. J. Reynolds cigarette advertising mascot shown here on a billboard, was controversial because, opponents said, he appealed to underage smokers. (Joel W. Rogers/Corbis)

moviegoers, and actors are often role models for adolescents. The use of tobacco by celebrities may encourage youths to smoke because youths often emulate the behavior of people they admire.

In recognition of the increased amount of smoking by youths, state health departments and consumer groups have devised methods to combat the effects of media exposure to smoking. For example, in 1998, Vice-President Al Gore unveiled the first nationwide advertising campaign since the 1960s to target adolescent smoking. The campaign, sponsored by the American Legacy Foundation, featured nine television advertisements involving celebrities, such as the musical group Boys II Men. These advertisements were designed to be hip, humorous, and fashionable. They focused on the adverse social effects, rather than the health effects, of smoking. The basis of these and other antismoking advertisements is that teenagers are more concerned with immediate, as opposed to intermediate or long-term, consequences of smoking.

Some states have been highly successful in decreasing the amount of smoking by adolescents. For example, in 1998, Florida launched a $44 million, youth-designed campaign that mocks tobacco advertisements and accuses tobacco companies of manipulation. Partly as a result of this campaign, Florida has seen a 54 percent reduction in smoking by middle-school students. Massachusetts, California, and Oregon also have initiated aggressive campaigns for smoking prevention.

Another smoking prevention tool is the Internet. Smoke Screeners have created a media literacy website that is designed to deglamorize smoking in the movies, and the Centers for Disease Control and Prevention have created an online source for information related to kids, teens, and smoking. Teenagers have also taken the initiative by forming the organization Students Working Against Tobacco (SWAT), which has a website dedicated to getting "the whole truth" to other teenagers.

An impressive amount of research suggests that smoking prevention interventions can assist in curbing the onset of smoking. In particular, school-based programs that teach social influence resistance skills have been related to significant smoking reductions among adolescents. Also, programs that focus on the development of self-image through means other than smoking, and on media literacy and normative expectations regarding smoking, have also proven beneficial. For example, the Life Skills Program, developed by the CDC (2000b), achieved a 44 percent reduction in smoking onset six years following the program. Additionally, Project Toward No Tobacco Use (otherwise known as Project TNT), which was also developed by the CDC (2000c), reduced smoking initiation among middle-school students by 26 percent over a two-year period. Finally, inoculation, a resistance tactic intended to make youths aware of the vulnerability of their antismoking attitudes, has been employed successfully by Michael Pfau and his colleagues (1994) to reduce the risk of smoking onset among adolescents who are in transition from elementary to secondary school.

Pechmann (1997), who offers advice for the design of antismoking messages, stresses the importance of showing the negative social, monetary, and physical appearance consequences of smoking. Pechmann also suggests placing advertisements on network television, on cable television channels that show rock videos, and on contemporary rock radio stations. While exposure to smoking in movies and in advertising can be influential for youths, so too can exposure to antismoking advertisements. For example, with regard to the influence of movie characters who smoke, Pechmann and Chuan-Fong Shih (1999) found that exposure to an antismoking advertisement before a movie encouraged youths to formulate negative thoughts about the subsequent movie characters who smoked.

See also: ADVERTISING EFFECTS; ALCOHOL ABUSE AND COLLEGE STUDENTS; ALCOHOL IN THE MEDIA; SOCIAL CHANGE AND THE MEDIA.

Bibliography

American Lung Association. (1999). "Teens Look at Tobacco Use in the Top 50 Movies of Each Year from 1991–1998. Thumbs Down! Thumbs Down!" Press Kit. New York: American Lung Association.

Botvin, Gilbert J.; Goldberg, Catherine J.; Botvin, Elizabeth M.; and Dusenbury, Linda. (1993). "Smoking Behavior of Adolescents Exposed to Cigarette Advertising." *Public Health Reports* 108:217–224.

Burton, Dee; Sussman, Steve; Hansen, William B.; Johnson, Carl Anderson; and Slay, Brian R. (1989). "Image Attributions and Smoking Intentions among Seventh Grade Students." *Journal of Applied Social Psychology* 19:656–664.

Centers for Disease Control (CDC). (2000a). "Tobacco Information and Prevention Sources (TIPS): Incidence of Initiation of Cigarette Smoking among U.S. Teens." <http://www.cdc.gov/tobacco/research_data/youth/initfact.htm>.

Centers for Disease Control (CDC). (2000b). "Programs that Work: Life Skills Training." <http://www.cdc.gov/nccdphp/dash/rtc/curric6.htm>.

Centers for Disease Control (CDC). (2000c). "Programs that Work: Project towards No Tobacco Use (Project TNT)." <http://www.cdc.gov/nccdphp/dash/rtc/curric7.htm>.

Evans, Nicola; Farkas, Arthur; Gilpin, Elizabeth; Berry, Charles; and Pierce, John P. (1995). "Influence of Tobacco Marketing and Exposure to Smokers on Adolescent Susceptibility to Smoking." *Journal of the National Cancer Institute* 87:1538–1545.

Glantz, Stanton A. (1997). "Tobacco Use Is Increasing in Popular Films." *Tobacco Control* 6:282–284.

Goldstein, Adam O. (1999). "Tobacco and Alcohol Use in G-Rated Children's Animated Films." *JAMA* 281:1131–1136.

Hazan, Anna Russo; Lipton, Helen Levens; and Glantz, Stanton A. (1994). "Popular Films Do Not Reflect Current Tobacco Use." *American Journal of Public Health* 84:998–1000.

Motion Picture Association of America. (1999). "1999 Motion Picture Attendance: Frequent Movie-Goers Make up a Larger Proportion of Teens than Adults." <http://www.mpaa.org/useconomicreview/1999summary/sld005.htm>.

Pechmann, Cornelia. (1997). "Does Antismoking Advertising Combat Underage Smoking? A Review of Past Practices and Research." In *Social Marketing: Theoretical and Practical Perspectives,* eds. Marvin E. Goldberg, Martin Fishbein, and Susan E. Middlestadt. Mahwah, NJ: Lawrence Erlbaum.

Pechmann, Cornelia, and Ratneshwar, Irvine S. (1994). "The Effects of Antismoking and Cigarette Advertising on Young Adolescents' Perceptions of Peers Who Smoke." *Journal of Consumer Research* 21:236–251.

Pechmann, Cornelia, and Shih, Chuan-Fong. (1999). "Smoking Scenes in Movies and Antismoking Advertisements Before Movies: Effects on Youth." *Journal of Marketing* 63:1–13.

Pfau, Michael, and Van Bockern, Steve. (1994). "The Persistence of Inoculation in Conferring Resistance to Smoking Initiation along Adolescents: The Second Year." *Human Communication Research* 20:413–430.

Roberts, Donald F; Henriksen, Lisa; and Christenson, Peter G. (1999). "Substance Use in Popular Movies and Music." Sponsored by the Office of National Drug Control Policy and the Department of Health and Human Services, Substance Abuse and Mental Health Services Administration. <http://www.media-campaign.org/publications/movies/movie_toc.html>.

Simmons Market Research Bureau. (1990). *Simmons Teenage Research Study.* New York: Simmons.

Smoke Screeners. (2000). "An Educational Program to Take the Glamour Out of Smoking in the Movies." <http://www.fablevision.com/smokescreeners>.

Students Working Against Tobacco. (2000). "Truth." <http://www.wholetruth.com>.

U.S. Department of Health and Human Services. (1994). *Preventing Tobacco Use among Young People: A Report of the Surgeon General.* Washington, DC: U.S. Government Printing Office.

MICHAEL PFAU
ERIN ALISON SZABO

U-V

▪ USE OF INFORMATION

"Information use" is concerned with understanding what information sources people choose and the ways in which people apply information to make sense of their lives and situations. This use can be instrumental (e.g., when a decision-maker uses financial data to inform a budget decision), or it can be affective, influencing how people feel (e.g., a person may use information gathered during a conversation with a friend to feel more motivated or better satisfied about a career choice). Information is defined as data (drawn from all five senses and thought) that is used by people to make sense of the world. Indeed, Brenda Dervin (1992) contends that information is only such when it is used by somebody.

The reasons for why people create information may not be the same as the reasons for why people use information. Information is interpreted and used differently (and often in unintended ways) by different individuals and groups. For example, the information that is provided in a radio broadcast may, in the view of the show's producer, have the primary purpose of influencing voters' decisions. However, that information may be used in an unanticipated or unwanted way; it may be used as a source of humorous commentary by a comedian, or it may be used as fodder for an alternative political viewpoint. The uses to which people put information depend on such factors as their existing knowledge, their affective state (i.e., mood and motivation), their intellectual abilities, and their existing skills (e.g., literacy) or physical disabilities.

One of the most prolific researchers in information behavior (i.e., all aspects of people's interaction with information), Tom Wilson (1999), considers information use to include people's physical and mental acts to incorporate information into their existing base of knowledge. Use of information is conceived as the final stage of a process that begins with recognition of an information need. Once the need has been identified, people search for information to meet that need, and then they apply or use the information that is found. This process is iterative and complex, and it is influenced by a number of factors.

Information Uses

People use information to seek meaning in a variety of situations. Sometimes they use information instrumentally, to do something tangible (e.g., to acquire a skill or reach a goal). Other times, information is used cognitively (e.g., to generate ideas). Yet in other cases, information is used in an affective manner (e.g., when an individual uses information to feel supported or to derive pleasure). Some researchers believe that people use information to reduce uncertainty, so that the more information that is provided, the greater the reduction of uncertainty. While this is sometimes true, information can also increase uncertainty about a particular issue or problem (e.g., about what political party to vote for or what career path to pursue). The World Wide Web is a good example of this because contradictory information can occur on different websites. These contradictions can leave a person feeling quite uncertain about how to make sense out of the information that they find.

People also use information to confirm or verify something that they know, to predict what may happen, and to develop or maintain personal relationships. Regardless of the labels that are used to describe the variety of uses to which information can be put, it is clear that the possible uses are as diverse as the number of individual people who are living in individual contexts and facing individual questions, issues, or problems. Moreover, one person may use the same information in two different ways, depending on personal circumstances. This is not meant to imply that information use is not predictable to some degree; variables that are internal and external to individuals certainly influence information behavior, including information use.

Contextual variables (e.g., whether the physical environment is comfortable) and the relative importance of an information need also affect people's decisions to make use of or to ignore information. For example, information about the quality of a local public school system may be ignored completely by a given person until he or she has school-aged children. A parent who is struggling to feed several children may pay more attention to information about subsidized lunch programs than to information about the overall educational quality of the school. This phenomenon is known as selective attention. People constantly make decisions about what information to monitor in an ongoing but relatively passive way, what information to seek in an active sense, what information to ignore, and what information to use. People may attend to information in a minimal way, simply storing it in memory until it becomes useful in the construction of some meaning at a later date. The reasons that people use to select certain information include psychological variables (e.g., personality characteristics), contextual variables (e.g., work roles or way of life), and social variables (e.g., social expectations or social norms).

People in all situations tend to use information sources that are convenient, that have been found to be useful in past experience, and that are believed to be trustworthy. Judgements about what makes a source trustworthy depend on a person's individual values, the person's particular situation, and the question or problem that the person is facing. People therefore develop habits of information use. For example, many North Americans habitually turn to the Internet for information. In all cultures, most people are in the habit of asking their friends and family for information.

People also seek emotional support from information providers, and then the judge the value of the information partly on the manner in which it is delivered. Thus, if an adolescent is given career-related information from a guidance counselor, that information is much more likely to be trusted and used if the counselor is viewed as a trustworthy person and if the counselor demonstrates concern for the feelings of the adolescent.

The importance of affect or emotional factors in information use is a large reason why personal communication (either face-to-face or technologically mediated) remains a primary source of information for many people. In workplaces, in families, and within adolescent peer groups, people seek information from others whom they trust and with whom they wish to strengthen social relationships. Thus, people may turn to a trusted family member for advice, or they may ask a question of an acquaintance or work colleague with whom they seek a social bond. On the other hand, when an individual wishes to avoid potential embarrassment or to maintain privacy, information may be sought from a more formal, impersonal source. Thus, people tend to minimize personal risk in their information seeking and use, and they sometimes feel the need to deceive others with regard to their information use in order to protect their self-image or to enhance their status or reputation. Somebody who needs information about a venereal disease, for example, is more likely to seek that information from a formal, anonymous source than from a family member who may be shocked by such a request. In a workplace, a person may, in an attempt to avoid appearing ignorant, deceive colleagues about the source of the information that was used to inform a decision; for example, a person might do this by giving the impression of having consulted several formal sources of information when in fact that has not been done.

Much has been written about types of information needs (i.e., what sorts of people in what situations need what sorts of information), about what kinds of information people seek, and about the processes that people use to seek information. Much of the research into the process of information seeking has focused narrowly on how people search for information via computers (i.e., the retrieval of information). Successful retrieval is equated with relevance to the user. Because relevance is subjective, it is difficult to predict what information will be found to be relevant or useful to people, except under specific conditions. Individual variation in cognitive or information processing style and situational factors (e.g., time constraints) have also been related to information use. For example, the familiar problem of information overload can cause cognitive confusion and force people to limit the information they use.

How people use formal information systems such as libraries is another question, although that area of research focuses on information seeking rather than on the actual use of the information that is found.

The Importance of Context

One of the most important aspects of information use is the context in which people's questions or information-related problems arise, sometimes called the "information use environment" (IUE). IUEs can be characterized by the following four major factors:

1. the people or context (e.g., a particular professional or special interest group),
2. the type of problem criteria used to evaluate information pertaining to the problem,
3. where a person seeks information (which influences, for example, access to information, experience using various information channels, and cultural rules and values),
4. and the way in which the person resolves problems.

For example, in an organization where problems tend to be unstructured and where creativity is encouraged, spending considerable time in conversation with colleagues to generate new ideas may be rewarded, thus suggesting that colleagues would be a primary source of information. In another environment, workers may face well-structured problems and find that particular online databases provide useful information. In that IUE, the use of the online information likely would be valued and rewarded. Those working in particular professions tend to use some information sources more than others; engineers and scientists rely heavily on print and electronic sources such as journals and books for their work, whereas organizational managers rely more on interpersonal sources such as colleagues and meetings. One cannot ignore the specifics of a situation, or the importance of specific work roles and their associated tasks, in determining the types of information that individuals will find useful.

The concept of IUEs and the importance of work roles and tasks fit well with what is known about information use by different professional groups. Health-care professionals have been found to use online information from Medline to make decisions related to patient-care, research, teaching, learning, administration, and consultations—all of which are task-related examples of information use. In all occupational groups, the factors that affect information use include perceived quality, availability, accessibility, and ease of use. Contextual factors that influence information use include an individual's seniority, experience, phase of work (or task), specialty, educational level, and professional orientation. For work-related information, while convenience might be a primary fact in choosing a source, informational quality is a primary factor in the final decision to make use of information.

Information use in daily life (i.e., non-work situations) has social dimensions as well. Identification with a particular social group affects people's selection of information sources that are considered to be normal or appropriate. The small social worlds that people tend to inhabit work very much like IUEs, creating a context of socially acceptable information sources and creating norms of interaction with information. It is only by studying a particular social group closely that the informational norms of that group can be identified. For example, Elfreda Chatman (1991) conducted a study of a group of janitors and showed that their mutual distrust limited interpersonal information seeking and use, while information obtained from newspapers and television was identified as being more useful to this group.

A similar emphasis on the importance of social context in relation to information use has been proposed by Reijo Savolainen (1995), who suggests that habitus (a concept borrowed from Pierre Bourdieu) strongly influences information behavior and use. The term "habitus" refers to people's disposition to behave in particular ways according to their beliefs and attitudes, the material resources to which they have access, their social capital (e.g., contact networks, rights to control others' activities), their cultural and cognitive capital (e.g., knowledge, learning styles, attitudes), and their current life situations (e.g., health, lifecycle stage). While these ideas have yet to be applied fully to information use, it is clear that a person's contact networks, for example, would have a bearing on the range and quality of information sources that are available to that person. It is also clear that people's use of information sources varies according to their education level, because this variable affects their skills and abilities, as well as their experience and comfort with particular information sources (e.g., online sources).

Barriers to Information Use

The reasons why people do not use information are many and complex. Laura Brick (1999) conducted a study of the non-use of information that was available in a workplace business library. She found that non-users were unaware of the information that was available to them, that they tended to delegate information searching to subordinates (who may or may not use the library), and that they were not information conscious (i.e., they did not see the need to obtain information for their daily tasks and decisions).

Barriers to information use in organizational settings have been the focus of much study related to knowledge management. Thomas Davenport (1997) argues that organizations often emphasize access to information that is potentially useful, rather than conducting thorough needs assessments to determine what information and what sources the organizations' workers actually find useful. Formal information systems in organizations are often poorly designed, making them challenging and inconvenient to use. Frequently, organizations underestimate the time that is required to implement an information system, and most important, the time that is required to teach workers how to use the system effectively. As a result, many organizational information systems are not integrated into existing workflow, so they remain peripheral to the workers' decision making. Optimizing information use in organizations requires attention to organizational culture and politics, as well. If workers tend to seek information from superiors in order to ingratiate themselves, eliminating that need by introducing a formal information system may disrupt established patterns of social interaction. Additionally, formal information systems may clash with established organizational practices such as information hoarding or filtering—two techniques that are used to establish and maintain organizational power.

Many personal barriers to information use have also been identified. Among these are not knowing what information is needed or available (i.e., people do not know what they do not know). People may not know what question to ask (e.g., a person may lack the necessary mental model or context of a problem to know how to articulate a request for help). People often do not know where to look (i.e., a person may have a question or problem but not know where to turn for help). People often do not know that sources exist (e.g., many people are pleasantly surprised by the availability of useful information in public libraries). The information needed may not exist (e.g., somebody may need a particular aggregate of data in order to make a decision, but that data has never been collected). A person may lack communication skills (e.g., a person may not have the language skills required to ask for help, or a person may display unusual social behavior that gets in the way of communication). A person may lack confidence or ability (e.g., government information available only through online kiosks will be inaccessible to people who lack the confidence or the technical skills to use computers). People may be discouraged by sources that they approach (e.g., they may encounter frustrating delays in getting the help they need, and simply give up, or they may receive inaccurate or inappropriate information). Finally, a common barrier is information scatter, which is confronted particularly in the case of complex information needs (when needed information is available only by using several different sources).

A lack of trust in an information source may prevent somebody from making use of that source. For example, Yin Zhang (1999) conducted a study of a technically savvy set of people (i.e., academics in the field of library and information science) and showed that only a minority is satisfied with electronic sources for research purposes. This is true largely because there are few useful Internet websites for research purposes, websites are unstable (i.e., they tend to come and go), and websites are not sufficiently reliable. These scholars who took part in this study believe that there is little quality control for web resources, and they feel the need to judge the authority and validity of these resources. They believe that the level of scholarship demonstrated in web resources is generally low and that the web is not well organized for retrieval (i.e., there is a need for better indexing and structuring, and there is a need for more standards). Furthermore, they point to a lack of social norms for using and citing electronic sources. Thus, for this group, these factors act as barriers to using the Internet for research purposes.

The Role of Information Literacy

More generally, people's use of information depends on their level of information literacy. Being information literate (i.e., having the ability to make efficient and effective use of information sources) implies a wide range of skills, and lacking any one of these could impede information use. To be information literate in the industrialized world in the twenty-first century, a person should have specific online searching skills (e.g., the ability to select appropriate search terminology, to construct a logical search strategy, and to evaluate information appropriately). In addition, people need to understand their needs in informational terms, know what information might help them, identify potentially appropriate sources, and understand how to evaluate the information that they find (i.e., on the basis of its authority and credibility, intended audience, quality or accuracy, objectivity, and scope). In order to be effective information users, people need to know how to organize and synthesize information logically (i.e., to construct meaning from it) and how to apply information to add value and create a quality product. In addition, people need to know how to share information appropriately and to use information and information technology responsibly and ethically.

All of these abilities require reasoning, the ability to use libraries and computers, critical thinking, creative thinking, communication, and social skills. Effective information use is also associated with self-efficacy (i.e., a belief that one can achieve a goal), an ethical stance, integrity, and trust. Thus, the three skill domains that are involved are the cognitive domain (e.g. skills in analysis, comprehension, synthesis, evaluation, explanation, and transformation), the affective domain (e.g., commitment, perseverance, confi-dence, curiosity, motivation), and the physical domain (e.g., operating tools such as computer hardware and software, and book indexes). When people are information literate, many of the barriers to effective information use may be overcome.

Making Information Useful

Barriers to information use also may be minimized by increasing the potential usefulness of the information itself. In addition to being relevant, information must ideally be accurate, precise, complete, reliable, communicated appropriately, timely, detailed, understandable, and consistent. However, even when information meets all of these criteria, there is still no guarantee that it will be used. Making use of information is an individual decision, and the use made of it may bear little resemblance to the information provider's intentions. It is apparent, for example, that regardless of efforts that are made to make information useful, people are more likely to use information that fits with their current understanding or point of view and to ignore information that challenges their closely held beliefs or values.

Information system designers have developed principles that are known to enhance the usefulness of information and to increase the probability of its being used. These principles include presenting information in a form and at a level that is familiar and comfortable to people. For example, consider attempts to dispense information about government programs and services to the inhabitants of a rural community in a developing country. Providing an Internet kiosk as a means of providing the information is less likely to lead to the use of that information by the local inhabitants than if local opinion leaders are used to relay the information in face-to-face encounters. If individuals or groups receive appropriate information via an appropriate channel, the chances of that information being useful are greatly increased.

Another way to enhance the usefulness of information (by increasing understanding) is to present the information frequently and in a variety of formats. For example, politicians use repeated advertising spots in a variety of media to increase the chances of people noticing them. Graphics are used in textual materials to enhance understanding, to provide additional information, and to increase interest. Appealing to different learning styles by using a variety of presentation methods will increase the probability of the information being used by the intended audience.

Summary

Information use has yet to be thoroughly researched. Nevertheless, it is generally accepted that information use is personal and therefore subjective and that it is naïve to assume that if people have access to information they will use it. People's use of various types of information sources varies according to individual factors such as their cognitive style and information literacy skills. Information use can be instrumental as in organizational decision-making, or affective, as when information is used to motivate. The importance of context and the specific task or question for which information is used are as important as individual factors in predicting information use. People's occupational or peer groups, their workplace settings and the tasks associated with those settings, and cultural norms and expectations all influence information use. People face a range of barriers to accessing and using information, including individual and structural barriers. However, attention to information provision and design of information systems can do much to ameliorate these obstacles.

See also: ECONOMICS OF INFORMATION; HUMAN–COMPUTER INTERACTION; INTERNET AND THE WORLD WIDE WEB; KNOWLEDGE MANAGEMENT; REFERENCE SERVICES AND INFORMATION ACCESS; RETRIEVAL OF INFORMATION.

Bibliography

Allen, Bryce L. (1996). *Information Tasks: Toward a User-Centered Approach to Information Systems.* San Diego: Academic Press.

Brick, Laura. (1999). "Non-Use of Business Libraries and Information Services: A Study of the Library and Information Managers' Perception, Experience, and Reaction to Non-Use." *Aslib Proceedings* 51(6):195–205.

Chatman, Elfreda A. (1991). "Life in a Small World: Applicability of Gratification Theory to Information-Seeking Behavior." *Journal of the American Society for Information Science* 42(6):438–449.

Davenport, Thomas H. (1997). *Information Ecology: Mastering the Information and Knowledge Environment.* New York: Oxford University Press.

Dervin, Brenda. (1992). "From the Mind's Eye of the User: The Sense-Making Qualitative-Quantitative Methodology." In *Qualitative Research in Informa-

tion Management,* eds. Jack D. Glazier and Ronald R. Powell. Englewood, CO: Libraries Unlimited.

Harris, Roma M., and Dewdney, Patricia. (1994). *Barriers to Information: How Formal Help Systems Fail Battered Women.* Westport, CT: Greenwood Press.

Kuhlthau, Carol C. (1993). *Seeking Meaning: A Process Approach to Library and Information Services.* Norwood, NJ: Ablex.

Marchionini, Gary. (1995). *Information Seeking in Electronic Environments.* Cambridge, Eng.: Cambridge University Press.

Savolainen, Reijo. (1995). "Everyday Life Information Seeking: Approaching Information Seeking in the Context of Way of Life." *Library and Information Science Research* 17(3):259–294.

Taylor, Robert S. (1986). *Value-Added Processes in Information Systems.* Norwood, NJ: Ablex Publishing.

Wilson, Sandra R.; Cooper, Michael D.; and Starr-Schneidkraut, Norma. (1989). *Use of the Critical Incident Technique to Evaluate the Impact of MEDLINE.* Palo Alto, CA: American Institutes for Research in the Behavioral Sciences.

Wilson, Tom D. (1999). "Models in Information Behaviour Research." *Journal of Documentation* 55(3): 249–270.

Zhang, Yin. (1999). "Scholarly Use of Internet-Based Electronic Resources: A Survey Report." *Library Trends* 47(4):746–770.

HEIDI JULIEN

V-CHIP

In an attempt to give parents more control over television content, the Telecommunications Act of 1996 mandated a change in the way new televisions sold in the United States would be manufactured. The act provided that within a specified time period (the deadline eventually becoming January 2000) all televisions with a diagonal screen size of thirteen inches or larger would contain technology permitting the blocking of programs on the basis of their ratings. This legislation was passed during a time when criticism of television content was increasing and there were several well-publicized incidents of youth violence that were variously attributed to the influence of television. Members of Congress, with leadership from Representative Edward Markey (D-MA), were seeking to provide parents with a way to deal with increasingly violent and sexual content without infringing on the First Amendment rights of the television industry.

Although devices permitting the blocking of television programs had been developed in the United States as early as the mid-1980s, the notion of television program blocking first entered the mainstream of public consciousness as the result of developments in Canada. In the early 1990s, Tim Collings, a professor of electrical engineering at Simon Fraser University, developed a television blocking device that he called the V-chip. Although the "V" in V-chip originally referred to "viewer" choice, the "V" has come to be associated in the United States with media violence in the minds of the general public.

The V-chip legislation did not mandate a specific rating system. However, it specified that if the television industry did not voluntarily produce its own rating system acceptable to the Federal Communications Commission (FCC), the FCC would appoint an advisory committee to recommend a V-chip rating system. The television industry developed the age-based "TV Parental Guidelines," which it released in December 1996. It then modified the system, as the result of public and political pressure, to add content indicators in July 1997. The rating system is designed to be applied to all forms of programming, with the exception of news and sports programs. The rating of a program is selected by that program's producers or distributors.

The V-chip works by reading a code that is embedded in the transmission of a program and is carried on line 21 of the vertical blanking interval (VBI), the same circuits that are also used to carry information for the closed captioning of programs. In addition to ruling on the acceptability of the rating system, the FCC had to approve a technical standard for the V-chip. Two issues regarding the design of the V-chip proved controversial.

The first issue was related to whether the V-chip would be mandated to read only the rating systems developed by the entertainment industry—the TV Parental Guidelines and the Motion Picture Association of America (MPAA) movie ratings—or whether it should be required to include other rating systems that might be developed by child advocacy groups, religious groups, or other organizations. Child advocacy groups favored the inclusion of more rating systems so that ratings might be based on criteria developed by child development experts, for example, and applied by people other than those who had a financial inter-

est in the programs being rated. Some free-speech advocates also promoted the capability of reading multiple systems, arguing that providing a government-sanctioned rating system is more coercive than permitting viewers a choice among rating systems. The entertainment industry argued for limiting the V-chip to the two systems developed by the industry, saying that to do otherwise would render the device overly complicated and unworkable. The FCC ultimately ruled that only the TV Parental Guidelines and the MPAA ratings would be mandatory. It did require, however, that the technology permit parents to block programs by both the age-based and content-based categories of the revised TV Parental Guidelines.

The second issue was related to whether or not the V-chip would permit parents to block unrated programs as well as blocking programs on the basis of their ratings. Because news and sports are not rated, and because it was anticipated that some producers or channels might choose not to rate their programs, child advocacy groups argued that blocking of unrated programs should also be a feature of the V-chip. Advocates for the television industry argued that the ability to block unrated programs would make television ratings mandatory rather than optional and that it could, in effect, result in the blocking of entire channels that were devoted solely to news or sports. The FCC did not require the V-chip to have the ability to block unrated programs. In response to consumer sentiment, however, some manufacturers decided to include this feature in spite of the fact that it is not required.

New television sets are shipped with the V-chip in the "off" mode. Parents may decide to use the V-chip by selecting which ratings they want blocked. Programs with these ratings will subsequently not be seen or heard on the television, unless someone chooses to override the blocking. The override is typically accomplished by entering a secret code number. In many sets, the channels that were blocked prior to the override return to the blocked mode after the television set is turned off. Many television sets provide other blocking features, independent of the V-chip, including the blocking of specific channels or the blocking of programs that occur at specific dates and times. Some systems also allow programs to be blocked by title.

Although hailed as a breakthrough by politicians and parenting organizations, the V-chip was not readily adopted by parents when it first became available. The slow adoption has been attributed to several factors. One is the lack of publicity for the V-chip and the understandable reluctance of the television industry to promote a product designed to limit its reach. Another factor is the complicated nature of the revised TV Parental Guidelines. Perhaps another impediment has been public perception that the V-chip is a crutch for lazy parents rather than a tool to help concerned parents more conveniently implement their decisions about what their children should watch.

In May 1999, the FCC set up a task force to ensure the effective implementation of the V-chip. This group has issued reports on the progress of the television industry with regard to the encoding of V-chip rating signals in programming and has encouraged publicity and promotion for the device.

See also: ANTIVIOLENCE INTERVENTIONS; FEDERAL COMMUNICATIONS COMMISSION; RATINGS FOR TELEVISION PROGRAMS; TELECOMMUNICATIONS ACT OF 1996; VIOLENCE IN THE MEDIA, ATTRACTION TO; VIOLENCE IN THE MEDIA, HISTORY OF RESEARCH ON.

Bibliography

Cantor, Joanne. (1998). *"Mommy, I'm Scared": How TV and Movies Frighten Children and What We Can Do to Protect Them.* San Diego, CA: Harcourt Brace.

Cantor, Joanne. (1998). "Ratings for Program Content: The Role of Research Findings." *Annals of the American Academy of Political and Social Science* 557:54–69.

Federal Communications Commission. (2000). "V-Chip Home Page." <http://www.fcc.gov/vchip>.

Kaiser Family Foundation. (1999). *How Parents Feel (and What They Know) about TV, the V-Chip, and the TV Ratings System.* Menlo Park, CA: Henry J. Kaiser Family Foundation.

Kunkel, Dale; Farinola, Wendy J. M.; Cope, Kirstie M.; Donnerstein, Edward; Biely, Erica; and Zwarun, Lara. (1998). *Rating the Ratings: One Year Out; An Assessment of the Television Industry's Use of V-Chip Ratings.* Menlo Park, CA: Henry J. Kaiser Family Foundation.

Price, Monroe E., ed. (1998). *The V-Chip Debate: Content Filtering from Television to the Internet.* Mahwah, NJ: Lawrence Erlbaum.

JOANNE CANTOR

■ VIDEO AND COMPUTER GAMES AND THE INTERNET

Since the 1970s, video and computer games have developed into one of the favorite leisure activities among children and adolescents. However, the rapid rise in the popularity of video and computer games went together with a corresponding increase in the debate about their effects. Advocates usually view the games as a benign activity, with great potential to promote children's problem-solving capacities, their eye-hand coordination, and spatial abilities. Opponents are concerned that the games displace other, more valuable activities, such as homework and reading. They argue that the games hinder children's social interactions because they involve a solitary activity. Other critics believe that the games hinder children's creativity because the child player must follow preset rules to succeed. And finally, it is claimed that the games glorify violence and cause callousness and aggression in children.

In academic research, usually no distinction is made between a "video game" and a "computer game." A video game is played on hand-held machines, such as a Game Boy, or on dedicated systems that are plugged into the television, such as Nintendo or Sega. A computer game is played on a personal computer. Since the mid-1980s, however, most games are released for more than one system. Because the content, the quality of graphics, and the degree of realism in video and computer games are comparable, it has become irrelevant to consider them as separate media. In this entry, therefore, the term "computer games" is used to refer to both video and computer games.

Different Types of Computer Games

There are many different types of computer games, each of which may have their own distinctive qualities and effects. Some games have the potential to foster children's creativity and problem-solving skills, whereas other games can be harmful for young children. In order to understand the effects of computer games, it is necessary to have some insight to the different kinds of games that are available. The six most common game types are adventure, role-playing, platform, action, simulation, and puzzle.

Adventure games usually involve an elaborate quest for something valuable, such as a princess or the Holy Grail. The player must solve various riddles and puzzles and overcome many traps in order to reach the final goal. Exploration plays a major role in this category, whereas reaction time is usually less important. Adventures for teenagers and adults may contain a great deal of violence. Some educational adventures aimed at very young children are especially designed to foster creativity.

In role-playing games, the player is required to take on the role of one of the central characters, for example, a wizard or a knight. If the player plays alone, the computer performs the other roles. If the game is played with other children, everyone has his or her own role. Role-playing games usually occur in a fantasy world. Like adventure games, success in role-playing games usually is affected by exploration and problem-solving skills rather than reaction time. *Dungeons and Dragons* is one example of the games that fall into this category.

Platform games are usually based on the principle of avoiding, chasing, or eliminating characters and objects while jumping onto platforms. Reaction time and eye-hand coordination are important requirements in these games, which usually contain a lot of action. Well-known examples of games in this category are *Mario* from Nintendo and *Sonic, The Hedgehog* from Sega.

The main aim of action games is to destroy as many characters and objects as possible. In a so-called beat-'em-up, the player uses his or her fighting skills to kill the enemies who appear on the screen. A well-known example in this category is the one-to-one fighting game *Mortal Kombat*. In a so-called shoot-'em-up, the player must shoot the characters or objects on the screen (*Doom* and *Wolffenstein* are examples of games that fall into this category). A modern beat-'em-up or shoot-'em-up is a journey through a virtual labyrinth with the aim of hitting a maximum number of targets, such as armored cars, dogs, or aliens. The latest generation games are three-dimensional. A player views the game from the viewpoint of the central character, which encourages involvement.

The aim of simulation games is to imitate real-life situations as well as possible while taking into account the problems and pitfalls that can occur in such situations. There are many types of simulations available, some of which involve complex planning and decision making. In flight simulators, the player flies an aircraft or attacks an enemy plane. In sports simulations, such as a soccer game, the player takes on the role of one of the soccer players, while the computer deals with the remaining characters. In a strategic war simulation (e.g., *Red Alert*), the player is in the military. Finally, in conceptual simulations (e.g., *Sim City 2000*), the player must build and govern a successful organization, city, or park.

Puzzle games are often quite challenging. In addition to requiring good eye-hand coordination, these games require the player to think quickly and use logic and reasoning to plan future moves. A well-known example in this category is *Tetris*.

The Macho World in Video and Computer Games

Most video and computer games are obviously made for boys. Mark Griffiths (1997) has pointed out that the majority of computer games are designed by males for males. Virtually all superheroes in computer games (especially the early ones) are forceful he-men with exaggerated macho characteristics. To the extent that females are present in the games, they consist of sweet princesses or helpless victims who must be protected or rescued from dangerous gorillas or other evil creatures. Females are usually depicted as a caricature: scantily dressed, with big breasts, curvaceous hips, and long legs.

In the more recent generation of games, females are more frequently portrayed in an active role. Some role-playing games for young children feature a female as the central character, for example, *Barbie Super Model* and *Belle and the Beast*. In some action games, players can choose a female warrior to act as their character. In the popular game *Tomb Raider*, for example, the merciless Lara Croft, a female archeologist, is the main character.

Does this shift to female macho fighters mean that girls feel comfortable with action games? There is no reason to believe that this is the case. The review by Griffiths (1997) of the literature on the demographics of video game use reports that males play video games significantly more often than females. According to Steven Schwartz and Janet Schwartz (1997), most games feature women in two extreme roles: victim or killer. Neither of these roles seems to attract girls.

Research on the playing of computer games suggests that until the age of eight years, boys and girls are equally attracted to computer games. This is understandable because many educational adventure games for young children are still "gender neutral." According to Jeanne Funk and her colleagues (1997), both boys and girls, as they mature, lose interest in these educational games. Boys then become interested in violent action games, and a much smaller number of girls start to play popular platform games and cartoon-like fantasy games. In fact, the time boys who are older than twelve years of age spend playing computer games is two to three times that spent by girls of the same age. Market research confirms these academic statistics. According to survey results published by Nintendo in 1992, 88 percent of the Super Nintendo players were males.

The considerable difference between boys and girls in their use of computer games has led to concerns among some researchers and educators. Patricia Greenfield (1984) has argued that, for most children, computer games are the entry point into the world of computers and technology. If children's computer literacy begins with playing computer games, it is a serious problem if girls get less opportunity to become familiar with these games. Therefore, Greenfield pointed out, there is an urgent need for computer games especially designed for girls. What kind of computer games would be appealing to girls? Research suggests that girls are less interested than boys in killing enemies. Girls are also less object oriented. They are less interested in devices, such as lasers, buttons, and futuristic weapons, which are common in computer games. According to Jack Sanger and his colleagues (1997), girls like real-life situations, and they are particularly interested in the development of relationships between characters. Girls are most interested in realistic, attractive characters, such as actresses, movie stars, male and female sports and music celebrities, and models. Games that take into account these preferences could stimulate girls to spend more time playing computer games.

The Effects of Video Games

Although there is still no consensus about the potential effects of computer games, many observers agree that the games might have both positive consequences (e.g., spatial ability, eye-hand coordination; creativity) and negative consequences (e.g., addiction, aggression).

Spatial ability refers to a child's competence in remembering the form of objects and understanding how these objects match with other objects or spatial positions. In virtually every intelligence test, a measure of spatial ability is included. Several studies have demonstrated that children who often play computer games perform better on tests of spatial ability. In a study by Lynn Okagaki and Peter Frensch (1994), a group of teenagers played the puzzle game *Tetris* for a total of six hours (in twelve separate sessions). None of the teenagers had had any prior experience with *Tetris*. After six hours of playing, the spatial ability of both boys and girls had improved. This benefit is not unique to puzzle games. Greenfield and her colleagues (1994) have demonstrated that other types of games also stimulate the spatial skills of the player.

Eye-hand coordination is the ability to execute rapidly with the hands what the eyes see. Eye-hand coordination is important for typewriting, but it is also important for operating a machine or navigating a plane. Some types of computer games, such as platform games and action games, require high levels of eye-hand coordination. The timing of the action is often a matter of split seconds. It is no surprise, therefore, that several studies have demonstrated that playing computer games improves children's eye-hand coordination.

Some parents and educators believe that computer games impair children's creativity because the games are played according to preset rules. They argue that children, who predominantly play rule games, do not get sufficient practice in "divergent" and "as if" experiences and that, as a result, their development of creative skills is impaired. Although it is important that children get the opportunity to practice divergent-thinking skills, it is wrong to suppose that all video and computer games have preset rules. In some computer games, children are given the opportunity to give free reign to their fantasies and ideas. They can draw, compose music, and create stories, and although nobody would recommend that parents should replace all real-life drawings and stories with computer-generated ones, there is little reason to assume that these computer games hinder children's creativity through lack of practice in divergent-thinking tasks. Many educational adventures or fantasy role-playing games are designed to foster imagination, and this is exactly what many game producers tell parents in their product information. Although no academic research has tested whether such computer games actually do what their producers claim, it is possible that educational computer games designed to foster imagination have a potential to encourage children's creative capacities.

A common argument against the playing of computer games is that it is addictive. Computer game addiction consists of a compulsive involvement in the game, a lack of interest in other activities, and physical or mental symptoms when attempting to stop playing (e.g., restlessness or aggression). There is some evidence that computer games displace other activities, such as television viewing and reading. However, for the majority of children, these effects are short-lived. A study by Gary Creasey and Barbara Myers (1986), in which computer game users were compared with nonusers, demonstrated that a newly introduced video game computer in the home mainly displaced television viewing and movie attendance. The study also found that early decreases in other activities, such as television viewing, started to disappear after several weeks when the games were no longer new. However, for a small group of children, interest in computer games does not wane after a few weeks. According to Griffiths (1997), there is no doubt that a small minority of children becomes addicted to computer games. For these children, playing computer games can take up considerable time that would otherwise be used for all kinds of valuable activities. Although many researchers have observed computer addiction, there is as yet no consensus about the prevalence of such addiction among children and adolescents.

Violence is a common theme in most computer games. According to Eugene Provenzo (1991), more than 85 percent of the leading Nintendo games has violence as a main theme. Since the mid-1980s, increasingly more computer games contain realistic and explicit violence aimed at humans. In a game such as *Night Trap*, for example, it is the goal to hang female characters on a meat hook. In *Carmageddon*, the player must run over and kill as many pedestrians as possible to earn points and credits. Because the new generation of computer games uses more explicit representations of extreme violence, the issue of whether playing violent games leads to aggressive behavior is ever more important. In the past, media effects researchers have progressively

Microsoft further strengthened the link between video games and the Internet when they unveiled on March 10, 2000, the video game console X-Box, which includes a 600-megahertz processor and a 3D graphics processor and is capable of playing digital video discs (DVDs) and connecting to the Internet. (Reuters NewMedia Inc./Corbis)

reached the consensus that exposure to television violence can result in aggressive behavior. Although there are some obvious differences between television viewing and the playing of computer games, the violence portrayed in both media contains similar characteristics. For example, both television programs and computer games often portray violence that is rewarded, justified, and realistic. It is no surprise, therefore, that a meta-analysis by John Sherry (1997) has demonstrated that playing violent computer games indeed encourages aggressiveness among players. According to Sherry's results, the effect of violent computer games on aggressiveness is dependent on the type of violence portrayed. Violence directed at humans leads to a greater effect than fantasy or sports violence.

The Internet

The Internet is the fastest-growing medium among both children and adolescents. According to online industry research, 54 percent of teenagers were expected to be online by the end of the year 2000, and this percentage is expected to grow rapidly in subsequent years. In North America, more than 13.7 million children and teenagers were expected to be online by 2001, with an increase to 36.9 million by 2005 (Nua, 2000).

The arrival of each new medium has brought public concern about its influence on children. The debate about whether the Internet is beneficial or dangerous for children is a controversial topic, and it is not guided by any academic research. Many teachers and educators agree that the Internet can offer children many educational opportunities. Children can learn about virtually any topic. In a survey study among nine- to twelve-year-olds that Patti Valkenburg and Karen Soeters (2000) conducted, information-seeking proved to be the second most important reason for using the Internet. One hundred and ninety-four children who were already online were asked why they used the Internet. Children reported that they often use the Internet to learn something, or to search for information related to their homework, hobbies, and idols.

Unlike television and computer games, which only involve the risk of exposure to inappropriate material, the Internet has two additional risks: harassment online and harassment offline. Harassment online refers to frightening or demeaning messages directed at the child. Harassment offline can occur when children give out their telephone numbers, addresses, or credit card numbers. In the above-mentioned survey, children were asked how frequently they had been confronted with unpleasant situations on the Internet. Approximately 14 percent of the children responded that they had experienced something unpleasant while using the Internet; 8 percent mentioned that they had been confronted with shocking websites, including horror and pornography; 3 percent mentioned that they had been threatened online by other children or adults; but none of the Internet users in this sample had experienced offline harassment.

Conclusion

It is evident that computer games and the Internet have positive and negative consequences for children. Whether or not children will benefit from computer games and the Internet depends to a large extent on how they use these media and what type of content is involved. When used improperly, computer games and the Internet can be problematic. When used in the right way, both computer games and the Internet can have a great potential for entertainment and education.

See also: CHILDREN'S CREATIVITY AND TELEVISION USE; COMPUTER LITERACY; COMPUTER SOFTWARE, EDUCATIONAL; DEPENDENCE ON MEDIA; GENDER AND THE MEDIA; INTERNET AND THE WORLD WIDE WEB; RATINGS FOR VIDEO GAMES, SOFTWARE, AND THE INTERNET; VIOLENCE IN THE MEDIA, ATTRACTION TO; VIOLENCE IN THE MEDIA, HISTORY OF RESEARCH ON.

Bibliography

Greasey, Gary L., and Myers, Barbara, J. (1986). "Video Games and Children: Effects on Leisure Activities, Schoolwork, and Peer Involvement." *Merill Palmer Quarterly* 32:251–262.

Greenfield, Patricia M. (1984). *Mind and Media: The Effects of Television, Computers and Video Games.* Cambridge, MA: Harvard University Press.

Greenfield, Patricia M.; Brannon, Craig; and Lohr, David. (1994). "Two-Dimensional Representation of Movement through Three-Dimensional Space: The Role of Video Game Expertise." *Journal of Applied Developmental Psychology* 15:87–103.

Griffiths, Mark D. (1997). "Video Games and Children's Behaviour." In *Elusive Links: Television, Video Games, Cinema, and Children's Behaviour,* eds. Tony Charlton and Kenneth David. Gloucester, Eng.: GCED/Park Publishers.

Funk, Jeanne B.; Germann, July N.; and Buchman, Debra D. (1997). "Children and Electronic Games in the United States." *Trends in Communication* 2:111–127.

Nua. (2000). "Internet Surveys." <http://www.nua.net/surveys>.

Okagaki, Lynn, and Frensch, Peter A. (1994). "Effects of Video Game Playing on Measures of Spatial Performance: Gender Effects in Late Adolescents." *Journal of Applied Developmental Psychology* 15:33–58.

Provenzo, Eugene, Jr. (1991). *Video Kids: Making Sense of Nintendo.* Cambridge, MA: Harvard University Press.

Sanger, Jack; Willson, Jane; Davies, Bryn; and Whittaker, Roger. (1997). *Young Children, Videos and Computer Games: Issues for Teachers and Parents.* London: Falmer Press.

Schwartz, Steven A., and Schwartz, Janet. (1994). *Parent's Guide to Video Games.* Rocklin, CA: Prima Publishing.

Sherry, John. (1997). "Do Violent Video Games Cause Aggression? A Meta-Analytic Review." Paper presented at the International Communication Association, Montreal, Canada.

Valkenburg, Patti M., and Soeters, Karen E. (2000). *Children's Positive and Negative Experiences with the Internet.* Amsterdam: University of Amsterdam, Department of Communication.

PATTI M. VALKENBURG

VIDEO GAMES, RATINGS FOR

See: Ratings for Video Games, Software, and the Internet

VIOLENCE IN THE MEDIA, ATTRACTION TO

Movies and television programs routinely feature violence, including everything from relatively minor scuffles to gory and gruesome encounters. The violent images in the mass media can be highly disturbing—they are often vivid and can be quite realistic. Moreover, violent depictions may produce unwanted consequences among viewers. Nevertheless, when it comes to entertainment, violence sells. Why would people knowingly expose themselves to images that are so horrific? Although this question has not received a great deal of attention, a number of theories have been offered to explain why individuals are attracted to violence in the mass media.

It should be noted that some of the theorizing that is relevant to this question comes from research that was designed to address similar, but different, issues. In fact, relatively little work has been conducted to determine what draws viewers to violent mass media. However, research does exist concerning attraction to horror films. Because horror films often include violence, research that uncovers why individuals are attracted to this content can help us understand why they are drawn to violent depictions. Nevertheless, the reader must keep in mind that some of the material reported in this entry is drawn from research that has not explored the attraction of violence *per se*. These deviations will be noted as they are discussed.

Theories that explain the attraction that individuals have to violent media can be grouped into two major categories: (1) those that reference the social motivations for viewing violent media and (2) those that cite the psychological processes that are responsible for viewing. In general, social motivations include viewing to obtain some kind of reward from society, such as the rewards people receive from conforming to socially appropriate roles. Psychological processes refer to the cognitive or emotional activities that lead people to view violent mass media to satisfy the demands of individual psychological makeup, such as viewing violence to satisfy one's morbid curiosity.

Social Motivations for the Viewing of Mediated Violence

Individuals are rewarded when they behave in a manner that is consistent with what society expects of them. For example, males are traditionally rewarded when they act strong, confident, and fearless, while females are rewarded when they act helpless and dependent on men. Males and females, then, may be motivated to conform to their gender roles to achieve these rewards. Some theorists argue that horror viewing provides a context in which males and females can perform their gender roles and experience the social rewards that follow. For example, when viewing a frightening film, males can act as though they are not bothered by what they see and demonstrate that they have mastered their fear. Females, on the other hand, can seek protection and cling to their male viewing partners when frightened. Because horror films often contain violence, it is possible that males and females may seek similar social gratification from viewing violent media.

Males are usually more avid viewers of violent media than females, however. Perhaps, then, the explanation offered above can only explain the popularity of violent media among males. For females, the rewards that are experienced as a result of conforming to gender roles may not compensate for the negative emotions that they experience during the viewing. In fact, research indicates that males experience more enjoyment from viewing frightening films than females do. For example, a study by Glenn Sparks (1991) showed that the more males experienced distress while viewing a film, the better they felt after viewing. However, female positive affect after viewing the frightening film was not related to levels of distress that were experienced during the viewing. Researchers suggest that the arousal that is produced from experiencing negative emotions while viewing a horror film intensifies the positive emotions that males feel when they are able to demonstrate mastery of their fears after the viewing. As a result, violent mass media may be attractive to males because it provides them with an opportunity to experience the rewards that are associated with displaying masculine qualities.

A different explanation for the attraction of males to violent mass media that also relates to social motivations is that males are taught that violence is somewhat acceptable for them and that they need to learn more about it to function properly in society. Females, on the other hand, are socialized to believe that acting violently or aggressively is not feminine. If males are taught that violence is relevant to them, then they may, as children, begin using violent media to understand better what it means to be male and how to enact male roles. Similarly, female lack of interest in violent media may stem from the fact that society will not reward females for being aggressive.

Some research suggests that gender differences in the attraction to violent media is most prominent with certain types of depictions. Specifically, in a survey by Joanne Cantor and Amy Nathanson (1997), boys were more interested than girls in television programs that featured the use of violence for a purpose, such as the restoration of justice. However, gender differences were not evident in the case of humorous, slapstick depictions of violence, such as those found in classic cartoons. These findings suggest that violence *per se* may not be universally attractive to males. However, violence that is used to restore justice may serve some function for boys and even adult males. Perhaps males are socialized to believe that the use of violence is acceptable to achieve justice; hence, viewing media content that features this kind of theme may help males learn how to use violence in a socially acceptable manner.

Other researchers suggest that adolescents who are poor students in school seek out violent mass media to achieve the social recognition and acceptance that they cannot gain from school. Keith Roe (1995) has argued that these adolescents create subcultures that share an interest in deviant media. Adolescent members of these subcultures gain the group membership, support, and valued identity that they are denied in other contexts. Research shows that, within samples of adolescents, there does seem to be a relationship between having a low academic standing and having an interest in violent media. It is possible, then, that the viewing of violent media may serve a social function for adolescents who have been rejected by or are unsuccessful in mainstream institutions.

Psychological Processes that Underlie the Viewing of Mediated Violence

In addition to the social motivations for the viewing of violence, individuals may seek out violence in the mass media to satisfy certain psychological needs. For example, aggressive individuals may be attracted to violent content in order to justify or to understand better their own behaviors. There is much correlational data suggesting that this explanation is correct. That is, the bulk of survey research indicates that individuals who have aggressive attitudes or behaviors are especially likely to view violence in the mass media and to choose violent content over nonviolent content. However, these kinds of data cannot rule out the alternative explanation that viewing violent media increases aggression in viewers.

Fortunately, other kinds of research have been used to gain more clarity on this issue. For example, an experiment by Allan Fenigstein (1979) demonstrated that inducing aggressive thoughts or behaviors in college-age male participants produced an increased interest in viewing violent films. In addition, a longitudinal survey by Charles Atkin and his colleagues (1979) measured children's aggression and exposure to violent television programs at two different times (with a time-span of one year between the surveys). This allowed the researchers to determine whether there was a relationship between being aggressive during the first wave of data collection and viewing violent television at the second wave of data collection, while holding prior violence viewing levels constant. In fact, Atkin and his colleagues found that children who were more aggressive during the first part of the study were more likely to watch violent programs during the second part of the study, regardless of how much violent television they had watched during the wave-one data collection. Taken together, this research suggests that adults and children who have aggressive dispositions are especially likely to seek out violence in the mass media.

Another psychological process that may underlie exposure to violent media is the subconscious desire to master one's own fears. This notion stems from a process of "repetition-compulsion" (introduced by Sigmund Freud), whereby anxious individuals are believed to select frightening stimuli repeatedly with the hopes of mastering their fears. In the context of the attraction to violent media, viewers who are particularly concerned about becoming a victim of crime or who are fearful of violence in general may expose themselves to violent material to try to lessen the intensity of their negative emotions via desensitization.

Research seems to support the notion that more anxious and fearful individuals are attracted to violent media. However, these individuals may not be equally attracted to all kinds of violent depictions. In particular, violent programs that feature happy endings in which justice is restored may be especially appealing to fearful individuals because they suggest that violent situations do not have to end in tragedy. In fact, a study by Jennings Bryant and his colleagues (1981) revealed that college students who were classified as anxious became less anxious after viewing a heavy diet of "justice-restoring" action-adventure programs. The therapeutic value of these kinds of violent programs may ultimately lead anxious individuals to purposefully select them to soothe their fears by witnessing reassuring outcomes. Some researchers have even suggested that violent media that provide happy endings may teach anxious viewers strategies for coping with violent situations. Feeling that they have gained the knowledge and skills for dealing with violence, these anxious viewers may experience some relief after viewing violent media.

Another psychological process that may underlie attraction to violent media is what many refer to as "morbid curiosity," wherein the attention of individuals seems to be innately drawn to violence. Perhaps this has evolutionary significance in that those human ancestors who paid attention to violence were more likely to survive. It is possible, then, that humans are naturally curious when it comes to violence and death. In fact, some research on horror suggests that a sheer "gore watching" motivation may be a primary reason for why individuals select horror films. For example, a survey by Deirdre Johnston (1995) found that high school students who were heavy viewers of horror films and had a preference for graphic violence reported that they were more interested than others in the way people die. Unfortunately, there are few other studies that directly speak to the possibility that the attraction to violent media is a manifestation of individuals' morbid curiosity.

Other research suggests that a host of personality traits underlie the attraction to violence in the mass media. For example, research by Ron Tamborini and James Stiff (1987) has shown that individuals who desire high levels of stimulation (often called "sensation seekers") are more likely to view graphic horror (which presumably con-

tains violence). The fright that these films produce may be experienced as pleasure by those who crave heightened levels of arousal and new sensations. Another personality trait that is relevant to viewing media violence is empathy. In another study, Tamborini, Stiff, and Carl Heidel (1990) found that nonempathic individuals are more likely to view media violence than are individuals who readily empathize with others. It could be that their tendency to avoid placing themselves in the position of others allows these viewers to enjoy the graphic violence. However, it has also been suggested that viewers who empathize or identify with the aggressors in media violence are attracted to this content. Johnston's 1995 survey revealed that adolescents who identified with the perpetrators of violence in horror films were more likely to have the gore-watching motivation that is associated with heavy viewing of these films. By seeing the violent situations from the perspective of the aggressor, these viewers avoid sharing the victim's negative emotions and may, in fact, vicariously participate in the aggressor's "triumph."

Conclusion

There are a variety of reasons why individuals may purposefully seek out violent content in the mass media. They might be attracted to this material to establish or fulfill specific social roles or to set in motion certain psychological processes that bring them comfort or pleasure. It is also possible that individuals are motivated by a variety of factors simultaneously. Given these possibilities, it is not surprising that violent content is attractive to so many different people and is such a staple of media entertainment.

See also: CATHARSIS THEORY AND MEDIA EFFECTS; DESENSITIZATION AND MEDIA EFFECTS; FEAR AND THE MEDIA; GENDER AND THE MEDIA; PARENTAL MEDIATION OF MEDIA EFFECTS; VIOLENCE IN THE MEDIA, HISTORY OF RESEARCH ON.

Bibliography

Atkin, Charles; Greenberg, Bradley; Korzenny, Felipe; and McDermott, Steven. (1979). "Selective Exposure to Televised Violence." *Journal of Broadcasting* 23:5–13.

Boyanowsky, Ehor O. (1977). "Film Preferences under Conditions of Threat: Whetting the Appetite for Violence, Information, or Excitement?" *Communication Research* 4:133–144.

Bryant, Jennings; Carveth, Rodney A.; and Brown, Dan. (1981). "Television Viewing and Anxiety: An Experimental Examination." *Journal of Communication* 31(1):106–119.

Cantor, Joanne. (1998a). *"Mommy, I'm Scared": How TV and Movies Frighten Children and What We Can Do to Protect Them.* New York: Harcourt Brace.

Cantor, Joanne. (1998b). "Children's Attraction to Violent Television Programming." In *Why We Watch: The Attractions of Violent Entertainment,* ed. Jeffrey H. Goldstein. Oxford, Eng.: Oxford University Press.

Cantor, Joanne, and Nathanson, Amy I. (1997). "Predictors of Children's Interest in Violent Television Programs." *Journal of Broadcasting & Electronic Media* 41:155–167.

Fenigstein, Allan. (1979). "Does Aggression Cause a Preference for Viewing Media Violence?" *Journal of Personality and Social Psychology* 37:2307–2317.

Johnston, Deirdre D. (1995). "Adolescents' Motivations for Viewing Graphic Horror." *Human Communication Research* 21:522–552.

Orbach, Israel; Vinkler, Edith; and Har-Even, Dov. (1993). "The Emotional Impact of Frightening Stories on Children." *Journal of Child Psychology and Psychiatry* 34:379–389.

Roe, Keith. (1995). "Adolescents' Use of Socially Devalued Media: Towards a Theory of Media Delinquency." *Journal of Youth and Adolescence* 24:617–631.

Sparks, Glenn G. (1991). "The Relationship between Distress and Delight in Males' and Females' Reactions to Frightening Films." *Human Communication Research* 17:625–637.

Tamborini, Ron, and Stiff, James. (1987). "Predictors of Horror Film Attendance and Appeal: An Analysis of the Audience for Frightening Films." *Communication Research* 14:415–436.

Tamborini, Ron; Stiff, James; and Heidel, Carl. (1990). "Reacting to Graphic Horror: A Model of Empathy and Emotional Behavior." *Communication Research* 17:616–640.

Zillmann, Dolf, and Wakshlag, Jacob. (1985). "Fear of Victimization and the Appeal of Crime Drama." In *Selective Exposure to Communication,* eds. Dolf Zillmann and Jennings Bryant. Hillsdale, NJ: Lawrence Erlbaum.

AMY I. NATHANSON

■ VIOLENCE IN THE MEDIA, HISTORY OF RESEARCH ON

Public controversy about violent content in the media has a long history that extends as far back as the first decade of the twentieth century in the United States. The earliest controversies revolved around depictions of criminality in the movies, and the very first case of movie censorship occurred in 1908, when the police in Chicago refused to provide a permit for the public display of the movie *The James Boys in Missouri.* Authorities objected to the content of the film because it focused on violent lawbreaking (Hoberman, 1998). The scientific study of the effects of media violence may not extend as far back as 1908, but it was only a few years later that media violence became a focus of the first major investigation of the content and effects of movies.

The Payne Fund Studies

As the popularity of movies grew in the 1920s, so too did public pressure on the movie industry to do something about the widespread concerns that were being voiced about the effect that movie depictions of sex and violence had on children. In response to this pressure, William Short, the executive director of the Motion Picture Research Council (a private educational group), invited a number of the most prominent scholars across various disciplines to design and carry out a series of studies into how movies affect children. The U.S. government was not funding such research at the time, so the researchers turned to private funding sources. The Payne Fund, a privately funded philanthropic foundation, agreed to provide the needed funding, and the studies were conducted between 1929 and 1932.

The studies produced under the Payne Fund were designed to answer a variety of questions, only some of which pertained to the study of media violence. One of the studies that did pertain to media violence was a large-scale content analysis conducted by Edgar Dale (1935). The results revealed that most—more than 75 percent—of the fifteen hundred films that were studied could be categorized as dealing with crime, sex, or love. The emphasis on crime was no surprise to critics of the movie industry, and these results served to fuel the public debate over the effect that movies have on audience members. Another study conducted under the Payne Fund was even more inflammatory in terms of the public debate. Herbert Blumer (1933) asked nearly two thousand people from different demographic groups to answer questions about their own personal experiences as a result of watching movies. Blumer did not reduce this data to any type of quantitative presentation; he simply presented what people wrote in response to the questions. In many cases, people reported having imitated movie characters and having integrated movie scenarios into their play behavior as children. By contemporary standards, the exclusive reliance on retrospective self-reports is a rather weak methodological technique. Nevertheless, Blumer's study had a significant effect on the controversy and helped keep the spotlight on the movie industry. That spotlight was also intensified with occasional news reports. For example, it was reported in 1931 that after viewing a violent movie, *The Secret Six*, a twelve-year-old boy in New Jersey shot another child in the head (Hoberman, 1998). According to the Motion Picture Association of America Production Code, put in place in the early 1930s, movies were not supposed to "lower the moral standards of viewers" or to encourage them to identify with criminals. However, the code was not enforced. When FBI Chief J. Edgar Hoover actually endorsed in the mid-1930s several movies that depicted gangsters and FBI agents, the controversy about movie violence tended to subside, but it reemerged again during the explosive growth of television. By the time the television age had arrived, research methods had matured and the U.S. government was more interested in providing funding for scientific studies. The controversy over media violence was about to enter a new era.

The Rise of Television

Television was introduced to the public in the late 1940s, but by 1950, only one in ten homes had a television set. As the proliferation of sets increased in the 1950s, another medium—comic books—was attracting attention for its violent content. In this case, a reputable psychiatrist, Frederic Wertham, wrote a book titled *Seduction of the Innocent* (1954), in which he reported the results of his study on the content and effects of comic books. His procedures for studying content lacked the rigor that is associated with modern scientific content analyses, and his conclusions about effects were not based on careful experimentation. Instead, the conclusions arose from Wertham's case studies of boys who had been referred to his psychiatric practice. Wertham's conclusions about the evils of violence in comic books were not necessarily shared widely among

Violence in the movies has long been a controversial issue, and this image represents the top ten "Thou Shall Nots" (including defeating the law and showing a dead man) issued by the Hays Office, the organization that was established in the 1930s to protect and uphold public morals through the creation of a production code. (Bettmann/Corbis)

scientists. Nevertheless, they elevated the media violence problem to national attention and caused changes in the comic book industry in terms of self-censorship. Rather than risk government intervention, the industry established its own review board to review comic book content prior to publication. The "seal of approval" from the review board was given only to those comic books that were deemed acceptable for children to read. Consequently, violent content decreased and parents came to rely heavily on the appearance of the seal of approval on a comic book's front cover to indicate that it was appropriate for children.

While the public was reading about Wertham's warnings of violence in comic books, they were also beginning to read regularly about "copycat" crimes that were reported in newspapers around the country. These reports seemed to suggest a disturbing capacity of television to stimulate imitative antisocial behavior. Wilbur Schramm, Jack Lyle, and Edwin Parker published a book, *Television in the Lives of Our Children* (1961), that argued that the apparent connections between tel-

Eric Hoffer, the "longshoreman philosopher," was a member of the National Commission on the Causes and Prevention of Violence. He was also the lead-off witness for the 1969 Senate Permanent Investigation Subcommittee hearings on campus disorders. (Bettmann/Corbis)

evision exposure and violence were not coincidental. Among other things, they documented the numerous examples of copycat violence that were reported in the news during the 1950s. Researchers were not the only ones to take note of these incidents.

In 1954, Senator Estes Kefauver, in his role as chairman of the U.S. Senate Subcommittee on Juvenile Delinquency, publicly questioned the need for violence on television. The National Association of Broadcasters (NAB) responded with a promise for research into the effects of violent content. It is not surprising that, since the NAB was not a research organization, it failed to deliver on this promise. Seven years later, not much had changed. The new chairman of the Senate subcommittee was Senator Thomas Dodd. Once again, the subcommittee raised the issue of television violence, but the broadcasting community showed little interest in contributing to any sustained research effort into the effects of media violence or in reducing violent content. In 1964, the Senate subcommittee strengthened its rhetoric and criticized the broadcasting community for the violence that was being disseminated. As the rhetoric grew hotter, the broadcast community grew even cooler to the idea of becoming involved in research. In

1969, the National Commission on the Causes and Prevention of Violence submitted a report that brought television violence under careful scrutiny. Data gathered by George Gerbner was prominently featured in this report. Unfortunately, while the commission report detailed the high prevalence of violent content and the negative attitudes of the public toward such content, little insight was offered about the actual effects that viewing violence had on subsequent attitudes and behavior.

The Report of the Surgeon General

Senator John Pastore was not satisfied with the conclusions that appeared in the report released by the National Commission on the Causes and Prevention of Violence. He bemoaned the fact that, although there was a surge in violence in the culture, there was still little data pertaining to the possible causal role that media violence was playing in fostering aggressive behavior. At Pastore's initiative, in his role as chairman of the U.S. Senate Commerce Committee's Subcommittee on Communications, the issue of media violence remained a top concern among lawmakers. In 1969, only a week after Pastore expressed his concerns in a letter to Robert Finch, the U.S. Secretary of Health, Education, and Welfare, the Surgeon General of the United States, William Stewart, was ordered by President Richard Nixon to initiate a new study into the effects of media violence. The project was facilitated by $1 million from the National Institute of Mental Health.

One incident that functioned to blemish the Surgeon General's eventual report on media violence (1972) concerned the naming of the advisory committee that would oversee the report. In a move that many observers found to be outrageous, the Surgeon General sent a list of forty names to the three major television networks (ABC, CBS, and NBC) and to the NAB, asking them all to indicate who would not be appropriate to serve on this committee that was supposed to conduct an impartial scientific investigation. According to Robert Liebert, Joyce Sprafkin, and Emily Davidson (1982), the rationale for this procedure was apparently based on the same practice that had been employed in the earlier Surgeon General's Advisory Committee on Smoking and Health. In that case, the tobacco companies were asked to eliminate the names of individuals who they thought might not be appropriate; in this way, the committee had hoped to prevent the possibility that the companies would later claim that the deck had been stacked against them from the beginning. In the case of the Advisory Committee on Television and Social Behavior, the opportunity to exclude researchers backfired and mired the final report in controversy. Although CBS did not suggest any names for elimination, the other networks did identify the names of seven researchers deemed inappropriate. Several of these names, including Albert Bandura and Leonard Berkowitz, were some of the leading scholars in the area of media effects and aggressive behavior.

The studies conducted under the auspices of the Surgeon General's effort were not coordinated or planned to cover the topic of television violence in any systematic way. Researchers who received grant money to study the problem were encouraged to take on their own research initiatives. Nevertheless, the final report, which included the results of twenty-three different projects, permitted the examination of a number of dimensions of the media violence question.

Content Analyses of Television

Gerbner (1972) contributed data from systematic content analyses of television to the Surgeon General's report. Using the definition that violence was "the overt expression of physical force against others or self, or the compelling of action against one's will on pain of being hurt or killed," Gerbner was able to compare the quantity of violence on network television in 1969. Quantities were provided by two earlier analyses that Gerbner had contributed to the report for the National Commission on the Causes and Prevention of Violence. The results of Gerbner's study indicated that violence on prime-time television occurred at the rate of about eight instances per hour—unchanged from the figures of his earlier analysis. (This rate has proven to be relatively steady over time since the study was done.) One area of concern indicated by Gerbner's data was an increase in cartoon violence during the Saturday morning time period directed at children. In fact, the data indicated that this time slot was the most violent of any on television.

Experimental Studies

One of the most important experimental studies in the Surgeon General's report was conducted by Robert Liebert and Robert Baron (1971). The purpose of the study was to investigate the potential for violent television to instigate aggressive behavior in children. Using children who ranged from five to nine years of age, the researchers randomly assigned the subjects to watch either a brief clip from a violent television show (*The Untouchables*) or an alternative clip of nonviolent sports programming. Following exposure to the television clip, the children were placed in a situation in which they could choose to help or hurt another child's progress at winning a game in an adjacent room. If they pressed a "help" button, they were told that it would make it easier for the child to turn a handle that would lead to success in the game. In contrast, if they pressed a "hurt" button, they were told that the handle would become hot for the other child in the adjacent room and would hinder progress toward winning. The results of the experiment revealed that children who had watched the segment from the violent show were significantly more likely to press the "hurt" button and to hold it down longer than were the children who had watched nonviolent sports program.

Aletha Huston Stein and Lynette Friedrich (1972) conducted another important experiment on young children who were from three to five years of age. In one of the relatively few longitudinal studies in the literature, these researchers observed children's free-play and classroom behavior during a two-week baseline period. They then randomly assigned children to watch either violent (*Batman* and *Superman* cartoons), prosocial (*Mister Rogers' Neighborhood*), or neutral programs for a period of four weeks. After the four-week treatment period, the behavior of all of the children was observed for two weeks. The major finding of the study was that children who had watched the violent cartoons were significantly more aggressive in their interactions than children in either of the other viewing groups. In a theme that resulted in much confusion in interpreting the overall findings of the Surgeon General's report, the authors reported that their result held only for children who had been rated above the median in aggressive behavior during the baseline observation period.

Reactions to the Report

The controversy that swirled around the release of the Surgeon General's report was started by the publication of a headline in *The New York*

Times on January 11, 1972, that declared that television violence was not harmful to youths. In the article that followed, the public was told that the Surgeon General's report had found evidence that the majority of young people were not adversely affected by television violence. Many of the researchers who were directly involved in the report's research took issue with the way in which the final conclusions were being communicated to the public. In view of the findings of many of the studies that showed that violence tended to increase aggressive behavior, even if the effects were sometimes limited to certain groups, the research community was upset because they thought the public was not learning what they needed to know in order to appreciate properly the risks associated with television violence. In the end, the Surgeon General's report functioned to draw close public attention to the television violence issue. It also motivated researchers to follow up on the report's findings and continue to study issues pertaining to the effects of media violence. In the decade following the publication of the report, significant progress was made in understanding the effects of media violence. As the science of media-effects research matured, there was a greater emphasis on understanding the particular theoretical mechanisms that might underlie the effects of violence.

Theories of Media Violence

The theories that have been applied to the study of violence in the media include catharsis, social learning, priming effects, arousal, desensitization, cultivation, and fear.

Catharsis

Even before the Surgeon General's report, Seymour Feshbach (1955) proposed a theory of media violence that, if supported, would have pleased Hollywood producers and set the public mind at rest concerning violent television. The idea of catharsis goes back to Aristotle, and Feshbach proposed that it might apply to the modern situation of watching violence on television. Just as Aristotle thought people could purge their feelings of grief by watching others grieve in a dramatic context, Feshbach thought that people could purge their feelings of anger and pent-up aggression by watching violence in a dramatic context. An early study by Alberta Siegel (1956), which used a *Woody Woodpecker* cartoon (as the example of a violent television show) to test the theory on nursery school children, failed to find any evidence for the catharsis hypothesis. The children who viewed violence tended to behave *more* aggressively, not less. Nevertheless, Feshbach and Robert Singer (1971) persisted with the catharsis idea and attempted to test it in a major field study that involved several institutional homes for boys. These authors accumulated some evidence that seemed to indicate that boys who were exposed to violent television programs behaved less aggressively than similar boys who watched nonviolent programs. Unfortunately for the catharsis hypothesis, this result was easily explained by noting that the boys who watched violent programs were also watching shows that they enjoyed; boys who watched nonviolent programs did not find these shows to be nearly so enjoyable and may have actually been provoked by the fact that their peers were permitted to see their favorite shows due to nothing more than the luck of the draw. Moreover, the internal validity of this experiment was also corrupted by the fact that some boys in the nonviolent program group protested so intensely about the elimination of one violent program (*Batman*) from their media diet that the investigators relented and permitted them to watch it. In the wake of these methodological problems, the catharsis theory was left floundering. Added to these problems was the accumulating evidence that exposure to violence was more likely to instigate violence than to diminish it.

Social Learning

Another early theory that was applied to the media violence controversy was Albert Bandura's theory of social learning (later referred to as social cognitive theory). Bandura (1963, 1965) emphasized that children learn behaviors from models in their environment who manage to capture a child's attention. Behaviors that the child attends to are "acquired" in the sense that children are able to reproduce these behaviors if they are motivated to do so. Not all acquired behaviors are eventually performed, however. Bandura drew upon the prevailing theory of the time and emphasized that the chief determining characteristic for the performance of a behavior was the extent to which the behavior was either rewarded or punished. In extending this notion to media violence, the theory predicted that aggressive behavior that was rewarded was much more likely to be copied or imitated than aggressive behavior that was punished. Bandura and his colleagues tested this formulation in several experiments. Children were typically exposed to a short film clip depicting aggressive behavior in a play context that was either rewarded or punished. Following exposure to the film clips, children were observed in free-play situations. Findings from these studies supported the theory in that children who saw aggressive behavior rewarded were more likely to behave aggressively than children who saw aggressive behavior punished.

Bandura faced a number of methodological criticisms from his studies that revolved around the measurement of key concepts. First, some scholars argued that the film clips used in these studies featured highly contrived scenarios that failed to resemble the sort of violent content that children might view on commercial television. Second, Bandura's definition of aggressive behavior included the number of times a child punched a large inflatable "bobo doll." The bobo doll, it was argued, existed for the sole purpose of being hit. Moreover, because the doll was inanimate, Bandura's notion of aggression was only "play" aggression. One could not assume that children who hit the bobo doll were actually under the impression that they were inflicting real pain on anyone. These limitations were addressed and overcome in subsequent research that, like the early studies, tended to show that viewing televised violence in the context of rewards could make aggressive behavior more likely in children.

Priming Effects

A major contributor to the early literature on the effects of media violence was Leonard Berkowitz. His theoretical formulation emphasized that media violence contained "aggressive cues" that could combine with a viewer's state of anger or frustration and trigger an aggressive response. In the 1990s, Eunkyung Jo and Berkowitz revised the theoretical language of the theory of aggressive cues to take advantage of more contemporary cognitive theory. Relying on the notion of "priming," these researchers outlined a position in which media violence is seen as a stimulus that primes thoughts related to aggressive behavior. Stated succinctly, their 1994 essay clearly specifies what could happen after exposure to media violence: "Under certain conditions and

for a short period of time, there is an increased chance that the viewers will (a) have hostile thoughts that can color their interpretation of other people, (b) believe other forms of aggressive conduct are justified and/or will bring them benefits, and (c) be aggressively inclined" (p. 46).

Brad Bushman and Russell Geen (1990) demonstrated the priming effect of media violence when they randomly assigned viewers to watch a movie that contained either high, moderate, or low levels of violence. Following the movie, when viewers were asked to list their thoughts, the viewers who had watched a violent film had significantly more aggressive thoughts than viewers of nonviolent film. In another study, Craig Anderson (1983) found that when people imagined themselves carrying out a particular action, they subsequently reported that they felt much more motivated to carry it out than if they had imagined someone else carrying out the action. Consistent with the idea of priming, Jo and Berkowitz (1994) commented on this result: "It is as if the thought of the particular action had, to some degree, activated the motor program linked to this action" (p. 48). It should be noted that the idea of priming effects runs directly counter to the catharsis hypothesis. Feshbach had believed that fantasizing about acting aggressively would reduce the likelihood of carrying out aggressive behavior. The priming hypothesis suggests exactly the opposite. In general, the decline of the viability of catharsis theory was directly linked to the many studies conducted by Berkowitz and his colleagues, which showed evidence for the instigating effects of exposure to media violence as well as for the priming process as a likely theoretical mechanism for these effects.

Arousal

While Berkowitz focused on the violent content in media messages, another researcher, Dolf Zillmann, believed that the capacity for violence to induce heightened levels of physiological arousal was also very important. In his theory of excitation transfer, Zillmann (1991) reasoned that arousal from viewing violence could intensify emotional reactions experienced immediately after the viewing experience. In cases where viewers experience anger subsequent to viewing an arousing program, the anger will be more intensely experienced and will be more likely to result in aggressive behavior. Many studies in the media context that are designed to test the excitation transfer hypothesis have revealed strong support for this formulation. Of course, one implication of the theory is that viewing media violence may also result in the intensification of positive emotions subsequent to viewing—if those positive emotions occur in reaction to some stimulus.

Desensitization

While most of the theories about the effects of media violence have attempted to shed light on the question about the extent to which viewing results in increased aggressive behavior, some research has focused on the question of desensitization to violence. According to the desensitization hypothesis, repeated exposure to violence results in emotional adjustment or saturation. Under this formulation, initial levels of excitement, anxiety, tension, disgust, and so on weaken with repeated exposure to violence. One of the most important consequences of this effect could be the reduced likelihood of a desensitized viewer to respond with a sense of urgency to violence in real life. While desensitization has been studied less frequently than instigation of violence, the research that does exist supports the idea that desensitization occurs.

Ronald Drabman and Margaret Thomas (1976) studied the desensitization hypothesis with children in an experimental context. After exposing randomly selected children to either violent or nonviolent television, they asked each child to monitor the activity between two other children presented on a video monitor. The child was instructed that if the activity of the children turned violent, they should seek out the experimenter for assistance. Children who had viewed television violence just prior to the monitoring task were significantly less likely to notify the experimenter when the interaction on the monitor turned violent. In addition, those children who did notify the experimenter took a significantly longer time to do so.

Cultivation

Gerbner's early contributions to the violence literature in the form of content analyses helped to form the basis for his theory of media cultivation. According to this view, viewers who watch large amounts of television content become cultivated into accepting the view of social reality presented in the television messages. Because, as the content analyses had revealed, the television world was one filled with violence, viewers who watch large amounts of television should come to believe that the world was a violent place. Specifically, because the incidence of violence on television suggests a more violent world than the one that actually exists, viewers who watch large amounts of television should adopt exaggerated perceptions of the occurrence of violence and should also come to fear criminal victimization more than viewers who watch smaller amounts of television.

Gerbner and his colleagues (1994) have presented evidence from sample surveys pertaining to the cultivation hypothesis. According to the theory, because cultivation is a gradual process, it cannot be studied by the experimental method. This feature of the theory poses some methodological difficulties in terms of being able to establish clearly the cause–effect relationship that the theory posits between television viewing and fear of criminal victimization. Sample surveys are inherently incapable of controlling all possible third variables that might contribute to the relationship between television viewing and any supposed cultivated attitude. Despite the fact that the theory and research pertaining to it have come under various attacks over the years, Gerbner has been a strong advocate of the perspective, and there appears to be enough empirical support to keep the theory viable.

Fear

Joanne Cantor (1998) and her associates developed a program of research demonstrating that viewing specific programs or movies that involve violence or the threat of harm often causes children to have nightmares or intense and enduring anxieties. The research also shows that there are important differences in the types of media stimuli that frighten children of different ages. These variations are based on the viewer's level of cognitive development.

Research Evidence and the Question of Causation

If there is a pivotal issue running through all of the research on media violence, it is the issue of causality. In the end, the challenge for the research community and the consumer is to evaluate the various kinds of evidence that have been presented, with a view toward formulating a reasonable conclusion about the effects of media violence. This evidence can be naturally occurring, the result of a survey, or the result of an experiment.

Naturally Occurring Data

Brandon Centerwall's 1989 analysis of crime statistics across several countries constitutes some of the most provocative data available on the question of whether television is related to an increase in violence in society. In 1945, prior to the emergence of television in the United States, the crime statistics show three homicides per 100,000 people. By 1974, that figured had doubled. This same sort of increase emerged in Canada. According to Centerwall, the relationship between the introduction of television in any society and the increase in homicides in not accidental. Instead, Centerwall believes it is a direct causal relationship. Of course, there is no way to establish an unequivocal case for causality with this type of data. Literally hundreds of changes occurred along with the rise of television, and those other changes could theoretically be related to increases in homicides. Centerwall's approach to this problem is to compare other countries that are similar to the United States in many of the ways that are known to affect the homicide rate. For example, he argues that South Africa is quite comparable to the United States on almost any variable of interest between 1945 and 1974—except for the fact that the South African government had a ban on television during this time period. In contrast to the doubling homicide rate in the United States, the rate in South Africa dropped by 7 percent. When South Africa lifted the ban on television in 1974, the homicide rate promptly increased by 56 percent during the next nine years. By 1990, the increase had grown to 130 percent—more than doubling in less than twenty years in nearly the same way it had done in the United States. Centerwall attempted to introduce careful controls in these comparisons in order to boost the integrity of his analysis. For example, he excluded all homicides in South Africa that could be attributed to racial tensions. Even with these controls, the data still show a relationship between homicides and the introduction of television. In the end, Centerwall claims that roughly half of all homicides in the United States result, in part, from exposure to television. The problem in evaluating this claim is that the method of analysis falls short of meeting the strict criteria for making causal claims.

David Phillips (1979, 1983, 1985) has also reported the results of a series of studies that appear to show a link between mass-media violence and violence in the real world. One line of studies attempted to show a connection between widely publicized stories of suicide and subsequent increases in the suicide rate, presumably as a result of direct imitation. Another line of studies attempted to show a link between the occurrence of heavyweight prizefights and subsequent increases in the homicide rate. Phillips's analysis is provocative but controversial. In addition to failing to meet the conventional criteria for establishing a causal claim, there are various anomalies in Phillips's data, and these anomalies defy clear explanation. For example, the main increase in homicides after prizefights seems to occur on the third day after the fight, but increases also appear on the sixth and ninth days following the fight. Phillips's analyses have been the subject of some major methodological disputes in the sociological literature. In the final analysis, the naturally occurring data pertaining to the effects of media violence is suggestive, but it is not conclusive.

Survey Data

The best survey evidence pertaining to media violence comes from longitudinal panel studies that relate early viewing of television violence to later incidents of aggressive behavior. This method has the advantage of examining the basic relationship between viewing violence and aggressive behavior in a context where the time-order of the variables can be firmly established. L. Rowell Huesmann and Leonard Eron (1986) have collected the best evidence of this type by studying subjects from the time when they were eight years old until they were thirty years old. The most important finding in this study was that young children who watched the highest levels of television violence were more likely to be involved in serious crime when they were adults. Huesmann (1986) summarized these findings by stating, "Aggressive habits seem to be learned early in life, and once established, are resistant to change and predictive of serious adult antisocial behavior. If a child's observation of media violence promotes the learning of aggressive habits, it can have harmful lifelong consequences. Consistent with this theory, early television habits are in fact correlated with adult criminality" (pp. 129–130).

Of course, as noted in the discussion of Gerbner's cultivation theory, the survey method, similar to the studies that rely on naturally occurring data, is limited in terms of drawing unequivocal conclusions about cause and effect. Added to this limitation is the fact that some other longitudinal surveys, after controlling for several different variables, failed to find a significant correlation over time between aggressive behavior and the viewing of violence in the media. Most notable among this group of surveys was one funded by the television industry and directed by J. Ronald Milavsky (1982), who was the vice-president of News and Social Research for NBC at the time. Taken together, the available survey data do suggest a relationship between aggressive behavior and the viewing of violence in the media. However, it remains impossible for researchers to argue for a clear causal link between the two variables based on this type of data.

Experiments

The experimental method is the only way, in principle, to demonstrate a causal relationship between two variables. In addition to some of the laboratory experiments mentioned above, there have been some notable field experiments that attempted to show, in more naturalistic settings, a causal relationship between aggressive behavior and media violence. One such study, by Ross Parke and his colleagues (1977), summarized the results of three field experiments that supported the notion that viewing violent films increases aggressive behavior. Although experimental research on the effects of media violence has become less prevalent than in the 1970s, the conclusions of more recent studies of this type reinforce the widely shared conclusion from earlier studies that support the idea that viewing violence causes aggressive behavior. Zillmann and James Weaver (1999) reported a study showing that violent films viewed on four consecutive days produced increased hostile behavior on the part of both males and females a day later, regardless of whether the subjects had been provoked to respond aggressively.

Conclusion

In the mid-1990s, a major new content analysis of violence on television was conducted. The National Television Violence Study was carried out by researchers from four U.S. universities. This analysis, which was funded by the National Cable Television Association but not subjected to industry control, reconfirmed the high levels of violence on television (including cable television). Moreover, reporting on the context features associated with violence, such as the prevalence of attractive perpetrators and the scarcity of depicted negative consequences, the report concluded that the way in which violence is typically depicted promotes imitation.

In 1994, Haejung Paik and George Comstock reinforced the causal conclusion in a meta-analysis of all studies pertaining to the question of media violence and aggressive behavior. Even researchers who have been cautious in reaching the consensus opinion among scholars lend credence to this conclusion. For example, in his review of the literature, Richard Felson (1996) was much more reluctant than most scholars to interpret the available evidence as being strongly supportive of the causal relationship. In the end, however, he stated, "I conclude that exposure to television violence probably does have a small effect on violent behavior for some viewers, possibly because the media directs viewer's attention to novel forms of violent behavior that they would not otherwise consider" (p. 103). With the causal connection being well established, the research in the late 1990s focused mainly on other types of questions, including why media violence is attractive, how program warnings affect children's desire to view violent content, how violent video games affect players, and how parents might intervene in the negative effects. These issues ensure that research on media violence will continue to be a vibrant area of scholarship.

See also: AROUSAL PROCESSES AND MEDIA EFFECTS; CATHARSIS THEORY AND MEDIA EFFECTS; CULTIVATION THEORY AND MEDIA EFFECTS; CUMULATIVE MEDIA EFFECTS; DESENSITIZATION AND MEDIA EFFECTS; FEAR AND THE MEDIA; NATIONAL TELEVISION VIOLENCE STUDY; PARENTAL MEDIATION OF MEDIA EFFECTS; RATINGS FOR MOVIES; RATINGS FOR TELEVISION PROGRAMS; SOCIAL COGNITIVE THEORY AND MEDIA EFFECTS; VIOLENCE IN THE MEDIA, ATTRACTION TO.

Bibliography

Anderson, Craig. (1983). "Imagination and Expectation: The Effect of Imagining Behavioral Scripts on Personal Intentions." *Journal of Personality and Social Psychology* 45:293–305.

Blumer, Herbert. (1933). *The Movies and Conduct.* New York: Macmillan.

Bushman, Brad, and Geen, Russell. (1990). "Role of Cognitive-Emotional Mediators and Individual Differences in the Effects of Media Violence on Aggression." *Journal of Personality and Social Psychology* 58:56–163.

Bandura, Albert. (1963). "What TV Violence Can Do to Your Child." *Look,* October 22, pp. 46–52.

Bandura, Albert. (1965). "Influence of Models' Reinforcement Contingencies on the Acquisition of Imitative Responses." *Journal of Personality and Social Psychology* 1:589–595.

Cantor, Joanne. (1998). *"Mommy, I'm Scared": How TV and Movies Frighten Children and What We Can Do to Protect Them.* San Diego: Harcourt Brace.

Centerwall, Brandon S. (1989). "Exposure to Television as a Cause of Violence." In *Public Communication and Behavior,* Vol. 2, ed. George Comstock. San Diego: Academic Press.

Dale, Edgar. (1935). *The Content of Motion Pictures.* New York: Macmillan.

Drabman, Ronald S., and Thomas, Margaret H. (1976). "Does Watching Violence on Television Cause Apathy?" *Pediatrics* 57:329–331.

Felson, Richard B. (1996). "Mass Media Effects on Violent Behavior." *Annual Review of Sociology* 22:103–128.

Feshbach, Seymour. (1955). "The Drive-Reducing Function of Fantasy Behavior." *Journal of Abnormal and Social Psychology* 50:3–11.

Feshbach, Seymour, and Singer, Robert. (1971). *Television and Aggression.* San Francisco: Jossey-Bass.

Gerbner, George. (1972). "Violence in Television Drama: Trends and Symbolic Functions." In *Television and Social Behavior,* Vol. 1, eds. George Comstock and Eli Rubenstein. Washington, DC: U.S. Government Printing Office.

Gerbner, George; Gross, Larry; Morgan, Michael; and Signorielli, Nancy. (1994). "Growing Up with Television: The Cultivation Perspective." In *Media Effects: Advances in Theory and Research,* eds. Jennings Bryant and Dolf Zillmann. Hillsdale, NJ: Lawrence Erlbaum.

Hoberman, J. (1998). "A Test for the Individual Viewer: Bonnie and Clyde's Violent Reception." In *Why We Watch: The Attractions of Violent Entertainment,* ed. Jeffrey H. Goldstein. New York: Oxford University Press.

Huesmann, L. Rowell. (1986). "Psychological Processes Promoting the Relation Between Exposure to Media Violence and Aggressive Behavior by the Viewer." *Journal of Social Issues* 42:125–139.

Huesmann, L. Rowell, and Eron, Leonard. (1986). "The Development of Aggression in American Children as a Consequence of Television Violence Viewing." In *Television and the Aggressive Child: A Cross-National Comparison,* eds. L. Rowell Huesmann and Leonard D. Eron. Hillsdale, NJ: Lawrence Erlbaum.

Jo, Eunkyung, and Berkowitz, Leonard. (1994). "A Priming Effect Analysis of Media Influences: An Update." In *Media Effects: Advances in Theory and Research,* eds. Jennings Bryant and Dolf Zillmann. Hillsdale, NJ: Lawrence Erlbaum.

Liebert, Robert M., and Baron, Robert A. (1971). "Short-Term Effects of Televised Aggression on Children's Aggressive Behavior." In *Television and Social Behavior,* Vol. 2, eds. John P. Murray, Eli A. Rubinstein, and George A. Comstock. Washington, DC: U.S. Government Printing Office.

Liebert, Robert; Sprafkin, Joyce N.; and Davidson, Emily S. (1982). *The Early Window: Effects of Television on Children and Youth.* New York: Pergamon Press.

Milavsky, J. Ronald; Kessler, Ronald C.; Stipp, Horst; and Rubens, William S. (1982). *Television and Aggression: A Panel Study.* New York: Academic Press.

Paik, Haejung, and Comstock, George. (1994). "The Effects of Television Violence on Antisocial Behavior: A Meta-Analysis." *Communication Research* 21:516–546.

Parke, Ross D.; Berkowitz, Leonard; Leyens, Jacques P.; West, Steven G.; and Sebastian, Richard J. (1977). "The Effects of Repeated Exposure to Movie Violence on Aggressive Behaviour in Juvenile Delinquent Boys: Field Experimental Studies." In *Advances in Experimental Social Psychology,* Vol. 8, ed. Leonard Berkowitz. New York: Academic Press.

Phillips, David P. (1979). "Suicide, Motor Vehicle Fatalities, and the Mass Media: Evidence Toward a Theory of Suggestion." *American Journal of Sociology* 84:1150–1173.

Phillips, David P. (1983). "The Impact of Mass Media Violence on US Homicides." *American Sociological Review* 48:560–568.

Phillips, David P. (1985). "The Found Experiment: A New Technique for Assessing the Impact of Mass Media Violence in Real World Aggressive Behaviour." *Public Communication and Behavior,* Vol. 1, ed. George Comstock. Orlando, FL: Academic Press.

Schramm, Wilbur; Lyle, Jack; and Parker, Edwin B. (1961). *Television in the Lives of Our Children.* Stanford, CA: Stanford University Press.

Siegel, Alberta E. (1956). "Film-Mediated Fantasy Aggression and Strength of Aggressive Drive." *Child Development* 27:365–378.

Stein, Aletha, and Friedrich, Lynette. (1972). "Television Content and Young Children's Behavior." In *Television and Social Behavior,* Vol. 2, eds. John P. Murray, Eli A. Rubinstein, and George A. Comstock. Washington, DC: U.S. Government Printing Office.

Surgeon General's Scientific Advisory Committee on Television and Social Behavior. (1972). *Television and Growing up: The Impact of Televised Violence.* Washington, DC: U.S. Government Printing Office.

Weaver, James B. (1991). "Responding to Erotica: Perceptual Processes and Dispositional Implications." In *Responding to the Screen: Reception and Reaction Processes,* eds. Jennings Bryant and Dolf Zillmann. Hillsdale, NJ: Lawrence Erlbum.

Wertham, Frederic. (1954). *Seduction of the Innocent.* New York: Rinehart.

Zillmann, Dolf. (1991). "Television Viewing and Physiological Arousal." In *Responding to the Screen: Reception and Reaction Processes,* eds. Jennings Bryant and Dolf Zillmann. Hillsdale, NJ: Lawrence Erlbaum.

Zillmann, Dolf, and Weaver, James B., III. (1999). "Effects of Prolonged Exposure to Gratuitous Media Violence on Provoked and Unprovoked Hostile Behavior." *Journal of Applied Social Psychology* 29:145–165.

GLENN G. SPARKS

■ VISUALIZATION OF INFORMATION

Visualization is defined in the *Oxford English Dictionary* as "the action or fact of visualizing, the power or process of forming a mental picture or vision of something not actually present to the sight." As the old adage "a picture is worth a thousand words" goes, visualization can be defined as a method that makes the best use of a person's perceptual abilities to observe, access, and understand data and information. Generally speaking, the purpose of visualization is to provide the user with not only a visual presentation and interpretation of the data and information but also a better understanding of the phenomenon behind the data and information. A more recent and domain-specific definition of visualization is given by the following: "Visualization provides an interface between two powerful information processing systems—human mind and the modern computer. Visualization is the process of transforming data, information, and knowledge into visual form making use of human's natural visual capabilities. With effective visual interfaces we can interact with large volumes of data rapidly and effectively to discover hidden characteristics, patterns, and trends" (Gershon, Eick, and Card, 1998, p. 9).

There are many ways to approach the concept of visualization. Edward Tufte (1990) categorizes visualization into three types: pictures of numbers (e.g., statistic graphs), pictures of nouns (e.g.,

maps and aerial photographs), and pictures of verbs (e.g., representations of motion, process, cause and effect). Visualization through computers can be portrayed as pictures and graphs, two-dimensional and three-dimensional images, three-dimensional models and simulations, animations, video segments, and so on. Visualization has been studied by a variety of scholars and researchers from such disciplines as art history, cognitive science, computer graphics, epistemology, graphic design, image processing, linguistics, semiotics, technical communication, and visual interfaces.

History of Visualization

The use of images to represent objects from the real world has a long history. As far back as 20,000 B.C.E., humans began to draw, paint, or carve images on cave walls to record and depict aspects of their experiences. For example, the Paleolithic cave paintings found in the Remigia Cave at La Gasulla in Spain vividly illustrate a group of hunters killing a wild boar. However, the use of graphs, pictures, and drawings was not restricted to the recording and depicting of objects; visualization also became an effective means for representing abstract concepts and communicating abstract ideas. The ancient Egyptian hieroglyphics are pictures that were used as a form of visual communication. The term "ideograph" refers to a symbol that is used to represent a concept in a pictographic language. In modern Chinese, for example, there are more than fifty thousand ideographs.

Visual representation of information has been helpful in assisting humans with the description, classification, analysis, and comprehension of the natural world. Astronomy, cartography, and meteorology were some of the earliest fields to use visualization techniques. For example, the astronomical images painted in the tomb of Pharaoh Seti I in 1290 B.C.E. describe the relationship between Egyptian astronomy and mythology. The earliest map to use a latitude/longitude grid was drawn in China in 1137 to depict the travels of Da Yu (Yu the Great). In the 1920s, American meteorologists began to use symbols and pictograms to represent such natural phenomena as hail, lighting, snow, and thunderstorms in their weather charts.

Ever since Leonardo da Vinci created perspective drawing in the 1400s, the technique has been used as the primary method for creating technical

The use of a pie chart or other forms of visualizing information can often help to enhance and clarify a business presentation.
(Jack Hollingsworth/Corbis)

graphics communications. In the late 1700s, Gaspard Monge developed the science of descriptive geometry, which provided the foundation for three-dimensional representations using two-dimensional media. Wilhelm Röntgen's discovery of x-rays in 1895 made it possible for humans to visualize what could not be seen with the naked eyes. The discovery also revolutionized the scientific fields of medicine and chemistry because it resulted in x-ray photography and chemical crystallography, respectively.

The Semi-Automatic Ground Environment (SAGE) system was the first time that computers were used for visualizing information. The system, which was developed in the United States in the mid 1950s, used interactive computer graphics combined with radar to track, analyze, and display aircraft positions on a cathode-ray-tube monitor. In 1965, Ivan Sutherland designed Sketchpad, a minicomputer drawing system. The field of computer graphics quickly developed to produce applications such as computer-aided

design (CAD), geographical mapping, and molecular modeling. With the development of more powerful computers, better software, and advanced interaction techniques, virtual reality became possible. Using this technology, it has become possible to explore information visually and interactively in real time.

A large variety of visualization techniques have been used for different applications. Some commonly used techniques of visualization include bar charts, pie charts, HiLo glyphs, XY diagrams, scatter plots, treemaps, contour plots, cone trees, fractal rooms, hyperbolic trees, and perspective walls.

Scientific Visualization Versus Information Visualization

Visualization can be divided into two areas: scientific visualization and information visualization. Scientific visualization primarily deals with data or information that describe physical or spatial objects (e.g., the human body, the earth, and molecules), and information visualization primarily visualizes data or information that is non-physical or abstract (e.g., text, hierarchy, and statistics). Both areas of visualization share the same goal of using visual representations via computers to access, explore, explain, organize, and understand the data and information.

According to I. Herman, G. Melanáon, and M. S. Marshall (2000), there are three essential differences between the two areas. First, the data or information that is visualized by scientific visualization is different from the data or information that is visualized by information visualization; the former often has an inherent geometry, but the latter does not. Second, the users of scientific visualization are different from the users of information visualization; the former are usually experts, while the latter may have different levels of expertise. Third, scientific visualization and information visualization have different computer requirements; scientific visualization demands the capability of complex computation and graphic representation, which is not always necessary with information visualization. Therefore, scientific visualization, a well-established yet relatively specialized field with a relatively small number of scientists, involves many visualization techniques, uses various software tools, and requires enormous computer resources to make data or information more accessible and comprehensible. Information visualization, one of the increasingly important subfields of Human–Computer Interaction (HCI), takes advantage of the graphical capabilities of the computer and the perceptual abilities of the user to process, interpret, and understand data and information visually.

Typical Applications of Visualization

Visualization of information has many practical applications, ranging from the visualization of simple numerical data to the visualization of complex molecular structures. Some typical applications of visualization techniques are those related to geography, software, medicine, education, information retrieval, data mining and electronic commerce.

Geographical information systems (GIS) were designed to collect, store, retrieve, manipulate, and display geographically referenced data. GIS visually helps users to gain new insights related to the data and to solve complex research, planning, and management problems. GIS software is developed all over the world, but three of the better-known products are Maptitude, GeoMedia, and MapInfo.

Software visualization uses computer graphics and animation to illustrate and present computer programs, processes, and algorithms. Software visualization systems are a way to help programmers understand their code in a more effective way, and they can also be used to help teach students how algorithms work in programming. There are many software visualization systems, ranging from Algorithm Animation to Visualization of Object-Oriented Programming.

The application of computerized imagery to the field of medicine has resulted in medical imaging techniques such as computed tomography (CT), magnetic resonance imaging (MRI), nuclear medicine imaging (NMI), and ultrasonography. These techniques visually magnify the subtle aspects of the diagnostic, therapeutic, and healing process of patients, thus allowing the members of the clinical staff (e.g., doctors, nurses, students, technicians, and managers) to handle medical data and information in a more intuitive and effective manner. Many medical visualization tools have been developed, but two of the more popular tools are Imaging Application Platform (IAP) and Medical Imaging Software Developer's Kit (SDK).

Visualization in education helps students using images to represent and comprehend concepts and ideas, reinforce understanding, develop critical thinking, and integrate new knowledge. Visualization is helpful for teaching and learning in language arts, mathematics, medicine, social studies, science, engineering, and so on. Visualization has been used as a helpful means in some new teaching paradigms, such as web-based courses, interactive classrooms, and distributed learning. Popular software of visual learning and teaching include a.d.A.M, ClassWise, and Inspiration.

Interactive two-dimensional or three-dimensional visualization techniques can enhance the information retrieval process by providing effective visual interfaces for users to use in navigating and manipulating large amounts of textual information. Visualization techniques also help the user to identify the relationships between documents and to refine the search results until relevant information is located. Two examples of software that are used for visualization in information retrieval are Visual Thesaurus and DR-

LINK (Document Retrieval using LINguistic Knowledge). Visual Thesaurus presents an animated visual display of semantic relationships between words. DR-LINK is an online search service that uses natural language queries to search a text database, facilitates information retrieval with various features, and outputs the results in different ways, including bar charts and graphs.

Data mining is the analysis of data for underlying relationships, patterns, and trends that have not previously been discovered. Visualization is used in data mining to provide visual interfaces during the data analysis process, visual manipulation of the data representation, and visual presentation of the mined data for a better understanding. Some examples of data mining visualization software are Spotfire, DEVise, and WinViz.

Visualization of marketing and advertising data in market analysis provides executives, managers, and researchers with a new way to query and explore the vast amounts of customer, product, and market data that are generated by customer relationship management. For the customers of electronic commerce, visualization can be used to make it easier for them to comparison shop through interactive visual interfaces. Cult3D, ecBuilder, and Webstores 2000 are three of the companies that develop software for use with electronic commerce.

Future Trends in Visualization

With the advancement of science and technology, visualization technologies will bring people new ways to view, analyze, and interact with data and information. Several trends in visualization provide a glimpse of its future potential.

First, new technologies are being developed for new applications. For example, virtual reality as a visualization tool can help build a simpler user interface that allows users to interact directly with data in a virtual environment (e.g., CAVE—a multiperson, room-sized, high-resolution, three-dimensional video and audio environment that allows the user to control visualization parameters). Object-oriented visualization environments can be built by visual programming with functional objects (e.g., interfaces and classes are shown in different colors). In addition, animation allows the viewing of discrete images in rapid succession for studying data that vary over time.

Second, the cost of visualization technologies is decreasing dramatically. As a result, more inexpensive, standardized software and hardware for information visualization will become available and affordable.

Third, there will be more collaboration among the producers and users of visualization products. For example, collaborative visualization will enable users to share data and information visualization processes via computer-supported cooperative work using collaborative technologies, such as Habanero, Microsoft NetMeeting, and Tango. In addition, the emerging visualization libraries created by corporate and academic research groups will provide a consistent cross-platform environment for the development of graphic products.

Fourth, more attention is being given to education for visualization. Both professional and academic communities are developing guidelines and teaching materials for visualization curricula and courses. These developments include books, videos, and websites.

Finally, universally recognized visual metaphors and conventions for structuring data and information in multiple dimensions will be developed.

Conclusion

Visualization, as a human perceptive ability and cognitive process, has existed throughout history, and it has evolved as humans have evolved. Visualization of information via computer technology has had an enormous effect on human society even though is has only a very short history. As society and technology advance into the future, the human quest into the nature of visualization and the visualization of information will lead to a better understanding of the relationships between information, visualization, technology, human cognition, and the natural world.

See also: COMPUTING; ELECTRONIC COMMERCE; GEOGRAPHIC INFORMATION SYSTEMS; HUMAN–COMPUTER INTERACTION; RETRIEVAL OF INFORMATION; USE OF INFORMATION.

Bibliography

Brown, Judith R.; Earnshaw, Rae; Jern, Mikael; and Vince, John. (1995). *Visualization: Using Computer Graphics to Explore Data and Present Information.* New York: Wiley.

Card, Stuart K.; MacKinlay, Jock D.; and Shneiderman, Ben, eds. (1999). *Readings in Information Visualization: Using Vision to Think*. San Francisco: Morgan Kaufmann.

Dong, Wei, and Gibson, Kathleen. (1998). *Computer Visualization: An Integrated Approach for Interior Design and Architecture*. New York: McGraw-Hill.

Friedhoff, Richard M., and Benzon, William. (1989). *Visualization: The Second Computer Revolution*. New York: Abrams.

Gershon, Naham; Eick, Stephen G.; and Card, Stuart. (1998). "Information Visualization." *Interactions* 5(2):9–15.

Herman, I.; Melançon, G.; and Marshall, M. S. (2000). "Graph Visualization and Navigation in Information Visualization." <http://www.cwi.nl/InfoVisu/Survey/StarGraphVisuInInfoVis.html#38950>.

Robin, Harry. (1992). *The Scientific Image: From Cave to Computer*. New York: Abrams.

Tufte, Edward R. (1990). *Envisioning Information*. Cheshire, CT: Graphics Press.

Ware, Colin. (2000). *Information Visualization: Perception for Design*. San Francisco, CA: Morgan Kaufmann.

SHAOYI HE

■ WEBER, MAX (1864–1920)

Max Weber was one of the founding figures of sociology. His work is important to students of communication for several reasons, including his methodological and theoretical innovations as well as a diversity of useful concepts and examples for the analysis of social behavior, economic organization and administration, authority, leadership, culture, society, and politics.

Weber grew up in Berlin, where his father was a lawyer and politicians and scholars were family friends. He studied law, economics, history, and philosophy at the universities in Heidelberg, Göttingen, and Berlin. He taught law briefly at the University of Berlin and became professor of economics at Freiberg in 1894 and then at Heidelberg in 1896. Depression and anxiety interrupted his career in 1898. He returned to his research in 1903 but did not hold another teaching post until just a few years prior to his death. All of his important work comes from the later period, including his most famous work, *The Protestant Ethic and the Spirit of Capitalism* (1904), and his studies of *The Religion of China* (1916), *The Religion of India* (1916), and *Ancient Judaism* (1917–1918). The masterwork, *Economy and Society*, was left fragmentary; it was edited and published posthumously in 1922.

Weber's work provides an example of historical and comparative social science that successfully negotiated between attention to theoretical concepts and empirical details. Rather than concluding an investigation with a generalization or theoretical claim—that all economic behavior is rational, for example—Weber would use the concept of rational behavior as a comparison point in conducting his research. In this way, his work explored particular differences and contingencies rather than generalizing across them.

Weber's work provides the origin of action theory as such. Weber defines action as meaningfully oriented behavior, and takes it to be the fundamental unit of sociological investigation. This is crucially important for communication studies, for it defines a model of social science distinct from behaviorism. Unlike behaviorism, in action theory the meanings that people have for their behaviors are taken to be crucially important. For example, "her arm went up" is a statement of behaviorism; "she raised her arm" is a statement of action theory. In behaviorism, all implications of meaning and motivation are avoided in favor of simple descriptions of physical events. In action theory, meanings and motives are the point of investigation. For students of communication, simple behavior is an important substratum of their investigations, but it is never enough. The study of communication without attention to motive and meaning can never be complete. Thus, Weber's example of a scientific approach to such problems is crucially important.

How could Weber claim a scientific approach to motives and meanings, which cannot be directly observed? His resolution of this problem has been widely admired and imitated. On the one hand, he combined logic, empathy, and interpretation to construct ideal types for the analysis of historical cases. He constructed, for example, ideal

Max Weber. (Archive Photos)

action theory and his methodological innovations. His analysis of economic organization and administration is the standard model of rational organization in the study of organizational communication. His studies of authority and leadership are important to students of both organizational and political communication. His studies in the sociology of religion explore the range of possibilities in the relation between ideas and social structures, a problem that continues to be at the heart of cultural studies. His contrasts of rational and traditional and his analysis of modern bureaucracy are starting points for analysis of modern industrial-commercial culture and communication and the effect of the media on culture and politics.

See also: CULTURAL STUDIES; MODELS OF COMMUNICATION; ORGANIZATIONAL COMMUNICATION.

Bibliography

Bendix, Reinhard. (1960). *Max Weber: An Intellectual Portrait*. Garden City, NY: Doubleday.

Gerth, Hans H., and Mills, C. Wright, eds. (1958). *From Max Weber: Essays in Sociology*. New York: Oxford University Press.

Weber, Max. ([1904] 1958). *The Protestant Ethic and the Spirit of Capitalism*, tr. Talcott Parsons. New York: Scribner.

Weber, Max. ([1916] 1964). *The Religion of China: Confucianism and Taoism*, tr. Hans H. Gerth. New York: Free Press.

Weber, Max. ([1916] 1958). *The Religion of India: The Sociology of Hinduism and Buddhism*, trs. Hans H. Gerth and Don Martindale. New York: Free Press.

Weber, Max. ([1917–1918] 1958). *Ancient Judaism*, trs. Hans H. Gerth and Don Martindale. New York: Free Press.

Weber, Max. ([1922] 1978). *Economy and Society: An Outline of Interpretive Sociology*, eds. Guenther Roth and Claus Wittich. Berkeley: University of California Press.

ERIC W. ROTHENBUHLER

type models of how the perfectly rational or perfectly traditional actor would make choices in ideal circumstances. These expectations would then be compared with what real people did in actual circumstances. When historical actors deviated from the ideal types, Weber did not take that as evidence of their cognitive shortcomings (their irrationality, for example) but as clues to additional concepts he needed to develop for further analysis. Working from the other direction, he interpreted historical records empathetically, striving to identify how the actors in a particular situation could have seen their action as a rational response to their circumstances. In this way, he was able to construct models of a range of types of rational action, opening up his theory to a greater range of human situations than either the behaviorists or the economists. Prayer, for example, as Weber pointed out, is rational behavior from the point of view of the faithful.

Weber's work also provides many useful concepts and examples for communication studies, in addition to the wide-ranging importance of his

☐ WEBMASTERS

Along with the emergence and growth of the Internet and the World Wide Web has come the creation of a new occupation: the webmaster. This person is responsible for publishing a website, which may be a single page or hundreds of thousands of pages. It is difficult to be precise about

A group of web-page designers work together to evaluate a design in their San Francisco office, which is located in an area that is home to so many high tech businesses that it is sometimes called the "Cybergulch." (Catherine Karnow/Corbis)

what a webmaster does, because the web itself is changing, and this in turn changes the way in which people use it. Some people consider the term "webmaster" to be an unnecessarily sexist term. Alternate terms include "webster," "web designer," and "information architect."

A key role for the webmaster is to be responsible for organizing the information at a website. Other people may decide on the content and provide excellent resources for the potential users of the website, but if those users are not able to find the resources that would interest them, then the work is in vain. Organization involves understanding the site as a whole and deciding on the best ways in which to help users get to the appropriate pages. Thus, organization is not just about how to arrange information within a single page; it is also about deciding how all the pages of a website will fit together. This is clearly a complex task.

In many ways, a webmaster is like the editor of a newspaper. Other people provide most of the content, but the editor has to arrange the content so that readers can find their way around the newspaper. A consistent house style is important in helping people to use a website. That means not just the style of writing but also the names that are used to describe parts of the website and the mechanisms that are provided to help the user to navigate within the website. Graphic design can be important in conveying an appropriate impression about the nature of the website and the organization that it represents. However, an obsession with flashy graphics, particularly animation, can make the website much harder to use, more confusing, and slower to download. Therefore, a webmaster must balance competing design interests.

It is important to remember that a website is intended to be used by different kinds of people with different needs. For example, in the case of a commercial website, the users may be people who work in the organization, regular customers, first-time customers, experienced web surfers, novices, people who have a specific thing that they want to find out about or buy, or people who want to browse around. A good design will help *all* users find their way around the website. A poor design will confuse users, which probably means that they will give up and go to a competitor's website instead.

Website design involves a lot of interaction with other people. This includes people who are going to write pages or provide text for the website and people who have opinions about what the website is for, how it should look, and what information it should provide. Inevitably, that means that the design process can be political because everyone thinks the things that they do are so important and crucial to the success of the organization that their pages should be directly featured on the home page and that they should be given priority at the top of any list of links.

In order to help users to find information within a website, the webmaster needs to consider issues of usability, which involves examining the existing website for potential sources of confusion. User testing of a website can reveal many problems, particularly where the designers have accidentally assumed more knowledge about the website than a casual user would have. If people do not realize that something is a link, they will not click on it. Support for navigation is especially crucial; otherwise, as users click around in a website, they may get a feeling of being lost.

The webmaster needs to be aware of the different ways in which people will use the website. For example, a website may be easy to use on a powerful computer with a big monitor and good network connections, but if the intended users are using less-powerful machines and poorer Internet connections, then the website should be tested in that environment as well. It may help to create text-only versions for some pages to make them easier to download over slow modems. Users who have disabilities should also be considered. For example, users who are visually impaired will have difficulties with graphical icons. However, additions to the Hypertext Markup Language (HTML) that creates the page can be made to describe in words what the graphic shows, so a text-to-speech browser can still be used. In addition to helping visually impaired viewers, this feature helps all users who simply prefer not to download graphics for rea-

sons of speed. Wider benefits often result when designs are created that bear in mind users who have specific disabilities.

Another important task for a webmaster is the maintenance of a website. New pages will be created and need to be integrated into the website so that they can be easily found. Existing pages may become obsolete, and links to other pages may no longer work. A webmaster should be concerned with the continual improvement of the usability and usefulness of the website. Traditionally, many webmasters focused on the technical aspects of a website (i.e., creating scripts for ordering products, managing backups of the data, and handling the server on which the website was hosted). However, the role of a webmaster has become much broader than that. A webmaster may now have a much more senior position that is responsible for creating an overall strategy for the website and then overseeing the work of others who are responsible for the more specific tasks that are involved in fulfilling that strategy.

Webmasters come from a variety of backgrounds, including programming, graphic design, librarianship, and technical writing. Because the web itself is still evolving rapidly, it is difficult to say which particular skills, backgrounds, or training will become the most crucial for finding employment in this occupation in the future. Clearly, a webmaster must understand how the web is used and how web-pages are constructed. That requires some familiarity with HTML. New design toolkits are always being developed, as are new protocols and technologies for providing access to different kinds of multimedia. Hence, the ability to learn these new technologies very rapidly is more important than knowledge of a particular technique that may quickly become obsolete. The skills of organizing information, interacting with different individuals and groups, and writing in a clear style will, however, always remain important.

See also: COMPUTER LITERACY; HUMAN-COMPUTER INTERACTION; INTERNET AND THE WORLD WIDE WEB.

Bibliography

Flanders, Vincent, and Willis, Michael. (1998). *Web Pages that Suck: Learn Good Design by Looking at Bad Design*. San Francisco, CA: Sybex.

Fleming, Jennifer, and Koman, Richard. (1998). *Web Navigation: Designing the User Experience.* Sebastopol, CA: O'Reilly & Associates.

Lynch, Patrick J., and Horton, Sarah. (1999). *Web Style Guide: Basic Design Principles for Creating Web Sites.* New Haven, CT: Yale University Press.

Nielsen, Jakob. (1999). *Designing Web Usability: The Practice of Simplicity.* Indianapolis, IN: New Riders Publishing.

Nielsen, Jakob. (2001). "Useit.com: Jakob Nielsen's Website." <http://www.useit.com>.

Rosenfeld, Louis, and Morville, Peter. (1998). *Information Architecture for the World Wide Web.* Sebastopol, CA: O'Reilly & Associates.

Sano, Darrell. (1996). *Designing Large-Scale Web Sites: A Visual Design Methodology.* New York: Wiley.

World Wide Web Consortium. (2001). "Leading the Web to Its Full Potential." <http://www.w3.org/>.

MICHAEL TWIDALE

■ WELLES, ORSON (1915–1985)

When Orson Welles's name is mentioned, the first thing that comes to mind is *Citizen Kane* (1941), which is still considered to be one of the best films in the history of motion pictures. However, Welles's "show business" success began long before (and continued long after) the creation of *Citizen Kane.*

Welles was born George Orson Welles on May 6, 1915, in Kenosha, Wisconsin. He was the son of Richard Head Welles, who became wealthy by owning wagon factories, and Beatrice Ives Welles, who was well known for her devotion to the arts and community involvement. Orson Welles was involved in theater from the age of three, when he played the role of "Trouble" in a production of *Madame Butterfly* at the Chicago Opera. By age ten, he had produced, directed, and starred in his own production of *Dr. Jekyll and Mr. Hyde.* In his young adult life, Welles produced *Macbeth* at the Negro Theatre in Harlem in 1936. Then, Welles, with the help of the Federal Theatre, formed the Mercury Theatre, for which *The Cradle Will Rock* was the debut production.

As radio became a successful entertainment medium, Welles made a smooth transition from theater to radio. He was involved in more than one hundred radio productions from 1936 to 1941. His productions ranged from classics such as *Hamlet*

Orson Welles displays many emotions during a 1938 radio broadcast. (Bettmann/Corbis)

(1936) and *Julius Caesar* (1938) to new shows such as *The Silent Avenger* (1938) and *War of the Worlds* (1938). *War of the Worlds,* an adaptation of the H. G. Wells novel, used fake news bulletins to announce that there were disturbances noted on Mars and then that there was a Martian invasion of Earth taking place. Although it was stated quite clearly four times during the broadcast that it was simply a radio drama, many listeners believing that Martians had really landed and were dispensing poison gas. As a result, panic struck from coast to coast. Phones rung off the hook at Columbia Broadcasting System (CBS) offices, some people flocked to churches to pray, and traffic jams were attributed to people fleeing areas where the Martians had "landed." However, myths surrounding the extent of the panic continue to exist. Stories abound about people committing suicide to avoid succumbing to the invaders and about other people dying of heart attacks from the shock of the Martian landing. None of these stories have ever been substantiated.

Sociologist Hadley Cantril (1940) studied the people who were most and least affected by the radio drama. Simply put, there was a direct correlation between the degree of panic and the amount of education and/or religious belief. The less educated and the more devoutly religious a listener was, the more often he or she believed the reports. Nothing major occurred in the regulation of the radio broadcast industry because of the event; Welles simply illustrated the power of the medium. The Federal Communications Commission issued a terse response saying the incident was "regrettable."

Citizen Kane, coming just a few years after Welles's *War of the Worlds* radio production, started a new chapter in the career of Orson Welles. *Citizen Kane* is remembered for a multitude of reasons, including that (1) it was Welles's first feature film, (2) he was only twenty-five years old when he made it, (3) the film featured many technical innovations, such as the creation of deep-focus lenses, the use of camera movement, and audio mixing, that had previously only been used in radio, and (4) the subject matter was highly controversial, since it was a thinly disguised biography of William Randolph Hearst, the newspaper mogul. The movie angered Hearst so much that none of the Hearst newspapers carried advertisements for the film and Hearst-employed film critics were harsh in their reviews. Other reviews were essentially good, but *Citizen Kane* was still a failure at the box office, and though it was nominated for nine Academy Awards, the movie won only the Best Original Screenplay award, which Welles shared with Herman J. Mankiewicz. *Citizen Kane* was voted the best film of all time in 1972 (and then again in 1998) by a panel of international film critics. In addition, film historians Thomas W. Bohn and Richard L. Stromgren, in *Light and Shadows: A History of Motion Pictures* (1975), wrote that *Citizen Kane* had the greatest influence on filmmaking since D. W. Griffith's *The Birth of a Nation* (1915), which had ushered in the art of storytelling in motion pictures.

Welles's second feature film, *The Magnificent Ambersons,* was released in 1942. The studio system made the film possible because Welles's style demanded extensive facilities, polished actors, and skilled technicians. For example, Welles filmed winter scenes in a cold storage locker, achieving the desired realism while still having complete control over lighting and camera positioning. Although *The Magnificent Ambersons* featured such

additional technical innovations, it has generally received less attention because it followed so closely on the heels of *Citizen Kane,* which was released only one year earlier. During his career, Welles directed fewer than twenty feature films (some of which were never completed) but acted in more than sixty. In his later years, he primarily served as a "voice" (i.e., he did voiceover narration, hosted various television shows, and provided voices for animated characters).

Welles's personal life included three wives and at least two other long-term relationships. Welles eloped with actress Virginia Nicholson in November 1934. They had a child, Christopher, in 1937 but were divorced in February 1940. Welles had an affair with Dolores Del Rio, another actress, while she was still married to Cedric Gibbons. Welles married Rita Hayworth, the actress, dancer, and "pin-up girl," in 1943. The couple had a child, Rebecca, in 1944, but were divorced in 1947. Actress Paola Mori was the next woman to marry Welles, in May 1955; Mori and Welles had a child, Beatrice, that same year. During Welles's later years, his female companion was actress and director Oja Kodar. Welles suffered a fatal heart attack on October 10, 1985, at age seventy.

Jonathan Rosenbaum wrote in a December 1996 article in *Cineaste* that there are probably two main perspectives about Welles's career. Rosenbaum contends that one view, which is most common in the United States, is that Welles's life is a bit of a mystery with some wondering why Welles did not live up to his potential, referring to *Citizen Kane* as his one and only major achievement. The other view, according to Rosenbaum, looks at Welles's life more compassionately, objectively considering a body of work—from theater to radio to film—and giving credit to Welles beyond focusing simply on *Citizen Kane.*

See also: FILM INDUSTRY, HISTORY OF; GRIFFITH, D. W.; HEARST, WILLIAM RANDOLPH; PARANORMAL EVENTS AND THE MEDIA; RADIO BROADCASTING, HISTORY OF.

Bibliography

Anderegg, Michael. (1998). *Orson Welles, Shakespeare, and Popular Culture.* New York: Columbia University Press.

Bazin, André. (1972). *Orson Welles: A Critical View.* New York: Harper & Row.

Bohn, Thomas W., and Stromgren, Richard L. (1975). *Light & Shadows: A History of Motion Pictures.* Port Washington, NY: Alfred Publishing.

Callow, Simon. (1997). *Orson Welles: The Road to Xanadu.* New York: Viking Penguin.

Cantril, Hadley. (1940). *The Invasion from Mars: A Study in the Psychology of Panic.* Princeton, NJ: Princeton University Press.

Naremore, James. (1978). *The Magic World of Orson Welles.* New York: Oxford University Press.

Rosenbaum, Jonathan. (1996). "The Battle Over Orson Welles." *Cineaste* 22(3):6–10.

Thomson, David. (1996). *Rosebud: The Story of Orson Welles.* New York: Knopf.

LAWRENCE N. STROUT

■ WILLIAMS, RAYMOND (1921–1988)

Blurring the distinctions between traditional academic boundaries, while focusing attention on aspects of culture usually silenced by the dominant society, Raymond Williams was a pervasively influential twentieth-century thinker. In more than thirty published books, and in hundreds of articles, Williams addressed questions of culture, communication, politics, literature, and drama. Working outside mainstream communication research agendas, two of Williams's books, *Culture and Society* (1958) and *The Long Revolution* (1961), became foundational texts in the development of a new political and intellectual tradition known today as British cultural studies.

Williams, born in Pandy, Wales, was the only son of Henry Joseph Williams and Esther Gwendolene Williams (neé Bird). He was raised in a socialist, working-class household; his father was a railway signalman, the son of a farm laborer, and his mother was the daughter of a farm bailiff. Williams attended the local elementary school, and when he was eleven years old, he received a county scholarship to attend King Henry Eighth Grammar School in Abergavenny. In 1938, Williams earned his high school certificate in English, French, and Latin and won the state scholarship to Trinity College, Cambridge. As a student at Trinity, he wrote short stories and political articles, reviewed films, and became editor of the student newspaper, the *Cambridge University Journal.* Williams rejected prevailing class boundaries and

Raymond Williams. (Archive Photos)

social positions in his writings on the stereotype of working-class boy as social misfit.

After two years at Trinity, Williams was drafted into the army, commissioned into the Royal Artillery, and sent to Normandy. The dehumanization of people that he observed during World War II had a significant effect on him, and when he was later recalled to service in 1951, he refused as a conscientious objector. Williams returned to Cambridge in 1945 and completed his degree. Financial responsibilities forced him to reject a graduate university fellowship, and in 1946, he instead began working in adult education as a staff tutor for the Oxford Delegacy.

Williams developed an affiliation with the New Left, a working-class labor movement that reacted to modern developments of industrial capitalism and emphasized popular education and popular culture. Considering popular culture to be a crucial site of struggle, Williams, in his articles and books, thought historically about cultural practices and explored issues of alienation and reintegration, along with the challenges of going between academic and working-class cultures. In 1961, Williams was appointed to a lectureship on the English faculty at Cambridge and later became a professor of modern drama. As a professor at Cambridge, Williams earned a reputation for supporting dissent, even that which was inarticulate, incoherent, or messy.

Two early influences on Williams were Marxism and the ideas of Cambridge literary critic F. R. Leavis. From Marxism, Williams gained an appreciation of the relationship between the system of production and culture, while from the ideas of Leavis, Williams received an understanding of the connections between art and experience. Politics was central to Williams's life and work; he wrote as a socialist for socialism and believed in the necessary economic struggle of an organized working class. He viewed his own political commitment as part of a long revolution, through which the system of meanings and values that contemporary capitalist society has generated must be defeated by sustained intellectual and educational work. For Williams, the long revolution was an integral part of the struggle for democracy and economic victory for the working class. Williams and other members of the New Left addressed fundamental Marxist theoretical questions regarding issues of power, class, domination, and exploitation. Ultimately, Williams rejected the economic and reductionist emphasis of traditional Marxism in favor of a Marxist cultural perspective that connected the realm of art and ideas to the entire material social process.

It is the centrality of culture, in each study of society, that is the common theoretical thread found in all of Williams's writings. Culture is viewed as a basic component of an evolving social process; nothing is static, fixed, or predetermined because all of life is an active and evolving process. Culture is a way of life, the lived texture of any social order. Williams rejected traditional boundaries between high culture and popular culture, insisted that culture is more than the visible sign of a special type of cultivated people, and called culture "ordinary" because it is fundamental to each individual in every society. Williams saw communication as an integral part of culture because ideas, meanings, experiences, and activities are transmitted through language, in the form of certain communication rules, models, and conventions. Language, he said, is a socially shared, reciprocal activity that is a basic element of all material social practices. Every society is somewhat different and creates its own traditions and meanings through an ongoing and active process of negotiation and debate.

In *Marxism and Literature* (1977), Williams outlined his own theoretical position—cultural materialism. Cultural materialism combines an emphasis on creative and historical agency that privileges experience as a fundamental part of any cultural analysis. It insists that all cultural practices, such as newspaper articles, poems, paintings, novels, political speeches, and buildings, be considered as practical communications that are created by a particular group of people or class in a historically specific place and time. Williams saw individuals as active participants who help to create their own culture, and he suggested that cultural practices should be studied along with historically specific social relations that relate to these practices.

While much of Williams's work thematically reflects his Welsh origin, his concepts are not culture specific; they address universal humanistic considerations. Throughout his career, Williams resisted traditional academic disciplines, categories, and boundaries. He did not distinguish between the imaginative and factual types of writing and insisted that both are cultural practices within an ongoing social process, produced by a specific society, in a particular historical time, under specific political and economic conditions. He considered *Culture and Society, The Long Revolution*, and his first novel, *Border Country* (1960), to be the integral parts of his trilogy on culture.

Often considered to be one of the great European socialist intellectuals, Williams remained politically engaged throughout his life. His writings liberate previously marginalized thought and provide historically based analyses of ideas that transcend race, class, gender, and cultural boundaries.

See also: CULTURE AND COMMUNICATION; LANGUAGE AND COMMUNICATION; SOCIETY AND THE MEDIA.

Bibliography

Eagleton, Terry, ed. (1989). *Raymond Williams. Critical Perspectives*. Cambridge, Eng.: Polity Press.

Inglis, Fred. (1995). *Raymond Williams*. London: Routledge.

O'Connor, Alan. (1989). *Raymond Williams: Writing, Culture, Politics.* Oxford: Basil Blackwell.

Williams, Raymond. (1958). *Culture and Society.* London: Chatto & Windus.

Williams, Raymond. (1960). *Border Country.* London: Chatto & Windus.

Williams, Raymond. (1961). *The Long Revolution.* London: Chatto & Windus.

Williams, Raymond. (1977). *Marxism and Literature.* Oxford: Oxford University Press.

Williams, Raymond. (1979). *Politics and Letters. Interviews with New Left Review.* London: Verso.

BONNIE S. BRENNEN

■ WILSON, HALSEY WILLIAM (1868–1954)

H. W. Wilson, founder of one of the first commercially successful bibliographic and indexing enterprises, contributed to the spread of bibliographic citation as a research practice, promoted the genre of reference publishing, and helped standardize library collections, especially in North American public and school libraries. Based first in Minneapolis, then in White Plains, New York, and later in New York City, by the time Wilson died the H. W. Wilson Company published more than twenty major indexing and reference services, including the *Cumulative Book Index* and the *Readers' Guide to Periodical Literature.* Wilson's business success resulted from a combination of factors: close attention to quality, efficient production methods, a unique pricing system, collaboration with his chief customers and his chief competitor, and the long-term dedication of talented key employees—many of them women. By 1998, one hundred years after its founding, the H. W. Wilson Company fully espoused digital technology, producing fifteen full-text databases, nineteen indexes, a website (http://www.hwwilson.com/) and many additional library-related publications.

Born in Wilmington, Vermont, on May 12, 1868, Wilson was the son of stonecutter John Thompson Wilson and Althea Dunnell Wilson, both of whom died of tuberculosis when Wilson was only three years old. The boy went to live with relatives on a farm near Waterloo, Iowa, and later studied at the University of Minnesota. In 1889, to help finance their studies, Wilson and his roommate started a business to provide textbooks to faculty and fellow students. The bookstore, which was located first in their bedroom and later in a university basement, prospered, and commerce overtook education. Wilson never graduated from the university, and after three years he bought his partner out of the bookstore.

In 1895, Wilson married university student Justina Leavitt, and together the couple expanded the business venture. Wilson began a current awareness service for customers, which helped them keep abreast of rapidly increasing numbers of new books. However, the lack of a single trade catalog made this task difficult. What he needed, Wilson decided, was a monthly cumulative list of new publications. Others (including Frederick Leypoldt of *Publishers' Weekly*) had attempted to provide a comprehensive trade catalog, but costs had always proved overwhelming. Wilson's new catalog—the *Cumulative Book Index* (CBI)—combined new entries with the old in each monthly issue throughout the year, culminating in a single cumulated volume. However, instead of discarding the Linotype slugs created for the initial entries, he cut costs by interfiling them for reuse in the cumulated numbers. Organized by author, title, and subject, the CBI eventually became the standard record of books published in English. In 1901, with the launching of his general periodical index—the *Readers' Guide to Periodical Literature* (RG)—Wilson created a similar publication for the fast-expanding magazine industry. By making accessible the articles that had hitherto been buried in journal back numbers, RG stimulated research practices that in turn demanded more specialized indexes. In response, Wilson went on to found the *Industrial Arts Index* (1913) and the *Agricultural Index* (1916) and to manage the *Index to Legal Periodicals* and the *Public Affairs Information Service.* Subsequent indexes included *Education Index* (1929), *Art Index* (1929), *Bibliographic Index* (1938), *Biography Index* (1946), *Play Index* (1949), and *Short Story Index* (1953).

Aware that his principal market consisted of libraries, Wilson consciously cultivated the goodwill and collaboration of librarians. He included periodicals in RG, for instance, only after carrying out regular opinion surveys among practicing librarians. The publications from Wilson also aided library collection development with the 1905 introduction of the *Book Review Digest,* followed by *Children's Catalog* (1909), *Standard Catalog for Public Libraries* (1918; later titled *Public*

1090 · WIRELESS TELECOMMUNICATIONS

Library Catalog), Standard Catalog for High School Libraries (1926), and *Fiction Catalog* (1942). Other publications for librarians included the journal *Wilson Library Bulletin* (1914), the *Sears List of Subject Headings* (first edited by employee Minnie Earl Sears in 1923), and the periodical index *Library Literature* (1936). These products contributed to a rationalization and standardization that helped shape library collecting, reference, and cataloging practices for decades.

Initially, Wilson's indexing ventures required subsidy from the old bookstore. Recognizing the need for self-sustainability, Wilson devised a pricing system intended to make his indexes affordable to large and small libraries and booksellers alike, while still achieving commercial viability. He called this system the "service basis," basing it on use rather than ownership. Instead of paying a flat fee for the number of volumes received, libraries paid a variable fee depending on the number of periodicals in their collection, a principle that foreshadowed pricing systems later adopted for digital databases. Wilson made another move to achieve sustainability when, in 1911, he reached agreement with his main competitor, Richard Rogers Bowker (by then publisher of *Publishers' Weekly, Library Journal,* and several indexes), to divide up the market and reduce overlap. Wilson undertook more frequent cumulations of CBI, added new journals to RG, and transferred to Bowker his directories of librarians and booksellers, while Bowker dropped some rival publications, including a periodical index.

Throughout his long career (which ended with his death on March 1, 1954), Wilson realized his visions with the help of several dedicated and ingenious women, including Justina Leavitt Wilson and employees Marion E. Potter, Edith Phelps, and Anna L. Guthrie. Firmly antiunion, Wilson ran his company as a "family," with himself the ever-present *paterfamilias.* Employees appreciated his unremitting hard work, austere lifestyle, and dedication to quality, and they rewarded him with their loyalty. Two symbols—a thirty-foot lighthouse atop a bronze book mounted on the roof of the company's building and a dime-store mousetrap on Wilson's desk—represented his striving for bibliographic enlightenment and his continual search for product improvement.

See also: BIBLIOGRAPHY; CATALOGING AND KNOWLEDGE ORGANIZATION.

Bibliography

"Halsey William Wilson." (1954). *Wilson Library Bulletin* 28(8):665–668.

Lawler, John. (1950). *The H. W. Wilson Company: Half a Century of Bibliographic Publishing.* Minneapolis: University of Minnesota Press.

Peet, Creighton. (1938). "A Mousetrap in the Bronx." *New Yorker* 14(37):25–28.

Plotnik, Arthur. (1973). "H. W. Wilson." In *Encyclopedia of Library and Information Science,* Vol. 10, eds. Allen Kent, Harold Lancour, and Jay E. Daily. New York: Marcel Dekker.

Plotnik, Arthur. (1978). "Wilson, Halsey William." In *Encyclopedia of Library History Biography,* ed. Bohdan S. Wynar. Littleton, CO: Libraries Unlimited.

Wilson, Halsey William. (1925). *The Bookman's Reading and Tools.* New York: H. W. Wilson Company.

Wilson, Halsey William. (1948). "Random Reminiscences." *Wilson Library Bulletin* 22(10):770–783.

CHRISTINE PAWLEY

WIRELESS TELECOMMUNICATIONS
See: Telecommunications, Wireless

WITTGENSTEIN, LUDWIG (1889–1951)

Among the foremost philosophers of the twentieth century, Ludwig Wittgenstein made important contributions to the philosophy of logic, theory of meaning, and philosophical psychology and methodology.

Wittgenstein was born into a wealthy Viennese family and began his education in engineering, before turning his attention to problems of mathematical logic and the philosophy of language. He studied with Bertrand Russell at Cambridge University, where he developed a unique perspective on emerging topics of analytic philosophy. He combined an extraordinary rigor of logical methods with a penetrating, uncompromising demand for clarity and philosophical justification of many aspects of logic and mathematics about which working theorists in the field, including Russell, were willing to take for granted. After World War

I, in which he served as an artillery officer in the Austrian army, Wittgenstein's reflections on logic and philosophy took a more ethical and aesthetic turn, due in part to his wartime experience, but also due to the influence of his early reading of the *Bible* and works by Arthur Schopenhauer and Leo Tolstoy.

Wittgenstein's philosophy is divided into early and later periods. In the early period, usually dated from 1912 to 1922, Wittgenstein was preoccupied with the task of developing a formal semantics for possible languages and the proper understanding of formal symbolic logic. He believed that language could only be meaningful if sentences are analyzable into ultimate atomic constituents that stand in one-to-one correspondence with possible facts that the sentences represent as a logical picture of the world. Specifically, Wittgenstein's *Tractatus Logico-Philosophicus* (1922) interprets all propositions as describing facts that collectively constitute the world. Sentences in colloquial language are conventional sign-system expressions for what on analysis in their transcendental symbolic aspects are concatenations of names for simple objects. Therefore, the meaning of a proposition is explained in Wittgenstein's early picture theory of meaning as a one-to-one correspondence between the articulated combinations of simple names that constitute fully analyzed propositions and the assemblages of simple objects that constitute the atomic facts that propositions describe. A proposition is true in Wittgenstein's analysis just in case the possible state of affairs it pictures actually occurs. Language, and with it all communication of information, is meaningful only insofar as it describes contingent empirical states of affairs. Wittgenstein limits meaningful expression to whatever can be said, which he distinguishes from the transcendental aspects of language that can only be shown by the picturing relation in the correspondence of simple names and simple objects.

The saying-showing distinction supports Wittgenstein's efforts to eliminate all traditional philosophical problems as literally nonsensical, which he argues cannot arise except through a misunderstanding of the logic and semantic requirements of language. The simple objects are the substance of the word, according to Wittgenstein's metaphysics of "logical atomism" in the *Tractatus,* because the same objects must exist in different configurations constituting different atomic facts in different, logically possible worlds. If it were not so, Wittgenstein argues, then there could be no extrasemantic foundation for semantics, and the meaning of a sentence would have to depend on the meaning of another sentence, in a semantic circle or infinite regress that contradicts the assumption that at least some language is determinately meaningful. All possible language in its symbolic aspect can be specified in terms of the sum total of logical combinations of names for all possible existent or nonexistent atomic facts interpreted as all possible combinations of simple objects. Wittgenstein describes the totality of meaningful expressions in a language by what he terms the general form of proposition, which he conceives as a truth functional operation on all elementary propositions that picture all atomic facts. The general form of proposition demarcates the class of all possible language, of all possible meaningful expressions, and, hence, of all meaningful thought. It thereby excludes as meaningless all efforts to use language to express ethical or aesthetic values (which Wittgenstein regards as one and indistinguishable), logical and mathematical form, forms of representation, the self as a subject of intentional states, religious awe and the sense of the mystical, whatever can be shown rather than said, and, finally, all traditional pseudoconcepts, pseudoproblems, and pseudopropositions of traditional philosophy. Wittgenstein concludes that there are no meaningful philosophical problems or philosophical theses and that the only proper task for philosophy is the clarification of meaning and the debunking of efforts to use language improperly to express anything that is not a logically contingent proposition about a logically contingent state of affairs.

After a seven-year hiatus, during which he taught schoolchildren in the Austrian Alps and worked on artistic and architectural projects, Wittgenstein decided that he might once again have something of interest to contribute to philosophy. In his later development, after 1929, Wittgenstein rejected the picture theory of meaning but continued to regard ethics as deeply rooted in common social practices or "forms of life." In his *Philosophical Investigations* (1953) and other posthumously published writings, on which he continued to work until shortly before his death, Wittgenstein regards philosophy as a kind of therapy for eliminating philosophical problems that arise through the misunderstanding of language. It is no part of philosophy to offer a positive doctrine of right and wrong, good and evil, but only to explain what Wittgenstein calls the "philosophical grammar" of these terms as they can permissibly be used in the language of ethics. The business of philosophy is to arrive at a correct understanding of meaning, rather than to formulate and defend substantive commitments to particular doctrines. As in the *Tractatus,* Wittgenstein in the later period resists the idea of philosophy as a discipline like pure science, which has a special subject matter and special methods of inquiry. Instead, he continues to see philosophy as a method of clarifying meaning in order to arrive at a perspective from which all traditional philosophical problems evaporate. The later Wittgenstein interprets meaning in terms of rule-governed "language games," in which linguistic and extralinguistic activities are fully integrated with ordinary nonphilosophical human purposes, and in which language is an instrument or tool whose meaning cannot be disassociated from its use in a language game.

See also: LANGUAGE AND COMMUNICATION; LANGUAGE STRUCTURE.

Bibliography

Baker, Gordon P., and Hacker, P. M. S. (1980). *Wittgenstein: Understanding and Meaning.* Oxford, Eng.: Basil Blackwell.

Baker, Gordon P., and Hacker, P. M. S. (1985). *Wittgenstein: Rules, Grammar and Necessity.* Oxford, Eng.: Basil Blackwell.

Black, Max. (1964). *A Companion to Wittgenstein's "Tractatus."* Ithaca, NY: Cornell University Press.

Fann, K. T. (1969). *Wittgenstein's Conception of Philosophy.* Berkeley: University of California Press.

Garver, Newton. (1994). *This Complicated Form of Life: Essays on Wittgenstein.* LaSalle, IN: Open Court.

Jacquette, Dale. (1998). *Wittgenstein's Thought in Transition.* West Lafayette, IN: Purdue University Press.

Kripke, Saul A. (1982). *Wittgenstein on Rules and Private Language.* Cambridge, MA: Harvard University Press.

McGinn, Colin. (1984). *Wittgenstein on Meaning: An Interpretation and Evaluation.* Oxford, Eng.: Basil Blackwell.

Monk, Ray. (1991). *Ludwig Wittgenstein: The Duty of Genius.* New York: Penguin Books.

Pears, David. (1987). *The False Prison: A Study of the Development of Wittgenstein's Philosophy,* 2 vols. Oxford, Eng.: Oxford University Press.

DALE JACQUETTE

▣ WORLD WIDE WEB

See: Internet and the World Wide Web

▣ WRITERS

Writing is essential to many professional careers but can also be a career itself. Most freelance writers of fiction, drama, or poetry must support their work with secondary jobs unless they have produced a bestseller or achieved an outstanding—and long-standing—reputation. Other types of writing are financially viable in commercial or academic settings. These include journalism; research in science, social science, and the humanities; literary criticism; philosophical essays and commentary; reviewing; scriptwriting in both film and television; and advertising and marketing. The importance of writing has increased as the Internet—with its various forms of e-mail, listservs, Usenet newsgroups, online publishing, and Web forums—increasingly dominates communications and extends the verbal mobility of an individual.

Some writers approach their craft as an art form and practice it in strict isolation; others approach it as a product, using teamwork strategies to brainstorm and articulate ideas into a final format. All writing depends on fluency of language, which begins in childhood and develops during primary, secondary, and graduate phases of education. Talent is only the beginning. Good writers evolve through effort, usually over a long period of maturation, but in their career they have an advantage over those who must employ physical skills that deteriorate with age. Theoretically, the wisdom that comes from experience will only enhance the skill, style, and scope of a writer.

One interesting way to discuss the enormous range of activity among writers is to divide writing into creative, factual, and interpretive forms, with generous allowance for combinations. The term "creative writing" is somewhat misleading, since creative and critical processes are involved in every kind of writing, but this is the term commonly used to cover the creation of poetry, drama, short stories, novels, and various other fictional genres. Creative writing depends on the freedom to blend the real and the imagined outside a framework of factual accuracy. Factual writing, on the other hand, requires objective fidelity to known facts—inasmuch as objectivity is individually and culturally possible. Factual writing can take the form of reporting or synthesizing information for news services, magazines, research journals, textbooks, and other nonfiction publications. Interpretive writing involves the critical analysis of fictional and factual texts, or of physical, sociopolitical, intellectual, psychological, cultural, and historical phenomena. The preparation and apprenticeship for these various kinds of writing vary, as do the careers connected with them.

The work of writing stories, poems, and plays traditionally has not required formal training. The best preparation for a writer is reading widely, writing constantly, and surviving the challenge of an unstructured career and income. The lifestyle of the writer of fiction has often been romanticized. In fact, self-discipline is fundamental, since the deadlines of a poet or novelist are generally self-imposed unless the individual is under contract—a happy situation that few attain without an established track record of publication. (Saul Bellow, one of the most successful and revered American novelists of the twentieth century, writes every morning without fail, consigning the rest of the day to teaching, reading, and other activities that stimulate and feed into his work. Similarly, renowned poet William Merwin maintains a daily writing schedule and fiercely protects his time and privacy to do so.) Since the financial rewards for young writers are precarious, and loneliness is more likely than public response, self-discipline depends on a deep commitment, even compulsion, to write for writing's sake. Moreover, writers shelve or throw away much more than they publish—there is a common saying that the wastebasket is a writer's best friend. Days, weeks, and even years may go by between truly productive periods. With persistent time and attention, however, writers are often surprised by unexpected ideas and solutions that seem to surface from subconscious processes.

The critical exercise of revising is as important as creating an initial draft, and some writers benefit from an editor or peer group to give them feedback on the clarity and effects of their work. Those who pursue a Master of Fine Arts (MFA) degree in creative writing have a built-in structure for this phase, in the form of professors who mentor them and fellow students who can form the nucleus of a lifelong network. The MFA not only provides these benefits within a context that allows time for concentrated writing, but also enables graduates to teach creative writing as a means of supporting their own work.

Whereas the MFA is optional for a successful career in creative writing, a master's degree in journalism has become essential for entering the profession of reporting, including news coverage in print and electronic media. Reporters are typically assigned a particular "beat" (e.g., the police station, city hall, and so on) or subject (e.g., education, culture, sports, politics) in which they investigate newsworthy events, interview witnesses, cultivate sources, and write up accounts based on fact-checking that is double-checked by editors before presentation on television or in print. The ethics of journalism have been subject to close scrutiny when reporters or feature writers make up what they do not know, attribute quotes inaccurately, or assemble composite stories based on representative but not actual situations. Ideally, the more knowledge a reporter builds in a particular area, the more reliable the information. Many other kinds of factual writing either depend on or benefit from the authority of a writer who holds a doctorate degree or has other advanced training. Some textbook publishers even refuse to publish a work written by a nondegreed author, no matter how experienced, and most academic journals assume specialized credentials for articles reporting on or summarizing research in science, social science, and the humanities.

An interesting contrast is the writing of advertisements, where truth and accuracy acquire a commercial standard of measurement, and success derives from effective persuasion rather than objectivity. Writers of advertisements use facts selectively to present products in their best light, competing for the attention of readers or viewers with quick, clever, repetitive, mnemonic phrases. An undergraduate degree in marketing or a Master of Business Administration (MBA) degree can boost a career in commercial writing, but a brilliant portfolio of sample advertisements may be just as convincing.

On a higher intellectual plane is the attempt to persuade readers of a theory through interpretive writing. Sociopolitical commentary, literary analysis, art criticism, and biblical interpretation are all examples of writing based on facts, documents, or data related to support a stated viewpoint. History depends on who is telling it, and interpretive writing, especially in areas such as biography, can edge close to creative writing when authors must use their imaginations to fill in the gaps of a life long gone. Writing a story, then, can take the form of creating, reporting, or interpreting—each process with patterns of its own—or an innovative blend of all three.

See also: EDITORS; INTERNET AND THE WORLD WIDE WEB; STORYTELLERS; STORYTELLING.

Bibliography

Barzun, Jacques. (1971). *Jacques Barzun on Writing, Editing, and Publishing: Essays Explicative and Hortatory.* Chicago: University of Chicago Press.

Bernstein, Theodore. (1958). *Watch Your Language: A Lively, Informal Guide to Better Writing, Emanating from the News Room of The New York Times.* Great Neck, NY: Channel Press.

Lamott, Anne. (1994). *Bird by Bird: Some Instructions on Writing and Life.* New York: Pantheon Books.

Strunk, William, Jr., and White, E. B. (1999). *The Elements of Style,* 4th edition. New York: Allyn & Bacon.

Welty, Eudora. (1983). *One Writer's Beginnings.* Cambridge, MA: Harvard University Press.

BETSY HEARNE

◼ WRITING

See: Alphabets and Writing; Literacy; Writers

X-Z

XENOPHOBIA
See: Intercultural Communication,
Interethnic Relations and

YOUTHS AND MEDIA VIOLENCE
See: Violence in the Media, Attraction to

ZOOLOGY
See: Animal Communication

Subject Index

Page numbers in **boldface** indicate article titles
Page numbers in *italics* indicate photographs
and illustrations
Key to codes: *f*=figure; *t*=table

A

AAM (American Association of Museums), 220, 625–626
AARP (American Association of Retired People), 577
Abacus, 175
ABC. *See* American Broadcasting Company
ABC Radio, 811
Abelman, Robert, 880
Abrams v. United States (1919), 344
Abramson, Herb, 854
Abramson, Paul, 719
Absent-Minded Professor, The, (film), 263
Absolute expression theory, 343
Abstraction of knowledge, 503–504
Abstracts, 75, 121, 428, 890
Academia, careers in, **1–3**
Academic achievement and children's television use, **3–8**, 1015–1016; *See also* Children's creativity and television use; Television, educational
Academic American Encyclopedia, 227
Academic journal editors, 276
Academic libraries, 533, 535–536, 541, 556–557
reference services, 867, 868, 869. 870
Academic research, 883
Academy Awards, 262, *263*, 264, 324, 338, 1086
Access (software), 177
Access to information. *See* Reference services and information access; Retrieval of information
Accountants, 96, 1022, 1038
Account executives, 1022, 1038
Accounting (conversation), 481
Acculturation, 453–454, 457, *457f*, 458
Acetate film, 734
Acid Rain database, 226
Ackoff, Russell, 584

ACM (Association for Computing Machinery), 178, 412
A. C. Nielsen, 826; *See also* Nielsen Media Research; Nielsen ratings
Acoustic cultures, 594
Acquisitions editors, 276
Acquisitions staff, television, 1039
Action theory, 1081–1082
Action video and computer games, 1059, 1060
Active listening, 488–489
Active mediation, 701, 702, 703, 704
Active responding, 489
Actors, 333
Acuff, Dan, 144, 146
A/D (analog-to-digital) conversion process, 864–865
Ada (computer language), 175, 177
a.d.a.m. (software), 1078
Adams, Sam, 660
Adams, Shawn, 926
Adaptive change, 455–456, *455f*
Adaptive stress, 453–454
Adaptors, 675
Addams, Jane, 243
Addiction to media. *See* Dependence on media
Addison, Joseph, 575
Addison-Wesley, 800
Addressable cable systems, 114
Adelphia, 91
Adjourning (group dynamics), 384
Adler, Peter, 454
Adobe Systems Incorporated, 967
Adoption of technology. *See* Diffusion of innovations and communication; Technology, adoption and diffusion of
Adorno, Theodor
    cultural studies, 200, 948
    culture industries, 209, 210, 211, 213, 215

D

Kennedy, John F.
    administration, 620
    assassination, 792–793, 1026
    presidential debates, 231, 232, 235
    television interviews, 619, 1026
Kennedy, John F., Jr., *581*
Kennedy, Joseph P., 640
Kennedy, Patricia F., 80
Kenney, Patrick, 289
Kensington Palace, *63*
Kermit the Frog (fictional character), *133*
Kernis, Jay, 825
Keyboard shortcuts, 414
Keystone Studios, 124, 125
KidsConnect service, 873
Kim, Young Yun, 454, 456, 456, 460, 461
Kimball, Penn, 499
Kinder, Donald, 288
Kinesics, 476, 675
Kinetographs, 274, 328
Kinetoscopes, 274–275, 321, 328, 563
King, Larry, 825
King Kong (film), 331
King World, 1034
Kingsbury Commitment, 995, 1005
Kinney Corporation, 845–846
Kinship terminology, 953
Klapper, Joseph, 944–945
Klein, Jon, 923
K-Mart, 836, 861
Knapp, Mark, 473, 475–476, 669, 374–875
Knight-Ridder, 652
Knots Landing (television show), 929
Knowledge, 568
Knowledge creation, 503
Knowledge gap, 233, 272
Knowledge management, 43–44, **501–506**, 567–568
Knowledge management, careers in, **506–508**; *See also* Chief information officers
Knowledge organization. *See* Cataloging and knowledge organization
Knowledge repositories, 588
"Knowledge" series (Machlup), 567, 568
Knowledge sharing, 503–504
Knowledge use, 504
Knowledge workers, 429, 430, 431, 432, 433, 434
KnowledgeJobs, 507
Knuth, Donald, 966, 967
Kohl, Helmut, 286, 287
Kopernik, Mikolaj, 697
Koppel, Ted, 1026
Korzenny, Felipe, 282–283
Kosovar refugee crisis, *1032*
Kotler, Jennifer, 302
Kotler, Philip, 933
Kozak, Michael J., 242
Krafka, Carol, 242
Krannich, Caryl, 592
Krannich, Ron, 592
Krelstein, Harold, 821

Kreps, Gary, 395, 775
Kretzmann, John, 161
Kroker, Arthur, 439
Krosnick, Jon, 288
Kruesi, John, 273
Ku-band satellites, 909, 911
Kubey, Robert, 237, 238, 602
Kuhl, Patricia, 510
Kuhn, Thomas, 697
Kukla, Fran, and Ollie (children's show), 1025
K'ung Ch'iu, 676
Kunkel, Dale, 129, 924–925
Kurtz, Paul, 698–699
Kuttschreuter, Margot, 940, 941

L
Labov, William, 949–950
Lacy, Stephen, 653, 656
Lafount, Harold A., 83
Laggards, 190, 248, 983
Lake Placid Club, 247
Lake Placid Education Foundation, 247
Lakoff, Robin, 317, 518, 955
Lamberton, Donald, 270
Lang, Tim, 183
Language acquisition, **509–513**, *511*, 515–516; *See also* Language structure
Language and communication, **514–519**
Language and culture, 518, 953–954
Language and diversity, 518
Language and gender, 955
Language and media, 956–957
Language and relationships, 518
Language games, 244, 479, 517, 1092
Language shock, 453–454, 455, 458
Language structure, 509–510, **519–524**
Lanham, Richard, 537
Lankes, David, 873
Lansford, Pennsylvania, 97–98, 107
Laptop computers, 173, 192, 999
Large dish antennas, *111*
Larson, Mary, 925–926
Lasswell, Harold, 525, 645, 915, 916
LATAs (local access and transport areas), 1006, 1010
Late majority adopters, 190, 248, 249, 983
Latin alphabet, 22, 25
Latour, Bruno, 22–23
Lau, Richard, 288
Laugh-O-gram Films, 262
Lauzen, Martha, 785
Lavalier microphones, 1044
Lawrence, D. H., 727
Layout designers, newspaper, 657–658
Lazarsfeld, Paul F., 200, 300, **524–525**, 915, 916
Lazio, Rick, 793
Le Guin, Ursula, 792
Leadership, 373, 375, 381, 388, 685, 692
Learned helplessness, 36, 37

N

NAACP (National Association for the Advancement of Colored People), 780
NAB (National Association of Broadcasters), 82, 86–87, 1068
Nader, Ralph, 824
NAEB (National Association of Educational Broadcasters), 763, 765
NAGPRA (Native American Graves Protection and Repartriation Act), 627
Naisbitt, John, 433
"Nancy Drew" series, 799
Napster, *195*
NARA. *See* National Archives and Records Administration
Narcissus, 593
Nardi, Peter, 352
Narrative filmmaking, 332–335
Narratives, 481
Narrowband, 112
Narrowcasting, 100
Narrower terms, 120
The Nashville Network (TNN), 100, 104, 1021
Nathan, Abie, *709*
Nathanson, Amy I., 31, 701, 703, 704, 1064
National Academy of Design, 616, 618
National Academy of Sciences, 88, 705
National Aeronautics and Space Administration (NASA), 58, *59*, 553, 908
National Agricultural Library, 544
National and University Library Ljubljana, 544
National Archives and Records Administration (NARA), 42, 44, 48, 49, 50, 544
National Association for the Perpetuation and Preservation of Storytelling, 968
National Association of Broadcasters (NAB), 82, 86–87, 1068
National Association of Educational Broadcasters (NAEB), 763, 765
National Association of Elocutionists, 156
National Association of Television Programming Executives, 1034
National bibliographies, 75
National Book Awards, 803
National Broadcasting Company (NBC)
  cable television, 92, 111
  color television, 1027
  culture industries, 210
  families and television, 302, 303
  FM broadcasting, 821
  high-definition television, 1028
  MSNBC, 105
  news, 100, 882, 1026, 1074
  ownership, 1021
  programming, 302, 1024, 1033, 1035
  radio broadcasting, 695–696, 820, 823, 902, 903, 1024
  ratings for television programs, 840
  satellites, 904, 905–906, 909
  Surgeon General media violence study, 1068–1069
  television broadcasting, 1018, 1024

National Cable Television Association (NCTA)
  National Television Violence Study, 634, 637, 838–839, 1074
  programming expenses, 92
  subscribers, 104
  workforce, 95
National Cancer Institute, 396, 397
National Center for Supercomputing Applications (NCSA), 365, 466
National Commission on Excellence in Education, 164, 560
National Commission on the Causes and Prevention of Violence, 1068, 1069
National Communication Association, 156, 317, 396, 689, 797
National Communication Association (NCA), 484–485, 486
National conventions, political, *286*
National Defense Education Act of 1958, 766
National Educational Television and Radio Center (NRTRC), 763
National Educational Television Association (NETA), 765
National Football League, 103
National Forum for Public Television Executives, 766
National Geographic (publication), 578, 720
National Information Infrastructure (NII), 164
National Information Standards Organization (NISO), 551
National Institute for Literacy, 435
National Institute of Mental Health, 634, 699, 1068
National Institute of Standards and Technology (NIST), 693, 893
National Institutes of Health, 396, 397, 530
National libraries. *See* Libraries, national
National Library of Medicine, 228, 396, 544
National Library of Spain, 529
National Library of the Czech Republic, 544
National Medal of Science, 88
National Museum of Natural History, 623
National Oceanic and Atmospheric Administration (NOAA), 359
National Online Manpower Information Systems (NOMIS), 227
National Opinion Research Center (NORC), 301
National Parent-Teacher Association, 634, 837
National Public Radio (NPR), 763–764, 765, 825
National Public Telecomputing Network (NPTN), 160
National/regional sales managers, 1038
National Research and Education Network (NREN), 164
National Science Foundation (NSF), 88, 291, 465, 530, 553
National Society for the Study of Communication, 156
National Storytelling Association, 968
National Storytelling Network, 70

R

V

X

Y

Z